ANCIENT SYNAGOGUE EXCAVATIONS AT KHIRBET SHEMA'

Joint Expedition to Khirbet Shema', 1970-1972.
"

THE ANNUAL OF THE AMERICAN SCHOOLS OF ORIENTAL
RESEARCH, VOLUME XLII

Edited for the Trustees by DAVID NOEL FREEDMAN

ANCIENT SYNAGOGUE EXCAVATIONS AT KHIRBET SHEMA', UPPER GALILEE, ISRAEL 1970–1972

ERIC M. MEYERS, Director of the Expedition,
Associate Professor of Religion, Duke University

A. THOMAS KRAABEL, Associate Director of the
Expedition, Professor of Classics, University of Minnesota

JAMES F. STRANGE, Associate Director of the
Expedition, Associate Professor of Religious Studies,
University of South Florida, Tampa

Drawings by JOHN F. THOMPSON, Architect

With contributions by REUBEN G. BULLARD, RICHARD S. HANSON,
MICHAEL L. BATES, HAROLD A. LIEBOWITZ, and
CAROL L. MEYERS

Published for the AMERICAN SCHOOLS OF ORIENTAL RESEARCH
by DUKE UNIVERSITY PRESS, Durham, North Carolina   1976

© 1976, Duke University Press
L.C.C. card no. 76–40864
I.S.B.N. 0–8223–0377–9
Printed in the United States of America
by Kingsport Press

This volume is dedicated to the memory of G. ERNEST WRIGHT, Biblical scholar, archaeologist, devoted teacher; and to NATHANIEL TFILINSKI, rabbi, inspector of antiquities, farmer. In their devotion to the history of their traditions, they have set models for generations; in their love of Eretz Israel, they have insured the study and safekeeping of its artifacts; in the dialectic of their seemingly disparate lives may perhaps be discerned the dynamics of Galilee which spawned a dual heritage no one has ever forgotten.

CONTENTS

LIST OF ILLUSTRATIONS

FIGURES

PLATES (following page 298)

PHOTOGRAPHS (following the plates)

PREFACE

The text of this manuscript was more or less completed in the summer of 1973, and no systematic attempt has been made to bring the notes up to date beyond the beginning of 1974. In addition, because of the large number of photographs and illustrations, a great deal of the graphic work could be done only after the text had been written. The entire manuscript was handed over to Duke University Press in the spring of 1974. For the graphic work the authors are especially indebted to Mr. John Menapace of Duke University Press and to Graphic Reproductions of Durham, N.C. A special word of gratitude is due Ms. Barbara E. Williams of the Duke Press for her painstaking work in page layout. The pottery plates were prepared by Gon-Graph Ltd. of Jerusalem, Israel. Mr. William Lessig of Duke Engineering Services inked a number of diagrams for publication. Statistical illustrations were in the main prepared by Dr. James Strange.

The task of pulling all of this material together has fallen essentially to the Director of the Expedition, whose proximity to the press made it most sensible. Dr. Carol Meyers of the Joint Expedition was an invaluable source of help in proofing the final manuscript. Mr. John Dowling, who served as general copy editor, has also been of enormous assistance.

Finally, mention must be made of the untimely passing of G. Ernest Wright, to whom this volume is dedicated. His contributions to Biblical Archaeology have illuminated all who are involved in this field of research. We shall miss him sorely.

January 1975   ERIC M. MEYERS

THE JOINT EXPEDITION TO KHIRBET SHEMA'
A PROJECT OF THE AMERICAN SCHOOLS OF ORIENTAL RESEARCH

THE SPONSORS

1970

DREW UNIVERSITY
DROPSIE UNIVERSITY
DUKE UNIVERSITY
HARVARD UNIVERSITY
LUTHER COLLEGE
THE SMITHSONIAN
  INSTITUTION
THE UNIVERSITY OF
  MINNESOTA

1971–1972

DROPSIE UNIVERSITY
DUKE UNIVERSITY
HARVARD UNIVERSITY
LUTHER COLLEGE
PRINCETON UNIVERSITY
THE SMITHSONIAN
  INSTITUTION
THE UNIVERSITY OF
  MINNESOTA

THE STAFF

1969 SEASON

Survey of Sites
Eric M. Meyers and Dean Moe

1970 SEASON

Project Overseer
G. Ernest Wright

Core Directory Staff
Robert J. Bull, *Senior Archaeological
  Director*
Eric M. Meyers, *Field Director*
A. Thomas Kraabel, *Associate Field
  Director*
Dean Moe, *Field Supervisor*

Architects
Sidney D. Markman
John F. Thompson

Surveyor
Charles Sherfesse

(1970 season, continued)

Draughtsmen
Cyrus Running, *Head Draughtsman*
Larry Rostad
Kay Wanous

Photographer
Hendrik van Dijk, Sr.

*Cambridge University Environmentalist
Team*
Eric Higgs, *Coordinator*
Tony Legge
Claudio Vita-Finzi
Derek Webley

Registrars
Vivian Bull
Dean Moe

Educational Director
Charles Fritsch

(1970 Season, continued)

Numismatist
Baruch Kanael

Epigrapher
Richard S. Hanson

Pottery Formatore
Moshe Ben-Ari

Area Supervisors
Frank Anders
Michael Goldwasser
Barbara Johnson
Harold Liebowitz
Carol L. Meyers
Dave Peters
James F. Strange

Nurse
Janice Kraabel

1971 SEASON

G. Ernest Wright, *Project Overseer*
Robert J. Bull, *Senior Advisor*

Core Directory Staff
Eric M. Meyers, *Director*
A. Thomas Kraabel, *Associate Director*
James F. Strange, *Associate Director*

Architects
John F. Thompson, *Head Architect*
Tom Blount, *Assistant*
John Machinist, *Assistant*

Draughtsman
Zipporah Schreiber

Photographers
Hendrik van Dijk, Sr.
Hendrik van Dijk, Jr.
Lee Sterner, Assistant

Numismatists
Baruch Kanael
Richard S. Hanson

(1971 season, continued)

Educational Director
Richard S. Hanson

Geological Consultant
Reuben Bullard

Registrar
Carolyn M. Strange

Pottery Formatore
Dean Schwartz

Area Supervisors
Sue Estroff
Diana Furmanik
John Gager*
Harold Liebowitz
Carol L. Meyers*
Daniel O'Conner
Olin Storvick

Nurse
Pauline de Cosse

1972 SEASON with further work at Meiron
G. Ernest Wright, *Project Overseer*

Core Directory Staff
Eric M. Meyers, *Director*
A. Thomas Kraabel, *Associate Director*
James F. Strange, *Associate Director*

Field Supervisors
Gideon Foerster (*Meiron*)
Harold A. Liebowitz
Carol L. Meyers (*Meiron*)

Architects
John F. Thompson, *Head Architect*
Genevieve V. Holubik, *Assistant*
Kenneth Schaar, *Assistant*
Warren Wilson, *Assistant*

* Also worked on rescue operations in ancient Meiron.

(1972 Season, continued)

Draughtsman
Phyllis S. Mangravite

Photographers
Milton J. Heiberg
Kati Ritchie, *Assistant*

Educational Director and Numismatist
Richard S. Hanson

Registrar
Pam Reierson
Janice Kraabel, *Assistant*
Carol Leiding, *Secretary*

Area Supervisors
Carol Andreini
Diana Furmanik
Susan Mayer †
Austin Ritterspach †
Marilyn Simon †
Marilyn Spirt †
Olin Storvick

Nurses
Janice Kraabel
Rita Hanson

† Worked in Meiron.

INTRODUCTION

The Joint Expedition to Khirbet Shema' is a project of the American Schools of Oriental Research (ASOR) and its affiliate, the W. F. Albright Institute of Archaeological Research in Jerusalem—conceived and initiated by the late G. Ernest Wright, who as president of ASOR in 1968 convened a group of scholars concerned with what Wright called "the archaeology of early Judaism." Realizing that great strides had been made in American archaeological circles for the earlier periods, they felt that Americans must also actively participate in the recovery of the material culture of Palestine in the Roman and Byzantine periods.

ASOR-sponsored excavations at Schechem and Tell er-Ras, at Ai, and more recently at Caesarea have begun to answer such a mandate: to apply the careful stratigraphic techniques of American archaeologists to later sites and, in particular, ancient synagogues. The early meetings at Harvard included Messrs. Meyers, Kraabel, and Kanael of the Joint Expedition, in addition to Professors Frank Moore Cross, Jr., Isidore Twersky, and Krister Stendahl; and consultations were held with Abraham Katsh, President of Dropsie University. It was not until the summer survey of 1969 by Meyers and Moe, in close cooperation with the Israel Department of Antiquities, that the idea really gained momentum with the selection of Khirbet Shema' as the most suitable site for excavation (see *ASOR Newsletter* no. 7 [1969–70], pp. 1–3, and infra photo I.1).

Several factors were at work in making such a selection, which many people at first thought unlikely and even improbable. First, the presence on the surface of well-cut and well-preserved architectural members suggested very promising finds, which had not gone unnoticed by the British in their 1881 *Survey of Western Palestine* (on pp. 246–47). Second, the very fact that no previous excavations had been conducted there raised hopes that the ancient materials would not be too badly disturbed. Third, Khirbet Shema' was situated in the heart of Upper Galilee, a region of major importance to Judaism of the talmudic period, but where few excavations had taken place.

Designed to interest scholars in a variety of fields such as Biblical Studies, Church History, Judaica, Classics, and Art History, the excavation of a single site was to have spurred a wider interest in both the historical and strictly archaeological problems which emanated from the materials uncovered by the excavation. In keeping with this interest the Joint Expedition from the outset sponsored an academic program for both undergraduate and graduate students. In most cases the sponsoring institution sent along a group of students together with a faculty member, and this group was in turn integrated into the broader academic program. Volunteers who came from nonsponsoring schools were in the main absorbed by the Duke University Summer School Program.

In other words, the Joint Expedition set out from the beginning to make known to American scholars and students the inner workings of an entire field which, except for the State of Israel, was largely being ignored. The authors do not contend that this volume in any way changes the situation which obtained in 1969, but if it in any way impresses upon students of Judaism in late antiquity the need to understand and use archaeological materials in comprehending the history of this period better, then we shall regard our work as at least a partial success.

As for the field work itself, it was divided as follows:

1970: June 23–August 25

Clearing and cleaning of site, surveying, laying out of grid, and preparation of a dirt road to the site up the western slope of the hill and through the Wadi Meiron all preceded the arrival of a staff of around thirty together with thirty-five volunteers, plus thirty hired laborers. The objectives of the first season were (i) to determine the limits and date of a building(?) west of a doorway with an incised eagle, (ii) to begin excavation of the main public building, which turned out to be the synagogue, (iii) to map all the tombs on the site and to excavate several of them, (iv) to attempt to record all of the surface architecture for a site plan, and (v) to prepare a new contour map at 5-meter intervals.

In addition, a team of environmentalists from Cambridge University, England, conducted ecological experiments on site with an elaborate flotation device, while the rest of their team combed the surrounding mountains and valleys collecting supplementary data which would further clarify the nature of the resources available to such a hill town.

1971: June 10–August 5 (see photo I.2)

The objectives of the 1971 season were (i) to complete excavation of the synagogue and its environs, (ii) to make soundings in the lower town on the eastern slope, (iii) to continue some tomb clearing, (iv) to excavate at least one cistern, and (v) to continue plotting the surface architecture. In addition to a staff of approximately twenty-five, some sixty student volunteers participated in the second campaign, while fifteen hired laborers had the onerous task of moving the tremendous stone fill which covered the topmost layers of the entire site. During this campaign the Joint Expedition was called upon by the Israel Department of Antiquities to undertake limited rescue excavations in ancient Meiron, since a planned expansion of a local school threatened the lower parts

of the ancient site. The Meiron areas were incorporated into the Khirbet Shema'
recording system and hence part of the Shema' Project. It was clear from the
outset, however, that so rich a site would soon demand the full attention of the
Shema' Project.

1972: June 11–August 10

Highest priority in the 1972 campaign was given to the task of restoring
the synagogue at Khirbet Shema'. Technical difficulties with heavy-duty lifting
equipment had prevented the completion of the excavation of certain internal
areas within the synagogue proper. Once restoration was completed, the staff
could proceed with its final objectives for Khirbet Shema' 1972, somewhat
pared down because of dwindling resources and because of a strong feeling
from both ASOR and Smithsonian officials in favor of publishing as soon as
possible. These objectives were (i) to clarify the stratigraphic relationship between the synagogue and the structures west and northwest of it, (ii) to excavate
further the building just north of the synagogue, (iii) and to complete final
plans of the site and buildings at Khirbet Shema'. In addition, a much larger
operation at Meiron was carried out, excavations now extending west up the
slope to the eastern end of the ancient synagogue of Meiron itself. These soundings and limited work at Meiron are reported elsewhere and separately from
the Shema' materials except where those materials especially illuminate or
clarify the Shema' finds. During the final seasons some seventy student volunteers participated with a staff of around twenty, together with a team of eight
hired laborers.

During these years the Joint Expedition made its headquarters at Moshav
Meiron. Without the help of the local inspector of the Israel Department of
Antiquities, Mr. Nathaniel Tfilinski, a resident of the moshav, setting up the
field quarters could never have been accomplished. His total familiarity with the
archaeological sites and material culture of Galilee also proved to be of invaluable assistance to the Expedition.

Also, to Mr. Eli Meironi, secretary of the moshav and manager of the Guest
Houses in which we lived for all three years, and to all members of the moshav
who made available the entire facilities of the community for our work, no
thanks are sufficient. Their assistance in every matter concerned with fielding
our Expedition will not be forgotten.

In addition, a special debt of gratitude is to be acknowledged to the National
Forestry Service (Qeren Qayemeth L'Yisrael) and the Conservation Department
(Shemurat Ha-teva), who rendered their assistance during the course of excava-
tion and in particular during the 1970 season.

Dr. Avraham Biran, Director of the Israel Department of Antiquities during the course of all our work, has been a constant source of help and assistance, together with his assistant Ms. Hanna Katzenstein. Their services extended far beyond the normal limits as they made every effort to accommodate the demands of our large volunteer program.

The authors also acknowledge with gratitude the assistance of Robert J. Bull during these years, especially during the 1970 season. David Noel Freedman, who served as Director of the Albright Institute of Archaeological Research in Jerusalem in 1969–70, helped in many ways in bringing the Expedition into the field. William G. Dever, who was next Director of the Albright Institute, has helped the Expedition in every way possible. He has made our affiliation with ASOR's Jerusalem affiliate, the W. F. Albright Institute of Archaeological Research, productive in the best sense and has helped keep our excavation office intact during the past several years when all the staff was busy in the States with other responsibilities. A debt to Mrs. Norma Dever is also acknowledged for her kind help in bookkeeping matters. Both Devers were especially helpful to the publication team during their stay in Jerusalem during the summer of 1973.

No words of appreciation can now be said to G. Ernest Wright, who as president of ASOR conceived this project and whose constant encouragement and sense of vision was a prime motivating force in all our work. Thomas Newman, Administrative Director of ASOR, has been invaluable with respect to the details of all matters pertaining to grants.

The Expedition kindly acknowledges the services in Israel of Mrs. Miriam Nir, year-round draftsman from 1970–73; and Ms. Dina Kastel, registrar 1972–73. Special thanks are due to Dr. Gideon Foerster for his interest in the project, his many consultations, and his presence in the 1972 Meiron campaign; to Dr. Dan Barag for his consultations on our glass and general assistance in matters archaeological; to Dr. Zev Yeivin for his frequent consultations; to Dr. Rachel Chachlili for her reading of parts of this manuscript; to Dr. M. Avi-Yonah for his many helpful suggestions; to the late Father Augusto Spijkerman, O.F.M., and Y. Meshorer, who assisted the authors in numismatic matters; and to Dr. M. Dothan for his abiding support and encouragement.

None of this would have been possible without a covering grant for 1970–72 of Foreign Currency Funds obtained through the Smithsonian Institution by ASOR. In this connection a special indebtedness to Mr. Kennedy B. Schmertz, Director of the Foreign Currency Program of the Smithsonian Institution and Mr. Kenneth D. Whitehead, Deputy Director, is gratefully acknowledged. For the final preparation of this volume the support of the Memorial Foundation for Jewish Culture is also acknowledged.

Among our list of academic sponsors, special thanks is acknowledged to the College of Liberal Arts and its Macmillan Fund, the Graduate School and the Office of International Programs of the University of Minnesota; to the Summer School and Office of the Provost of Duke University; to Harvard University and the Harvard Semitic Museum, through the generosity of Mr. John H. Meyer.

THE AUTHORS

July 30, 1973 (1 Av 5733)
Jerusalem
The Albright Institute

ANCIENT SYNAGOGUE EXCAVATIONS AT KHIRBET SHEMA'

COMPARATIVE CHRONOLOGICAL TABLE

Encyclopaedia of Excavations[a]		Sauer, *Heshbon Pottery*, 1971[b]		Kh. Shema' occupation
Hellenistic II	152–37 BCE	Late Seleucid	129–64 BCE	Stratum I: Hasmonean, 103–76 (37?) BCE
Roman III	180–324 CE	LR II–III	193–284 CE	Stratum II: LR 1, 180–284 CE
		LR IV	284–324 CE	Stratum III: LR 2, 284–306 CE
Byzantine I	324–451 CE	EB I–III	324–450 CE	Stratum IV: Byz 1, 306–419 CE
Byzantine II	451–640 CE	EB III–LB IV	450–640 CE	Stratum V: Byz 2, 419–640 CE
Early Arab	640–1099 CE	Pre-Umayyad–Early Abbassid	640–878 CE	Stratum VI: Arab, 640–850 CE
Crusader	1099–1291 CE	Late Crusader–Ayyubid	1187–1263 CE	Stratum VII: Medieval, 1150–1277 CE

a. See n. 7 to Introductory Note, below.   *b*. See n. 8 to Introductory Note, below.

INTRODUCTORY NOTE: KEY TO THE EXCAVATION

The recording system used in three years of excavation at Khirbet Shema'
assumed the keyed grid system shown on the overall site plan, fig. I.1. Analysis
of the data retrieved within this grid framework eventuated in the definition
of occupational "strata" or historical periods that are outlined in the Comparative Chronological Table on the facing page and discussed below. This Introductory Note is intended for the nonarchaeologist and for the specialist, both
of whom will want to understand the grid, the definition of a "locus," and the
resulting series of occupational strata.

The grid is essentially that used in tell archaeology.[1] The ruin was first
bisected by a north-south line through the British triangulation point, a fixed
metal marker of known elevation established by British surveyors at the end of
the 19th century. True north was determined by sighting from this point to the
northeast corner of the Yeshiva in Meiron. The line ran south to another point
just northwest of the mausoleum. The main east-west line was surveyed to
pass through the west doorway of what is now known to be the synagogue; the
balks along this line would provide a critical section through the synagogue and
the western terrace, first called Building B and Building A in our earlier neutral
terminology.[2]

These two lines divided the ruin into the NE, NW, SE, and SW quadrants.
Each of these quadrants was divided into 30 × 30 m plots called *fields*. The
fields were numbered as they appear in fig. I.1, with Roman numerals. Each
field was in turn divided into thirty 5 × 5 m plots referred to as *areas* or *squares*.
These are the plots excavated by the *area supervisor* and his/her team of volunteers.[3]

This grid system enabled us to give each area or square a unique numerical
designation. The reader will discover that the provenance of every artifact and
of all pottery is indicated by a number that includes the quadrant, field, area,

1. A similar grid is illustrated in Albright, *Archaeology of Palestine*, 16, fig. 2. (For full citation of works mentioned in these notes, see the Bibliography preceding the Appendixes in this volume.)

2. Building A lay on the western terrace just west of the Eagle Doorway or western entrance of the synagogue, which lay on the lower terrace. Building A turned out to be defined by a medieval wall on the north, which meant that there was no building there at all until after

the destruction of the synagogue. Building C was the designation of the large building just north and west of the synagogue that we have interpreted as a Bet-Midrash or guest house. See infra, ch. 3, section 21, and fig. 3.14.

3. It must be pointed out here that we did not rigidly adhere to our grid, but readily enlarged squares to 7.5 × 5m when circumstances demanded it. Cf. the discussion in Meyers-Kraabel-Strange, "Archaeology," 5f. For methodology, ibid. 5–8.

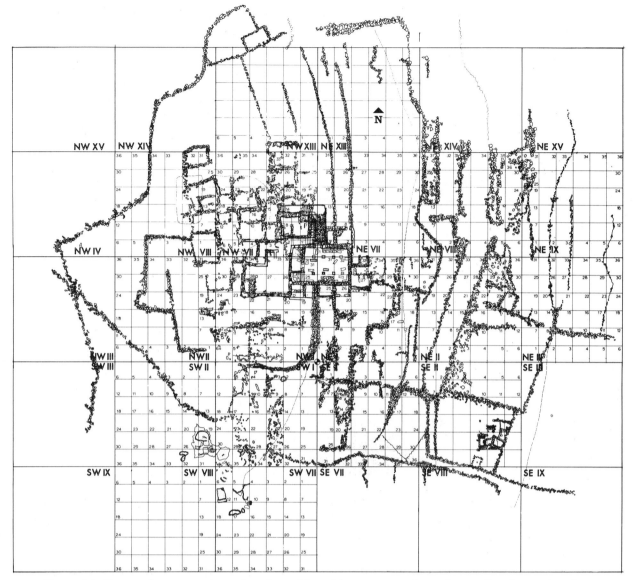

Figure I.1. Key to the excavation: site plan with grid squares and quadrants for the entire site.

and locus numbers. For example a sample number such as is found on our plate indexes indicating provenance can be broken down as shown in fig. I.2.

Every distinguishable three-dimensional feature excavated was termed a *locus* and given a locus number. In the field these numbers were usually five digits long; the first one or two digits were the square number and the last three digits referred uniquely to that square's loci in order of excavation. Thus L.24001 was the first locus excavated in square 24 of some field. Also L.24999 would be the 999th possible locus in that square. Thus L.24001 alone is not unique and requires the addition of quadrant, field, and square.

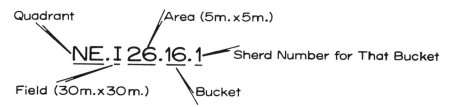

Figure I.2. How to interpret the index number assigned to items of the find.

There are certain locus number conventions. The locus number 00 refers to the modern cultivation layer. A few coins and other artifacts will be recorded as from specific squares, but from L.00. This means that they are from the surface or otherwise unstratified. An A or B after a locus number usually means that a single locus number designating a soil layer was divided into A and B at the level of interpretation because the artifactual material clearly implied that two layers were dug as one. In other words, two layers that could not be confidently distinguished in the field (because color, compaction, and particle size were not substantially different) could be distinguished later because material higher up in the locus was consistently later than the material on a lower elevation. On the basis of this evidence we realize now that there were two loci rather than one and use the convention of the A or B after the locus number.

An illustration of this situation is locus 1004 inside cistern C.1. This layer was dug as a single locus in the dark of this installation, but analysis of the coins and pottery indicated a clear chronological break within locus 1004. Therefore the layer was split into L.1004A and L.1004B of Strata IVA and IVB respectively.[4]

Another convention is the so-called "point one locus," a convention borrowed from the Tell Gezer excavations.[5] In this convention a decimal point and the numeral 1 are added to any locus number to designate material sealed under this surface. Thus, a paved floor may be noted as L.25018 in a given square, and the material sealed under the cobbles is called L.25018.1. Naturally this is crucial material, since the pavement "sealed" it off from later disturbances; this is the reason for the convention which calls attention to the locus.[6]

These conventions are well illustrated in the Locus List, appendix A in this volume, which will provide a convenient reference tool for those who wish to find in one place the most important information (except coin data, which are appended to the coin chapter) about the "critical loci," i.e., the loci we understand to be crucial primarily for chronology, but also as providing some sealed material to contribute to the ongoing discussion of the typology and chronology of ceramics.

4. Stratum IVA and Stratum IVB refer only to the history of the cistern and not necessarily to the history of the site.

5. Dever, Lance, and Wright, *Gezer I*, 11.

6. The only exception to this convention is in our coin list where only the last two digits of a locus are recorded. Since the coin list is organized by square there is no possibility of confusion.

The Locus List enables the specialist to locate in the text most of the relevant material from any critical locus. It also serves as an index to refer the reader to the places in the text where any particular critical locus is discussed. The list is organized by quadrant, field, and area (square). It also includes stratum (the second column). For us a *stratum* is a coherent cultural period or phase of occupation. Our tabulation of the strata of Khirbet Shema', in comparison to the chronological conventions of the *Encyclopaedia of Archaeological Excavations*[7] and to the more recent and more detailed work of James Sauer[8] on the chronology and ceramic typology of this period, is found above in the Comparative Chronology Table that opens this Introductory Note.

Stratum I or the earliest occupation at Khirbet Shema' is confined to the regnal dates of Alexander Jannaeus (Yannai) 103–76 BCE on the basis of numismatic and artifactual analysis. After a gap of more than two hundred years Stratum II appears, which seems to date from the accession of Commodus (180 CE) to Diocletian (284 CE), and which we call Late Roman 1. Stratum III, or Late Roman 2, dates from Diocletian to the earthquake of 306 CE, which destroyed the first synagogue. This period is followed in turn by Stratum IV, or the first occupation of the Byzantine period. Stratum IV ends with the destruction of the second synagogue by the earthquake of 419 CE. The second Byzantine occupation, Stratum V, dates from this earthquake to the Arab conquest of 640 CE. This leads us into the Arab-period occupation, Stratum VI, which lasts, to judge on the basis of coin and pottery evidence, up to the middle of the 9th century, or about 850 CE.

At this point we encounter another occupational gap. From about 850 CE, when the Abbassids are losing their grip on Palestine,[9] until the latter half of the 12th century, when our numismatic evidence begins again, Khirbet Shema' reveals no clear evidence for human occupation. Stratum VII, which is the medieval occupation, lasts therefore from ca. 1150 to 1277 CE, as dated on the basis of numismatic, ceramic, and artifactual analysis. This completes the archaeological and historical picture.

We are aware of the imperfections and built-in limitations of our system and beg the reader's indulgence. Doubtless the nonarchaeologist will find it cumbersome and the specialist think it too simple. Nevertheless, our aim is to enable the reader to move through the material with some ease while providing him with the tools to dig deeper into our evidence if he so chooses. The footnotes, appendixes, and Locus List are the point of entry for the specialist. The nonspecialist may generally confine himself to this key and the main text.

7. "Chronological Table of Historical Periods," in *Encyclopaedia of Archaeological Excavations in the Holy Land*, I, 3 (Hebrew).

8. J. A. Sauer, *Heshbon Pottery*, 3–5. We reprint portions of Sauer's table for reference and comparison and because it represents the latest work in the area of chronological terminology. We acknowledge that Sauer's chronological terminology is derived from a study of the "historical and archaeological evidence" of a single Transjordanian site,

yet it is the most detailed study to date and the significance of his results will only emerge in comparison with other sites both in Transjordan and Cisjordan.

9. We acknowledge a debt to Professor M. Avi-Yonah for pointing out this historical datum to the authors. Cf. Brockelmann, *History of the Islamic Peoples*, 131ff, on the disturbed political conditions in the Muslim Empire from 842 to 869 CE.

CHAPTER 1. KHIRBET SHEMA' IN UPPER GALILEE: THE HISTORICAL SETTING

1. THE SITE NAME

Located on one of the eastern spurs of Mount Meiron (Jebel Jarmaq) 760 m above sea level, Khirbet Shema' is about 10 km west of Safed and just south of the Wadi Meiron (see fig. 1.1).[1] This promontory or spur of Mount Meiron juts out northeastward from the southern end of the Mount Meiron massif, forming a village site naturally defended on three sides by its steep flanks. In fact the site is not easily accessible except from the southwest, following the 750-m contour line around in a half-circle to the northeast and Meiron, which is near the modern highway and presumably the ancient east-west trans-Galilee route. Its closest neighbor, ancient Meiron,[2] is separated from Khirbet Shema' only by the Wadi Meiron between them, and though the heavy rainfall of upper Galilee did not make water a great problem, both sites most likely made use of the spring of Meiron—not to be confused with "the waters of Merom" of the Bible (Josh. 11.5, 7).[3]

It seems clear that the translation of Khirbet Shema' (alternatively written Khirbet Sham' or Khirbet Sham'a)[4] as "the ruin of Shammai" must be fairly recent. The Arabic name with the *ayin* means "the ruin of the candle(s)." The inappropriateness of the name suggests that we look behind the Arabic name tradition for a more plausible explanation, though some might refer us to Elijah's Chair southwest of the site as that which might remind one of a candle.[5]

Neither the Arab geographers nor the Jewish travelers refer to the site by name. In fact it appears that for most of the Jewish travelers the tomb of

1. See *List of Historical Monuments*, par. 17, map co-ordinates 191/264. Air distance from Khirbet Shema' to Safed is approximately 5 km. (For full citation of works mentioned in the footnotes, see the Bibliography preceding the appendixes in this volume.)

2. Map coordinates 191/265.

3. For the biblical references and possible places of the famous battle there between Joshua and the King of Hazor and his allies, see Aharoni, *Land of the Bible*, 205–208. Aharoni rejects the view of others who place the battle near the Wadi Meiron and seeks to locate it further north at Tell el-Khureibeh (Marun er-Ras) 192/279. Ibid. 206, esp. nn. 82–86. Cf. the remarks of Avi-Yonah, "Meron." The large spring in the wadi was observed by Robinson, *Biblical Researches in Palestine*, 73, and identified by Klein, *Eretz Ha-Galil*, 130, n.17, as 'Ein Hatra, known in antiquity to have been the place of Rab Idi's home village. Though

there are many traces of ancient habitation in the wadi itself, no systematic survey of them has yet been made; this latter suggestion of Klein deserves further investigation. In the current Hebrew edition of the 1:100,000 map an 'Ein Shama' is noted just opposite Kefar Shammai, 192/263. It is noticeably absent from the English edition, though the old PEF map of 1:20,000 lists it as 'Ein es-Samu'i; see infra n.21.

4. Klein, *Eretz Ha-Galil*, 130, and also "Drei Ortsnamen," 273.

5. The suggestion that Khirbet Shema' might mean "ruin of a candle" first came to the attention of the authors from Zev Vilnay. Hayim Blanc of Jerusalem also orally proposed this possibility. The suggestion that this may somehow be related to the megalithic Elijah's Chair is the authors'. On the latter see Dalman, "Phönizische Grab," 195–199.

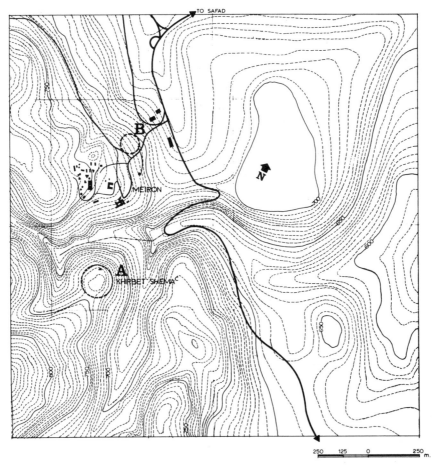

Figure 1.1. Topographic map showing the relation of
Khirbet Shema' to Meiron.

Shammai is simply located at Meiron with that of Hillel and others. It is not until
the 15th century that the mausoleum at Khirbet Shema' is specifically referred
to as that of Rabbi Shammai.[6]

But what is the origin of the tradition that places Shammai in Galilee? Our
earliest datable reference to Shammai's tomb in Galilee locates it in Dalton. This
is the opinion of Abiathar ben Elijah ha-Kohen (1040–1110 CE) as recorded in
Megillath Abiathar.[7] He reports a sacred tomb tradition of the 11th century
which places the tombs of Rabbi Josi ha-Galilee, Jonathan ben Uzziel, Shammai,

6. So Vilnay, *Holy Monuments,*264, citing an anonymous
traveler to Meiron in 1495 CE: "I saw the tomb of Shammai
and his wife, of blessed memory, buried in a single huge
stone the likes of which I have never seen, and underneath the great stone (mausoleum) is a tomb-cave of the
disciples of Shammai." The Hebrew itineraries of the 13th
to the 17th century are collected and translated in Carmoly,
Itinéraires. For Samuel bar Simson cf. ibid., 133: "Au bas
de montagne [de Meron] nous trouvâmes les sepulcres

de Hilel et de Schammai, ainsi que trois cent trente-six
autres tombeaux." Travelers' notices are also collected
in Ish-Shalom, *Holy Tombs,* 129–133; and Wright, *Early
Travels in Palestine,* 88f.

7. A. Kahana, *Literature of Israelite History* (Jerusalem,
n.d.) 163 (Hebrew). See also A. Assaf, "Abiathar Ben
Elijah Ha-Kohen," *Encyclopedia Judaica,* II, 72, and the
bibliography there.

and Hillel all at Dalton. But by the 12th century the tradition is transferred to Meiron, where it remains until shifted again to Khirbet Shema' in the 15th century. In this connection it is interesting that the shift to Meiron is not complete, for Gerson de Scarmela reports in 1561 that Rabbi Josi the Galilean and Rabbi Hillel are buried at Dalton, but adds "this Hillel is not Hillel the Elder."[8] Just four years later Uri de Biel will retain mention of Josi the Galilean at Dalton, but drop that of Hillel.

In other words we can discern with some degree of certainty three stages in the development of the Galilean Shammai tomb tradition and perhaps extrapolate a fourth, earlier stage: (1) A tradition places Shammai generally in Galilee, perhaps because of the flight to Galilee in 70 CE and the location of one of the twenty-four priestly courses there.[9] That is, in the folk reasoning the memory of the flight of the twenty-four priestly courses would eventually imply that the tomb of all the early sages must be located in Galilee. Similarly, since it was in Galilee that the rabbis reconstituted themselves after two devastating wars with Rome, later generations sought to validate their extensive settlements and activities there by ascribing burial shrines to venerated sages of long ago. (2) The first steps in localizing this tradition may be dated to the 11th century when at this stage of the tradition Dalton is recorded as the burial place of Shammai and others in the *Megillath Abiathar*. (3A) There is a partial transference of the tradition of the tomb of Shammai to Khirbet Shema' because of the anonymous traveler's notice of 1495; and as late as 1561 Gerson de Scarmela is still referring to the tombs of Hillel and Shammai in Meiron. But the transfer is apparently not yet complete; for Gerson the name of Hillel is still associated with Dalton: "this Hillel is not Hillel the Elder." (3B) A more complete transference of the Shammai-Hillel tradition to Meiron can be dated to the report of Uri de Biel in 1565. (4) The final stage is the transfer of the tomb of Shammai tradition to the nearby mausoleum of what comes to be called Khirbet Shema' in modern times.[10] What with the introduction of the feast of Lag B'omer into

8. Carmoly, *Itineraires*, 379. Identification of ancient Meiron with modern Meiron is only complicated by the itinerary of Benjamin of Tudela, who, when in Galilee, visits Tiberias, Tebnin (which he erroneously identifies with Biblical Thimnatha), Gush Halav, "Meroon, which is Maron," Alma, Qadesh, and then Dan. Tebnin is Crusader Toron far north, which is impossible given the distance of two (Spanish?) leagues or about 8.4 km in his text. In fact this distance would place him roughly at Hattin or perhaps Tabgha, depending on his road. Perhaps he means the otherwise unrecorded village of Tamra or Tomer "near Tsefat" (cf. Braslavi, "Land of Israel," 172), though this would be about double the distance. In any case his distances between Gush Halav, Meiron, and Alma conform to what we know of the topography, if we identify Meiron (Maron) with Marun er-Ras (191/278) and if he returns to Alma via Fara (193/274). In this case, we may have in Benjamin the earliest reference to the northern Meirun or Meiron, a medieval village perhaps

named after the great Meiron massif itself. According to Conder and Kitchener, *Survey of Western Palestine: Memoirs*, I, 202, this was a Moslem village in the 19th century. See infra n.21.

9. The twenty-four priestly courses are mentioned first in 1 Chronicles 24. Later references include M. Ta'anit 4.2; Tos. Demai 4.13. On the whole historical-geographical problem of the twenty-four associated villages see Klein, *Beiträge*, and *Eretz Ha-Galil*, 187ff. On inscriptions found at Ashkelon and Caesarea giving a list of the twenty-four villages see Avi-Yonah, "Caesarea Inscription," 45–57. A convenient bibliographical summary is found in Finegan, *Archeology of the New Testament*, 29. The only notice in the Talmud vaguely connected with the burial of Shammai, Tal.Bab.Hag. 22b, ignores the matter of locale and refers only to the graves of Beth Shammai where Rabbi Joshua prostrated himself.

10. It is possible that the mausoleum was seen as early as 1333 by Isaac Hello, who says that he saw at "Faravah,"

the Meiron area probably by 1300, it is not hard to imagine the kind of legitimation all these traditions assumed.[11]

Nevertheless an outstanding problem is the *ayin* in the Arabic name "Shema'." Several possibilities present themselves. (i) The Arab population heard the name "Shammai" (with an *aleph*) applied to the site, but such a word meant nothing to them, so they substituted the nearest Arabic word, *shema'*, "candle." (ii) The name "ruin of a candle" was already applied to the site by Arabs because of Elijah's Chair, or for some other reason now lost, and this appellation provided the linguistic link that drew Jewish travelers to locate the tomb of Shammai here. Other sites in Galilee contain the name "candle" or "candlestick": Kulat Shema', Neby Shema', Wadi Shema', and Shemat el 'Atikah ("the old candlestick");[12] but some of these names are most easily explainable as misunderstandings of earlier Hebrew or Aramaic names, perhaps even Canaanite. For example, it is difficult to understand Neby Shema', "the prophet candle," except as a linguistic shift from a proper name. Thus *The Survey of Western Palestine* suggests "Simeon" as the proper name behind Neby Shema'.[13] (iii) To elaborate on the *Survey*'s suggestion for Neby Shema', perhaps Khirbet Shema' means "the ruin of Simeon," the Simeon in this case being Shim'on bar Yochai, who is consistently located at Meiron in the medieval traditions. This would explain the *ayin* in the Arabic name,[14] though not the loss of the *nun*. To put it another way: it is quite clear that the tomb of Shim'on bar Yochai is located at Meiron as early as the 13th century. In the course of time the mausoleum at Khirbet Shema' must have been recognized for a brief period as the repository of his bones. Because there is no distinction in the pronunciation of Arabic between an *aleph* and an *ayin*, it was understood to be the final resting place of Shammai. But the form *shema* hung on in the tradition, as it stands to this day.

Of all the explanations set forth above it would seem that the one which

a village with a Jewish congregation, "an ancient sepulchral monument." This "Faravah" he mentions between Sa'sa and Dalton. This is most reasonably Ras al-Fawwar 1 km south of Khirbet Shema', called "Pere" on the Heb. 1:100,000 maps. Both Jacob of Paris and Gerson de Scarmela mention "Faravah" just after and just before Khirbet Hananyah ("Kfar Hanan" and "Kefar Inan," respectively). But there is no such "sepulchral monument" at Ras al-Fawwar, as the present authors can attest from a survey on foot in June of 1973, which strongly suggests that Isaac Hello was at Khirbet Shema' and simply confused the name.

11. The Arab geographer Dimashki (1300 CE) mentions Meiron (Mayrun) as a Jewish village with a remarkable cave with reservoirs that fill once a year on a "certain day." This day is "a feast day for the Jews." See Marmardji, *Textes géographiques arabes*, 197, Dimashki ms. 118. The Jewish travelers of the 13th to the 16th century also record wonders and miracles associated with pools and cisterns in the burial cave of Shammai and Hillel. For a discussion of the matter of water rituals and basins in Jewish tombs see Goodenough, *Jewish Symbols*, I, 103–110. Cf. the re-

marks of Avi-Yonah, "Meron," 1391, who notes that R. Moses Basola's mention (1522) is the earliest evidence for associating the festival of Lag B'omer with Meiron. The mention by Dimashki surely would push the date back to early medieval times.

12. See Stewardson, *Survey of Western Palestine*, ad loc.

13. Ibid. 132; and Conder and Kitchener, *Survey of Western Palestine: Name Lists*, 53.

14. The *aleph-ayin* exchange is endemic in colloquial Arabic. In Galilean Aramaic such a confusion was so common that a Galilean could not lead services in the synagogue since his pronunciation of these two letters was apt to be confusing. See Tal.Bab.Megillah 24b; Tal.Yer,Ber. 2. 4. Such a confusion lies behind the inscription found in the synagogue of Beth Shean: "May the artisan who did this *work* (spelled with *aleph*) be remembered for good." Bahat, "Synagogue at Beth-Shean," 57. For a more detailed discussion of this issue see Kutcher, "Studies in Galilean Aramaic," esp. p. 61; Dalman, *Grammatik*, 57ff., 99; and Mazar (Maisler), *Beth She'arim*, I, 9. The authors gratefully acknowledge their indebtedness to Jonas Greenfield for guiding them to several key sources.

must assume the loss of the *nun* in Shim'on is least likely. More probable is the one which presumes that the local Arabic-speaking population simply took over the traditions of Shammai and merely pronounced his name with an *ayin*. Whether the locals ever really thought of this site as the "ruin of the candle(s)" is impossible to determine, just as it is impossible to determine whether they ever understood "Shema'" to be the name of an individual. Though it is possible that the Jews took the tradition of the name over from the Arabs, with so much data on Shammai's tomb in the vicinity of Meiron, it seems far simpler to accept the opposite.

2. IDENTIFICATION OF THE SITE

In an earlier report the authors refused to either accept or reject the popular identification of Khirbet Shema' with Galilean Teqo'a[15]—mainly because of the preliminary nature of the numismatic and ceramic data available to the authors. However, it is now possible to accept this identification with some certainty. Such a proposal was first put forward by G. Dalman,[16] who soon afterward changed his mind,[17] only to return to his original position[18] after reading S. Klein's article on the subject.[19] Klein accepted the identification of Teqo'a with Khirbet Shema' and has been followed in this in more recent times by M. Avi-Yonah.[20]

Our examination of the literary sources which pertain to Galilean Teqo'a has been illuminated by three seasons of excavation, and though no external corroboration of the identification has been discovered during these years, the cumulative data, both archaeological and literary, weigh heavily in favor of such a proposal. In these discussions we have also accepted the identification of Meiron, probably the Meroth of Josephus, with ancient Meiron found just north of the Wadi Meiron.[21]

15. Meyers-Kraabel-Strange, "Archaeology," 5.

16. *Literarische Zentralblatt* no. 37 (1912), col. 1188.

17. Dalman, "Jahresbericht," 29; Gütterlin, "Tekoa," 45, n. 7.

18. *Theologische Literaturzeitung* no. 706 (1924).

19. Klein, "Drei Ortsnamen," 273, no. 3, and *Eretz Ha-Galil*, 130, 206ff.

20. *Macmillan Bible Atlas*, 141, 183. Though Avi-Yonah discusses Teqo'a of Galilee in *The Holy Land*, 203, he does not go into the question of the identification there. Vilnay, in *Holy Monuments*, fig. 95, lists Khirbet Shema' as Teqo'a, but adds a question mark. For an alternative view, namely, that Teqo'a is ancient Kisma, see Horaïn, *L'Identité de lieux de la Galilée*, 36.

21. In this we also follow Klein, *Beiträge*, 23–26, and *Eretz Ha-Galil*, passim. More recently Har-El, "The Zealots' Fortress," 123–130, has brought further evidence in favor of such a view. The demurrer of Avi-Yonah, *Holy Land*, 133, should be noted, however. Avi-Yonah would rather place Meiron further north at Marun er-Ras. His argu-

ment, however, depends on a number of other factors—identifying Bacca with Peqi'in, Thella with Tuleil, etc., all of which require further archaeological investigation. See supra n. 8. It should also be mentioned that Press, *Topographical-Historical Encyclopaedia*, IV, 979, places Teqo'a in modern Peqi'in. It is apparent that Press has confused Kfar Sumei' 179/265 with either Es-Samu'i 192.5/263 or with Khirbet Shema'. Kfar Sumei' in the estimation of the present authors has been properly understood by both Klein, *Eretz Ha-Galil*, 63, n. 58, and 154, 157, and Avi-Yonah, *Holy Land*, 130, n. 18, as Caparasima. Rabbinic sources are clear that this village demarcates the border between Sepphoris and Acre—so Tos. Gittin 1.3 and Tal. Yer. Gittin 1.2 and Tal. Bab. ad loc. The Talmudim have preserved the *mem* while the Tosephta has transcribed a *samekh*. The *Pratum Spirituale* of Moschus indicates that Caparasima belongs to Ptolemais. Press's other comments on this may be found in *Encyclopaedia*, II, 359, 471. Note that in "Kfar Sumei'" the Babylonian Talmud preserves an *aleph* and modern Arabic has preserved an *ayin*. Simi-

It is argued below that though the first synagogue of Khirbet Shema' was destroyed in the earthquake of 306 CE, which would presumably mean that it was built sometime in the latter half of the 3d century, there are many clear indications of earlier habitation at the site. A number of the tombs appear to be reused in late Roman times; a large wine press cut into bedrock, as well as other bedrock installations, appears to be earlier than the synagogues; the declivities in the synagogue clearly antedate the first building; bedrock cuttings around the synagogue also antedate its use; and terrace walls all over the site have been adapted to new uses in the heyday of the community, namely, the end of the 3d to the beginning of 5th century CE. All this evidence, though to be sure unaccompanied by decisive stratigraphic support, clearly points to a settlement at Khirbet Shema' at least in late Tannaitic times. Mindful of these considerations, we may proceed to the literary evidence.

3. THE LITERARY EVIDENCE

Klein[22] and others who have equated Khirbet Shema' with Teqo'a on the basis of literary evidence suggest that the town existed from late Hellenistic times onward. The new archaeological evidence from Khirbet Shema', though it includes a relatively high incidence of Hasmonean coinage, particularly from the time of Alexander Jannaeus, and hence suggesting some sort of limited occupation, is not extensive enough to justify understanding this site as a flourishing Jewish settlement providing pure olive oil for the Second Temple. This new datum has led us to a reexamination of the literary references to Teqo'a and to the conclusion that literary support for a Second Temple occupation at Teqo'a of Galilee is very dubious. Originally Klein had built his case around the following Gaonic citation:

Why do we celebrate eight days of Hanukah? . . . and why are there no more and no less than eight nights?

Because the Hasmoneans come from the tribal allocation of Asher, as it is written: [and Asher] "will dip his foot in oil" [Deut. 33.24].

His [Asher's] place is called Teqo'a, as it is written "Teqo'a is first in its quality of oil" [M. Men. 8.3], for out [of Asher] go forth the oils, and from there unto Jerusalem and back it is a trip of eight days. This is how they bring pure oil from there . . . and this is how the miracle of the eight days came about.[23]

Most commentators on Mishnah Menahot 8.3 have taken Teqo'a to be

larly the name of Sammu'i, near modern Kefar Shammai, is also written with an *ayin*, though *Survey*, I, 200, transcribes it with an *aleph*. All of this tends to support our discussion of the site name above, at least for Sammu'i, and possibly for Kfar Sumei' while surely attesting to the

prominence of Shammai traditions in Galilee. The *shin/samekh* exchange is also a common occurrence.

22. *Eretz Ha-Galil*, 21f.

23. The liberal translation is the authors'. See ibid. 2, nn. 1, 2, and Klein, "Drei Ortsnamen," 271, n. 2.

Judean Teqo'a.[24] The Babylonian Talmud, however, already influenced perhaps by the existence of a settlement in Galilee by that name, begins the discussion of this mishnah by relating it to 2 Sam. 14.2:

> "And Joab sent to Tekoa and fetched there a wise woman." Why to Tekoa?
> R. Johanan said, Because they were accustomed to olive oil, wisdom could
> be found among them.[25]

The Gemara continues with a baraita on Deut. 33.24 which also describes the territory of Asher as flowing "with oil like a fountain."[26] But then it continues with an elaborate story about the people of Laodicea, who were once in need of oil. First they appointed an agent who went to Jerusalem, but was told to go to Tyre. When he came to Tyre, he was told to go to Gush Halav. When he came to Gush Halav he was told to go to so-and-so in the fields, and this person gave him 100 manehs (myriad) of oil and was extremely kind to the agent. This story is repeated twice in the rabbinic literature.[27] The implication of the Gemara is that Teqo'a is understood to be in Galilee of Asher and near Gush Halav, an area famous for its olive-oil production in Amoraic times.[28] A similar confusion between "northern" and "southern" Teqo'a, also in a fairly early literary stratum, is apparent in the following mishnah:

> Nittai of Teqo'a brought dough-offerings from
> Be-ittur and they would not accept them.[29]

The attempts to identify Nittai's new home, "Be-ittur," are speculative, but point toward a location in the north,[30] where, presumably, his earlier home "Teqo'a" might then also have been located. Though Nittai could have come originally from southern Teqo'a—and whether Teqo'a was inhabited in late Second Temple times is a matter that can be settled only through further excavations[31]— it is more reasonable to assume that "Be-ittur" refers to the land of the Itureans in the Lebanon.

A Christian text, the *De vita prophetarum* of "Epiphanius," may be going back to Jewish traditions as early as the destruction of the Second Temple when it locates Amos's Teqo'a "in the land of Zebulon,"[32] in the north. By medieval

24. So, e.g., Danby, *Mishna*, and C. Albeck, *Mishnah* (Jerusalem 1953) ad loc.

25. Tal. Bab. Menahot 85b, Soncino trans., 517.

26. Ibid.

27. *Sifre Deut.*, ed. M. Friedman (Vienna 1864) 184a, and *Midrash Tannaim*, ed. D. Hoffmann (Frankfurt a.M. 1909), 220–221.

28. See Avi-Yonah, *Holy Land*, 203.

29. M.Hallah 4.10. In the context of the Second Temple, the simplest explanation for not accepting the dough-offerings is that they come from outside Eretz Israel. Albeck, *Mishnah*, 287, though he takes Teqo'a to be in Judea, notes that one could bring neither halloth nor terumah from outside Eretz Israel.

30. Klein, *Eretz Ha-Galil*, 22, and "Drei Ortsnamen,"

271, n. 4. In the latter he notes that both Schürer and Bacher remarked that Nittai or perhaps Mattai is a Galilean name. In the notice of Samuel bar Simson, 1210, in Carmoly, *Itinéraires*, 131 and 152, n. 67, Nittai's tomb is assumed to have been in Arbel in lower Galilee, though this tradition derives from Aboth 1.7, where Nittai is "the one from Arbel."

31. On southern Teqo'a see Avi-Yonah, *Holy Land*, 22, 54, 156.

32. So Radak (R. David Kimhi) on Amos 1.1 and 7.10, and also Dalman, "Jahresbericht," and Graetz, *Geschichte*, IV, 476, and nn. In the account of the prophet Amos, the word "Teqo'a" is glossed with "from the land of Zebulon" in a single manuscript of the *De vita prophetarum*, Cod. Paris, gr. 1115 (1276 CE), according to the thorough study

times, both the prophet and the wise woman of Teqoʻa were thought by some Jewish commentators to be from Galilean Teqoʻa.[33]

In other words, by Late Roman or Byzantine times at least, the mistaken notion that the Teqoʻa of Amos was in Galilee and near Gush Halav was fairly common. By later times an even greater confusion had taken place when commentators placed Amos and the wise woman of Teqoʻa in the north.

Other Tannaitic sources provide further details as to the geographical setting of Teqoʻa in Galilee and indeed tie it closely to the history of ancient Meiron, the traditional site of the ministry of R. Simeon bar Yochai. Moreover, Rabbi Judah the Prince, the redactor of the Mishnah, is reported to have studied with Simeon bar Yochai in Teqoʻa: "Rabbi said: When we learnt Torah at R. Simeon('s academy) in Tekoah, we used to carry up oil and towel from courtyard to the roof and from the roof to an enclosure, until we came to the fountain where we bathed."[34] Were it not for the fact that both the baraita and the tosephta which record the story of Rabbi's stay in Teqoʻa are so early, one would tend to dismiss them as legendary fabrications. But this tradition comes only a generation or two after the purported stay. This seems a rather brief time for such a story to evolve. The question must be asked, however, why Rabbi Judah does not himself include such a notice in his own edition of the Mishnah. Could it possibly be because R. Simeon's later career was too controversial to be included in a kind of normative work such as the Mishnah? These speculations do not gainsay the very weight and sheer existence of these traditions.

Anyone who has ever visited Khirbet Shemaʻ will have observed immediately how the houses of the town are built on the incline of the hill. Similarly, the

by Schermann, *Propheten- und Apostellegenden*. Schermann ascribes the addition to a geographical confusion on the part of the copyist and rejects earlier explanations which attributed the phrase to a misreading of lexical or geographical reference works by Epiphanius himself (p. 52; cf. 51–53). However, the addition "from the land of Zebulon" is a very specific one; it is more likely that the medieval copyists would not *add* it but would eliminate it as an "error" if they found it in manuscripts of the *De vita prophetarum* because they would know from scripture only of the "biblical" Teqoʻa in the south. If Schermann is correct in attributing the phrase to the copyist of Paris. gr. 1115, it may be that the copyists had become aware of the specific medieval Jewish traditions already noted which speak of a Teqoʻa in the territory of Zebulon, i.e., in the north. However, Schermann does not exclude the possibility that the *De vita prophetarum* is authentic; he rather indicates that proof either way is impossible. Thus the phrase could go back to Epiphanius himself, an accomplished linguist and scholar, a native of Eleutheropolis, less than 35 km from southern Teqoʻa, a man in a position to know something about "biblical" topography *as understood by* Christians and more specifically by Jews *in the 4th century*. The "mistake" in the text may go back to Epiphanius and derive from an identification of northern

Teqoʻa current in his time. However, there is a third possibility. Schermann determined that the *De vita prophetarum* derives its information about each prophet's life, manner of death, and place of burial from a Jewish source. He has analyzed its relations to the Jewish literature of the late Hellenistic and early Roman periods (*Apostellegenden*, 118–126). The reference to a Teqoʻa of Zebulon may have already been present in the Jewish source taken over and reworked by Christian writers perhaps as early as the 3d century, and/or by Epiphanius in the 4th century. The second and third explanations require a revision of Schermann's stemma of manuscripts (cf. ibid. 132), but the relation of manuscripts for this document is a complex one; and such a revision may well be in order on the basis of the information presented here, much of which was not available to Schermann himself.

33. So Radak (R. David Kimhi) on Amos 1.1 and 7.10.

34. Tal.Bab.Shabbat 147b, Soncino trans., 478. This baraita parallels the passage in Tos.Erubin 8.6, Zuckermandel, 147, line 24. Cf. also Tal.Yer.Erubin 8.6 and the interpretation of editors in Klein, *Sepher Ha-Yishub*, I, 157, where the enclosure is understood to be near a spring. From all these sources it is clear that the direction is down the hill where the spring was located, precisely the situation in the Wadi Meiron.

4th-century talmudic sage from Tiberias, R. Zeira, also notes the peculiar building techniques of the builders at Teqo'a of Galilee, who built one house over the next so that the lower one could use the foundations of the upper.[35] There is no other site from this period in the vicinity of Meiron and Gush Halav which is appropriate for such a manner of construction, or which has a spring so close to it.[36] So unique is the manner of construction that the Talmud compares it to Beth Shean.[37]

Since so many of the sources thus far used go back to the end of the 2d and beginning of the 3d century CE, precisely the period of Khirbet Shema' which has left only traces, it is important now to consider the further possibility that in that early period Khirbet Shema' (= Teqo'a) was a semidetached satellite settlement of Meiron, so that they were perhaps more than one community but not yet two separate villages. As a result, someone familiar with the locality might call it sometimes Meiron, sometimes Teqo'a (in the same way a young Harvard student today might call the place in which he lives and studies now Boston and now Cambridge). This suggestion had already been made by Dalman and was accepted later by Klein,[38] but neither recognized the full significance of this evidence for historical geography.

The interchange of these place names is found both in the Tosephta and in the Yerushalmi, in the laws concerning sabbatical release for the land; the two texts pertain to the eating of olives. The first specifies "that one may eat olives until they are gone in Teqo'a, R. Eleazar ben Ya'akov says, also those of Gush Halav."[39] The other mentions only Meiron and Gush Halav.[40] The apparent conflation of two traditions led Wilhelm Bacher to conclude that Meiron and Teqo'a were one and the same.[41] Given the archaeological realia, however, one might disentangle these traditions in a different way, somewhat as follows. Assume that Meiron, the older, better-known site is never labeled incorrectly, so that when the early sources say "Meiron" they mean at least our Meiron and sometimes also Teqo'a = Khirbet Shema', its not-yet-detached satellite. In this early stage "Teqo'a" also means the present site of Meiron and the present site of Khirbet Shema', perhaps with the latter location more in focus. Rabbi Simeon was the major figure for both communities (which were however not yet fully divided into two) and probably ministered to both. Later, Khirbet Shema' = Teqo'a became an independent town with its own synagogue, self-consciously

---

35. Tal.Yer.Baba Metzia 10.1, erroneously cited by Klein in "Drei Ortsnamen," 272, as Baba Batra 10.1, but later corrected in *Eretz Ha-Galil*, 130. This manner of construction can be observed in any number of Druse villages in the mountains of Galilee and even in the New Jewish Quarter of Jerusalem.

36. The spring by Meiron was identified by R. Tanchum Yerushalmi, a 13th-century Palestinian commentator, as the "waters of Meiron" of Joshua 11.5, a notion we have rejected following Aharoni. See supra n. 3.

37. See supra n. 35 and also Yeivin, "Survey" on the subject of towns in rabbinic times. Cf. also Krauss, *Tal-*

mudische Archäologie, I, 307, n. 286.

38. "Drei Ortsnamen," 273, n. 4.

39. Tos.Shebiit 7.15, Zuckermandel, 72, line 3.

40. Tal.Yer.Shebiit 9.2, baraita.

41. Bacher, *Agada*, II, 76, n. 2. Indeed, Bacher finds additional support in the *midrash* where R. Simeon bar Yochai took some of his students to "the wadi which was near Meiron, his city." *Midrash Tanchuma*, ed. Buber, Pikudei, par. 7. As we remarked above, Rabbi Judah the Prince is twice mentioned as having studied with R. Simeon in Teqo'a, Tos.Erubin 8.6, parallel to Tal.Bab. Shabbat 147b.

separated from the "mother city" Meiron. At *this* stage, one name would not do for both, and in the minds of those who knew the area, each town had its own label: one was "Meiron," the other "Teqo'a." Another possible way of understanding the situation is that Teqo'a was really an integral part of Meiron society in this early period and that for most people Teqo'a at this time merely conjured up the broader setting of Meiron and its environs, as the sources seem to indicate. One final shred of evidence reinforces in our mind the matter of identification of Khirbet Shema' with Teqo'a. In another baraita we find several metaphors used which supply additional geographical data: "Our Rabbis taught: Rich in possession (and) rich in pomp—that is a master of *aggadoth*. Rich in money (and) rich in oil—that is a master in dialectics."[42] "Rich in money" is transcribed in Hebrew literally as "one rich in rocks"—'*tyr sl'ym*. "Rich in oil" is transcribed in Hebrew as "a rich person is Teqo'a"—'*tyr tqw'*. "A master of dialectics"—*b'l plpwl*—is one "who by his creative powers is continually able to establish new points and evolve new principles, thus making his knowledge as continually productive as the possession of money and choicest oils."[43] In other words Teqo'a has its riches in its oil industry, learning, and rocks. If anything characterizes the topography of Khirbet Shema' it is the rocky ridge on which it is built, its creative use of bedrock, and extensive local quarrying. We have by now, it is hoped, sufficiently documented the former, that is, its almost legendary olive industry and learning, underscored in the above pun or wordplay.

Since stratigraphic considerations do not allow proposing a major settlement at Khirbet Shema' during the youth of Rabbi Judah the Prince, it seems most judicious to accept the theory that during this period Khirbet Shema' or Teqo'a functioned more or less as a suburb or satellite settlement of Meiron. Only in the course of time, when more and more settlers came to Teqo'a, built their inclining houses on the eastern slopes of the mountain, worked the olive fields, and increased their material possessions and personal wealth, did the villagers decide to erect their first synagogue. This event, we have proposed, took place sometime in the second half of the 3d century. It is probably during this expansionistic period that Teqo'a achieves its sense of independence from Meiron. In fact it may have been a sort of intercity rivalry, or perhaps just a remembrance of such a situation, that inspired the highly creative and innovative synagogue architecture that characterizes the material culture of Khirbet Shema'.

4. KHIRBET SHEMA' (TEQO'A) IN ITS REGIONAL CONTEXT
(See Fig. 1.2)

We would leave a quite inaccurate impression if we were to suggest that either Teqo'a or Meiron was not part of a much larger regional setting in Upper Galilee (Tetracomia). In this regard one can point to a number of Jewish villages

42. Tal.Bab.Baba Batra 145b, Soncino trans., 627.   43. Soncino, p. 627, n. 6.

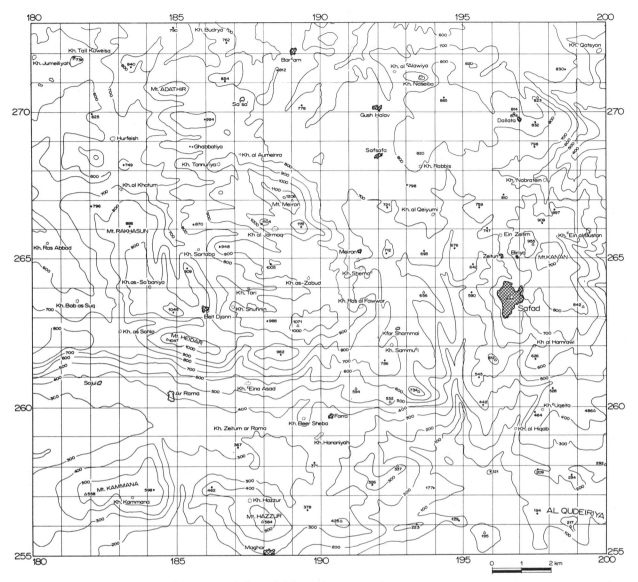

Figure 1.2. Topographic map of the Khirbet Shema' region.

in the immediate vicinity of Mount Meiron which define the extent and cultural continuity which tied them together.

Of the villages mentioned in the list of twenty-four priestly courses,[44] only three appear to be located in the general area: Meiron ($191^5/262^2$),[45] Tsefat (197/264),[46] and Yamnit, possibly to be identified with either Khirbet Yamma ($198^1/233^7$),[47] or Khirbet 'Ein Honi ($199^5/266$).[48] Though we are unable to ascer-

44. For references to literature see supra n. 9.
45. *List of Historical Monuments*, par. 17.
46. Ibid., i.e., modern Safed.
47. Ibid. par. 42.

48. Ibid. par. 17. Other sites outside Tetracomia but not too distant from Khirbet Shema' mentioned in the list of priestly courses include: 'Aylabo ('Elabun, 187/249), par. 37; Arbel (Khirbet Irbid, $195^5/246^7$), par. 38; Me'araya

tain the historical veracity of these notices, if we accept the identification of ancient Meiron with modern Meiron, then our very preliminary soundings tend to support an increase in population after 70 CE.

Other sites in the area which are clearly settled in the 4th century and tied into Khirbet Shema‘ Stratum IV include Meiron, Sa‘sa, Bar‘am, Gush Halav (perhaps the head village of Upper Galilee), Qadesh, Alma, and possibly Qatsyon. Further south one can mention Chorazin, Capernaum, et-Tabgha, Umm el-Ammed, Arbel, Tiberias, and Hammath-Tiberias.[49] Two other major sites which demarcate the boundary between Upper and Lower Galilee, Beersheba north (189/260), Khirbet Hananyah (189/259), and finally Sammu‘i (192/263) also may be added.[50]

This pattern only begins to change in the 6th century with the increasing dominance of Christianity. Large churches are erected before and during this century at Yarum (189/276), Suhmata (178/268), Hamita (166/276), Shavei Zion (158/265), Arab (182/251), Tabgha, and Capernaum, effectively encircling the Jewish area of Upper Galilee. The leading Jewish towns of the period are certainly Gush Halav, Nabratein (197/267), and Teqo‘a (Kh. Shema‘), and surely others unknown to us at present.[51] These occupy the center of Tetracomia and may form the last stronghold of the Jewish population.[52] On the basis of the 1974–1975 seasons at Meiron, it appears that the site was abandoned around 360 CE in the reign of Constantius II. (For further information see the forthcoming ASOR report.) Meiron was a major Jewish town by the beginning of the 2d century CE.

During the Arab period, Jewish communities continued to flourish in Galilee, though we know very little about them from literary notices. During the period from the Arab conquest to the middle of the 9th century, when occupation at Khirbet Shema‘ ceases, the large towns of Adhra‘ah, Qadas (Qadesh Naphtali), al-Lajjun (Legio—167/220), Akko, Taburiyyah (Tiberias) and Sur (Tyre) are mentioned by the Arab geographers.[53] We can only assume that life continued more or less the same after as before.[54]

During Stratum VII at Khirbet Shema‘, or the 12th and 13th centuries, Jewish life continued in spite of the rapidly shifting political fortunes of the

(Maghor?, 188/255), par. 34; and possibly Qabrite (el-Kabri?, 164/268), par. 5. Only further surveys and soundings can clarify the reliability of this listing.

49. For all of these consult the standard references, esp. Avi-Yonah, *Holy Land*, and his remarks in *Atlas of Israel*, IX/8, IX/9, as well as Saller, *Revised Catalogue*, which should be used with some caution, and Vogel, "Bibliography," 1–96.

50. This contention is based on the authors' visit to these sites.

51. Archaeological remains from synagogues at Bar‘am, Alma, Dalton, Sa‘sa, Baqa‘, Rosh Pinna, Khirbet Sara, Rama, Arbel, Sakhnin, etc., are not closely enough dated as yet except typologically to enable us to mention them here with certainty.

52. For a historical account of the social, political, and economic pressures on the Jews of the period cf. Avi-Yonah, *Geschichte*, passim.

53. Arab geographers' notices are collected in Le Strange, *Palestine Under the Moslems*, and Marmardji, *Textes géographiques*. See also the relevant section of the *Atlas of Israel*. Baladuri (869 CE) mentions as northern sites destroyed by the Arabs in 626–630 CE Baysan (Beth Shean), Susiyah (Susita-Hippos, 212/242), Afiq (Apheq), Jerash (Gerasa), Bayt Ras (Beth Rosh, Capitolina, 231/233), Qadas (Qadesh), al-Jawlan (Golan), Akkah (Akko), Sur (Tyre), and Saffuriyyah (Sepphoris, 176/239). Cf. Marmardji, 4.

54. For example, cf. the history of Nessana in the Negev after the Arab conquest. Kraemes, *Nessana III*, 28–35.

Crusaders, Fatimids, and Mamluks. Teko'a stood in Upper Galilee among Jewish settlements at Meiron, Gush Halav (Arabic "el-Jish," still its Arabic name), Alma, Biriat (just north of Tsefat), Safed (Tsefat), and Ahmya (203/261?). Tsefat is indeed the administrative center now, though Tiberias had been the provincial capital before the Mamluk period and evidently also the center of Galilean Jewry.[55]

What emerges from any examination of the data is that much yet remains to be done in Upper Galilee. Surface sherding and visits to these sites, however, reveal an astonishing continuity in material culture. Moreover, it is now possible to document the movement northward of the Jewish population after 70 CE, and it would appear that some major settlements in the region are in evidence by the 2d–3d century.[56]

Thus, when Khirbet Shema' is viewed in its broader regional setting, both its uniqueness and its commonality may be observed along a cultural continuum that extends from Galilee to the Golan.[57] As for Upper Galilee in particular, our work at Khirbet Shema' and frequent visits to other sites in the vicinity tend to support Avi-Yonah's contention[58] that Tetracomia was excepted from the 2d- and 3d-century Roman policy of urbanization because of the strength of its Jewish population, which refused to conform to Greco-Roman culture.

55. See Mann, 171, for a letter from the Rabbi in Safed (Tsefat) calling the heads of these communities to a meeting in that city. Also mentioned by Mann, 204, are 'Al'alwiyeh near Gush Halav and Akel, a dependency of Tsefat.

56. Esp. Qatsyon, Gush Halav, Chorazin, Capernaum, Tiberias, and certainly Meiron. Other such early sites may be identified with continuing archaeological research in

Galilee. See provisionally the first preliminary report on Meiron in *BASOR*, 1974. For a completely revised treatment the reader should consult Meyers-Meyers-Strange, "Excavations at Meiron, 1974–1975," forthcoming in *ASOR* (1976).

57. See infra ch. 7 on ceramics.

58. *Holy Land*, 112.

CHAPTER 2. THE ARCHAEOLOGICAL GEOLOGY OF THE KHIRBET SHEMA' AREA

Field work for the present study was carried out principally in the summer of 1970, when the writer was invited to participate in an investigation which was to be part of the excavational activity of Khirbet Shema'. Stratigraphic and structural studies were made in the field on the hill of the site as well as on the neighboring foothills and low areas in the region generally east of Mount Meiron. Local bedrock features were examined for quarry sites, rock cuttings, and rock structures which could have a bearing on the history of activities related to the occupation of Shema'. Regional studies were conducted in the area of Jish (Gush Halav) in the north and from Mount Hillel to the southwest of Shema' and extending east to the slopes of Safad. In addition to the field study, the writer analyzed lithic material, metals, and other objects in the excavation workrooms at Meiron and at the Albright Institute in Jerusalem.

1. THE GEOLOGICAL FRAMEWORK OF THE LEVANT (See Fig. 2.1)

The entirety of the Fertile Crescent from the Nile to the Persian Gulf lies between the Afro-Arabian shield on the south and the folded mountains of Iran, Armenia, and Turkey on the north. The central portion of this arc, the Levant, has been a coastal zone between this shield and the predecessor of the Mediterranean Sea throughout much of its geologic existence (since Cambrian time). Erosional products have been supplied to this pre-Mediterranean Sea (or Tethyan geosyncline) from this Afro-Arabian foreland. The shoreline shifted as marine waters covered the entire region from the ancient Mediterranean to the Mesopotamian–Persian Gulf areas from time to time. The ancient geography of the area is best understood from mid-Mesozoic time when the Nubian massif was above water and was undergoing erosion, shedding blankets of sand into the Levant to the north. Marine waters flooded much of the eastern Mediterranean area during the Middle and Late Cretaceous period and continued to cover the region into the Middle Eocene epoch, after which general emergence of the land took place.

The crustal movements which controlled the submergence and emergence

The author of this chapter is REUBEN G. BULLARD.

Miss Susan Rohaly deserves special mention for her excellent assistance in the field and as secretary. Much of the data incorporated in this study was gathered in geological laboratory research at the University of Cincinnati. The writer is grateful to the Core Staff of the Joint Expedition and expresses special gratitude for the interest of Eric Meyers, Director, Thomas Kraabel, Dean Moe, Robert Bull, and James Strange.

of the eastern Mediterranean from the Cretaceous period to the Miocene epoch were mostly vertical movements involving large areas of the crust of the earth. The character of these movements underwent an important change during the Miocene. Local folds began to develop in which the crustal stresses reached a maximum and resulted in faulting or a breaking up of crustal strata into blocks. Thus the framework was produced which continuing uplift and erosion have acted upon, giving rise to the peculiar sculpture of the region of Galilee in general and the area of Khirbet Shema' in particular.

2. THE GALILEE HIGHLAND

Galilee is situated between the Emek Yizreel on the south and the Lebanon border on the north. Its eastern margin is sharply demarcated by the abrupt sheer face of the Naftali Mountains, which border the upper Jordan Valley on the northeast, and by the plateau basalts on the southeast. The western margin is the northern coastal plain.

After Nubian sandstone deposition, an Early Cretaceous (Aptian) transgression covered the region of Galilee. Fine sands and clays, however, were increasingly replaced by carbonate deposition (giving rise to limestones) from the beginning of Aptian to the end of Albian time. By the Early Cenomanian, the carbonate lithic materials underwent dolomitization which very likely reflects conditions of warm shallow seas over the area. During the Cenomanian and Turonian (Late Cretaceous), considerable thicknesses (locally up to 1,000 m) of hard dolomite, limestones, and chalks were deposited over Galilee and elsewhere throughout the Near East. In Galilee two successive reef complexes developed in Late Cenomanian and Early Turonian time.

Crustal movements in the Late Cenomanian altered local conditions. The marine waters were enriched with silica, which now appears in the rocks as nodules of chert and geodes of quartz along with the silica replacement of carbonate sediments. From Late Cenomanian time into the Middle Eocene marine waters in the area were deep and became an environment which was very rich in planktonic foraminifera. These organisms gave rise to the uniform chalk strata which occur in the hills and mountains of Galilee.

During Late Eocene time, crustal uplift brought an end to marine water deposition. A general tilting of the region toward the southeast brought about the formation of an inland basin which extended to the area of Damascus.

Volcanic outbursts began in the subsiding basin after Middle Eocene time but before the Miocene; one of the centers of eruption is still in evidence to this day as Horns of Hattin. This activity was the beginning of extensive lava flows which were poured out intermittently throughout later geologic time (or the Eogene period). These sheet lavas composed of alkaline olivine basalt interfinger with sediments being deposited in the area. The extrusive volcanic activity finally

Figure 2.1.

GEOLOGIC MAP AND COLUMNAR SECTION
of the
MEIRON REGION, UPPER GALILEE

TOPOGRAPHIC & GEOLOGIC
ENVIRONMENT OF
KHIRBET SHEMAʻ

Contour Interval 25 Meters

0.0 0.1 0.2 0.3 0.4 0.5 km
Scale in tenths of a kilometer

LOCALITY

Kamon Dolomite	} — — — Mt. Haari
Lower Member Deir Hana FM	
Upper Member Deir Hana FM	— — — Mt. Meiron
Sakhnin Dolomite	— — — — — Mt. Peqiin
Yanuch Formation	— — — — — — Mt. Zevul

SCALE m	LOG	THICKN.	DESCRIPTION	FORMATION	STAGE	SERIES
480 460 440		A = 142.0+	A Sakhnin dolomite, dolomite, reefs	A SAKHNIN DOLOMITE kus	TURONIAN ?	UPPER CRETACEOUS
420 400 380 360		B = 81.5+	B Yanuch formation dolomitic limestone with chert, limestone	B YANUCH FORMATION kuy		
340		26.2	Chalky dolomite with chert and quartz geodes	UPPER MEMBER kudh₂	UPPER CENOMANIAN	
320		21.8	Limestone chalky dolomitic with some quartz geodes			
300		25.0	Chalk chalky limestone and dolomite with chert lenses and quartz crystals			
280			Dolomitic chalk yellow varved with quartz geodes and chert	Guide horizon		
260		14.1	Dolomite chalky and limey with chert			
			Chalk with quartz geodes			
240		59.8	Chalk and dolomitic chalk with some chert	LOWER MEMBER kudh₁		
220			Dolomitic limestone with chert			
			Dolomitic chalk			
			Chalky limestone and dolomite with chert and quartz			
200			Chalk			
			Dolomite chalk and limestone with chert and quartz			
			Dolomitic limestone well bedded with quartz geodes			
180		57.9	Dolomite chalky with chert lenses and quartz geodes			
160			Dolomitic limestone with quartz geodes			
			Chalky limestone with dolomite			
140			Dolomite grey hard	KAMON DOLOMITE kuk	LOWER CENOMANIAN	
		45.3	Dolomite limestone with quartz			
			Dolomite yellow			
			Limestone			
120			Dolomite grey well bedded with limonitic stains and calcite veins			
			Dolomite and chalk			
			Dolomitic limestone crystalline			
100			Marl, chalk			
		21.1	Dolomite grey with limonitic stains and quartz geodes			
80			Soil			
		22.8	Dolomite grey crystalline hard			
60			Dolomitic limestone soft			
40		25.2	Chalky sandy dolomite soft			
			Talus			
20		17.0	Dolomite crystalline hard			
0		14.1	Limestone, dolomite and dolomitic limestone transition zone	RAMA FORMATION	? Albian Vraconian?	?
			Limestone crystalline			
			Alternation of marl and lithographic limestone			

Modified from Shiftan, 1952 and Eliezri, 1959, by field observation in 1970 and 1971.

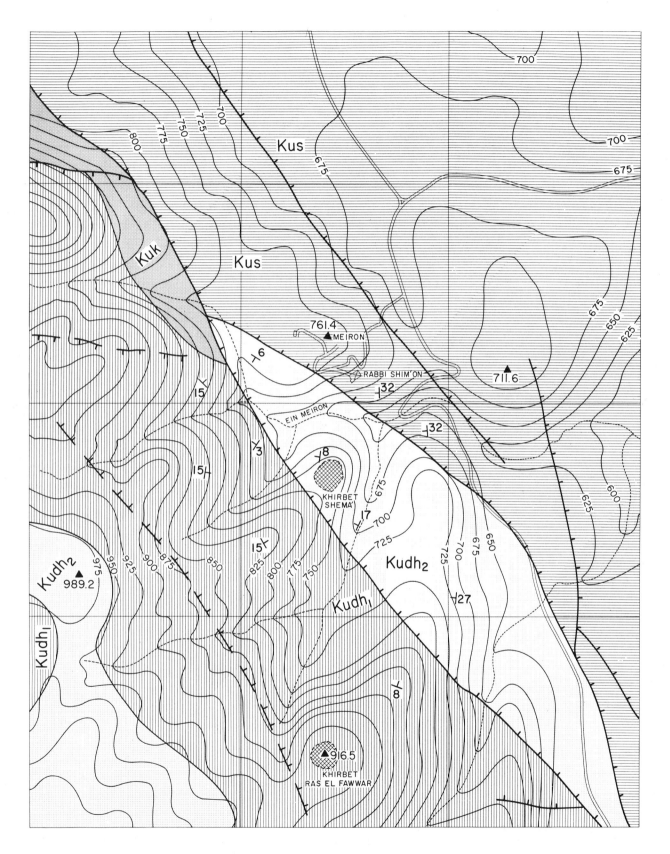

ended in a Plio-Pleistocene sheet basalt cover. These fissure flows, which covered the entire area of southeastern Galilee, extended east of the Jordan Rift Valley into the Hauran of southern Syria. Locally in the area immediately to the southeast of Jish (Gush Halav) another part of this regional volcanic activity occurred.

Late Cretaceous and Early Paleogene crustal adjustments in Galilee produced much of the folding which can be observed as upward curving or downward bending strata in the surface outcrops today. This folded crustal structure was modified in Neogene time by extensive block faulting which shows dominant northwest-southeast major trends. The fault block mountains of Galilee extend from Mount Tabor (588 m) to Mount Meiron (1,208 m) in the north and on into the region of Lebanon. Quaternary-Recent alluvium covers the basin between the fault block highs.

3. THE LOCAL GEOLOGIC SETTING OF KHIRBET SHEMA'

The site of Shema' is found on a northeast-trending spur among the foothills of Mount Meiron. Like other parts of Galilee, this area is also extensively faulted (see the accompanying geologic map, fig. 2.1) giving rise to extremely rough, mature topography into which wadis, often controlled by faults, have cut their steep-walled valleys. Bordering mountain blocks rise sharply from these valleys, and the region of Shema' is dominated by a central peak, Mount Meiron, 1,208 m, the highest elevation in the country. The high relief of this rugged area owes its character to the erosional history of the streams, which have been controlled by the base level established by the Jordan River and the Sea of Galilee to the east. The streams which drain the area thus seek their base level at more than 200 m below sea level.

The local rock is composed of strata of white to gray limestone which have undergone varying degrees of dolomitization. Sugary dolomitic limestone outcrops in beds which range from 0.3 m to 1.2 m thick up and down the eastern slope of the hill of Khirbet Shema' (see photo 2.1). Layers of chalk occur in thickness up to 1.5 m in sequences of chalky limestone, chert lenses, and vugs filled with quartz crystals. Interstratified units of yellow dolomitized chalk, containing bedded chert and quartz geodes, are also a part of the strata which form the hill on which the site was built.

The geologic environment of the site is also marked by evidence of faulting, as shown by the break in the outcrop pattern on the slope in photo 2.1 (the line indicated by X). The tombs excavated on the eastern slopes were cut into yellow chalky and dolomitic limestone which had been severely brecciated by fault-zone movements. This rock condition undoubtedly made the work of tomb cutting much easier.

Upslope about 0.3 km to the southwest from the site, the regolithic or weathered bedrock material is replete with quartz geodes weathering from strata of the lower member of the Deir Hana formation outcropping there (see the columnar section accompanying the geologic map, fig. 2.1). Almost universally strewn on the surface of the soil and weathered bedrock throughout the area were pendants and solution-sculptured remnants of the C-zone soil horizon features (see photo 2.2). Care was taken early in the excavation to demonstrate the natural origin of these lithic materials, which very strongly appeal to our desires to consider them as artifacts. These parent rock remnants occur as slope waste materials in archaeological environments where the bedrock has an impermeable crystalline nature.

Not only were probable quarry sites discovered on the northwestern slope of the hill of Khirbet Shema', but also the evidence of severe crustal sheering of the local rock along faults. The fault (tectonic) breccia (photo 2.3) shows the carbonate recementation of terra-rossa-rich fault gouge in the bedrock of the hill. Subsequent mechanical breakup of the surface rock undergoing physical weathering yields lithic materials which were available to the masons constructing the buildings of the site. Fault breccia was observed as chocking in walls and as smaller building-stone materials utilized and shaped in the wall construction on a minor scale in the buildings.

The soils of the slopes of the Shema' area are thin and vary from terra rossa conditions to rendzinate environments. X-ray diffraction analysis of three soil samples (using copper K_α radiation) showed that the dominant clay mineral in the terra rossa soils is kaolinite. This mineral when combined with varying amounts of silt and clay-sized quartz and other lithic materials affords a source for mud-brick manufacture (see below); and where streams have sorted and deposited sediment loads, as in the Wadi Meiron, alluvial-soil clays are available for ceramic manufacture (see infra photo 2.21).

While the terra rossa soils are found predominantly upon the harder, more crystalline limestones and dolomitic limestones, chalk bedrock material frequently gives rise to a calcareous rendzinate soil which contains minor amounts of palygorskite, a fibrous magnesian clay mineral which is abundant in the soils of the Shephela region of Israel. These soils, while giving rise to a very poor quality of ceramic material, were often mixed with stream-sorted temper composed of the wadi-worn bedrock sediment upon which the soils themselves occurred. Rendzinate soils occur in the Levant in areas where chalks and marls constitute the bedrock parent material.

Rock materials which appear higher on the Shema' foothill are locally cut with calcite veins, portions of which weather to become a part of the regolithic material mass wasting downslope. There is no question about the popularity of such materials among the inhabitants of Khirbet Shema'. Photo 2.4 shows a typical medium-cobble-sized fragment of vein calcite (travertine) which was a part of the slope material above the site. The most abundant use of this material was in the surface plasters used on the interior of the synagogue structures.

Pebble- to granule-sized crushed crystalline calcite was observed in these man-made materials, which will be described later.

Architectural materials

The lithic blocks which were quarried for use in the buildings excavated are all of local bedrock. They resemble the lithic components of the large mausoleum-like tomb structure which dominates the surface of the site on the southwest. The rock material is a micritic, partially dolomitized limestone with numerous tiny calcite veins running through it, generally subparallel to the regional stress directions as observed in the quarry sites. This rock material, typified in that used in the construction of the mausoleum (see photo 2.4), shows a weathering surface which lends its particular character to the monument and to many of the blocks of masonry exposed to the atmosphere on the site through time. The internal composition of this rock is shown in photo 2.5. Here the state of dolomite replacement of calcite is clearly observable. The rhombic crystals of dolomite can be seen forming in small vugs and cavities and veins within a rock matrix. The masonry of the synagogue, its walls, doorjams, lintels, and column bases are composed of this lithic material. Only exceptional architectural components are made of exotic materials not occurring at this site, and they are discussed by other writers in this report.

Special lithic materials and bedrock structures

Students of soil formation or pedologists are familiar with processes at work in the regolith by which rock becomes soil. They are not surprised to observe in hard and crystalline carbonate bedrock environments solution-sculptured and -smoothed remnants of the parent bedrock suspended in the soil material above the rock-soil interface. Many curious geometries have been observed by the writer within the excavation workings of archaeological sites in the Judean and Ephraim hills as well as in the hills of Galilee. Khirbet Shema' is no exception and resembles other areas in which such materials abound. It is not known how the original inhabitants of Shema' regarded such objects as those shown in photo 2.6 and others not illustrated. Whether they were ever used as tools or as cultic objects is also uncertain, but highly improbable. Students of material culture in contemporary excavations must use caution in arriving at hasty conclusions about the artifactual function of such objects. In all honesty, they must be regarded as fortuitously present in the total lithic and regolithic context of the site environment unless there is good evidence to demonstrate that the fact is otherwise. This writer has never observed such an instance.

While never as obvious or perhaps as definitive as the cut and polished rock section shown in photo 2.7, tomb interiors at the site studied by the author frequently intersected badly fractured, sheered, and crushed bedrock zones. No-where was this better illustrated than in Tomb 29 North, where the cuttings had intercepted a distinctive zone of faulting and brecciation. The powerful forces at work within the earth's crust are graphically illustrated in this and other specimens studied in the laboratory. Fragments of this rock, however, were as solid as the unbroken rock quarried elsewhere for construction purposes. There is no better illustration of the forces at work which gave rise to the geologic environment of Shema' than that which is illustrated here.

The massive character of the local rock layers lends itself well to tomb cutting. Various other structures that cut into the local rock are also instructive. Photo 2.9 shows the remains of a crushing facility, probably for grapes, to which the physical properties of the limestone and dolomitic carbonates lend themselves well. Not only does the rock material yield to the rock-cutter's chisel, but it possesses a high degree of impermeability to fluids, which enhances its usefulness for presses and for liquid storage. Then, too, the freshly cut carbonate surface becomes smoother, not only from the wear of its use, but also from rock surface/solution responses of carbonate materials to cold, rain, and surface waters.

Much of the surface rock material between Shema' and the city of Safad to the east is not of the physical character which lends itself well to this kind of installation. Indeed, rock surfaces on some of the neighboring spurs about Shema' are not at all suitable for such facilities as the one under consideration here. How much, if any, the amenability of gently dipping surface rock of the foothill spur of Mount Meiron on which Shema' was built attracted the first settlers to this site cannot be determined. It is certain, however, that the exploitation of the natural environment of the Shema' site by its occupants enabled them to achieve certain desirable objectives in their way of life. Flotation studies made upon selected occupational sediments show earths and sediments permeated with olive pits and olive-pit debris. Perhaps it is not unthinkable that the geologic environment played a role in the selection of this particular spur for the site of the structures and associated activities which made Khirbet Shema' what it was.

Although it was not included in the excavation plans for the recovery of the history of Khirbet Shema', the circular lime kiln (see photo 2.10) located on the wadi terrace in the valley on the eastern side of the hill of Shema' deserves mention. The structure is still nicely preserved, with the circular walls of the kiln silo still standing, showing only minor wasting of the upper part of the stones which compose the kiln. The reason for its preservation lies in the earthen embankment heaped up against the walls to prevent their slumping and to provide structural rigidity. The age of the kiln has not been determined, but it is certain that it is connected with the cultural history of the area. While it cannot be proved from any evidence observed that the kiln is contemporaneous with the occupation of Shema', it is not improbable that it was. The enormous quantities of plaster used to surface the interior of the synagogue would require large quantities of burnt lime. Such a commodity would not ordinarily be transported great distances, and its preparation at or near an inhabited area is normal.

The function of this circular structure as a lime kiln is undoubted. The stones which face inward are all highly calcined and in some cases there is minor fusing of the siliceous components of the rock because of the intense heat required to decompose carbonate rock. At normal atmospheric pressures a temperature exceeding 950°C is required to achieve the fugacity of carbon dioxide and the breakdown of the carbonate rock to form calcium oxide, the essential material in plaster. In a few places some nearly fused terra cotta hangs between the rocks, evidence of local soil clays used to set the wall rock materials as the kiln was being constructed and perhaps before the earth rampart gave additional support to the wall.

The loading doorway would serve as access not only for the laying of the timber fuel but also for the careful placement of suitable high-carbonate rock in layer-cake fashion as the kiln was being loaded. The same entryway would serve to facilitate the removal of the newly prepared lime before rainfall or dewfall could adversely affect the new product.

It is not surprising to the person who has had an opportunity to do much traveling in Galilee to observe the exotic lithic material shown in photo 2.11. The familiar dark rock which appears on the surface in southeastern Galilee and southwestern Syria is also found as an expression of lava flows which occur to the southeast of Jish (Gush Halav). This scoriaceous alkaline olivine basalt possesses myriads of gas bubbles which were released from the molten lava as it was about to solidify. The material, also correctly described as a highly vesicular basalt, occurred in the occupational levels of Shema'. Variations in the amount of bubbles and overall density of the rock were observed. There is no doubt of the desirability of this lithic material for certain functions of man.

The more dense, less vesicular basalt material was used in the construction of mills (see photo 2.12 for a microscopic thin section of millstone material). The lighter, more frothy lava (not to be confused with pumice) has been observed with faceted sides occurring as a consequence of use as a rubbing, rasping, or scraping stone utensil. The hard physical properties of basalt made it a popular lithic material out of which various tools could be fashioned. This impression is reinforced by the observation that basalt has a high frequency of occurrence in sites all over Israel and especially at Shema', where it does not occur in the local bedrock.

Among the small industrial occupations that occur in the history of Shema', one of the most intriguing is that of the smelting of iron. The evidence is clear that a smelting operation, perhaps on a very small scale, took place at or near the site. Photo 2.13 illustrates a crucible load which hardened in the form of its retainer upon cooling. The view is of the top of the slag-and-iron metal mass, the bottom of which clearly shows a convexity which is indicative of the crucible's form. There can be no doubt of the success of this particular smelting attempt. Photo 2.14 reveals quantities of iron metal suspended in the glassy slag matrix. Whether this represents the residue after most of the molten metal was drawn off or a chilling of the melt before all of its liquid metal content could be recovered cannot be determined. Not discernible in the polished-section photograph are small quantities of pyritic ore material unaltered by this particular smelting run. This poses interesting possibilities for the nature of the iron ore used in this local industry. Were attempts being made to work sulfide ores in addition to the more easily managed oxide iron ore sources?

An entirely unexpected lithic material was observed to occur on the surface of the site immediately before excavation began. The tufa shown in photo 2.15 is exotic to the Shema' environment. The occurrence of tufa, resulting from the precipitation of dissolved minerals on the vegetation growing around thermal springs, was not anticipated at this site. This exotic material may have originated around hot springs to the north of the town of Tiberias, where they were known to be active in the history of that city. The economic value of tufa for the inhabitants of Shema' is not clear, but it may have served a use similar to that of a soft tuff (not shown) found in the actual excavation of the synagogue. This latter material was considerably abraded and polished from being used as a mild rasping or rubbing stone, a function for which tufa also would be well suited. One is tempted to ask whether the presence of lithic materials suitable for mild abrasive rubbing and dressing might not suggest the preparation of sheepskin for parchment writing material, not an altogether improbable hypothesis.

4. MANUFACTURED CONSTRUCTIONAL MATERIAL AT KHIRBET SHEMA'

Since initial study began with the 1970 season, considerable attention has been paid to the plaster materials which occur in the buildings of the site. Plasters were observed on floors, seats, and walls of the main synagogue structure and in all of several hundred samples sent to the excavation workrooms for analysis. Selected samples were shipped to Cincinnati for continued study.

As a result of a careful review of all of these findings, a clear picture of the nature of the interior of the structure emerges. The wall and seats in the synagogue were constructed of local rock material and set in place with a straw-bound mud grouting. The interstone areas were then filled out with a coarse plaster material composed of calcined carbonate rock, often containing the ghosts of noncarbonate materials partially slagged when a silicate composition from the burning combined with a small-pebble- to granule-sized wadi sediment aggregate. The aggregate is composed of the detrital bedrock materials into which the local wadis cut their courses. The sediment is really a fingerprint of the geological environment of each stream. Thus it is not surprising to observe a composite of the local lithic materials mentioned above, subangular to rounded as a consequence of wadi transport, incorporated in the subsurface plaster mixture. Not all of this crude subsurface material was straw-bonded, perhaps because another subsurfacing operation was planned to go over it.

Nearly all the surface plaster observed from the synagogue structure was backed by a special subsurface preparation, a typical example of which is shown in photo 2.16. Layer B in this illustration is composed of a white calcium oxide lime plaster with minor charcoal flecks and incompletely calcined carbonate rock ghosts. Very little silicate slag was observed in this material, which suggests that nearly pure carbonate rock was used in the kiln load for the preparation of this plaster. Aggregate added to make up the subsurface material was less carefully selected than that for the surface plaster. While some instances of small pebble-size calcite crystal cleavage fragments were observed, this is the exception, and most of the lithic material is composed of granule- to small pebble-sized fragments of limestone, dolomitized limestone, chalk, silicified chalk, chert, quartz crystal fragments, carbonate-bonded terra rossa particles, basalt particles (probably derived from occupational wastage of basaltic utensils), all thoroughly blended with a straw or grass binder.

The abundance of the binder in the subsurface plaster shown at B in photo 2.16 is well illustrated in the subsurface-backing/surface-plaster interface shown in photo 2.17. The straw molds saturate the matrix. Several occurrences of the cellulose straw material still entrained in the plaster material were noted.

The surface plaster of the synagogue is quite different from the materials previously discussed. The upper section, A, of photo 2.16 shows a 5-mm surface-plaster section replete with crushed vein calcite crystal fragments or cleavage rhombs. These are very abundant in the plaster, constituting up to approximately 30 percent of its bulk. While a very minor amount of other aggregates, such as granule-size chalk and occasional ceramic fragments, was observed in the surface plaster, the calcite material was clearly dominant. A typical calcite aggregate found in the surface plaster is shown in photo 2.18. A somewhat tedious but rewarding extraction of the aggregate proves its deliberate preparation for the manufacture of surface plaster. Evidently, the calcite material provided a surface-plaster property of structural competence and rigidity which suited the builders' purposes. Calcite may have been chosen because of its nonreactivity with the slaked-lime plaster, which when moist would, within a short time after the surfacing was complete, recarbonate from atmospheric carbon dioxide. Moreover, there would be no reaction from the calcite material that would adversely affect the chemical or physical properties of the plaster surface. Perhaps less surface failure was experienced from spalling or flaking or cracking from the use of this lithic material, which could be obtained from sources in the immediate geological environment.

The plaster in the synagogue structures received additional attention from those who built and maintained these rooms. A hematitic red wash was applied to the plaster walls. Analysis of the red pigment shows the composition to be iron oxide, Fe_2O_3. The red wash has been sufficiently preserved to prove its presence as a deliberate surface decoration in the structure excavated. Early examination of the plaster in the excavation workshops suggested the presence of an orange-and-gray-colored wash on the plaster. Laboratory analysis at Cincinnati now confirms that the orange coloration, appearing on plaster fragments suspended in the occupational debris within the areas under excavation, is the hematitic red plaster, which has undergone partial soil leaching. Hydration of the iron oxide has lightened the depth of the red coloration. It is now understood that the gray coloration is due to contact with materials undergoing combustion, and the color is due in part to the dissemination of carbon particles in the plaster substance. This would occur if the surface were heated sufficiently to partially volatilize the straw subsurface binding. Smoke blackening is not to be ruled out in certain cases.

An additional plaster material was observed to occur in Locus 23001 (SE II.23.49). A crude plaster backing similar to that which was used for filling up masonry spaces in preparation for the type I and type III plaster discussed above, but with an entirely different surface covering applied. Type VI surface plaster, shown in photo 2.19, is unusual for the Shema' site. This plaster has a pink surface coloration, due not to the application of a wash but rather to the abundance of terra rossa particles added to the aggregate. About 25 percent of partially lithified subangular terra rossa fragments are added to this plaster, together with moderately well-rounded limestone, burnt limestone, dolomite, silicified limestone and chalk, terrestrial gastropod shell fragments, and minor crushed ceramic or mud-brick fragments in the granule- to sand-sized range, to make up the surface-plaster mixture. This surfacing was observed to possess good water-retention characteristics in a laboratory test. It is possible that the material surfaced a structure designed for liquid retention. It is the most resistent to abrasion of all the plasters observed.

The state of preservation of the structures of Khirbet Shema' precluded the occurrence of much mud-brick material. That which was observed, however, was instructive. Photo 2.20 illustrates the fact that mud-brick masonry was employed and that it was composed of a terra rossa soil material which occurs yet today in areas upslope on the spur of the site location. The aggregate present in the brick fragment is characteristic of the regolithic composition of the modern soils. The bricks were strengthened with a straw binder.

While not specifically considered to be constructional materials, several surface ceramic sherds were studied in the Cincinnati laboratory. Two examples briefly discussed are not characteristic of all of the pottery by any means, but are nevertheless informative. Photo 2.21 confirms the use of a terra-rossa-rich soil clay in ceramic preparation. The fragility of such material is illustrated by the copious use of grass binding shown in the ceramic section cut parallel or tangential to the direction of the wheel.

A different type of local ceramic is illustrated in photo 2.22, an example of carbonate-rich soil clay being tempered with a wadi sediment which is indigenous to the portions of streams which cross chalk or marl environments. This ceramic material may have been prepared from clays and sediments occurring in the area between Shema' and Safad.

5. CONCLUSIONS

The relationship of the occupants of Khirbet Shema' to their environment becomes a little clearer when we give attention to the materials which were a part of their culture. Like the people in other settlements in the Levant, the inhabitants of Shema' were dependent upon local resources for the commodities of their way of life. That they made good use of the economic geology of north-central Galilee cannot be questioned. We may even look with a higher degree of satisfaction at the microcosm of this site and the social and economic forces which operated to make it what it was. Perhaps it is not impossible to relive some of the more important moments of Shema' and examine the reason for its existence.

BIBLIOGRAPHY FOR CHAPTER 2

Eliezri, I. Z. "The Geology of the Beit-Jann Region Galilee, Israel." *Israel Journal of Earth-Science* 14 (1965) 61–66. The mapping was done in 1959.

Flexer, A.; Freund, R.; Reiss, Z.; and Buchbinder, B. "Santonian Paleostructure of the Galilee." *Israel Journal of Earth-Science* 19 (1970) 141–146.

Shiftan, Z. L. "The Geo-Hydrology of the Safad Region." *Bulletin of the Research Council of Israel* 1, no. 4 (1952) 5–19.

CHAPTER 3. THE SYNAGOGUE AND ITS ENVIRONS

1. BUILDING HISTORY: *Establishing a chronology*

The excavation of the first broadhouse synagogue in Galilee by the Joint Expedition is surely one of the most important aspects of the work at Khirbet Shema'.[1] The fixing of a date for that structure was a long and complicated process. Since the site is located on a spur of Mount Meiron where bedrock juts out everywhere, the occupational debris which has been deposited over the years is not as great as one finds at other ruins and at tells. Sealed remains, therefore, while not absent, are relatively sparse, and we are heavily dependent on them as well as upon ceramic typology and numismatic data to fix our chronology.

The task of dating was simplified by positive identification of materials associated with the first building; they had been buried and thus isolated during the rebuilding after the earthquake of 306 CE, which brought an end to Synagogue I of Stratum III (see sections 4 to 9 infra; the reconstructed building which the visitor to the site beholds is the last phase of Synagogue II of Stratum IV and represents only one of many phases in the cultural and architectural life of the settlement).

The clearest evidence for dating the "synagogues" at Khirbet Shema' comes from the few sealed loci of the 1971 and 1972 seasons. Even though these loci tell us mostly about Synagogue II, when they are combined with certain architectural and stratigraphic clues, a rather detailed history of both buildings emerges. Moreover, the data recovered from the entire site substantially strengthen the chronology proposed below, for it is difficult to imagine a thriving community without a central place of assembly. Cumulatively, therefore, the more general ceramic profile and numismatic picture from the entire site greatly assist in the task of dating.

Critical loci in the synagogue (see fig. 3.1)

The sealed fill within the bema (NE I.31, L.31022). When the interior of the *bema* was examined in an attempt to learn more about the architecture of Synagogue II (see fig. 3.2), it produced just enough coins and pottery to pinpoint

1. So Avi-Yonah, "Ancient Synagogues," 38. Credit for determining the general shape of this building goes to R. A. S. Macalister, in "Remains at Khurbet Shem'a," which provided a remarkable plan (pl. 2) at the beginning of this century. He did not recognize it as a synagogue, however; indeed, he had no suggestions as to its purpose (p. 198).

the date of its construction and thus the date of the building (see photo 3.1).

The *bema*, unexpectedly, proved to have a core of rubble and earth which was absolutely sealed by the stonework of the *bema* around and over it; contamination by later intrusions is virtually impossible. The fill (photo 3.2) contained pottery which was uniformly Late Roman (NE I.31.151 and 152) and two coins: R3854 is a virtually unworn coin of Constans, dating 337–341 CE, and R3855 is Hasmonean (103–76 BCE). Since the *bema* would be one of the last elements of the building to be installed, this information indicates that the repairs were complete and Synagogue II with a *bema* was in existence by the middle of the 4th century. If we assume that a new coin was either deliberately placed in the fill to signal the time of construction, or merely dropped at that time, the date can be moved back a decade.

The declivity in the northwest corner (NW VII.1, L.1052–1060). Sealed beneath more than a meter or so of debris, including large fallen architectural members, and extending nearly 2 m beneath floor level (see fig. 3.2, below) just north of column base no. 1, is a declivity that resembles a storage cave. Entered by four

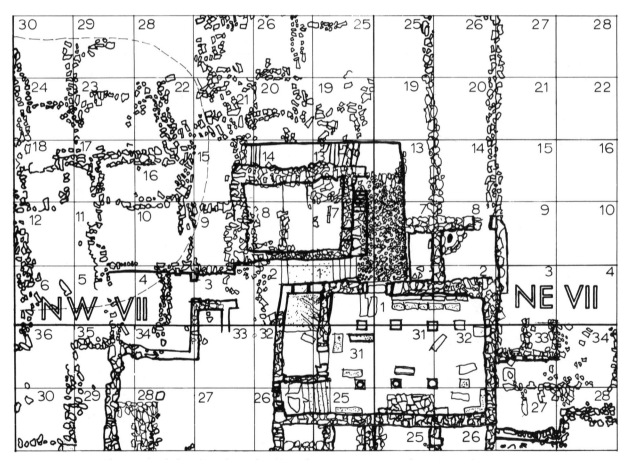

Figure 3.1. Close-up of the site plan, showing the synagogue and excavated areas.

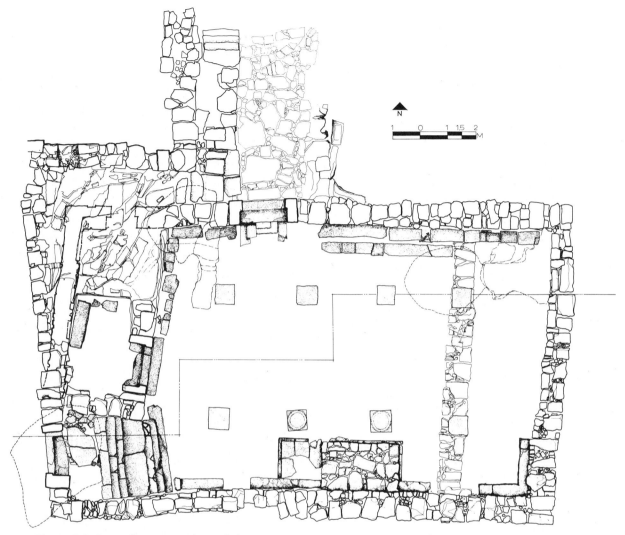

Figure 3.2. Stone-by-stone plan of the synagogue.

steps, each 15–20 cm high, the cave reaches a depth of about 80 cm beneath the cuttings in bedrock. Its mouth is 72 cm below the level of the top of column base no. 1, elevation 745.095. The soil loci recovered from here are L.1052–1060; their pottery reflects a homogeneous Middle-Late Roman horizon. At the lowest levels, however, earlier ceramic forms were to be found, together with one coin of Gratian dating to the later 4th century (R2183) deep in the fill (L.1060), and another coin dated to the emperor Hadrian, 119–38 CE (R2157), was also found in the fill (L. 1056). Great quantities of pithos sherds were also recovered here.

It is very likely that the cave was preexistent to both synagogues, as its typology and manner of construction suggest. Though its usefulness in providing a sealed locus beneath the floor level of the synagogue is of signal importance, it is also clear that the corpus of pottery here and the two coins inform us only of either the latest renovation of the synagogue floor or possibly of a thorough remodeling. The cumulative data here place this event in the late 4th century CE. Since the later coin of Gratian was found deep within the fill, it is obvious that the material above it must be at the very least as late as the coin.

What can have been the cause of so extensive a renovation in the second half of the 4th century? Since the fill in this declivity was full of clay and stone, it was introduced probably to prop up the floor in that corner. Heavy winter rains must have drained into that corner and undermined the floor and perhaps even pedestal no. 1 in the northwest corner, threatening the entire superstructure. We know that water drains into the building from the western threshold, which has channels cut into the slot for the door to drain water into the building. It is also possible that the damage was caused by the earthquake of 365 CE, coupled with excessive winter rains. The fill itself, however, comes from an Early-Middle Roman context, which suggests that the earlier materials might derive from a pre-synagogue phase of the declivity.

That is to say, the very nature of the cave suggests that it belongs typologically to the other bedrock installations and caves which antedate Synagogue I. Since no trace of purposeful storage was found in this declivity, it is wholly unlikely that it was dug during the period when Synagogue II was in use. It is probable rather that the mosaic above the declivity frequently needed attention and that in the late 4th century the northwest corner and possibly the entire floor of the synagogue were repaired; in the process, the workmen repacked the cave to provide a solid make-up for the new floor and part of the north wall. When the building collapsed, probably in the earthquake of 419 CE, this area was buried beneath heavy architectural fall and lay virtually undisturbed till our restoration effort in 1972.

The area west of the Stylobate Wall below floor level (NE I.32, L.32019, 32020). Though these loci are not "sealed" in the technical sense, since the final synagogue floor did not survive, the limited material recovered here, especially L.32020, which represents the material in the crevices of bedrock about 15–40 cm below floor level, should also help to secure the dating of the second building. The pottery is clearly earlier, Middle Roman to Late Roman, with a marked absence of Byzantine wares and forms. The two coins from these loci are of the 1st century BCE (Jannaeus) and 3d century CE (R2259 and R2195). The data are suggestive of an early-4th-century date for the second building, though they are certainly not conclusive. Nevertheless, to find such a ceramic and numismatic mix so deep below floor level has chronological significance. The absence of 4th-century coinage and Byzantine wares and forms thus tends to put the *beginning* of Synagogue II after 306 CE.

The area east of the Stylobate Wall, sealed beneath the plaster surface of the floor (NE I.26, L.26020; unsealed, L.26031). The most important evidence for dating

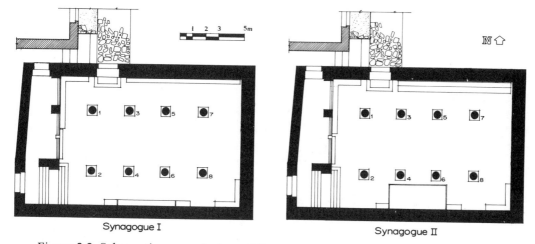

Figure 3.3. Schematic ground plan of Synagogues I and II.

the construction of the second synagogue comes from the southeast corner (see photo 3.3), where both the benches and a large patch of plaster flooring in front of the benches had been perfectly preserved. The surface was penetrated in 1971 and excavated in a single locus (L.26020) to bedrock, a depth of 90 cm below floor level. The pottery from here is homogeneous Late Roman. In an area which is no less "clean," although technically "unsealed" because it was not under the preserved plaster flooring (L.26031), were found two coins of Jannaeus (R2040, R2051), one of Nero, 58 CE (R2148), and one of Trajan, 104–107 CE (?) (R2041). All of this material, from a depth of 50 cm below floor level, was found with homogeneous Late Roman pottery and a marked absence of Byzantine wares and forms.

Once again the data are suggestive of a date for the beginning of Synagogue II around 300 CE. The absence of 4th-century coinage here is also significant.

Destruction by earthquake

It is argued below that the Eagle Doorway and the founding courses of the Western Wall existed—as indicated in the ground plan (fig. 3.3)—in the same alignment in Synagogue II as in Synagogue I. It is therefore important to note that pottery in the soil loci just west of the western entrance and below the level of the threshold is uniformly Late Roman (see NW I.32, L.3202, 32024, 32026, 32027). Other soil loci on the western terrace and associated with the latest use phase of Synagogue II also present a ceramic and numismatic picture that is entirely in accord with other data from the rest of the site.

The destruction date of Synagogue II of Stratum IV can be arrived at with some ease, since there is a sharp break in our coin evidence at Khirbet Shema' after 408 CE. Though most 5th-century coins are produced under Arcadius and

Honorius, early in the century, the best explanation for such a radical break in the coin profile is a sudden abandonment of the site;[2] this is further corroborated by the tumbled and badly shattered debris of Synagogue II. Dating by the closest "strong" earthquake[3] after that of 408 CE, we are able to conclude that Stratum IV occupation and Synagogue II came to an abrupt end in the earthquake of 419 CE. There is a "major" earthquake in 447 CE,[4] but it appears to be ruled out by the fact that there are no coins from the period between 419 and 447 CE. The probability that earthquakes are affecting the Meiron area is extremely high, since Safed is a major epicenter.[5]

The evidence for the destruction of Synagogue I by earthquake emerged dramatically in the course of excavations beneath the floor in the east end of the second building; here we recovered fragments of columns, capitals, and bases all shattered so badly that they could be used only as rubble building material or fill (see photo 3.4). Virtually all we know of the details of the first building comes from these architectural discards. A precise date for this event is provided by the fact that the only "strong" earthquake known for the 3d *or* 4th century is in the winter of 306 CE, a date well in line with the pottery and coin evidence from the site.[6]

The complete analysis of our coin evidence has provided one further piece of information on this point: although Synagogue I surely perished violently — and perhaps much of the rest of the village with it — the community must have remained on the site and quickly decided to rebuild, for there is no break in the coin evidence from the early 4th century. Life at Khirbet Shema' went on after the destruction of Synagogue I, but not after that of Synagogue II.

Strong corroborative evidence for abandonment after 419 CE comes from the authors' excavations at Meiron in 1971 and 1972, where there is also a radical break in the coinage in the early 5th century and no break in coinage around 300 CE.[7] Preliminary studies of the Meiron data, however, do not suggest a major dislocation of the kind we find at Khirbet Shema', where the situation in the synagogue building was such that an insecure column (especially column 1) could easily have brought down the entire structure.

Support for the 306 CE date may be provided by the break in coinage at Chorazin between 340 and 390 CE. The question must be then asked whether it was not the great earthquake of 306 CE which occasioned the statement of the Palestinian Christian, Bishop Eusebius of Caesarea Maritima, who described

2. So Y. Meshorer (orally, July 1973); but see his "Coins from the Excavations at Khorazin," where no such break is indicated.

3. See Amiran, "Earthquake-Catalogue," 225.

4. Ibid. A "major" earthquake is grade 9 and above, "strong" 7–8.

5. Ibid. 54–55, figs. 1–2.

6. See supra n. 3. Earlier the closest earthquake mentioned is dated 130 CE, later, 344 CE. The latter, however, appears not to have affected the site; it is not listed either as "major" or as "strong" by Amiran, "Earthquake-Catalogue," 51.

7. These remarks are based on the preliminary coin report of Richard S. Hanson of the Joint Expedition. For further details see the preliminary report on Meiron in Meyers-Meyers-Strange, "Excavations at Meiron," 22–25.

Chorazin as "desolate" (*eremos*) in his *Onomasticon*,[8] written around 330 CE.[9] What is quite clear is that occupation of the site was not interrupted until the middle of the 4th century, when a combination of factors may have led to the abandonment, possibly even the Gallus revolt of 351–352 CE, as suggested by Meshorer.[10] The sequence we suggest would then be a (partial?) destruction of Chorazin in 306 CE followed by final abandonment in the middle of the century. When viewed together with the evidence from Shema', especially in the light of our recent (1974–1975) work at Meiron, we may reflect that while a catastrophic earthquake may have affected wide areas of northern Galilee, it did not wholly impair the capacity of the people of Shema' and other parts of Galilee to persevere, to rebuild, and to reconstitute themselves as a community as soon as possible.

2. PRE-SYNAGOGUE INSTALLATIONS (See Fig. 3.4)

The town now called Khirbet Shema' antedates Synagogue I. There is clear evidence of earlier use of the space later occupied by this large building, and the earlier occupants are part of a community, not travelers or casual passers-by. The evidence for this is of course the *miqveh* later covered by the northeast corner of the building. We have not discovered where the people who constructed the *miqveh* worshiped—it may have been in Meiron or at an as yet unidentified location on the Shema' hill. If it was a smaller building on or near the site of the later structure, the excavations produced no evidence for it whatever.

Two of the three installations discussed in this section are exposed and still visible on the site: the *genizah* and the *miqveh*. The northwest declivity had to be filled in during the reconstruction of the building in 1972.

Three cavities in the bedrock are indicated with broken lines on fig. 3.4, one below the northwest corner of the building (NW VII.1), another beneath the northeast corner (NE VII.1) and the third directly below the western doorway (NW I.26). The two on the north are earlier than the building; the floor was laid

8. *Onomasticon*, ed. Klostermann, 174; cf. Finegan, *Archeology*, xv, 57. The comment is frequently repeated by later Christian writers; cf. the collection of texts in Baldi, *Enchiridion*, s.v. "Corozain."

9. Eusebius' statement is more trustworthy, perhaps, than statements of later Christian pilgrims who use similar language without visiting the site itself, assuming that the curse upon the city in Matt. 11.21–23 and Luke 10.13–15 had and still has its effect.

10. See Meshorer, "Coins," n.2, and Yeivin, "Khorazin." On other numismatic evidence, see Kloetzli, "Coins from Chorazin." One point in the Kloetzli article should be noted: the coins he discusses are from the ruins of the Chorazin synagogue, most of them in the southwest quarter of the building (fig. 1, p. 359); that most of the coins (66 of the 71 types) were minted after 306 CE indi-

cates that the synagogue lay in ruins for a considerable length of time, though not necessarily indicating a break in occupation before 350 CE. The statement by Loffreda, "Synagogue," 27f, that Eusebius furnishes a *terminus post quem* for the construction of the synagogue at Chorazin appears to be contradicted by Kloetzli's findings. Loffreda has recently repeated this assertion in "The Late Chronology," 37f; but note also Avi-Yonah's comments, "Editor's note," 44; we submit that the Shema' data permit a more likely reconstruction of the Chorazin evidence than Loffreda has given thus far. At Capernaum, 3.5 km away, the situation is somewhat different. The excavators V. Corbo and S. Loffreda indicated (orally, June 1973) that they have no evidence that this site was affected either by the 306 CE earthquake or by the two known for the first half of the 5th century.

over them and they were exposed thereafter (if at all) only during refurbishing and repair of the building. The more regular cavity under the western door was used by the synagogue community and was sealed only by the destruction of the building. As the last declivity in use, it will be discussed last.

The miqveh (ritual bath)

The northeast chamber (L.2029–2030) was discovered in 1971 during a probe under the synagogue floor to gather information about the date and construction of the building. As figs. 3.2 and 3.4 indicate, the bedrock slopes downward to the east so that the eastern quarter of the building had to be founded on an artificial terrace and the floor brought up to level with fill. Thus the north-

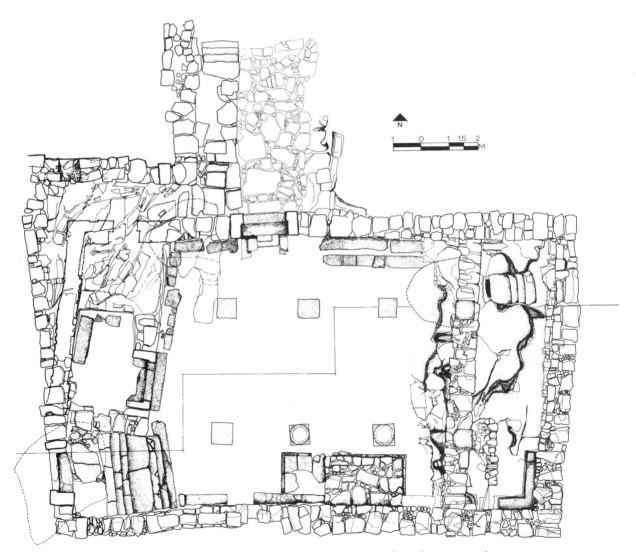

Figure 3.4. Synagogue ground plan, with detail of the *miqveh* at the east end.

east chamber runs back westward into the sloping face of the bedrock. At its deepest it is over 4 m below the synagogue floor. It is roughly egg-shaped in plan; the general impression is of a natural cave with man-made features, chiefly in the regularizing of the entrance, the cutting of a flight of shallow steps leading downward and inside the chamber (see photo 3.5), the preparation of a two-level bench on the right (north) side of the entrance, the deepening of the floor on the opposite side, and the provision of a small depression or sump at the west end of the chamber, opposite the entrance.

Two other features provide a clue to its use. First, the bedrock south of the entrance (visible in photo 3.5 and fig. 3.4 between the Stylobate Wall and the east wall of the building) appears to have been shaped so as to provide passage to the mouth of the stairway leading into the cavity. The shaping is rough (but no worse than that of the stairs) and part of the area is covered now by the foundations of the building so that certainty is impossible. Yet it appears that one approached the cavity along the terrace from the south and that anyone in the chamber was concealed by the bedrock on the north, south, and east. There may have been a similar entrance along the terrace from the north—note the line of bedrock under the floor of the adjoining room in photo 3.6. Certitude is not possible, however, since the area is now obstructed by the foundations of the northeast corner of the building. Second, a mortared channel (L.2039) ca. 45 cm wide was discovered running east-west just north of the entrance to the cavity, at the junction of the north wall and the Stylobate Wall in fig. 3.4. Traces of the channel were found also west of the Stylobate Wall. The cavity is too shallow to be a cistern or other storage installation and bears little resemblance to any of the tombs known from the site. The channel suggests a *miqveh*, and it is known that a similar channel conducted runoff rainwater into the larger *miqveh* on the east slope of the site. These two installations have other similarities also: both resemble bedrock caves which have been adapted to a more specialized use, both are entered via a narrow flight of steps cut into the bedrock, both have hollowed-out floors which may retain a quantity of water even today, both have benches cut in the bedrock above the water level, both utilize the bedrock to conceal occupants from view, both are cramped and awkward to use, and both are characterized by crude construction techniques, at least for the entrance and chamber. It is probable that the larger *miqveh* on the eastern slope is the later of the two and was built when the construction of the synagogue covered the earlier ritual bath.

The northwest declivity

The northwest declivity (L.1052–1060) is smaller and much shallower than the one discussed above; its deepest point is less than 2 m below the synagogue floor. A narrow slot in the bedrock (never more than 60 cm wide) begins just west of pedestal no. 1 and leads due north and down into the chamber, which is directly under the northwest corner of the building (see fig. 3.2). Four steps are provided, the smallest with a tread of ca. 15 cm and a riser of 9 cm; they are very crudely done and are the only worked surfaces apparent in the entire installation. These would have been useful only in the simplest kind of temporary shelter.[11]

The materials relevant for dating recovered from these two cavities have already been discussed; otherwise, their contents were the kind of detritus which might fall into any opening on the surface of an inhabited site: loose earth, pottery fragments, broken domestic items—and a roof roller in the northeast chamber or *miqveh!* Each cavity was directly under a substantial element of synagogue architecture: the northwest corner of the building is squarely over one, with the west doorpost of the north door not far off, and pedestal no. 4 is over the other; in spite of this, there is no indication that the builders of the synagogue tried to strengthen these potential weak spots by filling them tightly with stone. Their casual construction practices may have caused problems. It is likely that the floor over the northwest chamber had to be repaired owing to the insufficient rigidity of its bedding, and it is possible that the Stylobate Wall was built for the second building after the first had collapsed because of weakness in its foundation in just this area. The walls of the northeast corner show the most extensive rebuilding after that destruction.

The genizah

The third cavity visible in fig. 3.2 under the west door of the building is quite different from the two just discussed. They are cavelike in appearance, with a minimum of careful stonework; what we have called the *genizah* is more regular, the flat floor making right angles with the walls. The floor level is only slightly below that of the synagogue floor, so that the chamber is not *under* the main room of the synagogue but *next to* it.

The present entrance is on the north, a square opening 55 cm wide by 56 cm high, 38 cm above the floor of the Frescoed Room into which it leads (see photo 3.7). However, the chamber was earlier oriented not to the north but to the east. The original opening was apparently a square horizontal shaft 61 cm in both height and width; its bottom surface (still preserved) is 37 cm above the chamber floor and 104 cm below the ceiling. The bedrock above the north of this entrance was broken through at a later date, making a much larger, irregular opening which is now blocked on the inside with rough ashlars, and outside, on the east, by the heavy stairs which lead into the main building

11. This cavity may originally have extended somewhat farther to the south and west; the entrance "slot" just described appeared to continue in that direction, but because it passed under the benches against the west wall of the building and perhaps even under the wall itself it was not excavated.

from the west door. The bedrock dips down on the north and east sides of the chamber and becomes rather thin over the eastern and the later northern entrances; it is likely that the damage to the eastern opening took place during the construction of the stairway and that the rough ashlars had first to be laid into the opening to provide support for the stairway. The individual stairs are not cut from the bedrock but are composed of large, long ashlars laid on bedrock. The construction appears to have pierced the bedrock south of the original entrance as well; through the small opening which resulted (visible in the section, fig. 3.5), the back of one of the blocks which make up the stairway is clearly visible.

A glance at the plan of the synagogue and the section drawing depicting the cavity (figs. 3.2 and 3.5) makes clear the eastern orientation of the original cavity; not only was the entrance on the east, but the east side is also the highest (1.4–1.5 m), the chamber roof sloping down from there toward the south and west. There are no indications that this was originally a natural cave, as was the case for the cavities in the northeast and northwest corners. It appears to have been *cut* out of solid bedrock and to have had some human purpose from the beginning; yet it resembles none of the other subterranean installations—tombs, ritual baths, cisterns—elsewhere at Khirbet Shema'. Since it is earlier than the monumental stairway (for the earlier entrance is blocked by the stairway), it is at least earlier than the latest phase of the synagogue, when the stairway was surely in place. Indeed, the eastern access to the chamber could have been utilized by the synagogue community only in the unlikely circumstance that an earlier phase of the synagogue lacked the monumental stairway. Even then the opening would have been awkwardly low, almost at the level of the synagogue floor.

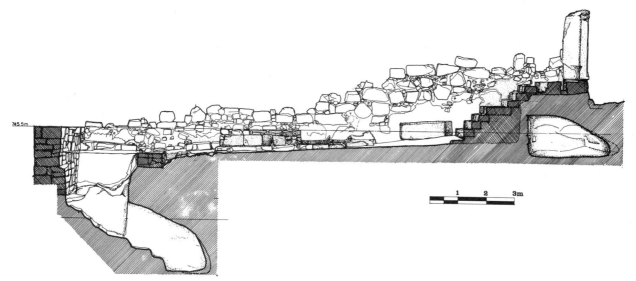

Figure 3.5. East-west elevation and section drawing through the synagogue.

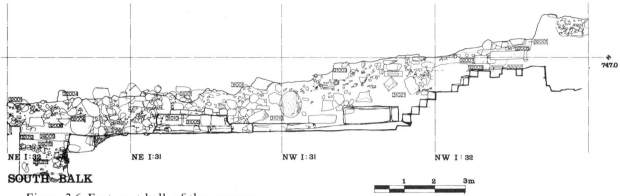

Figure 3.6. East-west balk of the synagogue.

Further, it could not have been constructed until the bedrock east of it had been cut away to form what is now the western end of the floor and the lower portion of the south wall of the synagogue; the natural surface of the bedrock visible in the south wall of the building at its west end (figs. 3.5 and 3.6) would otherwise have been higher than the top of the now blocked eastern access. The western portion of the south wall of the synagogue is known to antedate the eastern portion and therefore the building itself. A seam in the wall behind the *bema* is clearly visible 1.2 m east of the west end of the *bema* and indicates that originally the wall turned southward at that point and ran along the line of the terrace. Only when the building was constructed was the remainder (the eastern portion) of the south wall built; the eastern and western portions do not bond, indicating they are not contemporary. Therefore, the earliest attested use of the area now occupied by the southwest corner of the synagogue is a small terraced area in front of the opening leading to the chamber within, the entire complex of terrace wall, floor, and chamber cut from the living rock. At this stage the chamber was used for storage of some kind, probably in connection with the presses and other installations of the industrial area to the south. The terraced area east of it may not have been open (as in the reconstruction drawing); but if it was built up, all remnants of the walls and the roof were obliterated when the synagogue was built. It is unlikely that both chamber and terrace were connected in their use with the *miqveh* discussed above, since they are on different levels of the natural terracing of the site; however, their periods of use doubtless overlap.

When the first synagogue was constructed, the builders covered over the *miqveh* but made use of the other preexisting features; the terrace surface became part of the synagogue floor, and the terrace wall became part of the south wall of the building. It would have been a simple matter to seal off the chamber, since the west stairway would cover the chamber opening; instead, the small room (now called the Frescoed Room) was prepared, an opening was made in the bedrock between this new room and the chamber, and then the west stairway was installed. This sequence is determined from the fact that some of the stones used to block the earlier, eastern access to the chamber were inserted from inside. Thus the builders worked from the inside of the chamber as well as on the outside during the laying of the west stairway.

What plans did the builders have for this chamber when they fashioned a new access to it and thus made it an element in the synagogue? With its low ceiling and awkward entrance, it was suitable only for dead storage. However, the access could be carefully controlled, and indeed, the small opening could be covered to conceal the chamber completely. Such features strongly suggest that the chamber was intended by the builders to be the community's *genizah*, a place where sacred books and other articles used in the services could be properly disposed of when worn or damaged beyond usefulness. When the first building was violently destroyed, the chamber must have served its purpose; there is no indication that it was damaged in any way. Thus it probably continued as the *genizah* also in the second building.

The contents of the chamber, which date from the time of the synagogue, are discussed in section 18 below.

3. THE EARLIER SYNAGOGUE

While most of the information about these pre-synagogue installations at Khirbet Shema' was recovered in 1971, convincing evidence for an earlier synagogue and a clear impression of the building had to wait until the campaign of 1972. The probe beneath the floor in the northeast corner of the building in 1971 had been intended to provide information about what is now known to be the second synagogue. Coins, pottery, and other evidence sealed under the floor would provide a *terminus post quem* for the latest floor, and similar materials from the foundations could date them and thus the building. But the most important find of the 1971 probe was the ritual bath, earlier than any building known for this location!

While this work was going on, however, more and more evidence accumulated pointing toward a building earlier than the reconstructed present synagogue and later than the *miqveh*. A large stone (NE I.32, AF 18, photo 3.8) in the Stylobate Wall, 0.8 m south of the north pedestal, turned out to be the butt of a column, of a scale similar to the main columns in the reconstructed synagogue and with apophyge. Because it had been laid in at a slight angle from the horizontal, part of it had projected above floor level and had been roughly trimmed back. The drum had been rather carefully made—in contrast to the columns found above floor level, none of which was provided with an astragal, for example. Perhaps the earlier building had been a product of more skill and care, or perhaps more funds had been available for it.

A brief walk in the reconstructed synagogue provides further examples:

the doorposts of the northern and western entrances are as well made as anything in the building. The reason might be that special effort was taken with these particularly conspicuous pieces, except that the lintel for the north door is obviously cruder in workmanship (even though the menorah it bears is the one clearly Jewish symbol known to have been used to decorate and mark the building). The walls of the building for the most part are of almost unworked stone, but a few regular ashlars are visible, particularly just west of the north door; and two or three well-cut blocks with drafted margins were recovered from the debris of the building. Some capitals are obviously better done than others. One or two appear to be recut pieces—that is, earlier, more elaborate designs which perhaps were trimmed back less skillfully later because they had suffered some kind of damage.

But the south row of pedestals is the most convincing example: the two before the *bema* now are simple but well made, each topped with a circular plinth. The pedestal at the east end of the row is very crude, an ashlar of only approximately the same size as the other three; two horizontal grooves attempt to replicate the more elaborate decoration of the two central pedestals. It might be argued that these two are better cut because they are directly before the *bema*, except that the westernmost pedestal was like them originally but has been turned upside down! The explanation appears to be as follows: originally all the pedestals on the south were alike; then the easternmost was destroyed (and the westernmost perhaps damaged on the top). For some reason, only a crude copy could be provided for the destroyed pedestal on the east, so the west pedestal was turned upside down to "match" it, leaving the two finest pedestals as a pair alone in the most important location where the worship was focused.

The Menorah Lintel and the southeast pedestal are thus replacements for earlier architectural elements which had been damaged or destroyed. The destruction apparently shook the building to its foundations, perhaps displacing some of its foundations. The Stylobate Wall had to be repaired, and a damaged column drum was incorporated in it. The 1972 excavations to bedrock on both sides of that Stylobate Wall produced more fragments. Some, like the column drum, were in the building walls, indicating the extent of reconstruction necessary there. Others were not reused even in this way, but were simply dumped outside the building or beneath the floor. These fragments must come from a building which stood on the site of the present synagogue or very close to it, since no one would carry architectural members from somewhere else up the side of the hill of Khirbet Shema' only to use them in the rubble-and-earth fill of the floor. There is ample fieldstone nearby, wholly adequate for that! But the only location discovered on the site for such a substantial structure is the site of the present synagogue.

The most logical way of explaining the variety of evidence just rehearsed is to assume that the earlier building was in the same position and of the same general structure and dimensions as the present one: eight-columned, rectangular, with the main entrances on the north and west as now, and also oriented toward the south. It is highly likely that it too was a synagogue.

Its destruction was catastrophic, not gradual, to judge by the fracturing of some of the architectural members recovered. The most likely cause is an earthquake. The lintel of the north entrance was destroyed, as were some columns and the southeast pedestal. The Stylobate Wall was damaged, along with the northeast corner of the building, including the northern two-thirds of the east wall, an area bearing obvious signs of disturbance and rebuilding.

Though the earlier building may have had the same general plan, orientation, and columnation as the later, there were differences in interior furnishing as well as in quality of construction. The peculiar characteristics of the first synagogue, as far as they can be determined, are discussed in the next sections.

4. THE FIRST SYNAGOGUE: ENTRANCES

The two main entrances of Synagogue II are shown in fig. 3.3. These are also the original doors of the first building. It should not be surprising that they survived the earthquake of 306 CE which destroyed most of the rest of Synagogue I, since the south doorpost of the west doorway also survived the 5th-century destruction of Synagogue II and stands in its original position today. The north doorway endured the earthquake of 306 CE, but collapsed in the final catastrophe of 419 CE, bringing the Menorah Lintel down upon the synagogue floor. Both sets of doorposts remained at least partially exposed thereafter, unlike the capitals, most of which were soon protected from the elements by the windblown earth deposited in the ruins of Synagogue II.

In spite of the action of the elements for a millennium and a half, the evidences of competent workmanship on all four doorposts are clearly visible: the margins are straight and sharp, the moldings simple but well-cut. The design is an exceedingly common one; one suspects that the eagle-in-wreath motif on the south doorpost of the west door (fig. 3.7) was an especially ordered addition to a very standard pattern.[12] The masons appear to have been better artisans than planners; as photo 3.9 shows (cf. photo 3.10), the moldings at the base of the north doorposts have the same pattern, but the one on the east is a good deal higher than that on the west.

The doorposts at Shema' compare favorably with similar elements of the Meiron synagogue,[13] but there is an important difference in construction which may indicate something of the differences between these neighboring communities. At Meiron, the one wall still standing is built of ashlars throughout, in contrast to the roughly dressed fieldstone in the Shema' building. One would expect

12. Macalister, "Remains," 198, pl. 2, notes "another [circular] device, almost defaced" under the eagle-in-wreath; it has now completely disappeared.

13. In examining the ruins at nearby es-Samu'i (192/263), the excavators found a fragment of a doorpost identical to the one at Khirbet Shema'. Similar fragments have been found in the south and in the Golan.

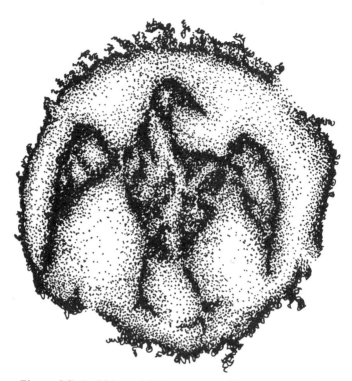

Figure 3.7. Rubbing of the eagle in a wreath, from the western synagogue entrance.

that communities would put the best they could afford into their synagogues. Ashlar is preferable to roughly dressed fieldstone, and most ancient synagogues —even the simplest ones—in the vicinity had walls of ashlar blocks. For some reason this was not done at Shema'. The walls of Synagogue I were not much better than those visible now from Synagogue II. Ashlars, some with dressed margins, were used around the north doorway of the second building; some are still *in situ*, others were found in the fill around the fallen doorposts. They suggest that this entrance was "framed" with ashlars, at least in the part of the wall which would be most readily seen by those entering the building. (There is no evidence of such construction around the west door, an indication perhaps that, at least in Synagogue II, the north door with its entrance area was the more important of the two.) It is unlikely that these random blocks are evidence that Synagogue I was constructed wholly of ashlar masonry; such a supposition would require that almost all of these blocks perished in the building's destruction and that Synagogue II was built from the foundations up, its walls containing almost none of the stone of the earlier structure.

Synagogue I also had certain well-cut pieces of exterior masonry, the doorways chiefly, but probably also the windows, now lost. The lintel with its huge menorah, recovered from beneath the fallen north doorposts, is shown by its inferior workmanship to be almost certainly from the second building; the only fragment which might come from a lintel of the first building is a scrap of bead-and-reel molding (AF 30 from NE I. 32, photo 3.4, extreme right) found discarded in the fill under the floor in the east end of Synagogue II. It is likely that all these pieces were done at the same time, by the same people and in the same style. The two doorways, for example, are of exactly the same dimensions, almost to the centimeter (see figs. 3.2 and 3.3). This fact and their other similarities make it highly unlikely that the entrances for Synagogue I were much different than what we have now from Synagogue II.

Further, all these pieces—the windows, lintels, and other lost elements as well as the doorposts and thresholds—were most probably done on the site, but by hired craftsmen. If village workers had had such skills, we would expect to see more evidence of it throughout the building. It is less likely that the worked pieces were brought completed to the site, either from a ruined building or from a stoneworks elsewhere; Shema' is probably too remote and its hillside site too precipitous for that.

5. THE FIRST SYNAGOGUE: THE TORAH SHRINE

In the partially reconstructed synagogue (fig. 3.10), plastered benches project from the east and west ends of the *bema*. Excavation within the *bema* showed that these are in fact elements of a single bench which ran along much of the south wall during a pre-*bema* phase of the building. Photos 3.1 and 3.2 show a section of this bench, plaster still intact, within the *bema*.

Dating evidence from inside the *bema* proves that it is an element of Synagogue II only; it marks a change in interior furnishing, but not in orientation. The earlier building always had an orientation toward the south, as is indicated by the fact that the south row of pedestals is clearly more elaborate than the north row. Its earliest phase *may* have lacked the plastered bench on the south wall, but it is equally possible that the bench is an original feature and not a later addition to the first building. In any case, the bench for Synagogue I and the *bema* for Synagogue II are well-attested elements of the interior of the building.

Excavations in 1972 provided evidence which suggests that sometime before Synagogue I was destroyed, a Torah shrine had been built against the south wall, partially covering the bench. As was indicated in the discussion of building phases above, elements of the first building which were damaged beyond use were dumped in the fill under the floor during the reconstruction after the earthquake of 306 CE; the 1972 excavations beneath the floor produced a number of architectural fragments which are necessarily earlier than the second synagogue and have no parallel in what was recovered from that second building. They include a clearly identifiable column base half the size of the present pedestals, and fragments which appear to come from a similar base or bases, as well as column and capital fragments of the same scale.

The base (NE I.32, AF 28, fig. 3.9 and photo 3.11) was recovered, in fill, 10 cm west of the Stylobate Wall (L.32018.1) and just beneath the level at which the floor of the second building had been laid. The base is 19 cm high, and while none of its sides is preserved to its full length, they were approximately 31 cm each. The column which the base supported would have been ca. 25 cm in diameter.[14]

Four important fragments were found together in the fill under the stone benches at the east end of the north wall of the building (NE VII.2, L.2034, bucket 84, photo 3.4). Three of them are from a small capital or capitals adorned with acanthus leaves. From the largest (AF 22) it is possible to determine that it

14. It is tempting to suggest that the other pedestal of the Torah shrine was a local copy of the one just discussed, but the evidence for such a copy is insufficient. Two joining fragments of an architectural piece of the same diameter as the top of our pedestal were recovered some ten meters apart in the fill under the floor west of the Stylobate Wall. They are NE I.26, AF 20, L.26029, and NE VII.2, AF 18, L.2033. When joined they are 16 cm wide, 9 cm high, and a maximum of 2 cm thick; the workmanship is less finished than that of the pedestal just discussed. They are the sort of thin splinters which might be produced if the round top of such a pedestal were struck a hard, glancing blow—but no other fragments were ever found.

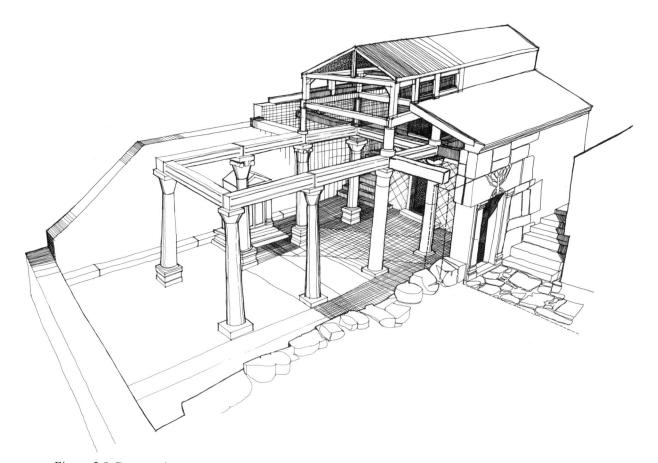

Figure 3.8. Perspective cutaway of the synagogue.

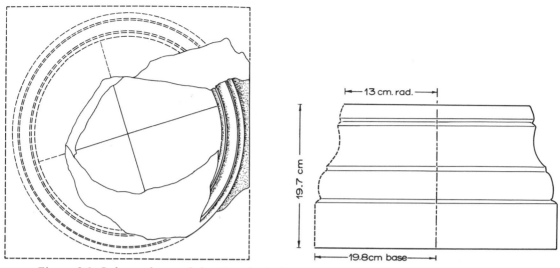

Figure 3.9. Column base of the Torah shrine.

fitted a column 22–24 cm in diameter. Another (AF 23) displays a smaller area of the lower surface of a capital of similar dimension, while a third (AF 21) preserves a small area of the decoration intact. Found with these was AF 20, a fragment with a comb-chiseled horizontal surface and, at a right angle to it, a double molding somewhat different from that of the base described above. Consistency was not a hallmark of this architecture, and this may be a fragment of the top of a base of the same size and purpose, or perhaps of the top of the column which rested on such a base. The diameter of the piece from which it comes would be about 25 cm.

In a neighboring square, another locus (NE I.32, L.32019), ten meters away and on the other side of the Stylobate Wall, produced a fourth fragment (AF 41) with acanthus decoration very similar to that described above and an undecorated segment of the bottom of another capital of the same diameter (AF 39).

Parts of the columns for such capitals and bases were also recovered (photo 3.8). The largest, AF 31 from NE VII.2, was built into the north wall of the building, east of the Stylobate Wall. Three more (NE I.32, AF 32, 37 and 40) were recovered from the fill beneath floor level. Each preserves enough of the drum to permit accurate measurement of the original diameter, 25 cm.

The dozen pieces just described were all badly battered, an indication of the swift violence with which the first building was destroyed. The base may not have fallen any great distance, since it would have been located at or near floor level, but whatever fell upon it broke off nearly a third of it; and the fragments of columns and capitals, which fell from greater heights, are shattered sometimes into jagged splinters. For this reason, some dimensions given above must be approximate, but it is certain that all the fragments are of the magnitude of architecture one would associate with a column diameter of 25 cm. This figure is less than half the average diameter of the columns and capitals recovered from above the floor and for the most part reerected. They were used in the second building, though most come from the first synagogue; and their diameters range from 47 to 62 cm. At the same time, pieces in the smaller scale are often more elaborately and usually more carefully done, suggesting that they come from an important and even central element of the building. This makes it unlikely that they are pieces of the roof supports or the gallery railing, two areas to which it has been suggested they might belong. Rather they are probably pieces of a Torah shrine destroyed with the collapse of the first building and replaced in the second building not with another shrine but with the *bema*.

Torah niches in walls are common in synagogues of the Roman and Byzantine periods in Israel[15] and the Diaspora,[16] and actual shrines or *aediculae* have been found in the 3d- or 4th-century synagogues of Dura-Europos on the Euphrates River, Sardis in western Asia Minor, and Ostia, the port of ancient Rome.[17] The Torah shrine or Ark of the Law is ubiquitous in Jewish religious art of the Roman and Byzantine periods,[18] a convincing indication of its importance in the life of the synagogue. These representations have a certain consistency which makes clear the standard features of such a structure. If visible, the scrolls are usually represented as resting on shelves and extending horizontally back into the *aedicula;* often only the scroll ends are to be seen. The double doors or curtains provided to cover the scrolls may be closed, concealing the scrolls completely, or they may be partially or fully open. They are flanked by columns supporting a gabled or rounded roof.[19] As is the case with other *aediculae* in ancient architecture, the surface or "floor" of the Torah shrine is higher than the floor of the room in which it stands, so that a small flight of stairs is customary before the curtains or doors. Fig. 3.8 suggests the appearance of the Torah shrine in Synagogue I; it is based on the standard pattern described above and on the fragments recovered in the 1972 excavations.

The earthquake which destroyed the first synagogue also shattered the shrine to such an extent that its elements were not reused but simply dumped in the subfloor fill. It is unlikely that Synagogue II contained a similar structure. All the fragments described to this point were found below the synagogue floor or built into its walls; thus they are from the first building, not the second. One might argue that the change from *aedicula* (in Synagogue I) to *bema* (in Syna-

15. Goodenough, *Jewish Symbols*, XIII, 150–51, "niche."

16. Ibid. Cf. references also on pp. 191–192, "Torah Shrine."

17. Dura: Goodenough, *Jewish Symbols*, IX, ch. 5 and the illustrations thereto, ibid. XI. Sardis: the best photographs and plans are now in Hanfmann, *Letters from Sardis*, esp. figs. 167f, 217. Ostia: Squarciapino, "The Synagogue at Ostia," passim.

18. For an exhaustive collection of the evidence see Goodenough, *Jewish Symbols*, IV, 99–144, and XIII, 191–192.

19. On the significance of the shell or conch motif frequently found between the roof line and the tops of columns, see R. Chachlili, "Sacred Architecture" and a forthcoming work in *BASOR*, preliminarily presented at the World Congress of Jewish Studies, Aug. 1973. Cf. *Jewish Symbols*, XIII, 179, "shell."

gogue II) is too radical to have happened in the relatively brief period—less than a generation—between the two buildings, so that there must have been an *aedicula* in Synagogue II as well. It would be possible to explain the absence of evidence by hypothesizing that no remains of a shrine were found from the second building because these would have been smaller, probably finer architectural fragments and were removed and reused by later occupants or passersby. However, the *bema* (which on this interpretation would have been a foundation of the *aedicula*) and the south wall are well preserved, and there is on them no trace of the existence of such a shrine. Even if every one of its architectural members had been removed, some mark of its location or foundation is to be expected. It is thus more likely that there was no stone *aedicula* in the second building as there was in the first, and that from the time the second synagogue was built, the space before the center of the south wall was occupied by a *bema* whose width and depth were as they are in the present structure.

On this interpretation, one question remains: What assumed the function of the Torah shrine in the second building? That is, where were the scrolls housed in the later synagogue? In most previous excavations, if a synagogue was provided with a *bema*, it also contained a Torah shrine or niche on the same wall, usually the side of the building closest to Jerusalem. Thus worshipers facing the *bema* at Dura or Beth Alpha or Eshtemoʻa also faced the Torah and the Holy City. And if the *bema* and the scrolls are on different sides of the building, as at Ostia, the Torah and not the *bema* is on the wall of orientation, closest to Jerusalem. Scholarly tradition thus would expect a housing for the Torah on the orientation wall, the south wall, at Khirbet Shemaʻ also. The wall behind the *bema* is never more than 90 cm thick and is preserved to a maximum height of 80 cm above the surface of the present *bema*. There is no evidence for a niche in the wall, nor does there appear to have been sufficient space for one.

But the shrine could have been wooden, fastened to the wall or standing on the *bema* against the wall; Jewish art provides many representations of the sort of double-doored chest which was customary for this purpose.[20] The actual wooden shrines have perished, of course; none has been found at Khirbet Shemaʻ or in any other excavation. But there is ample space on the present *bema*, and that is the likely location for any structure assuming the same function in the second building which the stone Torah shrine served in the first. And while it is unlikely that a stone *aedicula* could perish without leaving a mark behind, wooden shrines almost always vanish without a trace![21]

This explanation is already "unorthodox," of course; the usual understanding of the development of ancient synagogues requires that the wooden Torah

20. *Jewish Symbols*, IV, 99–144; Sukenik, *Ancient Synagogues*, 52f.

21. Those who postulate the existence of a wooden shrine or Ark of the Law in a specific synagogue usually base their statements on iconographic and literary evidence, not on actual finds, e.g., Capernaum, Chorazin, Barʻam, Meiron. Bits of bone and ivory found on the apse floor of the Maʻon synagogue were identified as remnants of a wooden ark. J. Pinkerfeld, "David's Tomb," 7, 14, 16.

shrine be always earlier than the *aedicula,* the assumption being that a wooden structure is less impressive than one made of stone. (On this interpretation, the full apse which characterizes the synagogues at Beth Alpha and Hammath by Gadera is the most impressive of all ancient repositories for the scriptures.) However, it would appear that the real question is not "wood or stone?" but one of impressiveness; this is not a matter of building codes, but of religious iconography and liturgical impact. The builders of Khirbet Shema' demonstrate a creativity and a certain freedom from the constraints of tradition, and there are indications that the level of expenditure was lower for the second building than for the first. If the resources or skills were not available to replicate the stone *aedicula,* the second building may have contained a splendid Ark of wood, textile, and other materials which stood on the *bema* and has perished without trace.[22]

6. THE FIRST SYNAGOGUE: BENCHES

The literary and the archaeological evidence agree that benches were a common feature of most ancient synagogues; indeed, in what Goodenough calls the "Galilean type" and Avi-Yonah the "earliest" type, benches are almost the only permanent interior fitting.[23] All the "broadhouse" synagogues fully excavated thus far have benches on at least two walls and always on the wall of orientation, closest to Jerusalem.[24]

The excavation of Synagogue II revealed a variety of benches from different periods and from both the earlier and the later buildings. Some are very late, e.g., those which make up the southernmost row along the north wall east of the north doorway; they are rough ashlars, one of astonishing length (2.4 m, NE VII.1, L.1010 = 2, L.2020), only approximately in line. Others are better cut and positioned, but still obviously secondary, e.g., AF 26 in NW I.31 on the south wall immediately east of the west stairway, set flush with the wall and placed rather carefully with small leveling stones beneath. All of these are clearly not integral to Synagogue II but were added later to increase its capacity.

A third group is the most likely to have come from Synagogue I and survived its destruction: the bench in the southeast corner of the building (see photo 3.12) and the one which runs behind the *bema* and protrudes from its east and west ends. They are made up of a number of roughly dressed ashlars (as photo 3.13 indicates) laid tightly against the already plastered walls of the building; they are covered both on the top and the front with another thick

22. An alternative hypothesis is that the Frescoed Room held some or all of the scrolls of Synagogue II. See infra section 18.

23. Goodenough, *Jewish Symbols,* I, 181–225; Avi-Yonah, "Ancient Synagogues," 32; generally on synagogue benches see Krauss, *Synagogale Altertümer,* 386–389, and Sukenik, *Ancient Synagogues,* indexes, s.v.

24. For Eshtemo'a, north and south walls, see Yeivin, "The Synagogue at Eshtemo'a," 43; for Susiya, north, south and west walls, Gutman et al., "Synagogue at Khirbet Susiya," 47; for Dura, all four walls in both the earlier and later building, see Goodenough, *Jewish Symbols,* III, figs. 593f.

layer of plaster. The bench along the south wall runs continuously for more than six meters. The *bema* of Synagogue II is built in front of it and over it; thus the bench antedates the *bema*. It also must have antedated the *aedicula* of Synagogue I and thus represents the earliest known phase of the earlier building. The *aedicula* was built over the bench as the *bema* was later. This seems certain from the parallels in other early synagogues and is not contradicted by the fact that the floor beneath and the wall behind the benches were found to be plastered. The craftsmen of Shema' commonly finished off a room with floor and wall covering *before* they laid in the benches, which were then plastered as well. The plaster behind the benches, therefore, does not come from an earlier, non-bench phase of Synagogue I.

The fourth group of benches is also plastered, like those just discussed, and they may all be contemporary, dating from Synagogue I. These are the bench in the northwest corner of the main room and the section of plastered bench against the north wall and just east of the north door (NE VII.1, L.1009). Here the plaster is damaged and the stone blocks more disturbed, so that it is no longer possible to say whether they are from Synagogue I or are attempts to replicate in Synagogue II the benching of the earlier building.

The destruction of Synagogue I took out the northeast corner of the building, damaging foundations there and eliminating everything at floor level and above. It is likely that the benches in this area, which were destroyed, were similar to those on the south which remained. The shock was violent enough to require some rebuilding of the Stylobate Wall as well. It is possible that the gap in the benching on the east end of the south wall resulted from this operation, when the bench was cut to get underneath it. Given the evidence of the other broadhouses, it would not be unusual to find benches nearly all around the room, as in the architect's reconstruction, fig. 3.3.

7. THE FIRST SYNAGOGUE: THE WESTERN WALL

"Western Wall" is a brief way of referring to that area of the synagogue— at whatever level—which is farther west than the lowest step of the western stairway. It was easily the most complicated part of the building to excavate, for habitation occurred intermittently here for centuries. The west wall and doorway of the synagogue survived the destruction of the rest of the building and were incorporated into a series of later structures. A curving wall (NW I.31, L.31002 = NW I.32, L.32006) had been attached to the western doorway of the destroyed synagogue to form a small building sometime in the Arab period; the wall stood over a meter high when excavation was first begun in 1970. Its founding level was 1.5 m above the synagogue floor, an indication of the time which had passed between the destruction of the synagogue and the later construction.

Quantities of domestic debris—basalt grinders, smashed Arab pottery—were also recovered at these higher levels.

This long history of post-synagogue construction together with the height of the bedrock and the skimpiness of the topsoil have eliminated all traces of the exterior wall in the northwest corner of the building and made it very difficult to trace the line of the west wall.[25] The unusual "broken" west wall in the ground plan, fig. 3.3, was not revealed in the excavations but is the product of a deduction from three solid pieces of architectural information visible in the synagogue plan, fig. 3.2: viz., (i) the west doorway threshold and stairs are all parallel to each other, but are not quite at right angles to the south wall of the building, (ii) the entrance to the Frescoed Room and the portion of the main room west interior wall north of that entrance are all in line, a line that is not quite perpendicular to the north wall, but (iii) the line is parallel to the mortared wall which is the west wall of the Frescoed Room. A face of bedrock *may* continue the line of the mortared wall to the north and may represent the line of the wall foundation at that point, but the bedrock is crudely worked and is disregarded for the present purpose. The reader may judge for himself on the basis of fig. 3.2, which shows the north end of the mortared wall and the entirety of the bedrock face.

The three pieces of evidence just listed prove that the west wall of the building was not a straight line, but bowed out slightly, breaking between the west stairs and the Frescoed Room. The result is an unusual plan on the west, but the explanation is surely to be found in the fact that the first building incorporates preexisting elements. To include them and to work with the bedrock in this area required the wall lines described here. The gallery too would have been parallel to the west interior wall of the main room and the mortared west wall of the Frescoed Room. This was all to the good, since the result is to make it face slightly toward the south wall of the building, the focus of worship in all periods.

The wall described above, with its massive stairway and its gallery canted slightly toward the wall of orientation, represents one of the most complicated pieces of synagogue architecture known from the ancient world also because of the complex way the terrain has been utilized in construction. The Shema' site is terraced, and the synagogue spans three terrace levels: while most of the floor has as its foundation the cut bedrock of one terrace, the east end of the building extends over the next terrace down. Thus the east wall and the eastern ends of the north and south walls are founded on the lower terrace. Like retaining walls, they contain the fill which forms the bedding for the eastern one-third of the synagogue floor.

25. This complexity and the difficulties involved in interpreting the evidence are both apparent in Meyers-Kraabel-Strange, "Archaeology," 10, fig. 5, where the tangle of later walls north of the western door appears to be the actual exterior west wall of the building; the stone-by-stone drawing, supra fig. 3.2, is more in line with what the actual walls must have been. We regret that our preliminary plan has also misled Avi-Yonah; cf. the simplified plan he gives in "Ancient Synagogues," 37.

The Western Wall area involves another terrace, the highest of the three. The west doorway stands upon it, and the western stairway leads from that level down to the main room of the synagogue, a drop of more than two meters from the threshold of the west door to the floor beneath the lowest step. Thus, just inside the synagogue's exterior west wall, there is an area much of which is almost three meters higher than the synagogue floor and which encompasses the western entrance and stairway, the chamber beneath the stairway, a small frescoed room in the center of the Western Wall area, and the bedrock outcropping upon which the northwest corner of the building is founded. These features in the Western Wall area provide most of what is unusual and even unique in this synagogue. They exist as a result of the creativity of the anonymous designer or designers of the building, who saw the three-level site as an asset, not a liability.[26]

When the builders approached the Shema' site, they realized that any entrance from the west would have to be located at the level of the upper terrace. Two features from earlier occupation were already present, possibly still in use: a man-made cavity cut westward into the bedrock and a small rock-cut terrace in front of it on the east. In brief, their decisions were the following: (i) to establish the west doorway directly over the storage cavity with a broad stairway leading from the doorway down to the level of the small terrace which now became the southwest corner of the floor of the new synagogue; in the process the original entrance to the storage chamber was covered; (ii) to cut a small room into the irregular, fractured bedrock just north of the storage chamber; and (iii) to erect a gallery for the synagogue at about the level of the upper terrace. The northern end of this gallery was founded on the bedrock outcropping at the northwest corner of the new building and it terminated at the south with a broad landing which served also as the first step east of the threshold of the west door. The stairway, chamber, and Frescoed Room may be located on the ground plan of the synagogue, fig. 3.3.

The gallery apparently occupied the same space and location in each building, and for anyone in the synagogue it must have been the outstanding feature of the Western Wall; however, relatively few elements of its structure were recovered in the excavations, perhaps because they would have been constructed chiefly of wood. A mortared wall (NW I.32, L.32008) supported the gallery on the west where it passed over the Frescoed Room; the rest of the flooring must have been founded chiefly on natural rock outcroppings (see photo 3.14).[27]

26. The contrast with the Meiron synagogue is startling and instructive: there a large knob of bedrock was selected as the site for a thoroughly conventional basilica, a duplicate of those at Bar'am (10 km) and Gush Halav (3 km) to the north; this simple design requires a flat surface, however — the latter two buildings are located in open fields — and to create this surface the Meiron builders cut a huge notch into the bedrock of the site and located the building in it. Thus, while the plan of the Meiron synagogue closely resembles those of its two northern neighbors at first glance, only the Meiron building has an entire wall of smooth-faced bedrock instead of more usual architecture! Compare Goodenough, *Jewish Symbols*, III, fig. 506 with figs. 505 and 519.

27. The rough working of bedrock which would have been under the north end of the gallery has already been discussed above.

On the north the quantity of rough bedrock still visible would be sufficient for this purpose. On the south the bedrock over the *genizah* and under the stairway was less ample and was supplemented with masonry by the builders. On the east there must have been a railing or perhaps a screen between the gallery and the main room of the synagogue; this would have been founded upon the lintel of the one entrance to the Frescoed Room and upon the interior west wall of the main room which was in line with it. The architectural details of the gallery floor and above were lost in the destruction of the first building, but the general appearance would be as shown in the architect's reconstruction, fig. 3.10.[28] Its dimensions, approximately 3 × 7 m, indicate that it would have supplemented the floor space of the main room by nearly 20 percent.

There is one obvious place to enter the gallery: from the south, after entering the building by the west door. However, if we assume that the gallery was for women, as most scholars do—though the serious objections of S. Safrai are yet to be adequately dealt with[29]—and that there was strict separation of the sexes in the Khirbet Shema' synagogues, we may view it as unlikely that men and women would enter the building by the same door, the women then turning north into the gallery, the men continuing down the stairs into the main room.[30] There may have been a barrier or wall at the south end of the gallery, blocking any access via the west door.

It appears likely that Synagogue II had a northern entrance to its gallery, since the passage running east-west between the synagogue and the North Building was regularized during that period, and the most obvious reason for such an improvement would be to provide relatively easy access to the north door of a "women's gallery." Without this east-west passage one would have had to clamber over rough bedrock to reach the hypothetical north door of the gallery from the entrance courtyard before the north door of the building. If there were a small north door to the gallery in Synagogue I, it could have been approached from the west only, where the terrain is relatively flat; or there may have been only the one entrance, from the south, via the building's west door.

On this issue, for the first building, there is no strong archaeological evidence either way. The bedrock in that area was so close to the surface and thus so exposed that all trace of the west end of the north wall has been lost; only a small depression in the bedrock remains, where the threshold of the small gallery door might have been laid—but perhaps only for the second building! This question apart, the gallery for Synagogue I must have been as de-

28. On the gallery, cf. Goodenough, *Jewish Symbols,* XIII, index s.v. "Balcony"; Krauss, *Synagogale Altertümer,* 355–357; the three works by Sukenik, *Ancient Synagogue of Beth Alpha,* 16–19; *Ancient Synagogue of El-Hammeh,* 72f. (literary references); and *Ancient Synagogues,* 47–49.

29. Safrai, "Was There a Women's Gallery in the Synagogue?" 329–338. In this article Safrai maintains that the literary sources do not permit the interpretation that women were excluded from the synagogue proper. On the contrary, he asserts, women and children participated in public worship and in the scriptural reading. Such is the case also for synagogues in the Diaspora.

30. On the question of the gallery, Chachlili (supra n. 19) maintains that it is absolutely characteristic of all synagogues, a view vigorously attacked by Safrai, 336f.

scribed above, in spite of the fact that no other ancient synagogue known from archaeological or literary evidence contained a gallery only on *one* side wall. For this site there was no other simple way the builders could have included a gallery while orienting the building to the south. And there is no other simple explanation for what was revealed in the excavation of this part of the site.

The Frescoed Room under the gallery received such a designation from the fact that traces of red paint were found on the plaster preserved on the lower levels of all four of its walls. This embellishment is an indication of the room's importance; a logical reason for that importance is that it was used to store articles in active use in the building, for example, certain *megilloth* and other objects connected with synagogue services or ritual. We have already educed evidence for a stone *aedicula* as the Torah shrine of Synagogue I. Thus the Frescoed Room was probably more important to Synagogue II than to Synagogue I and *may not have been* as elaborately decorated in the first building. It existed in both buildings, but it may have been a *frescoed* room only in the later.

It should also be made clear that there is no archaeological evidence from the room or the chamber south of it which pertains *only* to Synagogue I. Since both areas were in use until the last destruction of the building, this continual use obliterated any features peculiar to Synagogue I. Thus what can be said for

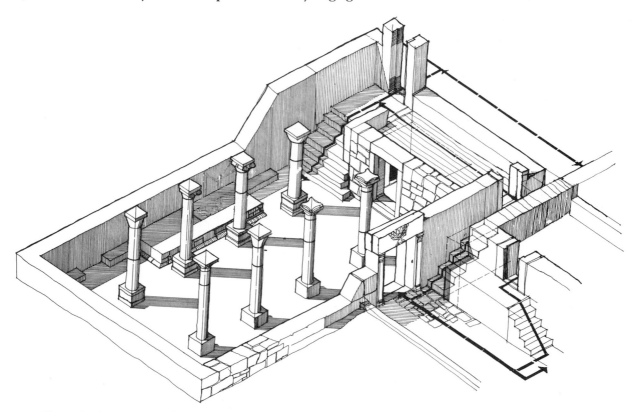

Figure 3.10. Isometric drawing of the synagogue, with traffic patterns.

this area for Synagogue I is based on comparisons with similar rooms associated with other ancient synagogues.

The general plan of the room is clear from the ground plan. It was over 2 m high, judging from the height of the doorpost and the preserved elevation of the mortared wall (NW I.32, L.32008) upon which the floor of the gallery above had been founded. The only entrance was from the east, from the main room of the building. The threshold and doorposts, still in place, show that the entrance was provided with a pair of doors which swung into the Frescoed Room. The placement of the locking hole in the threshold indicates that the doors were secured from outside, from the main room, at least in one phase of use. The doors would have been wooden, and each of the pair was nearly 2 m high and 0.75 m wide; they would have borne a striking resemblance to the tall, narrow double doors familiar from Jewish art in representations of the front of a Torah shrine.[31] However, any attempts to make a Torah shrine out of the Frescoed Room or to suggest one in its architectural details must pertain to Synagogue II; the *aedicula* on the south wall had this function in Synagogue I.

As the plans make clear, the Frescoed Room was wholly *within* the building and its only entrance is from the main room of the building. This is unusual, since most of the "side rooms" known from other ancient synagogues are beside or outside the building.[32] It is not always clear that they are an integral part of the synagogue complex; indeed, it is sometimes obvious that a room is used for synagogue purposes in one period, but not in another.

Not only is the Frescoed Room integral to the Shema' building, it must also have been an original element in the building. There is no way of building on this site, with its preexisting storage chamber (*genizah*) and small terrace, without dealing with the bedrock in this area. A close examination of the walls of the Frescoed Room reveals that none is of solid bedrock.[33] Each is to some degree built up with rough stone blocks, a procedure similar to that used in the walls of the main room. The bedrock over the chamber to the south proved to be quite thin in the east and north and at some point apparently collapsed at the northeast corner, suggesting that also in the area now occupied by the Frescoed Room the bedrock was fissured and uneven and sloped off to the east. The builders could either build up the area to the level of the footings of the gallery, or they could cut back the bedrock at the center of the Western Wall and add to the usable space of the building by creating a side room. They chose the latter alternative, in part perhaps because this was the only way the preexisting chamber could be utilized, now that its original access on the east was to be sealed off by the new stairway.

31. For example, the frieze from Peqi'in, west-southwest of Shema', published frequently, e.g., Sukenik, *Ancient Synagogues*, 54, fig. 13, and Goodenough, *Jewish Symbols*, III, fig. 573.

32. In addition to the standard collection of plans in Goodenough, *Jewish Symbols*, Sukenik, *Ancient Synagogues*, and the like, see now those in Avi-Yonah, "Ancient Synagogues," 36f.

33. The language of Meyers-Kraabel-Strange, "Archaeology," particularly at p. 15, gives a misleading impression and should be corrected.

We can only hypothesize the use or uses of the room within Synagogue I. The chamber to the south likely became the community's *genizah.* The Frescoed Room allowed easy access to it and in addition may have been used to store the *megilloth* which could not be accommodated in the *aedicula* on the south wall. Although a bit small for the purpose, it could have been used as a place to study and even to make copies of Scripture. However, it is equally likely that the room had no definite purpose in Synagogue I except to provide access to the *genizah* and as a handy place for miscellaneous storage. Its period of real significance may have begun only with the building of Synagogue II, to which time then the frescoed decorations should also be assigned. The *genizah* itself was a feature of the synagogue from its beginning, and it is reasonable that the secondary opening to it, from the Frescoed Room on the north, was also cut when Synagogue I was built. There would have been no access to the chamber otherwise, since the broad stairway leading into the building from the west blocked the chamber's original entrance.

8. THE FIRST SYNAGOGUE: THE COLUMNS

The pedestals, columns, and capitals in Synagogue II are taken, in large part, from the earlier building. Some had been damaged, however, and a few were beyond reuse so that replacements had to be made. Going on the general assumption that the first building was characterized by better workmanship than the second, it is possible to decide in many cases which elements come from Synagogue I.

In fig. 3.3 the pedestals are numbered 1 through 8, even numbers on the south row, smallest numbers to the west in each row. Thus the pedestal in the northwest corner is no. 1, the two before the *bema* are no. 4 (on the west) and no. 6. The pedestals on the north (nos. 1, 3, 5, and 7) are undecorated ashlar blocks of about the same depth and width but of varying heights. Simple and crude as they are, it appears that they are from Synagogue I; to argue otherwise would require that all four north pedestals from the first building were destroyed in the earthquake of 306 CE, an unlikely assumption in view of the fact that in the south row only one of the four had to be replaced. If the north row of pedestals was left plain in the first building, and all four in the south row looked the way nos. 2 and 4 do now, the intent must have been to mark the south wall as the important wall, the wall toward Jerusalem.

Three of the four south pedestals are original. No. 8 had to be replaced and no. 2 was turned upside down in an attempt to "match" it and to allow nos. 2 and 4 to be particularly distinctive, since they stood in front of the newly installed *bema.* Originally nos. 2, 4, 6, and 8 were provided with circular plinths and upper and lower moldings, as in the reconstruction drawing, fig. 3.8. Two plinth fragments which appear to be from damaged or destroyed pedestals have been recovered, one from under the floor of Synagogue II (AF 27, NE I.32), the other from beneath the floor of a room south of the building (AF 35, NE I.26).

The columns in Synagogue II are plain unfluted cylinders averaging 47–62 cm in diameter. One column fragment now in the Stylobate Wall (AF 18, NE I.32) has a slight concavity (see photo 3.8 and supra section 3.3), and the implication is that other columns in Synagogue I were similar. All seven capitals are round in plan, not square, at the point at which they meet their columns; what are here called "plinths" are also round (pedestals nos. 4 and 6), an exception to the usual square plinth of classical architecture. In the north row, however, the pedestals are perfectly plain and square, and it would seem likely that the columns with apophyges were located here, *if* we assume that a round plinth or the round bottom end of a capital would appear inharmonious next to the concavity. This is a twentieth-century judgment in harmony with the classical canons, and it is what the reconstruction drawing, fig. 3.8, shows. But Shema' builders have different preferences than we might expect at times, and they may have used concavities on all eight columns—perhaps even on both ends of each column!—because it suited them.[34]

The capitals are given the number of the pedestal they stand on or (in the case of no. 7) stand near in the reconstructed building. This may well be accurate for Synagogue II (see infra section 14) but it is no more than a convenience for Synagogue I, where there is no way of being sure where the capitals were placed.

If we may use workmanship as a criterion again, it is possible to be more accurate as to which of the capitals we have now are from the first building. To begin with, one of the seven still preserved is very uneven at the top; it is nearly certain to be a 4th-century replacement for a capital damaged beyond reuse in the destruction of Synagogue I. This capital, no. 2, is completely undamaged, probably because it had toppled into accumulated fill sometime after the collapse of most of the rest of Synagogue II; its irregularities are thus original, not due to damage. The other capitals have top and bottom surfaces which are parallel and relatively flat and thus made up for the instability of no. 2. A building with eight capitals as uneven as no. 2 would have been most unstable! We conclude that these six are from the first building and that no. 2 is the only one of the seven which is a replacement, done at the time Synagogue II was built.

Of the six original capitals, all but no. 4 and possibly the badly weathered no. 6 bear clear indications of recutting. No. 1 has a simple boss or projection at the center of what is now its north face, but a similar feature on the east has been removed completely and only traces remain on the west and south. No. 7 is

34. It should be noted that during reconstruction in 1972 the present column no. 1 was placed on its pedestal upside down for reasons of safety; stabilizing and repairing it would otherwise have been nearly impossible, since the break in that drum is toward what had originally been its base.

identical in basic design and surely belongs to the synagogue, even though it was recovered on the surface in the northwest corner of the site (NW VIII.19); it is broken at the top on two sides, but of the remaining sides one bears the same boss and the other has it removed.

These two capitals were probably of a simple Corinthian design to begin with, but the volutes and the acanthus decorations were trimmed away, probably because they were damaged in the collapse of the first building. This accounts for the shrunken appearance of the lower portion. Nos. 3 and 5 appear to have been more "Doric" in original design (all such classical labels fit this building only loosely), but also bear signs of reworking. No. 3 in particular has been recut so severely that its echinus has become concave.

Capital no. 4 is unusual in several ways: it is the only one for which there is something like proof that its present position is its original one. Note these two points: the two cylinderlike projections under the abacus are decorated with rosettes on only one end; the other end is plain, indicating that the other side of the capital was seldom seen. And the design with rosettes is unique to this building and almost unparalleled in synagogue architecture as a whole! This suggests that the capital would have had a place of honor, but one where the "back," without rosettes, would not show. Only locations nos. 4 and 6, in the center of the wall of orientation, fit these specifications. The capital shows signs neither of extensive damage nor of recutting. It displays none of the irregularity at the top which makes capital no. 2 potentially dangerous; on this basis, we assign it to Synagogue I.

If the badly weathered capital no. 6 be assigned to the first building also (with a bit less confidence, perhaps), the distribution of capitals would be as follows: two Doric, nos. 3 and 5; two vaguely Ionic, if the "cylinders" under the abaci of nos. 4 and 6 may be suggestive of volutes; and two Corinthian, nos. 1 and 7. No. 2 looks more like an unfinished Byzantine basket capital than anything else, but it may have been an attempt to copy still another classical order (Tuscan? composite?). It is quite different from the others we have and suggests that the two capitals missing from Synagogue I were a pair of some different style from the first six. This hypothesis would leave the first building with four "pairs" of capitals. We cannot be sure how they were arranged, but it is possible for reasons stated just above that no. 4 and thus also the other Ionic capital, no. 6, were where they are now, before the *bema*.

9. THE FIRST SYNAGOGUE: DESTRUCTION

Rumbling earth, toppling buildings, and ruined cities are a staple of the religious literature of the ancient Near East. The vividness of the language used must have come from first-hand experience. In such an earthquake, the carefully cut ashlars of monumental public buildings and the fieldstone of simple homes alike were vulnerable.[35]

Synagogue I was destroyed by the earthquake of 306 CE. The violence of the event and its effects may be gauged from the following examples:

(i) The foundations of the east end of the building were shaken to the point that extensive rebuilding was required for the Stylobate Wall, for the portion of the north wall east of it, and for most of the east wall. In the process, broken elements of Synagogue I were incorporated in the walls. The west end of the building is founded on bedrock and suffered less damage, but the lintel over the north doorway may have toppled off and been broken, since the present Menorah Lintel is clearly not original.

(ii) Many architectural members from Synagogue I were damaged to the point that they could not be returned to their original positions. One of the main columns of Synagogue I was found built into the Stylobate Wall just south of pedestal no. 7; it must have been discarded because it could not have been otherwise reused. Pedestal no. 8 was also damaged; if it was reused in the second building in some way, we have not been able to identify it, but the present pedestal no. 8 is clearly a crude copy of something better. And of course the entire Torah shrine was splintered to the point that its members could be used only as rubble in the fill below the synagogue floor.

(iii) The floor itself also required repair, either because of actual damage or because it and the fill beneath had to be removed in order to get at walls and foundations which required rebuilding. Afterward, as the excavation of this area has shown, fill was simply dumped in between the Stylobate Wall and the east wall and then a new floor laid over it. The fill included a great deal of Synagogue I plaster, particularly in the north, as well as the architectural fragments already mentioned. If some of the earth of the fill came from a destroyed domestic area, that would explain the quantity of pithos fragments also recovered.

In summary, the site must have looked something like this after the earthquake. The walls on the east end were displaced, some capitals damaged and at least one destroyed, at least one pedestal damaged and one column down, along with the lintel from the north doorway—all of which means that the roof also collapsed. The Torah shrine was shattered and the floor damaged by falling architecture. The doorposts still stood, along with the north and west stairways, and the gallery and the Frescoed Room survived thanks to the bedrock around them; but the rest of Synagogue I lay in ruins.

10. A SECOND SYNAGOGUE

After the devastation caused by the earthquake of 306 CE (described in section 9), very little of the synagogue was left. For the second building the basic

35. Generally Hermann, "Erdbeben." For Palestine: Amiran, "Earthquake-Catalogue."

plan remained the same. However, on the east the foundations themselves had to be rebuilt. The Stylobate Wall, partially dismantled, was repaired with fragments of broken architecture and wall blocks from the first building, some with bits of plaster still adhering to them. When this work was complete, quantities of earth were systematically dumped into the space below floor level and between the east wall and the Stylobate Wall, as is indicated by the tip lines noted during excavation in this area. Many bits of plaster and smaller architectural fragments from the earlier building were found scattered throughout this fill,[36] debris which provided us a great deal of information about the earlier building.

This reconstruction of the synagogue (and of the village) must have begun with little delay after the earthquake. There is no evidence that the site was abandoned even briefly, and evidence from the excavation of the *bema* suggests that the rebuilding was complete in the middle of the 4th century.

Sections 11 to 20 below describe the elements of this second synagogue as the excavations revealed them. For the most part these are visible in the partially reconstructed building on the site (fig. 3.8). With the assistance of other evidence from the history of synagogue architecture, they provide us with a detailed and accurate idea of the appearance of the actual structure, both interior and exterior, as shown in all of the architect's reconstruction drawings.

11. THE SECOND SYNAGOGUE: THE WALLS

The plan of Synagogue I was discussed above, along with the general outline of its walls. All our evidence indicates that the wall lines were the same for both buildings but that the walls themselves required partial dismantling and repair after the destruction of 306 CE. On the east the bedrock begins to slope downward below floor level just to the west of pedestals nos. 5 and 6, so that from there eastward the north and south walls extend downward and serve also as retaining walls to contain the fill which supports the synagogue floor in this area. Two phases are clearly visible in the east wall; its lower courses are finer, and on the west they project 14–19 cm beyond the upper courses, which are probably to be attributed to the rebuilding after 306 CE. The walls were inherently less stable here than elsewhere in the building because there was less support from bedrock. They appear to have suffered displacement again in the 5th-century destruction, since the present east wall bows out noticeably (see the plan, fig. 3.2).

The walls of Synagogue I apparently contained a number of ashlars, but were chiefly of roughly dressed fieldstone. The walls of the second building are wholly fieldstone except for a few ashlars still framing the north doorway. All are dry-laid with the exception of the interior west wall of the Frescoed Room; here mortar was required, since the "wall" is actually a shallow facing for the natural

36. Including two joining pieces found nearly ten meters apart; cf. supra n. 14.

rock and its structural function is to support the west side of the gallery floor above.

Much of the lower "walls" in the west end of the building is cut bedrock, as plans and photographs of that area indicate. For example, the wall behind the bench at the foot of the west stairway rises several meters as a solid face of bedrock before the building stones begin. Bedrock is used in the same way in the walls of the Frescoed Room and the west interior wall of the main room. In its wall construction, including the use of bedrock, the synagogue is quite similar to contemporary domestic and commercial structures on this site.

The synagogue walls, whether roughly dressed fieldstone, ashlar, or bedrock, were faced on the inside first with rough plaster, then with a finishing coat of fine plaster (see supra chapter 2). The Frescoed Room has painted plaster, and a few fragments of what might be painted plaster were recovered from excavations within the main room. Most of the plaster recovered was white, however, suggesting that most or all of the wall plaster was white as well. Patches of white plaster were found still adhering to the walls, particularly in the west, where the greater depth of fill protected them. They are most in evidence on the south wall above the west stairway, in the southwest corner of the building at the upper level next to the west doorway, and in the northwest corner at the lower level, where the plaster is laid over vertical bedrock surfaces.

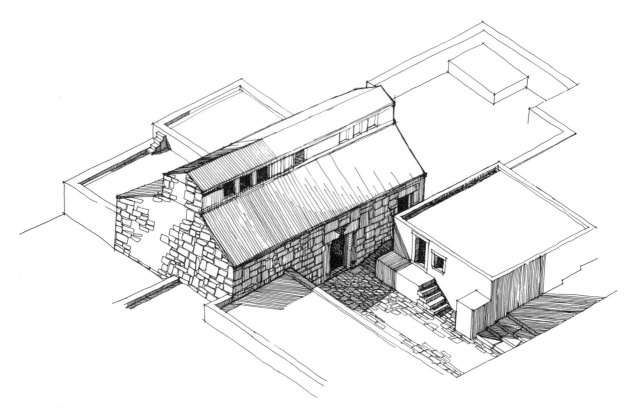

Figure 3.11. Clerestory synagogue reconstruction drawing, with the North Building.

Since it is called a "wall," the Stylobate Wall should perhaps be included in this section, even though no part of it was meant to be exposed. It is visible beneath pedestals nos. 7 and 8 in the synagogue plan, fig. 3.2. It abuts the north and south walls; that there is no seam in those walls at the points where the Stylobate Wall meets them indicates that the synagogue walls existed to their full length before the Stylobate Wall was built. At one point, when patches of plaster were found on some blocks of the Stylobate Wall, it seemed that it might earlier have been the east wall of a smaller building, perhaps a smaller, six-column synagogue. Closer examination showed, however, that the plaster must have been on the stones before they were laid into the wall, since nowhere does a single patch of plaster extend over more than one stone. These blocks had been used earlier in a plastered building and were reused in the Stylobate Wall. That earlier building may well have been Synagogue I, which we know supplied other rubble for incorporation into the later structure.

The Stylobate Wall served three purposes as part of the foundation of the synagogue: it bridged the cavity in bedrock which had once been a *miqveh*, it acted as a retaining wall for some of the fill under the floor, and—most important, perhaps—it served as a kind of stylobate for pedestals nos. 7 and 8, the only ones not founded on the bedrock itself. The instability of the building on its east end is obvious enough from the damage done there by the two earthquakes, but the damage would have surely been much more severe without the added strength and support which the hidden Stylobate Wall supplied.

The synagogue walls are not preserved to what might have been window level, and no architectural fragments from window openings have been recovered. It may well be that the main light source was not the windows, but a clerestory like that posited in the architect's reconstruction, fig. 3.11. Some such solution was probably required, since only on the east was there sufficient exposed wall to provide much room for windows; the west wall is limited owing to the rise of the terrace, and windows in the north and south walls would be obscured partially by the overhang of any roof.

12. THE SECOND SYNAGOGUE: FLOORS

Great quantities of tesserae were recovered from the very first day of excavation in and around the synagogue. They vary in dimension, and are not true cubes. In a random sample, two sizes predominated: 10 × 10 mm and 14 × 14 mm, with the third side of the tessera variously 2–4 mm less than the first two. Nearly all were white, the rest light gray, a very few dark gray. Their random dimensions and general irregularity suggest that they were locally produced. None was still in place, and only infrequently would a few cubes be found still bonded together.[37]

37. The largest area of mosaic appeared in NE I.26, L.26024 in the easternmost room immediately south of the synagogue. At first it was thought to be a section of intact floor, but it proved to be a patch of displaced mosaic from inside the building.

The complete destruction of the floor is to be attributed to the heavy annual rainfall in the region and perhaps to an inferior quality of bedding mortar. Rain falling on or near the ruined building would be channeled by the cut bedrock walls so that it sluiced across the floor and eastward down the slope, soon lifting all the cubes and eventually removing all traces of mortar as well.

Since tesserae were found throughout the building, it is likely that the entire main room except for the area east of the Stylobate Wall was paved, even though the subfloor in the western two-thirds of the building was already solid rock and would have needed no further surfacing. The pattern of the mosaic was monochromatic and likely quite simple, but nothing of its design could be recovered. The larger cubes may indicate later repair of the original floor, or they may have been used in borders and other less obvious parts of the room.

13. THE SECOND SYNAGOGUE: BENCHES

Except for the benches damaged in the collapse of 306 CE or dismantled in the reconstruction thereafter, all the benches of the first building are present in the second; yet these were not sufficient, and additions were made.

The benching which is most obviously new is that parallel to the north wall east of the north door, where a second row was added west of the Stylobate Wall (visible on the stone-by-stone plan, fig. 3.2). The main block of this new course is the broken 2.4-m ashlar on the east (NE VII.1, L.1010 = 2, L.2020). Its length suggests that it was intended as an architrave in the second building but was broken during the construction process and turned into a bench. Far shorter blocks were then lined up west of it to complete the new bench. All this made it difficult to use the original bench against the north wall, so the height of the latter was increased with a second course of blocks (NE VII.2, L.2006), some of which were found *in situ*. The result was utilitarian but recalls, except in its crudeness, the two levels of benches known from such familiar synagogues as those at Dura and Capernaum. At these sites and at Shema' the lower bench acted also as a kind of footrest for those sitting on the upper level; for backrests, worshippers sitting on the lower bench used the front of the upper bench and those on the upper bench used the synagogue wall.

The lower bench may have extended farther to the east; if so, it was dismantled by squatters after Synagogue II was destroyed and was reused in part to build a rough temporary north-south wall in the ruins (NE VII.2, L.2008). Similar circumstances would account for the fact that the second course on the bench attached to the north wall was incompletely preserved and that no benching appeared on the east wall except for the plastered bench in the southeast corner of the building, a holdover from Synagogue I.

The section of bench parallel to the north wall which is most clearly from Synagogue II is that which extends from the Stylobate Wall east to the corner of the building (NE VII.2, L.2006); the blocks here were neither plastered nor attached to the wall. In 1972 they were lifted and the area beneath (NE VII.2, L.2032–2038) was excavated to bedrock; during this process the mortared channel (NE VII.2, L.2039) which had fed the pre-synagogue *miqveh* was also revealed. The fill contained only Late Roman and some Middle Roman pottery and was deposited in such a way as to suggest that this entire area was badly disturbed in the collapse of Synagogue I and required extensive rebuilding both above and below floor level.

Because of the damage to the northwest corner of the building, it is impossible to be certain whether the benching there is new in Synagogue II or a remnant from Synagogue I. However, these benches too were plastered, suggesting that they are from the earlier building. There is no evidence that a second row of benches was installed here as was done east of the main door.

It may be significant that the only clear evidence of *added* benching (addition of a second row, elevation of the earlier benches) is on the wall opposite the *bema,* which was itself a substantial addition to the building. These innovations suggest a change in the synagogue service, in which the *bema* and the south wall and the events which take place in this area were given a new impressiveness and solemnity. If we agree with Avi-Yonah[38] that architectural changes in ancient synagogues reflect changes in the theological attitudes of those who build and use them, then we must ask what these new features at Shema' have to say about the religious life of this area in the latter 4th century.

14. THE SECOND SYNAGOGUE: THE CAPITALS

The columns, capitals, and pedestals of Synagogue I were described above. The rebuilding included as many of them as possible, with some changes and a minimum of outright replacement, as follows:

The pedestals on the north (nos. 1, 3, 5, and 7) apparently survived the 306 CE destruction undamaged. On the south, the pedestals were more elaborate and thus more susceptible to disfiguring damage. Thus the destruction may have been more severe. Pedestal no. 8 had to be replaced completely. The result is not impressive—an ashlar cube with parallel horizontal grooves that only vaguely suggest the molding of nos. 2, 4, and 6. In an effort to match the new pedestal, and perhaps because its circular plinth had been damaged, no. 2 was turned upside down, leaving the two center pedestals (nos. 4 and 6) with plinths, the two end ones (nos. 2 and 8) without them.

The columns were undamaged by the 306 CE destruction for the most part. The only drum known to have been so badly damaged as to defy reerection is AF 18, NE I.32, which was reused in the Stylobate Wall. Unfortunately this drum

38. Avi-Yonah, "Synagogue Architecture," 597f. Cf. infra, section 18, "Frescoed Room and Genizah."

was provided with an apophyge, and rather than try to replace it with an exact copy, the Synagogue II builders apparently decided to cut off any apophyges from the remaining drums. The result is that all the others recovered are straight-sided and perfectly plain.

The seven extant capitals have already been discussed in the attempt to determine the original appearance of the first building. To recapitulate, no. 8 is missing, no. 2 is the only capital which is obviously cut *de novo* to replace another irretrievably damaged in 306 CE, and the other six are all Synagogue I capitals, reused after their chipped and damaged areas had been trimmed back and cut away. Even now after recutting, it is clear that there were four pairs: nos. 1 and 7, 3 and 5, 4 and 6, and therefore probably also 2 and the missing 8.[39] This pairing is one evidence that the capitals in the *restored* building are located as they were in Synagogue II (and therefore in Synagogue I?), since it produces an interior pair and an exterior pair in each row of four columns. There are other arguments as well for the present arrangement. Nos. 1–5 were discovered within a few meters of their present pedestals. Nos. 4 and 6 are the most elaborate of the seven recovered, and for that reason belong immediately before the *bema*. Columns nos. 7 and 8 were in the extreme east of the building, where the buildup of fill was the shallowest; therefore one of their capitals is missing[40] completely and the other was recovered on the surface in the northwest corner of the site (NW VIII.19) where it had been moved for reuse. No. 6 was found one terrace to the east of the building, because the shallow fill in the east end also left it exposed.

The unparalleled pairing of capitals, which provides both symmetry and variety in overall effect, we can only attribute to architectural creativity, a characteristic of the community which was already apparent in the selection of a three-level site, the unparalleled two-door design, and in many details of construction. We can only speculate as to whether this creativity and openness were reflected in the religious life of the members of the community.

It is difficult to give specifics for the architecture at the second level, immediately under the roof. A number of small drums (average diameter ca. 35 cm) were recovered during excavation, some of which are presently lined up against the east wall of the restored building. These may have been used above the architraves as the architect's reconstruction, fig. 3.8, suggests.

39. Further study has thus proved incorrect the statement in Meyers-Kraabel-Strange, "Archaeology," 17, that "none of the eight capitals resembles any other."

40. Capital no. 8 for Synagogue II may have been AF 15 from NE VII.2 shown in the overall photograph (photo 3.34), lying against the east wall and immediately south of the opening to the *miqveh*, not far from its original find spot. It is 102.5 cm long and appears to have been cut from a column drum 50 cm in diameter; this diameter is preserved for the first 20 cm of its length, but then the column is cut back rather unevenly so that the diameter of the opposite end is only 43.5 cm. In two ways it resembles capital no. 2, with which it would be paired: their base diameters are very nearly the same (no. 2 is 43 cm) and they give the distinct impression of belonging to the second building but not the first. However, even for Synagogue II, this piece is rather crude; further, it has two notches which were cut at the same time the drum was re-cut, each 10 cm wide and 15 cm high, directly in line, one just under the 20 cm lip or molding at the "top," the other at the extreme opposite end, the "bottom." They have no obvious function in a "capital" and no parallels on capitals 1–7, or in the other drums.

15. THE SECOND SYNAGOGUE: THE BEMA

The platform or *bema* along the south wall was the focus of worship in Synagogue II. Its present dimensions are clear from the stone-by-stone plan, fig. 3.2 and photo 3.15. However, all of these can be misleading in one regard: the restored *bema* appears to have two levels, with the western third of the platform two courses lower than the remainder. Originally the entire platform was one level, nearly 70 cm above the mosaic floor (see photo 3.16). When Synagogue II collapsed, much of the architecture tended to fall toward the southwest corner of the main room. In the process, the west end of the *bema* was crushed by a 1.5-meter-long column drum (NE I.31, AF 5 = L.31008) and other, smaller pieces. During our consolidation of the *bema* in 1971, the damaged blocks were cemented in place in a manner which can be misleading until explained.[41] The only portion of the west end of the platform not destroyed was the lowest course with its heavy convex molding. Excavation in 1971 revealed that only the perimeter of this course was stone, as the stone-by-stone plan indicates (fig. 3.2). Still, the remainder of the *bema* appeared to be made up of solid stone, and we did not ask, in 1971, how such a substantial platform could be crushed even by falling column drums.[42] The situation was not clarified until a final probe in the center of the platform, at the back, against the synagogue wall, produced four important pieces of information. For Synagogue II we discovered the method and the date of construction of the *bema*. For Synagogue I we clarified the south wall benching and the make-up of the original floor. Essentially, the platform was solid only on the exterior; it had an earth-and-rubble core (see photos 3.1 and 3.2). The two lower courses of the perimeter were laid first, then fill was dumped into the interior, and finally the top of the platform was put on—slabs of stone some 20 cm thick. The lowest course may well be in reuse, since it does not appear to be prepared specifically for the *bema;* at the back, where it meets the bench from Synagogue I, it has been roughly trimmed to fit. In the front at the center another piece has been added, which lacks the convex molding of the remainder of the lowest course; this block may have been intended as a single step up to the top of the platform (nearly 70 cm above the floor) or simply inserted to extend the molding beyond its original span.

The *bema* is a common element in synagogues of the Middle Ages and later times.[43] However, relatively few are extant from the Roman and Byzantine periods, and only in the broadhouses do they appear in any way integral to the design. The major examples provide illuminating background for the use in

41. Meyers, "Hurvat Shema'," 59, shows the jagged west edge of the top of the *bema* before consolidation.

42. In Meyers-Kraabel-Strange, "Archaeology," 12f, we suggested that there were two phases to the *bema*, the original two courses, supplemented at a later date with the present top course, which elevated the platform by nearly 20 cm. This hypothesis was also based on the erroneous assumption that the *bema* was built of stone blocks throughout.

43. Cf. "Bimah," *Encyclopedia Judaica* IV, 1002–1006.

our building,[44] particularly for the relationship of *bema* to Torah shrine. As already indicated, the archaeological evidence at Shema' suggests that a stone *aedicula* or Torah shrine stood against the center of the south wall in Synagogue I, the location of the *bema* in Synagogue II. There is no evidence that a shrine of stone or of wood stood atop the *bema,* and some features of the Frescoed Room would lead us to believe that the scrolls were stored there in the second building. Do these architectural changes mean that worship focused on the place where the Torah was *stored* in the first building, but on the place from which it was read in the second? If there was a place of permanent storage for the Torah in the first building (at least in its latest phase), there must have been such storage also in the second. Must we locate it on the wall of orientation, the wall closest to Jerusalem, despite the lack of archaeological evidence? Or would the Frescoed Room on the west wall have been permissible?[45]

The comparative evidence points to the Torah shrine rather than the *bema* as the architectural element on which synagogue rituals focus. At the two recently investigated broadhouses south of Jerusalem, Khirbet Susiya and Eshtemo'a, both elements are on the north wall, the shrine above the *bema;*[46] here the two form an architectural unit. At Beth Alpha, however, the *bema* is an appendage to the apse which contained the scriptures and clearly is a later addition;[47] architecturally the apse dominates. In the remaining two examples, Beth She'arim and Ostia, the port of Rome, the situation is even more straightforward: the shrine and the platform are on opposite ends of the building, and it is the shrine which is on the "Jerusalem" wall. In both buildings the shrine is later than the *bema* and must mark a change in emphasis within the community. In the words of Sukenik, "as the synagogue came to occupy a more and more central position in Jewish life, there was a tendency to increase its impressiveness by the permanent presence of the most sacred ritual object, the Scroll of the Law."[48] The result in both buildings is awkward, with the shrine blocking access to a rear door, yet the very fact that community members were willing to put up with this awakwardness—indeed, *create* it by building the shrine—suggests that they felt it *necessary* to locate the Torah there.[49]

44. Generally on the literary evidence, Krauss, *Synagogale Altertümer*, 384–386; Sukenik, *Ancient Synagogues*, 57. But see the view of Goitein, "The Raised Platform in the Synagogue," 162, esp. n. z (Hebrew). Goitein argues that the *bema* was the place on which honored guests and members of the congregation sat. More probably the *bema* was the place on which and from which the scrolls were read during worship; so Meyers, "The Ancient Synagogue of Khirbet Shema'," 32f.

45. The larger question of orientation—never satisfactorily answered—has been recently addressed by Foerster, "The Synagogues at Masada and Herodium," 224–228. See also Avi-Yonah, "Ancient Synagogues," 42, Krauss, *Synagogale Altertümer*, 317–334, and Sukenik, *Ancient Synagogues*, 50–52.

46. Generally, Avi-Yonah, "Ancient Synagogues," 35. On Eshtemo'a, Yeivin, "Synagogue," 43–45. Susiya has a

second *bema* against the north wall and east of the shrine. Gutman et al., "Excavations," 47–52, esp. the plan on p. 47.

47. Sukenik, *Beth Alpha*, 13f; cf. 52–54.

48. Sukenik, *Ancient Synagogues*, 52. Generally on Ostia, Squarciapino, "Synagogue," 194, plan showing the *bema* against the northwest wall of the main room; p. 199, upper photograph. On Beth She'arim, Avi-Yonah, "Synagogue Architecture," 597; Goodenough, *Jewish Symbols*, I, 208. At Beth She'arim the remains of the relevant sections of the building are very badly preserved, and all interpretation is dependent on the report of the excavator; at Ostia, however, the remains are more abundant and evidence is completely clear.

49. "Synagogue Architecture," 597f. Utilization of the *bema* was not restricted to one kind of synagogue or one part of the world. It occurs in Palestine and the Diaspora,

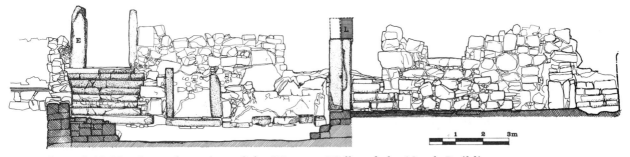

Figure 3.12. North-south section of the Western Wall and the North Building.

Does this mean that at Shema' the south wall of Synagogue II was provided with a Torah shrine in addition to the *bema*? It bears repeating that there was no mark on the surface of the platform to indicate that anything of wood or of stone had been installed upon it; yet the south wall is too shallow to contain a niche. Any Torah shrine on the "Jerusalem" wall would have to have been placed *on* the *bema*. A stone *aedicula* of some sort may be expected to have left some mark on the platform or on the wall behind it; if there was a shrine, it must have been of wood. Still, this is a time of transition, of "architectural experiments," as Avi-Yonah has recently stated. Synagogue II may have been an experiment in the placing of the Torah shrine, an experiment the details of which are no longer clear.[50]

16. THE SECOND SYNAGOGUE: THE WEST ENTRANCE (Fig. 3.12)

The doorposts and threshold of the west doorway (the Eagle Doorway) are still standing as they were in Synagogue I, but they have suffered serious damage due perhaps to the collapse of the building but also to exposure and to their incorporation in the rough structures of Strata V–VII, when the doorway was often blocked up. The lintel is missing completely, and the north doorpost is broken off at the top and split by a vertical fissure. The south half of the doorpost

and in all three general types of buildings. Cf. Avi-Yonah, "Ancient Synagogues," 32f; and Goodenough, *Jewish Symbols*, I, 179.

50. In the fourth stage of the synagogue at Sardis in western Turkey (according to Seager's reconstruction of the building history) the long, narrow main hall was divided into hall and forecourt by means of the insertion of the "shrine crosswall" provided with the usual three doors leading into the main hall. Two *aediculae* were installed against this wall, on the inside, one on either side of the center door. This construction occurs after the building had become a synagogue and is exactly contemporary with our Synagogue II; the Sardis building earlier, without the crosswall (Seager's third stage), may well have been in use by the Jewish community, and the additions which signal stage four were almost certainly done under Jewish auspices. The *aediculae* are surely in reuse, taken perhaps from an earlier public building. It is an indication of the

creativity and independence of this powerful Jewish community that it was not thought necessary to make these structures more closely resemble the "standard" Torah shrine. One must ask, however, why this Jewish community too carried out elaborate remodeling, no less extensive than Ostia's. Since the new plan placed two platforms on the (new) wall of orientation, the east wall, it seems likely that the same theological changes seen elsewhere are operating at Sardis as well, and that the two "shrines" were intended, one as the Torah shrine, the other perhaps as the *bema*. See Seager, "Sardis Synagogue," esp. 427, 429 (ill. 2), 433f. On this interpretation, the Eagle Table (whatever its precise function) in front of the apse at the west end of the building would be a holdover from the earlier orientation. A central *bema* may have been installed at a still later date (Seager, pl. 92, fig. 2, and p. 434), perhaps reflecting a decrease in the size of the community.

subsequently collapsed and a portion (photo 3.17) of it was reused in the post-destruction period. Consequently, the north doorpost is half as broad as the south in photos and plans of the building.

Of the two main entrances, this one on the west is surely the more impressive, with its wide staircase leading from a level halfway between floor and roof, down into the main room (see architect's reconstruction, fig. 3.10). The eagle-in-wreath design on the south doorpost may even indicate that in Synagogue I this was also the more important and perhaps the more heavily used entrance; there is no such decoration on the north doorposts.

But by the time Synagogue II was in use, the situation seems to have changed; at least there is no parallel on the west to the broad flagstone terrace in front of the north door. Pedestrian traffic in the town may have changed to the point that the north entrance was the more heavily used, but we suspect that a more important factor is the addition of the *bema* in Synagogue II. Its bulk made entrance from the west a bit more awkward; but—more important—the heightened impressiveness it lends to the south wall, or indicates for the south wall, probably made it less appropriate to approach the focus of worship from the side via the west door. Such an explanation is in line with conclusions already drawn from the arrangement of benches in the second building.

17. THE SECOND SYNAGOGUE: THE NORTH ENTRANCE

There are two obvious changes in the north entrance in Synagogue II. The first is the replacing of the original lintel (destroyed probably by the 306 CE collapse) with the Menorah Lintel (fig. 3.13 and photo 3.18), which in workmanship is clearly inferior to the doorposts and other elements known to have come from the first building.

The other change is increased impressiveness and elaboration of the entrance area (see photo 3.9), due to the growing preference of community members for entering the building from the north rather than from the west, and due also to the existence now of the North Building as an adjunct to the synagogue. The main route—a well-traveled route, to be sure—between the North Building and Synagogue II runs from the north entrance across the flagstone pavement and up the substantial stairway to the main entrance in the east wall of the North Building. The Menorah Lintel itself is an indication of the new importance of this area; it is a spectacular piece of religious iconography from a site whose architecture has produced no other such religious symbolism whatsoever.[51] It would be no surprise if further excavations revealed that only this lintel was decorated and that the lintel of the west door was left blank.

51. Unless the eagle on the west door be considered a specifically religious symbol; most recently on the use of the eagle as a Jewish symbol, see Kraabel, "Hypsistos," 89f.

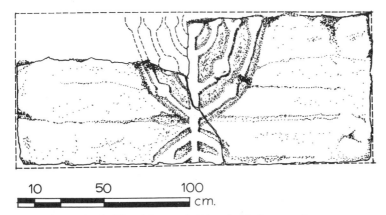

10   50   100

cm.

Figure 3.13. The Menorah Lintel of the northern synagogue entrance.

Excavations in the entrance area produced evidence of another method of heightening the impressiveness of the north entrance: quantities of exterior plaster were discovered in the fill (NW VII.1, L.1021, 1026) over the pavements and particularly in the junction of three architectural units: the synagogue north wall, the lowest level of the east-west stairway (NW VII.1, L.1017) between the synagogue and the North Building, and the southeast corner of that building. The area bounded by the north wall of Synagogue II and the east wall of the North Building was embellished with shining white plaster applied to these two walls and to the east end of the passage between the two buildings (for more on the entrance area, see infra, section 21).

Anyone passing through the double doors of the north entrance took three steps downward as he entered the building (see the north-south section, fig. 3.12). While this change in level may be due only to the exigencies of construction, it should be noted that the apse areas in certain later synagogues have a "lower space," probably in order to fulfill the verse, "Out of the depths I cry to Thee, O Lord" (Ps. 130.1).[52] It is not hard to imagine this Bible verse being used as a justification or at least an *ex post facto* "explanation" in a building in which the entire main room was well below the level of both main entrances.

A NOTE ON THE LINTEL WITH MENORAH OF SYNAGOGUE II[53] (NW VII:I.1)

In 1972, after the raising of the jambs of the north doorway of the synagogue, the rubble that had been buried under the jambs was cleared and the lintel that had once spanned these jambs was uncovered. The lintel had broken into at least three large fragments when it toppled onto the floor of the syna-

---

52. Avi-Yonah, "Synagogue Architecture," 598; cf. Sukenik, *El-Hammeh*, 75.

53. The authors are especially indebted to Ms. Carol L. Meyers for these observations on the Menorah Lintel.

gogue. Only the two largest pieces remain, but when put together they permit a total reconstruction of the lintel and its decoration. It is made of local limestone; its face is well-finished, but the other surfaces are less carefully made, indicating that they were not exposed. The face is a rectangle, 210 × 85 cm. In section it is roughly trapezoidal, the lower side measuring 30 cm and the upper side (slightly curved) measuring 43 cm. The rear surface is 67 cm high.

Carved in high relief in the center of the lintel is a large seven-branched menorah. There are no symbols or objects flanking it, nor is it set within a frame, garland, or wreath, nor is the lintel adorned with any molding. The representation of the menorah is the largest ever found on a synagogue lintel: it is 72 cm high and its branches have a spread of 80 cm. The branches curve gently upwards, and all end in cups. The central cup seems to be somewhat larger. Only the three right-hand cups are preserved, and each has a slightly different configuration, as if they were carved by a local artisan, perhaps unskilled, perhaps unused to creating monumental reliefs. The four outer branches (but not the three central ones) feature knobs or pomegranates partway up the branch. Again, these knobs are somewhat irregularly carved and asymmetrically placed.

The stand of the menorah differs substantially from the more or less standard tridentate or tripodal base. The outline of the base is triangular, but instead of three legs, five are present. This can be compared to the representation of a menorah on a Palestinian tombstone now in the Rockefeller Museum, which also has what is in effect a five-branched base.[54]

In short, the features of the menorah are somewhat irregular, the base unusual. The style is much cruder than that of the pilasters beneath. The Khirbet Shema' lintel thus seems to be the product of a local mason who decorated a large block, unfinished except on the front, with a menorah notable more for its size than for its concern with detail or style, yet certainly an embellishment to the synagogue the entrance of which it crowned.

18. THE SECOND SYNAGOGUE: THE FRESCOED ROOM AND GENIZAH (Photo 3.19)

The history of this area before Stratum IV has already been rehearsed. It remains here to describe the condition of the area when excavated, the finds insofar as they assist in explaining the room and the chamber, and their possible functions in Synagogue II.

Synagogue II collapsed in such a way that no heavy architecture fell into the Frescoed Room, although the floor just outside the door was littered with column fragments and capitals.[55] The small room with its high walls could still provide temporary shelter, and Byzantine and Arab sherds indicate that it was

54. Goodenough, *Jewish Symbols*, III, fig. 99.   55. See the photograph, in Meyers, "Hurvat Shema'," 59.

used by occasional squatters. As dust continued to blow in, the debris level gradually rose and the chamber began to fill.

Apparently a fault developed in the bedrock sometime after the site was abandoned, so that quantities of rainwater entered the *genizah* chamber each year. More than 150 buckets of water were removed from it during excavation, and most of the fill was removed as mud, which could be examined only when it had fully dried. The usual sifting was impossible at either stage, and the excavators were forced to break up the dried lumps with *patishim* and examine each one individually, a time-consuming and laborious process. What was recoverable was recovered, but some potential finds could be ruled out at the beginning; for example, anything susceptible to damage from regular submersions would long ago have been destroyed: wood, most writing materials, and some of the pottery and metal, including coins. Glass on the other hand would be able to withstand this kind of damage, and five substantial pieces, in addition to many smaller fragments, were found and registered (R1220, 1221, 1264, 1300 and 1740).

In general the finds span our Strata II–IV, with one piece of glass which goes back to Stratum I: the rim of a tiny sherd of cast bowl from the second century BCE. The glass from Stratum II consists of bases R1220 (infra ch. 8, pl. 8.7:23) and R1264 (very similar to R3294, (pl. 8.8:6) and rim R1221 (pl. 8.6:10). To this should be added the lamp fragment R1688 (pl. 8.9:7) from the first century. The coins are from the middle or late 4th century with the exception of R1550 (183–192 CE) and R1551 (98–117 CE).

During the use of this *genizah* it is unlikely that it was cleaned out thoroughly or frequently. It is also unlikely that while Synagogue I or Synagogue II stood and the Frescoed Room was intact, objects fell by chance into the narrow opening of the chamber. (When the site was abandoned and the Frescoed Room used temporarily by squatters, vessels and other materials were put in the chamber on occasion; hence the presence of some Byzantine and Arab pottery.) The early materials (coins, glass, lamps) were found in the chamber only because they were placed there deliberately; and they indicate that the *genizah* was in use throughout Strata III–IV and that the chamber was *put into use* as a *genizah* sometime in Stratum II, which would also be the time at which Synagogue I was built.

The finds in the chamber do not make it a *genizah*, but they are not such as to rule it out as a *genizah*. Rock-cut chambers are sometimes made to be used as graves or for domestic or industrial storage; nothing was found to suggest that this chamber was used in any of these ways. Secret chambers and treasuries are known from other synagogues,[56] and some provision for a *genizah* is incumbent

56. At Ma'on: pit in the pavement of the apse, called "the community chest" by Levy, 7; cf. 20. At Beth Alpha: a plastered cavity 80 cm deep, 100 cm long, 80 cm wide in the floor of the apse, containing 36 Byzantine coins and probably "the treasury of the synagogue," Sukenik, *Beth Alpha*, 13. At Hammath by Gadera the entire floor of the apse is 1.18 m lower than the surface of the upper step leading to the apse. Sukenik, *El-Hammeh*, 75, and pls. VII and VIIIa; cf. Goodenough, *Jewish Symbols*, I, 240; the apse may have been provided with a false floor, with the Torah shrine above the floor, and large cavity below, ample for both treasury and *genizah*. Cf. 'Ein Gedi, where a *genizah* is provisionally reported in Barag et al., "Second Season," 54.

upon any synagogue community.[57] The most famous Palestinian *genizoth* from ancient times are the pit in the floor of Masada synagogue[58] and the Qumran caves; but these are each the product of an emergency, and both are in climates such that their contents were preserved, proving the chamber a *genizah*. There is no way of proving that any of the side rooms or attached structures known for many Galilean synagogues was ever used as a *genizah*, since the climate has destroyed any manuscript materials which might have supplied that proof. But the probability remains. The preexisting chamber was ready at hand when Synagogue I was built. On the basis of archaeological data from Shema', parallels from other sites, and literary evidence, the designation of this chamber as the *genizah* and "treasury" or "community chest" for Synagogues I and II seems most appropriate.

The Frescoed Room is another matter. Its earlier history has been described in section 7 supra; its appearance as an element of Synagogue II is quite clear from the excavations (see the stone-by-stone plan, fig. 3.2, the north-south section, fig. 3.12, and photo 3.19). Both floor and walls are plastered, the wall plaster manifesting red-painted, apparently geometric decorations faded almost to invisibility. The one item of furnishing recovered was an unplastered stone bench, 166 cm long, 47 cm high, and 40 cm deep, against the north end of the west wall.

Two other features of the room are strongly indicated by the archaeological evidence. The entrance was through tall, narrow double doors which would have been squarely in the center of the west wall of the synagogue main room and which fastened from the outside. Pivot holes and locking holes are clearly visible in the threshold, and the height of the entry can be calculated from the dimensions of the south doorpost. In addition to the doors, one would expect a curtain or other closing over the opening in the south wall which led to the *genizah*, perhaps concealing it completely.

In trying to explain this room we do not propose to argue that it is an essential element of the synagogue, designed from the beginning for a particular purpose; both the room and the *genizah* chamber were utilized because they were *available*. The room remained from Synagogue I, but at that time it had not contained the scrolls (they were in the *aedicula* on the south wall) and for that reason was probably not specially decorated.[59] The chamber antedated Synagogue I; had it not existed under the west stairs, the community could have established a *genizah* elsewhere. We need not look for weighty reasons, theological or archaeological, for the origin of the Frescoed Room either. The question is

57. Generally, Habermann, "Genizah." It is also quite possible that a *genizah* would be used to store *matzoth* or wine for the festivals and shabbatot.

58. Yadin, *Masada*, 187.

59. At the end of this discussion it will be suggested that some, perhaps most, of the scrolls of Synagogue II might have been stored in the Frescoed Room, with perhaps only the Torah scroll in a small ark on the south wall. There is no reason why this could not have been done also in the first building, in which case the frescoes might also be from that time; if there were scrolls in the room in Synagogue I, then the decorations too should be from Synagogue I.

rather this: Since the room was there, how might it likely be used? For Synagogue I, specific uses were not obvious, and we gave only a few suggestions in discussing it. For Synagogue II, a building in which the *bema* now stands on the spot where the *aedicula* once stood, the answers are clearer.

If Synagogue II had a Torah shrine on its south wall, all trace of it has disappeared; yet every excavated synagogue which had a *bema* also had the remains of a permanent structure of some kind for the scriptures. Sometimes the *bema* and the shrine are on the same wall, the wall closest to Jerusalem (Khirbet Susiya, Eshtemo'a, Beth Alpha), sometimes each is on a different wall (Beth She'arim, Ostia). However, when shrine and *bema* are on different walls, the shrine and not the *bema* is on the wall of orientation. Thus we are not insisting that the Frescoed Room is the Torah shrine of Synagogue II, but only suggesting it, since there is no precedent for locating the shrine anywhere but on the wall of orientation.

Perhaps the strongest justification for the above hypothesis is that Shema' has already with Synagogue I a record of experimentation in design and is in a period of transition and experiment in synagogue architecture, with a building style, the broadhouse, which is itself a "transitional type."[60] The frescoes themselves indicate that the community had some special purpose for the Frescoed Room; why decorate *only* this space in such a way, if not because what it contained required it? In Synagogue I the scriptures are stored in a fine stone *aedicula;* Synagogue II had to have something equally fine, even if its location was unprecedented. (This would not have been the only instance of the inclusion in the Shema' building of elements and features not paralleled elsewhere.) Even if most of the community's scrolls were stored in the Frescoed Room (along with other articles used in the services), not all of them need have been there. As already suggested, there may have been a small shrine *on* the *bema* which left no trace behind. This last explanation has been made more attractive by the recent suggestion[61] that the shrine need not have been large enough to contain all the scrolls in use in the community. Something large enough to contain only the Torah scroll might have been sufficient, since on this hypothesis all other scrolls would be stored in a separate place which need not be on the wall of orientation. It would be enough to have the central Torah scroll in the symbolic position.[62]

60. Avi-Yonah, "Synagogue Architecture," 597.

61. By Dr. R. Chachlili, orally, June 1973.

62. Some representations of the Torah shrine in art show one container housing a number of scrolls, for example, Goodenough, *Jewish Symbols,* III, figs. 964–967, 973f, and an interesting Christian parallel, Galling, "Das Allerheiligste," 47f. However the space needed to contain multiple scrolls would be considerable and a large shrine like a closet, would be required; thus these representations are probably more symbolic than literal in their design (see, provisionally, Goodenough, *Jewish Symbols,* IV, 142–

144). There is also archaeological evidence that a good deal of space was required for all the scrolls a community used: the apses in Avi-Yonah's latest group, e.g., Beth Alpha, are quite spacious (Avi-Yonah, "Ancient Synagogues," 32; "Synagogue Architecture," 598–600), and the room added by the Zealots to the Masada synagogue is larger than our Frescoed Room (Yadin, *Masada,* 180–187, the "rear cell") and required major changes in the small building. In none of these buildings, including Shema', is the space used only for scrolls, but they would normally be the bulkiest single item. A container small enough to

On this variation of our original hypothesis, the small shrine on the *bema* would probably have been called the Torah shrine, but the Frescoed Room would have held the bulk of the scrolls.[63]

19. THE SECOND SYNAGOGUE: THE GALLERY

There were several new elements in the gallery on the Western Wall in Synagogue II; the most important was the north entrance to the gallery, installed probably at this time. The archaeological evidence for this doorway is minimal: a trace of a cutting in the bedrock which would have received its threshold (fig. 3.2). However, it is clear that the passage running east-west between the synagogue and the North Building was improved at the time of the second building, with a flight of stairs at the east end leading down onto the flagstones in front of the north door. This passage is so narrow as to be inadequate for substantial day-to-day communication from one part of the town to another; it is suitable only for occasional traffic. Yet the community went to some trouble to improve it with the regular flight of stairs. These stairs are not contemporary with the construction of the first building, since they now stand *in front of* the fine lower molding of the west doorpost of the north entrance (see photo 3.20).

The likely reason for such an addition is that there was something in the passage in the second building which was not there in the first. Since there was no entrance in the south wall of the North Building in this period, a small north entrance to the gallery seems the only feasible explanation. It is also in accord with the general principle requiring some separation of the sexes within synagogues. With this north gallery entrance, the women were able to enter the building without using the main west doorway.

The other new elements in the gallery were due to the effect of the earthquake of 306 CE. The gallery likely had a wooden floor in both buildings. It rested on bedrock at the north end and on the tops of the mortared west and south walls of the Frescoed Room and terminated at the north end of the upper landing of the monumental stairway, just inside the west doorway. This floor probably required renovation or replacement after 306 CE.

Certain small architectural members found in the main room of the syna-

fit on the Shema' *bema* and small enough to disappear without a trace might well have been too small to contain all the scrolls in regular use in the building.

63. In a study so indebted to the work of Goodenough, it should be noted that he once stated that "it is inconceivable that women would have been allowed to stand or pass above (a Torah shrine)," *Jewish Symbols*, I, 207. On the general hypothesis just advanced, the gallery of Synagogue II would be directly over the room containing the scriptures; if this synagogue had a separate place for women, the gallery is the most obvious. Were Goodenough absolutely correct in his statement, it would be a further argument for locating a small shrine, the one which actually contained the Torah, on the south wall. However, in modern times and earlier, synagogues have been constructed which have a portion of the women's gallery above the ark, e.g., the 1555 CE "Spanish Synagogue" in Venice (cf. Avi-Yonah, "Synagogue," plan 11, fig. 16). Goodenough had no ancient evidence which would substantiate his statement; it was an extremely well-informed guess, a "hunch"; but if the later examples reflect earlier practices, it was an incorrect hunch. The view that the Frescoed Room was used to store scrolls was previously advanced by Meyers, "Ancient Synagogue," 34.

gogue, just east of the gallery, may have been a part of the railing of the gallery or used in some other way in its construction. A small capital or pedestal, 42 cm on a side (AF 14, NW I.31) discovered on the floor next to pedestal no. 2 is surely from the second building, not the first; its irregular lines and rough technique are very much like those of pedestal no. 8, surely a product of the builders of Synagogue II.

Well-cut ashlars from the first building found in the west end of the main room and slightly farther north may also have been reused in the gallery. Some of the ashlars were a part of the north wall of the building (others are still in the wall) but the find spots of these other pieces suggest use near, therefore above, the west wall of the main room. Photo 3.20 shows these ashlars in the process of excavation (cf. photo 3.13).

20. THE SECOND SYNAGOGUE: DESTRUCTION (Photo 3.21)

The violence of the end of Synagogue II is strikingly clear from the tumble of main architectural members which began to be exposed as excavators neared the floor of the main room.[64] The building twisted in collapse, so that much of the debris fell toward the southwest. NW I.31, the square in that corner of the building, produced thirty major architectural fragments, including three capitals, two pedestals, and seven column drums! Another drum smashed the west end of the *bema*, and pedestal no. 4 was slightly displaced.

Most capitals and columns were found lying directly on the floor of the main room, indicating that the room was in use, not abandoned, at the time of the destruction. Columns 2, 5, and 7 fell a bit later after some earth had blown or washed in. Finally the north doorposts fell into the building, soon after the Menorah Lintel had toppled off; the doorposts pinned the lintel beneath them.

Other elements remained standing. The fractured bottom section of column no. 8 stood on its pedestal until an unknown vandal pushed it over between the 1970 and 1971 seasons. And the west doorposts suffered damage, but in the main never moved.

It is the graphic story told by this tumbled debris that makes it obvious that the building suffered a catastrophic blow which collapsed most of it instantly. An earthquake of some force would be required; the most likely is that of 419 CE.

21. THE NORTHERN ENTRANCE AREA AND THE NORTH BUILDING (Fig. 3.14): *NW VII.8, 9, 13, 14, and NW VII.1 (outside the synagogue)*

The archaeological history of the North Building, a generally square structure (6.55 × 6.50 m) just northwest of the synagogue, is unfortunately clouded

---

64. The litter of columns, capitals, architraves, and other debris is obvious in the pre-reconstruction photo- graph in Meyers, "Hurvat Shema'," 59.

by the fact that it was repeatedly reused into later Arabic times so that its internal soil layers and internal bedrock foundations yielded glazed wares down to the crevices in bedrock. On its imposing eastern face, the platform (L.1015) which was built to receive a stairway for its eastern entrance produced an important sealed locus (L.1016) relevant for dating its earlier use, which can be related to the synagogue (see photo 3.22). The steps (L.1017) which led up into the alley to the western terrace and perhaps to the gallery provide still another important architectural clue to the history of this entire area.

In the western sector of the building a crudely worked bedrock bench runs along the western and southern walls and is intercepted by another wall or bench in the middle which divides the room roughly in half. This dividing "bench" is composed of a row of headers laid on a cut bedrock foundation and is at roughly the same elevation as the benches on the southern and western walls. There is an interruption of this benching to provide access to the eastern section of the building. The distinct impression that this portion of the building provides is of an area used for study and conversation. One has only to imagine several coats of plaster on these benches to recover a sense of the orderliness of the arrangement, though no plaster has survived its extensive use in later periods. The manner of construction of the benching on the east is especially reminiscent of that in the synagogue proper.

Along the south wall of the North Building and just southeast of the eastern benching (see fig. 3.14), we excavated a small entrance with its pivot hole still *in situ*. Since the earth covering was minimal, there are no stratified deposits to help dating; the excavators have had to rely on architectural details to elucidate the chronological relation between it and the alley and stairway onto which it leads. A puzzling feature is that it opens abruptly into the northwest corner of the synagogue where we have postulated a gallery. It is therefore probable that this small entrance is late, Stratum V or later, i.e., not contemporary with the synagogue. It is difficult to imagine twenty or so individuals filing in and out of so narrow an opening while there was a much larger and imposing entrance to the North Building in the eastern wall. Moreover, the eastern side of the entrance includes a number of reused architectural fragments and the building technique closely resembles that of the later periods.

The steps (L.1017) to the alley postdate Synagogue I or Stratum III. They were laid in over the northern terrace flagstones in such a way as to obstruct partially the base of the western pilaster which had survived the destruction of the first synagogue building. The several finely hewn ashlars just west of the doorjambs are plastered on their outer face; this is unusually elaborate treatment for the walls of this site and is suggestive of the beginning of a passage. It is improbable that the original builders would so set these stairs as to obtrude upon the imposing northern entrance. Once again, the increasing narrowing of this alley as one approaches the putative entrance to the gallery suggests limited use, i.e., for communication in and around the synagogue; the heavier daily traffic between eastern and western parts of the town rather utilized the passage and stairway north of this building.

Along the eastern wall of the North Building and laid over the cobbled terrace is a platform which served as an entrance stairway to it. Since four stairs are preserved intact and the original threshold stone is preserved in the eastern wall, it is a simple matter to project two or three stairs and an imposing doorway here. Fortunately, the platform for the stairs had collapsed in such a way as to seal the debris inside it (L.1016). Of the five coins sealed by the destruction debris here the latest dates to the early 5th century, which precisely corresponds to the homogeneous ceramic horizon preserved, namely, Late Roman-Byzantine or Stratum IV. This leads to the unavoidable conclusion that the North Building was given its present orientation during the use phase of Synagogue

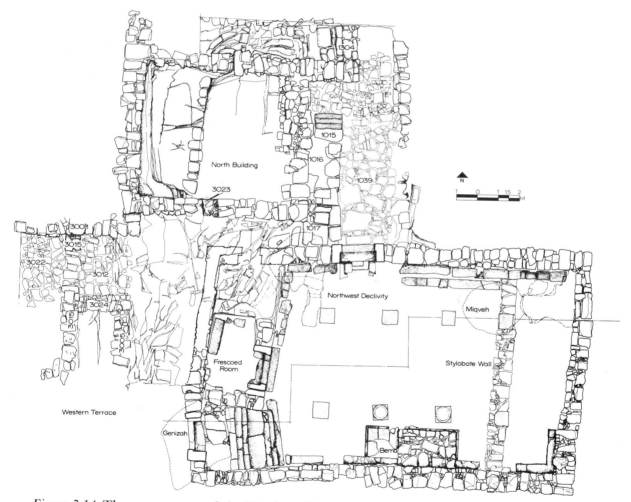

Figure 3.14. The synagogue and the North Building: stone-by-stone drawing.

II; before that time, the entrance might possibly have been on the north as is conjectured below.

It was quite clear during excavation, however, that the eastern wall had been in use over a very long period. A fallen doorjamb lay over the original threshold stone, which itself may be in secondary use. A Jannaeus coin was found beneath these two blocks (L.8002), but the pottery evidence is inconclusive. After removal of the upper block, a cleaning of the inner face of the eastern wall (L.8011) also yielded homogeneous Late Roman pottery, once again supportive of dating the North Building in its present form to Synagogue II of Stratum IV.

Several questions arise from the discovery that under the stairwell the flagstone surface (L.1039) did not fully extend to the east wall of the North Building, that a good deal of plaster was found sealed within the stairwell (L.1016), and that some plaster was found *in situ* on the exterior of the east wall (L.1002) of the building. The following solutions suggest themselves. Before the North Building became associated with the synagogue, its south and east walls may have existed (without the present entrances, of course) as retaining walls for a terrace north of the synagogue or as walls of an earlier building unrelated to the synagogue. On the latter hypothesis, the entrance to the building was in the north wall, where the discovery of a single large header laid over bedrock may mark the earlier doorway, later blocked. Finally, a building similar to the one we have now may have existed in the time of the Synagogue I, but with its entrance on the north.

The fact that the flagstones under the stairway are short of the east wall of what is now the North Building allows either of two explanations: either the wall was earlier and the terrace, when it was constructed later, was not laid all the way to the wall because the stairway was immediately to be built upon it, hiding the gap; or the terrace is the earliest of the three elements, but was cut at its western edge to receive the foundations of the wall.

Similarly, there are three possible explanations for the plaster in the fill inside the stairway: either the east wall of the North Building was plastered on the outside, and some of the plaster fell into the fill during the construction of the stairway; or plaster from the interior of the building fell over the eastern wall when the building suffered damage or collapse and remained there during the repair and the building of the stairway; or the east wall was plastered on the outside subsequent to the building of the stairway, and this plaster fell into the stairway after the abandonment of the building.

The few pieces of external plastering found *in situ* at the base of the east wall inside the stairway (L.1002) at the level of the first step, 746.46, pose a rather difficult matter. (The flagstone pavement leading to the northern entrance, L.1039, has an average elevation of 745.50.) Great quantities of plaster were discovered in the fill above the platform of the stairs; but the plaster *in situ* gives strong evidence that the North Building was plastered on its eastern external face, providing a sort of finished stucco look to the entire entrance area. These data tend to confirm the view that in the first synagogue period (Stratum III) this was some sort of building, not just a terrace wall; its main entrance was probably on the north, and it may not have been associated with the synagogue.

It is important to note that a wall to the east of the end of the flagstone pavement and opposite the North Building demarcated that side of the entrance court; it also served to mark the point at which bedrock falls off radically from this terrace level (see fig. 3.14). Most of this was removed during the 1970 season at a time when, because of mixed ceramic yields and other digging exigencies, this area was not properly understood. It seems quite unlikely, however, that this eastern side of the northern entrance area stood very high or that it too was plastered.

Along the north wall of the North Building yet another stairway (L.1304) was excavated (see photo 3.23), only four steps of which have been preserved. Laid in over bedrock, its lowest level was bounded on the south side by an eastern extension of the north wall which formed a rather formal entryway to the entrance area. It is at this point too that the flagstone pavement ends or is so disturbed as to leave no trace. Nonetheless, it is very significant to note that all coins here were of the 4th or 5th century and that Arabic sherds were completely absent. Because of the enormous amount of rock tumble to the northwest of the stairway we were unable to follow them out completely, but it is probable that these stairs connected the middle terrace with the upper area of the site and that they are contemporary with the second synagogue phase, when the North Building had its entrance on the east. It seems assured that this stairway, rather than the alley between the synagogue and the North Building, served as the main east-west circulation route.

Similarly, the debris accumulated in the entrance area was strikingly free of Arabic pottery, contrasting sharply with the finds inside the North Building. Such a contrast indicates that in the Arabic periods the inhabitants did not dig down to clear the courtyard; they were unaware of its existence. But in order to make use of the building they cleared debris in its interior down to bedrock.

Study hall and guesthouse (fig. 3.14)

Though it is clear that the flagstone pavement in front of the northern entrance area is to be related to the earlier synagogue structure of Stratum III, the dating from this complex informs us only of a use in Stratum IV. During Stratum IV access to the gallery could be gained in several ways. To judge from our limited soundings on the western terrace, access to the gallery from there was from the flagstones (L.3022, 3012) in the northwest, from the metaled earthen surface in the south, and by the western entry. In the north, access was via the alley stairs (L.1017). Such a circulation pattern would allow families from the major areas of the village easy access to the main public building of the community.

The situation for Stratum III is much more difficult to recover, since no sealed evidence from outside the building survived the destruction of Synagogue I. If we accept the fact that the ground plan of Synagogue II was substantially the same as Synagogue I, the situation would be virtually the same except for the stairs in the alley (between the synagogue and the North Building), which probably postdate Synagogue I. It is possible that there was a better stairway there in Stratum III, but no traces have survived. Persons from the north part of the site who wished to enter the gallery may have climbed up the north bed-rock from the north terrace, but it is more likely that they walked to the highest terrace via the staircase north of the North Building and from there headed south and entered the synagogue from the west. If so, the explanation may be that the inhabitants of Khirbet Shema' were going to great lengths to allow for separation of the sexes.

Similarly, when we attempt to understand the history of the North Building in Stratum III, with its main entrance on the north wall, we are hampered once again by the absence of sealed material of Stratum III here. The most attractive

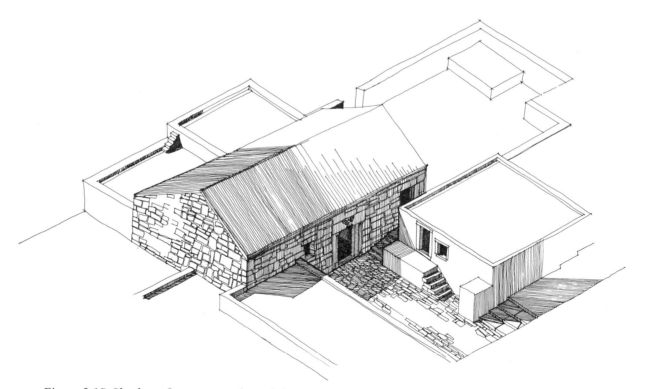

Figure 3.15. Shed roof reconstruction of the synagogue and the North Building.

theory would seem to be the simplest: that the North Building in this earlier phase had the same function as it did in Stratum IV, when its entrance was moved to the east wall and when the stairs to the gallery were laid in along its south wall.

The western third of the building resembles a kind of study hall or *beth midrash* (see photo 3.24).[65] The eastern two-thirds could well have functioned as a kind of guesthouse or *beth 'orhim* where travelers and distinguished visitors were given lodging.[66] To be sure, this building was repeatedly used after Stratum IV, but such a large structure, proximate to the synagogue and with a rather unique internal arrangement, can only be understood as an integral part of the synagogue complex. Though there is a major renovation of the North Building in Stratum IV, therefore, we would submit it did not change the use of the building as both study hall and guesthouse (fig. 3.15).

22. THE WESTERN TERRACE (Photo 3.25): *Areas west of the Eagle Doorway* (NW I.27 and NW I.28)

These two squares, situated west of the western doorway, constitute the western extension of the significant east-west balk which ran eastward through the synagogue itself; they were excavated in hopes of determining the relation of two standing pillars to the western wall of the synagogue (see photo 3.26). During the digging of these areas in 1970, however, only one surface was found, L.27007S and 28007S, at an elevation of ca. 747.68. The surface, a very rough "metaled" floor with beaten earth and small pebbles, lay just over the very uneven outcroppings of bedrock. The two standing piers were found to be elements of the surface architecture of Arabic periods (Strata VI and VII), and

65. A separate study hall is suggested by the Hebrew inscription from Dabbura in the Golan: "Eli'ezer ha-Qappar; This is the School (Bet Midrash) of the Rabbi," published by Urman, "Jewish Inscriptions," 21–23. The 170 cm length to the lintel on which the inscription is inscribed is rather short to go with the magnificent remains still found at the site. The Menorah Lintel at Khirbet Shema' is 210 cm long. On the sources for the Beth Midrash see Krauss, *Synagogale Altertümer*, 425, 438.

66. Hospitality toward the traveler and the stranger was an important precept in rabbinic Judaism, and facilities of a guesthouse proximate to the synagogue might be used for this purpose; so Klein, "Zur jüdischen Altertumskunde," 545–557, 603f; cf. also his "Neues zum Fremdenhaus der Synagoge," 81–84, the latter chiefly on the Stobi synagogue and other inscriptional evidence. The most famous is the Theodotus inscription (*CII*, no. 1414), which mentions a guesthouse in Jerusalem. More recently, D. Barag has identified a structure on the south associated with the 'Ein Gedi synagogue as a guesthouse, Barag et al., "Second Season," 54, and plan p. 52. Examples are located only a few miles from Khirbet Shema': an Aramaic inscription (*CII*, no. 979) from Rama, which mentions the gift by a Rabbi Eliezer of a guest-

house "before the gate," which Klein ("Zur jüdischen Altertumskunde," 554–556) interprets to be the gate of the local synagogue. For a different understanding of the text, see Ben Zevi, "A Third Century Aramaic Inscription," 94–96, and Marmorstein, "The Inscription of Er-Rame," 100f. Klein suggests that such a guesthouse was needed because Rama was on an important highway, a statement which might also be applied to Khirbet Shema' a few kilometers to the northeast. Klein (p. 556) also notes the reference Tal.Yer.Schekalim 7.5 to a guesthouse at Lubiya (190/242) in lower Galilee some 20 km from Shema'. The term used is *pwndqy* from the Greek *pandokeion*. Guesthouses and hostels for travelers are a common feature in many of the more remote areas of the Roman Empire in all periods; most of them were established by gentiles, of course, and even those established by Jews were not always in conjunction with the synagogue. However, Klein's evidence for the existence of a number of synagogue guesthouses allows the supposition that such buildings would be particularly useful at locations which attracted students and pilgrims, so that the utilization of the North Building occasionally or even chiefly as a guesthouse should not be excluded.

hence all speculation of a major building associated with the synagogue on the western terrace was finally dismissed.

In cleaning to bedrock in NW I.27 it became quite clear that although the bedrock intruded well above the surface, no effort had been expended to regularize it or cut it back. Cleaning the crevices of bedrock indicated how disturbed some of this area had been in the Arabic periods: Arabic glazed wares were found in the deepest crevices. Where the metaled surface was preserved, however, excavation revealed no Arabic sherds beneath, an absence indicating that it dated to Byzantine times—Stratum IV or Synagogue II.

The square 5 m to the west, NW I.28, was bounded on its western extremity by a wall 28003 running north-south, two to three courses high, founded on bedrock, and dressed only on its inner, eastern face. It continues north at least to square NW I.34. This wall was in use with surface 28007, which was disturbed by a pit 28004 in the northeast corner of the square dug in Arabic times, Stratum VI. Once again the pottery for the make-up of the surface was predominantly Late Roman and Byzantine, while of the fifteen coins, eleven were Roman specimens of the 4th and 5th centuries CE, one was a Tyrian coin of the 2d century CE, and three were coins of Alexander Jannaeus. Also found in the make-up of the surface in this area were large chunks of plaster which the geologist's field reading indicated were identical with some specimens of synagogue plaster debris, perhaps from the destruction or the rebuilding of the first building. This suggests that the western terrace and its surface 28007 postdate Synagogue I. It is of course quite possible with surfaces laid over bedrock that a similar rough external walking surface existed earlier, if we are to insist that the western doorway is original to the history of all the phases of the synagogue. Nonetheless, the evidence from these areas overwhelmingly relates to the final phase (or phases) of the synagogue or Stratum IV.

NW I.33, NW I.34 and NW VII.3 (fig. 3.14)

Just to the north of areas NW I.27 and NW I.28 we opened squares NW I.33 and NW I.34 with a view to further clarifying the approach to the western doorway and the occupation levels on the western terrace. NW VII.3 was sunk five meters further north of NW I.33 in an attempt to link up this terrace with the southern wall of the North Building. Both areas NW I.33 and 34 were greatly disturbed by later walls and debris from medieval times. So extensive was this disturbance that Arabic pottery was found deep in the crevices of bedrock and under many of the extant walls. In short, a clear link with the metaled surface in NW I.27 and 28 could not be conclusively established by soil layers. The north-south wall (L.28003) in NW I.28 was found to continue in square 34 and seems to have served as a sort of western boundary to the walkway or promenade of the western terrace.

Traces of a flagstone pavement (L.33012 and 33030) were found in NW I.33; but only to the north, in NW VII.3, could these flagstones be traced with certainty. Extending south and west from the southwest corner of the North Building, the well-worn cobbles were perfectly preserved (L.33012 in NW I.33). Sealed under sections of pavement (L.3020, bucket 27; L.3021, bucket 28), homogeneous Late Roman pottery was found, indicating a use contemporary with at least one phase of Synagogue II, or in Stratum IV. Associated with these cobbles in square NW VII.3 were wall 3001 to the north, the north-south wall and step 3015, and wall 3024. These walls and cobbles appear to form an entryway onto the western terrace, perhaps from the northwest quarter of the village (see fig. 3.14). From this entryway persons would descend to the western terrace, some turning right (south) and proceeding on to the metaled surface in NW I.27 and 28, while others could proceed straight ahead (east) to the gallery entrance on the north side of the synagogue.

In the 6th century or Stratum V (post-destruction period) this elaborate means of passage to and from the western terrace was blocked by wall 3005 in NW VII.3, which continued south as wall 33013 in NW I.33. This wall was provided with a finished face only on the east side, which implies a terrace wall. It may be that the easternmost wall of the western terrace was built at this time, in which case wall 3005–33013 served as the west side of an alley or narrow street that ran north. Since access to the northwest quarter of the town is blocked in this period, it is possible only to turn east at the north end of this alley to the narrow walkway between the North Building and Synagogue II. During this period the south entrance to the North Building may well have been built, after the destruction of the earthquake of 419 CE. This alleyway is rather crudely paved with large flagstones (L.3006 in NW VII.3) late in Stratum V when sufficient fill had washed in to make passage difficult during the winter rains.

West of wall 3005 a small east-west wall was built in Stratum V, 65 cm north of wall 3024; it generally resembles a grave (L.3013; L.3007 = the fill inside) though no trace of bones or grave goods were found. The use of this structure is problematic, but when it was built the cobbles beneath it (L.3012) were already covered by shallow fill (L.3014).

The traces of Stratum VI or the Arab period are extremely problematic, as everything was too close to the surface and subject to erosion. Only the north end of wall 3305 is clearly from this period, easily datable from the Arab pottery sealed under it; wall 3005 = 33013 was cut into from above, and the stones, visibly out of line with the originally north-south orientation of this wall, were set in, apparently using L.3024 as well. The new use of this wall is not recoverable.

In short, the most compelling theory regarding means of access to the western doorway of the synagogue in Stratum IV is that a flagstone pavement was laid over bedrock where the outcroppings make this a fairly easy task; but as the incline dropped, earth with a heavy limestone mixture was moved in to provide a sloping metaled surface up to the western threshold, which was considerably lower. If the gallery was used exclusively for women, those who came from the western terrace may have separated from their spouses outside at the northwest corner of the building, the men entering the west doorway and descending into the synagogue proper and the women using the gallery door in the alley. For families coming on the middle terrace, the men may have descended through the north entryway and the women could have used the alley to the west to ascend to the gallery. This is speculative, but one must account for the two great doorways plus the opening in the northwest corner of the synagogue. It is of course conceivable that the purpose of the alley was no more than to connect the two terraces, but its narrowness and its location virtually inside the synagogue complex make this explanation less probable.

23. ROOMS ADJOINING THE SYNAGOGUE

The rooms to be described in this section must first be distinguished from areas already discussed, in particular the northern entry and the North Building. In general the rooms discussed below were in use at least during the last stages of Synagogue II; and the first utilization of the space now called the North Room just north of the northeast corner of the building[67] surely antedates Synagogue I. Such early occupation of the other rooms is less likely. Much of this space evidently was still habitable after Synagogue II was destroyed; the cut bedrock floors and lower walls were used and reused many times over. This post-destruction occupation has obliterated much or most of the evidence from Strata II–IV. Excavation has told us most about the last phases of the use of these rooms, and it is chiefly those phases which this section presents. Given the frequent reuse of the spaces and the removal of earlier debris which often accompanied such reuse, we do not always have fixed chronological points to which to tie the periods of use of the rooms during the time Synagogues I and II stood. However, the plan of the general area makes it clear that these rooms *assume* the existence of the synagogue; they are ranged around the building on half its north side and all of its east and south sides and they all have a wall in common with the larger building. None communicated *directly* with the synagogue at any time, but their location was determined by that building's existence and at times some of them may have been pressed into service as its side rooms or "outbuildings."

(i) *Adjoining rooms south of the synagogue, upper level (photo 3.27)*

Excavations along the south wall of the synagogue revealed a series of four rooms which use the outside of the synagogue wall as their north wall. They do

67. The North Building is thus immediately west of   the terrace before the northern door; the North Room is east of that terrace.

not communicate directly with the synagogue and appear to have been private rooms or shops contemporary with the synagogue, and perhaps earlier.

The two rooms on the upper level are a part of the upper terrace of the synagogue area, the terrace at the level of the gallery and the western entrance area. South of the synagogue, the eastern perimeter of that terrace is a north-south terrace wall; it antedates the synagogue, since it was constructed as a unit with the east-west terrace wall which later became the west end of the south wall of the synagogue. The west room has as its west wall the southern extension of the exterior west wall of the synagogue, which contains the west entrance (the Eagle Doorway) of the building.

From west to east, the arrangement is as follows: wall NW I.26, L.26003 (this wall also contains the Eagle Doorway), west room, north-south wall NW I.25, L.25006, east room, the terrace wall NW I.25, L.25004 = NE I.25, L.25015 (see the Introductory Note, fig. I.1, Key to the Excavation). Further, the west, north, and east walls of the west room and the west and north walls of the east room are, at the bottom, cut bedrock; the interior vertical face shows the wall to be cut bedrock at the bottom, a built wall above—just as is the case with the south and west walls of the main room of the synagogue. The chief difference is that in the southern adjoining rooms, the bedrock is not also cut horizontally to form the floors; rather, the bedrock under the floors of the rooms is irregular and in places has been hacked away. Finally, there is no pattern of relationships between the elevations of the floors inside the synagogue and those in the adjacent rooms to the south. The clear implication is that these rooms in their earliest phase are contemporary with the synagogue, perhaps even earlier, and that they were not related in use to the synagogue. They may have been originally constructed, in connection with the pre-synagogue chamber that we have called the *genizah,* for domestic or industrial purposes which have been wholly obscured by a series of later reuses. With their substantial bedrock-and-stone walls and their location near the central area of the town, it is unlikely that the rooms were ever unoccupied for long.

The rooms on the upper terrace were excavated fully only at the north, where they have a wall in common with the synagogue. The west room of the upper terrace is 3.25 m wide (east-west) and contained the following loci of NW I.26: 26005, 26009, 26014, 26018, 26019, 26029. The one clear surface in the room is a cobbled floor, L.26018 (photo 3.28); the pottery and glass (L.26019) beneath indicate that it is contemporary with Synagogue II. The pottery above is later, indicating continuing or intermittent use after the destruction of the building. Below this surface, at bedrock level, a rough niche has been cut into the north wall; it could never have been more than a few centimeters above the lowest surface, and its purpose is unclear.

The west and east rooms on the upper level are separated by a wall 55 cm wide (NW I.25, L.25006). In the lower portion of the wall the height of the bedrock varies, but it is never less than 0.5 m with the remainder made of hammer-dressed fieldstone. A notch has been cut in the bedrock some 40 cm wide and 30 cm deep, 0.5 m from the north wall, and the beginnings of another notch are visible just north of the south balk. Both are roughly done but clearly deliberate. There are no corresponding notches or supports on the west wall of the west room or the east wall of the east room.

The east room on the upper level was excavated as NW I.25 in 1971. Its east and west walls are preserved to an average height of 2ʻ m above the lowest point in the room. It is 2.6 m wide, east to west, and uses the terrace wall (L.25004 = NE I.25, L.25015) as its east wall. No surface comparable to the cobbles (L.26018) of the next room was found here. The absence of a clear surface is probably to be explained by the layer of heavy rock tumble found throughout the square, directly on the irregular bedrock at points where it was higher, somewhat above the bedrock wherever it dipped down; the soil (L.25007) under this tumble contained plaster and large sherds of Late Roman–Early Byzantine pottery. The terrace wall appeared unusually thick at this point (1.9 m); the reason, we discovered, is that it had been supplemented on the west with an outer row of stones founded on this tumble. All this suggests that at the time Synagogue II was destroyed, some of the debris fell into the east room, smashed through the thin earth or stone surface there, and buried the objects in the room. Later occupants of the space did not clear out the tumble, but built upon it.

These rooms were excavated not so much to learn everything possible about them as to ascertain the kind of structures adjacent to the synagogue. Had the wall between the rooms (L.25006) been exposed southward to its full length, we would have learned more about both rooms. At present, they do not appear to have been associated with the synagogue, despite the fact that someone went to the unusual length of cutting their lower walls from bedrock just as was done with the synagogue walls. The original rooms may have been related to the pre-synagogue installations known from this part of the site; but their substantial walls made them obvious candidates for occasional and long-term reuse and this has eliminated that early evidence.

(ii) Adjoining rooms, south of the synagogue, lower level (photo 3.29)

The two rooms adjacent to the south synagogue wall on the lower level give every indication that they were in use together. They are approximately the same size, their surfaces in the period of Synagogue II were apparently at the same elevation, and both have entrances to the south, opening onto a path or road which came from the west (via an opening in the terrace wall) and would have permitted communication with the two upper-level rooms (described immediately above) and with the upper terrace.

The west room was excavated in 1970 within NE I.25, and the east room in 1971 and 1972 as the southern part of NE I.26. The arrangement is as follows:

west wall, i.e., the terrace wall (NE I.25, L.25015 = NW I.25, L.25004), west room, common north-south wall (NE I.25, L.25025), east room, east wall (NE I.26, L.26041). The north wall in both rooms is the south synagogue wall: NE I.25, L.25003 = NE I.26, L.26002. The east-west wall on the south is NE I.19, L.19021 = NE I.26, L.26042. The area immediately south of NE I.25 was excavated in 1970 as NE I.19, and some of its material is also relevant in this section.

In this area, the bedrock slopes down to the east to such an extent that the walls of the east room are founded *on* the bedrock; but in the west room the north and west walls and the west portion of the south wall are of cut bedrock in their lower portions, similar to what was found in the rooms on the upper level and in the synagogue itself. As in the upper-terrace rooms (but not in the synagogue), the bedrock was not also cut horizontally to form the floor surface.

In general, the cut bedrock strongly suggests that the west room was built at the time of the construction of Synagogue I. Its west wall is earlier, of course, since it is originally a terrace wall which bonds with the east-west terrace wall (NW I.26, L.26004 = NW I.25, L.25002) which later became the west end of the south wall of the synagogue (see section above). To build Synagogue I, this east-west terrace wall was extended east (NE I.25, L.25003 = NE I.26, L.26002) to what became the southeast corner of the building. At that time or soon thereafter, the bedrock in the space that is now the west room was cut away to form a vertical face under the north (L.25003) and west (L.25015) walls and also to form the lower portion of a new east-west wall on the south (L.19021).

The east room was probably constructed at the same time, since its south wall (L.26042) bonds with the wall between the rooms (L.25025) and the south wall of the west room (L.19021), built when the space south of the synagogue wall was turned into the west room. Further, the major surfaces in the rooms (L.25042 in the west, L.26022 on the east) have precisely the same elevation, 743.9.[68]

The east room's surface is cobbled (see photo 3.29). In the west room the surface found was compacted earth, on which was discovered the most beautiful small object of the entire expedition: a carefully carved carnelian (ch. 8, pl. 8.11:24; and photo 8.7). Other finds in this locus and just above it suggest domestic occupation, or more likely, a small shop. It appears that occupation in the west room came to an end suddenly, at about the time Synagogue II was destroyed. The fact that the east room has a cobbled surface may indicate use different from that of the west room with its floor of hard-packed earth. Neither room is of sufficient size to be a dwelling unit. They were probably small shops of

68. Thus they are considerably lower than was the floor of the synagogue itself, just on the other side of the rooms' common north wall. The Stylobate Wall in the synagogue is at 744.7 at its top. Since the Stylobate Wall runs beneath the easternmost pair of pedestals, this figure may be taken as the elevation of the surface upon which the mosaic floor in the synagogue was laid.

the kind one would expect near a center of pedestrian traffic like the synagogue; the concerns of the east shop required a stone floor, those of the west shop did not.

(iii) Adjoining rooms north of the synagogue

The rooms described here are contiguous to the synagogue on the north and east of the flagstone entrance area before the north door. The space west of that entrance is occupied by the North Building, discussed in section 21 above. The entire area is in the center foreground of photo 3.30.

The area is bounded on the north by a path or stairway which provided access to the north entrance area of the synagogue, much as the path south of the south rooms led via an opening in the terrace wall from the lower to the upper level in that area. The entire area under discussion was in use before Synagogue I, since it is related to the pre-synagogue *miqveh* and other cut bed-rock installations; at that time the flat, somewhat irregular bedrock may have been open space as far to the west as the pre-synagogue storage chamber which later became the *genizah*. All the walls in the foreground of fig. 3.1 have been built on bedrock which had already been worked for one purpose or another. The north-south wall in the foreground of photo 3.30 (NE VIII.1, L.1018), for example, rests on two different levels of worked bedrock. The same cutting may also be seen on the other side of the wall. The bisecting of this space with a north-south wall is done after the north wall of the synagogue has been constructed.

The excavated squares in this area are (west to east) NE VII.1, 2, and 3. The north wall, bordering the path and stairway mentioned above, is L.2043 = 3007. The north-south wall parallel to the synagogue's east wall but a meter farther east of it is 3002; the north-south wall which abuts the north synagogue wall, bonds with wall 2043 = 3007, and bisects the area is 1018.

The area between 1018 and the north entrance of the synagogue was not fully excavated, but extensive probing revealed pits and other regular cuttings in the bedrock which are probably from the pre-synagogue period: NE VII.1, L.1020-1026. The use of this area (2.95 m east-west, 3 m north-south) in the time of the synagogue cannot be fully understood without further excavation, but it is possible that it was a part of the larger entrance area of the building and was filled in to the level of the entrance area terrace. Surely there was no communication to the east, since wall 1018 is without openings or doorways, and a stairway to the level of the synagogue entrance area would probably have blocked any entrance to the north.

The room just to the east (the North Room), however, is contemporary with Synagogue II; it is the largest and most important area discussed in this section (see photo 3.31). It is large enough to have been a private dwelling, but its proximity to the synagogue and to its more important north door suggest that it was the common property of the synagogue community. The floor was in part cut bedrock from the earlier period, but chiefly flagstone pavement, NE VII.2, L.2015 = NE VII.3, L.3009. This pavement was built up to the mouth of a spacious pre-synagogue storage pit cut in bedrock and visible in photo 3.31. The bedrock here (L.2018) is at elevation 743.96; the pavement is built up with fill until its upper surface is at 743.83. The storage pit (L.2017) consists of a main chamber directly under the opening and a subsidiary chamber to the north. Both are roughly elliptical in plan, the larger 1.85 m wide, 1.65 m long, and 0.84 m deep, the smaller 1.00 m wide, 1.10 m long, and 0.80 m deep. For the builders of the North Room, it offered substantial storage capacity, and they laid in the floor in such a way as to take advantage of it.

The room also had low stone benches running along the north and south walls (L.3008 and 3001), a feature also found in the North Building and in the synagogue itself. Finally, the North Room is securely dated: pottery under a clearly undisturbed area (L.3009.1) beneath the pavement was uniformly Late Roman. At the same time, the east wall (L.3002) contains some very regular ashlar blocks of the type we have been associating with Synagogue I. The collapse of that building made the ashlars available for reuse; thus the wall and therefore the room belong probably to the Synagogue II period. At that time, in the later 4th century, the community appears to have required more capacity in the synagogue (witness the added benches; cf. supra section 13) and outside it, hence the utilization of the North Building on the west and the North Room on the east, both flanking the north entrance to the synagogue, apparently the more important entrance in this period.

(iv) Adjoining rooms east of the synagogue (photo 3:32)

The pattern which we have already seen on the south and north of the synagogue continues on the east: a series of smaller structures or rooms is attached to the exterior walls of a town's large, central public building. The synagogue provides one substantial, ready-made wall for these smaller installations, and the traffic generated by the synagogue assures that these smaller rooms too are in the center of things. When the east end of the synagogue was founded upon an artificial platform projecting out onto the lower terrace, it took little time for community members to realize what the location on the lower terrace now had to offer.

The area immediately east of the synagogue (NE I.33 and NE VIII.3) differs from those described above in one regard, however: the east wall of the synagogue offered much greater protection for squatters and more permanent residents one terrace below; even today the remnants of the wall rise over 2 m above the surface just to the east. The result was frequent use, rebuilding, and reuse.

Figure 3.16. A systems approach to the reconstruction of Building B of the Khirbet Shema' complex, *by* John F. Thompson.

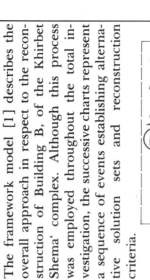
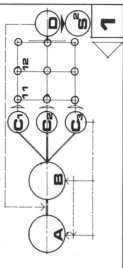
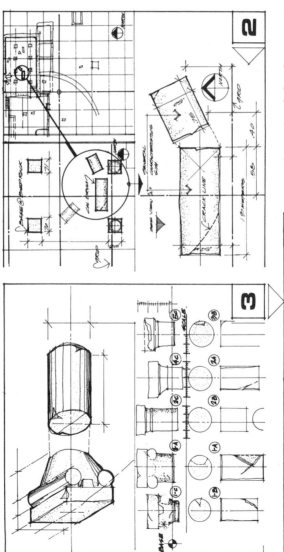

The framework model [1] describes the overall approach in respect to the reconstruction of Building B, of the Khirbet Shema' complex. Although this process was employed throughout the total investigation, the successive charts represent a sequence of events establishing alternative solution sets and reconstruction criteria.

Area A of the framework model [1] represents a general information gathering phase. During this phase information, including descriptive analysis, was gathered and recorded at various scales of influence. Physical relationships such as proximity, destruction patterns, inventories of sizes, textures, and physical similarities were developed, along with other relevant information dealing with Building B and its environs. [2] and [3]. Concepts and preconceptions generated through discussions with various experts were recorded during all phases of work. These were later evaluated against the criteria developed during the investigative process.

Although the basis body of information relevant to the field of investigation was constantly being modified, an attempt at synthesis was begun during phase B, the fundamental grouping phase in [1]. After the establishment of trial groupings of architectural elements, final groupings were generated that satisfied known or assumed physical and social criteria, [4] and [5].

In order to establish a total reconstruction picture (D of [1]) major structural, environmental, technological, social, and chronological groupings were evaluated and compared (Areas C_1, C_2, C_3, etc. in [1]). The result was a solution set that would satisfy continuing detailed investigation into such areas as possible roof configurations and the sequence of construction and destruction phases, [6], [7], and [8]. Continued testing of the schematic reconstruction appeared necessary only to the new archaeological and "architectural" data generated during the course of work at the site. The influences of the surrounding buildings and major circulation corridors formed a part of this testing phase, [9]. Upon reevaluation and modification of the tentative reconstruction set (D of [1]) a solution set (S^2 of [1] and [10]) was established in conjunction with alternative reconstruction drawings. This became necessary because of the lack of substantial quantitative structural elements required for criteria satisfaction. In addition, extensive catalogues were prepared for use during the actual reconstruction of the synagogue by the Israel Department of Antiquities in cooperation with the staff of the Joint Expedition to Khirbet Shema'.

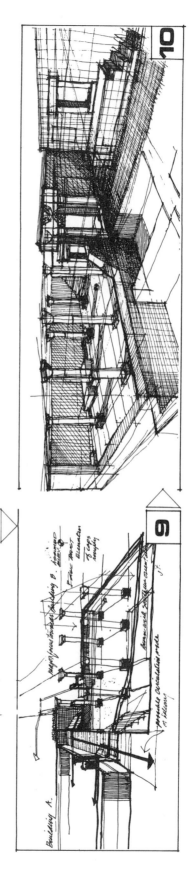

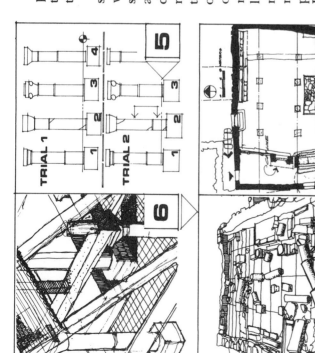

The main east-west wall in this area is NE I.33, L.33002, 0.5 m wide. It abuts on the east wall of the synagogue at 2.25 m north of the southeast corner of the building and is preserved to the same height as the east synagogue wall at the point where they meet; but its height drops 1.5 m in the first 5 m of its length, probably as the result of the quarrying of its blocks for later structures.

This wall and the east wall of the synagogue are the only substantial walls in this area; the east-west wall (L.33002) is slightly later than the synagogue itself, but surely dates from the time of the building's use. It is a building wall, not a terrace wall, and suggests that this terrace below the synagogue had substantial structures on it, contemporary with Synagogue II, perhaps earlier. The area south of this wall was not excavated.

The only candidate for a surface from the synagogue period is the cobbled L.33008 (NE I.33), built against the two walls just described, but nothing more can be determined about the structure which went with it. The walls built on it and the other surfaces in this area are a part of the post-destruction occupation. Immediately to the north, excavations east of the synagogue and of the North Room tell a similar story—indications of use contemporary with the synagogue, but wholly disturbed by later occupation (NE VII.3, L.3004–6, 3010–13, 3015–20).

24. POST-DESTRUCTION OCCUPATION

There is little real stratigraphic evidence to help us understand the occupation at Khirbet Shema' immediately after the massive earthquake of 419 CE. As will be clear from our coin report, coin populations of the mid to late 5th century are absent, though that may not imply complete abandonment. Yet it is difficult to imagine what kind of domestic or industrial occupation could characterize a century during which no one dropped a coin.

The first concrete evidence for human occupation is to be found in the 6th century. Even at this time, however, the paucity of coins is quite striking in view of the considerable numbers of coins from the 4th and 5th centuries. Though it is not clear what structures might be associated with these coins across the entire site, it is evident that most come from within fill high in the debris of the ruins. Such find spots imply visits by casual visitors, though it is possible that at least one or more families continued to live here, perhaps to tend the olive trees or vineyards, and that the six coins of the 6th century represent their losses during the end of the Byzantine period.

The next evidence for clear occupation is again largely from coins, but this time reinforced by the presence of pottery also of the 8th and 9th centuries. Again there are only five coins for the entire site—not enough to conclude anything about the character of the occupation.

Nevertheless the ceramic and coin finds appear to concentrate in the vicinity of the synagogue. That is, long after the synagogue had collapsed and had silted full from the winter rains, these people of Stratum VI came upon the scene.

At this juncture it is impossible to say just what the extent was of the Early Arab period occupation. From our scanty remains, which include the North Building and areas to the west and north of it, we can say that occupation confined itself to the top of the hill at Khirbet Shema'. Not even one stray Ummayad coin was found on the lower slopes or in the soundings in SE II.

Our coin evidence is much too thin to draw any hard chronological conclusions, but it appears that occupation begins with the 8th century and ends by the mid-9th century, i.e., during the period of difficulty on the part of the Ayyubids in maintaining their empire.

The same propensity for occupying the very top of the hill is also characteristic of the Mamluk occupation. In this case (Stratum VII) we have much more pottery and coins and building remains so that it is plain that virtually the whole of the area directly upon the synagogue site and west, northwest, and north of it was occupied as a tiny village. The lower slopes remained devoid of houses or other domestic or, for that matter, industrial installations.

Since this stratum was open to the top and modern disturbances, it is also in a fragmentary condition. However, it is possible to say that the structures to the north of the synagogue were in use during this period, as witness the Crusader coin inside the grain bin in NE VII.3. The houses to the east of the synagogue also yielded considerable late material, as did the North Building and the western terrace. Within the synagogue proper there appeared a sheepfold or other temporary structure with walls one stone wide and one course high still extant. This enclosure ran east from the interior wall of the synagogue and then turned south to the south wall in a butt joint. One stone of this wall is visible in the east-west section drawing at the surface in square NE I.26.

One fascinating bit of evidence about the dietary habits of the Stratum VII people is revealed from the bone evidence they left.[69] Analysis of the bones indicates that the most popular animals for slaughter were goats, sheep, and cows, which is what one might predict from knowledge of the Middle East today. But two surprises turn up in the next group. This group, the animal bones of the second most numerous type in Stratum VII at Khirbet Shema', comprises the following, in descending order: bird, pig, sheep, and gazelle. This is surprising on two counts: the appearance of pig and the appearance of gazelle.

It must be emphasized that we do not know the ethnic or religious make-up of the population at Khirbet Shema' in the 12th and 13th centuries CE, but the probabilities are great that they were either Moslem Arabs or Eastern Jews. Either way, pork is proscribed from their diet. Of course, it is also possible that

69. Animal bones were identified by Mr. Jeffry Schwartz of Columbia University. Only the 1970 bones were so identified, and the analysis below confines itself to the Stratum VII bones. The authors recognize the difficulties inherent in interpreting Stratum VII on the basis of bones alone. However, given the total fragmentary nature of the surface architecture, it was deemed necessary to include this information here.

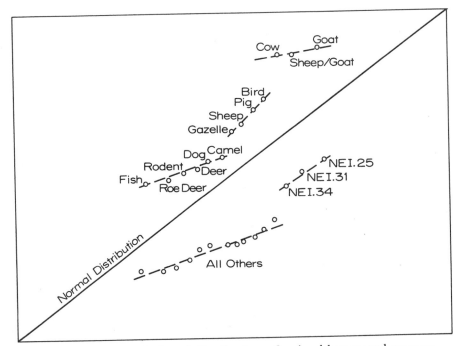

Figure 3.17. Normal plot of distribution of animal bones and squares.

Khirbet Shema' was settled by Christians in this period; but since Shema' appears to have been a dependency of the nearby large village, Meiron, it seems to follow that our site would also be Jewish.

Whatever the case may be, that these are pig bones is incontrovertible.[70] Likewise gazelles formed a significant part of the diet; no one would predict this from modern data, since gazelles are absent from the region today.

Finally we might note that a small percent of the bones are of camel, dog, deer, rodent, roe deer, and fish in that order. Since there are very few of these bones, it is impossible to draw any conclusions about diet from them. It seems even more unlikely that people in this region were slaughtering dogs and camels than that they were eating pigs and gazelles. The reader is referred to fig. 3.17 for a plot of distribution of animal bones at Khirbet Shema'.

A bit more information can be gleaned from the animal bones of Stratum VII.[71] It can be seen from fig. 3.17 (normal plot of animal bones—normal plot of squares) that squares NE I.25, NE I.31, and NE I.34 separate out as bone-rich in comparison to the rest of the squares. If we look at these squares on the site plan, we see that NE I.25 is just south of the synagogue, NE I.31 is wholly

70. According to Schwartz it is unlikely that these are wild boar bones, as the structure is characteristic of domestic pigs.

71. The authors gratefully acknowledge the aid of Mr. George Levenbach of New Providence, N.J., who executed the following statistical analyses in considerably more depth and detail than are presented here. Mr. Levenbach is an engineer by training, but has worked professionally with other engineers and scientists as a statistician for some years. Mr. Levenbach has supplied the technical references herein.

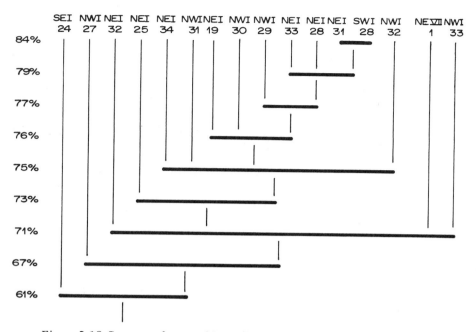

Figure 3.18. Squares clustered by animal bone abundances.

inside the synagogue, and NE I.34 is the easternmost square excavated outside the synagogue.

Two of these squares furnish data that correlate with this circumstance. NE I.32 is the first square east of the sheepfold or other structure mentioned in the western end of the ruined synagogue in Stratum VII. It is reasonable to assume that the fill here, for that is what it is, is also a repository for middens thrown down from the occupational area on the western terrace. On the other hand NE I.34 is inside a Stratum VII house (in its last use), or more likely, the courtyard of that house. It is yet to be seen why NE I.25 would be bone-rich, but the simplest explanation is that it, too, yielded important data from refuse or midden layers.

We tried to squeeze further information from these bone counts by applying cluster analysis using a similarity matrix. This appeared to be a fruitful tack to take, especially in view of the growing popularity of this technique among some American archaeologists.[72]

For the specialist we might say that the matrix is constructed with the squares as rows and the animal types as columns. For each square the percentage of animal bones for each type of animal is calculated. (The total number of bones in any given square is 100 percent.) From the "abundance" matrix we can derive a "similarity" matrix by applying the "O" multiplication for these

72. The bibliography of such efforts has burgeoned considerably in the past few years. For a recent effort at application of cluster analysis on archaeological evidence from Israel the reader is referred to L. D. Smith, "Cluster Analysis."

matrices as described by Kendall.[73] We use the similarity matrix as input for a computer program based on Johnson's "minimum" approach to obtain the tree illustrated in fig. 3.18.[74] From this tree we see that our three squares mentioned above are only 73 percent similar, though NE I.34 and NE I.31 are slightly better than 75 percent similar.

No clear pattern emerges from analysis of this cluster diagram. At 75 percent we can adduce nine similar squares, but they are not contiguous, nor do they cluster around recognizable architecture, industrial areas, or agricultural centers. We therefore present the tree for those to analyze who may wish to pursue the matter.

In any case we can say with confidence that during Stratum VII the occupation was quite thin, confining itself to the top of the hill in the vicinity of the synagogue, though of course by that time it would not be known to the population that there had ever been a synagogue.

73. Kendall, "Incidence Matrices."   74. Johnson, "Hierarchical Clustering Schemes."

CHAPTER 4. SOUNDINGS IN THE SOUTHEAST QUADRANT AND OTHER AREAS

One of the objectives of the expedition for the 1971 season was to carry out soundings on the lower terraces of the eastern slope of the hill. This was realized in SE II in three areas: the cistern (C-1), squares 17–19 and 22–24 of SE II (the "commercial/industrial area"), and the *miqveh* or T-17. In addition, attention was given to cleaning and recording the large wine press cut into the surface bedrock just north of the mausoleum (see Introductory Note, Key to the Excavation). The press lay within fields SW I and SW II but was recorded simply as the "press." Thus a total of four areas yielded important architectural and artifactual evidence for reconstructing historical and cultural patterns at Khirbet Shema', primarily during Strata IV and V.

1. THE CISTERN

This water installation is illustrated in fig. 4.1.[1] It is a typical cone-shaped hollow cut into bedrock in SE II.22. It measures 5.59 m deep and 3.44 m wide at the bottom. At the very bottom, centered directly under the top entry is a shallow declivity 56 cm wide × 30 cm deep. This depression is visible in fig. 4.1 and in photo 4.1; it serves to allow the users to dip out the last bit of water during dry periods.

Evidently the citizens of Teqo'a knew that the porosity of the bedrock required sealing, as the inside of the cistern is well-covered with two coats of lime plaster (see photo 4.2). This plaster contains ground sherds and tiny stones as a binder.

Excavation of the material inside the cistern showed a history of use and abandonment in two strata of three phases. These represent two uses (phases) in Stratum IV and one use (phase) in Stratum V.[2] Stratum IVA is the first use of the cistern as revealed by the debris within. This use is distinguished from that of Stratum IVB on the basis of the coins. Fig. 4.2 illustrates relative coin depths

---

1. The squares in SE II were not numbered according to the grid, for non-archaeological reasons. The first square excavated was number square "1," which made the next square north "7" as in the regular grid. Later, we numbered that square SE II.1A. Equivalencies are as follows:

SE II.1A = SE II.22
SE II.1 = SE II.23

SE II.7 = SE II.17
SE II.8 = SE II.18

2. It is impossible to conjecture when the cistern was first cut, as the puddled silt and clay in the bottom cannot date from the earliest use of the cistern unless it was never cleaned. For the preliminary report on the cistern see Meyers-Kraabel-Strange, "Archaeology," 21. (For full citation of works mentioned in the footnotes, see the Bibliography preceding the Appendixes in this volume.)

in the cistern (expressed simply as registration number) plotted against date. Clearly there are two groups of coins, one group from 325–306 CE and another group from 375–408 CE.[3]

The simplest explanation for this clear grouping is that the silt and clay that settled on the floor during the active use of the cistern for water storage (L.1004 and L.1005) accumulated during two distinct periods. We term these periods Stratum IVA and IVB. Therefore, L.1005 and L.1004A belong to Stratum IVA. L.1004B belongs to Stratum IVB.

After Stratum IVB, the cistern was abandoned and partially covered. During this period small stones and other loose debris fell in or were casually thrown in, forming a small mound on top the earlier clay and silt that settled out of the

3. Coin R1363 is worn smooth and can only be dated generally to the 4th century. The other coins with nar- rower date ranges do group themselves as indicated in the text.

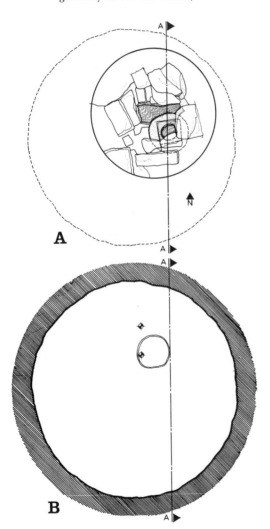

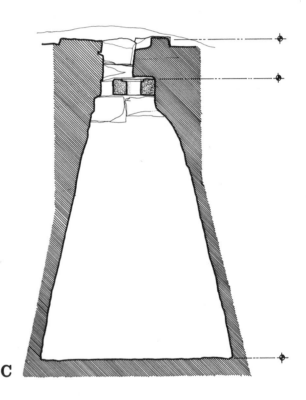

Figure 4.1. Plan and section of the cistern.

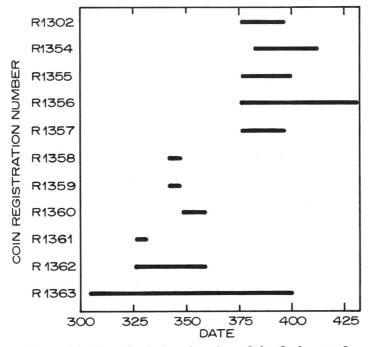

Figure 4.2. Plot of relative elevation of the find spot of coins in the cistern, against date.

water (see photo 4.3). One might say that this small hole really was used mainly as a receptacle for refuse by the few citizens that remained. These layers comprise L.1001, L.1002, and L.1003. They have all the characteristics of naturally laid layers, including few artifacts or pottery.

The pottery from the cistern is illustrated in fig. 4.3. Simple visual inspection of that figure shows that by and large the forms found inside were suited to drawing or dipping water: namely, cooking pots or jars. In fact, cooking pots and various kinds of small jars are represented by more than half the sherds found in the cistern. This is not surprising in view of the need to lower a vessel by a string from the cistern mouth into the water. What may be surprising is that no juglets were found, which can only mean that they were never used for drawing water, or at least that they were used so rarely that none were broken at the cistern.

As for the cooking pots found, here we need only point out that there are two clear types. Those illustrated infra, pl. 7.15:15, 20–23, are the earliest type, as they are found in the lowest locus, L.1005 *beneath* the coins of the earlier group (325–360 CE). Thus this type of pot cannot date later than the first half of the 4th century at Khirbet Shema'. On the other hand, the globular cooking pots illustrated infra, pl. 7.16:25–27, were not found in L.1005 and therefore must represent vessels dating *after* the middle of the 4th century CE.

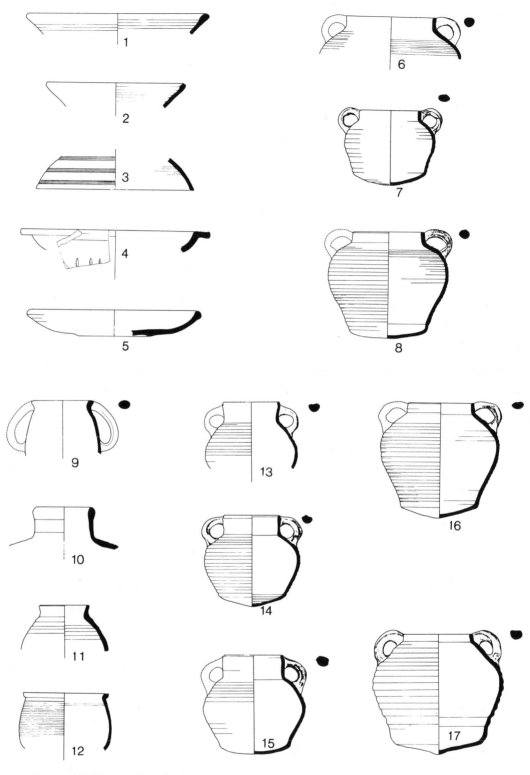

Figure 4.3. Composite of selected cistern pottery, 1:5.

A surprising number of terra sigillata sherds were found, including one complete reconstructed form (infra, pl. 7.23:24). Of course, these could not be used for dipping water, so it is reasonable to assume that they represent casual throwaways. This would also be the case with the unique bowl or cup in pl. 7.19:1 and the singular cooking pot or jar in pl. 7.19:17.

Artifacts include glass (31 registered fragments) and various iron implements such as a knife blade (R809), a nail (R638), and an ivory pin (R 639). Some of these are illustrated in the artifact plates for ch. 8.

The differentiation between coins and pottery clearly implies the double use mentioned above. What we did not discuss was the correlation with the known historical events in the Galilee at this time.

We know of two major events of prime importance that might correlate with the gap in the cistern coinage of 360–375 CE. The first is Gallus's revolt in the middle of the century, or about ten years before the latest coin in the earlier group.[4] It is unlikely that Gallus's revolt directly affected Teqoʻa, or any other town in upper Galilee for that matter, as evidently the Byzantine troops marched from Akko-Ptolemais to Tiberias via Sepphoris or more likely Legio. That is, Teqoʻa may have been forced to accommodate refugees from lower Galilee, but it seems doubtful that a disruption in the use of the cistern would occur. On the other hand, the earthquake of 362 CE may have been just destructive enough to disrupt life in the village for a few years. It is also possible that this earthquake would be an event of sufficient magnitude to cause interior remodeling of the synagogue.

Though the coin evidence for the break in use of the cistern seems incontrovertible, we must point out that such a dislocation in village life did not leave any clear evidence anywhere else in our excavations. Therefore, the gap from 360–375 CE may be purely accidental and due to the localized vagaries of life in and around field SE II at Khirbet Shemaʻ.

2. THE INDUSTRIAL QUARTER

This area, comprising five squares, was only partially excavated during the 1971 season. Because of curtailment of available funds in 1972, the area was not touched again. Therefore, not enough material was unearthed to allow more than a preliminary report.

Excavation proceeded first of all in square SE II.23 (see fig. 4.4) because the great quantity of stone fall there implied substantial architecture. Shortly the excavation team found southern and western walls of a small room (L.23007 and L.23006 respectively) only 50 cm below the rocky fall. These two, together with the north wall (L.23010) and the east wall (L.24021), form a small room

---

4. For a convenient summary of what can be known of this revolt see Avi-Yonah, *Geschichte*, 181–187, map 2.

3.6 × 2.3 m that we call room A. The walls average ca. 65 cm thick and stand now less than 50 cm high.

One gains entry to this room from the north. The door is only about 70 cm wide and is located ca. 1.50 m from the west inside corner of wall 23010. Outside the door to the east are the remains of a staircase. Anyone who walked up these stairs (with risers 20–25 cm each) would be entering the house about 1.60 m above floor 23014. This is a bit low for a house, so this room may have been a storeroom in its last use, as the storage jars found smashed on floor 23014 seem to imply. On the other hand, the inner faces of the walls of room A are furnished with small stones, as can be seen in photo 4.4. This suggests that this is certainly not a basement but is in regular use, as the doorway itself would imply. That is, it may have been built originally as a public room or shop.

The uppermost earthen floor inside was identified as L.23014. Upon it were found the whole smashed jar (infra ch. 7, fig. 7.10) and the restorable terra sigillata plate, infra, pl. 7.23:25, together with other sherds not restorable.

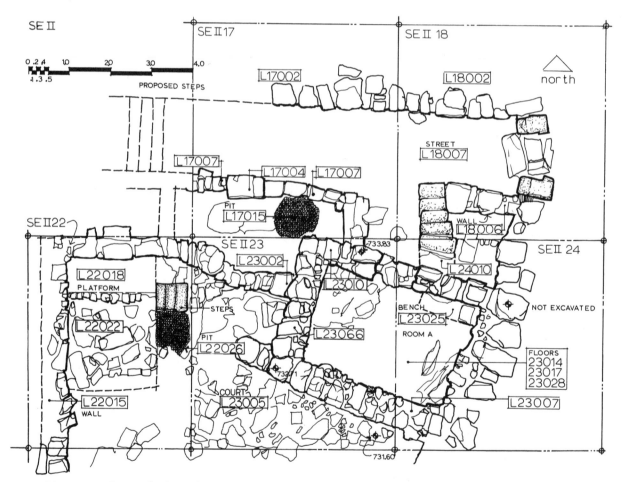

Figure 4.4. Ground plan of SE II.

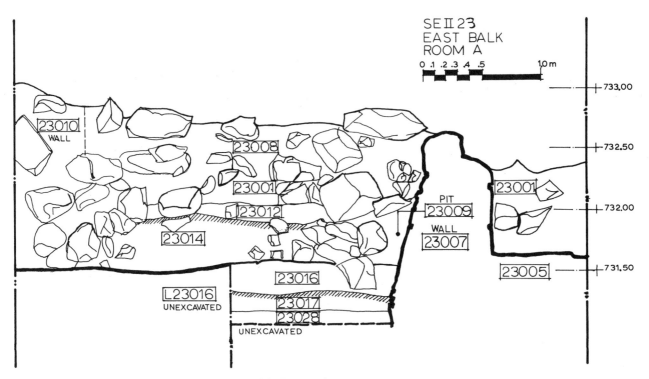

Figure 4.5. Section drawing of SE II.23, Room A.

Five coins of 4th to early 5th century date were also found in this debris. Thus the latest date of use for floor 23014 would be early 5th century, or just before the earthquake of 419 CE (see fig. 4.5).[5]

Directly under floor 23014 lay fill 23016, which doubtless simply leveled up the area for floor 23014 (see fig. 4.5). However, 14 cm below that was floor 23017, which also yielded three 4th-century coins and some pottery, including the storage jar collar (see, pl. 7.21:28, and see also photo 4.5). Slightly higher than floor 23017 in the northwest corner of the room was bedrock, which ran in front of the door. In the northeast corner of the room at the same elevation as bedrock (el. 731.43) appeared a low bench of six stones 0.42 × 1.10 m against wall 24010. The bench and bedrock are visible in photo 4.4.

Resting upon floor 23017 was an almost intact amphoriskos (see p. 237 and, pl. 7.23:26). It was lying in the southwest corner, probably where it was left, perhaps having been dropped by its owner, which would account for its broken base.

Fourteen centimeters below floor 23017 lay another candidate for a floor, L. 23028, found in the south center of room A. At a slightly lower elevation in the southwest corner of the room, but also beneath L.23017, was L.23019, which

5. From the section drawing (fig. 4.5) inside room A, one can see that floor 23014 was cut by pit 23009 just north of wall 23007. Fall that comes from the destruction and abandonment of wall 23007 is found within this pit. Therefore, it is possible that 23014 was used as a sort of courtyard after room A collapsed. However, it was not eroded, nor does it reveal other characteristics of an *outside* floor.

had all the earmarks of decomposed bedrock, i.e., virgin soil. Even so, it yielded most of a lid illustrated infra, pl. 7.17:5.

Thus the full history of occupation of room A includes two and perhaps three floors, though this is not as secure a conclusion as we might wish—not all the material could be dug to bedrock. In any case, the lowest floor (L.23028) lies 2.10 m below the putative ceiling. This is ample headroom for a room in regular use. The door giving onto the street in SE II.17 and SE II.18 may suggest earliest use as a shop with living quarters above.

The "street" mentioned above (L.18007 = L.17009) runs east-west through squares 18 and 1. On the north it is bounded by wall 17002 = 18002, but on the east it terminates in a regular doorway in wall 24021 (= L.18021) with about 1 m between the door posts. The door would open to the west, which normally implies that the area west of wall 21021 is *inside* a building or courtyard.

What we have tentatively called a street is only about 1.60 m wide just inside the doorway in wall 24021 (between walls 18002 and 18006) but widens to slightly more than 2 m in square 17. This is the area between wall 17002 (L.18002) to the north and low wall 17007, which effectively screened pit 17010 from passers-by.

This particular declivity and the similar installation L.22006 in square 22 seem rather enigmatic as they now stand. Since the northwestern corner of the room (the bond joint of walls 23066 and 23010) is built slightly over pit 17015, it is evident that this rock-cut chamber must antedate the room. Similarly, in square 22, platform 22022 is built slightly over pit 22006, which suggests that the latter antedates the former.

The function of these two rock-cut pits is difficult to assay. Neither is plastered, so it is doubtful that they held liquid. On the other hand, in their present configuration, it would be difficult to seal them if grain were stored in them. L.17015 is 1.22 m deep, but L.22006 is closer to 2 m deep.

The fill within these chambers (L.22003, L.22004, L.22005, L.22006 and L.17010, L.17011, L.17012, L.17013) did not yield much early material. Nevertheless some of the most distinctive ceramics of SE II were found in pit 22006 (see fig. 4.7): the unique bowl in pl. 7.18:3; the two pieces of terra sigillata of pl. 7.23:14, 23, as well as two sherds from basins with folded rim in pl. 7.17.15–16; and the base for an amphoriskos illustrated in pl. 7.23:26. On the other hand the ceramics from pit 17015 are quite prosaic, mainly a few sherds of storage jars as in pl. 7.20:46.

The amount of pottery in pit 22006 suggests deliberate fill taken from the town dump. The only other area in SE II that yielded such a striking accumulation of pottery was the fill between platform 22022 and wall 22031 (see photo 4.6) in close proximity to this pit. This fill was excavated as L.22018 and L.22020 and yielded the other basin with folded rim, infra, pl. 7.17:19, and the neck of a large storage vessel in pl. 7.24:13, among many sherds of Galilean bowls.

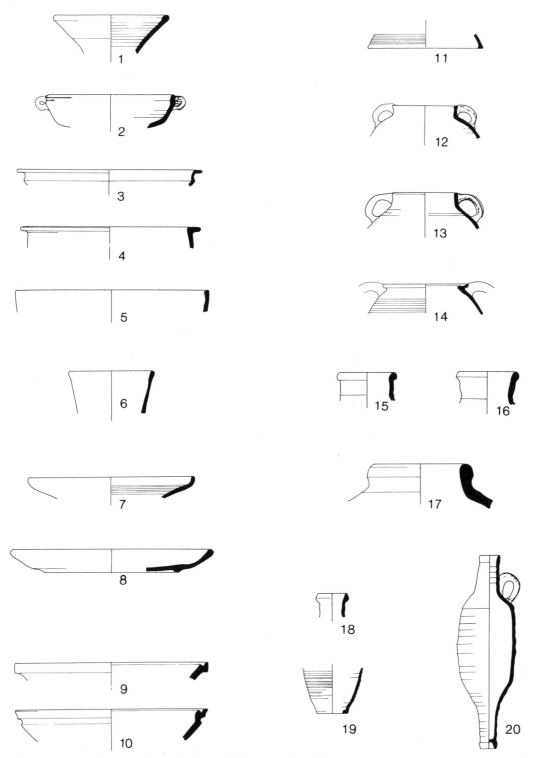

Figure 4.6. Composite of selected SE ceramics, 1:5.

The difference in ceramic content between the two pits and the similarity in the fill of pit 22006 and that area north of the platform simply suggests fill taken from two separate locations. It may also suggest (as does the difference in orientation of the walls in the west of the excavated area from those in the east) that the architecture in the east of the excavated area in SE II (and perhaps wall 17002 = 18002 in the north) has nothing to do with room A.

Outside room A to the west and south is a typical courtyard surface (L. 23004 and 23005) just above bedrock. It was partially paved (L.23005) but was otherwise compacted clay. It yielded little artifactual material, but must date early in the use of the area.

The artifactual content of the debris in SE II included a surprisingly large number of coins, almost all of which dated to the 4th and early 5th centuries. This substantial increase in the coin population surely implies at least a commercial aspect to life in this area. That is, some commodity was bought and sold (bread?). The coins also clearly show that life here began primarily in the early 4th century and terminated with the earthquake of 419 CE. Yet earlier coins are present in sufficient quantity to imply possible earlier occupation.

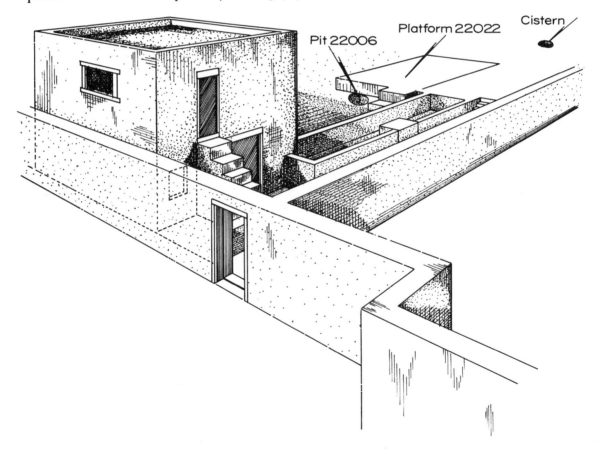

Figure 4.7. Perspective drawing of SE, looking to the southwest.

Other data indicating earlier occupation are spatulate lamp nozzles from L.22018 (fill north of platform 22022) and L.23001 (surface accumulation). The nozzle in L.23001 likely washed down from higher areas to the west, but the one in L.22018 is in deliberate fill. Of course, the original provenance of that fill is not known, and the latest material is 4th to early 5th century. Nevertheless we need not assume that the fill was transported any great distance to be placed in the cavity north of platform 22022. That is, it is most likely that this Herodian nozzle is from earlier occupation close by.

At present it is impossible to propose any final answers to the question of what use this area was finally put to. Furthermore, at present the architectural relationship of the cistern to this complex in SE II remains unresolved. Since it lies roughly in line with the street it may be integral to this industrial quarter, including room A; but only further excavation would enable us to say. Nevertheless for a possible reconstruction of the area in perspective the reader is referred to fig. 4.7. The staircase that leads up to the cistern is pure conjecture, but would explain the differences in elevation between the cistern mouth and the street (see photo 4.7).

3. THE RITUAL BATH OR MIQVEH (Photo 4.8 and Fig. 4.8)

This impressive installation was first excavated in 1970 as "Tomb 17," since what we are now calling the "pre-lavatorium" was located during the tomb survey.[6]

T-17 lies about 11 m west of wall 18021 of the industrial quarter in SE II. It was cut into bedrock as one of the most important features of a large irregular enclosure. This enclosure is bounded on the west by wall 18021 and its northern and southern extensions for a total north-south length of about 124 m. A singular semi-elliptical wall encloses the rest of this space forming a field about 124 × 132 m. Total area would be in excess of 6000 square meters or 1.5 acres.[7] It is impossible to say at this juncture what this great enclosure might be. The simplest hypothesis is that perhaps originally it consisted of agricultural terraces into which later the ritual bath and Tomb 29 (among others) were added.

This installation itself is divided into two chambers with an entryway from

6. See our report in Meyers-Kraabel-Strange, "Archaeology," 21–25.

7. On our site plan (supra Introductory Note, fig. I.1, Key to the Excavation) the enclosure is not drawn completely. The two walls running off the plan in SE IX and NE III are the southern and northern ends, respectively of this great semi-elliptical wall. The setting described here revises our earlier comments in Meyers-Kraabel-Strange's caption to fig. 10; clearly the wall to the west is more likely a terrace wall, as we noted on p. 23. Nevertheless the bath would still be outside the city as referred to in M. Mikvaoth 8.1. Note that rabbinic law does not require a

menstruant to bathe outside the city. An inference that it does is not intended in Meyers-Kraabel-Strange's comments (pp. 23–24) pertaining to M. Mikvaoth 8.1. Rather, the issue concerns a *miqveh* of unknown origin found outside the city walls. The fact remains that this installation assuredly had an earlier history, which is lost to us, but in all probability is associated with water. The mishnah in question deals specifically with such a pool or cistern and its suitability for use as a *miqveh*. Hence if a *miqveh* of unknown origin is found outside the city walls, it is fit even for a menstruant. The authors gratefully acknowledge the advice on this matter of Rabbi Emmanuel Feldman.

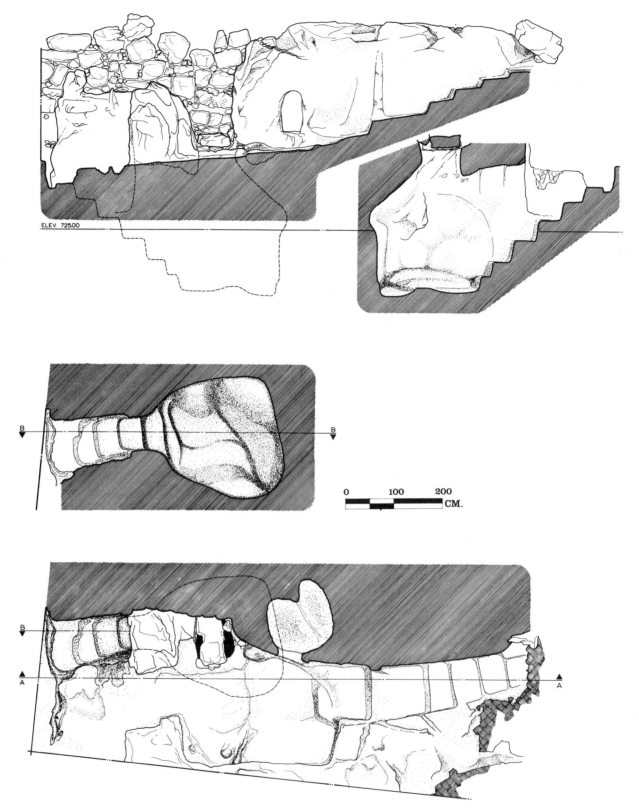

ELEV. 725.00

0   100   200
CM.

Figure 4.8. Ritual bath plans and sections.

Figure 4.9. Proposed reconstruction of the ritual bath.

the east that opens onto a forecourt associated with the first chamber (see fig. 4.9). West of this 2.75 × 2.00 m forecourt, the bedrock is cut to resemble doorposts (note the clear jamb on the east side; the jamb on the west had badly disintegrated). As one proceeded westward through the door he would be within a small roofed chamber (2.35 × 1.60 m.) that formed the approach to the lower chamber down and to the right 180°. That is, we have three clear architectural areas: the approach staircase, the forecourt with its pre-lavatorium, and the inner vestibule with its underground bathing chamber (see fig. 4.9). Though it is not clear in either our plans or photo 4.8, the western end of this installation terminates in a wall well-faced on the inside with small stones. No plaster was found in the washed-in fill, an absence which implies that the stone facing did not hold plaster.

The last step of the approach is provided with a channel cut into the step to collect rainwater. The channel ends in a shallow sump or settling basin before flowing directly into the overhead hole of the lower chamber. (photo 4.9).[8] This lower, well-plastered bathing chamber (photos 4.10, 4.11, 4.12) is approached by seven steps and is about 2.40 m long × 2.35 m wide at the back. At step 6 the chamber is ca. 0.90 m wide, forming a roughly trapezoidal chamber. The 3-m-high walls provide no obstacle for a menstruant's total immersion.[9]

The smaller chamber or pre-lavatorium is well suited for *hafifah* or cleansing of the hair before ritual immersion.[10] This chamber, about 1.0 m high, would require the bather to assume a squatting position. This demand throws light on the whole idea of *hafifah* as practiced at Khirbet Shema' (Fig. 4.8).[11]

Parenthetically we might add here that our interpretation of this installation as a *miqveh* or ritual bath seems simplest for several reasons: (i) The exterior approach staircase, forecourt, inner vestibule, and roof seem inappropriate for

8. The sump meets the requirements of M. Mikvaoth 4.1 for clean water.

9. According to M. Mikvaoth 1.7 the bath must hold 40 *seahs* of rainwater. For variations in this measure in Mishnaic and Talmudic times see A. Ben-David, "Ha-Middah ha-Yerushalmit." Our chamber would hold at least 10.38 m³ of water if filled to a depth of 1.5 m.

10. See M. Mikvaoth 9.1–9.3 and the Gemara, Niddah 66b.

11. See Meyers-Kraabel-Strange, "Archaeology," 25.

a village cistern, the alternative interpretation. (ii) The total capacity of the lower chamber when filled to the height of the middle step would be one-third the capacity of cistern 1, which is 30.5 cubic meters when filled to a height of ca. 4.3 m. This seems small by comparison. (iii) There is no ready explanation for the upper chamber, if we assume that the whole is a cistern. Storage jars or cooking pots for dipping *could* be kept there, but then we need to ask for possible motivation, which seems difficult to find.

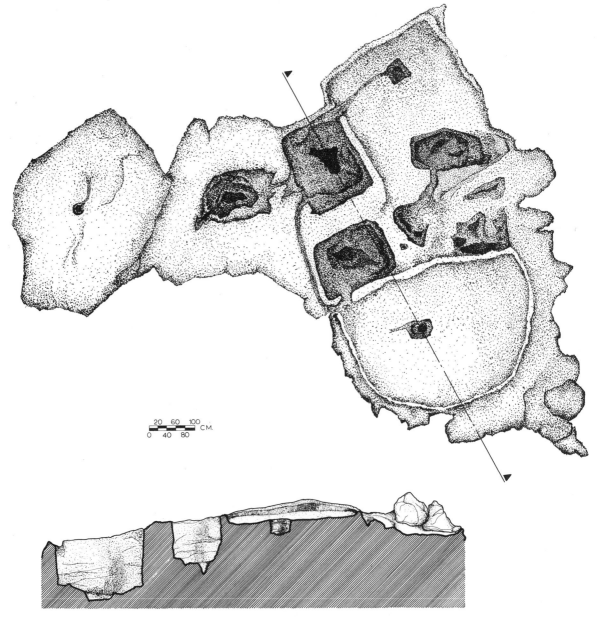

SECTION

Figure 4.10. Plan and section of the wine press.

The pottery from T-17 is typical of the 4th to early 5th centuries, or Stratum IV. Of course, we need to remind ourselves that this material is washed in from higher up on the hill, but even the lowest levels yielded the same ceramic horizon. What may be significant is that by far the most common pottery forms in the *miqveh* were "Galilean bowls" and storage jars. Globular cooking pots were not as much in evidence as one might predict from the profile of the entire site or from the profile of SE II (see Table 4.1). However, frequency count of storage jars was exactly that of SE II, eleven meters up the hill. Only one coin, that of the Hasmonean period, was found. Very little artifactual evidence was found in the water-washed fill.

Table 4.1. COMPARATIVE TABULATION OF CERAMIC TYPES

	Site	SE II	C-1	T-17
Galilean bowls	39.8%	20.0%	7.7%	50.0%
Bowls, everted lip 1	3.8	1.4	0	7.1
Bowls, everted lip 2	3.6	1.4	0	1.8
Cooking pots, hor. handles	1.6	1.4	0	0
Cooking pots, globular	12.4	20.0	46.2	1.8
Lids	1.8	1.4	3.8	0
Basins, lipped	0.8	4.3	0	3.6
Misc. bowls	1.8	7.1	0	1.8
Arab bowls	2.6	0	0	0
Cooking pots, folded rim	0.5	1.4	0	0
Misc. jars or cooking pots	3.1	0	11.6	3.6
Jars	14.5	21.4	3.8	21.4
Juglets	8.2	5.7	0	3.6
Terra sigillata	3.3	12.9	11.6	0
Storage jars	1.7	1.4	0	0
Basins	1.3	0	0	0

It seems simplest to conclude that this installation was in use during Stratum IV or the height of occupation at the site. Precisely when it was cut we cannot say, but a date around the turn to the 4th century seems most reasonable in view of the ceramics. It evidently went out of use at the time of the earthquake in the early 5th century.

4. OTHER AREAS

Another major area of interest of the Expedition was the focus on agricultural practices of the ancient inhabitants of Khirbet Shema'. Consequently the wine press just north of the mausoleum was cleaned and recorded in the 1971 season (see photo 2.9). This press is cut into bedrock and covers an area 11.2 m east-west and 9.6 m north-south for a total area of nearly 64.5 square meters (see fig. 4.10).

The main pressing area is shown in the northeast of the plan. This ca. 4.0 × 2.7 m area is ringed by a groove to collect the freshly squeezed grape juice and conduct it to several collecting and settling basins. These drain into one another, as is evident from the plan, in such a way that the last basin would collect the purest fluid and that most suitable for making a clear wine.

Since this installation is cut directly into surface bedrock, it cannot be dated by associated artifacts. The soil and other debris that had washed into the basins was disturbed and contained modern or near-modern material. It is possible that the press was used as late as the Turkish period. Exactly when it was cut can no longer be determined. The upright stone posts of a screw-type press are still visible northeast of the wine press (see photo 4.13). It is possible that the whole complex of structures in the southern half of NW I and the northern half of SW I is another industrial complex devoted to vintage.

Finally, mention must be made of two upper millstones located at the site. One is built into the neck of cistern 1 and the other lies on the surface in SW I.2 (see site plan, supra Introductory Note, fig. I.1, Key to the Excavation). Both stones suggest the presence of a grain-grinding industry, as one might expect. The stone in the cistern must date to the Stratum IV or active use of that installation, but the surface stone could date to any period; morphologically it resembles the one in the cistern neck.

The results of our soundings in SE II and other areas thus suggest that the ancient inhabitants of this village busied themselves with the main elements of an agricultural economy. It is not clear at all that they engaged in industry, such as ceramics, glass blowing, or forging. Rather the picture that emerges is of a largely agricultural (but not necessarily pastoral) economy in the Roman and Byzantine periods. Doubtless the same picture held true during the later Arab-period occupations.

CHAPTER 5. THE TOMBS

1. THE MAUSOLEUM (Photo 5.1, Figs. 5.2, 5.3, 5.4)

The great monument of Khirbet Shema', which for centuries had guided pious pilgrims and visitors to the putative tomb of Shammai,[1] was for the purposes of recording labeled T.M.[2] In the necropolis of the community it commands the center of attention; and though it is not situated in the center of what appears to be the main cemetery of the settlement—namely, the string of tombs along the eastern incline of the mountain to the northern point of the hill—it is highly unlikely that its history is to be understood apart from the remainder of those tombs and apart from the history of the settlement itself (see fig. 5.1).

Indeed, the strategy of digging tombs dictated that we relate T.M. to the ruins of the site. Unfortunately, excavation soon revealed that the great mausoleum was built virtually on bedrock. Soil layers up against T.M. were wholly disturbed. Foundation stones beneath the lower story of T.M., however, were plastered over to level the monument (see photos 5.2, 5.3), though the material might better be described as a kind of mortar or cement.[3] Though the overwhelming number of sherds recovered from sections up against all sides of T.M. were Late Roman and Byzantine, contemporary with the major periods of occupation, enough intrusive material was found to urge utmost caution in arguing its date from ceramics. In the absence of such data we must simply conclude that though without parallel, the Mausoleum does fit into the typology of Jewish tomb monuments in late antiquity and that there is no evidence to suggest the noncontemporaneity of T.M. with the synagogue and environs. Whether T.M. dates to the earliest or latest phase of the history of settlement is impossible to determine. Nonetheless, it can be asked whether the town itself may not have grown up around the Mausoleum. If such might have been the case, then T.M. would date to the earliest settlement.

---

1. See the authors' earlier remarks in Meyers-Kraabel-Strange, "Archaeology," 3, 20–21, esp. n. 1, where a bibliography is given. (For full citation of works mentioned in the footnotes, see the Bibliography preceding the Appendixes in this volume.)

2. Dalman, "Phönizische Grab," 195–199, has attemped to relate T.M. to Phoenician megalithic tombs, a line of argument without substantiation. Dalman evidently had in mind the tombs and monuments reported, for example, in Perrot and Chipiez, *History of Art in Phoenicia*, 142–251. He also relates an Arabic tradition which refers to the monument as "house" and also mentions the more familiar Arabic "sirir" or "bedstead," Guérin, *Description géographique*, II, 433–434. The authors found no evidence however, to link the so-called Throne of Elijah or Dalman's "Messiasthron," which lies further west up the mountain, to the settlement at Khirbet Shema' (photo 2.2).

3. This plaster was described by geologist R. Bullard as "clean white calcium oxide plaster with medium sand-sized to fine-pebble-sized grits, with moderate well-rounded chert, limestone with angular calcite rhombs, burnt limestone fragments and milky quartz . . . the aggregate has a potential source in the stream deposits at the base of the hill."

Clearance of the lower chamber revealed even more modern disturbances dating to recent years, when it was apparently used as a storage room for a shepherd. Its *kokh*-type entryway, with a beautifully cut threshold stone, suggests that it was at one time used as a bone repository for secondary burials. The great massive block in the center of the monument is cut to receive two corpses, skulls oriented toward Jerusalem. It might well represent the place of primary interment for heads of families with the lower chamber serving as the place to which they were ultimately collected in a secondary burial.

The entire Mausoleum offers the impression of a *domus aeterna, Fenstergrab,* or free-standing sarcophagus,[4] and when viewed together with T-1 beneath it (photo 5.4), may well represent the *nephesh* of a larger subterranean tomb

4. Avigad, *Ancient Monuments,* 66–73. For "eternal house" see Goodenough, *Jewish Symbols,* I, 75f.

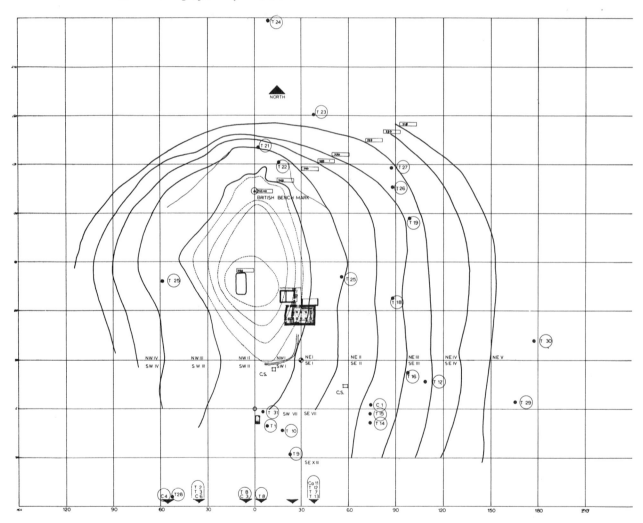

Figure 5.1. Contour map showing locations of tombs.

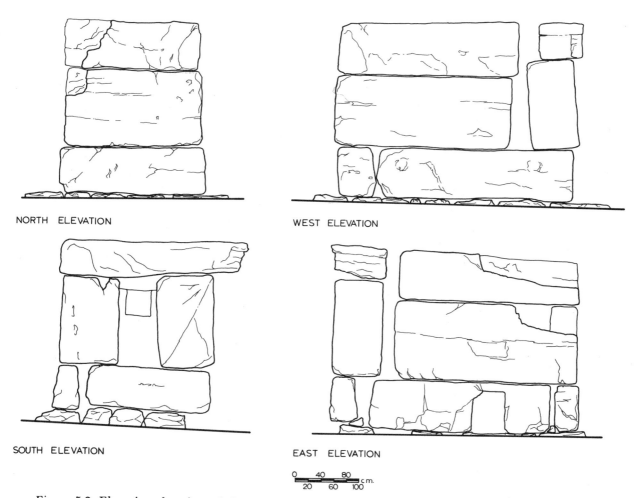

NORTH ELEVATION

WEST ELEVATION

SOUTH ELEVATION

EAST ELEVATION

```
0      40    80
                  c m.
   20    60   100
```

Figure 5.2. Elevation drawing of the Mausoleum.

complex (including perhaps even T-31 slightly to the northeast), the kind we find in Jerusalem.[5] The erection of such an imposing structure (height 2.60 m, width 2.40 m) was itself a major engineering feat; several badly weathered lugs on the western side of the middle block indicate that ropes were used to move the great stones from a quarry very nearby.[6]

One final point bears mentioning regarding T.M. and its placement in the larger context of the settlement of Khirbet Shema'. Situated on the southwestern extremity of the town, it is strikingly proximate to the synagogue and virtually contiguous with the industrial quarter of the town, especially the large wine press (see supra Introductory Note, fig. I.1, Key to the Excavation). Since all evidence points to the contemporaneity of T.M., T-1, and T-31, all in this industrial sector, one is forced to ponder the rabbinic injunctions to place tombs downwind

5. See Finegan, *Archeology*, 191ff; Avigad, *Ancient Monuments*, passim.

6. Geologist Bullard has confirmed the proximity of a quarry and has noted that the weathering of T.M. is the same as that found on the long-exposed architectural members of the synagogue.

SECTION A

SECTION B

0 40 80 cm.
20 60 100

Figure 5.3. Section drawing of the Mausoleum.

and beyond the city limits, not to ask how priests could have avoided this vital part of town.[7] In the absence of data that would justify assigning these tombs to dates either before or after the major periods of Jewish occupation, one is forced to conclude that ritual issues such as these did not impede the work of the town planners and architects of Khirbet Shema'.

2. TOMB SURVEY

The objectives of Field T for the 1970 season were three: (i) to survey the site and locate as many ancient tombs as possible in two or three days; (ii) to select one or more tombs for stratigraphic excavation; and (iii) to accumulate from the excavation a corpus of datable material to illuminate the history of the site. From the outset we anticipated that only robbed tombs would be found, but the hope was that those robbed in antiquity would still yield pottery and other artifacts useless to ancient robbers.

A total of thirty declivities were located and assigned numbers serially.[8] These included tombs, caves, collapses, and at least one cistern (and a few rock-cut graves); they were all plotted, for the sake of completeness. Location of all tombs is given on the site plan (see fig. 5.1). Distances were chained in the field from three reference points on the site and from other plotted tombs. Distances are therefore uncorrected for topography and include cumulative error. T-29 was plotted from surveyor's notes.

T-1: A rock-cut tomb, its entrance 10 m east of the Mausoleum, the most

7. See especially Semahot 4 for the laws pertaining to the priestly defilement and the broader discussion of Zlotnick, *Tractate "Mourning,"* 110–118. See also M. Baba Bathra 2. 9, Tal.Bab.Ta'anit 16a.

8. Numbers are given serially, more or less, in order of the original recording, with the prefix "Ca" for cave, "C" for cistern, and "T" for tomb, rock-cut opening (possible tomb), rock-cut grave, or collapse. Collapses are included on the grounds that they may be tombs or cisterns.

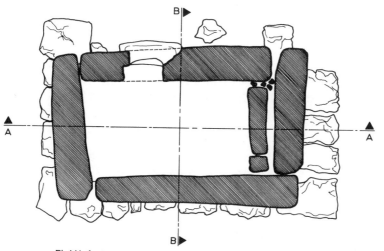

PLAN 1 (LOWER CHAMBER)

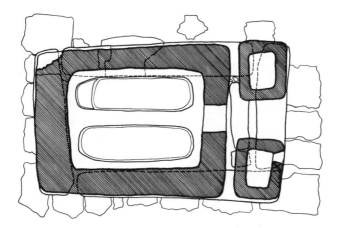

PLAN 2 (MAIN CHAMBER)

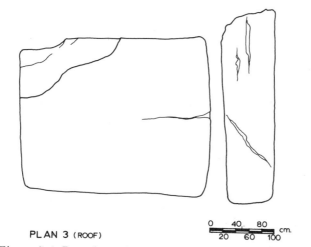

PLAN 3 (ROOF)

Figure 5.4. Drawing of the Mausoleum indicating three
levels of construction.

prominent landmark on the site. T-1 is also 10 m east and 10 m south of the reference point just north of the Mausoleum.

T-2: A shaft-type tomb 110.5 m south of the Mausoleum. Late Roman sherds were found near but not in the shaft, the top of which faces north.

Ca-3: A cave 7 m east of T-2, facing northeast. Its proximity to T-2 suggests that it may have been used for burials. There are more Late Roman sherds on the surface above and to the south.

Ca-4: A vertical bedrock outcropping, with perhaps two rock-cut entrances facing east. It lies 43 m south of T-2. The rock facing forms a rough arc, with one opening in the center and the other 2.25 m northward. There appears to be another opening at the center of the chord of the arc, since a rather large tree is growing there out of what is otherwise bedrock.

Ca-5: A cave 37 m east of Ca-4, with a large amount of shrubbery at the opening, suggesting a large root system. There is much Roman-Byzantine pottery on the terrace above the opening.

Ca-6: A large cave about 150 m south of Ca-5. There is no clear evidence of occupation or use for burials, though the ceiling appears to have partially collapsed. The present floor has been silted to within 0.50 m of the ceiling at the entrance. The mouth faces eastward and is about 4.0 m wide.

T-7: A small opening facing east, 60.5 m east of Ca-3. There is a large amount of brush at the entrance, but the visible corner of the opening may be rock-cut. It is silted full.

Ca-8: A cave at the base of a 3-m-high outcropping 26.5 m east of Ca-3. There is a large amount of brush at the entrance that was partially removed. It is not clear whether the cave was rock-cut. The opening is 0.36 m high × 2.87 m wide.

T-9: An open and empty rock-cut grave 27.0 m southeast of the Mausoleum. The grave is oriented east-west and measures 0.47 × 0.69 m.

T-10: A covered, rock-cut grave 19.7 m east of the Mausoleum. The cover stone was slipped westward, probably for robbing. The cover stone is 1.41 × 0.75 × 0.35 m.

A pottery survey of the peak south of Khirbet Shema' indicated that the pottery was of very mixed date. It was therefore decided to confine the survey to the site of Khirbet Shema' proper. In the course of this pottery survey, however, a possible tumbled-down wall was found 10 m south of T-2 and Ca-3. There was also a small "tumulus" 15 m southwest of T-2, with one cup-hole in the bedrock 2 m northward. The tumulus is severely scattered, with surface sherds of Early Bronze or Iron II type. Also there was found near the south summit a possible ancient road leading southward and upward through a cyclopean wall to a large flat open place, perhaps an animal enclosure, military encampment, or "high place."

Ca-11: A cave 73.9 m east of T-3 at the base of a 3-m-high outcropping of bedrock.

T-12: A possibly rock-cut opening 18.5 m north of Ca-11. It is 0.80 m high ×
0.60 m wide. A small niche cut (?) outside to the left is 0.27 m wide × 0.29 m high.

T-13: A small hole at the base of bedrock out of which is growing a tree with
a 30-cm trunk. The hole is 37.6 m south of T-12.

At the base of the peak south of Khirbet Shema' is a winter spring that runs
directly into the wadi. This suggests that there may be seasonal prehistoric
occupation in the vicinity. Chert flakes have been found on the slopes of the
Wadi Shammai.

T-14: On the hill of Khirbet Shema', 76.3 m. east of the mausoleum, there is
a fallen-in cave, tomb, or cistern (a collapse). It measured 0.68 m wide × 0.46 m
deep.

T-15: This appears to be a stone-lined vertical shaft of a cistern or well,
6.7 m north of T-14. The top is roughly elliptical, 1.22 × 1.16 m. (There is a
clear cistern 6.3 m north of T-15 with a Roman grindstone in the mouth, photo
4.2. Its opening is 0.96 × 1.05 m. It was designated C-1. See supra, ch. 4, section 1.)

T-16: A collapse 21.6 m east of the cistern just mentioned, representing
again a cave, tomb, or cistern.

T-17: Later identified as Ritual Bath.

T-18: A square, rock-cut opening 77 m north of T-17 and 16.2 m west of
the same. This niche is 1.10 m high × 0.76 m wide and presently 0.80 m deep
into bedrock.

Ca-19: A shallow cave 46.5 m north and 8.5 m east of T-18. Roman-
Byzantine sherds are in abundance in front. The cave is silted full. It is 0.92 m
high × 2.27 m wide × 1.37 m deep.

T-20: A small, square-topped opening 49.5 m east of Ca-19. It is 0.38 m
high × 0.41 m wide and almost completely filled with soil and 1-cm stones.
Roman-Byzantine sherds are in front.

Ca-21: A vertical shaft 167.7 m north and 4.3 m east of the reference point
immediately north of the Mausoleum. The shaft is 3 m deep × 0.74 × 1.10 m.
and opens northward at the bottom. This bottom opening is 0.39 m high ×
2.11 m wide, opening northeast at the bottom of a 3-m outcropping. It is likely
a natural formation.

T-22: A rock-cut tomb 11.20 m southeast of Ca-21 facing east. The opening
is now 1.45 m wide × 0.40 m high, though it was badly cut out in the north side
in a robbing operation. It contains two arcosolia with three graves each, a niche
for secondary burial, and one *kokh*. It was cleaned for drafting during the season.

T-23: About 38.3 m east of T-22 is an almost vertical outcropping about 5 m
high. At its base is a tomb entrance with a possible sealing stone shattered *in situ.*
This entrance is roughly semicircular, measuring 0.90 m high × 1.74 m wide.
The present depth of the entrance is 5.4 m. Inside and to the right is an opening
0.50 m high × 2.77 m wide that leads to a room that is 4.0 m in diameter. Inside
and to the left of the outside entrance is another opening, 0.70 m wide, partially

blocked by fallen and washed-in debris. This opening leads into another roughly circular room 2.3 m in diameter. Some of the rock debris seems to be associated with the robbing operation, and the tomb has been visited in modern times. There is considerable soil washed into all three rooms.

Ca-24: A cave on the northern face of the Khirbet Shema' hill 79.0 m east by north of T-21. The cave opening is 2.20 m wide × 0.32 m high. The maximum present depth of the cave is 1.90 m, though the blackened roof is partially collapsed, blocking entry. The ceiling shows clear adze marks, and the blackening implies occupation rather than inhumation.

T-25: A clear rock-cut tomb 76.8 m southwest of the British triangulation point on the north end of the hill (Fig. 5.5). The tomb is therefore on the west side opening westward. The present entrance is 0.92 m high × 1.30 m wide, somewhat enlarged by the robbing operation. The broken seal stone still lies at the entrance. Outside to the right of the entrance is a rock-cut niche in the vertical facing that is 0.76 m high × 0.99 m wide and is cut 0.94 m into the rock, perhaps the remnant of a burial. There are also traces of a *kokh* to the left of the entrance.

The main chamber is rectangular and measures 5.60 m east-west and 5.30 m north-south. Twelve or perhaps thirteen *kokhim* extend outward from the walls. There is a great deal of washed-in soil and rubble. Some of the picking at the entrance may be modern.

T-26: An open rock-cut grave 86.0 m east and 4.0 m north of the British triangulation point. The grave is oriented east-west with the west end cut out when robbed. Present internal dimensions are 0.63 m wide × approximately 1.20 m long. The cover stone is missing, though a nearby stone block 0.80 × 0.31 × 0.34 m may have formed part of the cover.

T-27: A rock-cut tomb 85.5 m east and 10.4 m north of the British bench mark. The entrance leading westward into the outcropping appears to have communicated with the main chamber through a horizontal shaft about 2 m long. The roof of this shaft is now cut away revealing an inner opening at the west end. This second entrance is 0.60 m high (presently) and 0.68 m wide.

The main chamber is oriented east-west, 4.01 m on that axis and 3.25 m north-south. There are 12 *kokhim*, with the *kokh* just north of the entrance enlarged and rounded as though for secondary burials. A vertical robbing shaft communicates with one of the western *kokhim*. An arched lamp niche is cut high and south of the entrance. Presently the main chamber is filled with soil and rubble to within about 1.4 m of the ceiling.

T-28: A square-cut opening with shoulders as though to receive a sealing stone, 72.4 m southwest of the reference point directly north of the mausoleum. This entrance is quite close to the new road on the west face of the hill.

The visible top of the opening is 0.61 m wide, though it is filled to within 0.10 m of the top. Excavation would be complicated by a tree that grows out of the opening's south side.

The bedrock on the west face of the hill of Khirbet Shema' is so badly fissured that it holds little promise for tombs other than T-25 and T-28.

T-29: A small hole cut into bedrock associated with two close-by collapses, 58.1 m east of T-16 or 178 m east of the reference point north of the Mausoleum. This opening is 2.9 m north of one collapse and 6.3 m north of another. Clearance of brush from the opening revealed that the opening is a robber hole cut into the north chamber of a double tomb. This two-chambered tomb was therefore designated T-29 North and T-29 South and was excavated.

T-30: A square-cut opening 38.6 m west by north of T-29. It is partially blocked by a stone 0.55 × 0.35 m. The mouth of the opening is 0.60 m wide and partially filled.

T-31: An arched opening 2 m east of the reference point just north of the Mausoleum. This opening is silted to within 0.20 m of its top, but it closely resembles the arched opening to T-1.

The immediate results of the survey thus included seven clear tombs, nine caves, five square-cut openings, three rock-cut graves, two collapses, one cistern, and four indeterminate openings. Later excavation of T-17 indicated that it is a *miqveh*. These data are presented in tabular form in Table 5.1.

Note that T-29 is really two interconnecting tombs. Thus, counting T-29

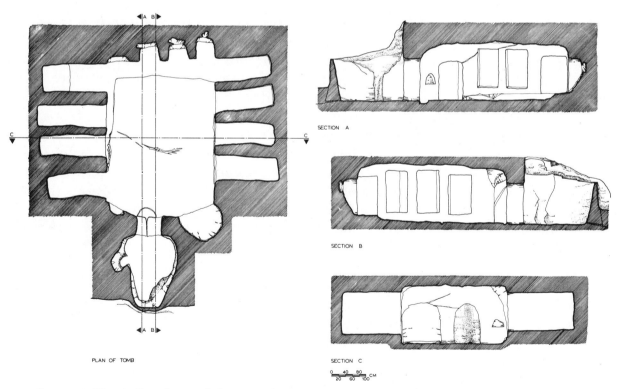

PLAN OF TOMB

SECTION A

SECTION B

SECTION C

Figure 5.5. Tomb 25: plan and three sections.

Table 5.1. SURVEY OF TOMBS AND OTHER OPENINGS AT THE SITE OF KH. SHEMA'

Tombs	Caves	Rock-cut Openings	Rock-cut Graves	Collapses	Cisterns	Indeterminate
T-1	Ca-3	T-18	T-9	T-14	C-1	T-7
T-2	Ca-4	T-20	T-10	T-16		T-12
T-22	Ca-5	T-28	T-26			T-13
T-23	Ca-6	T-30				
T-25	Ca-8					
T-27	Ca-11					
T-29	Ca-19					
T-31	Ca-21					
	Ca-24					

South and T-29 North as two tombs, we have nine clear tombs. If we then add T-20, T-28, and T-30 as "probables," we have perhaps twelve excavatable tombs. Finally, addition of the graves, collapses, and cistern raises the total count to eighteen possibilities, of which six were excavated or cleaned. It is quite possible, however, that another survey with a larger crew would uncover numerous other tomb-sites, especially in the Wadi Meiron itself, which was excluded from this survey.

3. THE EXCAVATION OF T-4

T-4 was selected for excavation because its form (two entrances into a vertical rock face) seemed classic and because its filled-in state promised that a corpus of pottery might be preserved there. Therefore a 1.53 × 2.00 m square was set against the face of the outcropping, located so that the northern entrance would be bisected by a balk. No pottery or artifacts were found in the loose, black (7.5 YR 3/2) surface soil, which did not appear to be occupation debris. The square was extended southward one meter to bisect the southern entrance with a balk also. After 0.50 m of soil was removed, it became clear that the northern opening was a dead end, so efforts were concentrated on the south entrance.

After a total of 0.82 m of soil had been removed it was obvious that the southern entrance too was naturally formed. Its peaked configuration was due to water wash and not rock cutting. Consequently T-4 was abandoned, especially as there was no pottery.

4. THE CLEANING OF T-1 (Photo 5.4)

Tomb 1 was not excavated, since it contained only modern debris to a depth of only about 10 cm. It was cleaned and drawn and proved to be most interesting (fig. 5.6).

Tomb 1 is a *kokh*-type tomb which originally included a small antechamber (1.90 × 2.95 m) that communicated with the main chamber by a square door opening, 1.02 m high × 0.63 wide. The antechamber contained two rock-cut sarcophagi (1.64 × 0.82 m), now largely destroyed; and another entrance to the left behind the sarcophagus (0.77 m high × 0.75 m wide) was square-cut and communicated with a small chamber probably cut for secondary burial or perhaps simple inhumation. This chamber is 0.82 m high × 1.15 m wide × 2.15 m long.

At the north corner of this antechamber is an irregular opening that leads eventually to the main chamber also, though its configuration certainly suggests secondary cutting and even robbing. This opening is 1.10 m high × 0.72 m wide and continues to the northeast about 2.10 m to a very rough dead end. The northwest side of this rough cutting penetrates into the main chamber as a roughly arched opening which is 1.13 m high × 1.30 m wide at the bottom.

The entrance to the main chamber is 1.02 m high × 0.63 m wide, with about 7-cm shoulders to receive a door or sealing stone. Two shallow steps lead down into the main chamber, which is oriented east 24° south, or approximately south by southeast. This main chamber contains a rock-cut bench about 0.35 m wide and about 0.28 m high on four sides. Ten square-topped *kokhim* open out from this main chamber. Evidently none were cut to receive sealing stones. These

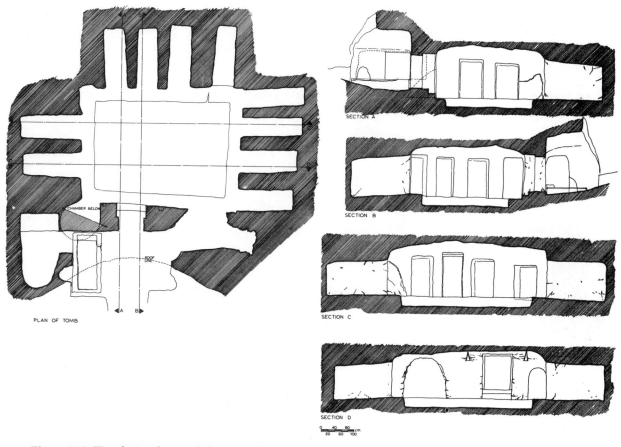

Figure 5.6. Tomb 1: plan and four sections.

kokhim average 1.08 m high × 0.64 m wide × 1.75 m long. In the south corner of the main chamber is a low arched door 0.90 m high × 0.55 wide leading to a small, irregularly shaped chamber possibly intended to receive secondary burials.

This tomb was thoroughly rifled in antiquity and has been visited so often in modern times that no burial goods or pottery remain. It is undecorated, and no inscriptions were in evidence.

5. THE CLEANING OF T-22 (Photo 5.5, Fig. 5.7)

T-22 also contained a thin layer of debris with signs of modern visitation, including candles and tins. It is an arcosolium-type tomb with one *kokh* and two rock-cut sarcophagi. The exterior entrance is so badly cut from robbing that it is impossible to recover its dimensions. It opened into a small antechamber 2.00 × 3.16 m that contained the two rock-cut sarcophagi to the right and left of the entrance. The right sarcophagus is shattered almost beyond recognition. The

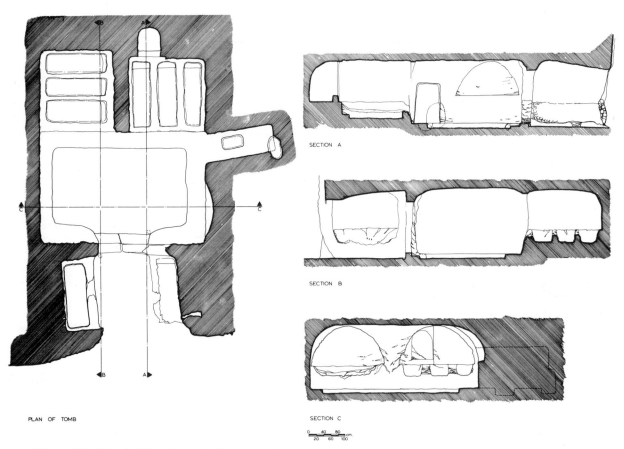

PLAN OF TOMB

SECTION A

SECTION B

SECTION C

Figure 5.7. Tomb 22: plan and three sections.

left one is 0.88 × 1.90 m. Technically speaking these are trough graves, as they are not entirely free-standing.

The doorway to the central chamber (photo 5.6) lies south of the central axis of the tomb. The entrance is 1.34 m high × 0.65 m wide; the latter dimension is uncertain. This entrance gives directly onto the main chamber, which is 4.57 × 3.00 m, the entrance being on the long side. The floor of the main chamber is depressed 10 cm, forming a 0.43-m-wide "bench" on four sides. The north wall contains a clear arcosolium-type arch, though it is too shallow (0.18 m maximum) for a body. The ledge of the arch is about 0.70 m above the floor and 1.71 m long. The arch itself rises to a maximum of 0.91 m above the ledge. The peculiarly narrow ledge may have originally carried an ossuary, though no traces of any remain.

The west wall of the tomb contains two arcosolia, each with three trough graves, shouldered to receive cover stones that are now missing. The southern of the two is 2.15 × 2.00 m and the other is 1.98 × 2.07 m. An interesting thing about these arcosolia is that the three graves in the southern arch are oriented north-south, while the three in the other arch are oriented east-west (photo 5.7). There is a bone niche in the northern arch 14 cm above the top level of the graves. It is arched, 0.75 m high × 0.57 m wide, and is cut back into bedrock 0.65 m.

Ordinarily one does not expect *kokhim* and arcosolia together, but the northwest corner of the main chamber contains a *kokh* cut 1.95 m deep. It is 1.10 m high × 0.75 m wide, dimensions which compare favorably with those of the *kokhim* in Tomb 1. More interesting are the two niches inside the *kokh*, evidently for secondary burials or ossilegium. One niche is on the center axis of the *kokh*, 45 cm back from the entrance, 0.61 × 0.54 × 0.20 m deep. The other niche is cut 20 cm into the back wall of the *kokh* and is east of center, cutting 25 cm into the east wall. Its total dimensions are 0.61 × 0.36 × 0.65 m *high*, in which it only cuts 15 cm below the floor.

Tombs with arcosolia are well known and are in use from the Late Hellenistic period on; they are especially common in the Roman period.[9]

6. THE EXCAVATION OF T-29 NORTH (Figs. 5.8, 5.9)

The discovery of Tomb 29 included the bonus that it was really two interconnecting tombs. Therefore the objectives in excavation included collecting archaeological evidence to clarify the history of the cutting and use of these two tombs.

The method was first to set a small probe (2.15 × 0.70 m) on the eastern, downhill side of the opening to excavate the outside soil to bedrock and gain en-

9. Examples are known at Tell en-Nasbeh, Rehovot, and of course at Beth She'arim and the Tomb of the Kings, which contain both arcosolia and *kokhim*. These typological parallels suggest a 2d to 4th century CE date.

trance to the interior fill. In the course of this exterior excavation it became clear that this was probably a robber hole, as its morphology was irregular and it was located at the southeast corner of the tomb. In fact it was discovered that this entrance cut through the end of one of the *kokhim* (L.04, *kokh* 1), which had its entire roof removed, forming a roughly north-south trench leading to this robber hole (see photo 5.8).

After clearance of the entrance an east-west probe (L.03) was excavated along the axis of the tomb 0.25 m from the north wall and 1.00 m wide extending the length of the main chamber. This probe exposed the east-west stratigraphy of the fill and revealed that there were bone chips 0.82 m off the floor

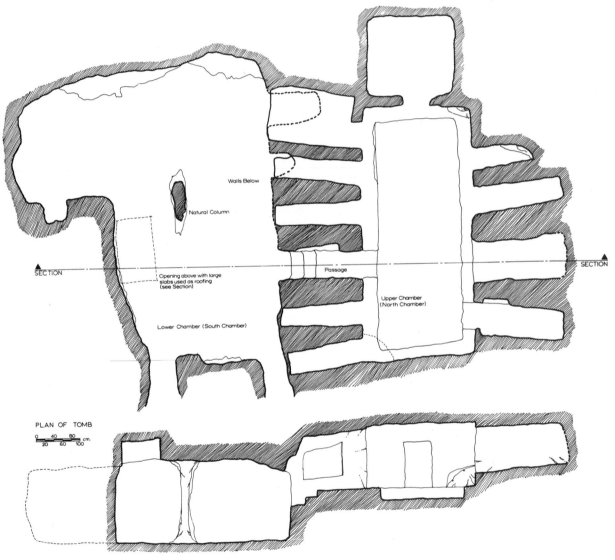

Figure 5.8. Tomb 29, north and south chambers: plan and section.

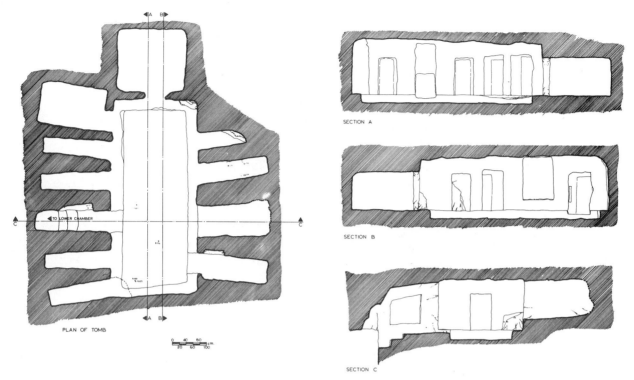

SECTION A

SECTION B

SECTION C

PLAN OF TOMB

Figure 5.9. Tomb 29, north chamber: plan and three sections.

and disarticulated long bones 0.50 m above the floor, the latter associated with skull fragments.

The fill of this probe was in five main layers composed of soil alternating with scree (see fig. 5.10). The topmost layer (L.03, 7.5 cm thick) was dark brown (7.5 YR 4/3) surface soil wash penetrated by insect borings, evidently laid while the tomb was open. The second layer was subangular scree thrown from *kokh* 9 sometime in antiquity as ceiling fall. This layer lensed out in all directions from the *kokh* and was not found 1.24 m south. The third layer was again the same dark brown soil laid over a long period of time when the tomb was open. The worn sherds in it implied water deposition. There were a few long bones in this layer, in complete disarray.

Another layer of limestone was found directly above the floor in front of the east bench, though 1.00 m south of the bench it rested upon the bottom soil layer. This limestone layer was composed of small cobble- to silt-sized weathered dolomitic limestone. It was laid rapidly and is associated most probably with a robbing operation, namely, the cutting of the hole in the southeast corner of the main chamber.

That there were no artifacts or bones in the layers of limestone supports the suggestion that these layers accumulated as ceiling fall from *kokh* 9 and as quarrying scree from the robbing operation respectively.

The bottom layer of soil, about 10 cm thick, was composed of very pale brown (10 YR 7/3) clay to fine silt-sized particles (L.06). In geologist Bullard's opinion it was laid by atmospheric settling when the tomb was sealed, i.e., in use. In this layer were found many disarticulated bones, a whole lamp (491, infra ch. 8, pl 8.10:2), skulls, iron nails, a few tiny glass fragments, and very few sherds.

A north-south 1-m-wide probe cut along the east wall confirmed the major outlines of the stratigraphy of the east-west probe, though the scree was absent in the southeast except atop the bench. The balks of these two probes reveal that the fill generally entered from the southeast corner, as all soil layers (not the scree) peak there (see fig. 5.10). This is also true of the bottom layer of very pale brown soil, which is 0.37 m thick in the southeast just in front of the benches. In the bottom layer in this probe were many disarticulated long bones, two lamps (489, 490, infra pl. 8.9:6,2), a nail fragment, glass body fragments, and a few sherds. This bottom layer was assigned L.06.

Bones and pottery appear to be concentrated in two main layers: in the very pale brown layer on the floor (L.06) and in the dark brown layer *above* the lowest limestone layer to about 50 cm above the floor and 2 m into the tomb, then following the contour of the fill down westward until it merges with L.06. In other words, two periods of ossilegium are represented: one in the earliest use locus of the tomb and one evidently associated with the robbing, as the latter "use" lies above the limestone layer associated with robbing. The bones never represent articulated skeletons, but only scattered long bones and fragments, with complete skulls found only in the bottom locus. The lack of skulls in the upper bone layer may be associated with the violence of robbing, in which bones were thrown and the fragile skulls were crushed.

When the stratigraphy of the main chamber had been well established in these two probes, the rest of the main chamber was excavated in sections, one layer at a time. The intact lamp, R 491, was found 8 cm above the floor in the southeast of the tomb. This lamp was associated with many more disarticulated bones (photo 5.9).

The *kokhim* were numbered 1 to 10 clockwise (photo 5.10), beginning at the southeast corner at the robber entrance. Following are the data of their dimensions and contents.

Kokh 1 (L.04, 1.82 × 0.50 m) now opens to the sky, since its roof was cut off in robbing or quarrying. Its bottom is filled with plastered stones, and the opening into the tomb was once sealed with plastered stones. There are still two 35-cm stones *in situ* that formed that seal. Such sealing suggests that villagers tried to repair and reuse the tomb at some time. This *kokh* was devoid of objects or pottery.

Kokh 2 (L.17, 1.05 m high × 2.00 × 0.52 m) was filled with dark brown soil to a depth of 0.90 m at its mouth. This fill sloped steeply to the rear, where it filtered out of a small hole into Tomb 29 South. The small hole is 32 cm in diameter. This *kokh* yielded few bones and only two tiny glass fragments. There were considerable quantities of worn sherds, presumably washed in with the fill.

Kokh 3 (L.18) is very interesting, as it was cut originally as a *kokh* 0.85 m high × 1.98 × 0.62 m. Later it was cut through at the end and converted into a passageway. Two steps were cut into its south end 1.10 m from its opening, the back wall was cut out from 0.75 m above the floor and cut back 0.50 m. The two walls were "dimpled" 32 cm on the west and 15 cm on the east, and the ceiling was raised to a total height of 1.57 m. This included lowering the floor 10 cm, which necessitated cutting into the south bench.

This *kokh* likewise contained dark brown soil, to a depth of 0.66 m in front, that yielded much worn Late Roman and Early Byzantine pottery, a small iron ring (483), and another small metal ring with three fragments of iron chain attached (482).

Kokh 4 (L.15: 1.06 m high × 2.05 × 0.58 m) yielded only a chert blade 2.1 ×

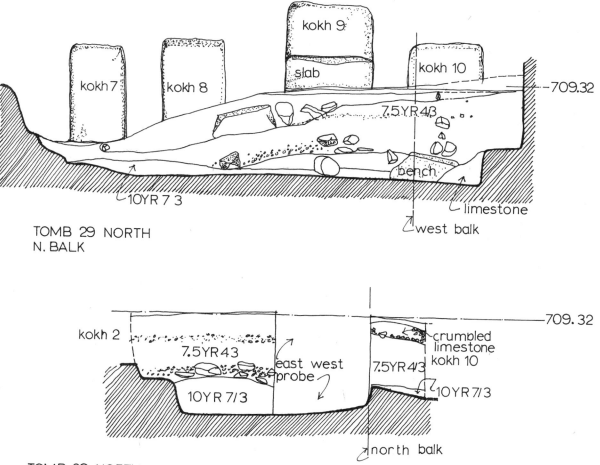

Figure 5.10. Tomb 29 North, north and west balks.

2.5 cm from its 9-cm-deep fill. It was also cut through in its south end by a small 25-cm hole.

Kokh 5 (L.14, 1.12 m high × about 2.00 × about 0.55 m) contained a heap of bone fragments piled at the back. There were no artifacts, though again the fill yielded many worn sherds.

Kokh 6 (L.13) was surprisingly large. Its entrance was cut into the east side of its axis and measured 1.15 m high × 0.50 m wide. The internal dimensions of the *kokh* were 1.10 × 1.90 m. This type with the door to one side is common and is found for example in the Tomb of James in the Kidron Valley. The fill seemed to be slightly yellower here (10 YR 4/4), though still dark brown. The floor was covered to a depth of only 3 to 9 cm, but yielded many disarticulated bones and bone fragments in the back plus three small metal rings (481, 487, and one with attached link, 480), an iron nail (488), and four unclear lamp fragments (503).

The bone chamber (L.16) was clearly intended for secondary burial and contained 17 to 22 cm of bones and bone fragments (photo 5.11). The chamber was 1.10 m high × 1.87 × 1.68 m. Its floor was covered by 9 cm of fine decayed limestone, sterile of either objects or pottery. The door opening was on the central axis and measured 1.02 m high × 0.57 m.

Kokh 7 (L.12) is the smallest of all, 1.05 m high × 1.17 × 0.52 m, which may suggest that it was intended for an ossuary or for secondary burial. It contained no pottery or objects. Its floor was covered by less than 1 cm of finely divided limestone from the floor itself; there were no bones.

Kokh 8 (L.11, 1.07 m high × 2.03 × 0.63 m) contained 2–3 cm of crumbled limestone above 12 cm of dark brown soil. The limestone layer contained nothing, but the fill yielded a most interesting combination of objects. There was a heap of disarticulated and broken long bones 0.52 m from the back concentrated on the east side. The bones were within the fill from 6 to 12 cm above the floor. Then 0.77 m from the back on the east side and 8 cm from the pile of bones lay a small lamp (479, infra ch. 8, pl. 8.10:3). The lamp was 11 cm above the floor and 5 cm from the east wall. On the opposite (west) side of the *kokh* were two large (9 cm in diameter) iron rings (371, 372), 0.69 and 1.11 m from the back, or 0.42 cm apart. The iron rings lay 12 cm above the floor in the fill. Within the fill at the same level were two iron nails (369, 370). The associated pottery included very small undistinguished sherds with some Late Roman–Early Byzantine sherds, including one 4th-century bowl rim. That these objects were found above the floor suggests that either the tomb was in use while open, which is extremely unlikely, or that this *kokh* contained a wooden coffin, no trace of which now remains. Presumably the coffin would have been opened and disturbed in the robbing operation. As the wood decayed while the tomb was open, the lamp, iron rings, nails, and bones were deposited in the fill.

Kokh 9 remained unexcavated because of the enormous ceiling slab that rested upon its fill. This *kokh* was unique in more than one respect, however. Its floor was cut about 30 cm *above* the level of the benches, while in general the other *kokhim* were cut at bench level. Its door also was 1.20 × 0.90 m, the largest of all. Since the original entrance to the tomb is not on the central axis of the main chamber in the east wall as one might expect, and since this opening seems to be cut deliberately high and wide, it is probable that this represents the original entrance.

Kokh 10 (L.10) is rather unique also in that its internal width does not match the width of its entrance. The opening is 1.20 × 0.50 m, while immediately inside, the *kokh* enlarges to a maximum width of 0.80 m and narrows again to 0.52 at the back. Its length is 2.07 m. There is also a sort of niche cut into its western wall beginning 20 cm into the *kokh* and 32 cm above the floor. This rather free-form niche is 0.46 m high × 0.60 × 0.10 m deep into the wall.

The washed-in soil filled *kokh* 10 to a maximum depth of 1.17 m in front and sloped steeply down to the rear (north). This fill contained an iron nail (368) and one lamp fragment (504) with rather many well-worn Late Roman–Early Byzantine sherds.

Final clearance revealed that the main chamber was oriented east-west and was 5.62 × 2.55 m. The ceiling averages 1.70 m in height. There is a rock-cut bench on four sides that averages about 34 cm wide and 28 cm high. There is a bone chamber or charnel room on the central axis of the west side, while six *kokhim* open northward and four more give onto the south. The stone is cut fairly smooth and the entire tomb has a finished appearance, except in the northwest corner and in *kokh* 7, the loculus nearest that corner. This is probably because the workmen ran into an especially hard fold of rock that cuts across both that corner and the rear of *kokh* 7.

The tomb yielded 36 buckets of pottery. Three of these came from the entrance probe (L.01), which also contained an iron fragment (41), a rather worn ostracon reading "BR" ("son of . . .") in Aramaic (407), and a glass fragment (3). Fourteen pottery buckets came from the upper layers of fill inside the tomb, from which came seven glass fragments (477, 478, 69, 68, 67, 278, 812), one iron fragment, four iron nails (141, 142, 143, 145), and the usual worn, approximately 4th century CE pottery. The lowest layer yielded five small buckets of pottery, four lamps (476, 489, 490, 491), a glass fragment (204), a bead (367), a lamp fragment (505), and a small metal ring (366). There were no coins.

The four lamps on the floor were not resting as though part of the burial goods, but were tumbled about with bones. Two were found together (489, 490), and in fact one was on top of the second, which was upside down. The others were on their sides within the fill. Only the lamp in *kokh* 8 seemed relatively undisturbed. Since this disarray is associated with the bottommost layer, the simplest interpretation is that tomb robbers hastily dug through the human and artifactual remains in each *kokh*, sweeping them out onto the floor of the main chamber. This accounts for the random appearance of bones and lamps.

7. THE EXCAVATION OF T-29 SOUTH

This tomb was first entered through *kokh* 3 of T-29 North. It is most interesting because of its form and because of certain internal peculiarities. The tomb was found to have outside fill extending only halfway into the main chamber, so its form could be seen almost completely. It is roughly L-shaped, with the long leg oriented east-west (see fig. 5.8). This leg is 6.72 m long × 3.8 m wide, with two entrances on the east wall at the southeast and northeast corners. Each entrance proved to be 0.70 m high × 0.60 m wide. The long leg was cut first, as is evidenced by the slightly raised floor of the short leg, which is oriented north-south. This secondary enlargement extends another 2.24 m south and is 2.5 m east-west. The tomb contains one shallow *kokh* 0.75 m high × 0.43 × 0.52 m wide in the east wall of the short leg. There are another two *kokhim* in the north wall of the tomb, with traces of the initial cutting of a third. These two *kokhim* are roughly cut, about 0.80 m high × 1.25 × 0.70 m wide, and 0.75 m high × 0.70 × 0.53 m wide.

Another interesting feature is the roughly cut stone column left in place 1.4 m from the south wall and 3.00 m from the east wall. It is roughly elliptical in cross section (0.90 × 0.30 m). Just south of this column is a vertical shaft cut into the ceiling of the tomb (see fig. 5.8). This unexpected feature is 1.20 × 2.20 m and is covered by six stone slabs. These slabs are chinked with smaller stones and plastered (photo 5.12). The plaster contains body sherds laid flat and covered by a final 1-cm layer of fine plaster that makes an effective water barrier. Finally, stones were plastered into place above this layer, though the entire shaft above the slabs were not filled with plastered stones. Instead, the remainder of the fill was rubble and soil.

The peculiar morphology of this tomb, with a vertical shaft, roughly cut interior, and two horizontal entrances, suggests that it was originally intended as a cistern. Its nearest parallel is the large cistern at the end of the staircase at the Tomb of the Kings in Jerusalem, which likewise contains a free-standing column, two front entrances, and a vertical shaft.[10]

Evidently workmen in T-29 South accidentally cut through to T-29 North in four places: *kokhim* 1 to 4 are all cut through in their south ends. The shortness of the *kokhim* in the south tomb may therefore be due to their abandonment when T-29 North was encountered. This accidental penetration would imply either that the workmen did not know of the existence of the north tomb or that they miscalculated their distance. The first seems more likely.

The excavation of T-29 South was initiated by first removing the surface soil from the top of the vertical shaft, though the plaster and slabs were not removed. The two collapses that marked the entrances were excavated to bed-

10. Finegan, *Archeology*, 199f, and photograph top of p. 200.

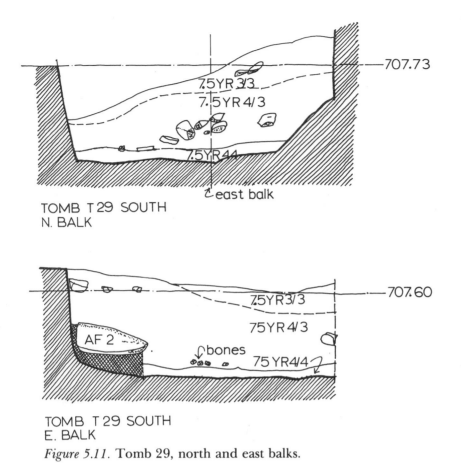

TOMB T 29 SOUTH
N. BALK

TOMB T 29 SOUTH
E. BALK

Figure 5.11. Tomb 29, north and east balks.

rock, when it was seen that they were essentially rock-cut troughs. The southern entrance had stones plastered above the entrance proper, perhaps in an attempt to prevent collapse of the rubbly facing. The northern entrance was discovered to have cut through the end of *kokh* 1 of the north tomb, as mentioned above.

The interior fill of T-29 South was excavated by probes to discover the stratigraphy. The east-west probe excavated just inside the south entrance was designated L.06 (see balk, fig. 5.11). Its section shows that the fill had tumbled through the entrance into the long leg to the foot of the column. Its maximum depth was 1.21 m at the entrance. It was dark brown (7.5 YR 3/3) and contained numerous pottery sherds; it grew lighter toward the bottom.

This fill did not contain as many bones as the fill in the north chamber (T-29 North), though there were two rather neat piles of bones in the west end of the probe 9 cm above the floor. These piles marked the beginning of the bottom layer or use locus (L.06, color 7.5 YR 4/4). At this level were also found two lamps, Kennedy type 5 (492, 493, infra pl. 8.9:3,1). Though the two entrances had been opened in antiquity, there was no crumbly limestone layer as in the northern chamber.

A north-south cross probe (L.07) was excavated across the fill 1.25 m west of the two entrances in the east wall (see balk, fig. 5.11). This confirmed the stratigraphy of the fill, showing the progressive lightening of the fill from 7.5 YR 3/3 to 7.5 YR 3/4 to 7.5 YR 4/4 (from dark brown to brown). The bones in the bottom layer were not nearly so neatly gathered as in L.06. The north end of this probe also came upon an 8-cm-diameter iron ring near the floor (405) of a type virtually identical with that of rings found in *kokh* 9 of the north chamber. Also in the north end of the probe was found a large stone that proved to have the general configuration of a seal stone. It was 0.93 × 0.67 × 0.37 m. Resting against the bottom end of this stone was a large ashlar 0.28 × 0.28 × 0.95 m. Its size and proximity to the stairs cut into the end of *kokh* 3 of T-29 North suggest that it served as the bottom step, though it is now dislocated. The southern chamber is about 0.80 m lower than the northern chamber, and the last rock-cut step in *kokh* 3 is a rather long 0.70 m above the floor. The block would effectively divide this step in two.

The three *kokhim* yielded no objects. Only the easternmost *kokh* in the north wall contained fill, but it held no objects. The other two loculi contained small heaps of bone fragments.

This fill within the tomb and above the layer associated with the earliest use yielded 17 buckets of sherds, mostly very worn and small. However there was a significant amount of restorable Arab pottery and some Byzantine. This fill also contained two glass fragments (455, 459), two beads (457, 458), two iron nails (406, 403), four small metal rings (399, 400, 401, 500), and a few lamp fragments (507, 405, 486).

The use locus on the floor was found throughout the tomb. In the west end the bones lay *upon* and *within* this soil of settled, silt-sized particles, though in more or less complete disarray. The evidence of careful ossilegium was in the three *kokhim* (no skulls) and in the entrance probe (photo 5.13), though even there the skulls were not necessarily associated with the long bones.[11]

The bottom layer associated with the use of the tomb (L.06, L.12) yielded 13 buckets of pottery, most of it well-worn, though none of it appeared to be Arab. Geologist Bullard pointed out that the soil in the use locus was puddled from standing water. Thus at least some of the pottery in the use locus could have been washed in, at least some of the small sherds.

Besides the pottery the use locus contained one glass bead (361), one glass spindle whorl (279), one fragment of a glass vessel (456), two iron nail fragments (360, 362), one small metal ring (363), one large (8-cm) iron ring (405), one worn Late Roman coin, one lamp fragment (484, infra pl. 8.9:5), and three lamps (404, infra pl. 8.9:8, 492, 493).

11. Perhaps the skulls did not endure; often bones from various parts of the body decay at surprisingly diverse rates in various contexts. Secondary burials in which the skulls are separated from the long bones and which date to Herodian times are reported at Ramat Rahel. See Stekelis, "A Jewish Tomb-Cave at Ramat Rachel," 25. Cf. also Meyers, *Jewish Ossuaries*, 9ff.

The worn coin appears to date generally from the 4th century CE. The lamp fragment 484 is of the round type with depressed discus, repeated *ovulo* decoration around rim, no handle, and short rounded nozzle, though one spatulated nozzle was found in L.08 in the fill. All the intact lamps and the lamp fragments are of the same type as lamp 484, and lamp 493 is virtually identical with one found at Beth She'arim, even to the flat, raised area around the wick hole.[12]

The homogeneity of the lamps is clearly suggestive of a 2d to 3d century CE first use of this tomb, which is parallel to the first use in Stratum II of Tomb 29 North. That is, the north and south chambers show use side by side during the 3d century at least, and it is reasonable to assume that they were in use during the 4th century as well.

In this connection we must mention that all the burials in Tomb 29 South were disarticulated. In the long leg of the "L," bones were found in rather neat heaps, often without skulls. In the shallow *kokh* in the southwest of the tomb (*kokh* 1) was a small heap of bones, as was the case in loculi 2 and 3. This strongly suggests that this south chamber of Tomb 29 only served as a charnel house for secondary burial. In the 2d and 3d centuries some of the lamps associated with primary inhumation—presumably in the north chamber—were brought in with the bones, but for the later period virtually none were found.[13]

A reconstruction of the history of the cutting and use of the two tombs suggests as many as six stages:

(1) The first cutting and use of Tomb 29 South as a cistern, perhaps as early as thirty years prior to the beginning of Stratum II, or 150 CE, if we are to take seriously the parallel to the cistern in the Tomb of the Kings in Jerusalem.[14] In this stage it would be rectangular in plan, with one or two walk-in entrances on the east and a vertical shaft in the ceiling on the south side.

(2) The cutting of Tomb 29 North, intended as a tomb, which accidentally cuts into the cistern, probably late in the second century (Stratum II). The workmen decide to incorporate the south chamber.

(3) The enlargement of the cistern (T-29 South) at the southwest, the sealing of the ceiling shaft, and the attempts to cut loculi 1, 2, and 3, with an incipient attempt at a fourth that just began and immediately cut into *kokh* 4 of the north chamber. At this point the decision was made to use the south chamber as a charnel house, which necessitated converting *kokh* 3 of the north chamber into a connecting hall.

Also at this time *kokh* 1 of T-29 North was accidently broken into, perhaps

12. Avigad, "Excavations at Beth She'arim, 1954," 204–210, fig. 3, no. 1. Note the area around the wick hole and the volutes on either side; also the discussion of these lamps and their putative 2d–3d century CE dates in connection with Tomb 29 North.

13. "Virtually," because only one lamp fragment (679) could be interpreted as from a later lamp. It is quite undistinguished in form, as it is only 4 cm long from the break through the center of the wick hole to the opposite edge on the long axis. It is about 5 mm thick, like later (4th-century?) lamps.

14. For the received opinion of the original owner of the tomb—Queen Helena of Adiabene—and the date ca. 50 CE, cf. C. Watzinger, *Denkmäler Palästinas*, II, 65; Finegan, *Archeology*, 199f. It is attractive to move the date of our cistern earlier to match that of the Tomb of the Kings, but then it would be difficult to answer the question for whom it was intended.

when enlarging the north entrance to T-29 South (or even adding it). This loculus was then sealed at its north end with plaster and stones.

(4) The continuous use of both chambers side by side with T-29 South as the charnel house and T-29 North as the tomb for primary burial. This north chamber also has a small charnel house of its own in the west wall. It is possible that two or more families used this unique double tomb throughout the life of the settlement until the earthquake of the 5th century, that is, during our Strata III and IV.

(5) Discovery and robbery of the north chamber, perhaps in Stratum V or VI.

(6) Gradual filling in of both chambers, now open to casual visitors. The Arab pottery in the south chamber suggests that it silted in last, perhaps because its chamber was the larger. During this time an earthquake dislodged a stone slab from the entrance to T-29 North, sealing this entry.

The dating of the tomb and its use rests upon dating its form and the material within it. As for the tomb type with *kokhim*, it is known from Hellenistic times all the way to the 4th century CE, a span of six to seven centuries. The pottery, however, gives us an insight into the periods in which the tomb was in use.

The earliest forms are lamps 489 and 490 from just off the floor. These lamps, with round bodies, repeated relief *ovolo* decoration (often with two double axes on opposite sides of the fill hole), broken discus, and no handle, and most clearly paralleled at Huqoq, where the material dates to the 2d century CE.[15] Further 2d-century CE parallels are found in the Cave of Letters, though the fragmentary nature of the lamps makes it impossible to determine whether they are of the type with broken discus.[16] One must note finally this type of lamp in Cave 1 at Qumran, though reconstructed, correctly, with small fill hole, especially no. 13 illustrated in the excavators' fig. 8. This lamp is dated to 70 CE.[17]

We can deduce an evolution of style and design from Qumran to the Cave of Letters to Huqoq and then finally to our site. That is, lamps of this type have very clear decoration with well-prepared clay and hard firing at these other earlier sites, but our two examples show an effacement of design that suggests a long history of making molds from lamps (cf. particularly number 489, which is virtually smooth.) This leads us to posit a late-2d-century or even early-3d-century date for these lamps at Khirbet Shema', and therefore for the first cutting and use of Tomb 29 North.[18]

Lamp 476 off the floor of the main chamber is clearly a 4th-century type. Again the best-dated parallels are from Beth She'arim, with their terminus in the mid-4th century. Thus we appear to have a 4th-century use of the tomb, though whether early or late is impossible to say.

15. B. Ravani and P. P. Kahane, "Rock-Cut Tombs at Huqoq," fig. 4, nos. 5 and 6, and pp. 128ff.
16. Yadin, *Finds*, fig. 42, B.I, 3.1, and II.12, p. 114. Cf. also Bar-Adon, "Expedition C," 29, and fig. 1.8, for a variant form of the same date.

17. Barthélemy and Milik, *Discoveries*, fig. 8.
18. Cf. Avigad, "Excavations," 259, fig. 31; he dates these lamps to the 2d and 3d centuries CE, but more "widespread" in the 3d. Unfortunately he does not cite evidence for this conclusion.

Lamp 491 is also off the floor, found in a secondary context. That is, it was found heaped with human bones on the floor in such a position vis-à-vis the floor and bones as to suggest that it had been thrown out of its *kokh* with the associated bones by robbers, as was also the case with lamp 476.[19]

This lamp is not easily paralleled except possibly at Beth She'an cistern III of house IV, where such a parallel is dated 491–610 CE.[20] This date seems very high when its similarity to lamp 479 in *kokh* 8 is taken into account.

Lamp 479 is bilanceolate or leaf-shaped, with impressed decoration in the form of a wreath and circles. The flat, backward extending handle is decorated with three impressed lines. There is a circle around the fill hole. It was found *in situ* on the floor of the *kokh* 7 cm from the west side and 75 cm from the back. On the other wall of the *kokh* were two iron rings (371, 372) about 9 cm in diameter, apparently from a coffin or ossuary, though all the bones in this *kokh* were found pushed together at the back—at the nearest, 6 cm from the backmost ring. This pattern may suggest some kind of disturbance of the material in the *kokh*, but the lamp seems to belong here.

Its nearest datable parallels seem to date from the 3d or 4th centuries CE. Evidently this is generally so for such lamps from Pella.[21] The examples from Tomb 8 are dated to the 3d–4th centuries on the basis of parallels to the whole homogeneous corpus in the tomb. Unfortunately there are no coins or inscriptions to give us a secure date.

However, other parallel material is securely dated. One specimen of this lamp type occurs at Beth She'arim, which has a *terminus* of 351/2 CE or mid-4th century.[22] Others are rather frequently found at Nazareth.[23] In this case a significant number of fragments of a lamp of just this type were sealed under a mosaic and must therefore be dated before 427 CE. Therefore the lamp of this type (479) and the larger similar model from off the floor (491) would appear to date securely to the 4th century. Their terminus at the end of the 4th century or beginning of the 5th cannot yet be securely established.

This leaves us with a use span from the late 2d or early 3d century CE to perhaps the end of the 4th century or even the beginning of the 5th, a span which precisely parallels the occupation of the site in Strata II, III, and IV.

The question of the date of the robbery is more difficult. Since lamps 476 and 491 are on the floor, we must presume that the entry occurred after the Stratum IV use. The robbers also presumably found *kokh* 1 plastered up at one

19. Avigad, *Beth She'arim*, III, 213. See also fig. 24.4–5 for parallels in form, but not in specific decoration. Further Avigad, "Excavations," p. 33.6–10 for the same form of lamp and technique of decoration but dissimilar motif.

20. Fitzgerald, *Beth-Shan*, pl. 36.16, with impressed wreath decoration and about 9.5 cm long. The example from Tomb 29 North is about 10.4 cm long and decorated with impressed circles.

21. Smith, *Pella*, I 215–216; pl. 60:52, 53, 96, with wreath decoration; pl. 65:258, with the same decoration from tomb 6; pl. 78:291, 386, 372, 290, from tomb 8.

No. 386 is most similar to Khirbet Shema' lamp 479. See also pl. 83:56 (photograph) from tomb 2, level 3, for a specimen with wreath only.

22. Avigad, "Excavations," 205–239; pl. 33, no. 13 (stylized decoration).

23. Bagatti, I, 196, fig. 81.1–14. The handles have one groove (one example), two grooves (three examples), or three grooves like ours (one example). All are decorated with the wreath or double-wreath motif as near as one can tell from the photographs.

end and cut through both the southeast roof and wall *and* into *kokh* 1, completely removing the roof of the loculus. This would also explain the position of lamps 489 and 490 on the floor directly in front of *kokh* 1 and the open loculus. Unfortunately the robbers left no material to date their forced entry, so we can only hypothesize that it was late in the history of the town, perhaps in Stratum VI or even later.

8. THE CLEARING OF TOMB 31 (Photo 5.14, Fig. 5.12)

Tomb 31 was recorded in the survey of Conder and Kitchener: "A tunnel with an arched roof has been driven into the rock, and at the end a sarcophagus has been excavated in the floor, where it is slightly wider."[24] Their figure records a depth of 11'6" or 3.50 m.

Our cleaning of this unique tomb indicated that it was roughly rectangular in plan, but the wall at the entrance was not parallel to the back wall. Thus the depth along the south wall was 2.60 m, whereas along the north wall the depth is 3.60 m. The width varied from 2.00 m at the front to 1.70 m at the back for a small chamber. Perhaps the most interesting and seemingly unique feature of this tomb was its rock-cut, vaulted ceiling, visible in fig. 5.12, section A. This essentially makes of the tomb a simple rock-cut barrel vault and may be unique in tomb architecture.[25]

The false doorway outside the tomb to the south (see photo 5.15 and fig. 5.12, section B) could be interpreted either as a symbolic entrance to the netherworld or as simply unfinished cutting of another tomb. The manner of sealing this tomb is something of a problem, because all trace of an east or entry wall is missing now. But reference to fig. 5.12, section B, reveals that the roof overhangs about 30 cm. A wall can be built from the rock-cut area in front of the tomb to fit under this overhang, though building it is not without architectural problems.

The pit graves are common to Roman and Byzantine tombs all over the Levant. Presumably the cover stones of these three graves were long since robbed off. Only the small pit on the north wall appears unusual, and it is most reasonably interpreted as a repository for bones in secondary burial.

9. SUMMARY AND CONCLUSIONS

It is clear that Khirbet Shema‘ was able to support a fairly extensive necropolis during its earlier history,[26] a point which would tend to support our suggestion that Teqo‘a in Stratum II is tied closely to the history of Meiron. Tomb architecture is most easily paralled from Beth She‘arim, and it is likely

24. *Survey*, I, 247, and figure in the text.
25. Obviously the vaulted arcosolia with two or three graves at Beth She‘arim are roughly parallel to Tomb 31, but none of the catacombs are single, simple barrel vaults with pit graves.

26. It is important to note that we found no tombs to go with the Arab or medieval occupation of Strata VI and VII.

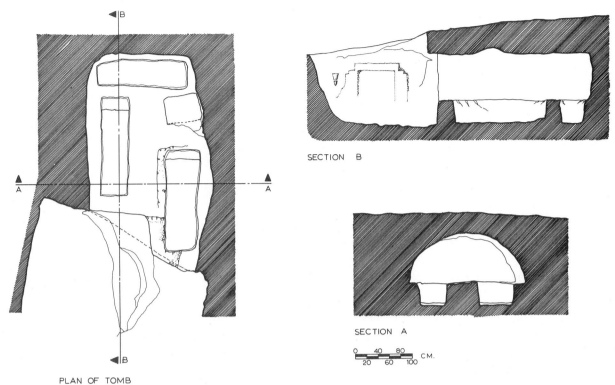

SECTION B

SECTION A

0 40 80 CM.
  20 60 100

PLAN OF TOMB

Figure 5.12. Tomb 31: plan and two sections.

not without significance that this western Galilee site provides the best parallels in many ways to our tombs.

Though we have slight evidence for coffins, we have a good deal for secondary burial. The fact that nearly all of the tombs at Khirbet Shema' have been rifled in antiquity or in more recent times, however, urges us to use the data with caution. Nonetheless, the abundant evidence for ossilegium at this site suggests that the custom of secondary burial, just as at Beth She'arim, has special importance.[27] Nothing indicates that bodies have been reburied here from other sites, however. Rather, painstaking effort was expended to insure proper burial in what most probably were family tombs.

In sum, one might simply observe that nothing seems anomalous or otherwise odd about the burial customs at Khirbet Shema' in respect of burial goods, inhumation, or tomb architecture, though we have certainly indicated unique features in architecture. Everything points to a cultural horizon of a simple, Jewish Galilean village with the usual burial practices.

27. See Meyers, *Jewish Ossuaries*, 10–11, 71–92. The absence in these pages of a bone report is due to the fact that the Ministry of Religion attempted to halt our tomb digging. In a compromise arrangement, all human bones were handed over to the ministry for reburial before it was possible to study them.

CHAPTER 6. NUMISMATIC REPORT

During the first three seasons of excavation, Khirbet Shema' yielded 550 coins representing Ptolemaic, Seleucid, Tyrian, Hasmonean, Roman imperial and provincial, Byzantine, Islamic, and European mints that span more than sixteen centuries of time (see fig. 6.1). The majority of these coins are in fair to good condition and all were found scattered about the site, for, to this date, no hoards have been discovered there. Less than one fourth of the total number are truly difficult to identify, and most of those can be classified as to type and dated within a century. The sum total are to be published at a later date. For the present, we would like to offer a report that will indicate something of the numismatic evidence we have and produce a general outline of its character.

Since these coins can assist us greatly in the dating of our site, we are dedicating another chapter to an analysis of the data as they relate to that matter. Independent of that, however, we would like to describe what we have found and deal with other pertinent or interesting information that is brought to light. To aid us in this discussion, we have reproduced illustrations of some specimens, in plates 6.1 to 6.5. In as many cases as possible we have cited information for one or two coins typical of a group and omitted the specific descriptions of other coins of the same type.

In identifying the Late Roman coins, we have relied heavily upon the volume by Carson, Hill, and Kent.[1] For Jewish-Palestinian coins we have made particular use of Meshorer's recent volume.[2] Other crucial bibliographical material will be referred to at appropriate points.

With some necessary overlapping, we shall proceed chronologically, beginning with the earliest types. The information in the top line of the description includes the registry numbers by which our artifacts are recorded for our own use.

1. PTOLEMAIC AND SELEUCID COINS

The oldest coins found at Khirbet Shema' are a small number of Ptolemaic and Seleucid specimens that were minted in the Levant or, in some specific

In this chapter the text is by RICHARD S. HANSON, *Professor of Religion, Luther College, in cooperation with* MICHAEL L. BATES, *Associate Curator of Islamic Coins, The American Numismatic Society, New York City. The identification of Greek, Roman, and Jewish coins is by Professor Hanson and* BARUCH KANAEL, *formerly of Haverford College; the identification of Islamic, European, and Crusader coins is by Mr. Bates.*

1. Carson, Hill, and Kent, *Bronze Coinage.* (For full citation of works mentioned in the footnotes, see the Bibliography preceding the Appendixes in this volume.)
2. Meshorer, *Jewish Coins.*

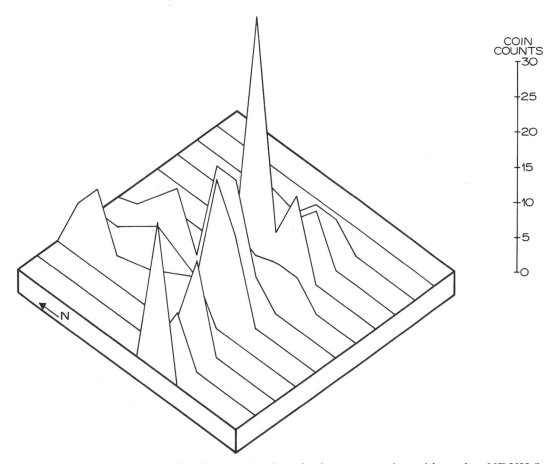

Figure 6.1. Isometric frequency distribution of 4th and 5th century coins, with peak at NE VII.2.

instances, in the city of Tyre. There are three specimens of a Ptolemaic type which seems to be of the 3d century BCE. Two are bronze; one is orichalcum and is described as follows.

> *Pl. 6.1:1, R626.* Ae, 18 mm, 5.00 g.
> *Obv*: Zeus/Amon Re facing right with lion's skin headdress.
> *Rev*: (PTOLE)MAI(OYB)ASI(LEŌS); eagle, wings open with thunder bolt in claws.[3]

A fourth specimen is similar except that the eagle has half-folded wings. It appears to be a coin of Ptolemaios IV or V, which places it in the 2d century BCE.

The Seleucid coinages of Tyre have been helpfully treated in three monographs of the American Numismatic Society: no. 10, *The First Seleucid Coinage of Tyre,* by Edward T. Newell; no. 34, *The Second and Third Seleucid Coinages of Tyre,* by Edgar Rogers; and no. 73, *The Seleucid Coinages of Tyre,* by Edward T.

3. As illustrated in Seaby, *Greek Coins*, 192.

Newell. Relying on these works particularly, we can identify a few coins with the Apollo-like bust of the ruler facing right on the obverse and a palm tree with two clusters of fruit on the reverse. There are five such specimens on which the Greek title BASILEŌS is inscribed to the right of the tree, and on some of those the date is also visible. We have selected two for illustration.

Pl. 6.1:2, R 1369. Ae dilepton, 13 mm, 1.77 g.
Obv: bust of Demetrius II.[4] *Rev:* palm tree with inscription at right reading BASILEŌS. Date in lower field. ĒXR (168 = 145/4 BCE).

Pl. 6.1:3, R1497. Ae dilepton, 13 mm, 1.78 g.
Obv: diademed bust of Alexander I (?). *Rev:* palm tree with inscription to the right, arching downward from top to bottom: BASILEŌS. Date in lower field: ĒXR (168 = 145/4 BCE).

One other coin that is not as clear seems to be a specimen of the same type, while another appears to have a portrait of Demetrius I on the obverse, which would date it to 162–151 BCE. What may be the earliest of these Seleucid coins features the bust of Antiochus IV (175–164 BCE) on the obverse and a strutting horse moving to right on the reverse. One dilepton with an unclear bust on the obverse appears to be a Seleucid coin as well. On the reverse is the standing figure of a naked Apollo, with some inscription at the right reading, from top to bottom, (BA)SILE(ŌS). It is likely a coin of Alexander I (152–144 BCE).

Another type is seen in the following specimen.

Pl. 6.1:4, R1494. Ae dilepton. 13 mm, 1.58 g.
Obv: bust of Seleucus I (?) with lion headdress, facing left. *Rev:* palm tree with an archer's bow to the right and some Greek inscription visible between the two, reading top to bottom: ....)S(....

One other specimen, very worn, belongs to this group by virtue of its flan, giving us a total of eleven specimens.

2. COINS OF THE CITY OF TYRE

The earliest coins of the independent city of Tyre (an era that begins at 126/5 BCE) are four, with the head of Tyche resplendent in turreted headdress facing right on the obverse and a war galley on the reverse. No inscription is visible on any of these, and that is a pity, for they are a dated series. Earliest in type is our largest specimen (21 mm, 3.44 g), which belongs to the 1st century BCE. The other three belong to the 1st century CE.

A palm tree reverse is found on several of our Tyrian coins, with the turreted bust of Tyche on the obverse.[5] Some of these may be earlier but wherever

---

4. By comparing portraits in Gardner, *British Museum Catalogue*, pl. XVII.

5. Hill, *Greek Coins of Phoenicia*, VI, pl. XXI, for examples.

a date is visible, they are of the 1st or 2d century CE. One, which has the Tyrian monogram and the inscription IERA as well, is to be dated at 64/5 CE. Two others are less well preserved and should be dated to the period 104/5–166/7 CE. Only one specimen is too worn to classify as either early or late. We illustrate with our clearest specimen.

Pl. 6.1:5, R2266. Ae, 16 mm, 2.49 g.
Obv: turreted bust of Tyche facing right. *Rev*: palm tree with inscription around from left upward: ......IERAS. Date across field: DLS (234 = 108/9 CE).[6]

The head of Melqarth on the obverse forms a common type of Tyrian coin, with some version of a war club, butt end downward, on the reverse. The earliest specimen, with bearded bust, has a date of 3/2 BCE. A more common type in our group is the beardless bust on the obverse, with the Tyrian monogram at the top of the club.[7] There are four specimens of two similar types.

Pl. 6.1:6, R2312. Ae, 21 mm, 9.87 g.
Obv: laureated bust of Melqarth facing right. *Rev*: club downward, inscription imposed on the two sides: MĒTRO/POLEŌS/APS *Lsr* (in Phoenician); oak leaf around. The date is 155/6 CE.

Pl. 6.1:7, R1376. Ae, 22 mm, 11.78 g.
Obv: bust of Melqarth right. *Rev*: club downward, inscription imposed on both sides: (MĒTRO)/POL(EŌS)/ĒO(S *Lsr*); oak leaf around. The date is 152/3 CE.

Exceptional to the bronze coins listed above is one silver half-shekel with beardless bust of Melqarth on the obverse and a crude eagle with wings outspread and the Greek inscription, TYROYIE(RASKAIASYLOY), on the reverse. It belongs to a series that lasts from 125 BCE to 56 CE and is likely an early specimen of that series.[8]

Three other coins appear to belong to the Tyrian-Seleucid group but are too damaged to be clearly identified. One has a Tyche bust on the obverse. Another, less surely of this group, exhibits only a strutting horse on the reverse. One coin the size of a dilepton appears to have the bust of Apollo on the obverse, while the reverse preserves the bottom portion of a bull moving left. It could be a coin of Seleucus II (246–226 BCE), but this is uncertain.

Besides these thirty-six coins spanning the late 3d century BCE through the 2d century CE, there are five Tyrian city coins of the Roman colonial era. They range in date from Caracalla (211–217 CE) to, possibly, Claudius II (268–270 CE). We shall deal with them in section 4 below, devoted to Roman coins.

It is significant, we think, that the earliest five centuries' worth of numismatic evidence uncovered at Khirbet Shema' shows a steady supply of coins

6. See ibid. nos. 338–55, pl. XXXII.3.
7. See ibid. nos. 356–60, pl. XXXII. 1, 4, for examples.

8. See ibid. no. 44, pl. XXIX, 18, 19, and pl. XXX for examples of this type.

emanating from Tyre. It would seem to indicate that this area of Upper Galilee was somewhat within the orb of Tyrian commercial influence. After all, these people could have been getting coins from points south that were actually nearer or as near. Why should most of the coins in the first two centuries of the Common Era come from Tyre and how did it happen? We would suppose that it has to do with the marketing of their limited exports of one agricultural product: they were selling olives or olive oil at the Tyrian market. In exchange they received Tyrian coins.

3. HASMONEAN COINS

A surprisingly large number of Hasmonean coins were found at Khirbet Shema'—all of them bronze, as one would expect, and almost all of them minted by Alexander Yannai. Following the precedent set by Y. Meshorer, we shall list them by type.

There are six specimens of a type described by the following two examples.

Pl. 6.1:8, R2061. 14 mm, 1.75 g.
Pl. 6.1:9, R1533. 15 mm, 2.39 g.
Obv: anchor surrounded by the Greek inscription: BASILEŌS ALEX-ANDROY and with a circle of dots around that. *Rev:* star with eight rays and the Hebrew letters, *yhwntn hmlk*, placed between those rays.[9]

There are three and possibly two more specimens of a type described by this example.

Pl. 6.1:10, R1303. 13 mm, 1.44 g.
Obv: anchor surrounded by the inscription: BASILEŌS ALEXANDROY. *Rev:* star with eight rays, within a circle.

There are six and possibly two more specimens of a type ideally described by J. Naveh in his article, "Dated Coins of Alexander Jannaeus," *IEJ* 18 (1968) 20–25. These are the only coins of Yannai which bear dates, but unfortunately none of ours are well enough preserved to give us that information.

Pl. 6.1:11, R393. 12 mm, 0.86 g.
Pl. 6.1:12, R2051. 12 mm, 0.90 g.
Obv: anchor within circle, inscription around: BASILEŌS ALEXANDROY. *Rev:* eight-pointed star within circle of dots; Heb. inscription around (illegible; could be either *'lksndrws* or *yhwntn hmlk*).[10]

Pl. 6.1:13, R552. 10 mm, 0.45 g.
There are nine specimens and possibly one more of the simple type in which the obverse has an anchor within a circle and the reverse, a star within a circle

9. Meshorer, *Jewish Coins*, no. 8.   10. Ibid. no. 9.

of dots. Similar to these is one of a type in which the star on the reverse is placed within a circle.[11]

There are thirteen specimens of a type in which the obverse is filled with Hebrew script within a wreath and the reverse consists of double cornucopiae with pomegranate between and a circle of dots around. Five of these are clearly coins of Alexander Yannai, with varying amounts of Hebrew inscription visible enough to read. Four other specimens clearly read Yehohanan and, though it is still a debatable matter, we would surmise that they are coins of Hyrcanus II. As pointed out by Meshorer, it is more a matter of assumption than proof that any coins were minted prior to Alexander Yannai. Four specimens of this type are so illegible that we cannot safely specify the ruler who minted them. We give two examples with relatively legible inscriptions.[12]

> *Pl. 6.1:14, R632.* 13 mm, 1.43 g.
> Inscription on the obverse: *yhw/ntnhk/hnhgl.....*
>
> *Pl. 6.1:15, R1332.* 14 mm, 1.56 g.
> Inscription of the obverse: *yhwn./.hkhnh/gdlw../r....*

Besides these coins, which can be clearly identified as Hasmonean, there are twelve unclear specimens which we would have to assign to the Hasmonean group if pressed to a decision, giving us a total of 42 to 54 Hasmonean coins in all. The quantity is rather amazing when we consider that they represent a span of time scarcely more than the ruling dates of Alexander Yannai (103–76 BCE). Our ceramic evidence would not support the conclusion that there were a large number of persons at Shema' during the 1st century BCE. Nor is it sufficient to say that it indicates the great quantity of coins minted by Alexander during his reign—though that must be part of the explanation. When we first encountered these coins and were finding them together with Roman coins of the 4th century CE, we explained to ourselves that the Jewish inhabitants of this site were so ardent in their feelings toward the Hasmonean age that they were keeping and using those coins for five centuries beyond the time that they were minted. And that must remain a possible explanation for their presence in some later layers of debris. But still another explanation is needed and it has been suggested that Alexander used this site (and others nearby) as a staging area for his troops when he conducted his northern campaigns.

It is difficult to explain the presence of this numismatic evidence in the face of the absence of ceramic evidence from the same period. In the face of it, we must bear in mind the fact that we have a small number of Ptolemaic and Seleucid coins from an even earlier date and a steady supply of coins from Tyre going back into the 2d century BCE. This evidence can only suggest that there were people living at our site well before the Common Era.

---

11. Ibid. nos. 10, 11.

12. See ibid. nos. 12–29, for various examples of this type.

4. ROMAN COINS

The sizable quantity of Roman coins uncovered at Khirbet Shema' fall into the following distinct categories: (i) coins minted in Palestine for the procurators and the Jewish kings, (ii) 1st and 2d century imperial coins, (iii) colonial coins of the 3d century, (iv) 3d century antoniani and, (v) coins of the era of Constantine the Great and his successors (4th and 5th centuries CE).

4.1 The coins of the procurators and the Jewish kings

We have one specimen of a coin of Herod Archelaus (4 BCE–6 CE). On the obverse we see double cornucopiae. The inscription is not visible, but should read, $\overline{\text{ERO}}$/D/OY. On the reverse there is a war galley and, again, the inscription is not visible, but should read ETHNA/RCH$\overline{\text{E}}$/S.[13] We have one specimen of a coin on which the obverse displays Agrippa I facing right, with a turreted bust of Tyche on the reverse. The date: 37–44 CE. One coin bears the inscription of Nero.

Pl. 6.2:1, R2148. Ae, 15 mm, 2.63 g.
Obv: (N)ER(O)NO(S) within wreath. Rev: palm branch with Greek letters to both sides reading (L)EKA(ISA)ROS (year 5 = 58 CE).[14]

We have two coins of Domitian minted for Agrippa II. On both we see the bust of Domitian facing right on the obverse. The reverse of one reveals the Greek inscription, ETOK....(year 24) AGR(IP). The other is described below.

Pl. 6.2:2, R633. Ae, 15 mm, 2.92 g.
Obv: bust with a portion of the legend visible: ....(D)OMITKAI... Rev: palm tree with Greek letters at each side of the trunk reading ET KE/(B)AS A(GG). (Date: 81 CE).[15]

Texture and size of flan suggest that two more coins belong to this Palestinian group, but both are too pitted and worn to identify.

4.2 Roman imperial coins of the 1st to 2d century C.E.

Pl. 6.2:3, R613. Ar, 17 mm, 3.04 g.
Obv: bust of Vespasian with portion of legend: .....SCAESVESP....... Rev: TRPO....with the standing figure of Jupiter on a rostral column. The coin was minted between 75 and 79 CE.[16]

---

13. See ibid. 59b.
14. For similar coins, see ibid. pl. IX, coins of Herod Antipas (4 BCE–39 CE).
15. See ibid. no. 130.
16. Similar, but not identical to Mattingly and Sydenham, Roman Imperial Coinage, II, no. 254, where the obv.

Pl. 6.2:4, R1551. Ae, 18 mm, 3.42 g.
Obv: bust of Trajan with Greek inscription around: (AYTSAINEPTR) AI(AN)OSSEBTER. *Rev*: double cornucopiae with palm branch between. Inscription: TIBERK AYET (Tiberias, year 81 = 99/100 CE).[17]

Pl. 6.2:5, R2157. Ar, 17 mm, 2.81 g.
Obv: laureated bust of Hadrian with the legend HADRIANVSAVGVSTVS. *Rev*: Ceres (or Venus?) standing, with the inscription, C O S I I I around.

In addition to coins cited above, we have one very worn, small brass coin which may be a coin of Nerva (96–98 CE), a military issue of the Fourth Legion, overstruck on a coin of Nero with the stamp NYEA, and a bronze coin of Hadrian with a Greek inscription on the obverse reading, AYGRAADR (IANOKAISSEB) and the emperor standing to left with spear in hand on the reverse.

4.3 Roman colonial coins of the 3d century C.E.

The earliest specimen in this group is a coin of Septimius Severus.

Pl. 6.2:6, R585. Ae, 22 mm, 4.66 g.
Obv: bust of the emperor; inscription illegible. *Rev*: Minerva with spear and the letters, ... V O C ... , inscribed around.

Another coin appears to have the bust of Septimius Severus on the obverse, but it is too worn and faint to permit a sure identification.

One coin displays a rather clear bust of Caracalla with some inscription visible (IMPMAV.......G). On the reverse, the emperor is sacrificing leftward at a small altar, with an inscription around which seems to read: COLTYR...... CPIII.[18] Another also appears to have the bust of Caracalla on the obverse, but the reverse is too unclear to identify.

We have one handsome billon tetradrachma of Elagabalus.

Pl. 6.2:7, R1331. Ar, 24 mm, 15.11 g.
Obv: bust with AYTKMA ANTŌNEINOS and the symbols, b b, at the bottom. *Rev*: eagle with head turned left; LS E at the top, a star between the legs at the bottom. Inscription around: ĒMARCHEIN ATOSTOB.[19]

A second coin of Elagabalus is bronze with Latin script. The inscription on the obverse reads: IMPMAV AN TONINVSAVG. On the reverse we see a figure of Astarte placing her ring on a trophy as she is crowned by Nike; on the left, a palm tree; on the right, a murex shell. Inscr. around: T(V) IO RVM.[20] A third

legend reads IMPCAESARVESPASIANVSAVG.

17. This coin is illustrated in Kindler, *Coins of Tiberias*, no. 6.

18. This reverse is similar but not identical to Hill, *Greek Coins of Phoenicia*, pl. XXXII.8.

19. Much as pictured in ibid. pl. XXXVII.2, where such a coin is attributed to Caracalla. The late A. Spijkerman attributed our coin to Elagabalus.

20. As in ibid. pl. XXXIII.2.

coin is virtually identical to this, but is less well preserved. On a coin of Elagabalus minted in Petra we see a reverse that features horned oxen moving right.

Pl. 6.2:8, R1404. Ae, 18 mm, 3.91 g.

Three coins of the colony of Bostra have similar portraits on the obverse. The clearest one is a bronze drachma which reads IMPCMAVRSEVALEXAN and is, hence, a coin of Severus Alexander (222–235 CE).[21] Another, far more worn, is quite surely the same, but a third coin of this type is thicker and heavier and may have a portrait of Elagabalus or even Commodus (180–192 CE) on the obverse.

There are two tetradrachmas which appear as follows.

Pl. 6.2:9, R2102. Ae, 26 mm.

Obv: bust of Philip II (244–249 CE) facing right with radiate crown; portion of legend legible: IMP(MIVLPHILIPPVSAVG). *Rev:* Apollo standing full front with head left toward an altar of fire; inscription around: COLTVRO MET.

Pl. 6.2:10, R1310. Ae, 25 mm.

Obv: laureated bust on one who appears to be Claudius II (268–270 CE) facing right; the legend is not readable. *Rev:* a galley with three figures in it, the one in the center standing larger than the other two; inscription around: COLTVR(O MET).

4.4 *Antoniani of the 3d century C.E.*

Pl. 6.2:11, R2079. Ae, 20 mm, 3.12 g.

Three of our antoniani are of Gallienus (253–260–268 CE). In each case the obverse inscription reads GALLIENVSAVG. On the reverse of one we see Virtus standing left and the inscription: VIRTVSAVG. On the reverse of the second, Securitas stands to the left and the inscription reads: SECVRITPERPET H. The date range for both of these is 260–268 CE. The reverse of the third reads SALVSAVGG E and features the figure of Salus facing left. The date range is 253–260 CE.

Pl. 6.2:12, R2072. Ae, 22 mm, 2.93 g.

There are possibly two specimens from the reign of Valerianus (253–260 CE). One is rather clear. The obverse inscription reads IMPCPLICVALERI (ANVSAVG) and on the reverse we see a goddess standing left and the inscription, FORTVNAREDVX. The other is much less clear and, therefore, not certainly a coin of Valerian. There appears to be a figure of Apollo on the reverse.

Pl. 6.2:13, R592. Ae, 21 mm, 1.99 g.

There are three identical antoniani of Probus (276–282 CE). One is in good condition. The obverse inscription reads IMPCMAVRPROBVSPFAVG. On

---

21. A coin similar to those illustrated in Hill, *Greek Coins: Arabia, Mesopotamia and Persia,* pl. III. 15 or IV. 7.

the reverse we see Jupiter giving Victory to the emperor, with the inscription around: CLEMENTIATEMP. Mint mark: K XXI.[22]

There are two coins of Maximinian from the years 285–305 CE. One is quite clear. The obverse inscription reads IMPCMAMAXIMINIANVX and on the reverse we see Jupiter giving Victory to the emperor, with the inscription around: CONCORDIAMIL(ITVM).

4.5 *Coins of the era of Constantine the Great and his successors*

Beginning with the time of Constantine the Great, the quantity of our numismatic evidence multiplies considerably, reflecting either a great increase in the supply of coins or an increase in the population at Shema'—or both. To facilitate reporting the quantity and the variety, we shall tabulate by the names of emperors wherever that is most convenient; but, since the reverse legends become more and more significant for identification and for dating as the period proceeds, we shall divide our evidence after that kind of data beginning with the date of 324 CE.

a. *Licinius I (307–324 C.E.)*

Pl. 6.3:1, R636. Ae, 17 mm, 1.67 g.
Within a total of six coins, we find four types. On one coin, the bust is facing left with an obverse inscription that reads DNVALLICINLICINIVSNOBC; on the reverse we see Jupiter standing, while the inscription reads, IOVICON-SERVATORICAESS, and the mint legend, (SM)ANT. This could possibly be a coin of Licinius II, but if it is of Licinius I as we think, it is prior to his elevation to the title of Augustus.

On two specimens the bust faces to the right and the obverse legend reads, IMPCVAL(LICINIVSPF)AVG; on the reverse we see a phoenix to the left of a seated figure, and the inscription around reads, IOVICONS ERVATORI XIII SMANE.[23] The size is Ae3. On one specimen the obverse legend is IMPLICI-NIVSAVG and on the reverse there is a camp gate with the legend, PROVIDEN TIAEAVGG, around. The size is Ae2.

Pl. 6.2:2, R1325. Ae, 20 mm, 2.62 g.
There are two specimens with the obverse legend IMPLICINIVSPFAVG, and with SOLIINVI CTOCOMITI on the reverse, with Sol standing to left.

b. *Constantine the Great (306–337 C.E.)*

Pl. 6.3:3, R629. Ae, 20 mm, 2.16 g.
Pl. 6.3:4, R1538. Ae, 19 mm, 2.41 g.

---

22. Similar to Mattingly and Sydenham, *Roman Imperial Coinage*, II, pl. V. 16.

23. As in Reece, *Roman Coins*, no. 882 (pl. 54).

There are four specimens of a type minted in 308–320 CE, in which the reverse features Sol standing left with globe in hand and with a star to the right.[24] Other details vary on each, as does the placement of the letters in the legend, which reads SOLI INVICTO COMITI. On three of them, the obverse legend reads IMPCONSTANTINUVSAVG. On the fourth, the title IMP is absent. The size of all is Ae2.

Pl. 6.3:5, R1320. Ae, 18 mm, 3.03 g.

From the period 324–330 CE come three specimens representing two types. On the reverse of one we see a camp gateway with two towers and a star above.[25] The legend reads PROVIDENTIAEAVGG; the mint legend, SMANT. Another specimen of this reverse type is far less well preserved. On the third coin, the reverse consists of a circle with VOT/XXX within and the legend, DNCONSTANTINIMAXAVG around, with SMHB beneath.

Pl. 6.3:6, R565. Ae, 18 mm, 2.78 g.

One coin of Helena, the empress facing right, with the legend FLHELENA AVGVSTA around, belongs to this group and was minted in 324–330 CE. On the reverse we see Pax standing left, holding a branch in the right hand, with the legend SECVRITAS REIPVBLICA around. The mint legend reads SMANTA.[26]

Pl. 6.3:7, R1565. Ae, 17 mm, 2.76 g.

There are three examples of an VRBS ROMA coin minted in 330–335 CE. On the obverse is the helmeted bust of Roma facing left, with the inscription around. On the reverse we see the wolf with twins and two stars above. In one instance, the mint legend appears (SMKA). The size of all three is Ae3.[27]

Pl. 6.3:8, R1368. Ae, 15 mm, 1.23 g.

There are two specimens of an Ae3 coin in which the reverse features two soldiers with two standards between and the legend, GLOR IAEXERC ITVS.[28] Both have as the obverse legend, CONSTANTINVSMAXAVG. The date span is 330–335 CE. There are six specimens of the Gloria Exercitus type on which there is only one standard between the two soldiers.[29] All are Ae3. The date span for these is 335–337 CE. It is interesting to note that none is exactly like any other in every detail. From mint to mint and from time to time, the dies differed.

From the period 337–341 CE come three specimens of commemorative coins which portray the veiled bust of Constantine on the obverse with the legend DVCONSTAN TINVSPTAVGG around. On the reverse is a quadriga—in one

24. Similar to ibid. no. 836 (pl. 52).

25. As in ibid. no. 839 (pl. 52) or 876 (pl. 54), or Carson-Hill-Kent, *Bronze Coinage,* no. 12 (pl. I).

26. A coin of this type is illustrated in Reece, *Roman Coins,* nos. 877, 878 (pl. 54), or Carson-Hill-Kent, *Bronze Coinage,* no. 65 (pl. II).

27. As in Reece, *Roman Coins,* nos. 885, 886 (pl. 55), or Carson-Hill-Kent, *Bronze Coinage,* no. 65 (pl. II).

28. As in Reece, *Roman Coins,* no. 884 (pl. 55), or Carson-Hill-Kent, *Bronze Coinage,* no. 60 (pl. I).

29. As in Reece, *Roman Coins,* no. 890 (pl. 55), or Carson-Hill-Kent, *Bronze Coinage,* no. 1028 (pl. I).

case, with CONSA beneath.[30] One Ae3 specimen shows Pietas veiled and standing to right, with (V)N(M)R in the field.[31] The date for this coin is 341–346 CE. Of the same date is a coin with Aequitas, winged, standing left, holding a balance and a transverse scepter. The inscription (IVST VENER MEMOR) is worn away.[32]

The Gloria Exercitus coins, which begin in 330 CE, were minted for or by the sons of Constantine as well as on his own behalf. To begin our series of 4th–5th century Roman coins as divided by reverse types, we shall begin with the Gloria Exercitus series that were minted for the sons of Constantine.

c. *Gloria Exercitus: two standards (330–335 C.E.)*

Pl. 6.3:9, R2240. Ae, 17 mm, 1.91 g.
Pl. 6.3:10, R1347. Ae, 17 mm, 2.02 g.
Pl. 6.3:11, R1306. Ae, 17 mm, 2.44 g.

In addition to the two mentioned above as coins of Constantine I, there are six specimens of this type. Four are coins of Constantine II and two of Constantius II while he still bore the mere title of NOBC.

d. *Gloria Exercitus: single standard (335–341 C.E.)*

Pl. 6.3:12, R595. Ae, 14 mm, 1.38 g.

In addition to the six mentioned above as coins of Constantine I, there are thirteen more specimens of this type. All are Ae3. Four of these are of Constantius II, and eight specimens are in bad enough condition to prevent identification of the bust portrayed. One coin has the helmeted bust of Constantinopolis facing left on the obverse.

e. *Victoriae D.D.AUGG.Q.N.N., Victoria Augustorum or Vict. Aug.: two Victories vis-à-vis, each with a wreath in hand (341–346 C.E.)*

Pl. 6.3:13, R1308. Ae, 15 mm, 2.52 g.
Pl. 6.3:14, R1359. Ae, 14 mm, 0.94 g.

Five Ae3 coins are of this type. Two, with readable obverse legends, are coins of Constans. One is quite surely of Constantius II and two others are worn beyond recognition on the obverse. The full legend, VICTORIA AVGVSTORVM, is found on one coin of Constans, while the same figure of Victory moving left with wreath held before appears on the obverse of two other coins whose legends are worn away. The portrait on the obverse seems to be that of Constantius II. All are Ae3.[33]

f. *VOT/XX/MVLT/XXX within wreath (341–346 C.E.)*

Pl. 6.3:15, R2003. Ae, 16 mm, 0.55 g.

30. As in Reece, *Roman Coins*, nos. 891, 892 (pl. 56).
31. As in ibid. no. 893 (pl. 56).
32. As in Carson-Hill-Kent, *Bronze Coinage*, no. 1469

(pl. I).
33. See ibid. no. 630 and 140 (pl. I), or Reece, *Roman Coins*, no. 902 (pl. 57), for similar examples.

Pl. 6.3:16, R1358. Ae, 15 mm, 1.73 g.

One coin of this type bears the image and title of Constans. Six other specimens are coins of Constantius II and seven others are too worn to permit further identification. Indeed, some of the latter could be from a later time (specifically, ca. 383 CE, when this formula was used by Gratian, Valentinian II, Theodosius I, and Arcadius).

g. *Fel Temp Reparatio (346–361 C.E.)*[34]

Pl. 6.3:17, R1558. Ae, 20 mm, 3.34 g.
Pl. 6.3:18, R2080. Ae, 22 mm, 4.98 g.
Pl. 6.3:19, R1360. Ae, 17 mm, 1.97 g.
Pl. 6.4:1, R2328. Ae, 22 mm, 4.34 g.
Pl. 6.4:2, R581. Ae, 18 mm, 3.87 g.
Pl. 6.4:3, R541. Ae, 17 mm, 2.40 g.
Pl. 6.4:4, R2052. Ae, 16 mm, 1.38 g.

We excavated an uncommonly large number of coins of this description at Khirbet Shema': no fewer than 56 specimens. Earliest in the series are two coins of Constantius II on which the FEL TEMP REPARATIO legend is accompanied by the emperor at the right standing over two victims. Both coins are Ae2. The other specimens all feature the emperor attacking a fallen horseman with his spear. Five are Ae2 coins of Constantius II and 43 are Ae3 coins of Constantius II or unclear as to the identity of the emperor portrayed. Three specimens are quite clearly coins of Constantius Gallus, which dates them to 351–354 CE. One rather clear Ae2 coin reads DNVLCLCONSTANTI-VSNOBCAES on the obverse. A second Ae2 specimen has the features of Constantius Gallus and the letters, ...NOBCA....., legible in the legend which surrounds it. A third specimen, Ae2 in size, is possibly of Gallus, but the legend is unclear. Of the great number of Ae3 coins in this group, some are possibly coins of either Gallus or Julian. Three Ae3 coins are by inscriptional evidence clearly of Julian Caesar and the period, 355–361 CE.

h. *Spes Reipublice (355–361 C.E.)*

Pl. 6.4:5, R1557. Ae, 14 mm, 1.29 g.

Four coins of Constantius II and Julian Caesar are of this type, the reverse of which features the emperor standing left with standard or spear in arm and a globe held before him.[35]

i. *Virtus Exerc Romanor (360–363 C.E.)*

There are from one to five coins of this category. All are Ae3 and none are

---

34. See Reece, *Roman Coins,* pl. 58 or Carson-Hill-Kent, *Bronze Coinage,* pl. II, for a variety of examples.

35. As pictured in Carson-Hill-Kent, *Bronze Coinage,* no. 2504 (pl. IV), or Reece, *Roman Coins,* no. 940 (pl. 60).

in good condition. The reverse figure of either Virtus or the emperor leading a captive to the right is all that can be seen.

j. *Vota coins of Julian (361–363 C.E.)*

The vota coins of Julian have the formula, VOT/X/MVLT/XX. We have two possible specimens but both are so worn on the obverse as to make our identification uncertain. If they are not coins of Julian, they must come from a later period, namely, 425–450 CE. Both are Ae3.

k. *Securitas Reipublicae coins of Julian (361–363 C.E.)*

One specimen of this type is clear enough to be attributed to Julian and another is a likely candidate. Both are Ae3. As will be seen below, the Securitas Reipublicae legend reappears in 367–383 CE.

l. *Vota coins of Jovian (363–364 C.E.)*

Pl. 6.4:6, R1514. Ae, 15 mm, 1.46 g.
We have three Ae3 specimens of the VOT V formula. Only one clearly bears Jovian's legend on the obverse. The other two can be identified only by the reverse.

m. *Securitas Reipublicae, period of 364–383 C.E.*

Pl. 6.4:7, R2183. Ae, 17 mm, 2.83 g.
Six specimens of this category can be identified as to emperor and, hence, dated with some precision. One is quite likely, but not surely, a coin of Valens (364–378 CE) and a second coin, reading DNVAL... on the obverse, is either of Valens or Valentinian I (364–375 CE). One coin is more surely of Valentinian I and three specimens are of Gratian. Seven other coins are quite surely of this Securitas Reipublicae type, but unclear as to obverse date. All are Ae3.

One Ae3 coin that is either of Valens or Valentinian I belongs to this time period (364–378 CE) but is totally unclear on the reverse.[36]

n. *Gloria Romanorum (364–408 C.E.)*

Pl. 4:8, R1571. Ae, 14 mm, 1.19 g.
One Ae3 specimen belongs to Valentinian I and, to judge from the portrait, a second as well. One is an Ae3 coin of Valens. On all three of these, the reverse features the emperor dragging a captive to the right. One other specimen with unclear obverse is also of this type.[37]

Pl. 6.4:9, R1476. Ae, 21 mm, 5.26 g.
Pl. 6.4:10, R634. Ae, 22 mm, 4.28 g.

---

36. With Victory standing to left, holding wreath and palm, as in Carson-Hill-Kent, *Bronze Coinage*, no. 527 (pl. III).

37. Similar to ibid. no. 897 (pl. III).

A rather good Ae2 specimen features the bust of Valentinian II on the obverse (375–392 CE) with a crested helmet such as one sees on Constantinopolis or Roma. The reverse, unlike the above, has the emperor in a galley with Victory at the helm.[38] Another Ae2 coin with this same set of figures on the reverse has Theodosius I (379–395 CE) on the obverse.

Pl. 6.4:11, R1334. Ae, 15 mm, 1.74 g.

A Gloria Romanorum coin with three emperors standing is represented by seven Ae3 specimens.[39] One seems to bear the image of Theodosius I on the obverse. Two others, one quite surely and the other only apparently, are coins of Honorius from 393–395 CE. One has the bust of a child, which may mean that it is a coin of Theodosius II and from as late as 408 CE. One other, with a youthful bust, may be a coin of Theodosius II as well—if not of Arcadius or Honorius. Two coins are insufficiently clear on the obverse to be further identified, but do have the three emperors standing on the reverse. There is one specimen of a Gloria Romanorum type with two emperors facing. It is a coin of Honorius or Theodosius II.

o. *Salus Reipublicae/e (313–393 C.E., 402 C.E., and later)*[40]

Pl. 6.4:12, R1498. Ae, 14 mm, 1.21 g.
Pl. 6.4:13, R674. Ae, 13 mm, 0.86 g.
Pl. 6.4:14, R1364. Ae, 14 mm, 1.13 g.
Pl. 6.4:15, R1332. Ae, 12 mm, 1.66 g.
Pl. 6.4:16, R550. Ae, 13 mm, 1.18 g.
Pl. 6.4:17, R1335. Ae, 12 mm, 1.20 g.

The Salus Reipublicae/e coins are usually small. Twenty-three of our thirty examples are Ae4 and the rest are all Ae3. Seven are coins of Valentinian II (375–392 CE). Three are inscribed with the name of Theodosius. One is most likely a coin of Theodosius I (379–395 CE) and another, with the bust of a child, must be a coin of Theodosius II, but from very early in his long reign (408–450 CE). A third features the bust of a youthful figure and, therefore, is likely a coin of Theodosius II as well. Six specimens are coins of Arcadius (383–408 CE).

There are fourteen more coins of the Salus Reipublicae type—some with no more than the figure of Victory moving leftward on the reverse—that could have been minted by any of the rulers of the period. Quite likely later than most of the rest of the series is one Ae4 coin which appears to have the bust of Johannes (423–425 CE) on the obverse. The portrait may, on the other hand, be that of Arcadius.

p. *Vota series of 378–383 C.E.*

One Ae3 specimen has the formula, VOT/V/MVLT/X, within the wreath

38. Similar to ibid. no. 2165 (pl. III).
39. As in ibid. no. 2214 (pl. III).

40. See ibid. nos. 1105, 837, 840 and 527 (pl. III) for various examples similar to ours.

and is likely of Theodosius I (379–395 CE). Four Ae4 coins bear the formula, VOT/X/MVLT/XXX. Two, and probably one other, are coins of Theodosius I. One appears to be a coin of Arcadius (383–408 CE).

q. *Virtus Exerciti*

One surface find produced an Ae2 coin with Victory hailing the emperor and the legend, VIRTVS(EXERC)ITI clearly inscribed on the reverse. It is a coin of Honorius (395–408 CE). Another coin, Ae4 in size, also bears that reverse legend, but the figure, badly worn, seems to be nothing more than Victory. The obverse inscription clearly reads DNARCADIVSPFAVG, which dates it to 313–408 CE.

r. *Other reverses with the Victory motif*

VICTORIA AVGGG, with figure of Victory dragging a captive to the left, forms the reverse of one Ae4 specimen that bears the name of Theodosius on the obverse. It is a coin of Theodosius I from the period 378–383 CE. Our latest Roman coins are small and rather badly preserved. One group of four features the figure of Victory moving left but with no inscriptional evidence intact. The only safe thing to say is that they come from the late 4th or very early 5th century CE. One coin with Victory moving left may be a coin of Theodosius I with Spes Romanorum on the legend. One specimen which may be a coin of Valens (364–378 CE) shows the emperor facing, head right, with an upright spear in his arm to the left. The inscription, were it visible, should read RESTITV TORREIP. It is an Ae3 coin minted in 364–367 CE.

s. *The cross within a circle: an early 5th century type*

The cross within a circle appears on the reverses of five coins. The obverse legend identifies one as a coin of Arcadius (383–408 CE). The other four may be of the same time period or from the reign of Valentinian III (425–455 CE), in which case the legend should read SALVS REIPVBLICAE, were it preserved.

t. *Miscellaneous late coins*

Four coins, none of them clear enough to identify very specifically, show the standing figure of the emperor (or Virtus?) with a shaft propped in hand to the right. They are not necessarily late, but the fact that they are small suggests it. Two Ae4 coins show two Victories facing, with the legend, VICTORIA AVGG, around. We would suggest that both were minted under the auspices of Valentinian III (425–435 CE) and are, likely, our latest coins.

Besides the identifiable coins listed above, there are 128 coins in bad condition which must surely come from the 4th to 5th century period, judging from texture of metal and the size and shape of the flans. This gives us a grand total of 361 coins from the era of Constantine the Great and his successors through to sometime early in the 5th century CE when the supply ceases and the first significant gap in our chronology of coins occurs. None of our latest Roman coins can be very surely dated beyond 435 CE, while the earliest Byzantine coins (see below) begin at the end of the 5th century CE. Judging from numismatic evidence alone, then, one could conclude that there was no population at our site during the last three quarters of the 5th century CE.

5. BYZANTINE COINS

Only six Byzantine coins were uncovered at Khirbet Shema'. The earliest of these is a follis of Anastasius I (498–518 CE). The obverse legend reads (DN) ANAS(TASIVSPPAVC) and within it we see the diademed bust of the emperor facing right. On the reverse we can clearly see the large M, but barely make out the cross above and the stars to either side in the field. CON appears beneath.

There are two coins of Justin I (518–527 CE). One is a small coin (diameter 17 mm) with the emperor facing on the obverse and DN.... of the legend visible. On the reverse we see the legend VICTOR(I AAVCCCA) and an angel facing in a robe with a long cross in his right hand. The other coin is a follis with DNIVSTI.... and the head of the emperor facing right on the obverse. All that appears clearly on the reverse is the large M which designates it as a follis.

There is one follis of Justinian I, the armored bust of the emperor facing right on the obverse with DNIVST(INI)ANVSPPAVC around. On the reverse we see a star to the left and a cross both above and to the right of the M, with CON beneath. Less clear than the above is a follis with the M on the reverse and ANNO written vertically to the left. Nothing else is clear enough to read. On the obverse are two figures facing as if seated, but very unclear. We would judge it to be a coin of Justin II (565–578 CE). One other follis is quite surely of Justin II. On the obverse are the two figures, Justin and Sophia, seated and facing, and we can make out .....IVS..... of the legend. The reverse is in excellent condition. There is the large M, with ANNO written vertically to the left and X (year 10) to the right. Above is the cross and between the legs of the M, the monogram $\overline{\text{B}}$. Beneath: NIK. The date is 575 CE.

Pl. 6.5:1, R2309. Ae, 28 mm, 13.44 g.

Another follis of Justin II is also quite clear on the obverse, where we see the emperor and Sophia seated and DNIVSTINVSPPA around. On the reverse: M with cross above and A beneath, ANNO at the left, II at the right, the mint mark KYZ at the bottom. The date is 572/3 CE.

One fragment of a penta- or decannummium is surely Byzantine, but there is nothing by which to further identify it.

6. ISLAMIC COINS

Thirty-seven Islamic coins were found at Khirbet Shema'. All those which are datable can be ascribed either to the years 700–830 or to 1156–1277 CE. It would be unsafe, however, to draw conclusions based on the absence of coins from the intervening three centuries. That period was one in which copper coins were hardly struck at all in Syria, while silver coins of Syria are rare up to the mid-11th century and almost nonexistent thereafter until about 1175 CE. Given the rarity of coins in these two metals, their absence on the site is probably a result of chance. The European coinage found at the site falls within the second of the two Islamic periods.

Geographically, nearly all the coins can either be attributed to Syrian mints or are presumably Syrian. The only non-Syrian coins from the first chronological group are three 'Abbassid dirhams from Cairo, Baghdad, and Isfahan; in the second period only a 12th-century fals of Anatolia. The Syrian mints known to be represented are Tyre, Damascus, Aleppo, and Hamah. The first of these is surprising, considering the date of the coin; the latter three are quite predictable, inasmuch as these three cities produced the bulk of Syria's coinage in the 12th and 13th centuries. The regional or local nature of the late Islamic coinage contrasts strongly with the international character of the European coinage of the same period found at the site. None of the latter comes from Syria, and only one coin comes from the Near East.

6.1 *Umayyad coins*

The earliest Islamic coin from Khirbet Shema' is an anonymous fals bearing simple religious legends only, without mint or date, a common type. It may most plausibly be attributed to a Syrian mint in the first two decades of the 8th century (Ae, 14 mm, 1.40 g).[41]

6.2 *'Abbassid coins*

a. *al-Mansur (136–158 H./754–775 C.E.)*

Pl. 6.5:2, R2207. Ar, 25 mm, 2.93 g.
Dirham, Madinat al-Salam (Baghdad), 151 H/768 CE. Usual inscriptions, as BM I, 48, no. 71.[42]

b. *al-Ma'mun (193–218 H./809–833 C.E.)*

Two dirhams and one Syrian copper are the latest 'Abbassid coins to be found on the site. The dirhams, of well-known types, were struck in the Iranian city Isfahan, 204 H/819–20 CE (Ar, 25 mm, 1.23 g),[43] and in Misr (Cairo), 214 H/829–30 CE (Ar, 24 mm, 1.73 g).[44] The fals is of great numismatic interest.

41. J. Walker, *Muhammadan Coins*, II, 209–210, nos. 631–639.
42. Lane-Poole, *Oriental Coins.*
43. Lavoix, *Catalogue des monnaies*, I, 220, no. 904.
44. Ibid. I, 367, no. 893.

Pl. 6.5:3, R2135. Ae, 14 mm, 1.07 g.

Obv: in central field, the *shahada* in three lines. *Margin: duriba hadha'l-fals bi-sur. Rev: Muhammad/rasul/Allah/'adl. Margin: sana sitt wa-tisa'in wa-mi'a.* The reading of the legends on the Khirbet Shema' specimen is supplemented by comparison with other examples of the same issue in the collection of the American Numismatic Society and in a private collection. There is mention of another example in Tiesenhausen,[45] where, however, the reading of the mint is questioned; the date was read 166, and the last word of the reverse field inscription was misread. The coin is now to be attributed without doubt to Sur (Tyre), 196 H/811–812 CE. No other Islamic issues of this city are known until the time of the Fatimids (10th century), excepting the coppers of the year 200 H/815–816 CE with the mint Sur al'Maumuniya, which is probably the same as Sur.

6.3 *Seljuk of Rum*

The only coin of this Anatolian dynasty is a fals of Qilij-Arslan b.Mas'ud (551–588 H/1156–1192 CE) without mint or date (Ae, 19 mm, 1.85 g).[46]

6.4 *Ayyubid*

a. *Salah al-Din (564–589 H./1169–1193 C.E.)*

One dirham and three coppers may be attributed to this ruler, the "Saladin" of the Crusaders. The inscriptions on the dirham are partly effaced, but the type is the ordinary one of Hamah or Damascus, while the date is 58x H/1185–93 CE (Ar, 23 mm).[47] The coppers can all be attributed to Damascus, although the mint name is not always legible. There is one struck in the name of the Zengid Isma'il b. Mahmud as putative overlord from about 571–573 H/1175–1178 CE (Ae, 22 mm, 5.58 g)[48] and two of the year 586 H/1190 CE (Ae, 23 mm, 5.18 g and 22 mm, 5.72 g).[49]

b. *al-'Adil Abu Bakr (596–615 H./1200–1218 C.E.)*

Seven coins of this ruler were found. The single dirham lacks both mint name and date, but is the usual interlaced trilobe type of Damascus, 599–607 H/1202–1211 CE (Ar, 19 mm).[50] There were also six coppers of this ruler, of a single type characteristic of Damascus. Not all have a legible date or mint name, but some may be more precisely dated on the basis of minor variations. In order they are: 598 or 599 H/1201–1203 CE, 607 or 609 H/1210–1213 CE,

45. Tiesenhausen, *Moneti*, p. 266, no. 2598.
46. Lane-Poole, *Oriental Coins*, III, 49, no. 93.
47. Type of Lavoix, *Catalogue des monnaies*, III, 180, no. 472.
48. Type of Lane-Poole, *Oriental Coins*, IX, 308, no. 608.
49. Type of ibid. IV, 74, nos. 279–283.
50. Type of ibid. 97, no. 358 (pl. IV).

608 H/1211–1212 CE, 608 H/1211–1212 CE, 6xx H/1204–1218 CE and two which are undatable.[51]

c. *al-Kamil Muhammad (615–635 H./1218–1238 C.E.)*

Pl. 6.5:4, R520. Ae, 19 mm, 2.74 g.

The single coin of this ruler is of some numismatic interest. A similar fals was published by Lane-Poole,[52] but the second line of the obverse was illegible on his specimen. On ours the last two words are clearly *Nasir al-Din.* Our specimen can also be dated 634 H/1236–1237 CE, but the mint remains unknown. It is certainly Syrian, probably from Damascus.

d. *al-'Aziz Muhammad of Aleppo (613–634 H./1216–1237 C.E.)*

Although its mint and date are effaced, a fals of this ruler with the name of the caliph al-Mustansir can be attributed to Aleppo, 623–634 H/1226–1237 CE (Ae, 22 mm, 3.47 g).[53]

e. *al-Salih Ayyub (637–647 H./1240–1249 C.E.)*

This ruler is represented only by a Syrian fals with mint and date effaced or lacking (Ae, 18–20 mm, 3.37 g).[54]

6.5 *Mamluk coins*

Pl. 6.5:5, R591. Ae, 21 mm, 1.70 g.
Pl. 6.5:6, R589. Ae, 18 mm, 2.30 g.
Pl. 6.5:7, R2015. Ae, 15 mm, 1.58 g.

The only Mamluk ruler to whom Khirbet Shema' coins can be attributed is al-Zahir Baybars (651–676 H/1260–1277 CE). His one dirham has mint and date effaced but is probably attributable to Hamah, about 666–673 H/1267–1275 CE (Ar, 24 mm, 3.33 g).[55] The nine coppers are all very similar and can be attributed to Damascus on the basis of style.

6.6 *Unattributed*

Pl. 6.5:8, R1382. Ae, 21 mm, 0.71 g.

Seven specimens were in too poor condition to be attributed. Of these, four are apparently Mamluk, possibly Baybars; two others can be ascribed to Syria, 13th–15th century, with the balance of probability in favor of the 13th. One disc is quite mysterious and may not be a coin at all.[56]

51. Type of ibid. 102, no. 372; Lavoix, *Catalogue des monnaies*, III, 234–235, nos. 612–614.

52. Lane-Poole, *Oriental Coins*, IV, 114, no. 419.

53. Type of ibid. 89, no. 331.

54. Like ibid. 118, no. 430?

55. P. Balog, *Coinage of the Mamluk Sultans*, 97, nos. 64–66.

56. Ibid. 105–106, nos. 98–99, 101–102.

7. MEDIEVAL EUROPEAN COINAGE

The European coinage found at Khirbet Shema' can all be dated between 1162 and 1250 CE and is thus contemporary with the second and latest group of Islamic coins. The European coins, however, contrast strongly with the Islamic coins of the same period in that none of them were struck in Syria. Four are from Europe itself: two from France and two from Sicily. One was struck at Damietta in Egypt.

The earliest (which may, of course, have been in circulation for some time before reaching Khirbet Shema') is a billon denier of Hugh III, Duke of Burgundy 1162–1192 CE, struck at Dijon. *Obv*: UGO DUX BURGDIE. *Rev*: DIVIO-NENSIS.[57] The other French coin, also a billon denier, appears to have been struck by William I of Chauvigny (1203–1233 CE) at the fort Chateauroux. The coin certainly belongs to one of his immediate predecessors or successors at that fort, if not to him.[58]

> *Pl. 6.5:9, R2016.* Ae, 17 mm, 0.62 g.
> *Pl. 6.5:10, R2090.* 17 mm, 0.61 g.

Two Sicilian issues in the name of the Emperor Frederick II (1197–1250 CE) were found. One, a copper denaro, is a known type, attributed by Sambon to 1243–1248 CE.[59] The other is a half-denaro, with obverse inscription IMPERATOR·ROM and reverse IERSP·ET·SICIL·R. A half-denaro with these inscriptions is apparently novel, although a corresponding denaro is known as well as half-denaro of the same period with a variant inscription. Sambon attributes this type to 1247–1250 CE.[60] The single Crusader denier was struck at Damietta in Egypt during the occupation of that city by the Crusaders in 1219–1221 CE (the Fifth Crusade). A known type, it bears the name of John of Brienne, King of Jerusalem, as regent for his daughter Yolande (1212–1225 CE), and the mint, DAMIATA.[61]

One European coin is so Byzantine in character that we at first tried to seek its identity in catalogues of Byzantine coins. It is a *grosso* of Marino Morosini, Doge of Venice in 1249–1253 CE. The obverse, which shows St. Mark facing the doge with vexillum and DUX between, bears the inscription, MMAVROC/SMVENETI. The reverse is inscribed with IC XC and shows Christ seated facing on a square-backed throne.[62]

57. Variant of Poey d'Avant, *Monnaies féodales*, III, 196, no. 5658 (pl. CXXX, no. 16).
58. Cf. ibid. I, 274, nos. 1959–60 (pl. XXXI, no. 16).
59. A. Sambon, *Normanni*, 102, no. 36.
60. Cf. ibid. 104, nos. 51, 53.
61. G. Schlumberger, *Numismatique*, 93 and pl. III, no. 31.
62. The coin is to be seen in *Corpus Nummorum Italicorum*, VII, 34, no. 16 and tav. II. 7. This was pointed out to us by William E. Metcalf, Assistant Curator of Roman and Byzantine Coins at the American Numismatic Society.

8. SUMMARY AND CONCLUSIONS

The coin data reveal three kinds of information useful to the archaeological task of unraveling the mysteries of Khirbet Shema': (i) information to assist in dating the levels of occupation we disclosed, (ii) information regarding the commercial ties of the site during its various periods of occupation, and (iii) information concerning political ties, domination, and events.

If it were coin evidence alone that informed us of the times of habitation, we should say that the first period of occupation began in the 1st century BCE or even earlier. Our very earliest coins are three Ptolemaic specimens which may come from the 3d century BCE and, in addition to that, there is a group of Seleucid coins from the 2d century BCE. It would be rash, however, to suggest that occupation began that early, for we can be reasonably certain that coins were kept in circulation long past the time when they were struck. The earliest settlers at Shema' may well have had coins a hundred years old in their purses when they came.

The significantly large number of coins of Alexander Yannai must suggest something more than the quantity of coins struck by that ruler. The quantity is so large that we can only suggest a significant number of persons either camping or living at the site in the 1st century BCE.

The steady supply of coins that begins with the 2d century BCE coins minted by the Seleucid rulers in Tyre continues without interruption until a goodly supply of Roman coins begins to replace them in the last half of the 3d century CE. This suggests steady, though moderate to small, occupation of the site all through those four centuries. Then, with no break in supply whatever, the quantity swells in the 4th century CE and remains at a significant high into the first quarter of the 5th century CE. All through the period that begins with Constantine the Great, we have a supply that tallies out at about three coins to represent each year of habitation. (For the first two centuries of the Common Era, by contrast, we find about one coin for every eight years of occupation and for the 3d century CE, about one for every five years.) This can only represent a period of more intense occupation.[63]

The absence of coins from ca. 425 CE to the end of the 5th century CE

---

63. That no coin hoard has been found can be called into question by the coin density plot illustrated in fig. 6.1 (Khirbet Shema' 4th to 5th century coins). There is a noticeable peak in NE VII.2 that calls for explanation. Upon examination of the field books it seems that this great density of coins was discovered outside the synagogue just north of the great North Wall of that building. That is, fifteen of the 4th to 5th century coins found all stem from L.2022, which was soil-sealed under two stones designated L.2024. These two stones lay beneath a cobbled floor, L.2015. According to the weekly report of the Area Supervisor, the coins lay "all on bedrock" in association with the foundation course of the north synagogue wall. In view of the stratigraphic evidence from within the synagogue, this must imply that bedrock was exposed during the first century of use of the synagogue, but that pavement 2015 was put down late in the history of this room to the north. (Excavator's note.)

suggests that the site was abandoned during that period, and the supply that begins with a follis of Anastasius I (498–518 CE) ends with a coin that cannot be dated later than 602 CE. Yet this 6th-century occupation is represented by no more than six coins. Another gap occurs at this point, and then we have a series of six to nine Islamic coins that span the period 695–824 CE—presenting us with the same sparsity in supply that we found for the Byzantine period.

The supply of Islamic coins that begins with four specimens struck by Salah al-Din (earliest specimen: 1175–1178 CE), ends with ten coins of Baybars I (1260–1277 CE) and comprises only thirty-three coins, five of which are European and Crusader types. The period lasts for one century and the supply is only one-ninth of that for the comparable period of ca. 325–425 CE, when our supply is greatest. The final period of habitation at Shema' would seem to have been small, relative to the population that occupied the site in its heyday of activity and construction.

The most notable bit of information regarding the commercial ties of our humble site is the fact that we find a steady supply of coins minted in Tyre from the 2d century BCE through half of the 3d century CE. This suggests that the meager exports of the people who lived at Shema'—likely limited in stuff to olives and olive oil—were in the direction of Tyre, where payment was made in coins struck at that commercial city. The large quantity of Hasmonean coins breaks into this with a countersupply that may represent a political policy rather than a market to the south at the time they were introduced.

Where mint evidence is perceivable, the greatest single source of coins in the 4th century CE is Antioch. This may not be significant commercially, for it may only indicate that Antioch replaced Tyre as a minting center at that time. The most common source of coins in the Islamic periods of occupation is Damascus.

It is interesting, though not surprising, that European/Crusader and Islamic coins occur together at our site. The two sorts must have enjoyed equal currency at Shema' and other sites in the land. As far as common trade was concerned, a coin was a coin, no matter what governing power had minted it and as long as there were no restrictions against its use.

The most interesting political data supplied by our coins is the presence of a large quantity of coins minted by the Hasmonean rulers and, particularly, Alexander Yannai. For the most part they are so miserable in quality that only a patriotic Jew could have loved them. Unlike the coins of Tyre, which are generally impressive for their size if not for their quality, these coins can only reflect the eagerness of Yannai to declare himself sovereign in an emphatic way. Coins are a means of declaring political power and a way to spread political propaganda, and this was even more true in the centuries that precede the development of mass media of communication such as the printing press. Because they passed from hand to hand rapidly and thus reached many people, coins were a most effective device for letting the world know that sovereignty was asserting itself. Yannai minted huge quantities of coins in conjunction with his efforts to win and control the old territories of the glorious Kingdom of David.

There seems to be evidence, though it is shaky and hard to control, that these coins were used as currency for an unbelievably long time at Shemaʻ. Some of them are worn to near nothing by handling, and many occur in proximity to coins from as late as the 4th century CE. Could it be that our site was the home of Jewish folk who valued the memory of the days of autonomy so much that they kept the old Hasmonean coins in hand or even in usage that long? In juxtaposition to this suggestion, we must note the complete absence of coins of either of the Jewish revolts.

The story of conquests and rule by great powers is also told by our coins: the shift from the rule of the Ptolemies to the rule of the Seleucid kings, the entrance and rule of Rome, the shift of Roman power from west to east and the establishment of Byzantine rule, the invasion of the Islamic powers and the changes of leadership that occurred among them, and, finally, the coming of Christian Crusaders to the land. This is all general knowledge shared by all our readers, however; there is no need to rehearse that story.

The mint marks on coins tell something of a story. We have far from enough information, owing to the worn or damaged condition of most of our coins, but there is enough to see some interesting shifts in the provenance of the Roman coins of the Constantine and post-Constantine era. More than half of the coins of the mid-4th century CE (ca. 325–375) came from Antioch, and the rest tend to come from mints to the north such as Heraclea or Cyzicus. At the end of the 4th century, however, there is a noteworthy rise in the number of coins minted in Alexandria. Apparently the center of control for our area was lessening from Antioch and northward and increasing from the south. Or does the shift in some way reflect the rebellion against Gallus that occurred in mid-century? It would seem too delayed for this explanation.

It is notable that Tyre ceases to be a source of coins after the middle of the 3d century CE. Apparently the Romans took away the privilege of minting at that point.

As one might well expect, the bulk of our Islamic coins were minted in Damascus. There is one coin each from Tyre, Baghdad, Cairo, and Aleppo, but twenty coins from nearby Damascus.

CHAPTER 7. CERAMICS

1. INTRODUCTION

These pages present the most important pottery evidence from the 1970, 1971, and 1972 seasons of excavations. Since we have chosen to publish ceramics only from our major loci, this chapter is by its nature no exhaustive analysis of the pottery data. Rather it is an examination of ceramics from loci that are either sealed or considered critical for dating structures. Therefore we do not expect to be able to present the complete evaluation of pottery types or a complete seriation analysis of the various kinds of vessels. Instead, the chapter is intended first of all to present the evidence we draw upon for our chronology, and secondly to make a contribution to dating pottery types and their development from loci with associated coins.

2. "GALILEAN BOWLS"

"Galilean bowls" are illustrated in fig. 7.1 and pls. 7.1–7.10. Generally they are shallow, with flat or shallow conical bases or perhaps convex bases, sometimes with carination between the rim and the base. They often occur with decorative internal ribbing. The rims occur in several varieties, often being clearly differentiated from the body by a more or less sudden thickening. They are known with and without handles and in later forms with vestigial handles.

These bowls have been rather fully discussed by Loffreda, who calls them "cooking bowls of family T."[1] Loffreda notes sixteen sites in Galilee and the Golan where they have been found, and this localization is the reason for our name. To Loffreda's list may be added Pella in Transjordan and finds of surface sherds by the present authors at Bar'am, Sammu'i, Gush Halav, Ras al-Fawwar, Beer Sheba North, Khirbet Hananyah, Arbel, Tubah, and Umm el-Ammed, all in upper Galilee. To the Golan sites can be added Daburiyyeh (212/272), Deir Qerukh (220²/256⁹) and Fakhurah (214⁸/267⁴). Finally, one must note the absence to date of this form from published sites in the south, including Samaria, Jerusalem, Bethany, and Ramat Rahel.[2] Loffreda has distinguished six main

1. Loffreda, "Evoluzione," 237–263, and V. Corbo et al., *Sinagoga*, 18–21. (For full citation of works mentioned in the notes, see the Bibliography preceding the Appendixes.) Loffreda's complete treatment of the Capernaum pottery was received too late to be incorporated here, but it is included in the Bibliography for reference purposes.

2. The term "Galilean bowl" is more accurate than our earlier label "Shema' bowl" used in Meyers-Kraabel-Strange, "Archaeology," 27, fig. 12, but even this new name is provisional and will be set in quotation marks. Its appearance in the Golan does not warrant changing the name to acknowledge its presence there, since it is possible that these bowls were manufactured in Galilee at ancient Sogane (modern Sikhnin) and ancient Kefar Hanania (modern Khirbet Hanania). Cf. Avi-Yonah, *Holy Land*, 255.

Table 7.1. NUMBERING SYSTEM FOR BOWL DESCRIPTIONS

First digit   1—one groove in rim
                       2—two grooves in rim
                       3—rounded rim
                       4—flat rim

Second digit   1—no clear line of division between rim and body (both near same thickness)
                       2—clear line of division (different thicknesses)

Third digit   1—two vertical loop handles
                       2—two small pierced handles
                       3—two vestigial "ear" handles, no opening
                       4—two vestigial handles as small (ca. 8 mm) lumps
                       5—no handles

Fourth digit   1—flat base
                       2—round base
                       3—carination to shallow conical base

Fifth digit   1—no internal ribbing
                       2—internal ribbing

The places of digits are reckoned from the left. A zero in any place means that the information for that feature is not known.

types of our "Galilean bowl."[3] However, relying on a careful typological analysis we can distinguish at least eight main types from rim analysis alone, and several others can be differentiated on the basis of differing styles of handles and bases.

To reduce verbal descriptions to a simpler format we have converted the description of a bowl into a five-digit number, with the digits separated by periods. Each digit refers to one variable in the morphology of the vessel—rim type, rim treatment, handles, base, and internal ribbing. These numbers are used only in the sequence analysis itself; in the discussion of each type we will rely on the usual word description. The numbering system is given in Table 7.1.

Logically it is possible to describe $4 \times 2 \times 5 \times 3 \times 2 = 240$ types of "Galilean bowls" with this schema, but not all possible combinations occur. In fact very few vessels were complete enough to determine base type, so seriation analysis was performed mainly on the rims, which appear to be diagnostic.[4]

Table 7.2 shows equivalences for Loffreda's types of the "Galilean bowl" compared to the typology at Khirbet Shema'.

One can readily perceive that, on the basis of rim type alone, the Capernaum six types overlap into at least eleven types from the Khirbet Shema' evidence. At Khirbet Shema' we perceive four main types of rim, each with two subtypes that appear to be reasonably well separated in terms of frequency of occurrence

3. Loffreda, "Evoluzione," 240–248, and Corbo et al., *Sinagoga*, 56–60.

4. The small amount of Meiron material is published here only as an aid to sequence analysis. The complete pottery, coins, and stratigraphic analysis will be published in our forthcoming final report. See also supra ch. 3, n. 7.

Table 7.2. EQUIVALENT TYPES OF "GALILEAN BOWL"

Loffreda	*Khirbet Shema'*
Type 1	1.1.5.1.1 or 1.1.5.2.1
Type 2	1.2.2.2.2
Type 3	2.1.1.2.1
Type 4	2.2.2.3.2 or 2.1.2.3.2
Type 5	3.1.4.3.2 or 3.2.4.3.2
Type 6	4.1.4.3.2 or 4.2.4.3.2

to justify classifying them tentatively as subtypes. The four rim types are these: rim with single groove, rim with double groove, rounded rim, and "flat" rim. The second variable is the presence or absence of a more or less pronounced difference between the rim and the body of the vessel, a difference most easily illustrated in the case of the rounded rims. These two variables give us $4 \times 2 = 8$ types of "Galilean bowl," classified on this basis of rim only (1.1, 1.2, 2.1, 2.2, 3.1, 3.2, 4.1, 4.2). See fig. 7.1.

Thus Loffreda's first four types correspond generally to the Khirbet Shema' bowls except for an overlap at types 3 and 4. That is, from his drawings we can see that his type 4 has both our 2.1 and our 2.2 types: 2.1 is represented in his fig. 5 by numbers 1, 2, 4, 10, 11, 13, and 15. For all of these the transition from body to rim is more or less smooth. The remainder exhibit a more or less abrupt change in thickness. Number 10 also has carination to a reconstructed round base, but that is another matter. Loffreda's type 6 can be divided into clearly round rims and flat rims, not to mention the transition from body to rim. "Flat" rims (4.) are represented in his fig. 7 by numbers 5, 9, and perhaps 25, and in his fig. 8 by numbers 6, 7, 11, 12, 13, 14, and 16. We will return to this problem in our discussion of the evolution of these forms as we can perceive it at Khirbet Shema'.

Typology and chronology

Type 1.1, the earliest form of these bowls attested by our stratigraphic and coin evidence, is evidently the rim with one groove and no clear distinction between the rim and the body (see fig. 7.1). The earliest stratigraphic context for this type is found in our rescue operation at Meiron in square MI.2, L.2019, which constitutes the make-up underneath floor 2018.1. This locus contained six coins, of which two were clearly 3d-century CE and one specimen of a Tyrian coin that may be of the 3d century. Certainly the coins sealed in floor 2018.1 and 2016.1 above this locus provide a terminus in the early 3d century. These rims are not found in contexts clearly datable to the 4th century CE, which implies that they were no longer manufactured after some date during the 3d century. This type of Galilean bowl varies in radius more or less continuously in our

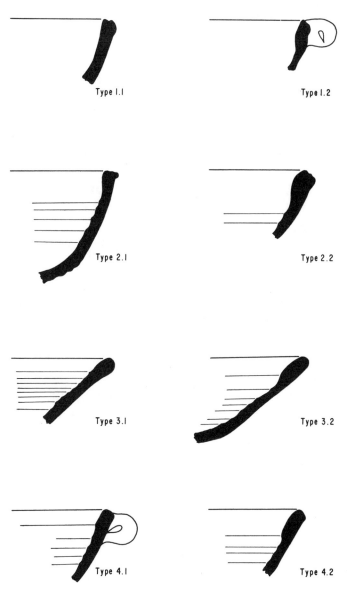

Figure 7.1. Types of "Galilean bowl" rims.

examples from about 4.5 to 14.5 cm. That is, the bowls are not clearly differentiated into subtypes on the basis of radius. There is also a certain irregularity of stance and molding that suggests that this type stands at the end of its development, which is consistent with our date for its appearance before mid-3d century CE and with Loffreda's early chronology.[5]

Type 1.2, another early type of rim, is distinguished from type 1.1 only by

5. Loffreda, "Evoluzione," 251–254; also idem, *et-Tabgha,* fig. 31:11.

the clear distinction between thickened rim and thinner body (see pl. 7.1:14–30). It is slightly more abundant in MI.2, L.2019, but does not entirely vanish in the 4th century CE. This rim type, however, is relatively more abundant in the 3d century at Meiron, MI.2, L.2015 (fill), 2014.1 (floor), and 2011 (floor) than type 1.1. This may suggest that this bowl type is a later variant of type 1.1.[6]

Type 2.1, bowls with two grooves and no clear distinction between rim and body (see pl. 7.2:1–23), are very abundant in their 3d-century context and evidently continue to be manufactured through the 4th century, judging from their relative abundance in NW VII.13, L.13003. There is a greater population for this type than for either type 1.1 or type 1.2, which may suggest that it has slightly later origins.[7]

Type 2.2, with double-grooved, distinctly thickened rim (see pls 7.2:24–34, 7.3:1–16, 23–27), cannot be simply a variant on type 2.1, since it is found relatively commonly in the 3d century and then drops out of sight at Khirbet Shema' in 4th-century contexts. Its pattern of decline in the 3d century and absence in the 4th century most closely resembles that of types 1.1 and 1.2, which may suggest that this type is a variant of these two rather than of type 2.1.[8]

Type 3.1 shows a very simple rounded rim that is generally thicker than the body, but the transition from rim to body is so gradual that no clear distinction between rim and body can be made (see pls. 7.4:1–32, 7.5:1–32, 7.6:1–2, 4–9). This form starts abruptly in Meiron, MI.2, L.2015, which must date, to judge on the evidence of its coins, to the mid-3d century at the latest, confirming Loffreda's "type 6" *terminus post quem*.[9] This is our most abundant variant of the "Galilean bowl" through the beginning of the 5th century CE from all over Khirbet Shema'. In view of its great abundance in late contexts, it may represent the end of the evolution; but see below.

Type 3.2 varies again from the preceding type by the sudden transition from thickened rim to body (see pls. 7.6:3, 10–30, 7.7:1–32, 7.8:1–24). The form starts at the same time as type 3.1 and seems to have the same life on our site, though it occurs in relatively fewer examples than type 3.1. This rather strongly implies that types 3.1 and 3.2 are merely variants of one another, with 3.1 somewhat predominating.[10]

Type 4.1 is a short-lived variant, so it appears, on 1.1 (see pls. 7.8:24–30, 7.9:1–14). This bowl with "flat" rim and no clear division between thickened rim and body occurs in several subtypes, depending on the angle between the flat edge and the axis of the body as it appears in section. But it is not at all clear from our evidence whether these subtypes are significant variants of the basic bowl rim with one flat surface. What is clear is that the common overhanging lip on the outside of the rim is closest in form to type 1.1, the rim with a single

6. Loffreda, *et-Tabgha*, figs. 30:1, 4, 31:11.
7. Ibid. figs. 30:5, 31:10.
8. Ibid. figs. 30:6, 31:13–14, 18.

9. Loffreda, "Evoluzione," 257; cf. also idem *et-Tabgha*, figs. 30:8, 31:21.
10. See Loffreda *et-Tabgha*, figs. 30:7, 31:23, 25, 33:35–36; also Smith, *Pella*, I, pl. 28:1237.

groove and unclear transition from rim to body. In other words typologically and stratigraphically it appears that 1.1 and 4.1 belong together, for both types virtually disappear after about the middle of the 3d century. It is also significant that virtually no parallels to this rim can be found.

Type 4.2, on the other hand, illustrated in pls. 7.9:15–28 and 7.10:1–19, reaches its *floruit* after the mid-3d century and appears to be in decline only by the end of the 4th and beginning of the 5th, i.e., after the dominance of types 3.1 and 3.2. Therefore it is impossible to view this form merely as a variant of 1.1, though it may well be descended from 2.2, which it also resembles typologically.[11]

As for *bases*, it is very difficult to make any statement about the types on our "Galilean bowls," since only three specimens could be reconstructed from rim to base, and none were recovered anywhere intact. Yet one can see that type 1.1 has curving outer walls, which suggests a concave base. A few examples, however, have a steeply sloping body, which implies either carination to the base or a flat base or both (see pl. 7.3:19–20). The only complete bases we have are on rim types 2.1 (pl. 7.3:19–20) or 3.1 (pl. 7.6:3, but cf. pls. 7.2:33, 7.3:27, 7.6:26–28). As one can readily see, the former is flat and the latter is a shallow cone with a flattened point and sharp carination between base and body.[12]

Handles were manufactured in three major types on "Galilean bowls" from our site.[13] These are full loop handles, small loop handles, vestigial "ear" handles, and simple lumps of clay. The loop handles are attached vertically at the rim and on the body and are clearly functional.[14] The largest example we have extends from the body 17 mm, though two examples, now broken, could have been larger. The maximum vertical measurement is 25 mm. The most striking fact about these handles is that they are found only on rim types 2.1 and 2.2, or those with double grooves, but they are far and away most abundantly associated with rim 2.1, the double-grooved rim with no clear distinction between rim thickness and body. Chronologically, therefore, these full loop handles appear to continue from the early 3d to the end of the 4th century CE, or for the life of the "Galilean bowl" type 2.1.

The second type of handle—the small, still functional vertical loop—is distinguished from the type 1 handle in that the hole in the loop has almost disappeared, so close are the attachments for the two ends of the handle.[15] This handle is most often attached vertically at the outer edge of the rim and then to the body just below the rim. No more than a string could be passed through the resulting hole. The handle extends from the body a maximum of 15 mm on our

11. Cf. Loffreda, *et-Tabgha*, fig. 30:2 (without handles) and Smith, *Pella*, I, pl. 28:1209.

12. Parallels appear in Avigad, "Excavations," 210, fig. 3:11, though with a more pointed base than ours. See also Bagatti, *Nazareth*, fig. 226:3 and 13 with convex base.

13. See our numerical taxonomy, supra Table 7.1.

14. Other examples occur at Capernaum. Loffreda,

"Evoluzione," fig. 4:4 and 16, on a rim type 2.1, exactly as at Meiron and Khirbet Shema'; Bagatti, *Nazareth*, fig. 226:4 on rim type 1.1.

15. Also at Capernaum. Loffreda, "Evoluzione," fig. 5:15, 16 and on rim type 1.1 and 1.2; fig. 5:15 on rim type 2.1; fig. 6:1 on rim type 2.2. See Bagatti, *Nazareth*, fig. 226:1.

pottery, and its maximum vertical measurement is 20 mm, though most commonly the latter measure is 15 mm. This handle occurs, though infrequently, on all types except 2.1, 2.2, and 3.2. It may be an accident that it does not appear on type 2, since otherwise this type overwhelmingly has handles of type 1 (and also a few of type 3), and type 2 handles appear typologically to be midway in evolution between types 1 and 3. Then also at Capernaum these handles definitely occur on rim types 2.1 and 2.2,[16] implying an evolution of handles on types 2.1 and 2.2 of the first three handle types.

The simplest and least functional handle type is missing on rim type 2, but this too may be accidental, since type 2.1 bowls in particular occur at Khirbet Shema' at the end of the 4th century in sufficient quantities to suggest manufacture, or during the period of greatest popularity of type 4 handles.

Type 3 handles are simply vertical discs of clay, concave on both sides from pinching when wet, and no longer functional.[17] They are generally attached outside the rim continuing down about 15 mm from the top of the rim. They may extend horizontally as much as 15 mm from the rim. These handles are clearly conventional and stylized, that is, vestigial. The potter no longer understands the function of this attachment as anything other than decorative, or perhaps simply as a traditional element in bowls of this type.

Type 3 handles are found on all "Galilean bowls" except 3.1 and 3.2, which is surely not accidental, particularly in view of the parallel evidence cited from Beth She'arim and Capernaum. The distribution published of type 3 handles from these two sites is virtually identical, except that there are no illustrations of bowls with these handles of rim type 2.1. This may be accidental. A chronology of type 3 handles is not simple to deduce. They occur in the 3d century on rim 1.1, but not on the equally 3d-century rim type 4.1. However, they do not appear on 3.1 or 3.2 type "Galilean bowls," an absence which implies that their life is effectively over; that is, they are no longer a live option for a new form such as 3.1.3.2 in the mid-3d century CE.

Type 4 handles are simply small wads of clay pressed onto the rim of almost exclusively type 3.1 and 3.2 "Galilean bowls."[18] (One example is known on a type 4.2, if the rim is correctly identified.) These pieces of clay seldom extend more than 8 mm horizontally from the rim and are the last remnants of a handle tradition; that is, there is virtually no rationale left for affixing such a piece of clay to the rim except as a potter's tradition.

It should be clear from the above discussion that all types of "Galilean

16. See supra n. 10.
17. These are illustrated at Beth She'arim by Avigad, "Excavations," fig. 3:10, on a rim type 1.2 or perhaps 4.2. They also appear at Capernaum. Loffreda, "Evoluzione," fig. 3:10, on rim type 1.1; fig. 3:11, on rim type 4.2; and fig. 6:6, on rim type 2.2.

18. These vestigial handles have been published from Beth She'arim (Avigad, "Excavations," fig. 3:11, on a rim type 4.2); from Nazareth (Bagatti, *Nazareth*, fig. 226:3 (?), on a rim type 3.2, and p. 287, an example "of the same mould as No. 13", of rim type 3.2 also); and Capernaum (Loffreda, "Evoluzione," fig. 8:13, rim type 3.2, and fig. 8:5, rim type 3.2).

bowls" occur with handles at Khirbet Shema'. One must hasten to add, however, that only types 2.1 and 3.2 are unambiguously associated with virtually one handle type. Types 1.1 and 3.1 are also significantly correlatable with one handle type each. Therefore it is possible to deduce a correlation between rim type and handle type from the relative abundancies of their occurrence. The handle types that predominate, with their rim types, can be summarized as follows:

(i) Single-grooved rims with no clear transition to body generally have vestigial "ear" type handles, where handles occur. On the other hand bowls with single-grooved rim, and a clear distinction to the body, generally have no handle. However, when this type is provided with a handle, it is a small loop or an "ear" handle.

(ii) Double-grooved rims, with no clear distinction to body, generally have full loop handles, when handles are found. But the double-grooved rim with a

Table 7.3. VARIETIES OF
"GALILEAN BOWLS" AT MEIRON
AND KHIRBET SHEMA'

1.1.2	(few)		3.1.2	
1.1.3	*		3.1.4	*
1.2.2	(few)	1.2.5	3.2.4	*
1.2.3	(few)			
			4.1.2	
2.1.1	*			
2.1.3			4.2.2	
			4.2.3	
2.2.1		2.2.5	4.2.4	
2.2.3				
			4.2.5	

* Predominant types with handles.

clear distinction to body either has no handle or may have a loop or an ear handle.

(iii) Simple rounded rims virtually always occur with the smallest vestigial handle, when the handle is found.

(iv) So-called "flat" rims, that is, rims with a flattened edge all around and with no clear distinction to body, generally have no handles, but when handles are found, they are small vertical loops with tiny holes. The variant with a clear distinction to body generally has no handle either, but when a handle occurs it is a small loop, "ear," or vestigial lump of clay.

Thus our "Galilean bowls" at Meiron and Khirbet Shema' occur in the sixteen varieties of Table 7.3 (horizontal lines divide rim types).

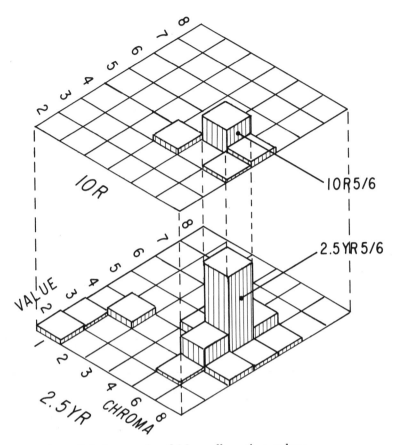

Figure 7.2. Isometric of Munsell section colors of "Galilean bowls."

Wares

Section color of "Galilean bowls" is surprisingly constant, in view of the length of time that these forms were manufactured and in use. Exterior and interior color varies more widely than section color because of vagaries in stacking and firing. Interestingly enough, differences in section color correlate with forms, as will be indicated below.

Fig. 7.2 illustrates variations in section color. The figure is an isometric view of two pages from the *Munsell Soil Color Chart*[19] with columns of each chip corresponding to the relative abundancies of "Galilean bowls" of that specific color. It is immediately apparent that most of these bowls are 2.5 YR 5/6 ("grayish reddish orange") or 5 R 5/6 ("grayish red"), though to the untutored eye they appear orange in hue. The small variations in chroma from 4 to 8 and in

19. Color names are from the National Bureau of Standards Circular 553 (1955), 16–31, a list of names approved by the Inter-Society Color Council and now in use by the Munsell Color Company, manufacturer of the *Munsell Soil Color Charts* (Baltimore 1971). For another use-ful list see the comparative tabulation of Munsell soil color names and the conventions of the Japanese Industrial Standard in M. Oyama and H. Takehara, *Standard Soil Color Charts*, 14–20.

value from 3 to 6 are probably caused by variations in duration of firing, temperature, and stacking. A significant number of these bowls are found of color 2.5 YR 2/1, 3/1, or (mainly) 4/2, "grayish reddish brown." The darkest color, 2.5 YR 2/1 or 3/1 ("dark grayish reddish brown"), is associated wholly with rims 1.1, 2.1, and 4.2. The slightly lighter color of 2.5 YR 4/2 is wholly associated with rims 1.1, 2.2, and 4.1.

The first and most striking anomaly in these data is that rounded rims are entirely missing from the tabulation of *darker* section colors. That is, our latest rim type is not represented. This suggests a certain evolution of firing technique in which the earliest forms (1.1, 2.2, 4.1) are often fired darker (2.5 YR 4/2 predominantly, though also 2.5 YR 2/1) than the later "grayish red" forms. Those that continue from early to late in our stratification (rims 2.1 and 4.2) are also occasionally fired 2.5 YR 3/1, another dark shade. Since the firing is all the way through the sherd (we are dealing with *section* color), it is not a question of stacking, but of kiln temperature. Earlier forms are evidently sometimes fired at a lower temperature than later forms.

A very few sherds of "Galilean bowls" exhibit section color of dark reddish gray (5 RP 3/1), dark bluish gray (5 PB 3/1), or dark purplish gray (5 P 4/1). These also are four earliest forms, since these colors occur exclusively with rims of types 4.1 and 1.1, both of which are found in use in contexts dated prior to the middle of the 3d century CE at Khirbet Shema'.

Grit or temper is present only in white, black, and gray particles, and any given bowl usually included two types. Most commonly the clay for these bowls has added to it a few small white and black or white and gray grits (temper). That is, the clay is not very plastic and does not require much temper. Generally "Galilean bowls" are fired hard. There are a significant number that are fired medium, and these bowls are commonly those with "some" or "many" small white grits. That is, it appears that the potter prepared his clay in advance with greater density of temper in anticipation of medium firing. Only rim types 2.2, 3.1, 3.2, and 4.2 are ever medium fired, but this does not correlate well with the chronology. Rim 2.2 is early, while 3.1 and 3.2 are late. Furthermore the life of rim 4.2 extends over the entire 3d, 4th, and early 5th century period at Meiron and Khirbet Shema'. Thus from our data alone no clear pattern emerges for firing hardness and chronology.

Chronology and evolution of types

Since we have the stratified remains for only two centuries at Khirbet Shema' and Meiron—namely, the 3d and 4th/5th centuries CE—we cannot reconstruct the entire evolution of these sixteen types of bowls; however, some generalizations do seem at least tentatively possible.

It seems fairly clear from our evidence that "Galilean bowls" of types 1.1

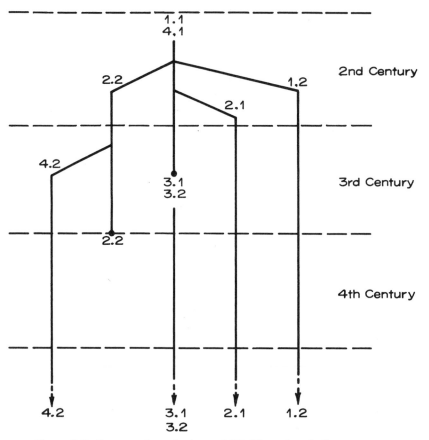

Figure 7.3. Proposed evolution of "Galilean bowls."

and 4.1 are the earliest. These two rim types may be ancestors of 2.1. Type 2.1 continues to exist to the end of the 4th century, but 4.1 evolves into 3.1 and 3.2 by mid-3d century. Rims of types 1.2 and 4.2 may appear about the same time early in the 3d century, again as descendents of 1.1. In this case rim 1.2 begins to die out, but 4.2 seems to continue side by side with 3.1 and 3.2 to the close of the 4th century.

These suggestions can be schematized as in fig. 7.3. Such a pattern of evolution is similar to but not identical with Loffreda's from Capernaum. Probably only more excavations, ceramic analysis, and publications will complete the picture.

3. BOWLS WITH EVERTED LIP (Pls. 7.10:20–29, 7.11 and 7.12:1–27)

Bowls with the lip everted are only about one-fourth as plentiful at Khirbet Shema' as the "Galilean bowls" discussed above. They are just as surely types of domestic pottery as the "Galilean bowls," for they virtually never occur in SE II, the "industrial area." These bowls occur in two main types. Type 1 is a shallow bowl with sharp carination between lip and base (see pls. 7.10:20–29, 7.11:1–20).[20] Type 2 is a deeper variety with no carination but rather a smoothly rounded body (see pls. 7.12:1–27).[21] Since none of our examples of either major type could be reconstructed to the base, we can only presume that both models were originally manufactured with rounded or concave base, judging from the concavity of the sides.[22] Some of our examples are provided with two vertical loop handles attached either at the outer edge or below the rim and onto the body.

Type 1 is tentatively divisible typologically into three groups that have chronological significance: Group A (types 1.1 and 1.2), Group B (types 1.3 and 1.4), and Group C (type 1.5). These are illustrated in pls. 7.10 and 7.11 and fig. 7.4. Their inner relationships will be discussed below.

Type 1.1 is rather rare at Meiron or Khirbet Shema'. Its everted lip curves out to the horizontal from the roughly vertical body. On the four specimens we publish in pl. 7.10:20–23, the lip extends about 14 mm on the average from the body and forms a concavity at the join. The carination is so sharply defined, at about 14 mm (average) below the 5 mm-thick lip, that it suggests a metal proto-type, though we need not assume that one ever existed.[23]

The four examples on pl. 7.10 are rather uniform in diameter, since three have diameters of 28.4 cm, 29.0 cm, and 33.2 cm. The last and largest is 36.0 cm in diameter, which yields an average of 31.7 cm for all four vessels, with average wall thickness of 4.5 mm. This type is found in L.2019 at MI.2, which must date in the late 2d or early 3d century CE. Otherwise it occurs in early 4th-century to early 5th-century contexts, but its *terminus ante quem* cannot be determined from our site.

Type 1.2 differs from the preceding type mainly in that in profile the body from lip to carination yields generally a much more vertical stance (see fig. 7.4, and pls. 7.10:24–29, 7.11:1–4). The lip is still horizontal but does not protrude more than 10 mm from the body. The connection between lip and body is still rounded, but by and large there is more definition to the connection. Finally the stance of the body below the carination suggests a deeper vessel. The carination begins about 20 mm below the lip and is far less sharply formed than in type 1.1. One vessel has two vertical loop handles (pl. 7.10:27).

In the ten examples we publish, one can detect two subtypes, clearly distinguishable by diameter and body thickness. The dominant type 1.2A (pls. 7.10:24–29, 7.11:1) has an average diameter of 31.1 cm. Body thickness is about 4 mm. On the second subtype, 1.2B, on the other hand (pl. 7.11:2–4), the mean is a much larger 43.3 cm. Body thickness has increased to about 6 mm,

20. These vessels are called "tegami a labbro spongente" by Loffreda, "La ceramica," 60. Our type 1 is illustrated in the same article, fig. 2, nos. 1–3.

21. These are also illustrated in Loffreda, "La ceram-ica," fig. 2, nos. 4–7.

22. Loffreda illustrates the one complete vessel from Capernaum in "La ceramica," fig. 2, no. 1. Note its rounded or concave base.

23. There are no other signs of a metal prototype for this vessel. Type 1.1 is not illustrated in the finds from Capernaum.

presumably in response to the increased load demands on the vessel.[24] Our evidence at present is too meager to enable us to define the significance of these subtypes.

These two varieties of type 1.2 occur at Meiron in L.2015 of MI.2, dated by coins to about mid-3d century. They are also found at Khirbet Shema' in square NE I.32, which contains much 3d century pottery beneath the synagogue floor. About half of the specimens occur also in 4th-century contexts, which may suggest that this type begins in the mid-3d century and continues to be produced through the 4th century to some unknown *terminus,* perhaps after 450 CE.

Type 1.3, on the other hand, can be distinguished from the two preceding types (i) by the sharp angle on the outside of the vessel between the out-turned lip and the body and (ii) by the gentle carination between lip and base (pl. 7.11:5–8). Average diameter is 27.0 cm, and the wall thickness averages 5 mm. These vessels occur both in largely early 3d-century contexts at Khirbet Shema' (NE I.32; L.32016) and in later clear 4th-century contexts such as T-17. Thus the life of type 1.3 of the vessel in question may span at least 150 years and perhaps even longer, though it occurs so seldom that chronological generalizations must be quite tentative.

Type 1.4 (pl. 7.11:9–12) is singularly interesting in that the concavity between lip and carination is as in type 1.1, but the lip extends only about 10 mm from the body as opposed to about 14 mm in type 1.1. Perhaps more striking yet is the difference in rim profile. The profile of 1.1 resembles a "lazy S," whereas that of type 1.4 reveals a more vertical stance. To put it more directly: in type 1.1 the body and rim form one continuous curve from the carination upwards; in type 1.4 the body first slopes *inward,* then assumes the vertical, and finally curves outward to form the lip. Type 1.4 is also much deeper than 1.1, but the slope of the body below the carination is the same as in the other types. Only type 1.1 is as shallow as Loffreda's bowl no. 986.[25] The diameter of these bowls is sensibly constant, holding pretty generally to 28.1 cm except for one that measures 41.5 cm in diameter. The former diameter is close to Loffreda's average of about 30 cm for the group.[26] None of these occur with handles in our excavations. Wall thickness averages 4.5 mm. Type 1.4 has been found in largely early 3d century contexts at our sites (e.g., NE I.32; L.32016), but not earlier. It also occurs in very clearly 4th and early 5th century contexts at Khirbet Shema', again suggesting a long life for a variant on the theme.

Type 1.5, the latest type, reveals no new traits (pl. 7.11:13–19). Diameter averages 28.5 cm and wall thickness 4.5 mm. Its everted lip more closely resembles the slightly dished, horizontal rim of type 1.3, but its gentle carination more closely resembles that of type 1.2. It seems reasonable to suggest that this rim may be a descendent of these two varieties. One example of this bowl occurs

24. Our type 1.2 in its second subtype may be at Capernaum. Loffreda, "La ceramica," fig. 2, no. 2.

25. Ibid. fig. 2, no. 1.
26. Ibid. 62.

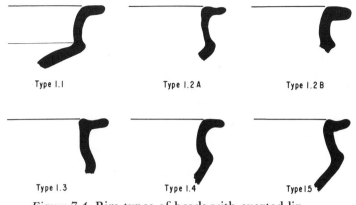

Type I.1   Type I.2 A   Type I.2 B

Type I.3   Type I.4   Type I.5

Figure 7.4. Rim types of bowls with everted lip.

with two high vertical loop handles, attached at the lip and at the carination (pl. 7.11:17). There is a slight groove in this handle that is missing from the handle on type 1.2 illustrated in pl. 7.10:27.[27] Type 1.5 bowls occur wholly in 4th to early 5th century contexts and must represent the end of the typological evolution at Khirbet Shema' and Meiron; but we will return to that later.

If we look at all the type 1 bowls just from the point of view of average diameter and wall thickness, we see that they form a distinct group except for type 1.2B, which is quite large and heavy in comparison to the others. Types 1.1, 1.2A, 1.3, 1.4, and 1.5 range in average diameter from ca. 26.0 cm to ca. 32.0 cm, a narrow range with a median of 29.3 cm, quite close to Capernaum's average of about 30 cm. Wall thickness for these five types averages 4.5 mm. Type 1.2B, therefore, is quite out of character in terms of average diameter (43.3 cm) and wall thickness (6 mm). Its great diameter and heavy walls set it apart from the others and suggest a distinctive use. Unfortunately, we have too few examples to come to definitive conclusions on this point.

Ware or fabric of these bowls is sensibly similar to that of "Galilean bowls." Section color is mainly 2.5 YR 5/6 ("grayish reddish orange") or 10 R 5/6 (same) almost exactly the same as for the "Galilean bowls." Our sample is small, but there may be one or two significant variations from this similarity. Type 1.1 bowls with everted lip are largely 10 R 4/6 ("moderate reddish brown") in color, or one step lighter. Likewise type 1.5 seem to be mainly 2.5 YR 6/8 ("moderate orange") in section color, or one step darker *and* two steps lighter in chroma. The former need not be a significant difference, but the latter may imply that later in the development of these bowls, firing is less careful or kiln conditions less constant.

Almost all varieties of this carinated bowl include "few," "small," "black and white" grits and are hard fired. The only significant deviation from this norm is

27. Grooves in vertical handles seem to be most abundant in our 4th–5th century jars and juglets, for example.

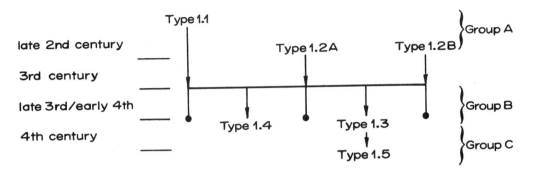

Figure 7.5. Possible evolution of everted-lip bowls.

again with type 1.5, which uses *"many,"* "small," "black and white" grits and is *medium* fired. Again this correlates with chronology and suggests an evolution of firing methods and preparation of clay. That is, in the later period the clay is prepared for medium firing with many grits and perhaps a partial reduction atmosphere in the kiln, though the same color effect might be obtained by stacking. Evolution of this form is not unambiguously clear from the Khirbet Shemaʻ and Meiron evidence, but we can formulate a hypothesis to fit the data into a framework (fig. 7.5). As the figure suggests, we find one type in use at Meiron in the late 2d century which is joined in the 3d century by a second type (with two subtypes). From these two major types (1.1 and 1.2) evolve two other types (1.3 and 1.4), though types 1.1 and 1.2 continue to be used side by side with them. Only in the 4th century is there evidently a reduction in the number of new types to one, namely, type 1.5. This final type is also used side by side with types 1.3 and 1.4.

Published parallels are difficult to find. At Heshbon there is a type of small carinated 3d-century bowl that may be related to this form, though the rim is inverted and the carination not nearly so sharp.[28] Also two similar bowls with sharp carination and with concave lip were found in tomb I at Huqoq.[29] These appear to have a diameter of about 13 and 19 cm each, and one has two vertical loop handles. Kahane does not discuss these two vessels except to mention "fragments of jars and cooking pots (fig. 3:1, 3, 5–7),"[30] which suggests that he regards these vessels as cooking pots. All the material found with these vessels from the upper layer of the central pit he dates to the early 2d century at the latest,[31] which presumably dates these vessels. They may therefore be ancestors of our carinated bowls.

Further earlier varieties have been published from Ashdod.[32] All three have handles, and the diameters are ca. 17 cm and 17 cm and 19 cm, or somewhat smaller than ours generally. In their earlier discussion of this type[33] the ex-

28. Sauer, *Heshbon Pottery*, fig. 2, nos. 68–70; see text p. 26. No. 70 on fig. 2 similar in color to many of ours, 2.5 YR 5/6 (red).

29. Ravani and Kahane, "Huqoq," fig. 3:3 and 7.

30. Ibid. 123, "The Central Pit."

31. Ibid. 134–135.

32. Dothan and Freedman, *Ashdod I*, figs. 11:2 ("cooking pot"), 13:3 ("cooking pot"); Dothan, *Ashdod II–III*, fig. 24:4 ("casserole").

33. Dothan and Freedman, *Ashdod I*, 30.

cavators mention parallels from Samaria[34] and Qumran[35] that fit their later chronology of Stratum 2 in the 1st century CE. Again these vessels may form the ancestry of our types but are not directly parallel. Their later discussion dates the form to "the later half of the second century [BCE]" and suggests that the rim is upcurving to receive a lid.[36] Their parallels are from Samaria[37] and Athens[38] and suggest a broad geographic distribution for the ancestors of the Khirbet Shema' types.

Strangely enough, when we turn to the Galilean sites that furnished the clearest parallels for our "Galilean bowls," namely, Beth She'arim, et-Tabgha, and Khirbet Kerak, we find no similar material. However, the present authors have personally retrieved sherds of these carinated bowls in surface surveys at Umm el-Ammed and Gush Halav and in great quantities at Khirbet Hananyah. It is just possible therefore that, if ancient Kfar Hananyah was indeed a pottery manufacturing center for Upper Galilee, this bowl was locally manufactured at that site.

Nazareth, also, furnishes four examples of the bowl with everted lip and carination.[39] On 224:5 and 6 plus 225:5 carination is quite sharp, and the lip appears to extend 10–15 mm from the body. The single example with a handle shows it to be attached like ours, but it is quite flat in section. Unfortunately these vessels come from mixed contexts.

Finally we note that at Capernaum the stratigraphy and associated coins indicate that this form, which Loffreda calls "A1," must begin in the middle of the 3d century and continue at least through the greater part of the 4th.[40] This chronology parallels almost exactly our chronology from Meiron and most exactly Khirbet Shema', except that type 1.1 begins *before* mid-3d century and type 1.5 runs on into the beginning of the 5th century, giving us a very long three-century life for this form in all its subtypes.

The second type of bowls with everted lip (type 2) appears to be rather deep, judging from the stance of the walls in the sherds we have recovered (see pl. 7.12). Unfortunately none of these examples have survived to the base or could be so reconstructed, so our typology must rely virtually on rim analysis alone. These vessels may well be varieties of cooking pots, but their relative scarcity at both Meiron and Khirbet Shema', especially in the face of the great abundance of globular cooking pots, rather suggests that the typical vessel is simply a deep serving bowl, though of course it could certainly have lent itself to cooking.[41]

We can readily distinguish only two types. The first, type 2.1, has an in-

34. Crowfoot et al., *Samaria-Sebaste* no. 3, fig. 72:8 (our type 2.2); idem, *Samaria-Sebaste* no. 1, fig. 176:3a (globular cooking pot).

35. De Vaux, "Fouilles au Khirbet Qumrân," fig. 3:2 and 6, but actually a closed form—namely, a jar, of the Herodian period.

36. Dothan, *Ashdod II–III*, 61.

37. Crowfoot et al., *Samaria-Sebaste* no. 3, fig. 41:20.

38. Thompson, "Two Centuries of Hellenistic Pottery," 311–450, fig. 121:E141 (type 2.1).

39. Bagatti, *Nazareth*, figs. 224:4–6, 225:5.

40. Loffreda, "La ceramica," 63f.

41. Loffreda assumes their function as "pans." "La ceramica," 60ff.

verted lip at a stance and with a slight concavity that suggest it was intended to receive a lid. This supports the interpretation of a cooking pot, though again it must be pointed out that this is an extremely rare form at either site. It is impossible to give more than an estimate of the depth of this vessel from our examples on pl. 7.12. No. 2 on pl. 7.12 probably does not exceed 5–9 cm in depth, though no. 1 probably does exceed that figure considerably. On the other hand there is a marked regularity in diameter and wall thickness that strongly supports the contention that they are indeed all of a single type. Outside diameter ranges from 18.5 cm to 28.5 cm, with a mean of 23.5 cm. Wall thickness averages about 4 mm. No. 2 on pl. 7.12 is equipped with two vertical loop handles roughly elliptical in section. The handles are attached *beneath* the lip, which is sure evidence for a lid.

Examples of this form occur in clear 4th-century context at Khirbet Shema' and once at Meiron in a late-2d-century context. The 4th-century occurrence could also be deduced from the ware or fabric of this vessel, since it is similar to the forms discussed above. Section color ranges from "dark reddish orange" to "moderate orange": 10 R 4/8, 10 R 5/6, 2.5 YR 6/6, or 2.5 YR 6/8. Surface color is also a shade of orange, namely, 2.5 YR 6/6 ("grayish reddish orange"). These vessels are generally hard fired and self-slipped, and the clay contains few, small, white and/or black grits. However, there are a few sherds that suggest a subtype of ware that contains many, small, white grits and is medium fired.

The second subtype of this vessel (type 2.2) is far more plentiful than type 2.1. Its everted lip is roughly horizontal and sometimes, but not always, slightly dished as though to receive a lid. It is possible that other significant subvarieties of this rim can be detected, but at present we see no more in our limited data (pl. 7.12:9–27). These cooking bowls range continuously in outside diameter from 18.5 cm to 37 cm, an impressive range. Depth is impossible to gage. Wall thickness is quite constant as well, ranging from 2 mm at the thinnest (pl. 7.12:18) to 6 mm near the top (pl. 7.12:23). One of these (pl. 7.12:19) is quite unique in this respect in its surprisingly constant thinness, namely 2.5 mm.

Ware for type 2.2 is somewhat more varied than for type 2.1. Section color tends to be the usual "grayish reddish orange" (2.5 YR 5/4, 5/6, or 6/6; 10 R 5/6), though exterior color varies much more widely: 2.5 YR 5/4, 5/6, 6/3, 6/4, 6/6 and 7/3. However, 2.5 YR 6/6 ("grayish reddish orange") is the most common exterior color. This too is a self-slipped form. By far the most common (50 percent of examples) grit color, size, and distribution are "black and/or white," "small," and "few," and about 75 percent of the vessels are hard fired. The minority that are medium fired seem to have a "few" or "some," "small," "white" grits. In other words, there are two main ware types in terms of grit color, size, and distribution together with firing: (i) a few, small, black and white grits hard-fired, and (ii) a few or some, small, white grits medium-fired.

Type 2 forms occur in clear 4th-century contexts at Khirbet Shema', though no. 12 on pl. 7.12 occurs in a clear post-mid-3d-century locus at Meiron (MI.2., L.2015); also no. 7, a type 2.1 of late-2d-century context (MI.2, L.2019). This *may* suggest that type 2.1 of the bowls with everted lip is slightly earlier than type 2.2, but only further stratigraphic and stylistic analysis of other similar pottery will finally tell. In other words, judged on the basis of our evidence, these two variations of the bowl with everted lip and *no* carination could perhaps be manufactured from the late 2d century to the early 5th CE (type 2.1) and from the mid-3d century to the early 5th (type 2.2).[42]

Type 2 is not a well-attested form in Galilee except at Capernaum. Yet the type at Capernaum with downturned lip is absent from our corpus.[43] What this may mean is not immediately obvious. A clear earlier example of this type, a vessel with handles, has been found by the excavators at Ashdod, Area A, Stratum 2,[44] which again ends at 70 CE. Another was found in Area A in their later seasons (1963, 1965) and is dated by Kee to the end of the 2d century BCE.[45] Its handle is attached partially to the *top* of the lip, unlike our examples, though otherwise it would be a clear type 2.2. A vessel in the same tradition but with in-turned *and* out-turned lip was also found in Area A at Ashdod and is assigned to the same date.[46]

The so-called Roman 4 pottery from Samaria-Sebaste furnishes one parallel for a type 2.2 bowl with everted lip and no carination.[47] However, its lip appears to extend 4 cm from a round, heavily ribbed body, which surely implies that it is an Early Roman example, a dating which fits the context of the other pottery published with it.[48]

The published material from Qumran includes no examples of this form, nor does the material from the Wadi Muraba'at.[49] No parallels are present at Huqoq,[50] and none, surprisingly enough, in the 3d- and 4th-century tombs from western Galilee reported by V. Tzaferis[51] and V. Sussman.[52]

However, at least one such rim (type 2.2) is published from Nazareth.[53] This was used as a cooking pot, since it was found "blackened on rim and in body below the neck."[54] This rim was found in silo 48c, which appears to be of a Byzantine or 4th/5th century context, judging from its lamps.[55]

Jerash furnishes at least five examples of this type with everted rim and no carination, all from tombs.[56] Unfortunately, little of the Jerash pottery has any

42. This is similar to Loffreda's chronology at Capernaum. "Type A2" (our type 2.1 and 2.2) begins in the Early Roman period and begins to die out in the mid-3d century, or 63 BCE–250 CE. Our span is smaller, ca. 150 CE–425 CE.

43. Loffreda, "La ceramica," fig. 2:7.

44. Dothan and Freedman, *Ashdod I*, fig. 11:1, called by the excavators "cooking pots."

45. Dothan, *Ashdod II–III*, fig. 24:3, text p. 61.

46. Ibid. fig. 24:7, text p. 61.

47. Crowfoot et al., *Samaria-Sebaste* no. 3, fig. 72.8.

48. The excavators do not date this group except relatively. Ibid. 304.

49. See esp. de Vaux, "Fouilles" 83–106; idem, "Les grottes de Murabb'at," 245–267.

50. Ravani and Kahane, "Huqoq," 121–147.

51. Tzaferis, "Tombs in Western Galilee."

52. Sussman, "Ancient Burial Cave at Rehovot."

53. Bagatti, *Nazareth*, fig. 225:9.

54. Ibid. 285.

55. Ibid. figs. 234 and 235.

56. Fisher and McCown, "Jerash-Gerasa 1930," fig. 38:19 (diameter 21 cm), but with down-turned lip; fig. 41:98 (diameter 22 cm); fig. 42:13 (diameter 20 cm), 16 (diameter 25 cm).

chronological control, since no associated coins were found except in tomb 8 (fig. 41), of which "two belonged to the first century, one was Arabic, and two were illegible."[57] Nevertheless a glass balsarium[58] from tomb 9 is doubtless of 2d century date in spite of the excavators' date of the 4th/5th century.[59] Furthermore the pottery from these tombs does not have the typological earmarks of Byzantine pottery, but of Middle Roman pottery at the latest. Therefore, if this suggestion is correct, the cooking bowls with everted lip and no carination from Jerash should also date to the period 180–324 CE.

The type 2 form is noticeably absent from the Roman and Byzantine strata at Pella, though "Galilean bowls" do occur in the Byzantine stratum.[60] It is difficult to conclude anything from lack of evidence, but two interpretations are possible: (i) the form was confined to Cisjordan in these periods, or (ii) the form had already died out before the early 6th century when the church was built. The latter interpretation is attractive in view of the presence of "Galilean bowls," albeit rarely, and considering the presence of cooking bowls with everted lip at Jerash/Gerasa.

The excavations at et-Tabgha have also turned up two examples of rims of type 2 vessels,[61] both from Level IV, i.e., sealed underneath "pavement a" and bedrock. This "level" or stratum appears to date somewhere in the second half of the 3d century CE, for Loffreda dates the construction of "pavement a" to about 400 CE.[62] This date fits in well with the chronology of this form at Meiron and Khirbet Shema', though it seems odd that so few sherds from this vessel type were recovered.

From the foregoing parallels one can see that the type 2 vessel appears to have had a long life. Its antecedents at Ashdod date as early as the late 2d century BCE, though an Early Roman date may be preferable in view of similar material from Samaria-Sebaste. In any case we have ample parallels with a measure of chronological control to confirm that this is largely a Galilean and upper Transjordanian vessel that was manufactured from the 2d to the early 5th century CE, though it surely reached its *floruit* in the early 4th century.

4. COOKING BOWLS WITH HORIZONTAL HANDLES

This form, illustrated in pls. 7.12:28–29 and 7.13:1–10, is predominantly late at Khirbet Shema', but not entirely so. It is clearly an open cooking pot, sometimes roughly hemispherical, with inward or horizontally beveled rim. Sometimes it is ribbed on the exterior, and it is reasonable to assume that all varieties had two horizontal handles. Diameter ranges from 20 to 30 cm. Depth

57. Ibid. 564.
58. No. 96 in the glass catalogue, ibid. 542.
59. Cf. the discussion of the glass from grave 10 at Pella together with Kraeling's misdating of the same type of glass at Gerasa in Smith, *Pella*, I, 214.
60. See supra p. 170.
61. Loffreda, *et-Tabgha*, figs. 31:22, 32:22, diameter about 20 cm.
62. Ibid. 97.

cannot be exactly ascertained from our unreconstructable examples, but probably was not greater than a 2 : 1 ratio of width to depth.

We appear to have two distinct varieties of this cooking bowl at Khirbet Shemaʻ, distinguishable by the stance of their bodies. One variety, type 4.1 (pls. 7.12:28, 7.13:1–5), is rather shallow and roughly hemispherical, with the horizontal handle attached directly below the invariably horizontal rim (except for pl. 7.13:5). Type 4.2, on the other hand, has only a slightly rounded body, with the more or less vertical sides curving inward at the horizontally or inward-beveled rim. Handles are attached at or 1–1.5 cm below the rim (pls. 7.13:6–10, 7.12:29).

The ware for these vessels is all of one kind, generally, in that all are hard fired and all use small grit. More than two-thirds use black and white grit, but they are about equally divided between "some" and "many" in distribution. Yet this is sensibly more grit distribution than for the pottery forms we have just discussed. The ware for these is also more porous and gritty than that of previous forms. Nevertheless all examples to date are self-slipped, though color is not uniform.

Section color on these sherds is either quite dark (e.g. 5 PB 4/1, "dark bluish gray") or somewhat lighter (e.g., 10 R 5/6, "grayish reddish orange"). Only one vessel has the 10 R 5/6 color (pl. 7.12:29—NE I. 19.70.3), and that is a reading on one side of the pot. On the other side the color is 10 R 4/1 ("dark reddish gray"). Exterior color also yields the same variety, in fact at least one unit value or chroma different for each sherd. Nevertheless it is clear that the average color, the Munsell chip around which the section colors appear to cluster, is 5 YR 5/3, a variety of reddish brown.[63]

The provenance of the bowls of these types is outside the synagogue, for example in NE I.19, a house built up against the south wall of the community's worship center. The layer in question, however, L.19070, is from the last use of the house or Stratum VI. Unfortunately no coins were found in this locus or in the loci above and below it to date it absolutely, except relatively later than the destruction of the synagogue, i.e., post 417 CE. Two examples were found in L.13003 of NW VII. 13 and one of L.13002. This gives us some encouragement with respect to chronology, as the locus beneath contains the late-4th/early-5th-century coins and the fill above contains one 8th-century coin. It is therefore reasonable to say that this locus contains material of occupation between the 5th century and the early 8th century and probably early in the period or Stratum V. This puts this form as early as Middle Byzantine. One sherd of a vessel of type 5.2 (pl. 7.13:6) occurs in a clearly late-4th-century CE context in SE II.1, L.1008. This gives us a chronological range from the late 4th century to perhaps as late

63. A random sampling of exterior color for 35 sherds of type yields the following: (1) for type 4.1—2.5 YR 6/4, 5 YR 6/3, 5 PB 3/1; (2) for type 4.2—2.5 YR 3/1, 2.5 YR 5/4, 5 YR 4/4.

as the 7th century, though one sherd (pl. 7.13:1) occurs in a later context, Stratum VII. But this sherd could well be earlier.

This is the picture of the *terminus post quem* from Capernaum.[64] The *terminus ante quem* is harder to define, but may become clearer below in our discussion of parallel material. Cooking bowls published from Capernaum occur in contexts after the middle of the 4th century CE,[65] but only of type 5.1. We cannot as yet speculate about the meaning of the absence of other types, but it may be accidental, as only fifteen sherds of type 4.1 were found at all of Khirbet Shemaʻ.

One such cooking bowl, probably also type 4.1, is published from et-Tabgha, with a diameter of some 25.5 cm, from B2, the second water installation ("Job's Oven"), dated by Loffreda to the late 4th to early 5th century CE.[66] It is rather similar to two sherds from NE I.19, L.19070 at Khirbet Shemaʻ, illustrated in pl. 7.13:9–10, though it has no handles.

When we turn to Khirbet Kerak we find at least six examples published[67] of three different rim types. Khirbet Kerak pl. 54:10 has a beveled rim with two horizontal, raised loop handles attached just at the level of the rim. Pl. 54:11 is similar, though much shallower, with rim beveled outward, and both these examples feature a carination 25 mm below the rim, a characteristic missing from the Khirbet Shemaʻ pottery. On the other hand Khirbet Kerak pl. 54:13 is quite similar to our pl. 7.13:9 or 10, and perhaps also to 7.13:6, though 7.13:10 has the usual horizontal handles. Three other examples of this cooking bowl are reproduced in the same volume, pls. 33:4, 33:7 (= 53:24), and 33:9. The examples in pl. 33:4 and 9 have flat rims, but the bowl in 33:7 (= 53:24) has a curious kind of groove as though for a lid of a specific type. Its handles are also attached to the outside of the rim so that the attachments extend *above* the rim but not *onto* it. This allows a lid to seat properly. Two of these rims are from the "pre-church" stratum, two from the "church" stratum, and two from high up in the fill in the trench east of the church. Though there is little or no control on the chronology of the material from the soil layers under, within, and above the church, these contexts suggest an approximate life for this vessel at Khirbet Kerak from the 4th to the 6th century CE. This would not be out of the question for this form at Khirbet Shemaʻ.

A single sherd of a vessel of this type has been published from the synagogue finds at Maʻon (093/082) in the south of Israel.[68] It was found in a 6th-century context, as is made clear by the coins.[69] In this case the rim is beveled inward with the upturned horizontal handle fastened just below the rim.

Three examples of this vessel type have been published from the synagogue excavations at Beth Shean,[70] but, neither specific provenance nor probable

64. Loffreda, "La ceramica," 65; "Synagogue," 21.
65. Loffreda, "La ceramica," fig. 2:9 = our type 4.1.
66. Loffreda, *et-Tabgha*, fig. 56:252 (=57:2) and p. 149. For a question of the date of this stratum see p. 150f.

67. Delougaz and Haines, *Khirbat al-Karak*, pls. 33:3 (= 54:11), 33:4, 33:7 (= 53:24), 33:9, 54:10, 54:13.
68. Levy, "Excavation Report," fig. 6:8.
69. Rahmani, "Small Finds and Coins," 18.
70. Tsori, "Synagogue at Beth-Shean," fig. 9:3–5.

date is given. One must therefore assign them in general to the "Byzantine" stratum of the structure, or generally to the 5th–6th century. Further examples of the same date have been found in the house of Kyrios Leontis at Beth Shean.[71] These are distinguished by their inward-beveled rim with a slightly overhanging lip on the *inside* of the pot. The two horizontal, raised handles are attached just below the rim.

By far the most comprehensive discussion of this form in the literature to date is that of Saller in the Bethany publication.[72] He produces four examples in the figures, only one of which clearly parallels our forms. [73] Saller notes that sixty-six examples of the rim with horizontal handles were registered from the caves in the grove.[74] The coins from the grove include nos. 38, 40, 41, 43, 44, of a late Byzantine date (491–578 CE) and nos. 55, 57, of Umayyad date (661–750 CE).[75] These data suggest a 6th to 8th century date for the form in question, though the handles *below* the rim may be typologically later, i.e., Umayyad, while the vessels with horizontal handles mounted *at* the rim may be earlier, i.e., Byzantine. Saller notes Byzantine use of this form from Mount Nebo, Jerash, Jericho, Beth Shean, and Jerusalem, and Umayyad use from the citadel at Amman, Khirbet en-Nitla, Alayiq, and Khirbet Mefjer.[76] The latest date is quite interesting; Baramki reports that this form was in widespread use in the mid-8th century at Khirbet Mefjer when the earthquake occurred and *may* have continued in use until medieval times.[77] It must be pointed out here that on these vessels of his ware 18b, which he dates to the 12th–13th centuries,[78] handles appear lower down the body, as on Bethany 48:3338.

A more recent discussion of this form appears in the Pella publication by R. H. Smith.[79] In his treatment of the Palestinian parallels to the Pella corpus of cooking pots with "roughly hemispherical shape (sometimes with a flattened bottom) and a pair of opposing horizontal handles"[80] he points out a dominance of this cooking pot type in the Late Byzantine period at Ramat Rahel, which is in accordance with the Pella data. Thus, though the history of development of this vessel is not yet known, it seems clear enough that it is first made in the Byzantine period (perhaps late 4th century, witness Khirbet Shema' pl. 7.13:6 from Stratum IV) and continues in use through the 8th century and doubtless later.[81] The Khirbet Shema' evidence therefore fits quite well into the early part of this framework, since all but two of our examples come from Strata V or VI.

71. Tsori, "House of Kyrios Leontis," fig. 5:9–10.
72. Saller, *Bethany*, 246f.
73. Ibid. fig. 48:3338 (= 119:11, but with horizontal handles 9 mm *below* the rim), fig. 48:4003 (type 4.1), pl. 47:8–9 (also handles below the rim).
74. Ibid. 246.
75. Ibid. 347–349.
76. Ibid. 247, nn. 30–38.
77. Baramki, "Kh. el Mefjer," 71, ware 18a, esp. fig. 13:1, 3, 6–9.

78. Ibid. 71. Another clue is the lack of ribbing on the ware 18b vessels, fig. 13.
79. Smith, *Pella*, I 224, 230; cf. pls. 30:1127 = 1128 = 1328, 43:1314(?), 45:1281, 1284; 69:481 (dated 522–675 CE); 91D:1129 (color photo).
80. Ibid. 230.
81. Cf. Baramki, "Kh. el Mefjer," fig. 13:1–6, 8–9, 11–13 (8th century); fig. 12:26 (12th–13th century?); de Vaux and Steve, *Fouilles a Qaryet el-'Enab = Abu Gosh*, B:17–19, 25–26.

5. COOKING VESSEL WITH FOLDED LIP

This cooking pot type is illustrated in fig. 7.6. Only one example was found, almost intact, from NW VII.9 in a Stratum VII (medieval) context, 1150–1277 CE at Khirbet Shema'.

The outside rim diameter of this vessel is 19.5 cm, while its maximum height is probably not in excess of 30 cm. It is of a dark brown ware, very gritty, and medium to hard fired. This particular specimen is blackened on the outside from use. The pot is roughly bag-shaped, probably with a rounded base. The rim is round on top with a lip folded outward. Two handles are attached 17.5 mm below the out-turned lip. These handles are straps of clay with two shallow longitudinal grooves. The handles are attached horizontally so as to form an arch tilted down slightly and ca. 5 cm wide. These are roughly in the tradition of the horizontal handles of the form discussed above in section 4.

No parallels to this vessel have been found so far in Palestinian or Syrian contexts, though parallels to certain *elements* in the vessel can be noted. At Bethany, for example, several handles are described that approximate these

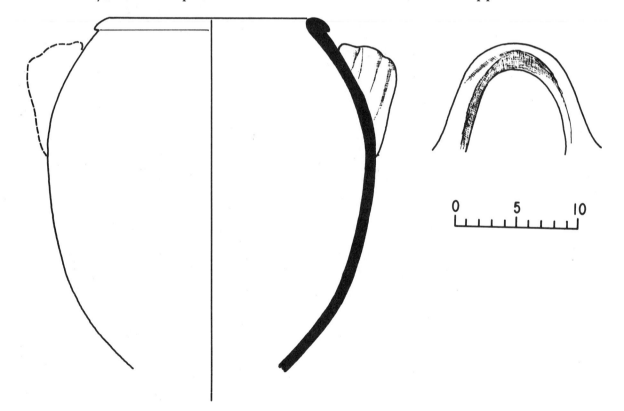

Figure 7.6. Drawing of a complete cooking pot from NW VII.9, 1.3.

handles,[82] though most are tilted *upwards*. Saller does not attempt to narrow the dating within the wide range implied by the term "medieval." The folded rim has been published on a collar of a water jar from a Crusader building at et-Tabgha,[83] with parallels from Emmaus[84] and Abu Gosh.[85]

Neither rim nor handles are characteristic of the late wares from Khirbet Mefjer or Khirbet Kerak, but certain elements, or their later developments, are found in the Mamluk pottery at Pella. The same outfolded rim is found on jar 915 from tomb 7 in IIH in the East Cemetery.[86] The Khirbet Shema' handle type as such is not illustrated, but a later development in which the strap is tilted edge-up is attested on cooking pots from the same tomb.[87] All these Pella examples date to the 14th–15th century.

In any case it appears clear that this specific cooking pot, though so far unparalleled, is probably not unique, since elements of its form are fairly well known. This may be only one of many that were lost from our thin, unsealed medieval stratum by erosion and human disturbance.

6. GLOBULAR COOKING POTS WITH NECKS

By far the most common type of Roman to Byzantine cooking pot in Palestinian sites is the form with globular body, short neck, and two opposing handles.[88] This type has been found in abundance at Khirbet Shema' and Meiron and in fact can be tentatively divided into at least five subtypes, though not all these subtypes are yet firmly established in the repertoire of Roman and Byzantine pottery.

Type 1.1 (pl. 7.13:11–18) is a subtype characterized by a double groove in its rim, which also exhibits a turned-out horizontal lip. Generally the neck is vertical, though in about one-third of our samples the neck is splayed outward. The neck ranges from 14 to 18 mm in height, for an average height of 15.8 mm. The diameter of the mouth of these vessels of type 1.1 ranges from 10.4 to 20.8 cm. Interestingly enough, the diameter does not range more or less continuously, but at least in our small corpus increases by sudden increments. That is, we have three groups by diameter: nos. 11, 12 and 14 on pl. 7.13 have an average diameter of 19.2 cm, with a range of 17.6 to 20.8 cm; nos. 13, 15, and 16 on the other hand, average 13.3 cm in diameter and the range is 13.2 to 13.6 cm; finally, nos. 17 and 18 average 10.7 cm, while the range for the two is 10.4 to 11.0 cm.

82. Saller, *Bethany*, 429f, "Medieval Period"; fig. 55: 7326.

83. Loffreda, *et-Tabgha*, fig. 43:106 = 44:9.

84. B. Bagatti, *Emmaus*, fig. 25.

85. De Vaux, "Céramique masulmane," pl. F and fig. 32.

86. Smith, *Pella*, I, pl. 70:915.

87. Ibid. pls. 76:917, 905; 77:821, 483.

88. For the Hellenistic forebear to this Roman and Byzantine form see Lapp, *Palestinian Ceramic Chronology*, 184–188, esp. type 71.1B dated 200–100 BCE. Cf. also Kahane's discussion of this general type pot in "Pottery Types," 129f and Wampler's helpful remarks in McCown and Wampler, *Tell en-Nasbeh I-II*, 30f and paragraphs 8ff.

The surface of these vessels is perfectly smooth, with no rippling or ribbing on the upper part of the body, which is as much of these pots as we have.

The provenance of these vessels at Khirbet Shema' is a more or less random distribution around the ruin; i.e., they exhibit no special pattern in their distribution on the site. All came from Stratum IV contexts, however, with the possible exception of pl. 7.13:11 and 14, which may be part of the earlier material in these mixed loci, or Stratum III. If so, the chronology of this form at Khirbet Shema' would range from as early as 284 CE to as late as 417 CE or later. It is significant that only one sherd of this type, which we do not publish here, stems from MI.2 or a 3d-century context: MI.2.44.18, L.2016.1, before 250 CE.

Parallels are not plentiful, but et-Tabgha furnishes us with possibly two.[89] Fig. 31:19 from level IV has a diameter of 10.4 cm and a neck height of 13 mm, which is most similar to our pl. 7.13:18 and 19. It dates to the 4th century, exactly within our Stratum IV. Fig. 56:260 from basin B2 at et-Tabgha has a diameter of 13.6 cm, closest to our pl. 7.13:13, 15, and 16. Loffreda suggests a Late Roman to Early Byzantine date, or the 4th and 5th centuries CE for the entire corpus from basin B2.[90] This seems to accord with the same pottery forms in a Stratum IV context at Khirbet Shema'.

This type of cooking pot is called type P2 in the preliminary report on the excavations at Capernaum.[91] In the photograph one can see the rim grooves, smooth surface, and everted lip. Loffreda dates this form at Capernaum from as early as the end of the 1st century CE to well into the 4th century. This is earlier than we have at Khirbet Shema' or Meiron, but the 3d- and 4th-century use is exactly parallel.

From Pella we find a neck of this pot type from "the Byzantine Stratum of IIA in the East cemetery."[92] Its diameter is ca. 13 cm, closest to our pl. 7.13:13, 15, and 16. Its date would presumably match that of "Phase I" of the West Church Complex or about 530–610 CE.[93] This is rather surprisingly late in view of the usual life of ceramic forms, but its singularity at Pella may in fact suggest that it is an earlier form strayed into a Late Byzantine context.[94]

This rim type is well represented in the finds from the vaulted cisterns of the Temple of Zeus at Mount Gerizim.[95] The seven pots there are described as generally of orange-red ware, fine paste, few or no white grits, and light ribbing to surface-smoothed. Diameters range from 15.0 to 19.0 cm, with the average 16.0 cm. Neck height is uniformly about 23 mm. There are differences from our type 1. The neck on these Mount Gerizim pots is usually slightly outflared. The body slopes downward more steeply than in our type 1 and seems to be almost straight in section as far as it is preserved. Diameter is somewhat greater

89. Loffreda, *et-Tabgha*, figs. 31:19 (= 32:19) and 56:260.

90. Ibid. 150.

91. Loffreda, "La ceramica," fig. 9:2, pp. 71f.

92. Smith, *Pella*, I, pl. 44:1257, pp. 222, 223.

93. Ibid. 164.

94. It seems significant that this type does not turn up in Transjordan south of Pella.

95. Bull and Campbell, "Balatah (Schechem)," 2–40, fig. 11:1–7. Pottery descriptions, p. 19. Description of the stratigraphic and numismatic context, pp. 15f.

than our average in either type 1.1 or 1.2. The neck is also generally higher in the Mount Gerizim vessels. Nevertheless, in rim type, surface treatment (when smooth), handle section, and ware, they are generally parallel to our type 1.2 and type 2, if grooved. These pots are nicely dated to 250–350 CE on the basis of the forty-one associated datable coins.

Another earlier parallel to this cooking pot type is afforded by the excavations at Chorazin.[96] Only one example, without handles, is published from Locus 50, the southeast room of Building B. Yeivin notes the absence of handles and refers the reader to Hamilton's excavations in Jerusalem for a parallel.[97] According to Yeivin's context this sherd could date anywhere from the 2d to the 4th century CE, the same dating as our evidence indicates.

Two clear examples of this cooking pot type have been published for Khirbet Kerak.[98] These are in the 6th-century stratum, but their ware descriptions resemble ours so far as one can hazard a comparison.[99] Perhaps they are 5th-century examples of this cooking pot type in what is ultimately a predominantly 6th-century stratum.

An example of what appears to be a complete type 1.2 cooking pot comes from tomb 70 at Nazareth.[100] This vessel is about 17 cm in outside rim diameter and about 21.5 cm in overall height, but with a neck only 9 mm high, rather short in comparison to our type 1.2. The body is smooth all around except for a few ribs just above the midpoint of the body and a few centimeters below and 4 cm out from the center of the base. It has a round base and flat handles and is well fired. Bagatti thinks this pot type is characteristic of loculi tombs, but dates the use of this particular tomb from the 2d to the 7th century CE. Doubtless his implied early date is correct, but it still falls reasonably well within the Khirbet Shema' chronology.

Chronology for this form, then, stretches from sometime in the early 3d century to the beginning of the 5th century at least. It is possible that this type was manufactured both earlier and later than our evidence so far allows, as the evidence from Pella and Khirbet Kerak may suggest.

Type 1.2 (pls. 7.13:19–26, 7.14:1–21, 7.15:7, 7.16:15, 24) is a subtype differentiated from type 1.1 solely by the *lack* of the grooves on top of the rim. In other words, one would normally explain the typological relationship between

96. Yeivin, "Khorazin," fig. 9:5. Yeivin seems to think that his rim ordinarily appears without handles. If the entire collar was recovered without handles, then surely he is right.

97. Namely, Hamilton, "North Wall," 1–54, fig. 21:4. This is, however, a collar from a jug and seems an unlikely parallel. Rather, the complete cooking pots illustrated in Hamilton's figs. 6:9 and 16:7 seem more appropriate parallels, except that the stance is vertical rather than outward flared. Fig. 6:9 is dated by Hamilton, p. 11, to the 3rd-4th century CE on the basis of parallel material from Mount Ophel, specifically from rooms 33, 35, 36, and 37, pl. 13. Unfortunately there is clearly an admixture of Arab pottery in the form of glazed wares from room 36, pl. 13:37–39, and in incised decoration on a red-ware strainer, pl. 13:41. The "North Wall" cooking pots mentioned above (figs. 6:9 and 16:7) nevertheless provide good parallels in rim treatment and have the shouldered bulge as our pls. 7.15:20–23 and 7.16:25–27, though they are without ribbing except on the bottom of the "North Wall." Example from fig. 16:7.

98. Delougaz and Haines, *Khirbat al-Karak*, figs. 53:32 (= 33:15), 53:33, both from the "church" level.

99. Ibid. fig. 53:32 is of "dark red fabric, thin," and fig. 53:33 is of "reddish brown compact fabric."

100. Bagatti, *Nazareth*, fig. 192:17 and p. 233.

1.1 and 1.2 by saying the 1.2 is the simpler and probably, therefore, later version of type 1.1. Surprisingly enough, though, our evidence does not indicate that this is so. We noted earlier that only one sherd of type 1.1 is from a 3d century context at Meiron, but no fewer than 23 out of 32 published examples, or about 72 percent of type 1.2, were discovered in the 3d-century context of MI.2. In fact, enough of these sherds were found in L.2019, an early 2d century CE context, to indicate clearly that type 1.2 begins before 150 CE. Furthermore, they are common in Stratum IV at Khirbet Shemaʻ, but so rare in Stratum V as to indicate that their *terminus ad quem* must be ca. 419 CE. This reckoning gives us an approximate 275-year life for this form and in effect makes type 1.1 logically a short-lived variant of type 1.2. Since this conclusion seems to violate the assumptions by which typological and seriation analysis operates, we have to assume that further excavation and publication of ceramic evidence will ultimately illuminate the difficult problem here.

One point that should bolster the hypothesis that types 1.1 and 1.2 are allomorphs is that both types are of sensibly identical ware. Section color is 2.5 YR 5/6 ("grayish reddish orange") in about 60 percent of the cases. Likewise, exterior color is largely the same (34.6 percent of the cases), though 19 percent are 2.5 YR 6/6 and another 19 percent 2.5 YR 6/8 ("grayish reddish orange" and "moderate orange," respectively). The side of the pot that fired darker because of stacking is gaged 2.5 YR 6/1 (3.9 percent), 2.5 YR 5/1 (7.7 percent), or 2.5 YR 4/1 (7.7 percent), all varieties of "grayish reddish brown" (see fig. 7.7).

Almost all examples of type 1.1 and 1.2 cooking pots are hard fired (85 percent) except for the few that are medium fired. More than half (58 percent) are of a single grit size and frequency, namely, "small" and "few." About one-fourth use black grit, another third use white grit, and slightly more than one-third (39 percent) use black *and* white grit. The remainder use gray grit or all three choices.

Thus, the potter prepared his clay in a traditional manner for the entire period of manufacture of this vessel. He used some, small grit (either black and white, white, or black in order of preference) and generally fired these pots hard. His kiln was always fired up to about the same temperature (colors in the 7.5 YR or 10 R range are rare, indicating the constancy of firing). At the current state of the data it is impossible to distinguish type 1.1 from 1.2 by ware.[101]

Type 2 cooking pots are rather diverse in rim treatment but can be divided typologically into at least four subgroups: type 2.1 (pls. 7.14:22–24, 27–28, 7.16:18) is a cooking pot subtype with a wide mouth and a rim grooved on the interior and slightly out-turned neck; type 2.2 (pl. 7.15:1–4, 10) is a subtype

101. There is a slight but insignificant decrease in neck height for type 1.2: average is 14.9 mm within the range 12–16 mm. Subtype diameters also group at 10.2 cm, 15.5 cm, and 21.2 cm (as compared to 10.7 cm, 13.3 cm, and 19.2 cm for subtype 1.1).

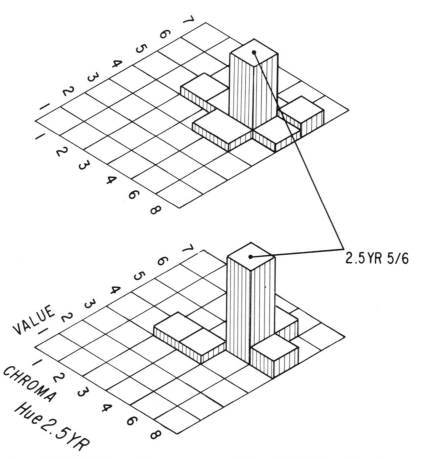

2.5 YR 5/6

Figure 7.7. Globular cooking pots, types 1.1 and 1.2, Munsell section
color. Above, exterior color; below, section color.

with a more widely flaring neck, generally of smaller diameter than type 2.1;
type 2.1 averages 18.7 cm in diameter, whereas type 2.2 averages 14.0 cm.

Ware of type 2.1 is relatively the same as that of type 2.2. Section color of
type 2.1 averages 2.5 YR 5/6 ("grayish reddish orange"), while that of type 2.2
averages 2.5 YR 5/5, hardly a significant difference. Exterior color of type 2.1
averages 2.5 YR 6/6 ("grayish reddish orange") to 7.5 YR 7/3 ("brownish pink")
on the darker side. Exterior color of type 2.2, on the other hand, averages 2.5
YR 5/4 ("light reddish brown") to 2.5 YR 4/1 ("grayish reddish brown") on the
darker side (see Table 7.4). About half of both subtypes use some, small grit and
are hard fired. Grit is mostly white (about two-thirds of our examples); otherwise the potter used black and white grit.

Provenance of types 2.1 and 2.2 is largely Meiron, MI.2 of an early 3d-
century CE date. A few examples come from Khirbet Shema', however, and the
Meiron parallels suggest a largely 3d-century date for all examples, though

Table 7.4. COMPARATIVE TABULATION OF TYPE 2 COOKING POT WARES

Cooking pot type:	Type 2.1	Type 2.2	Type 2.3	Type 2.4
Illustration	Pls. 7.14:22–24, 27–28, 7.16:18	Pl. 7.15:1–4, 10	Pl. 7.15:6, 8 18	Pl. 7.15:6, 13 14
Average diameter (cm)	17.8	14.0	17.5	13.5
Average neck height (mm)	24.	20.3	19.	28.7
Description	Wide mouth, rim grooved on interior, slightly turned-out high neck	Wide mouth, no groove, more widely flared, low neck	Wide mouth, low neck, triangular to simple rim, outflared neck	Wide mouth, high neck, simple rim, slightly outflared neck
Dominant wares	22 2	22 2	22 <u>2221</u> 1 4222	1 2 <u>4231</u> 1 2 121
Section color	2.5 YR 5/6	2.5 YR 5/5	5 PB 4/1 2.5 YR 5/5	5 PB 4/1 2.5 YR 5/5
Exterior color	2.5 YR 6/6 7.5 YR 7/3	2.5 YR 5/4 2.5 YR 4/1	2.5 YR 5/3	2.5 YR 5/5
Dates (century CE)	3d–5th	3d–5th	3d–5th	3d–5th

enough (unpublished) examples come from clear Stratum IV contexts to indicate that this is a 3d to early 5th century form.[102]

Published parallels to type 2.2 are not to be found, and parallels to type 2.1 are difficult to locate; but Smith observes that this form (perhaps also the low-necked varieties of our type 3) appears to be transitional between cooking pots with high neck ("rim neck") and neckless cooking pots.[103] He publishes two examples[104] of ware color 2.5 YR 6/8 and 5 YR 5/4, i.e., reasonably close to ours, but *slipped* in another color: 10 YR 4/1 ("brownish gray") and 2.5 YR 4/2–6 ("grayish reddish brown" to "strong brown"). The difference may correlate with their later date in the 6th century CE.

102. Unpublished examples include the following:

Stratum	Provenance	Locus	Section	Exterior	Ware
IV	NE VII.3.25.6	3018	10 R 5/6	5 YR 5/6	white, small, many, medium
IV	NE I.32.60.1	32018.1	2.5 YR 4/1	2.5 YR 4/1	white, small, few, hard
IV	NE VII.2.81.2	2032	2.5 YR 6/6	2.5 YR 6/6	b. & w., small, few, hard
V	NE VII.1.49.1	1021	2.5 YR 5/6	2.5 YR 6/6	b. & w., small, many, hard
VI	NW I.33.47.8	33022	5 PB 4/1	2.5 YR 5/4	white, small, some, medium

103. Smith, *Pella*, I, 224.

104. Ibid. fig. 28:1218, 1271.

A cooking pot similar to type 2.1 is found at Bethany.[105] Saller does not discuss this form, but from the illustration it appears to be unribbed, with slightly out-turned rim and with an 11.6-cm-diameter neck.

Finally we note one possible parallel from the pre-church level at Khirbet Kerak.[106] This vessel is ribbed and deeper than ours, but its low neck, thin wall, and "dark red fabric" may place it in the same general ceramic tradition as our type 2.1 (or possibly type 3) cooking pots. It would date prior to 450 CE, if Kraeling's remarks still hold for the chronology.[107]

Types 2.3 and 2.4 of this form (pl. 7.15:5–6, 8–9, 11, 13–14, 18) represent something of a "miscellaneous" category, but concentrate mainly on vessels with simple rim[108] and out-turned or outflared neck. Some of these resemble type 2.2 rims and necks without the internal groove on the rim—namely, nos. 6, 8, 9, 11 and perhaps 18—and are designated type 2.3. Furthermore, others resemble type 2.2, also without the interior groove on the rim, namely, nos. 5, 13, and 14. Consequently it seems prudent to refer to this type as a subtype of type 2. However, the necks of these vessels are consistently shorter than those of types 2.1 and 2.2, which induces us to hold them separate as subtypes for the time being, particularly in view of the similarity in dates for certain vessels in types 2.1 and 2.2 and types 2.3 and 2.4.

The four vessels that we designate type 2.3 come from three different chronological contexts—the first half of the 3d century (pl. 7.15:6), the 4th to early 5th century (pl. 7.15:8–9), and the 7th to 9th century (Stratum VI, pl. 7.15:11). But the stratum designation for the last sherd is misleading, for only one sherd of Stratum VI was found in bucket 29; the remainder were predominantly LR in field reading, which is our Stratum IV. Thus we have one early-3d-century sherd and three from the 4th to early 5th century for type 2.3, almost exactly parallel to the dates for type 2.1.

The average outside diameter of the necks of these four vessels is sensibly constant, ranging from 14.0 to 21.6 cm for an average of 17.5 cm. This compares favorably with the average diameter of 17.8 cm for type 2.1 (pl. 7.14: 22–28). However, the average neck height is 19 mm, as compared with the estimated average neck height of 24 mm for type 2.1.

We tentatively classify three rims as a subtype, type 2.4 (pl. 7.15:5, 13, and 14). Their high, outflared necks immediately call to mind type 2.2 (pl. 7.15:1–4). The average diameter of these three rims is 13.5 cm, as compared with 14.0 cm for type 2.2—significantly similar. But again the estimated average neck height of type 2.4 is in excess of 28.7 mm, whereas that of type 2.2 is 20.3 mm— significantly less. Therefore, though 2.3 is similar to 2.1, and though 2.4 re-

105. Saller, *Bethany*, fig. 48:5168.
106. Delougaz and Haines, *Khirbat al-Karak*, fig. 53:36 (= 33:6).
107. Ibid. 20f.

108. Even the casual eye can see that pl. 7.15:6 and 9 are not simple rims, but they are included here for convenience.

sembles 2.2, differences in neck height and rim treatment indicate that they must be held as distinct subtypes, at least tentatively.[109]

Ware of type 2 (subtypes 2.3 and 2.4) is somewhat varied. The average exterior color is 2.5 YR 5/3, a variety of light reddish brown for type 2.3, and 2.5 YR 5/5 for 2.4, between light reddish brown and grayish reddish orange. The exterior color ranges smoothly from 1 to 6 in chroma and from 4 to 6 in value. Also the hue ranges from 10 R to 10 YR, but about two-thirds of all pots are 2.5 YR in hue, with only one 10 R and one 10 YR. The section color occurs in two distinct hues for both subtypes: 5 PB 4/1 ("dark bluish gray") or 2.5 YR 5/5, the transition color between light reddish brown and grayish reddish orange. About one-third of the vessels are of the former color and are always medium fired, though the vessels that are "yellow-red" (2.5 YR) in section are almost equally divided between hard fired and medium fired.

In other variables the wares divide rather distinctly. Type 2.3 vessels of section color 5 PB 4/1 are predominantly made with some or many, small to medium, white grit. Those of section color 2.5 YR 5/5 use mainly some, small, black and white grit. On the other hand type 2.4 cooking pots of medium or large section color 5 PB 4/1, use many, small, black and white grits. Those of section color 2.5 YR 5/5 use few or some, small, black grits.

Clear parallels of these pots are not to be found at northern sites such as et-Tabgha, Capernaum, Nazareth, Shavei Zion, Pella, or Khirbet Kerak, nor are they found south at Jericho, Bethany, Jerusalem, or Tell en-Nasbeh. Our dating evidence for the last two subtypes is therefore our coins, which securely place these two cooking pot types in the 3d to early 5th century CE.

Type 3 cooking pots (pls. 7.15:15–16, 20–23, 7.16:1, 3, 7–23) are characterized by a simple rim and a low vertical neck; more than one-third exhibit heavy ribbing. Four have been reconstructed (pl. 7.15:20–23) and show their maximum diameter above the center, a sharp turn to the base, and concave to slightly pointed base.[110] The low neck averages 13.7 mm high within the range 12 to 16 mm. The diameter appears to exhibit two means of 8.6 and 10.0 cm, within the range of 8.4 to 11.2 cm.[111] Thus this pot type is the single most cohesive group in ranges of neck height and diameter. It is a dominant group in numbers.

Two of our published examples of type 3 come from 3d-century contexts, namely, pl. 7.16:7 and 23, both from MI.2, L.2015, and L.2011 respectively, or post-250 CE. Almost all the remainder are from Stratum IV contexts, and some are from areas almost without admixture of earlier materials, such as SEII. or C-1, L.102, 104, and 105. Two sherds occur in a clear Stratum V context,

109. In this connection it should be mentioned that subtype 2.4 doubtless had handles as on pl. 7.15:4, as did all examples of type 2.

110. Pl. 7.15:22 is of different proportions but of the same general description.

111. Pl. 7.15:18 from NW I.34.9.11, L.34007, Stratum VI, is surprisingly thick (6 mm minimum) and the handles quite large to classify it easily as subtype 2.3. We leave it out of the calculations of average diameter.

namely, pl. 7.15:21, 23 from the cistern. But these are refuse layers directly upon the material from the last use of the cistern in Stratum IV; therefore, it is reasonable to suppose that these whole (repaired) pots are from early in the 5th century, perhaps before 425 CE. The rim illustrated in pl. 7.16:21 is from a Stratum VI context, but the field reading for this specific bucket does not include Arab pottery; that is, this sherd is Byzantine at the latest, as its thickened rim may already suggest, but probably not later than the 5th century. Therefore the chronology of type 3 appears to extend from mid-3d century to early 5th century, with its *floruit* in the 4th century CE. There may be a few examples, a statistical "tail," extending through the 5th century.

Parallels to our type 3 are rather rare. Two possible examples are published from Chorazin, dated to the 2d–6th century CE.[112] Chorazin fig. 9:1 from L.10 most closely resembles our pl. 7.16:3, though the handles on the Chorazin pot rise somewhat higher. Chorazin fig. 9:2 from L.59 resembles our pl. 7.16:13. Yeivin's general "Roman-Byzantine" date fits our chronology well.[113]

Interestingly enough, type 3 pots do not appear in the reports of either Capernaum or et-Tabgha, an absence which seems odd in view of the presence at Meiron, Khirbet Shema', and Chorazin. Perhaps it reflects their nature as public sites.

On the other hand, Pella may offer at least one type 3 cooking pot, also from the "Byzantine Stratum of IIA in the East Cemetery."[114] However, it is ribbed, slipped, and 5 YR 6/6 ("light brown") and the handles rise rather high above the simple rim, which may imply a 6th-century date for this example, as does its context, though Smith prefers a date "quite early in the Byzantine period" because of general similarities to cooking pots from the Tell er-Ras cisterns.[115]

Another and geographically less distant parallel is found at Gush Halav (el-Jish) just north of Khirbet Shema'. A cooking pot from a loculus tomb cleared in July of 1937 delivered up at least one complete cooking pot that is similar to our type 3 in form, though the rim cannot be clearly seen in the photograph.[116] The pot appears to have a rim diameter of about 12 cm, a neck of 20 mm, and an overall height of about 17 cm. It seems to have a simple rim and ribbing all over the body, and its maximum body diameter above its center like our type 3. Unlike our type 3, however, it appears to have a flat base. Its handles rise above the height of the rim, but are evidently not attached to the top of the rim but to the side of the collar just below the rim. Makhouly dates the tomb to the 4th–5th century, but the juglets illustrated in his pl. 30:1e–g are clearly 6th-century, judging from their parallels at Khirbet Kerak and elsewhere. The lamp with

112. Yeivin, "Khorazin," fig. 9:1, 2.
113. Ibid. 151.
114. Smith, *Pella*, I pl. 43:1327, p. 223. Its rim may have a slight exterior lip, in which case it is really most similar to our type 1.1 or 1.2.

115. Ibid. 223. But Bull's pots are more clearly related to our cooking pot type 1.1 or 1.2 because of their pronounced external lip. See supra p. 194.
116. Makhouly, "Rock-Cut Tombs at el-Jish," 45–50, pl. 30:2c. The cooking pot in question is from "chamber B," the second tomb, containing 17 loculi.

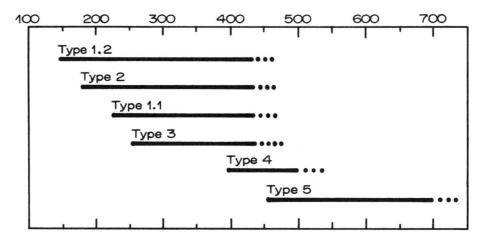

Figure 7.8. Date ranges for globular cooking pots at Khirbet Shema'.

trough between fill and wick holes must also be as late. Yet his general date for the tomb may be right for the cooking pot in question.

Type 4 cooking pots with short neck (pls. 7.15:12, 19, 7.16:25–27) comprise only five examples from our corpus. Characteristically their rims are lightly grooved on the outside and they feature a vertical to slightly outflared neck. The neck averages 27.8 mm in height within the rather narrow range of 25 to 32 mm. Diameter averages a small 9.4 cm, with a range of 8.4 to 11.2 cm. These are by far the smallest cooking pots as a type in our corpus. All are ribbed on the body and have the same base and body shape as the whole type 3 cooking pots. The necks of these vessels bear a strong general resemblance to types 2.2 and 2.4 cooking pots and may be variants of type 2. The lack of ribbing on 2.2 and its generally earlier date may in fact suggest that type 4 is a descendent of that earlier form.

These five vessels are predominantly Byzantine in date. The examples of pl. 7.16:25–27 all come from the cistern—no. 26 from Stratum IV, and the other two from Stratum V. Thus an early 5th century date for the first appearance of these cooking pots seems assured. The latest date when they still appear is difficult to ascertain. The vessel of pl. 7.15:19 comes from a generally Stratum VI context (NW I.33. L.33022), but again the specific bucket of pottery in question was read "R-B," i.e., no Arab or Stratum VI pottery was in evidence. Therefore it seems best to confine the end of the use of type 4 pots to early Stratum V. Consequently this pot type dates almost wholly to the 5th century CE.

Cooking pots at Khirbet Shema' (and from MI.2 in Meiron) thus appear in about five major types, or four if type 4 is taken to be the later evolution of type 2. The *terminus post quem* of these forms has been fairly easy to deduce from our own dated stratigraphy, but by and large the *terminus ante quem* still eludes us. In any case the chronological range of the various cooking pots is presented in fig. 7.8.

7. LIDS OR COVERS

Lids are illustrated in pl. 7.17:1–14 and represent well-known forms from various Roman and Byzantine sites in Galilee and beyond. Various types are shown in the plate, but two subforms are distinguishable by rim treatment. That is, either the rim is horizontal with a small inner lip or no lip (nos. 1–11) or there is a pronounced out-turned lip (nos. 12–14). The variety of stances, surface treatments (ribbed, wet-smoothed, or self-slipped) and depths reveal a variety of types that we cannot systematize typologically from such a small corpus; we will only point out that those with exterior lip are all of the same low stance.

Doubtless all forms originally exhibited handles such as are illustrated in pl. 7.17:1–3, but no handles could be mended with enough other sherds to reconstruct an entire form. Note that no. 3 has a steam hole in the top, a not uncommon feature of lids or covers.

Ware of these forms is surprisingly constant, though not all come from the same stratum. The dominant section color is 5 YR 5/3 or 2.5 YR 5/3 ("light grayish reddish brown"). Exterior color ranges widely in hue from 5 R to 7.5 YR, but average value/chroma is 4/3 or 5/3; therefore the range is from (light) grayish red to (light) grayish brown.[117] Grit size and distribution and firing are quite constant: small, medium grits and medium fired. Grit is black or black and white. One handle sherd of a rather odd lid that we do not publish, since we could not establish its radius, was 10 R 6/8 in section ("moderate reddish orange") and 10 R 5/6 in exterior color ("grayish reddish orange"). Its provenance is NE I.32, L.32016, a mixed locus with material from Strata III–VI.

Diameters of the covers illustrated in pl. 7.17:4–11 are of two distinct means: 15.8 cm for nos. 4–5 and 23.8 cm for nos. 6–11 (range is 14.5 to 28.5 cm). The lids with outside lip (pl. 7.17:12–14) are also of two diameters: 14.0 cm for no. 12, and 22.0 cm for nos. 13–14.

Chronology of this form ranges almost as broadly as that of the cooking pots from Khirbet Shema'. The earliest context is that of pl. 7.17:1 from Meiron, a post-250 CE locus. Three examples, nos. 2, 3, and 5, are from clear Stratum IV contexts. Five more examples, nos. 4, 6, 7, 9, and 14, are Stratum V or Middle-Late Byzantine in date. Finally, no. 13 comes from a Stratum VI locus, but is doubtless Byzantine. The latest that our material could date would be at the end of Stratum V, or early 7th century, a dating that would give us a very wide chronological range for this material; but the range can doubtless be shortened by the discussion of parallel material below.

117. Strictly speaking, average hue would be about 2.5 YR.

Precise parallels to our lids are difficult to find, but the House of Kyrios Leontis at Beth Shean furnishes one example, though startlingly great in diameter (40 cm).[118] It is rather similar to our pl. 7.17:14 in rim treatment, though its fine ribbing, about 1 cm vertical smooth area just above the rim, and large diameter make it less immediate a parallel. Tsori assigns it a "Roman-Byzantine" date, which accords reasonably well with our chronology.

Lid 1193 at Pella is rather similar in diameter to our cover of pl. 7.17:5, though the Pella lid has a different stance and broader ribbing.[119] It comes from the west church complex and therefore is 5th-century at the earliest. Other lids from Pella, as well as lids from Khirbet Kerak[120] and Capernaum[121] all have the same stance, in which the lid rests upon a "lid device," whereas ours must rest upon a horizontal or nearly horizontal rim. However, the exterior treatment of the cover in our pl. 7.17:6, with bands of four incised lines each all around parallel to the rim, is also found at Khirbet Kerak.[122] It is impossible to gage rim stance from the photograph, but the "pre-church" provenance of pl. 14:36 suggests a 4th–5th century date.

From Bethany comes at least one cover with horizontal rim such as ours.[123] This lid is complete and features a knob handle unlike any of ours. Its diameter is ca. 28 cm, about the same as our pl. 7.17:9–11, and its smooth exterior near the rim and "red-brown" ware is not dissimilar to ours. Unfortunately we can only assign a date to the lids from Bethany of the Roman through Arab periods.

The excavations at Khirbet en-Nitla furnish us with Byzantine material from the 4th to the early 7th century. Lids that resemble ours in flat, horizontal rim, but all with extended lip on the exterior, are published by Kelso, with no notation of provenance.[124] Their walls are much thinner than ours and they are heavily ribbed. Rather a better parallel is afforded by the lid termed "Arabic," also from Khirbet en-Nitla.[125] This lid is ca. 14.0 cm in diameter, almost exactly that of our pl. 7.17:12. It also has the same stance and wall thickness, though the rim is more sharply defined and the lip is thinner than ours.

The dating evidence from Khirbet en-Nitla is sparse, but there are two important types of data. (i) Coins indicate a 4th to 5th century occupation with a peak in the 6th, followed by a steep drop in the 7th and 8th centuries. No coins of the 9th century were identified. (ii) No Arab glazed or molded vessels were found.[126] The excavators' general dates are doubtless correct, but we may refine them somewhat in the light of the above considerations. That is, Byzantine occupation lasts from the 4th century to perhaps as late as the Persian in-

118. Tsori, "House of Kyrios Leontis," fig. 9:17.

119. Smith, *Pella*, I, pl. 28:1193 (= color photograph 90c), p. 224.

120. Delougaz and Haines, *Khirbat al-Karak*, pl. 54:16–17; cf. Fitzgerald, *Beth-Shan*, III, pls. 30:13 and 31:12.

121. Loffreda, "La ceramica," fig. 12:4.

122. Delougaz and Haines, *Khirbat al-Karak*, pl. 43:34, 36.

123. Saller, *Bethany*, fig. 48:3996, p. 277.

124. Kelso and Baramki, *New Testament Jericho*, 34 (type 11A) and pls. 16 and 28, nos. 25 and 57.

125. Ibid. 36 ("type 27"), pls. 17 and 28, no. N17.

126. Ibid., coins on p. 52 and absence of Arab glazes, p. 35.

vasion, with a peak in the 6th century. Arab-period occupation is sparse and perhaps confined to the 7th and 8th centuries, *before* the introduction of the ubiquitous green glazes sometime in the 8th century, maybe until the Ayyubid conquests of the mid-8th century.

The point of the preceding paragraph is to predict a reasonable date for Khirbet en-Nitla cover N17. Since the "Byzantine" lids are only generally parallel to our pl. 7.17:12–14, and the "Arab" lid under discussion more satisfactorily parallels our lid of Stratum V, it seems reasonable to ascribe the Khirbet en-Nitla lid to the 7th century and ours to the end of our Stratum V, or early 7th century.

A cover of the same general low stance, horizontal rim, but with no lip is found at Mount Nebo.[127] Schneider seems to think it Byzantine, but its date is in doubt.

Finally we mention a similar lid from Khirbet Mefjer of ware 18a.[128] This is of a "coarse, dark red ware"[129] and ribbed, but the ribbing extends from the presumed knob handle to within about 3 cm of the rim. Thus a 3-cm band is smooth, exactly as in the Bethany example. Baramki dates this "ware" to the 8th century, which implies that the Khirbet Shema' lids may indeed date as late as the early 7th century anyway. Thus we have lids that date from perhaps 275 CE to 625 CE at our site. The form doubtless continues later elsewhere.

8. BASINS WITH FOLDED RIM

This type of open vessel is illustrated in pl. 7.17:15–20. Unfortunately no complete or reconstructable examples were found, but the characteristic rims easily isolate this basin. The most striking feature of the ceramic form is the compound curve of its rim. This folded rim provides a continuous handle built into the rim for transport of the vessel, as Loffreda and Bagatti have noted.[130] The base of the vessel can be determined only from parallels. Those found at Nazareth and Beth She'arim (see below) are manufactured with convex bases, ribbed or smooth. Diameter of all our examples is quite constant and ranges from a minimum of 20.5 cm to a maximum of 29.5 cm. The majority are very close in diameter, however, and range from 27.5 to 29.5 cm (pl. 7.17:15–19) for an average of 28.0 cm. Rims on our few vessels seem to come in three clear subvarieties. The first subtype exhibits a deep groove on top of the rim and is illustrated in pl. 7.17:5; the second features a double fold (nos. 16–17 and 20), and the third a wide groove *below* the rim (nos. 18–19).

These vessels come largely from T-17, the *miqveh*, and SE II, the industrial-commercial area. The provenance strongly suggests that what we have here is

127. H. Schneider, *Mt. Nebo*, vol. 3, fig. 14:1, and vol. 2, pl. 157:8. See vol. 3, 121. Diameter is 20.5 cm, close to that of our pl. 7.17:13.

128. Baramki, "Kh. el Mefjer," fig. 13:17.
129. Ibid. 71.
130. "La ceramica," 69; *Nazareth*, 287.

not household pottery but vessels for public or commercial use.[131] Chronological context at Khirbet Shema' is wholly Stratum IV. Thus the life of this vessel type is confined to the 4th and early 5th century at our site, though it could have a longer life elsewhere.

Parallels are well attested at Capernaum, Nazareth, Beth She'arim, and Kafr Kanna, with rather similar vessels found at Pella and Chorazin. The published Capernaum vessel[132] resembles our pl. 7.17:18 most closely, though the former basin is about 30 cm in diameter as compared with 26.5 cm for the latter. Loffreda dates it to the 3d and 4th centuries CE. One Late Roman example from Nazareth[133] is complete with a rounded or convex ribbed base, as is the base on the one published from the cisterns at Beth She'arim, though the latter is additionally equipped with three handles on the bottom forming a tripod base.[134] Loffreda mentions vessels of this type from Kfar Kanna as well as other examples from surface survey at er-Ras, Sepphoris, and Khirbet Kanna.[135]

The Expedition to Pella has published a Byzantine vessel of diameter 22.5 cm that is rather similar also to our pl. 7.17:18, though the rim is rounded on top and notched on the inside.[136] Also a 2-mm-wide band of three grooves is cut into the body all around, slightly over 1 cm below the rim. The color also, though the vessel is hard fired, is a neutral gray, N4, but like our vessels it has a rim that appears to double as a sort of continuous ledge handle. Its date may be 5th or 6th century and the type may be a descendent of a Transjordanian type of this basin.

A similar function must be assigned to rims on two vessels published from Chorazin, though otherwise they are not similar to ours.[137] These are deep bowls from building C (L.59) of the 4th century CE whose strongly everted rims are well formed for use as a kind of horizontal handle. Their diameters are 36 cm and 27.5 cm. Thus it appears that the practice of forming the rim to serve as a handle is not confined to our vessel type.[138]

We must mention here a rim from Samaria-Sebaste that is not unlike our pl. 7.17:18. The vessel in question has a diameter of 28 cm, exactly right for our evidence, but only the rim has been preserved. It is an example of "miscellaneous red wares." Crowfoot describes it as "Glaze dull. Decoration of 'nicks' on body."[139] It is possible that the Samaria rim represents an ancestor of our form that derives from large, late sigillata wares of the east.[140] From the parallels it is possible

---

131. Loffreda notes that none of the examples from Capernaum were blackened from use on fire (ibid.). The same is true of ours.

132. "La ceramica," fig. 12:1.

133. *Nazareth*, fig. 231:7. Others are fig. 231:9–10.

134. Avigad, "Excavations," fig. 3:4; "third century and first half of fourth" on p. 209.

135. Loffreda, "Kafr Kanna," 328–348 (not illustrated); cf. also "La ceramica," 70.

136. Smith, *Pella*, I, pl. 43:1310 (not discussed in the text) from the "Byzantine stratum of IIA in the East Cemetery."

137. Yeivin, "Khorazin," fig. 8:19–20 and p. 151.

138. Doubtless other vessels are provided with outturned or everted rims for the same reason.

139. Crowfoot et al., *Samaria-Sebaste*, III, fig. 83:3 and p. 344.

140. Cf. Hayes, *Late Roman Pottery*, 210, form 198.

to conclude tentatively that this is a Galilean form of the 3d to early 5th century. It would be interesting to find its point of manufacture and discover whether its use extends into the Golan or southwards in Cisjordan.

9. LOCAL DEEP BOWLS

In pl. 7.17:21–29 are illustrated three general types of small bowls that appear to be largely without parallel. The first type consists of the two bowls with exceptionally thick walls that were made either skillfully by hand or less skillfully on a wheel. The slight irregularities in diameter, stance, and surface wiping suggest the latter. Perhaps they were products of the potter's apprentice or even entirely locally made. These two are discussed together despite their obvious differences in form because of their similarities in ware, manufacture, and firing. They both appear in a 4th to early 5th century context and in the same square, though different loci. Their diameters and depths are respectively 16.5×9 cm and 16.5×8 cm. Wall thickness is ca. 7 and 6 mm respectively.

It is possible that these bowls were used as small lids. The excavators at Shavei-Zion have a small bowl, of outside rim diameter 18 cm and wall thickness a surprising 8 mm, which they publish as a lid. Its stance and carination 8 cm below the rim recalls our pl. 7.17:21,[141] but it exhibits a simple rim.

The vessel of our pl. 7.17:22, on the other hand, with everted rim and round base, resembles a bowl found in room 20 of the excavations in the Tyropoeon Valley in Jerusalem.[142] The bowl in question is of outside diameter about 15 cm, with gracefully everted rim like our no. 22, but with a flat base. It was found with a lid inscribed *Anastasiou*. The ware of the bowl is not described. The vessels illustrated in the Tyropoeon plate are labeled "Pottery from the Street Level" and are clearly mixed in date from 6th to 9th century at least. If so, then this bowl would be a Late Byzantine form at the earliest. It is not at all clear that our bowl and the Tyropoeon bowl are related except in form. The point is that the latter is clearly a bowl.

A bowl of almost the same type as the one from the Tyropoeon Valley of diameter ca. 12 cm is found in a 5th-century context at Ramat Rahel.[143] It is of brown-red ware with large white and gray grits. Its provenance suggests a use as part of the domestic pottery of the Byzantine monastery.

Pl. 7.17:23 illustrates a singular, very thin-walled bowl with everted, downturned rim, 17.2 cm in diameter. It is self-slipped, uses few, small, white grits, and is hard fired. It is manufactured with great skill, as is attested by the 2-mm-thick walls, thorough preparation of the clay, and hard firing. There is no core, and it is the same 2.5 YR 5/6 ("grayish reddish orange") on the exterior and in-

141. Prausnitz et al. *Shavei Zion*, fig. 11:12 (see also fig. 11:9, with handle and carination) and p. 41.
142. Crowfoot and Fitzgerald, *Tyropean Valley*, pl. 15:23.

143. Aharoni, *Ramat Rahel 1961–62*, fig. 22:12, discussion of context, pp. 14ff. See also *Ramat Rahel 1959–60*, figs. 17:8, 3:1.

terior *and* in section, a testimony to the preparation, stacking, and firing of the kiln. It comes from a Stratum VI context, but there is no way of deciding whether it is Byzantine or Arab, since the ware is common to both periods.

Two bowls of similar rim treatment and diameter are illustrated in pl. 7.17:24–25. The rim is pinched inward so that it bulges slightly on the interior. (This is more pronounced in no. 25 than in no. 24.) Diameters are 18.5 cm and 17.5 cm. The ware of no. 24 is rather different from that of no. 23. The section color is 10 R 5/6 and 4/1 ("grayish reddish orange" and "dark reddish gray"), while exterior and interior color is 10 R 6/4 ("light reddish brown"). The color difference may imply that this bowl is fired at a slightly lower temperature than 17:23. The first bowl of the two, no. 24, is from a Stratum III context, whereas the second, no. 25 is from Stratum IV. It is impossible to draw evolutionary conclusions from two examples.

The bowl with curious rim illustrated in pl. 7.17:26 is about 16 cm in diameter. Its rim is both inverted and everted. It comes from a Stratum III context at Khirbet Shema'. An *Umayyad* example with slightly concave walls but of the same diameter from Pella[144] is medium fired, with a neutral gray core, and 10 YR 6/2 ("light grayish yellowish brown") in exterior color. The late date of the Pella bowl seems odd in view of our early context. It may simply be a later descendent of the same type.

A 5th-century bowl also from Pella is manufactured with the same rim but is 30 cm in diameter.[145] The section color is 2.5 YR 5/6 ("grayish reddish orange"), while the exterior color is 2.5 YR 6/8 ("moderate orange"), significantly brighter. The parallels to the rim into the Umayyad period may suggest a surprisingly long life for this form.

The last three bowls in pl. 7.17 are all uniformly about 12.5 cm in diameter, with wet-smoothed exterior, simple rim, and almost identical ware. They all also stem from SE II, and no. 29 is from one of the pits. The depth of these three exceeds 6 cm, 5 cm, and 6.5 cm respectively. Their great depth in comparison to their diameter, their steeply sloping sides, thin ware, and simple rim all point to a use as large cups or deep bowls associated with the industrial or commercial character of SE II. They probably had flat bases. Their chronological context is 4th to early 5th century at SE II. Since all of them, few as they are, are found in our commercial-industrial installation, we may conclude that they are specially manufactured for use in this and similar installations.

Rather similar vessels that are clearly cups (though called "bowls" by the excavators) were found in the Byzantine monastery at Ramat Rahel in a 5th-century context.[146] They are of rim diameter only 8 cm and height 6 cm, much smaller than ours, but of the same general morphology, including simple rim. Cups of nearly the same diameter are known from Dhiban (Dibon) in Trans-

144. Smith, *Pella*, I, pl. 30:1157 and p. 232.
145. Ibid. pl. 42:1302 and p. 222.

146. Aharoni, *Ramat Rahel 1961–62*, fig. 22:8–10; see n. 119A.

jordan.[147] These are 10–12 cm in diameter, with various surface treatments in accord with their suggested post-550 CE date. Unfortunately they come from wind- and water-laid layers against the south defense wall, but they are likely examples of domestic pottery. Their steep, thin walls recall our vessels. Their buff ware with white slip is far removed typologically from ours.

The lack of other vessels of specifically parallel features in ware and surface treatment implies that the three in pl. 7.17 are perhaps of a type unique to Khirbet Shema'. The lack of parallels for neighboring sites tends to corroborate that view, though of course the picture may change with future archaeological investigations.

10. BOWLS

This section comprises the discussion of the bowls from pl. 7.18:1–25.[148] These are largely Stratum VI and VII vessels except for numbers 1–5 on the plate.

Pl. 7.18:1. This small bowl is only 12 cm in diameter and is rather thin-walled, about 3.5 mm at maximum. It is ribbed below its inverted, simple rim and has the general morphology of 2d-century-BCE Hellenistic bowls without this example's ribbing. The section color is 2.5 YR 4/6 ("strong brown"), while the self-slipped exterior is 2.5 YR 5/3 ("light grayish reddish brown), though the interior is a darker 2.5 YR 4/1 ("grayish reddish brown"), probably due to stacking. The bowl is hard fired, with few, small, black and white grits. It is from a 4th to early 5th century context.

Only two examples of this bowl type were found,[149] indicating its relative rarity. An almost identical parallel is published from Capernaum,[150] of diameter 12.4 cm and walls 6 mm, but otherwise the same, even to the heavy ribbing. Its date is presumably 4th–5th century. Four similar bowls are known from the excavations at the monastery in Jerusalem,[151] noted by Loffreda above. They are ascribed to the Early Roman period, which is logical in view of their smooth sides, and therefore are ancestors of our bowls.

A good later example of such a bowl type comes from Mount Nebo; it is of buff ware with slight ribbing on the interior and exterior.[152] According to Schneider the bowl is "rather roughly fashioned," which *may* suggest a Late Roman or Byzantine date, though he does not suggest a date for this form. But since in 1935 the excavations concentrated in the Atrium, its surrounding rooms, and the monastery, all of which are Byzantine at the earliest according to the

147. Tushingham, *Dibon*, fig. 10:57–67; descriptions p. 151; discussion of the Byzantine pottery pp. 74–76.

148. For the most comprehensive discussion to date on these Hellenistic bowls see Kelso and Baramki, *New Testament Jericho*, 27, no. 81, "type 12."

149. The other example is less complete and unpub-

lished from NE I.26.47.3, L.26029 of the same ware, diameter, and wall thickness.

150. Loffreda, "La ceramica," fig. 12:3 and p. 95. Loffreda indicates it may be used as a lid.

151. Bagatti and Milik, *Dominus Flevit*, fig. 32:15–18.

152. Schneider, *Mt. Nebo*, III, fig. 6:7 and pp. 67, 70.

coins,[153] it seems reasonable to assign this bowl to the 4th–5th century, i.e., contemporary with ours.

A clearer parallel is offered by the Bethany publication.[154] This bowl (actually from Jericho) is 11.4 cm in diameter, with about 4.5-mm-thick walls, and has a flat, disc base. It is of "red-brown ware with numerous white grits," roughly similar to ours, at least in color. Its base would not form a convenient handle, if it were used as a cover. Since its sides are plain, it probably has a date earlier than our pl. 7.18:1; indeed it is properly in its "clear late Hellenistic to early Roman context." Perhaps this one from Jericho and the others from Jerusalem and elsewhere form the ancestors of our later bowl, though the example from Mount Nebo is roughly contemporary.

Pl. 7.18:2–4. These three bowls appear to be all of a type. They have inverted, simple rims and are of ware not unlike that of "Galilean bowls." Diameters are 28, 23, and 24 cm for an average of 25 cm. All stem from clear 4th to early 5th century contexts. No clear parallels could be found,[155] which may again suggest that these bowls were manufactured "on order" largely for use in SE II and similar installations.

Pl. 7.18:5. This bowl is unique at Khirbet Shema'. It is a rather large bowl that does not have steeply sloping sides and therefore may be rather shallow. Its simple rim is furnished with a deep groove on the outside and a design on the outer edge of the rim that resembles rouletting, though it is incised. Ware for this bowl is very similar to that of the foregoing vessels, and it stems from Tomb 29 North, the pale brown layer of dust on the floor of the tomb. Thus, the bowl could date from the 2d to the 5th century according to the lamps found with it. No parallels to the bowl have been found.

Pl. 7.18:6–8. These three Arab vessels represent one type of our so-called white ware at Khirbet Shema'. These shallow vessels are decorated with an incised horizontal groove or grooves, below the simple rim and incised repeated zigzags. Section color averages 10 YR 8/3 ("pale orange yellow"). The vessels are soft fired and relatively thick walled for their diameter. Diameters are 12.6 cm, 14.0 cm and 10.0 cm. Exterior color averages 7.5 YR 8/3 ("brownish pink"), though to the uncritical eye it looks "buff" or "off-white." Ware is generally soft to medium fired and uses many, small, black grits or few, small to medium, white or black and white grits. This is one of the few vessel types that are ever soft fired. The provenance of these three bowls at Khirbet Shema' is Stratum VI (630–850 CE) for no. 6 and Stratum VII (1100–1250 CE) for no. 7. No. 8 essentially resembles no. 6 and therefore is likely of the same period—Stratum VI.

Large amounts of this ware were excavated at Khirbet Kerak, where it was termed "soft buffware."[156] Unfortunately the excavators' discussion of this ware

153. Ibid. 1.

154. Saller, *Bethany*, fig. 53:2–54 ("2–54" is the registration number of the bowl) and p. 255.

155. But see Bagatti and Milik, *Dominus Flevit*, fig.

27:15–16 for deeper bowls, roughly similar, of Late Hellenistic (?) date.

156. Delougaz and Haines, *Khirbat al-Karak*, p. 37. No examples of this ware occur at Samarra.

Table 7.5. TABULATION OF KHIRBET MEFJER "WHITE" WARES

Ware	Color	Hardness	Decoration	Date CE
2	gray	soft	barbotine	
			incised geometric	12–13
2a	cream, reddish	hard	incised	12–13
3	buff	hard	ribbed	12–13
6	cream	soft	smooth	9–10
12–12a	cream	soft	combed	12–13
14	grayish or cream	(– ^{a})	rouletted bands	9–10
15	pinkish	(– ^{a})	incised criss-	
			crosses	8
19	(– ^{a})	very soft	white or pink slip	12–13
			painted br., geom.	
20	cream (molded)	soft	molded geometric	9–10

^{a} Information is not given.

does not mention its chronology or provenance. The section color ranges from "light buff and drab" to "light tan" and "pinkish buff"[157] and is thus similar to that of our bowls. A sherd from Khirbet Kerak similar to our pl. 7.18:6 comes from the surface.[158] It is included with "light buff sherds with plastic decoration," or "Khirbet Mefjer Ware," pl. 41:12. The sherd in question is incised with two parallel lines in a zigzag pattern.[159] The two parallel lines below a horizontal groove are rather inversely similar to the decoration on our pl. 7.18:8. The Khirbet Kerak sherd could date from 630 to 800 CE or 1075 to 1200 CE, according to the coins.

Our pl. 7.18:7 features clay pellets attached alternately between the zig-zags that themselves move back and forth between two lines parallel to the slightly everted rim. This decoration is quite similar to that of a Khirbet Kerak sherd from a jar illustrated on the next plate (42) and perhaps to that of a bowl or other open form also on pl. 41.[160] No date is given, but again it must be 630–800 CE or 1075–1200 CE, judging from the coins.

Of course the most famous find-spot of this general ware is Khirbet Mefjer itself, where light buff fabrics are classified as ware 2, ware 2a, ware 6, ware 12, ware 12a, ware 14, ware 15, and possibly ware 19.[161] The specific characteristics of these wares differ somewhat, but their variables are tabulated in Table 7.5 (wherever Baramki gives them).

Only ware 15 of the 8th century CE according to Baramki appears to parallel our pl. 7.18:8 in stance and general method of decoration, namely, incised criss-crosses between horizontal (incised?) lines.[162] It is impossible to tell from the

157. Ibid.
158. Ibid. pl. 40:7.
159. Ibid. pl. 41:12.
160. Ibid. pl. 41:10. Discussion of this ware as "Khirbat Mefjer ware," 37 ff.

161. Baramki, "Kh. el Mefjer," 65–103.
162. Ibid. fig. 10:11–13, particularly no. 11. Ware description is on p. 70. These are all somewhat larger vessels of diameter ca. 13.5 cm, 16.0 cm, and 14.5 cm as compared to our pl. 7.18:8, diameter of 10.0 cm.

Table 7.6. SAMARRA "WHITE WARES"

Ware	Color	Hardness	Decoration
I.A	light yellow	(not given)	simple incisions or hatching
I.B	yellowish white	hard	appliqué bands, incised
II.A	bright yellowish white	hard	stamped, impressed
III	(not given)	(not given)	combing, applied pellets
IV	(not given)	(not given)	barbotine, combing or incisions

small sherd of our no. 8 whether the decoration is zigzag or crisscross, but it is definitely incised. The only "white" ware from Khirbet Mefjer that carries appliqué or "barbotine" decoration is ware 2 of the 12th-13th century CE. This therefore parallels our pl. 7.18:7, which also comes from our Stratum VII of the 11th-12th century CE.

If the only datable "white wares" were from Khirbet Mefjer, then we would tend to date our Khirbet Shema' bowls to the medieval period. However the 9th-century ceramics from Samarra in Syria also include white wares, some with the same decorations as Baramki's putative 12th to 13th century wares. A tabulation of the Samarra unglazed ceramics that appear to be classifiable as "white wares" is presented in Table 7.6.

It must be remembered that Sarre and Baramki evidently do not always mean the same thing by "barbotine." Sarre reserves the term for low-relief decoration, while Baramki evidently also means applied pellets or knobs of clay. In any case this gives us pottery closely dated to 838–883 CE though not necessarily lying within the same cultural sphere as Khirbet Shema'.[163]

The Khirbet Shema' bowls under discussion are soft rather than hard, pinkish rather than yellowish, and incised rather than combed. The Samarra incising seems to be multiple rather than simple. In other words, our forms have more affinity with Khirbet Mefjer than with Samarra. Yet Samarra yields a sherd with attached pellets between combed X's that is essentially the same decorative idea as our pl. 7.18:7.[164] It appears to be a small, deep bowl, perhaps like Khirbet Mefjer's fig. 10:11–13.

If the relative dates from the coinage at Khirbet Kerak (1075–1200) and Khirbet Shema' (1150–1277) are secure, and if Baramki's and Hamilton's dates of the 12th and 13th centuries at Khirbet Mefjer can be made to stick, then our no. 7 can be dated between 1150 and 1200 CE, second half of the 12th century. On the other hand, if the ceramic affinities are with Samarra, then we must look to the 9th century for the date of these bowls.

In this connection we must add that no. 6 may be intrusive in its context and actually date from Stratum VII above the Stratum VI cobbles between which it was found. If it is intrusive, its apparent stylistic affinity with the late "white" wares at Khirbet Kerak is not so surprising.

163. Sarre, *Keramik von Samarra*, 101.   164. Ibid. pl. IV.9 = sherd 59, p. 16.

Pl. 7.18:9. This is the rim of a bowl with rather thin walls (4 mm), sharply defined rim of diameter 20.2 cm, and an incised horizontal line 8 mm below the rim. Its depth cannot now be estimated. The section color is 5 YR 7/4 ("light yellowish brown"), but the interior and exterior are glazed 2.5 Y 6/6 ("dark yellow"). Ware is hard, while the clay includes many, small, *brown* and black grits. The brown grits may be grog (ground-up sherds). This sherd comes from an otherwise clear Stratum VI (640–850 CE) context, but its monochrome yellow glaze on both interior and exterior bespeaks a medieval origin. Therefore it may well be intrusive in the locus in which it was found, for overlying it is later mixed material continuing to modern times. In any case the sherd is unique at Khirbet Shema'.

Its nearest typological relative in the literature would be the so-called "metallic wares" from Crusader sites in the Levant. These are characterized by red ware and a form that is "thin and precisely turned, with clearly defined edges."[165] Our rim no. 9 could be from a carinated bowl in which the rim sherd broke off just above the carination. The ware is dated 12th-13th century.

Unfortunately this ware is usually glazed green or brown. "Orange-yellow" glazes characterize so-called "glossy ware" of the same date. However, it is not out of the question that such a glaze could appear on such a form; yellow glaze appears on Syrian pottery of the 9th-10th century according to Florence E. Day.[166] She discusses Abbassid bowls (750–950 CE) that are "bright mustard-yellow" (her no. 9) and "dull yellow" (no. 10). These bowls are differentiated from ours in that the glaze runs down the outside only 1 or 2 cm.

Yellow glazes also are known at Khirbet Mefjer, though not monochromatic glazes. Baramki assigns them to the 9th-10th century.[167] Finally we mention monochrome yellow glazes from Pella in Transjordan.[168] The bowls in question, from tombs 2 and 7, do not resemble ours, but are glazed 5 Y 6/8 ("dark yellow") over a white slip. Smith dates this bowl to the (presumably) *early* 13th century. In other words yellow glazes are well known from the 9th to the 13th century CE, but they are best known as monochromatic glazes in the medieval period. It seems most likely that our rim is of that period (Stratum VII).

Pl. 7.18:12–13. These two medieval Arab (Stratum VII) bowls are of strongly similar ware and decoration. They feature vertical, thickened rims and sharp carination, 15–20 cm below the rim. Diameters are 20.8 and 27.0 cm, the first with walls of 3 mm and the second with walls of 6 mm. The bowls are slipped in white to receive the brown and yellow glaze: at least two horizontal bands of yellow relieve the dark plainness of the brown interior, though judging from parallels, the bottom held a geometric design. The glaze is applied up to the rim

165. Mackay, "Pottery from Corinth," 249–320, no. 5.
166. F. E. Day, "Islamic Glazed Wares" in Delougaz and Haines, *Khirbat al-Karak*, 40–48, esp. 45. See also Sarre, *Keramik von Samarra*, sherds 116–119, 122–124, etc.
167. Baramki, "Kh. el Mefjer," fig. 11:2, 7, 8, of "ware 16a"; see also p. 70.
168. Smith, *Pella*, I, pls. 72:1001, 58:401.

on the interior of no. 13, but spills over outside on no. 12. The exterior is an unglazed 5 YR 5/2 or "light grayish reddish brown." Ware is 10 R 6/8 ("moderate reddish orange") in section or "red" to the casual observer. The bowl was fired hard with the clay prepared with many small gray and red grits.

The larger, thicker bowl (no. 13) is from a clear Stratum VII context, while no. 12 is from a surface locus and therefore probably Stratum VII also. This places these forms in the 11th to 12th century CE at Khirbet Shema', or between 1150 and 1277 CE.

Yellow- or brown-glazed decoration is commonly dated 11th to 12th century at Khirbet Mefjer.[169] Likewise at Bethany this glaze type (though not the pattern) is attested on bowls of different form dated to the 12th and 13th centuries.[170]

The *form* of this bowl type is well attested in Crusader contexts of the 12th and 13th centuries CE, as at Emmaus, though the Emmaus bowls on p. 104 are not glazed.[171] Glazed forms, also yellow or brown, are illustrated on p. 129.[172] This is dated from the 12th to the middle of the 13th century, or exactly parallel to ours. Likewise such bowls are well known from Abu Gosh, where they are dated to the 13th and 14th centuries.[173] The same forms and glazes also appear at al-Minyeh,[174] and at 'Atlit of the same date,[175] plus other Palestinian sites also of the 13th to the 14th century.[176]

Finally we must note a similar bowl from Pella,[177] of diameter 21 cm, with ware of section color 2.5 YR 6/6 ("grayish reddish orange"). It was slipped "white" (actually 7.5 YR 8/4 or "pale orange yellow"), then glazed in 2.5 YR 4/8 ("strong brown") with a hatched, geometric design in 2.5 Y 8/4 to 5 Y 7/4 ("grayish yellow"). In this case there is one horizontal yellow band on the interior at the carination and another on the rim, though it is a bit irregular. Smith dates it to the 13th century on the basis of the parallels we cite above.

Thus it seems assured that this form must occur at the end of Stratum VII at Khirbet Shema'. That is, this vessel type must have been used during the first three-quarters of the 13th century at our site.

Pl. 7.18:15–16. These two sherds illustrate a very common green-glazed bowl type in Palestine, Syria, and beyond. The example we publish is about 19.5 cm in diameter and perhaps 8 cm deep. Its ware is red, but it is then slipped in white on the interior and glazed "yellow green" (5 GY 6/8) or what appears brilliant moss-green to the casual observer. The rim of this bowl comes from a context that must be dated Stratum VI (640–850 CE) at the latest.

Parallels to these green-glazed bowls are known from all over Syria-Palestine,

169. Ibid. fig. 11:7–8.
170. Saller, *Bethany*, fig. 55:5548 and p. 281.
171. Bagatti, *Emmaus*, 104; fig. 23:1–8.
172. Ibid. fig. 31:11–14.
173. De Vaux and Steve, *Abu Gosh*, fig. 32:12, 14, 18, and p. 139.
174. Puttrich-Reignard, *Die Palastanlage von Chirbet el-Minje*, 29 and fig. 16–17.

175. Johns, "'Atlit; Stables," 53 and pl. 27.
176. The best discussion to date of these and other parallels is de Vaux and Steve, *Abu Gosh*, 139f. Another more recent example is from the House of Kyrios Leontis (Tsori, pl. 46:4B).
177. Smith, *Pella*, I, pl. 72:494, color photo pl. 93, and p. 239.

as the type was popular in the early Arab period. Examples are known from Bethany,[178] Khirbet Mefjer,[179] Beth Shean,[180] and Jerusalem,[181] to name only a few sites. The discussion of monochrome-green Umayyad glaze by F. E. Day in the Khirbet Kerak report remains the most useful discussion to date. In fact she confines this type to the period 650–750 CE or specifically to the Umayyad epoch.[182] If this is correct, then our bowl must date toward the end of Stratum VI or perhaps the 8th century.

Pl. 7.18:18. This rim resembles those of nos. 12–13 and 17. It is a green-glazed bowl with outside diameter of 28.5 cm, simple vertical rim, and carination between 4.5 and 5.0 cm below the rim. Ware is 2.5 YR 5/4 ("light reddish brown") in section. A green glaze (2.5 GY 5/8) covers both interior and exterior. The bowl is fired hard, and the clay is prepared with many, small, white grits. This bowl occurs in a clear Stratum VI or Early Arab context. This accords well with its green glaze, which is usually ascribed to the Umayyad period (see above).

A possible parallel from Khirbet Mefjer features the same ware ("16a") which is evidently "red," sensibly the same as ours.[183] This area is dated 9th–10th century by Baramki.

Pella furnishes another possible later example of one bowl from a group of a dozen glazed bowls from tomb 7 in the East Cemetery.[184] It is much smaller, being only ca. 18.5 cm in diameter, but it is 2.5 YR 6/6 ("grayish reddish orange") in section color, close to ours. It is slipped white and glazed 5 GY 7/6 to 7.5 GY 4/6 (yellow-olive green) inside and running over the rim outside a few centimeters. However, its rim is about 9 mm thick, while ours is 6 mm or less.

Smith dates his entire glazed corpus to the 13th century CE especially arguing from evidence of C. N. Johns from 'Atlit.[185] He is doubtless right for his corpus, but our bowl just as clearly dates 850 CE at the latest, judging from the early Arab wares found with it. Thus it seems reasonable to conclude that this general bowl type, with simple vertical rim, carination, and (probably) ring base is manufactured continually to the medieval period. Our own example cannot date later than the mid-9th century.

Pl. 7.18:23–24. These two sherds represent two rim types and a ring base of another green-glaze bowl type, this with black line decoration. The larger bowl is a little less than 33 cm in diameter at the simple rim and perhaps 10 cm deep. Form is approximately hemispherical, if the rim and base illustrated come from similar vessels. The vessel is of red ware slipped in white, then glazed green after a design of parallel lines is cut into the slip. The glaze that settles into this

178. Saller, *Bethany*, fig. 55:2961 and p. 277, though the rim is somewhat inverted.

179. Baramki, "Kh. el Mefjer," figs. 11:1 (but with a disc base), 11:4 (especially), 11:5–6 dated by Baramki 9th–10th centuries.

180. Fitzgerald, *Beth-Shan*, III, 37.

181. Crowfoot and Fitzgerald, *Tyropean Valley*, pl. 13:39, but white ware and disc base.

182. Day in Delougaz and Haines, *Khirbat al-Karak*, 42f. Note her *caveat* on the use of the Kh. Mefjer ceramic dates, n. 30.

183. Baramki, "Kh. el Mefjer," fig. 11:9.

184. Smith, *Pella*, I, fig. 72:973.

185. Ibid. 239. Cf. Johns, "Excavations at Pilgrim's Castle 'Atlit," 145–164; "'Atlit; Stables," 31–60.

Figure 7.9. Completed pattern of a brown on yellow glazed medieval bowl.

incised line fires greenish-black to form a variety of "graffiato" decoration. Provenance of these sherds is probably Stratum VI.

Day points out that the Abbassids (750–950 CE) improved on the Umayyad monochrome green glazes by the simple expedient of cutting designs into the white slip before glazing, i.e., by inventing "sgraffito" or "graffiato" pottery.[186] The earliest these forms could date would therefore be mid-8th century CE. This is especially clear at Samarra.[187] However "sgraffito" wares are best known from medieval contexts such as 'Atlit or even the later occupation at Corinth.[188]

De Vaux describes a sherd from Abu Gosh which exhibits floral designs cut into the slip and covered with green glaze. He dates such ware to the 13th century on the basis of parallels from el-Minyeh, 'Atlit, Emmaus, Khirbet Mefjer, Egypt, and Syria.[189]

Finally we cite a clear parallel from Bethany. This bowl of diameter ca. 28.0 cm and depth ca. 7 cm is fired ware with a "creamy slip" and a light green glaze over straight, curve, or spiral incised lines. Saller observes that it is quite common at Bethany.[190]

In this connection we do well to point out that the bowl in photo 7.1 is of

186. In Delougaz and Haines, *Khirbat al-Karak*, 41.

187. Sarre, *Keramik von Samarra*, pl. 27:4 with green-flecked glaze. Sarre thinks the origins of this design are Chinese.

188. See supra n. 157, also Johns, "Medieval Slip-Ware," 137–144, pls. 49–56, though not all illustrate sgraffito decoration. See also Mackay, "Pottery from Corinth," 249–320.

189. De Vaux and Steve, *Abu-Gosh*, 139, nn. 2–7.

190. Saller, *Bethany*, fig. 55:5548 and p. 281.

the same type as pl. 7.18:17 in form, but nos. 23–25 in decoration. In this case the bowl was found in NE VII.1.51, L. 1024 or a Stratum VII context. It is decorated with a six-pointed star and spirals and glazed *yellow* with brown-painted (not incised) design (see fig. 7.9).

This pottery is well dated to its appearance at the Palestinian sites mentioned above, but its manufacture and use at al-Mina in northern Syria can be shown to be between 1200 and 1268 CE. This is exactly in line with our late Stratum VII at Khirbet Shema'.[191]

11. NECKLESS COOKING POTS WITH FOLDED RIM

These vessels are illustrated in pl. 7.18:26–29, though only rims survive. The rim is turned upward in two cases to form a "lid device" or a concave ring for receiving a cover. Outside rim diameter ranges from ca. 12.5 cm to ca. 21.5 cm for an average of about 17.0 cm. No. 29 has two handles mounted below the rim and doubtless on the body, and it is reasonable to assume that they all had two such vertical handles and surely all were ribbed.

Section color averages 5 YR 5/4 ("light brown"), but exterior color ranges from 2.5 YR 5/2 ("light grayish reddish brown") to 7.5 YR 6/8 ("dark orange yellow"), though the latter is generally a bright spot on one side of the vessel due to uneven firing conditions in the kiln. Average exterior color is 5 YR 5/4 or the same as section color. The ware is prepared with a few or very few, very small to small, white or black and white grits. All our examples are medium fired.

These vessels stem predominantly from a 4th or 5th century context at Khirbet Shema'. It is even possible to ascribe no. 27 to a 5th-century context on the basis of associated finds. It is just possible that the rim with lid device (nos. 26, 29) is earlier than the downturned rim, but we have too few examples to make many far-reaching conclusions.

Exact parallels are not easy to come by, but pots with rather similar rims that are folded out twice ("convoluted") are known from Pella.[192] Typologically they appear to be Late Byzantine descendents of our pots. Pella also includes at least one such that appears to *precede* our form typologically, though not chronologically.[193] This rim is everted without being squeezed into the clay of the body. Similar examples continue into the Umayyad period at Pella, showing a long continuous history of the form.[194] This rim features a groove on the outside.

This same folded, grooved rim is known at Khirbet Kerak.[195] More to the point, however, is the example of Late Roman "soft tan" ware on Kerak pl.

191. Cf. Hobson, "Later Al Mina Pottery," 115–116. Also Lane, "Medieval Finds at Al Mina," 19.

192. Smith, *Pella,* I, pls. 43:1242, 1246, 1249 and 42:1295, and fig. 68, p. 223. The same rim is found at Beth Shean. Fitzgerald, *Beth-Shan,* III, pl. 31:3–4, dated 5th–6th century. See also Tsori, "House of Kyrios Leontis at Beth-Shean," fig. 7:11.

193. Smith, *Pella,* I, pl. 28:1271.

194. Ibid. pls. 30:1118, 91D:1119, 1109.

195. Delougaz and Haines, *Khirbat al-Karak,* pls. 33:5 and 54:14, p. 33. See also pls. 33:6, 53:39 for forms like ours.

53:39 which rather closely resembles our pl. 7.18:26. It is of "pre-church" provenance and therefore perhaps contemporary with our Stratum IV, though that is by no means assured.

We can also find the same tradition in Transjordan at Dhiban.[196] The vessels in question have (inside?) diameters of 10 cm, 16 cm, 12 cm, and 17 cm. The examples from Dhiban are within our range. They date to 575–600 CE according to the excavators and therefore represent a later form, but not necessarily a later development of this form.

Thus it appears that this cooking pot type is generally known in the 5th and 6th century particularly, and even into the Umayyad period, but mainly in Transjordan. Our examples may well be among the earliest known vessels of this form, for they appear to start in the early 5th century.

Finally it must be noted that it can hardly be accidental that all our clear parallels to this cooking pot are from eastern Palestinian or near Transjordanian sites. None are published from Capernaum, et-Tabba, Chorazin, Nazareth, Beth Shean, Samaria, or a host of other sites. Both the presence and absence of forms is instructive and suggests an original manufacturing center in the vicinity of the Sea of Galilee.

12. MISCELLANEOUS OPEN FORMS, JUGS, AND COOKING POTS

The vessels in pl. 7.19 illustrate a group of forms that occur quite frequently at Khirbet Shema'. They are cup or deep bowl (no. 1), vessels almost "hole-mouth" in form, sometimes with low neck (nos. 2–8), two-handled jugs that are also likely varieties of cooking pots (nos. 9–22), and larger jugs, perhaps for storage (nos. 23–32). It is possible that nos. 24–25 and 27 are from storage jars.

Pl. 7.19:1. This graceful, small, deep bowl or cup was found in the cistern. It is about 12.5 cm in outside rim diameter and may have been ca. 10 cm deep. Its date is probably second half of the 4th century CE.

Pl. 7.19:2–8. These vessels illustrate a type of everted rim on pots of various size from diverse chronological contexts. No. 6 dates as early as the 2d century CE, while no. 5 is from Stratum V. The remainder stem from early Arab contexts, except 7.19:2, whose context is medieval.

Parallels are not numerous, but can be found. Perhaps the earliest is an open-mouthed vessel from Chorazin that resembles rather closely our no. 8.[197] The vessel in question is described as having "sandy ware, well fired" and ascribed to L.50, the southeast room in Building B. Yeivin dates the group with which it is published to the 2d–6th century CE.[198]

A 6th-century parallel to our no. 3 comes from Pella.[199] Its provenance is

196. Tushingham, *Dibon*, fig. 9:16–19, descriptions p. 147.

197. Yeivin, "Khorazin," fig. 9:9 and p. 151.

198. Yeivin's parallel is a neckless storage jar from the Tyropoeon Valley, pl. 14:30, of rim diameter ca. 15.5 cm. Its wall appears too thick to provide a close parallel.

199. Smith, *Pella*, I, pl. 43:1252 and p. 224.

the "Byzantine Stratum IIA in the East Cemetery." This pot is 2.5 YR 6/8 ("moderate orange") in section *and* exterior color, while the outside is smoke-blackened from use. It is hard fired, and Smith presumes that it had a handle or handles. It is doubtless 6th-century.

Another Pella pot resembles our no. 5. It comes from the "Byzantine stratum of Area I, the West Church Complex."[200] This vessel is larger than ours, since its diameter is ca. 18 cm with walls half the thickness of ours. Section color is 10 YR 6/8 ("dark orange yellow") and slip color is 10 YR 4/1 ("brownish gray"). It is to be dated to the 6th century or late in our Stratum V.

Bethany furnishes a Byzantine parallel to our pl. 7.19:7.[201] The Bethany example is actually the everted, sharp rim of a fairly large pot of outside rim diameter ca. 12 cm as compared with a diameter of ca. 14.5 cm for our no. 7. Unfortunately Saller does not assign it a date, and our vessel is unstratified.

The material from Emmaus is dated by Bagatti to the medieval period, but several jugs of similar everted rims like ours have been published from there.[202] These jugs are with handles except for a surviving fragment on fig. 29:6. The vessels are dated to 1150–1250 CE, almost exactly our Stratum VII. These must therefore represent medieval descendents of our type.

The parallels tend to confirm the rather wide time span covered by this rim type at Khirbet Shema'. Doubtless an evolution of forms could be deduced if sufficient numbers had been found, but the small number of our examples precludes such an analysis.

Pl. 7.19:9-14. These six vessels appear to be all of a type despite some differences in handle size and rim treatment. Diameter for nos. 9–10, 12–13 is very close to 10.5 cm. The other two pots are 12.8 cm and 6.4 cm in diameter, to give three groups. The larger diameter for no. 11 correlates with its date, as it is the only one from Stratum IV. All exhibit slightly flared high neck, simple rim, and steeply sloping sides. As a group they date predominantly to the early Arab period but must begin in the 5th century or so, to judge from the context of nos. 10 and 11.

Pl. 7.19:15-22. This is a group of somewhat miscellaneous jugs and cooking pots, all distinguished by an outflaring or everted simple rim forming a short neck. Probably all had two vertical handles much like nos. 19–20. The handles on no. 17 seem to be mounted upside down, but a globular, Byzantine cooking pot from Khirbet en-Nitla features handles mounted the same way.[203]

Stratum IV is represented by nos. 15, 17–20, 22, six examples. They do not form a homogenous group. On the other hand are nos. 16 and 21 from Stratum VI. Stratum V is not represented.

No. 21 is a clear example of an Arab-period vessel with barbotine decora-

200. Ibid. pl. 28:1271 and p. 224.
201. Saller, *Bethany*, fig. 43:5124.
202. Bagatti, *Emmaus*, fig. 29:6–8.

203. Kelso and Baramki, *New Testament Jericho*, pl. 27:N33 and p. 34, no. 121.

tion on the handle such as is best known from Khirbet Mefjer.[204] This vessel is 10 R 7/3 ("light grayish reddish brown") in section and 7.5 YR 7/3 in exterior color (ditto), an example of our "white ware." This is similar to Baramki's "ware 20," though his is soft fired and ours is hard fired. Such decoration on a vertical handle of a vertical-necked jar comes from Chorazin. It is "gritty ware, light and hard-fired."[205] Yeivin dates all his Arab pottery to the 9th–10th century.

Pl. 7.19:23–32. These represent a variety of jugs, as demonstrated by their handles, and a number of other vessels that may be jars, e.g., nos. 24, 25, 27.

Stratum IV rims are illustrated in nos. 25, 28, and surely 29 on the basis of its resemblance to 28, though the latest material in its locus is Stratum VI. Stratum V is represented by a single, unique rim, no. 27. Stratum VI vessels are in the majority: nos. 24, 26, 30–31. No. 32 is the only medieval rim in this group. It is from a very large vessel of diameter ca. 20 cm and with 2.5-cm-thick handles.

13. JARS

There are two major types of jars found at Khirbet Shema', with much overlap into the Meiron material, as one might expect. In addition, there are perhaps three other types represented less frequently. Finally, there are a variety of other rims that suggest other types, but there are too few of each to classify satisfactorily.

Pl. 7.20:1–3. These three jar rims all stem from the earliest locus in Meiron, MI.2, and therefore represent our earliest jars from the late 2d century CE. All three are similar in ware and workmanship but not in form. The first simple rim is rolled outward from a thin wall that is already turning to the body. The second two are evidently folded, slightly out-turned, and rather more sharply defined at the top. Two other examples like nos. 2–3 were found in NE I.32., L.32016, a fill mixed with material from Strata IV-VII and surely earlier strata, as witness these forms. These resemble Late Hellenistic jars of a variety called "rounded rim" by Lapp, excavated at Beth-zur, Samaria, and other sites.[206] They are dated as late as 100 BCE, but not later. A better ancestor for our no. 1 is perhaps provided by Lapp's type 21 "large jars," particularly "A" from Beth-zur and Shechem.[207] This form is of the same date. The rim type in our no. 1 is found at Capernaum.[208] There it is described as having pink ware, many grits, and "light firing," with an almost black slip inside and out. There is no suggested date for this particular jar, but the ensuing discussion seems to imply a 4th to 5th century date.

Type 1, pls. 7.20:5–16, 33–51 and 7.21:1–4. This jar type is ubiquitous at Khirbet Shema' and is well represented at Meiron. Mainly necks and handles of

204. Baramki, "Kh. el Mefjer," fig. 5:15 for handle decoration; but see fig. 15:9 for "ware 20" of the 9th–10th century.
205. Yeivin, "Khorazin," fig. 9:21. For date see p. 156.

206. Lapp, *Palestinian Ceramic Chronology,* 148, type 11.
207. Ibid. 157.
208. Loffreda, "La ceramica," fig. 4:2, p. 77.

this form were excavated, and no complete specimens of this particular type could be recovered. The rim is somewhat peculiar in that it is both everted and inverted. That is, at the top of the neck the rim turns outward, so that, viewed from the exterior at least, it appears to have a rolled rim. Just below this eversion, however, the rim turns inward as much as 4 mm before turning straight downward to form the collar. This inversion is sometimes visible on the collar outside, forming a constriction below the rim.

Generally, though not always, the bottom of the collar is formed with a distinct, sharp edge all around, sometimes called the drip ring, though it is not clear that it was always functional. These rims average ca. 10.0 cm outside diameter and the neck is 4.0 cm high or more.

Ware is quite regularly prepared and fired the same in these jars. Section color averages 2.5 YR 5/2–3 ("light grayish reddish brown") or 5 PB 5/1 ("bluish gray"), two distinct colors, though ware is almost always fired medium hard. Exterior color averages 5 YR 6/4 ("light brown") for all examples, since the ones with dark core do not exhibit significantly darker exteriors. For almost all these jars clay is prepared with small, black and white grit, but the potter does not clearly favor any consistent distribution of the grit ("few," "some," or "many").

Provenance of these type 1 jars is of more or less random distribution about the site. The context is largely Stratum II at Meiron (17 percent) or Stratum IV at Khirbet Shema' (52 percent). The remainder are found in later contexts; but it is not clear that they are being used in Stratum V, for example, as so few occur there. Chronology of this form begins, then, about 200 CE at Meiron (one sherd in L.2019 at Meiron is too few for chronological conclusions) and runs on into the 5th century.

This jar is well paralleled at Capernaum, where specimens are divided morphologically into two types, "type 2" and "type 4."[209] Though the two types from Capernaum are present in our material, we did not adopt Loffreda's division because we could find no chronological or ware differences. Loffreda points out that his type is a variant of type 2, and he can say no more than that it belongs to the Roman period.[210]

Our type 1 jars are also paralleled at et-Tabgha, where they occur in unstratified material near corner A (the northwest corner) of edifice E 1 and in basin B2.[211] Loffreda dates this pottery to the 4th-5th century CE.

One complete example of our type 1 jar and one preserved with handles are published from Nazareth.[212] The one complete example is from cistern 4F and the other from limited excavations in the Church of the Annunciation (area 25). These have straight sides with heavy ribbing most of the way down. On the bottom, ribbing is quite wide to the concave and slightly pointed base. Handles are mounted on the shoulder and are almost circular. They exhibit two

209. Ibid. fig. 4:1, 6 and pp. 75ff.
210. Ibid. 79.
211. Loffreda, *et-Tabgha*, figs. 35:38, 40, 56:261.
212. Bagatti, *Nazareth*, fig. 217:3-4, pp. 265ff.

or three longitudinal grooves. Bagatti dates these generally before the Mount Nebo pottery and after or during the Huqoq and Beth She'arim ceramics. This must mean 3rd–5th century.

One further possible complete example of this type comes from Beth Shean with the corpus from the summit and western slope.[213] This jar is 50 cm tall as compared with 43 cm for the Nazareth example, but both are 30 cm thick through the middle. The Nazareth jar also sports more prominent shoulders than the vessel from Beth Shean. The rim and collar are the sticking point, however, as the inversion below the eversion is missing from the Beth Shean example, and this jar has a pronounced drip ring in the drawing. Nevertheless, it is already the case that Beth Shean has produced 6th-century pottery, and this jar may therefore be a later example of this type.

We have no clear parallels to this specific rim type from sites in Transjordan or from more southern sites, including the "Roman 4" pottery from Samaria. It is, therefore, a working hypothesis of this expedition that type 1 jars are manufactured in Galilee and only a limited number were exported in the 3d, 4th, and early 5th centuries.

Type 2, pl. 7.20:17–31. These collared rims are in the same general tradition as our type 1, but with significant differences. Dimensions are quite constant, average outside diameter at the rim being ca. 9.5 cm. The overwhelming majority range between 8.8 and 10.6 cm. Only two—nos. 22 and 26—are smaller, and both are slightly less than 7.0 cm in diameter, representing perhaps a subgroup of this jar type. Collar height is a virtually unvarying 4.0 cm, a testimony to the mechanical potting for this jar type.

Ware is quite constant as well, being generally medium fired with clay prepared with many, small, black and white grits. Section color ranges between 10 R 5/6 and 2.5 YR 5/6 ("grayish reddish orange") while exterior color is lighter, ranging between 10 R 6/3 and 2.5 YR 6/3 ("light grayish red" to "light grayish reddish brown").

The rim is characterized by a thinly folded-over exterior, often with a shallow constriction or groove outside, within the sharply defined area of the fold. There is often a suggestion of a drip ring at the bottom of the collar. Stance varies from the generally vertical to slightly outflaring. No complete specimens of this jar could be recovered, so we publish only the collars. No. 26 reveals that the body was ribbed.

Chronology of these forms is virtually identical with that of type 1, though type 2 is only half as abundant as type 1. Roughly one-third of these rims stem from the 3d-century context at MI.2. About five-eighths or somewhat more were excavated in Stratum IV contexts at Khirbet Shema'. The rest occur in later strata, but generally in mixed fill, which indicates that they probably were not

213. Fitzgerald, *Beth-Shan*, III fig. 32:18.

being produced past the early 5th century. Therefore, the range early 3d to early 5th century seems reasonable for the use-span of these jars at our two sites.

Type 2 jars are well known at Capernaum, where they are Loffreda's "type 3."[214] He observes that these rims are rare in the synagogue and quite rare in the octagon, but he dates their first appearance to the end of the 3d century and the beginning of the 4th, 50 to 100 years later than they appear at Meiron. He notes their conspicuousness in the Early Roman period at the Herodium and their Byzantine occurrence at Khirbet Kerak.[215]

Type 2 jars also appear at et Tabgha from level IV of pavement a of edifice E 1 and from trench I in Basin 2. Both occurrences are dated to the 4th–5th century, our Stratum IV.[216]

Well-dated examples are also known from Tell er-Ras on Mount Gerizim, again from the vaulted cisterns in front of the Temple of Zeus, likely used as a church at the time.[217] A series of these reveal a typological development from a sharply defined fold (as in pl. 10:2–3, 5–7) to only a suggestion of that feature (pl. 10:1, 4, 13–14). These are dated 250–350 CE by associated coins.

Further examples are known from Samaria, from the "Roman 4 pottery."[218] These wares are undated except indirectly by their homogeneous grouping. There is a preponderance of Early Roman wares in the group, and the Samaria jar is slightly ribbed and *buff-slipped,* a feature that may also mark it Early Roman or Middle Roman.[219]

A somewhat similar rim occurs on a jar from Beth She'arim catacomb 13, hall 2, of light reddish brown ware.[220] The collar features the folded rim but is 12.5 cm in diameter with a height ca. 4.25 cm. The folded part of the rim is ca. 2.5 cm wide as compared with ca. 1.5 to 1.8 cm on our jars, and no drip ring is in evidence. Thus, though this jar appears to belong to this pottery tradition in general typology, it is significantly, but perhaps only locally, different. This jar is presumably to be dated to 200–350 CE with the entire corpus, according to Avigad.

Rims that are similar to Beth She'arim (and ours) in the fold and constriction at the point of the fold, but of various stances, are found at Dhiban in a 6th-century context.[221] Three are 10 cm in diameter and one is 11 cm, sensibly close to ours, but it is not clear that they are all collared rims. Fig. 12.28 in that publication is nevertheless quite similar typologically to our type 2 except that the stance slopes inward. It is of "light brown ware, black and white grits" and has a rim diameter of 10 cm. There is a quite clear drip ring. Its date of 575–600 CE places it chronologically with a similar jar from Khirbet Kerak.

214. Loffreda, "La ceramica," fig. 4:4, pp. 75ff.
215. Ibid. 79.
216. Loffreda, *et-Tabgha*, figs. 31:17, 56:257.
217. Bull and Campbell, "Balatah (Shechem)," 32, fig. 10:2–9, 12–14.
218. Crowfoot, *Samaria-Sebaste*, III, fig. 72:3.

219. On occasion slip can only be detected by thin section analysis. Therefore color differences that are attributed to slip sometimes need to be accepted with caution.
220. Avigad, *Beth-She'arim*, III, fig. 94:1, p. 147.
221. Tushingham, *Dibon*, fig. 12:6–9, 28, descriptions p. 155.

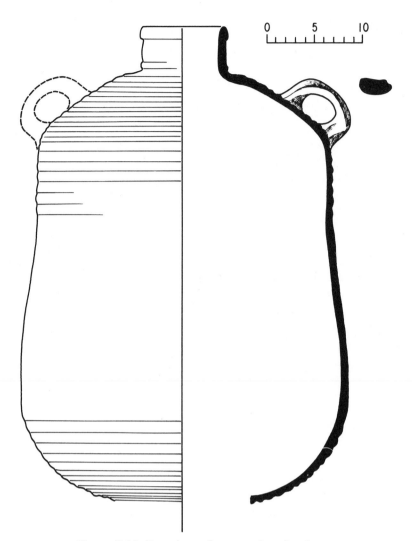

Figure 7.10. Drawing of a complete jar from
SE II.23.34, L.23017, 1:4.

Another Transjordanian parallel emerges at Pella, again from the 6th-century Byzantine Stratum of the "West Church Complex."[222] In this instance the fold is less dramatic in that the constriction or hollow in the fold is missing. Diameter is only about 8.5 cm, with neck height less than 3 cm. The drip ring is only a conventional feature, a slightly raised ridge. Ware is 2.5 YR 5/4 or "light reddish brown," but the jar is slipped 10 YR 4/1 or "brownish gray." It is hard fired.

Finally, we note the appearance of a type 2 jar in almost complete form at Khirbet Kerak, in this case from tomb 4.[223] In this example the rim is ca. 9 cm

222. Smith, *Pella*, I, pl. 29:1187.

223. Delougaz and Haines, *Khirbat al-Karak*, pl. 55:4.

in outside diameter and the collar 5 cm high, both dimensions differing significantly from our norm. The body is ribbed at the attachment of the handle, but smooth elsewhere. There is no sign of a drip ring. Ware differs also; it is of "soft brownish fabric." None of ours were soft fired. Its appearance in the tomb is indeed fortunate, since coins from the tomb date 529–575 CE. If we assume that the occupants are roughly contemporary, then a mid- to late-6th-century date for this jar is not out of line and may account for its alternative ware.

From our parallels it appears that our type 2 jar may begin as early as 200 CE, though 250 CE is a more comfortable date (the single sherd from MI.2., L.2019, may be intrusive), and continues perhaps as late as the end of the 6th century. Its absence in Late Byzantine sites such as Mount Nebo, Bethany, Ramat Rahel, and Shavei-Zion indicates that the type has largely run its course by this time. Its period of life seems to reach a peak perhaps in the 4th century CE.

Geographical distribution also appears to be significant. So far clear parallels are known from sites clustered on the northwest and southwest shores of the Sea of Galilee, as far south as Tell er-Ras, as far west as Beth She'arim, and as far north as Meiron. Transjordanian use is also important. The absence of this jar type at Nazareth becomes all the more noticeable as that would be near the geographic center of this Cisjordanian area. In any event it appears that we are dealing with a largely northern and possibly Transjordanian form that reaches its period of greatest popularity in the 4th century CE.

Type 3, pl. 7.21:5–16, 28, fig. 7.10. These jars could be understood as variants of type 1 and 2. The first subtype 3.1 (nos. 5–9 and fig. 7.10) are characterized by rounded, everted rims and vertical to outflaring stance. Average outside diameter is ca. 9 cm, and average collar height is a bit less than 4.5 cm.

The second subtype, 3.2 (nos. 10–16, 28), on the other hand features a variety of rim treatments, but in general rims are more angular than rounded and about the same stance. Outside rim diameter occurs in two groups averaging ca. 8 cm (nos. 11–13, 15) and slightly more than 11 cm (nos. 10, 14, 16, 28). Neck height is not significantly disparate, averaging slightly more than about 4 cm for all these vessels.

It is surely not accidental that all sherds published of type 3 (except for two from Meiron) were found in SE II (including the cistern) the *miqveh* (T-17) or Tomb 29 east of the *miqveh*. Though at least two other (unpublished) sherds rather similar to these were found in NE I.19 and NE I.26 in 1972, the striking preponderance of sherds from the area around SE II calls for explanation. It is just possible that the irregularity of treatment of these rims is precisely what led the potter to sell them for commercial or other non-household use. That is, the householders may have as much preferred jars of a regular form then as they do today.

The two sherds from Meiron are from a post-250 CE context. Fully 80 percent of these jars stem from a Stratum IV context, however. Thus, to judge from our evidence alone, these jars must date to ca. 250–425 CE.

At Beth She'arim appears a jar rim similar to our type 3.1, pl. 7.21:5.[224] In this case the jar is restored about halfway to the base and reveals heavy ribbing and a reinforcing ring around the jar at the base of the handle. This pottery is from the cisterns (at the Zeid Farm) which Avigad dates to the 3d century and the first half of the 4th.

The same jar appears in Jerusalem in Hamilton's excavations against the North Wall near the Damascus Gate.[225] The jar rim in question is from sounding A against the north tower, from what Hamilton calls the "Late Roman-Byzantine" levels. Many sherds of this "late" type were found at 9.00 to 9.40 m below datum. Most of the coins found were above this level and mainly were dated after 513 CE. It is reasonable to assign this jar to the same or more likely an earlier period.[226]

Loffreda publishes a jar similar to our no. 9, from Capernaum.[227] It is described as light brown—almost pink ("carne"). Interestingly enough it is *slipped* white inside and out, according to Loffreda, and is well fired. The slip is a bit of a puzzle, but doubtless the general date is pre-5th-century CE.

Hamilton also publishes a sherd similar to our no. 11 of type 3.2 from his Jerusalem excavations.[228] This particular collared rim is from the lowest layer of Shaft B and occurs with clear Herodian vessels. That seems to place this jar in the 1st or early 2d century CE, in which case it may well be an ancestor of our form. It is ca. 11 cm in outside rim diameter with a 4 cm collar. This is a much larger collar than ours (compare diameter—ca. 7 cm) and that may be attributable to its early date.

Our same rim is found at Tell er-Ras on Mount Gerizim, the cisterns, and exhibits the same irregularity of rim treatment—more angular than rounded. All the pottery in these cisterns is dated by Bull to 250–350 CE.[229]

Pella produces two rims that are very similar to our pl. 7.21:12–14 or type 3.2.[230] The first is a rim as simple as our no. 12–10 cm as compared with 8 cm in diameter. It is also darker in section (10 YR 4/3) and is slipped "dark reddish gray" (5 R 4/1–2). It is of Umayyad date, which probably accounts for these differences. Nevertheless it enables us to see that our ribbed jar of this type survives a long time. The other Pella jar is quite similar to ours in ware and section profile, though it is between the two in diameter. It is 2.5 YR 5/4 in exterior color ("light reddish brown") and 2.5 YR 4/1 in section ("grayish reddish brown"). It is 6th century in date and therefore later than ours, but it is clearly in the same ceramic tradition.

224. Avigad, "Excavations," fig. 3:6.
225. Hamilton, "North Wall," fig. 6:6 and p. 10.
226. For a 6th-century rim not unlike this one, cf. Aharoni, *Ramat Rahel 1961–62*, fig. 34:7.
227. Loffreda, "La ceramica," fig. 4:9 and p. 77.
228. Hamilton, "North Wall," fig. 14:4.
229. Bull and Campbell, "Balatah (Shechem)," fig. 10:10–11, 15.
230. Smith, *Pella*, I, pls. 31:284 and 29:1201.

Fig. 7.10 illustrates the almost complete jar of type 3.1 from SE II.1.34, L.1017. Rim outside diameter ca. 9 cm, and the collar is the proverbial 4 cm in height. This vessel is ribbed on the shoulders and bottom, but is smooth on the slightly concave sides. The neck features a low drip ring. This clear 4th to early 5th century jar is parallel in rim treatment to a jar from the cistern at Beth She'arim.[231] The cistern jar is also ribbed on the shoulder and is ca. 30 cm in diameter just below the handle, almost exactly the diameter of ours. This yields a clear 3d to early 4th century example of this jar type in western Galilee.

Three recent examples from mixed fill at Samaria also feature ribbing on the shoulders (fig. 7:21), but the diameters are a bit disparate: ca. 9 cm, 11 cm, and 11.5 cm; also the last-mentioned has a slight added ring around the center of the collar.[232] Hennessy did not assay a date for these jars; but their presence high up in the fill argues for a late date, and certain vessels appear to be Late Roman to Early Byzantine (though Herodian and Middle Roman vessels are surely present).

Finally there is a clear example of this collar—though with rather exaggerated drip ring—from the mausoleum at the foot of Tell Rosh Ha-'Ayin (Ras el-'Ain) northeast of Tel-Aviv. The rim is 9 cm in diameter, and one can see the beginning of ribbing on the body below the collar.[233] Eitan dates this jar and the chronologically similar pottery found with it (the second group) to the last half of the 3d and first half of the 4th century CE.

From this comparative evidence one might conclude that this is easily the most widespread jar type found in Khirbet Shema'. Its date span is also quite wide, but there is a discernible peak in the 4th century between 250 and 400 CE. Presumably this marks its time of maximum manufacture and use.

Type 4, pl. 7.21:17–23, 32, and fig. 7.11 (complete Arab jar). These jar rims are all of a type generally, though no. 21 may be a jug. Their rim diameters are of two averages: ca. 8 cm (nos. 17, 20) and ca. 11 cm (nos. 18–19, 22–23, and fig. 7.11). Neck height is generally about 5 cm. Ware is fairly constant. Section color is 2.5 YR 7/4–6/1 ("light reddish brown" to "light grayish reddish brown"); exterior color is 2.5 YR 7/4 or "buff" to the casual eye. Clay is prepared with few, small, red and white grits, and the jars are medium fired, often with a gritty feel.

Only one of these jars could be reconstructed to reveal the complete form (fig. 7.11). In this case we are dealing with a surface find and therefore perhaps a medieval jar, but it is definitely in the same tradition. This jar has the straight collar with simple rims and thickening of the rim on the inside. The bag-shaped body is ribbed only from the bottom of the collar to the reinforcing ring below the high, rounded handles. Walls are smooth and without sudden changes in

231. Avigad, "Excavations," fig. 3:7.
232. Hennessy, "Excavations at Samaria-Sebaste, 1968," 1–21, figs. 7:21, 6:4, 6.

233. Eitan, "Excavations at the Foot of Tel Rosh Ha'ayin," 49–68, fig. 15:5, Eng. summary pp. 6*–7*.

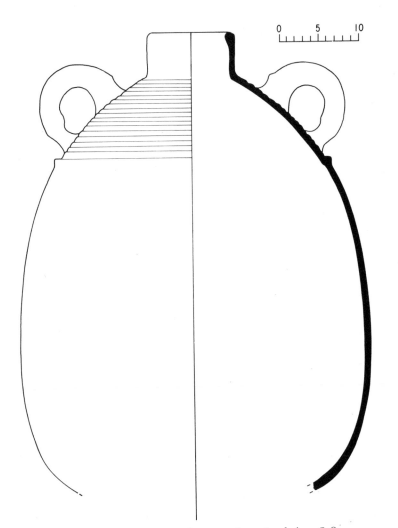

Figure 7.11. Drawing of a complete Arab jar, 2:9.

direction as they round off to the doubtless rounded base. Maximum outside diameter is 44 cm and estimated height about 60 cm.

The form of the complete Byzantine jar is well illustrated in the Ramat Rahel volumes.[234] These are large, bag-shaped jars with the greatest diameter near the concave base. For example in the Ramat Rahel vessels, maximum diameter occurs at 25 percent of height or 30 cm up on a 120-cm-high jar. Ratio of width to height averages very close to 9 : 10, and jars are commonly in excess of 1 m high. Our late jar from fig. 7.10 has a width to height ratio of about 7.5 : 10. These Byzantine jars are generally ribbed all over the body, though combed decoration exists.

These jar types occur in predominantly late contexts at Khirbet Shema',

234. Aharoni, *Ramat Rahel 1959–60*, fig. 4:5, 7; idem, *Ramat Rahel 1961–62*, figs. 8:11, 9:4–8, 24:1–8.

ranging from Stratum IV to early Stratum VI. The range is therefore 4th to 8th century, but their peak at our site is evidently in Stratum V, the 5th to 6th century.

Pella furnishes us with several 6th to 8th century examples of this jar type.[235] The Byzantine jar collar is 2.5 YR 6/8 in section ("moderate orange") and slipped 5 YR 4/1 ("brownish gray"). The Umayyad specimen is "neutral gray" in section, slipped 7.5 YR 5/2 ("light grayish brown") and then glazed 7.5 YR 6/4 ("light brown"). The glazing separates it from ours, as none of ours are glazed.

Likewise from Bethany we find at least one example of such a Byzantine jar,[236] and other examples are known from Ramat Rahel dated to the 6th century,[237] Mount Nebo, also of the 6th century,[238] and Emmaus, dated as late as 1150–1250 CE.[239]

These jars occur at many other sites, and their distribution and chronology is fairly well known. They are found north and south in the Holy Land and dated predominantly in the 6th century, though their descendents survive as late as the 12th, if Bagatti's forms from Emmaus are in fact later developments in the same ceramic tradition.

Pl. 7.21:24–25. These two cups are unique in our corpus and from the same locus of the same square. Though they are not from the same vessel, they are surely from the same vessel *type.* These are extremely thin walled (2 mm and 3 mm respectively), 8 cm in diameter, and of the same ware. The walls curve gently inward, and the cups probably had round bases.

These cups are in mixed loci within the synagogue, but they occurred only with Late Roman and Byzantine pottery, and their wares betray more affinity with Byzantine ceramics at Khirbet Shema' than with the Arab or medieval wares higher up in the fill. Therefore, the Stratum VII designation of the fill is misleading in their case.

Cups rather of this type are known from Dhiban in Transjordan from area V5.[240] These are of "fine metallic buff ware, overfired to dark gray[!] . . . burnished or polished on outside." This is labeled "Byzantine," but the parallel they adduce is from Khirbet Mefjer, of 8th-century date. An incurved cup of diameter 10.1 cm and estimated height 7.4 cm comes from Mount Nebo. Wall thickness appears to be about 3–3.5 mm. Schneider is unsure about the dating but points to the Khirbet Mefjer cups as a *terminus ante quem.*[241]

A cup from Bethany is of almost identical stance to ours, though ware resembles more closely that of Dhiban.[242] It is slightly more than 11 cm in diameter and ca. 9.5 cm high (complete) with walls perhaps 3 mm thick. Saller suggests no date for this form other than the general period 6th-8th century.

235. Smith, *Pella,* I, pls. 29:1262, 31:1141.
236. Saller, *Bethany,* fig. 39:7051 (see p. 206), fig. 41: 7312 (see p. 209), both dated "Late Byzantine."
237. See supra n. 204.
238. Schneider, *Mt. Nebo,* III, fig. 2:5.

239. Bagatti, *Emmaus,* fig. 24:4, 8.
240. Tushingham, *Dibon,* fig. 5:10, description p. 136.
241. Schneider, *Mt. Nebo,* III, fig. 13:14 (no. 503), description p. 116, discussion pp. 117f.
242. Saller, *Bethany,* fig. 53:5889 and p. 272.

More helpful in dating are perhaps the Bethany cups of same form and diameter ca. 8.5 cm, or sensibly closer to ours. These must be examples of the monk's eating utensils from the 6th-century monastery.

Thus it is likely that these cups are 6th-century at Khirbet Shema'. They are a popular form, but perhaps rare because considered a luxury item in ancient post-destruction Teqo'a.

14. JUGLETS AND MISCELLANEOUS CLOSED FORMS

Plate 7.22 brings together necks and bases of a variety of small juglets and other closed forms. Not all can be clearly paralleled from any Palestinian source, so only those vessels represented elsewhere will be discussed.

Pl. 7.22:1. This seems to be actually a small cup not unlike those drawn in pl. 7.21:24–25. The difference is that the walls of this vessel slope inward to about 4.0 cm below the rim, where the direction changes. Small balls of clay appear to have been smoothed onto the lip as a decorative element, but in no regular pattern. Rim diameter is slightly less than 9 cm, while the walls at their thickest are about 4 mm at the simple rim.

Provenance of this sherd is SE II.1, but from a locus that is unsealed at the top—and indeed from the first bucket in the first locus! Therefore it may be a stray sherd from the later strata, as in fact its decoration seems to suggest.

The only parallel of note is from Khirbet Mefjer.[243] This is an 8th-century cup of a hard, thin metallic ware (ware 10) without decoration. Since our only parallel is of the Arab period, it is even more probable that the cup from SE II is also of the Arab period.

Pl. 7.22:4. This rim and portion of a handle from a juglet is a well-known form in Early Roman contexts, though in this case it is from Stratum IV at Khirbet Shema'. Our example is of a light red, rather sandy ware that is well fired. This is Lapp's type 31.ID-E.[244] These juglets are therefore known from Qumran and Alayiq, though also from the Tyropoeon Valley.[245] Most recently these have been found at Heshbon, dated "Early Roman."[246]

Pl. 7.22:5. This juglet is rather similar to our no. 6 also, though no. 5 is from a much earlier context. That is, vessel no. 5 is from Stratum II.1b in Meiron square MI.2, early 3d century. It bears a resemblance to Hamilton's Herodian juglets from the excavations against the north wall of Jerusalem, but only somewhat so. There is also an affinity with the 6th-century Jerusalem juglets with nicked decoration known from Khirbet Kerak, among other places.[247]

Pl. 7.22:7–8. These two sherds are surely of the same general juglet type. Their most obvious characteristic is the sharply downturned rim, which gives the

243. Baramki, "Kh. el Mefjer," fig. 7:21.
244. Lapp, *Palestine Ceramic Chronology*, 163.
245. Ibid. Cf. also Crowfoot and Fitzgerald, *Tyropean Valley*, fig. 12:25.

246. Sauer, *Heshbon Pottery 1971*, sherd 24, p. 19, fig. 1.
247. Cf. Delougaz and Haines, *Khirbat al-Karak*, pl. 34:1–6; pl. 56:8–12.

effect of a down-hanging collar at the top of the neck. The earliest context for this sherd at Khirbet Shema' is Stratum IV, while no. 8 occurs in mixed fill with Stratum VII material. It is reasonable to suppose that it dates to Stratum IV at the earliest.

This juglet cannot be directly paralleled by material published from other Galilean sites. However, similar rims are known from juglets from Ramat Rahel that are clearly part of the 6th-century repertoire.[248] Yet this sherd, at least as represented in no. 7, is of Stratum IV or the early 5th century at the latest. Therefore, the juglets from Ramat Rahel must represent later developments of this vessel type.

Pl. 7.22:11–12. These two rims and partial neck of the same vessel type are slightly out-turned or everted at the sharply pointed (in section) triangular rim itself. No. 12 is from Stratum IV; no. 11 is from mixed fill. Ware is hard, with the clay prepared with some, small, white grits. Section color is 5 PB 3/1 ("bluish gray"), while the exterior color is 5 YR 4/1 ("brownish gray"). Exterior is self-slipped and smooth-wiped.

A rim rather similar to our no. 11 has been published from Bethany.[249] It is 5 cm in diameter compared to our 6 cm. More important is the actual form of the rim, which is considerably more sharply defined. Its general morphology would suggest that it is Early Roman in date, though Saller does not discuss this particular rim. These rims are also similar to those of pilgrim flasks, as is readily apparent from those illustrated from Bethany.[250] The two flasks in question exhibit an outside rim diameter of ca. 4.5 cm and Saller also assigned them an Early Roman date.

Thus it is difficult to conclude what vessel type these two rims represent, but at least the parallels from Bethany suggest an earlier date than our context. On the other hand, it is quite possible that our rims are indeed 4th-5th century and not earlier, but represent a later development of the earlier rim treatment.

Pl. 7.22:15. This very small juglet rim is intriguing in its execution, as it features a pinched, raised ring all around, marking the bottom of a kind of collar. The outside diameter of the ring is greater than that of the mouth, which is only slightly greater than 3 cm at its simple rim. Between rim and ring the collar is constricted to form a kind of continuous concavity.

This rim is from a clear Stratum IV context in NE I.26, though this square yielded much earlier material. It so happens, however, that the clearest morphological parallel is from Khirbet Mefjer, a vessel dated by Baramki to the 9th-10th century.[251] We must point out, however, that a similar collar, though wider at top than at rim, is known of probably Roman date at Bethany (see the discussion below of pl. 7.22:16–17).[252] In any case this rather odd-shaped rim and collar cannot be later than the early 5th century at our site.

248. Aharoni, *Ramat Rahel 1961–62,* fig. 7:25.
249. Saller, *Bethany,* fig. 58:4643.
250. Ibid. fig. 45:4–5.

251. Baramki, "Kh. el Mefjer," fig. 4:2.
252. Saller, *Bethany,* fig. 58:4996 and p. 309.

Pl. 7.22:16–17. These two juglet rims are generally similar in form to the preceding rim in that they too have the pinched, raised ring around the bottom of the collar. However, these two are only ca. 2 cm in diameter. The generally outflaring body of no. 16 suggests that the body is globular, though whether it has a flat base or round base must remain conjectural.

It has already been mentioned above that the closest parallel to these two juglets is from Bethany.[253] The Bethany example, however, has twice the rim diameter of our juglets. Otherwise it is morphologically identical, even to handle attachment at the raised ring. Saller describes the ware as "rather thick red ware with tiny white grits and with a yellow slip over the exterior." This description probably places the juglet in the Late Roman period. Our two juglets are clearly Stratum IV at the latest, though no. 17 from the north chamber of Tomb 29 could reflect the 2d–3d century use of that tomb.

Pl. 7.22:20. This is a rather unique top to a juglet from a Stratum IV context at Khirbet Shemaʻ. Its walls are rather thick for its diameter—walls of 6 mm as compared with an outside rim diameter of slightly more than 3 cm (compare wall thickness of 4 mm and diameter of 4 cm for no. 13). Its distinctly cup-shaped top is reminiscent of globular juglets of Early Roman date of Lapp's type 31.[254] However, its incised decoration, thick walls, and ware betray a later date.

Unfortunately the only morphological parallel to date is medieval, a jug of outside rim diameter 5.5 cm from Emmaus.[255] Nevertheless, the parallel is instructive, for it allows us to see the survival or, more likely, the renascence of this rim type on a related closed form.

Pl. 7.22:28. This Stratum VI juglet is distinguished by its "white ware," incised and barbotine decoration, and thin walls. It is evidently the top of a small jug that doubtless had a handle. Its outside rim diameter is ca. 6 cm, while the walls are a thin 3–3.5 mm.

Such juglets or jugs are not unknown in Palestine, and Khirbet Mefjer has at least one example in "soft gray ware with incised and barbotine decoration."[256] The juglet in question has an outside rim diameter of 8.5–9.0 cm. Baramki identifies this vessel as a sample of "ware 2," which he describes as "thick, yellowish, creamy" and dates to the 12th and 13th centuries. Though the date is too late in comparison to ours, its form is similar.

Perhaps a parallel closer in time to ours is that found on the terrace at Beth Shean.[257] Of course it is in mixed Byzantine and Arab material, but surely it is not as late as the Khirbet Mefjer example, if the latter is correctly dated.

This general rim type is known as white ware from Samarra.[258] These are all undecorated juglets with one handle, tall necks, and double-carinated, cylindrical bodies. Sarre describes the ware as "thin, yellowish-white clay," or

253. Ibid.
254. See supra n. 245.
255. Bagatti, *Emmaus*, fig. 28:13.
256. Baramki, "Kh. el Mefjer," fig. 15:13.
257. Fitzgerald, *Beth-Shan*, III, pl. 30:2.
258. Sarre, *Keramik von Samarra*, fig. 7, and p. 5.

essentially the same as our "white ware." The valuable characteristic of the Samarra pottery, of course, is that it represents a 9th-century corpus, though more of palace wares than peasant wares. That is, the Samarra pottery overlaps with our Stratum VI pottery in the first part of the 9th century.

Pl. 7.22:30. This heavy, thick-walled stump juglet base is from the *miqveh* (T-17). The less than 3-cm-diameter flat base first rises vertically and then enlarges to a globular body. The base is quite similar to bases of juglets with nicked decoration from Khirbet Kerak,[259] among other places. These also are very close to 3 cm in diameter at the bottom, though the body is rounder than our vessel. Wall thickness of our juglet (or pitcher) is 6–8 mm, which is significantly thicker than the 5-mm walls of the juglets and pitchers from Khirbet Kerak.

The Khirbet Kerak parallels are closely datable to the mid to late 6th century on the basis of associated coin evidence. Thus our base would be about 100 years earlier, but in the same general pottery tradition.

Pl. 7.22:43–45, 50–52. These bases, presumably of jugs or pitchers, are approximately all of a kind. They are thin-walled (3–4 mm), with rounded (no. 43), concave (nos. 44–45), or flat bases (nos. 50–52). More importantly they are all examples of our "white ware" from Stratum IV (no. 50), Stratum VI (no. 51), and Stratum VII (no. 43). That is, since no. 43 occurs in mixed fill of which the latest pottery is Stratum VII, we have a possible range from the late 5th to the mid-9th century CE.

One base of this general sort also of white ware is known from Samarra. If it has a concave base (the drawing does not indicate a section) it most closely resembles our no. 45. If on the other hand, it has a flat base, then it most closely resembles our no. 52.[260] It is 9th-century in date.

Later (?) examples of the same general vessel type as at Samarra come from Khirbet Mefjer. The vessels in question are generally one-handled, long-necked jugs. The examples at Khirbet Mefjer are of "ware 21," described by Baramki as generally of "gritty buff" paste and dated by him to the 12th or 13th centuries.[261] But this date may be called into question both by his own stratigraphic evidence ("under the burn layer") and by the parallels from Samarra.

Ware of these pots is generally the same. Section and exterior color is 5 YR 7/3 ("grayish yellowish pink").

15. RED WARES (Pl. 7.23:1–25)

These forms vary somewhat in color, ware, and form, but are all in the tradition of the eastern red wares that range in color from red to orange to brown or purplish brown. Clay is finely levigated or elutriated.[262] The surface

---

259. Delougaz and Haines, *Khirbat al-Karak,* pl. 56:8–12, 34:1–6.

260. Sarre, *Keramik von Samarra,* fig. 7:1.

261. Baramki, "Kh. el Mefjer," figs. 15:19–20, 14:7, 9(= our pl. 7.22:52).

262. For a description of this process of preparing fine

appears polished because of self-slipping in fine clays, or simply because it was indeed polished. But it is self-slip, i.e., the slip is of clays identical to that of the body of the vessel. Thus we are not dealing technically with signed or stamped white-clay wares with fine red or brown slip but with later developments in the same tradition.[263]

Though there is a certain amount of small variation in clay preparation and firing of the vessels, they tend to be distinctly uniform in color, grit size and distribution, and firing. Section color averages 5 YR 5/5 ("light brown"), though there is a range from 2.5 YR 4/8 to 10 YR 5/1. Exterior color varies much less, ranging from 2.5 YR 6/8 to 7.5 YR 7/4 in our examples, for an average exterior color of 5 YR 7/6 ("moderate yellowish pink"). This latter color can be popularly described as rather "light orange."

The clay is generally prepared with a few, small, white grits, though a significant minority use medium grit. Surprisingly enough these plates are generally medium fired at Khirbet Shema‘. Usually we assume that terra sigillata is hard fired. This slight difference in manufacture may point to a local rather than exotic origin.

Pl. 7.23:1. This is a shallow bowl of outside rim diameter ca. 28 cm. It is of orange ware with repeated, incised decoration on the exterior below the rim. The decoration is rather irregularly worked, i.e., not rouletted or otherwise mechanically produced. It stems from the cistern, a clear Stratum IV context at Khirbet Shema‘.

Parallels to this vessel are fairly easy to find. First our bowl resembles Hayes' "form 45" of African red slip ware, of which one example is from es-Zib (Roman Ecdippa, north of Akko) and perhaps more closely "form 59" of the same ware, which has no Palestinian examples.[264] Hayes dates the former to 230/40–320 CE and the latter (type A) to 320–380/400 CE. Both sets of dates match our context well.

A bowl with similar decoration but with slightly different rim is known from cistern 51 at Nazareth. Unfortunately this find spot does nothing to fix its date.[265]

A rim of essentially the same type, though decorated with grooves all around, is published in the Capernaum preliminary report.[266] Its radius is not given, though Loffreda describes it as a "quite large bowl" of bright red ware. It was fortunately found beneath the Byzantine mosaic of the Octagon, which must place it in the 5th century at the latest.

Again the same general form is known at Chorazin, in this case with half-herringbone nicks outside below and upon the out-turned rim, also done by hand.[267] Outside rim diameter is slightly more than 23 cm. The vessel is glazed

clays see Hodges, *Artifacts*, 20.

263. Cf. Hayes, *Late Roman Pottery*, 2–12, for an account of this ceramic tradition in the various regions of the Roman Empire.

264. Ibid. fig. 11:9, p. 63, and fig. 15:1, p. 98.

265. Bagatti, *Nazareth*, fig. 227.14. For discussion of context see pp. 70–72.

266. Loffreda, "La ceramica," fig. 3:13 (1673, labeled "1671" on figure by error).

267. Yeivin, "Khorazin," fig. 8:3 and p. 151.

red on the inside and on the rim. Ware is "sifted clay, well fired." No date is given by Yeivin for this piece, but its find spot inside the *miqveh* implies a date before the 7th century.

Other examples of this form are known from Jerusalem[268] and Bethany.[269] That is, this is a well-attested bowl in the Palestinian terra sigillata corpus. However the date span is not well known, though it may be generally inferred from the examples above to be from the 4th to perhaps the 6th century CE. The Khirbet Shema' form would therefore date early in this range.

Pl. 7.23:2–4. These three rims are generally all of a type. A molding appears below the rim proper, giving the likeness of a "collar" all around. None of our examples are decorated, and none could be reconstructed to the base, but doubtless they were provided with some type of footed or ring base such as is illustrated in nos. 12–25. Diameter ranges from ca. 21 to 26 cm for an average of slightly less than 24 cm.

Two of these bowls are from Stratum V, 419–600 CE. No. 3 comes from mixed fill of Stratum VII date at the latest. But these rims probably date to an earlier period. Such bowls are well represented in the Palestinian Late Roman to Byzantine period. First, one may note that this is essentially Hayes' "form 3C" of his "'Late Roman C' ware," which includes in this case an example from Silet edh-Dhar, north of Samaria. This particular Palestinian bowl has a ring base rather like our no. 15 and is 25 cm in diameter. Hayes dates this form entirely to the late 5th century, specifically 450–490 CE, somewhat early within the date range of our Stratum V.[270]

Capernaum has yielded two rims of this type.[271] They are illustrated by Loffreda but not discussed. However, their general context would suggest a Late Roman to Byzantine date.

From Nazareth come four published examples of this rim type, though with rouletted decoration in the "collar."[272] They are of outside rim diameter ca. 21, 22, 24, 27 cm, for an average of 23.5 cm. Bagatti dates these examples to the 3rd–4th century by analogy with certain pieces from the cisterns at Beth She'arim.[273]

A color photograph of a section of such a rim of diameter 18 cm is reproduced in the Pella publication.[274] The sherd comes from the West Church Complex, Area I E, Level 37, the Byzantine stratum. Interestingly enough, this level yielded two coins of the 4th century and one of the 7th, probably of Constans II (641–668 CE). Smith is of the opinion that the latter coin is intrusive.[275] Whatever the stratigraphic origin of the coin, it appears from plan 3 that level 37 belongs to the Umayyid-Abbassid stratum, which can only mean that we are

268. Hamilton, "North Wall," fig. 8:5.
269. Saller, *Bethany*, fig. 49:4039 (red glaze from grave "d" of tomb 71) and fig. 49:3081 (light brown surface).
270. Hayes, *Late Roman Pottery*, fig. 67:7 and p. 333.
271. Loffreda, "La ceramica," fig. 3:5.

272. Bagatti, *Nazareth*, fig. 227:9.
273. Ibid. 294, n. 3 = Avigad, "Excavations," 210, fig. 3:16–19, none of which appear at Khirbet Shema'.
274. Smith, *Pella*, I, pl. 90B:1225.
275. Ibid. 157.

dealing with washed and blown-in accumulation after the Byzantine occupation. The sherd is therefore "free-floating" chronologically, but it is improbable that it should be post-Constans II.

Another more closely dated example was found at the House of Kyrios Leontis at Beth Shean. Tsori dates this "red ware" rim, which has a diameter of nearly 30 cm, to the 3rd–4th century,[276] which corresponds to his Stratum VI.

An example of this rim type with rouletting is known from Bethany but is not dated.[277] Similar rims are known at Dhiban[278] and at Khirbet Kerak,[279] where they must date to the 6th century at the latest.

The cumulative parallel evidence, therefore, suggests a date span for this bowl in Palestine from the 4th to the 6th century, though early 7th century manufacture and use are not impossible. No particular geographical pattern is evident from this same evidence, however; the implication is that manufacturing centers were widely scattered.

Pl. 7.23:5. This is a bowl of rim diameter about 24.5 cm. The rim of this vessel also resembles a "collar," though without the concavity of the form in nos. 2–4. It was only found in SE.II at Khirbet Shema', though near the surface of square 1. The body is decorated with shallow diagonal nicks done by hand with a blunt tool. These nicks average 3–4 mm long × 1 mm and are too irregular to have been rouletted or even cut from a pattern.

Section color was the most yellow of all the terra sigillata vessels, at 10 YR 5/1 ("brownish gray"). Exterior color was a slightly redder and more chromatic, 7.5 YR 6/4 ("light brown"). Clay shows few, small, white grits, and it is medium fired.

Of all Hayes' forms, this rim most closely resembles his "form 99C" of African red slip ware.[280] Hayes adduces one example of this bowl from Nesaana (pl. 48, shape 11) of diameter 19.0 cm.[281] He dates the form to ca. 560/580–620 CE, a century later than our Stratum IV.

A 4th–5th-century example of the same type, of smaller diameter (19 cm), is published from et-Tabgha.[282] The bottom edge of its molded rim is more sharply defined than ours.

A faintly similar rim with footed base is known from Bethany, though of diameter a surprisingly large 30 cm.[283] It is of light brown ware covered with a red slip. Saller does not attempt to date this bowl, though a Byzantine date seems reasonable. It is only distantly morphologically related to ours.

From the synagogue excavations at Ma'on (094083) comes a small corpus

276. Tsori, "House of Kyrios Leontis," fig. 6:5.
277. Saller, *Bethany*, fig. 49:3330. Bagatti publishes what may be one of these rims from Beitin in his article "'Terre Sigillate' in Palestina," 70–75, fig. XVI:5.
278. Tushingham, *Dibon*, fig. 11:1–10.
279. Delougaz and Haines, *Khirbat al-Karak*, pl. 52:11 (a surface find); pl. 52:10–13, all of "'Late Roman' Red Ware."
280. Hayes, *Late Roman Pottery*, fig. 28:22 and p. 155.

281. With reference to diameter it is important to note that Hayes' examples range from 18.0–19.2 cm averaging just over 18.5 cm. This is significant because of the narrow range of diameters and because it is 7 cm smaller than ours. Thus, the resemblance may be circumstantial, particularly in view of the 6th-century date for Hayes' form.
282. Loffreda, *et-Tabgha*, fig. 56:250 = fig. 57:1, p. 149.
283. Saller, *Bethany*, fig. 49:5355, p. 259.

of 6th-century pottery including a "rim of bowl, pseudo–*terra sigillata*, with incised decoration."[284] The bowl is reconstructed with a ca. 24.5-cm diameter and features the same decoration as our no. 5 just below the rim, but tilted 90° from that on no. 5. This particular sherd was found among the debris in the apse. Five coins of Justin I (518–527 CE) were also found there and seem to be clearly related to the use of the building.[285] It is therefore reasonable to assume that this bowl is no earlier than the early 6th century.

Though the Ma'on sherd provides the closest morphological parallel to our bowl, its date seems too late. On the other hand the material from Capernaum and et-Tabgha seems to corroborate more closely our date.

Pl. 7.23:6–11, 24, 25. These eight vessels are all similar in their simple rim treatment. Generally there is a thickening of the rim, though not always. Only two of the complete forms could be reconstructed on paper, namely, nos. 24 and 25. A low ring base is characteristic of all the completed forms, as witness nos. 12–23. Average diameter is slightly less than 30 cm, ranging from 23 to 29.5 cm. Exterior color averages 5 YR 7/8 ("moderate orange") and section color 5 YR 6/6 ("light brown"). Clay is prepared with some, small, white grits and is medium fired.

These bowls are not found as such in Hayes' corpus of Late Roman sigillata forms. Nevertheless examples not unlike these are known at Nazareth (rather like no. 7 here), Capernaum (similar to no. 9), and Chorazin (most comparable also to no. 9).[286] According to their contexts, these parallels would date to the 3d to 5th century CE.

The two bowls on pl. 7.23 that are completed to the base (nos. 24 and 25) can also be roughly paralleled at these same sites, though now Khirbet Kerak replaces Capernaum. In this case the sherds represented must date from the 4th to the 6th century.[287]

The most striking datum from our parallels is that all are from the Galilee area. It is quite possible that these specific terra sigillata bowls are from some ceramic center in Galilee and sold only in a restricted market from Nazareth eastward to the western shores of the Sea of Galilee and perhaps beyond. It will be most instructive to see where else these vessels will be found in future excavations.

16. AMPHORISKOI (Pl. 7.23:26–27)

One intact amphoriskos and several sherds were unearthed at Khirbet Shema', almost all in SE II, which is of itself very significant. The one intact

284. Levy, "Excavation Report," pp. 6–13, fig. 5:10.
285. Rahmani, "Small Finds and Coins," p. 18.
286. Bagatti, *Nazareth*, fig. 227:6; Loffreda, "La ceramica," fig. 3:3; Yeivin, "Khorazin," fig. 8:7 (though with external incised decoration).

287. Bagatti, *Nazareth*, fig. 227:7; Delougaz and Haines, *Khirbat al-Karak*, pl. 52:59 (of "hard granular brownish red" ware); Yeivin, "Khorazin," fig. 8:12 (but of a low base with interior rouletting).

example is ca. 27.5 cm tall and just under 9 cm in diameter in the middle. It is equipped with one loop handle. This particular amphoriskos is not perfectly symmetrical, but is otherwise rather uniformly thrown in respect of wall thickness, which is quite close to 5 mm. The base is a narrow 2.5 cm in outside diameter, whereas that of pl. 7.23:27 is a slightly greater 3.5 cm.

Ware of these two published examples is quite constant. Section color is 5 YR 5/6 ("light brown") with exterior color 7.5 YR 7/4 ("light yellowish brown"). They are not slipped; color difference is due to the firing. Clay is prepared with a few, small, white grits and is medium fired.

We have already mentioned the provenance, SE II. To be specific, this pot was found lying upon floor 1017 adjacent to wall 1007 (see p. 109 and photo 4.5). The other base fragment of another amphoriskos was found in SE II. 22, or inside "cistern" 22006, in its fill. This gives us a clear end of Stratum IV context for both pieces.

Such a base as our pl. 7.23:27 is published from Nazareth and termed a "bottle" by Bagatti. It was found in cistern 51, which was not reported by its strata.[288]

Another pair of fragments is reported from Beth She'arim, catacomb 13, halls 2 and 8. The top half with single handle is brown, but the bottom is reported to be of yellowish gray ware, which implies that the fragments are from two vessels, as do their find spots. Avigad does not hazard a guess as to date but refers to tomb 157 at Gezer, which contains Byzantine ceramics.[289]

A possible amphoriskos stems from Bethany. The base in question is 3–3.5 cm in diameter, with the typical concave base. It is classed with "Late Byzantine and Early Arabic" pieces.[290]

This is evidently a fairly rare piece in Palestine, as the lack of parallels suggests. It may be only associated with oil commerce, which would account for its absence from so many sites. In any case its appearance at Khirbet Shema' is clearly 4th to early 5th century in an industrial-commercial area.

17. LARGE STORAGE VESSELS AND BASINS

Among the characteristic sherds endemic to our site were certain thick, rather poorly formed pieces of quite large jars and basins. The jar rims, illustrated in pl. 7.24:1–13, are of a fairly uniform section color, averaging 5 YR 5/3 ("light grayish reddish brown"). Similarly, exterior is slightly lighter and slightly more chromatic, averaging 5 YR 6/4 ("light brown"). Clay was prepared in one of two ways: either with some, medium and/or large grits or with many, small *and* large inclusions. Evidently the potters used almost any grit on

288. Bagatti, *Nazareth*, fig. 220:4 and p. 279. Cistern 51 is discussed on pp. 70ff.

289. Avigad, *Beth She'arim*, III fig. 94:12A and 12B and p. 147. See also Macalister, *Gezer I–III*, pl. 109:1.

290. Saller, *Bethany*, fig. 62:412, p. 311.

hand to reduce the plasticity of the clay, as these bits may be black, white, gray, or red. All are medium fired. There is some evidence that clay preparation correlates with point of manufacture, for the vessels from the early strata at Meiron appear uniformly to include the many, small *and* large grits mentioned above. It will perhaps be interesting and worthwhile to investigate more thoroughly the manufacturing technique of these vessels, but that is beyond the scope of the present volume.

Outside rim diameters reveal two groups: pl. 7.23:5–7, 13, average just under 16 cm, while the other jar rims average just over 22 cm. Likewise wall thickness for nos. 5–7 and 13 averages just over 14 mm, while the others feature walls ca. 16 mm thick.

The rims of these large jars are so diverse as to suggest local, perhaps home, manufacture. In other words, they were likely made by the householder at home of local materials. Their large size necessitated thick walls, but their medium firing makes it improbable that they ever stood alone. Rather more likely, when in use they were partially buried in the ground.

These vessels stem from an early context at Meiron, but predominate at Khirbet Shema‘ in Stratum IV. We also have a significant number from Stratum VI, the occupation of the Arab period. It is impossible to predict the stratum from rim treatment or clay preparation alone as yet, however. In any case, the manufacture and use of these vessels spans the 2d to perhaps as late as the mid-10th century at our sites.

Such vessels are well known at Capernaum, and Fr. Corbo reports that he finds them in predominantly 4th and early 5th century contexts.[291] Meanwhile Loffreda has not published any in his preliminary report.[292] Otherwise it is difficult to discover any published examples of such jars. It may be that other excavators have yet to publish their own. Until they do, it will be difficult if not impossible to hypothesize about origins of the form, extent of manufacture and use, or specific function.

Pl. 7.24:14–21 and fig. 7.12. The drawings illustrate some of the main types of large basins found at Khirbet Shema‘. These generally have flattened simple rims with thick bodies. No. 17 features a band of appliqué decoration about 13 mm below the rim. Doubtless all had thickened, flat bases as illustrated in no. 15 and fig. 7.12.

Two of these vessels are peculiar in the stance of the rim, which slopes *inward* (nos. 18–19). Furthermore no. 18 originally was supplied perhaps with two handles about 4 cm below the rim. Unfortunately they (it?) broke off long ago and their form can no longer be reconstructed, though presumably in fig. 7.12 we are looking at the upper attachment of a vertical handle. This is the only form in pl. 7.24 that exhibits a handle.

291. Oral communication from F. Corbo.

292. For "ceramica grossa" see Loffreda, "La ceramica," pp. 93–95.

We can divide these vessels typologically into three groups: Group 1 is illustrated in nos. 14, 17, and 21 and fig. 7.12. The type is of flat base and rounded sides sloping upward to a flattened rim. Outside rim diameter ranges ca. 34–48 cm, with an average of ca. 41 cm. The wall averages 14.5 mm thick. *Group 2* is illustrated in nos. 16–20 and features a rounded body sloping upward to a rounded rim with a slight external lip. The rim is in vertical stance. These vessels range in diameter from about 24.5 cm to slightly over 41 cm, with an average of nearly 33 cm. *Group 3* is made up only of two basins, nos. 18 and 19, with sides sloping inward to a simple or flattened rim. No. 18 is almost a jar, with the suggestion of a neck, while no. 19 is reminiscent of the hole-mouth jars of much earlier periods, though it is not a true hole-mouth.

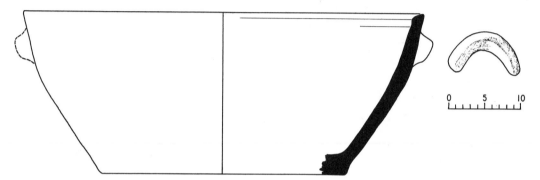

Figure 7.12. Drawing of a flat basin, 1:5.

Section color is fairly constant, around 2.5 YR 5/3 ("light grayish reddish brown"), though occasionally the vessels are fired with a much darker core averaging 5 PB 3/1 ("dark bluish gray"). Exterior color averages 5 YR 6/4–7/4 ("light brown" to "moderate yellowish pink"). Clay has been prepared predominantly with some, medium, white grits, though many variations occur.

These vessels occur almost wholly in our Stratum VI, the Arab occupation. One basin, no. 17, stems from a Stratum VII context but is unique in that stratum and therefore likely earlier. Likewise no. 19 from the south chamber of Tomb 29 is probably washed in, since it was found high in the fill, L.29009.

Thus, these basins are probably datable to a century and a half between 700 and 850 CE at our site. Furthermore the vast majority were found in NW VII.7,8, and 13, three squares north of the synagogue. In fact, the North Building was almost wholly contained in NW VII.8, while NW VII.7 contained mainly about 2 m of debris above the street at the north entryway of the synagogue. Thus these vessels are extremely localized and shed much light on the type of occupation of our site in Stratum VI. It may be that they are associated with an industrial rather than a domestic installation in these squares.

Some good typological parallels to one of our basins in particular come from

Khirbet Mefjer.[293] These resemble our pl. 7.24:17 even to the decoration. They exhibit the same sides, sloping outward to a flattened rim. Diameters are 18.5 and 27 cm, as compared with our larger ca. 34.5 cm outside rim diameter. However, Baramki dates these to the 12th–13th century. From Capernaum also come similar basins of several sizes, but of entirely different rim treatment. Loffreda does not date these basins, but presumably they are before ca. 450 CE.[294]

Therefore, though the evidence is slim, it appears that such basins are known in the Arab period. It is possible that so simple a form endures to the 12th–13th century, as Baramki's analysis seems to suggest, but we must move here with caution, applying Day's *caveat* about the dates of the Khirbet Mefjer forms.[295]

18. CONCLUSIONS

It is possible to deduce a certain amount of information about the extent of use of some of the pottery forms discussed in this chapter because of the discussion of parallels from other sites. Of course, the hypotheses we bring forward must remain provisional for the moment; our discussion has not attempted to be so much exhaustive as representative. Nevertheless certain tentative geographical patterns do emerge and should not go unnoticed.

First, one must point out here in one place the forms that seem to be uniquely northern or Galilean. These are "Galilean bowls," bowls with everted lip (pls. 7.10:20–29; 7.11; 7.12:1–27), globular cooking pots with necks of our type 3 (pls. 7.15:15–16, 20–23, 7.16:1, 3, 7–23), basins with folded rim (pl. 7.17:15–20), jars of our type 1 (pls. 7.20:5, 16, 33–51; 7.21:1–4) and the terra sigillata bowls in pl. 7.23:6–11, 24–25. That is, there is some evidence that at least six of our ceramic types may be of Galilean or at least north Palestinian provenance. This is an important inference, because, just as some forms may be unique to the north, one might expect to find in the south certain forms unique to the south. Indeed, Late Roman and Byzantine pottery may be as clearly divided between northern and southern Palestinian forms as are the Early and Middle Bronze ceramics, to name only two periods. There may even be more regional varieties that we do not yet recognize as such. Until a more or less complete corpus of Roman and Byzantine ceramics is published, however, the existence of separate lines of development in the north and the south must remain no more than a hypothesis, at best a theory.

One might note other possible patterns, particularly with the later forms. For example, parallels to our cooking bowls with horizontal handles (pls.

293. Baramki, "Kh. el Mefjer," fig. 12:1, 3, of "ware 19," dated by Baramki to the 12th–13th century.

294. See Loffreda, "Synagogue," pp. 37–42.
295. See supra n. 182.

7.12:28–29, 7.13:1–10) seem to be well represented in the Jordan rift, in the Jerusalem area, and in Transjordan but absent or rare elsewhere. This observation bears further investigation. Furthermore, the plain green glazes also seem to be best represented in the Jordan Valley and Jerusalem, whereas the graffiato green glazes spread westward to the coast.

On the other hand, one is struck by the number of forms that find parallels as far south and east as Dhiban in Transjordan and as far south as Jerusalem in Cisjordan. It is clear that the residents of Khirbet Shema' had access through trade to ceramic forms found all across Palestina Prima and Secunda, though these are not the dominant forms represented at the site. That is, from the ceramic evidence alone it appears first of all that Khirbet Shema' belongs in a regional trade network which is the main strand in its cultural contact. But secondly, it must be said that Khirbet Shema' clearly participated in wider trade—and presumably cultural—contact.

CHAPTER 8. THE ARTIFACTS

In plates 8.1 to 8.11 appears a selection of artifacts from Khirbet Shema'. We only publish material from our major loci (but even then not everything) or objects of intrinsic interest, even if surface finds.

By far the most frequently found artifactual material was glass (52 percent of all registered artifacts, i.e., 2154 items other than coins). This was a bit of a surprise, for we had hypothesized that the site was that of a fairly poor, isolated village and that glass would be more characteristic of city life, as in Tiberias. Nevertheless, as one can see from fig. 8.1, the amount of glass found is not out of line with what one might predict in proportion to the other materials represented.

In fact, from the normal plot by material in fig. 8.1 the reader can see that by and large two groups of artifacts are represented. Group 1, the most frequently appearing material, consists of objects of glass, iron, and ceramic. "Ceramic" is probably underrepresented because many lamp fragments would be processed as "pottery" rather than as "artifact." Group 2, which consists of material that occurs with less than 5 percent frequency, is made up of basalt, bronze, bone, chert, copper, brass/wood (both appearing at the 0.08 percent level) and lead/silver (at 0.04 percent). There is less basalt than one might predict from the other frequencies, but basalt is also a useful material that would be "mined" from an ancient site by later visitors.

We will rely on this normal plot of fig. 8.1 to indicate the relative grouping of artifact materials, but not for important conclusions about the type of occupation of the site. This plot will be a useful tool in comparing statistical profiles of other Galilean sites to Khirbet Shema' in the future.

1. IRON (PLS. 8.1:17–27; 8.2:1–9, 11, 13–14, 8.3:2–5, 7–21, and Photo 8.1)

The iron objects were almost all in poor condition because of the severe winters in Upper Galilee. The arrowheads, or more properly boltheads, in pl. 8.1:17–24 are medieval. The other iron objects are such as are commonly found at Byzantine sites everywhere, e.g., Beth She'arim, Khirbet Kerak, and Bethany.[1] The coffin rings in Tomb 29, two of them from the same coffin in the north chamber, are interesting. The iron nails are self-explanatory. From fig. 8.2 one can see that NW I.31 and NE I.31 were highest in relative frequency of iron artifacts.

---

1. See the parallels cited in the keys to the plates.

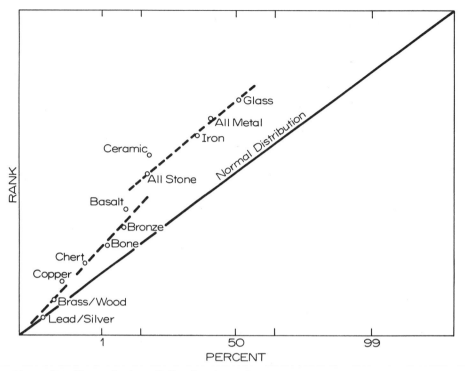

Figure 8.1. Normal plot of distribution of artifact materials.

2. BRONZE (PLS. 8.1:1–16, 8.2:10, 12, 8.3:1,6, and Photo 8.2)

Bronze objects account for only 2.6 percent of all our registered objects and are thus rarer than one might expect. Cosmetic tools or kohl sticks (and one kohl spoon) were well represented, though not in the tombs. Other jewelry or decorations in bronze are well known in the Byzantine period and are found at our site in Strata IV–V. For example, the rings in pl. 8.1:11–14 are quite similar to those known at Bethany, though we could have cited other publications for parallels.

The ring illustrated in pl. 8.1:14 and photo 8.2 is clearly engraved with a twice repeated design, but we can make no real sense of it. It cannot be read successfully either as paleo-Hebrew or as Cufic. In the meantime we might take it to be two animals grazing, but really it remains an unresolved enigma.[2]

The bronze ball (pl. 8.1:15) probably decorated a wooden door.

The bronze ring (pl. 8.3:6) may have been sewn to clothing; compare the iron rings of similar diameter from Tomb 29 (pl. 8.3:2).

2. The authors wish to thank Frank M. Cross, Jr., of Harvard University, D. N. Freedman of the University of Michigan, and M. L. Bates, Associate Curator of Islamic Coins at the American Numismatic Society for their assistance in attempts to read the ring. Richard Hanson is of the opinion that "the design is a stylized version of two palm branches. That motif is popular in the area and would be appropriate to a ring for personal use. Indeed, some of the examples on Herodian coins are not too far from this execution."

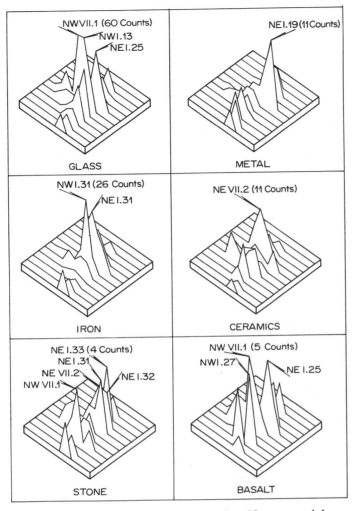

Figure 8.2. Relative distribution of artifact materials at Khirbet Shema'.

3. GLASS (PLS. 8.4, 8.5, 8.6, and 8.7, 8.8:1–16, 8.11:13–22, 24–25)

Our earliest glass is that illustrated in pl. 8.4:1–9. This is Late Hellenistic glass, ground and polished on the outside, often with a horizontal groove or grooves cut on the inside. This glass is best represented in Palestine at Tel Anafa, though it is known as far south as at Nessana in the Negev.

This is the main type of artifact we have to go with our Hasmonean coins. That is, we have no *pottery* (except for the lamp in pl. 8.10:4) and we publish here *all* fragments of these bowls. In other words, these glass sherds represent less than 1 percent of all glass recovered, a fact which should indicate its relative rarity at Khirbet Shema'.

Fig. 8.2 shows that the counts for glass fragments are exceptionally high

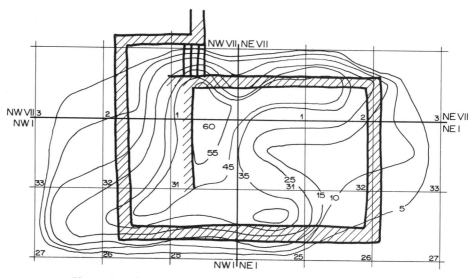

Figure 8.3. Contour density plot of glass fragments in the synagogue and environs.

in NW VII.1, NW I.31, and NE I.25. If we translate this information into a contour density plot for the eighteen squares around the synagogue we get a drawing like fig. 8.3. In this case the contours were located by means of an ordinary desk calculator routine *before* the outlines of the synagogue were superimposed. It is strikingly evident that one of the highest concentrations of glass occurs within the northeast corner of the worship area of the synagogue, i.e., east of the inside wall and inside the north wall.

Such a high concentration demands explanation. Examination of the data reveals that almost 30 percent of the glass recorded from square NW VII.1 was actually found outside the synagogue, north of the synagogue wall. But even if the count is 45 and not 60 in the extreme northwest corner, it is still 55 in the next square south, NW I.31, which lies wholly within the synagogue. Thus, we still must account for such a high peak.

Clearly this glass stems either from the putative women's gallery or from the Frescoed Room, which otherwise lies one square west in NW I.32. The likely explanation is that some of this glass was stored in the Frescoed Room at its last destruction, but the rest may have washed down from the gallery area. Since the winter rains have washed eastward from NW I.32, and since it is unlikely that the sherds washed across the Western Wall, it seems most probable that at least some of these sherds represent remains of vessels stored in the Frescoed Room during the use of Synagogue II.

On the other hand, there is a simple explanation for the glass peak in NE I.25, which localizes atop the *bema* in the drawing. Actually, about 20 percent of this glass is from outside the synagogue in the house built against the south wall. Thus this is a false peak.

The date range for our glass is largely 4th to early 5th century CE, Stratum IV. There is a small amount of earlier glass (Hellenistic, already mentioned, and Early Roman) and another sprinkling of 6th century CE forms. In the main, though, our glass chronology follows Stratum IV both in our own stratification and in cross-dating from other sites.

4. CERAMIC (PLS. 8.8:19, 29, 32, 8.9, 8.10, 8.11:1–12, 30–32)

4.1. *Ceramic lamps*

This class of artifacts is largely made up of lamps, which are shown particularly in pls. 8.9, 8.10, and 8.11:1–6, 8, and 12–17. The earliest of these may be the Hellenistic lamp shown in pl. 8.10:4. There is one feature that may indicate a later date for this lamp, however—the high loop handle. Such a handle is ordinarily characteristic of 6th century CE lamps. But its find spot underneath a very large stone on the western terrace implies an early date; that is, it was found in almost sterile fill above bedrock and under the stone. It evidently washed in, but long before the later material (including 8th century CE green glazes) above it. Another like it is known from Samaria. The Samaria lamp was found in summit strip 1 in level II, between the Iron II material and the Early Roman debris. That is, it is doubtless Late Hellenistic, as the Samaria excavators believe. Our example of this lamp, then, goes with the Hasmonean coinage and molded glass of Stratum I.

Next in chronological order we mention the two Herodian lamp nozzles in pl. 8.11. This is virtually the entire corpus of these nozzles from our site. They come from surface loci or from Stratum IV loci (four similar ones we do not publish). Only the nozzle illustrated in pl. 8.11:12 comes from a locus with a clear man-made function, the fill between platform 22018 and wall 22031 in SE II.22. This fill was more pottery than soil. It clearly stemmed from earlier occupational debris. Though we cannot guess what type of occupation goes with these nozzles, it is undoubtedly scant and thin.

The 2d to 3d century CE lamps in pl. 8.9 have been discussed as a type in chapter 5 above. What we have not discussed is their provenance in areas other than Tomb 29. As a matter of fact, these lamps are distributed in and about the synagogue. They may be associated with the rock cutting prior to Synagogue I or more likely are contemporary with the construction of Synagogue I.

The later lamps fit precisely into our Stratum IV. That is, they are 4th to early 5th century CE lamps, as is supported by evidence from Beth She‘arim above all. It is significant that no clear 6th century CE lamps are present.

Perhaps the most interesting lamp base is that shown in photo 8.3 and pl. 8.10:10. The menorah with branches is virtually identical with that published in Avigad, *Beth She‘arim*, III, fig. 93.2. Both are 3.15 cm long in internal diameter and could be formed from the same mold, though the relief in our example is slightly less sharp, suggesting that it is made from a mold that was made from a lamp identical to the Beth She'arim example.

The top of the Beth She'arim lamp is not illustrated in the Avigad volume, but it resembles ours in pl. 8.10:1. That is, in form it is probably 6th or early 7th century CE, though it could run as late as the 8th century. Our lamp was found one meter above the floor in the southwest corner of the synagogue beneath the Arab house; therefore, it is probably 6th–7th century CE.

4.2 Note on the lamp base with menorah (pl. 8.10:10, photo 8.3)[3]

On the bottom of the lamp, with an oval base, is depicted a menorah, highly unusual in several respects:

(i) It has only five branches, rather than the more usual seven found in Jewish art in antiquity. However, there are many exceptions to the standard seven-branched form: e.g., a graffito at Beth She'arim[4] has a five-branched menorah; a tombstone near Zoar has one nine-branched, one five-branched, and one possibly three-branched menorah; a Palestinian tombstone of unknown provenance shows eleven branches;[5] an ossuary now in the Rockefeller Museum depicts five branches;[6] the Monteverde catacomb has five-, nine-, and eleven-branched menoroth on tombstones;[7] several lamps are known to have five-branched menoroth, and a menorah on a bronze zeal from Avignon has five branches;[8] a semicircular block in the Tiberias Museum has a five-branched menorah.[9]

The sporadic appearance of non-seven-branched menoroth perhaps reflects the work of artisans or sponsors who wished to adhere to the Talmudic injunction against copying the Temple candelabrum: "A man may not make . . . a candelabrum after the design of its candelabrum. He may, however, make one with five six or eight [branches], but with seven he may not make it even though it be of other metals."[10]

(ii) It has a bar across the top, in itself not an unusual feature. However, protruding from the bar above the central arm is a projection that perhaps represents a lamp or flame. None of the side arms has such a projection; and the presence of only the central projection seems to be unparalleled. (Note, however, that a central projection from the five-branched candelabrum on an arched lintel fragment from Capernaum[11] forms the center or heart of a shell motif radiating upwards from the bar.)

---

3. Section 4.2 is by Carol L. Meyers.
4. Goodenough, *Jewish Symbols*, III, fig. 61. (For full citations of works mentioned in the footnotes, see the Bibliography preceding the Appendixes in this volume.)
5. Ibid. fig. 96 and fig. 99.
6. Ibid. fig. 158.

7. Ibid. figs. 707, 727, 729, 730.
8. Ibid. figs. 939, 942, 945, 946, and fig. 1012.
9. G. Foerster, "Some Unpublished *Menorah* Reliefs from Galilee," pl. xxvi:4.
10. 'Abodah Zarah 43a. Cf. Menahoth 28b and Rosh Hashanah 24a-b.
11. Loffreda, *A Visit to Capharnaum,* 69, fig. 43.

(iii) There is no base or stand for the menorah. This is not so uncommon, but it would be more usual for some sort of tripodal base to appear.

(iv) The associated symbols, one on each side of the central trunk, are puzzling. At first glance they seem to be two palm branches or lulavim. However, they are not identical representations, the right-hand figure having several more branches than the one on the left. Possibly, the latter is an alternate ethrog called *Rübe*.[12] If so, this would be a unique combination.[13]

In short, the type of menorah represented on this lamp base has a combination of features that are all unusual or unique. There is a possibility that this may not even be a Jewish symbol. However, that seems unlikely: the details are aberrant (perhaps because the menorah as a symbol is so widely diffused by this time) but the basic form is that of menorah with bar and two associated symbols.[14]

4.3 *Miscellaneous ceramic objects (photo 8.4)*

We only mention a variety of other ceramic artifacts such as the button (pl. 8.8:19), the bead (pl. 8.8:29), the spindle whorl (pl. 8.8:32), the strainer from an Arab period (pl. 8.11:9), the stopper cut from a sherd (pl. 8.11:7) and one of two identical crosses impressed on terra sigillata (pl. 8.11:10 and photo 8.4). The latter two parallel roughly the stamps illustrated in Hayes' *Late Roman Pottery* but are unique enough to imply Palestinian manufacture. That is, crosses stamped or impressed on the bottom of terra sigillata vessels are well known in the Late Roman and Early Byzantine periods in the Levant. Loffreda reports many types of terra sigillata stamps, including two similar to ours. Loffreda's fig. 2:14 resembles our pl. 8.11:10 (cf. his fig. 3:10), though ours is much less carefully manufactured. Both of his are from level II, the Late Roman to Early Byzantine periods.[15] Hayes dates his stamps on "Late Roman C. Ware" from the mid-5th to the 7th century CE, or late in our Stratum V. From fig. 8.2 one can see that NE VII.2 is highest in ceramic artifacts.

The ostraca illustrated in pl. 8.11:30–32 are the only examples of inscribed material from the whole site. Unfortunately, they are not particularly informative. Pl. 8.11:32 reveals only two letters "BR" incised on a well-worn sherd, probably of a closed form judging from the manufacturing lines on the inside. Doubtless, it read originally "_____ son of _____." That is, it gave the name of the owner of the pot.

5. STONE (PLS. 9.8:17–18, 31, 33–34, 8.11:23, 26–29, and Photo 8.5)

These are a variety of items of lithic origin which constitute about 6.2

---

12. Cf. Lietzmann in Beyer and Lietzmann, *Torlonia*, 19–21.

13. Goodenough, *Jewish Symbols*, IV, 146f.

14. If this analysis of the menorah lamp base be correct, it could mean that Jews still occupied Khirbet Shema' long after the synagogue was destroyed.

15. Loffreda, "Stampi."

percent of all registered artifacts at Khirbet Shemaʿ. Distribution about the site appears to be random, as is plain from fig. 8.2. For the purposes of the normal plot "all stone" includes basalt, chert (flint), and seldom occurring materials such as agate, chalcedony, and carnelian.

The bowl rim in pl. 8.8:18 is unique at Khirbet Shemaʿ as far as we now know. Unfortunately, it was found in surface debris.

The spindle whorls illustrated in pl. 8.8:31–34 are largely stone and are well paralleled at Pella and elsewhere.

Fragments of basalt grinders and querns were found all over the site, as can be seen in fig. 8.2. Unfortunately, none were in well-stratified early contexts, so we publish one vessel and one grinder (pl. 8.8:18, 8.11:28).

6. BONE AND IVORY (PL. 8.8:20–28 and Photo 8.6)

Only 1.3 percent of our artifacts were of bone or ivory. A certain ambiguity in identification remains, for without laboratory procedures it is usually impossible to distinguish the two.

The bone or ivory artifacts that are of special interest are the pin from the cistern (pl. 8.8:24), the comb fragment from the surface of the ruin (pl. 8.8:28), and the Hellenistic scarab (pl. 8.8:27 and photo 8.6).

This corpus of published artifacts represents about 12.8 percent of our total registered inventory. The main pattern that emerges from the total is exactly that of a small Galilean village with a minimum of wealth. The only real surprise is the amount of glass. We may find that the distribution profile in fig. 8.1 is entirely normal for sites far beyond the Galilee. That is, it may be that glass on the order of 50 percent is entirely reasonable.

7. SELECTED SMALL FINDS[16]

7.1 *Red carnelian gem (pl. 8.11:27, photo 8.7)*

During the 1970 excavation season a red carnelian, carved intaglio, oval ringstone was found in the fill (L.25042) just above the floor of a room (NW VII.25.47) just south of the synagogue. The accompanying finds from the Stratum IV locus suggest a probable date for the deposition of the gem.[17] However, the production of the gem may antedate the date suggested by the archaeological context, since gems were frequently retained for many years.

The gem, the only piece of cut jewelry from the site, is perfectly preserved.

16. The author of section 7 is Harold A. Liebowitz. He wishes to thank Barry Gittlen, Marilyn Simon, and James Weinstein, with whom he discussed aspects of this study, for their comments and valuable suggestions. Yet, in no way are they responsible for possible errors in fact or interpretation.

17. For a full discussion of the stratigraphy of the locus, see supra ch. 3, section 23 (ii).

The plain back and the carved intaglio face of it are slightly convex, and the sides slope gently. The design features a bust of Athena, with the bust in three-quarter view and the head, which faces left in the impression, in profile. The figure wears a crested, undecorated Attic helmet without a cheekpiece. Athena's long, straight nose continues almost on a straight line with the small portion of the forehead left uncovered by the helmet. The ridge of the eyebrow is prominent and serves to set the facial features off from the forehead and helmet. The V-shaped eye is schematically rendered. Contrary to normal practice, no attempt was made to render the upper and lower lids. The lips are slightly parted and the chin is small. The cheekbone is rather prominent, but otherwise the planes of the face are simplified and the head is idealized. Shoulder-length, sparse, but gracefully undulating strands of hair descend at the side of the neck where they emerge from behind the neckpiece of the helmet. The shoulders are narrow and the buttonlike breasts are small. The goddess's attire cannot be identified with assurance, since the execution of the figure becomes impressionistic below the shoulders. Yet, the figure appears to wear a chiton and to be draped with an overgarment which covers her left shoulder, leaving her right shoulder bare. The possibility exists that the overgarment is the aegis usually worn by Athena, but it lacks the scalelike quality and snakes generally associated with the aegis. However, since the clothing in general is rendered superficially, the absence of these details need not be conclusive.

Though more care was taken in the rendering of the head and helmet than in the rendering of the shoulders and chest, the overall quality of the gem is excellent. The details of the helmet are cut with precision and the silhouette is masterfully drawn. While the modeling is generalized, it is sensitive and controlled.

Athena is frequently featured on Roman imperial gems (late 1st century BCE to 4th century CE). Yet practically all of the Athena gems may be assigned to one of the following four major types, depending either on the figure's stance and gesture or on the amount of the figure portrayed.[18] Type I: full-length, standing figure assuming one of a variety of poses;[19] type II: full-length seated figure, usually with left arm bent at the elbow and right arm extended;[20] type III: bust in three-quarter view and head in profile;[21] type IV: head in profile. The Khirbet Shema' gem is typical of type III. Each of the types can be further subtyped, but types III and IV are of paramount interest here. The most obvious variable is the type of helmet worn by the goddess. While in the vast

18. See for example, H. B. Walters, *Catalogue of the Engraved Gems and Cameos in the British Museum* (London 1926), nos. 1347–1380; Gisela M. A. Richter, *Catalogue of Engraved Gems: Greek, Etruscan and Roman* (New York 1956) nos. 268–273. Athena is also portrayed as a full-length running or advancing figure, but this type is rare. See for example the gem in the Thorvaldsen Museum in Copenhagen in Paul Fossing, *Catalogue of the Antique Engraved Gems and Cameos* (Copenhagen 1929) pl. VIII. 607, and Walters, nos. 1357, 1363.

19. The variations occur primarily in the placement of the left hand (held aloft with a spear and a shield in it, or resting on the shield) and in the kinds of attributes in the extended right hand (Nike or some sort of vessel).

20. Walters, no. 1366, pl. xix; Richter, no. 270, pl. xxxix.

21. Walters, nos. 1372, 1373, 1375; Richter, no. 273.

majority of instances the Corinthian helmet is worn, the Attic helmet is infrequently worn. Indeed, there are few examples of Athena in a crested Attic helmet, and none of these represent true parallels to the Khirbet Shema‘ gem.

Anticipating the possibility of the existence of regional variations, the writer compared the Khirbet Shema‘ gem with gems discovered in Palestine. Eleven Athena gems were found on the surface in the vicinity of Caesarea Maritima.[22] Eight of the gems feature a standing Athena (type I).[23] One of the gems features her sitting (type II)[24] and two of the gems feature the bust of Athena (type III).[25] However, in both of the busts, Athena wears the Corinthian helmet, while on the Khirbet Shema‘ gem she wears an Attic helmet. Moreover, both of the Caesarea gems are stylistically crude in comparison with the Khirbet Shema‘ gem. Therefore parallels for the Khirbet Shema‘ gem have to be sought from among gems of unknown provenance now in museums and private collections.

The closest, yet unsatisfactory, parallels are provided by two gems in Munich. One belongs to type III and the other to type IV. The type III gem, dated to 2d-1st century BCE, features Athena dressed in a chiton and a crested Attic helmet and wearing her aegis over her right shoulder.[26] In spite of the superficial resemblance, this gem differs significantly in style from the Khirbet Shema‘ gem. While the Munich gem is linear in style, the Khirbet Shema‘ gem is more finely and softly modeled. The folds of the chiton of the Munich gem are rendered by V-shaped and zigzag lines, and the details of the helmet are rendered by raised bands. The Athena on the type IV gem, dated to the 1st century BCE,[27] wears an unadorned, crested Attic helmet similar to the one worn by the Khirbet Shema‘ Athena. The Munich and the Khirbet Shema‘ gems are also similar in the summary treatment of the eye; only the upper lid is rendered. Nevertheless, the overall stylistic treatments of the head differ in the two cases. On the Munich gem, the nose is larger and more articulated, the lips are closed and fleshier, the chin is prominent and jutting, and in general the face has a more masculine quality. Moreover, the workmanship of the Munich gem, while displaying a greater interest in modeled surfaces, is not as fine as that of the Khirbet Shema‘ gem.

While few parallels for Athena busts or heads with crested Attic helmets exist among the intaglio gems, the percentage of Athena busts in crested Attic helmets is higher among cameos. A fine cameo in the Thorvaldsen Museum in Copenhagen[28] portrays Athena in a crested Attic helmet decorated with an

22. Anit Hamburger, "Gems from Caesarea Maritima," ‘Atiqot 8 (1968) nos. 32–42.
23. Ibid. nos. 32–39.
24. Ibid. no. 40.
25. Ibid. nos. 41, 42.

26. Elfriede Brandt, Antike Gemmen in Deutschen Sammlungen, vol. I, part 2 (Munich 1970) no. 978, pl. III.
27. Elfriede Brandt, Antije Krug, Wendula Gercje, Antike Gemmen in Deutschen Sammlungen, vol. I, part 3 (Munich 1972) no. 2180, pl. 189, and p. 15.
28. Fossing, no. 1938, pl. XXIII, and p. 263.

olive wreath and spiral ornaments. See also the cameo featuring Athena in a crested Attic helmet and aegis in the Metropolitan Museum,[29] and the cameo double portrait of Julia, daughter of Augustus, featured as Athena, and Livia, featured as Hera, in the British Museum.[30] Julia wears an unadorned Attic helmet, a chiton fastened at the shoulders and an aegis covering her left shoulder.

It is difficult to date the Khirbet Shema' gem with certainty. The stratum in which the gem was found provides only the *terminus ad quem*. The gem can conceivably represent an heirloom and date to a much earlier period. Dated and datable coins, which usually aid in the dating of Roman gems, are of no help in the dating of Athena gems since (with the exception of the early Attic period) the treatment of Athena on the coins reveals no particular stylistic progression.[31] Furthermore, the gem cannot be securely dated on stylistic grounds. It is possible to date securely Greek gems on stylistic grounds, but it is far more difficult to obtain secure dates for Roman gems on stylistic grounds. While the Greek gems are characterized by a continuous evolution of styles, the Roman gems are copies of Greek originals of different periods and show no stylistic progression.[32]

However, on the basis of the 1st century BCE parallels and on the basis of the excellent quality of the gem, I would suggest a 1st century BCE to 1st century CE date for the gem. Beginning with the 2d century CE, there is a perceptible decline in the quality of carved gems.[33] Gems begin to assume amuletic functions in which aesthetic considerations are secondary.[34] The basically crude assemblage of gems from Caesarea, dated by Hamburger primarily to the 2d and 3d centuries CE, represents such a collection of amuletic gems.[35]

The suggested early date for the gem is less problematic than may be imagined. Note that a significant number of Jannaeus (103–76 BCE) coins were also found on the site, though there is limited pottery. Like the coins, the gem appears to represent an object of value retained for many years, but in the instance of the gem, not for its historical worth, but for its aesthetic value.

7.2 Scarab (*pl. 8.8:27, photo 8.6*)

A well-preserved scarab was discovered during the 1970 season in an unstratified surface locus (NE I.34.9, L.34001).[36] The scarab is of ivory or bone and shows traces of green glaze. Stratigraphic evidence provides no clues to its date, but scarabs were frequently retained for many years.

29. Richter, no. 607, pl. LXVI, p. 604.
30. Walters, no. 3584, pl. XL, and p. 337.
31. Cf. Hamburger, 8.
32. Gisela M. A. Richter, *The Engraved Gems of the Greeks, Etruscans, and Romans*, part II. *Engraved Gems of the Romans* (New York 1971) 5, 8.
33. A. Furtwängler, *Die Antike Gemmen*, III (Berlin

1900) 359. See also Walters, p. vi.
34. Walters, p. vi. Cf. Hamburger, 2, 3.
35. Cf. Hamburger, 3–5.
36. While the material in L.34001 is predominantly Late Roman–Byzantine, there are sufficient quantities of Arab sherds here to place the use phase of the associated floors and walls in the post-destruction period. The

The scarab is pierced lengthwise for placement either on the swivel of a finger ring or on a string to be worn as a pendant. A typical thickening surrounds the pierced opening at either end of the scarab. The scarab is straight-sided and has a convex back and a flat base. The schematically yet well-cut back and sides are incised with details of the back and legs of a beetle. The undivided elytra is set off from the prothorax, head, and clypeus by a deeply incised line. The prothorax is reduced to a narrow band extending from side to side, with two transverse lines incised at each end. The head and clypeus are schematically rendered by two incised lines extending from the outer incision of the prothorax to the outer forward edge of the scarab. The space between the incised lines broadens as the lines proceed to the outer edge of the scarab, where the clypeus is schematically represented by two sets of short incisions.

The legs of the beetle, rendered by incisions, are highly stylized. Yet, the abstract pattern ultimately derives from more traditional treatments of beetles' legs. In the traditional treatment, the front legs slant forward, and the center and rear legs slant backward. The front legs of the Khirbet Shema' scarab are represented by a slightly oblique shallow incision near the front end of the scarab, the center legs by a short, deep vertical incision, slightly posterior to the prothorax, and the rear legs by a long diagonal incision starting at the center of the scarab and slanting towards its lower rear extremity. The three incisions are connected by a slanting incision near the top of the scarab extending from the top of the front legs to the top of the rear legs. In place of the border normally found at the base of scarabs, there is a second, slightly slanting incision extending from front to back and connecting the front legs, center legs, and rear legs. Another incision extends from the upper slanting incision to the rear edge of the scarab. This line appears to have no naturalistic counterpart and was made for compositional purposes.

Four signs are cut into the base of the scarab. Only two of the signs are legitimate hieroglyphs: the 𝔰 *nefer* and the O *ra*. These signs are separated by the head of a long-horned ibex (?) with its horns swept back and bent. The remaining sign appears to represent the head of a horse. The two legitimate hieroglyphs (*nefer-ra*) imply good luck and are frequently found on Hyksos scarabs. These signs appear in isolation on a Twenty-Fourth Dynasty scarab in the Cairo Museum.[37] The meaning of the remaining two signs, which dominate the intaglio design by their size and antithetical back-to-back placement,[38] remains totally obscure. While deer are featured on several Egyptian scarabs,[39] they are represented as full-length figures and not merely as heads.

scarab, it would appear, has simply been preserved in late fill.

37. Percy E. Newberry, *Scarab-Shaped Seals* (Catalogue général des antiquités égyptiennes du Musée du Caire, nos. 36001–37521), (London 1970) no. 36596, pl. V.

38. Back-to-back flowering reeds placed on either side of a central sign are found on several Egyptian scarabs (ibid. pls. XVI, XVII).

39. W. M. F. Petrie, *Button and Design Scarabs* (London 1925) nos. 864–875, pl. XIV.

The scarab is obviously not Egyptian. It differs from Egyptian prototypes in the treatment of the back[40] and legs[41] and in the inclusion of two non-Egyptian hieroglyphic signs. The scarab is also unparalleled by scarabs from beyond the Egyptian borders.

The unique character of the scarab precludes the possibility of dating it on the basis of parallel stylistic traits. Yet, it is virtually certain that the scarab cannot postdate the period when scarabs ceased to be produced in Egypt and elsewhere. Since there are no stylistic parallels to enable us to date the Khirbet Shema' scarab, it would be reasonable to date it to the latest phase in the production of scarabs.

While scarabs become less popular in the Egyptian Late Period than they were during the New Kingdom, their production continues in Egypt until the end of the Pharaonic period. Several scarabs of the Thirtieth Dynasty are known.[42] However, the production of scarabs appears to have ceased early in the Ptolemaic period.[43.]

Outside of Egypt, the scarab, which had gone through various stages of development, persisted somewhat longer than in Egypt. Beyond the borders of Egypt, three basic types of scarabs, classified primarily on the basis of the design on the base, developed. These are scarabs with Egyptianizing motifs, scarabs with orientalizing motifs, and scarabs with Greek motifs. The Egyptianizing scarabs were most popular in Syria and Palestine. Their apparent persistence in Palestine into the Hellenistic period is evidenced by their discovery in Hellenistic contexts in 'Atlit.[44] There is no evidence for the continued existence of scarabs in Palestine into the Roman period.

The scarabs that are characterized by oriental motifs appear to have had a similar history. Only the scarabs with Greek motifs had a somewhat longer history. The practice of decorating the back of a stamp seal with the beetle

40. The style of the head and clypeus of the Khirbet Shema' scarab accords somewhat with the style of a type given a range in date by Alan Rowe from the Hyksos period to the Nineteenth Dynasty. *Catalogue of Egyptian Scarabs, Scaraboids Seals, and Amulets in the Palestine Archaeological Museum* (Cairo 1936) pl. XXXII.18. However, Rowe does not indicate the treatment of the prothorax, which on the Khirbet Shema' scarab is atypical of Egyptian scarabs. The style of the head and clypeus on the Khirbet Shema' scarab is also related to the style of the head and clypeus on a Hyksos scarab published by Newberry (n. 37) no. 36805, pl. xx. But the prothorax on the Hyksos scarab is not reduced to a narrow band.

41. On Egyptian examples, the front legs are usually extended forward and the center legs and rear legs are usually extended backward. The tops of all three sets of legs are placed close together. For a fine illustration of the legs of the beetle on Late Period scarabs, see two of the scarabs from the tomb of Tamwetamani, son of Shebitku (664–653 BCE), from the cemetery of El Kurru in Dows Dunham, *The Royal Cemeteries of Kush: El Kurru* (Cam-

bridge, Mass. 1950) pl. XLVIII. F.I. A similar treatment of the legs is found on Phoenician, Greco-Phoenician, Archaic Greek, and Etruscan scarabs; cf. John Boardman, *Archaic Greek Gems* (London 1968) fig. 1, p. 15.

42. W. M. Flinders Petrie, *Scarabs and Cylinders with Names* (London 1917) 33.

43. M. Pieper, "Die Siegelung in den griechischen Papyri Ägyptens," *Aegyptus* 14 (1934) 245–252, esp. 249. Isolated examples continue into the Roman period, but these have not been published with illustrations. Pieper cites the possibility that one scarab discovered by Petrie at Tanis may date to the period of the Roman Empire (ibid. 249). Perhaps his reference is to a seal or amulet with the head of Ptah and a scarab back found in the "early Roman age site" on the west mound at Tanis; see W. M. Flinders Petrie, *Tanis*, part I, 1883–1884 (London 1885) 35. Petrie also noted the existence of a large white marble scarab inscribed with the name of Antonius and dated to the Roman period (supra n. 42).

44. C. N. Johns, in *Quarterly of the Department of Antiquities in Palestine* 2 (1932) 44ff.

shape spread to Greece and Etruria. The majority of the seals from 6th century BCE archaic Greece have beetle backs.[45] In the 5th century BCE the beetle shape was generally superseded by the scaraboid.[46] The beetle back was also popular among the Etruscans, who continued to use the motif even after it was abandoned by the Greeks from whom it was borrowed.[47] The scarab shape continued in use into the Roman Republican period (3d to early 1st century BCE). However, in this period, the scarab shape, largely superseded by the ringstone, is rarely used. It is found only on Roman Etruscanizing gems.[48] Thus, it appears that the beetle back persisted in the classical world after the Egyptianizing and orientalizing scarabs ceased to be produced in the Levant.

The Khirbet Shema' scarab, though differing from Egyptian and Egyptianizing scarabs in the manner of treatment of the back and legs, and by the introduction of non-Egyptian hieroglyphic signs, is attributable to the Egyptianizing class of non-Egyptian scarabs. Since this class does not appear to have persisted beyond the Hellenistic period, a late Hellenistic date is the latest period to which the Khirbet Shema' scarab can reasonably be dated, although an Early Roman date cannot be absolutely ruled out.

45. Cf. Boardman, *Archaic Greek Gems,* 13. See also H. R. Hall, who notes that by the 6th century the scarab had become the typical type gem. *Catalogue of Egyptian Scarabs, etc. in the British Museum* (London 1913) IX.

46. John Boardman, *Engraved Gems: The Ionides Collection* (London 1968) 15.

47. Boardman, *Archaic Greek Gems,* 13, and idem, *Engraved Gems,* 14.

48. Richter (supra n. 32) 11.

CHAPTER 9. RESPECTUS

Though the excavations at Khirbet Shema' uncovered but a fraction of the material culture left behind by the ancient inhabitants of Teqo'a, the data here presented offer a striking glimpse into the world of the Galilean sages in the period which gave birth to the Palestinian Talmud. To be sure, these data do not tell a complete story, and for this reason from the outset the mute stones have been related to literary remains which survived somewhat more intact. The picture which emerges from the three seasons of excavation is one of a thriving Jewish village set somewhat apart from the encroaching Greco-Roman culture which was engulfing most of Syria-Palestine except for Tetracomia (Upper Galilee).

Numismatic evidence has indicated that Teqo'a and Meiron had close commercial ties with the municipality of Tyre. Ceramic data have proved that the cultural ties of Teqo'a and Meiron stretched beyond Galilee eastward into the Golan. These factors must be given judicious consideration in considering the kind of architectural eclecticism which has come to symbolize the uniqueness of Khirbet Shema'. But once again, not all the ceramic forms exhibit the kind of cultural continuity that ties this site into a much broader cultural continuum. Many of these anomalies derive from the fact that not enough work has been done in Galilee.

The meager remains of Stratum I leave unresolved the question of the Hasmonean occupation in this part of Galilee. But several hypotheses must be proposed. Coins of Alexander Jannaeus have turned up in significant numbers at Khirbet Shema' and Meiron: he is not known to have campaigned in precisely this area, but he may well have brought his troops along the trans-Galilee north-south route which bypasses the Wadi Meiron and camped there briefly. While most of Upper Galilee was annexed in the Judaizing campaign[1] of Aristobulus I it is not at all clear that the Meiron area was brought under Hasmonean control until Jannaeus.[2] We know from Josephus that Jannaeus took Mount Carmel and Gabaa to the west—and like Khirbet Shema'–Meiron, Carmel also had very close ties with Tyre—and subjugated the fortified cities of Gilead to the east and the Valley of Antiochus to the northeast. While not specifically mentioned by Josephus, Jannaeus could well have used the Meiron area as a launching pad or camping area for his northern exploits.

---

1. Josephus, *Antiquities* XIII, 11.3 (318–319), but especially in Iturea. Cf. *War* I.3.3–76.

2. *Antiquities* XIII, 15.4 (395–397); Avi-Yonah, *Holy Land*, 69.

Stratum II occupation, though far greater, is still rather limited. Khirbet Shema' is not a thriving village in the late 2d century CE. From the earlier ceramic evidence scattered about the site from this period, particularly "Herodian" lamp nozzles, it can only be said that Khirbet Shema' was settled at this time and may have looked to Meiron as its cultural center during this period. Because of the thin cover in this site, however, stratified material from this Middle Roman horizon is very uncommon. This datum is a major consideration in explaining the "apparent" slow spread of Jewish villages after Bar Kochba in the north.[3] That is to say, further digging at Khirbet Shema' and at other sites could well produce greater quantities of evidence from this period than we have thus far been able to uncover. But even at Meiron, where the sheer quantity of earlier material from this period is far greater, only limited amounts of stratified earlier material have been recovered, as in MI.2.

Sometime in the latter part of the 3d century CE sufficient numbers of people had settled at the site to require the building of a place of worship. In our nomenclature this activity occurred in Stratum III and resulted in Synagogue I. This structure has already been described, and though its history was short, its importance in the history of early synagogues cannot be gainsaid. Its basic ground plan remained the same in Stratum IV when the community resolved to rebuild their sanctuary and homes. This period, although it lasts only a little over a century, provides us with most of the details of everyday life at Khirbet Shema'; and it is from this period that we come away with the sad details of another catastrophe, the earthquake of 419 CE, which brought an abrupt end to the life of the community. Strata III and IV together span nearly a century and a half.

The *miqvaoth* of Strata II and IV indicate that the inhabitants of Teqo'a Ha-Galilit were deeply concerned with matters of ritual purity and cleanliness. On the other hand, the proximity of the Mausoleum and other tombs to the *yishub* (settlement) itself raises problems regarding purity which we have been unable to resolve.[4] As for the synagogues, it is certainly clear by now that the builders and town fathers who commissioned them were not constrained by conventions of architecture that were operative at neighboring sites. Both our buildings are broadhouses: this important fact has reopened the entire question of the development of Galilean synagogues, but its implications for an explana-

3. It is just possible that the dearth of clear late 1st and early 2d century material in Galilee is suggestive of an alternative interpretation of the alleged move northward of the Jewish population of Judea. Dr. H. Thomas Frank has pointed out to the authors that the move northward after the First Revolt in 70 CE and Bar Kokhba in 135 CE may not really come to a head until the 3d century CE. Therefore, if he is right, the earliest remains in Galilee would appear late in our Stratum II. This idea is worthy of more serious attention and investigation by serious scholars of the period both from the point of view of the archaeological data and a new look at the literary evidence. But see the forthcoming *ASOR* report of Meyers-Meyers-Strange on Meiron for later information (see supra chapter 1, n. 56).

4. It should be remembered, however, that since so many tombs have been robbed it is impossible to say in every case what is contemporary with what. We have suggested above that the Mausoleum is contemporary or at least in use with either Synagogue I or II, but this is purely conjectural.

tion of the religiosity of the inhabitants are still unclear. We have already suggested that such innovation might be interpreted as an attempt on the part of the Teqo'ites to establish an identity apart from their neighbors at Meiron. On the other hand, the fact that local artisans were used, as most surely in the case with the Menorah Lintel, may sufficiently account for some of the unique features of decoration.

Whatever reasons may be offered to account for the uniqueness of the synagogues, it is useful to reiterate the several salient architectural features and to assess their implications for synagogue typology: (i) the absence of the triple façade facing towards Jerusalem, heretofore thought to characterize "early" Galilean synagogues; (ii) the broadhouse ground plan, hitherto only known from the south and outside Palestine without internal columnation; and (iii) the unique internal arrangement with respect to the placement of the scrolls.

Other aspects of the placement of the synagogue clarify its function in the life of the community. We have already noted that the Shema' synagogue is not erected on the highest spot of the town and that one must enter it by stepping down. However, its very situation in the heart of town, with a main street running right up to the northern entrance—a feature already predicted by R. A. S. MacAlister[5]—indicates the centrality of the building in the town plan. That such a fact reflects to a great extent the religious sensibilities of the inhabitants seems to be quite certain. With private homes and domestic installations attached to the very walls of the synagogue, we may discern both the desire to integrate the synagogue into the life of the community as its main focus and at the same time understand an equally strong desire to set the synagogue apart from the profane aspects of everyday life.

A synagogue site is sacred because of what occurs there, namely, a meeting between God and His people. It is not surprising then that of all rabbinic legislation the Talmud provides so few details about the synagogue itself. There is no tractate on how to build a synagogue; many details are provided by the literature, but in an almost casual way.[6] Thus, to impose rigid typological views on the development of the synagogue building is perhaps to impose standards and conventions that were not at issue. The Shema' building, if anything, is a hybrid between the basilica and broadhouse; and while in terms of excavated remains it provides a stunning exception to the dominant pattern of ground plans, its anomalies perhaps should not be exaggerated.

When we consider other cultural indicators, especially ceramics, the general picture is the same: while many forms appear to be unique, there is also ample evidence for close ties to other parts of Galilee and the Golan. This may simply suggest frequent trading between these areas, stretching as far west and north as Tyre, but it also underscores the fact that Jewish towns and villages in these

5. "Remains at Khurbet Shema', Near Safed," pl. 2.
6. A. J. Heschel, "Symbolism and Jewish Faith," in *Religious Symbolism*, ed. F. Ernest Johnson (Port Washington 1955) 58.

areas shared many elements of material culture quite apart from the religious sphere. That many such ceramic forms are not found in the south points to regional differences whose full significance is not yet apparent.

One final matter: in Upper Galilee we find little evidence in this period for Hellenistic influence—little Greek and only limited representational art[7]—yet there must have been participation in the prevailing Roman-Byzantine culture. The rather unique adjustments of Khirbet Shema' to the prevailing culture cannot be properly understood as of the present owing to the limited amount of chronologically fixed data. The finds do raise some very serious questions, however, about post-Constantinian Palestine, especially when viewed against the regional evidence as a whole. The great flowering of Jewish material culture in this same period—usually thought to be a time of stress and growing tension between Jews and Christians—seems to suggest that the restrictive legislation against Jews had a far more limited impact than was thought heretofore.

Thus, while the evidence of Strata III–IV has thrown fresh light upon the development of the synagogue building and has afforded a new glimpse into Jewish life of Upper Galilee, it has likewise raised new and broader issues which may only be better understood through further archaeological work.

With regard to the later occupations, on the other hand, we can say even less. It is clear that the thriving village of Stratum IV is replaced by much more meager structures. The extent of occupation is considerably restricted, and the life of the community must therefore have been far less vigorous. Village life, if there was such in Stratum V, for example, must have been only a poor reflection of the bustle of Stratum IV. And even though the tempo of life picks up in Stratum VI and ultimately Stratum VII, the decline of the material culture itself suggests that our site is gradually disappearing from view as a viable alternative living space for residents of Upper Galilee during the centuries of the Arab period.

7. Avi-Yonah, *Holy Land*, 112.

BIBLIOGRAPHY

Aharoni, Jochanan. *The Land of the Bible: A Historical Geography.* Translated by A. F. Rainey. Philadelphia, 1967.

Aharoni, Yohanan. *Excavations at Ramat Rahel: Seasons 1959 and 1960.* Rome, 1962.

Aharoni, Yohanan. *Excavations at Ramat Rahel: Seasons 1961 and 1962.* Rome, 1964.

Albright, William Foxwell. *The Archaeology of Palestine.* Harmondsworth, 1951.

Amiran, D. H. Kallner. "A Revised Earthquake-Catalogue of Palestine." *Israel Exploration Journal* 1 (1950/51) 223–246.

Avigad, N. *Ancient Monuments in the Kidron Valley.* Text in Hebrew. Jerusalem, 1954.

Avigad, N. *Beth She'arim: The Archaeological Excavations During 1953–1958,* vol. III. *The Catacombs 12–23.* Text in Hebrew. Jerusalem, 1971.

Avigad, N. "Excavations at Beth She'arim, 1954." *Israel Exploration Journal* 5 (1955) 205–239.

Avi-Yonah, Michael. "Ancient Synagogues," *Ariel* 32 (1973) 29–43.

Avi-Yonah, Michael. *The Atlas of Israel.* Jerusalem, 1970.

Avi-Yonah, Michael. "The Caesarea Inscription of the Twenty-Four Priestly Courses." In *The Teacher's Yoke: Studies in Memory of Henry Trantham,* edited by E. Jerry Vardman and James L. Garrett, Jr. Waco, Texas, 1964.

Avi-Yonah, Michael. "Editor's Note." *Israel Exploration Journal* 23 (1973) 43–45.

Avi-Yonah, Michael. *Geschichte der Juden im Zeitalter des Talmud in den Tagen von Rom und Byzanz.* Studia Judaica: Forschungen zur Wissenschaft des Judentums, II. Berlin, 1962.

Avi-Yonah, Michael. *The Holy Land from the Persian to the Arab Conquests (536 B.C. to A.D. 640): A Historical Geography.* Grand Rapids, Mich., 1966.

Avi-Yonah, Michael. "Meron." *Encyclopedia Judaica,* XI.

Avi-Yonah, Michael. "Synagogue." *Encyclopedia Judaica,* XV.

Avi-Yonah, Michael. "Synagogue Architecture in the Classical Period." In *Jewish Art: An Illustrated History,* edited by Cecil Roth. New York, 1961.

Bacher, Wilhelm. *Die Agada der Tannaiten.* 2 vols. Strassburg, 1890, 1903.

Bagatti, B. *Excavations in Nazareth,* vol. I. *From the Beginning to the XVIIth Century.* Jerusalem, 1969.

Bagatti, B. *I monumenti di Emmaus el-Qubeibeh e dei dintorni; risultato degli scavi e sopralluoghi negli anni 1873, 1887–90, 1940–44.* Jerusalem, 1947.

Bagatti, B. "'Terre sigillate' in Palestina nei secoli V e VI." *Faenza* 39 (1953) 70–75.

Bagatti, B., and Milik, J. *Gli scavi del "Dominus Flevit,"* part I. *La necropoli del periodo Romano.* Jerusalem, 1958.

Bahat, D. "The Synagogue at Beth-Shean: Preliminary Report." Text in Hebrew. *Qadmoniot* 5 (1972) 55–58.

Baldi, D. *Enchiridion Locorum Sanctorum.* Jerusalem, 1955².

Balog, Paul. *The Coinage of the Mamluk Sultans of Egypt and Syria.* New York, 1964.

Bar-Adon, P. "Expedition C." *Israel Exploration Journal* 11 (1961) 25–35.

Barag, D.; Porat, Y.; and Netzer, E. "The Second Season of Excavations in the Synagogue at En-Gedi." Text in Hebrew. *Qadmoniot* 5 (1972) 52–54.

Baramki, D. C. "The Pottery from Kh. el Mefjer." *Quarterly of the Department of Antiquities in Palestine* 10 (1940–42) 65–103.

Barthélemy, D., and Milik, J. T. *Discoveries in the Judean Desert I: Qumran Cave I.* Oxford, 1955.

Ben-David, A. "Ha-Middah ha-Yerushalmit." *Israel Exploration Journal* 19 (1969) 158–169.

Ben Zevi, J. "A Third Century Aramaic Inscription in Er-Rama." *Journal of Palestine Oriental Society* 13 (1933) 94–96.

Beyer, H. W., and Lietzmann, H. *Jüdische Denkmäler,* I: *Die jüdische Katakombe der Villa Torlonia in Rom.* Studien zur spätantiken Kunstgeschichte, IV. Berlin-Leipzig, 1930.

"Bimah." *Encyclopedia Judaica,* IV.

Braslavi, J. "The Land of Israel in the Hebrew Translation of Basnage's 'Histoire des Juifs.'" Text in Hebrew. *Eretz Israel* 6 (1960) 168–173.

Brockelmann, Carl. *History of the Islamic Peoples.* Translated by Joel Carmichael and Moshe Perlmann. New York, 1947.

Bull, R. J., and Campbell, E. F., Jr., "The Sixth Campaign at Balatah (Schechem)." *Bulletin of the American Schools of Oriental Research* 190 (1968) 2–40.

Carmoly, Eliakim, ed. and trans. *Itinéraires de la Terre Sainte des XIIIe, XIVe, XVIe et XVIIe siècles.* Brussels, 1847.

Carson, Robert; Hill, P. V.; and Kent, J. P. C. *Late Roman Bronze Coinage,* part I. *The Bronze Coinage of the House of Constantine,* A.D. *324–346.* London, 1965.

Chachlili, Rachel. "Sacred Architecture and Decoration in the Hellenistic-Roman East." Text in Hebrew. Ph.D. dissertation, Hebrew University, Jerusalem, 1971.

Colt, H. D., ed., *Excavations at Nessana,* I. London, 1962.

Conder, Claude Reignier, and Kitchener, Horatio Herbert. *The Survey of Western Palestine: Arabic and English Name Lists.* London, 1881.

Conder, Claude Reignier, and Kitchener, Horatio Herbert. *The Survey of Western Palestine: Memoirs of the Topography, Orthography, Hydrography, and Archaeology.* 3 vols. London, 1881–1883.

Corbo, V.; Loffreda, S.; and Spijkerman, A. *La Sinagoga di Cafarnao dopo gli scavi del 1969.* Jerusalem, 1970.

Crowfoot, J. W., and Fitzgerald, G. M. *Excavations in the Tyropean Valley, Jerusalem, 1927.* London, 1929.

Crowfoot, J. W.; Crowfoot, G. M.; and Kenyon, K. M. *Samaria-Sebaste: Reports of the Work of the Joint Expedition in 1931–1933 and of the British Expedition in 1935,* no. 3. *The Objects from Samaria.* London, 1957.

Crowfoot, J. W.; Sukenik, E. L.; and Kenyon, K. M. *Samaria-Sebaste: Reports of the Work of the Joint Expedition in 1931–1933 and of the British Expedition in 1935,* no. 1. *The Buildings at Samaria.* London, 1966.

Dalman, Gustaf Hermann. *Grammatik des jüdisch-palästinischen Aramäisch nach den Idiomen des palästinischen Talmud, des Onkelostargum und Prophetentargum und der jerusalemischen Targume.* 2d ed. Leipzig, 1905.

Dalman, Gustaf Hermann. "Jahresbericht des Institutes für das Arbeitsjahr 1911/12." *Palästina Jahrbuch* 8 (1913) 1–63.

Dalman, Gustaf Herman. "Phönizische Grab und der Messiasthron bei Meron." *Zeitschrift des Deutschen Palästina-Vereins* 39 (1906) 195–199.

Danby, H. *The Mishna, Translated from the Hebrew with Introduction and Brief Explanatory Notes.* Oxford, 1933.

Delougaz, P., and Haines, R. *A Byzantine Church at Khirbat al-Karak.* Chicago, 1960.

deVaux, R. *See* Vaux, R. de

Dever, William G.; Lance, H. Darrell; and Wright, G. Ernest. *Gezer I: Preliminary Report of the 1964–66 Seasons.* Jerusalem, 1970.

Dothan, M. *Ashdod II–III: The Second and Third Seasons of Excavations 1963, 1965, Soundings in 1967.* Figures and Plates. *'Atiqot* 9–10 (1971).

Dothan, M., and Freedman, D. *Ashdod I: The First Season of Excavations.* Jerusalem, 1967.

Eitan, Avraham. "Excavations at the Foot of Tel Rosh Ha'ayin." *'Atiqot* (Hebrew Series) 5 (1969) 49–68.

Encyclopaedia of Archaeological Excavations in the Holy Land. Prepared by the Israel Exploration Society and Massada Ltd. Text in Hebrew. 2 vols. Ramat-Gan, 1970.

Finegan, Jack. *The Archaeology of the New Testament.* Princeton, N.J., 1969.

Fisher, C. S., and McCown, C. C. "Jerash-Gerasa 1930." *Annual of the American Schools of Oriental Research* 11 (1929–30) 1–59.

Fitzgerald, G. M. *Beth-Shan Excavations, 1921–1923: The Arab and Byzantine Levels.* Publications of the Palestine Section of the Museum of the University of Pennsylvania, vol. III. Philadelphia, 1931.

Foerster, G. "The Synagogues at Masada and Herodium." Text in Hebrew. *Eretz Israel* 11 (1973) 224–228.

Foerster, G. "Some Unpublished *Menorah* Reliefs from Galilee." Text in Hebrew. *'Atiqot* 7 (1974) 77–80.

Frey, P. Jean-Baptiste. *Corpus-Inscriptionum Iudaicarum: Recueil des inscriptions juives qui vont du IIIe siècle avant Jésus-Christ au VIIe siècle de notre ère.* 2 vols. Rome, 1936, 1952.

Galling, K. "Das Allerheiligste in Salomos Tempel; ein christlicher 'Thoraschrein,'" *Journal of Palestine Oriental Society* 12 (1932) 43–48.

Gardner, Percy. *British Museum Catalogue of Greek Coins: The Seleucid Kings of Syria.* Bologna, 1963.

Goitein, S. D. "Ambol–The Raised Platform in the Synagogue." Text in Hebrew. *Eretz Israel* 6 (1960) 162–167.

Goodenough, E. R. *Jewish Symbols in the Greco-Roman Period.* 13 vols. New York, 1953–69.

Graetz, Heinrich. *Geschichte der Juden von den ältesten Zeiten bis auf die Gegenwart.* 11 vols. in 13. Leipzig, 1897–1911.

Guérin, V. *Description géographique, historique et archéologique de la Palestine,* part III: *Galilée.* 2 vols. Paris, 1880.

Gutterlin, W. "Tekoa." *Palästina Jahrbuch* 17 (1921) 31–46.

Gutman, S.; Yeivin, Z.; and Netzer, E. "Excavations in the Synagogue at Khirbet Susiya." Text in Hebrew. *Qadmoniot* 5 (1972) 47–52.

Habermann, A. M. "Genizah." *Encyclopedia Judaica,* VII, 404–407.

Hamilton, R. W. "Excavations Against the North Wall of Jerusalem, 1937–1938." *Quarterly of the Department of Antiquities in Palestine* 10 (1940–42) 1–54.

Hanfmann, G. M. A. *Letters from Sardis.* Cambridge, Mass., 1972.

Har-El, M. "The Zealots' Fortress in Galilee." *Israel Exploration Journal* 22 (1972) 123–130.

Hayes, J. W. *Late Roman Pottery: A Catalogue of Roman Fine Wares.* London, 1972.

Hennessy, J. B. "Excavations at Samaria-Sebaste, 1968." *Levant* 2 (1970) 1–21.

Hermann, A. "Erdbeden." *Reallexikon für Antike und Christentum,* V.

Hill, G. F. *British Museum Catalogue of Greek Coins: Arabia, Mesopotamia and Persia.* London, 1922.

Hill, G. F. *Catalogue of the Greek Coins of Phoenicia.* London, 1910.

Hobson, R. L. "The Later Al Mina Pottery." *British Museum Quarterly* 11(1937) 115–116.

Hodges, Henry. *Artifacts.* London, 1968.

Horaïn, C. M. *L'Identité de lieux de la Galilée.* Ghent, 1963.

Ish-Shalom, Michael. *Holy Tombs: A Study of Traditions Concerning Jewish Holy Tombs in Palestine.* Studies in Folklore and Ethnology, V. Text in Hebrew. Jerusalem, 1948.

Johns, C. N. "'Atlit; Stables at the S.W. of the Suburb." *Quarterly of the Department of Antiquities in Palestine* 5 (1936) 77–94.

Johns, C. N. "Excavations at Pilgrim's Castle, 'Atlit (1932)." *Quarterly of the Department of Antiquities in Palestine* 3 (1934) 145–164.

Johns, C. N. "Medieval Slip-Ware from Pilgrim's Castle, 'Atlit (1930–31)." *Quarterly of the Department of Antiquities in Palestine* 3 (1934) 137–144.

Johnson, S. C. "Hierarchical Clustering Schemes." *Psychometrika* 32 (1967) 241–254.

Kahane, P. "Pottery Types from the Jewish Ossuary-Tombs Round Jerusalem." *Israel Exploration Journal* 2 (1952) 125–139.

Kelso, J. L., and Baramki, D. C. *Excavations at New Testament Jericho and Khirbet en-Nitla. Annual of the American Schools of Oriental Research,* 29–30 (1949–51).

Kendall, D. G. "Incidence Matrices, Interval Graphs and Seriation in Archaeology," *Pacific Journal of Mathematics* 28 (1969) 565–570.

Kindler, Arie. *The Coins of Tiberias.* Tiberias, 1961.

Klein, Samuel. *Beiträge zur Geographie und Geschichte Galiläas.* Leipzig, 1909.

Klein, Samuel. "Drei Ortsnamen in Galiläa." *Monatsschrift für Geschichte und Wissenschaft des Judentums* 67 (1923) 270–273.

Klein, Samuel. *Eretz Ha-Galil.* Text in Hebrew. Jerusalem, 1945.

Klein, Samuel. "Neues zum Fremdenhaus der Synagoge." *Monatsschrift für Geschichte und Wissenschaft des Judentums* 77 (1933) 81–84.

Klein, Samuel. *Sepher Ha-Yishub.* Text in Hebrew. Jerusalem, 1939.

Klein, Samuel. "Zur jüdischen Altertumskunde: das Fremdenhaus der Synagoge." *Monatsschrift für Geschichte und Wissenschaft des Judentums* 76 (1932) 545–557.

Kloetzli, G. "Coins from Chorazin." *Liber Annuus* 20 (1970) 359–369.

Kraabel, A. Thomas. "Hypsistos and the Synagogue at Sardis." *Greek, Roman, and Byzantine Studies* 10 (1969) 81–93.

Kraemes, C. J., Jr. *Nessana III: Non-Literary Papyri.* Princeton, N.J., 1958.

Krauss, Samuel. *Synagogale Altertümer.* Berlin-Vienna, 1922.

Krauss, Samuel. *Talmudische Archäologie.* Grundriss der Gesamtwissenschaft des Judentums. 3 vols. Leipzig, 1911.

Kutcher, J. "Studies in Galilean Aramaic." Text in Hebrew. *Tarbiz* 21 (1950) 192–205.

Lane, A. "Medieval Finds at Al Mina in North Syria." *Archaeologia* 87 (1937) 19–78.

Lane-Poole, Stanley. *Catalogue of Oriental Coins in the British Museum.* 10 vols. London, 1875–1890.

Lapp, P. W. *Palestinian Ceramic Chronology 200 B.C.–A.D. 70.* New Haven, 1961.

Lavoix, Henri. *Catalogue des monnaies musulmanes de la Bibliothèque Nationale.* Paris, 1887–1896.

Le Strange, Guy. *Palestine Under the Moslems: A Description of Syria and the Holy Land from A.D. 650 to 1500.* London, 1890.

Levy, S. "The Ancient Synagogue of Ma'on (Nirim): Excavation Report." *Bulletin: Louis M. Rabinowitz Fund for the Exploration of Ancient Synagogues* 3 (1960) 6–13.

List of Historical Monuments. Prepared by Israel Department of Antiquities. Text in Hebrew. Jerusalem, 1964.

Loffreda, S. *Cafarnao II: la ceramica.* Jerusalem, 1974.

Loffreda, S. "La ceramica della Sinagoga di Cafarnao." *Liber Annuus* 20 (1970) 53–105.

Loffreda, S. "Evoluzione di un piatto-tegame secondo gli scavi di Cafarnao." *Liber Annuus* 19 (1969) 237–263.

Loffreda, S. "The Late Chronology of the Synagogue of Capernaum." *Israel Exploration Journal* 23 (1973) 37–42.

Loffreda, S. "Scavi a Kafr Kanna." *Liber Annuus* 19 (1969) 328–348.

Loffreda, S. *Scavi di et-Tabgha (Lago di Tiberiade).* Jerusalem, 1970.

Loffreda, S. "Stampi su terre sigillate di Cafarnao." *Liber Annuus* 21 (1971) 286–315.

Loffreda, S. "The Synagogue of Capharnaum: Archaeological Evidence for Its Late Chronology." *Liber Annuus* 22 (1972) 5–29.

Loffreda, S. *A Visit to Capharnaum.* Jerusalem, 1972.

Macalister, R. A. Stewart. *The Excavation of Gezer I–III.* London, 1912.

Macalister, R. A. Stewart. "Remains at Khurbet Shem'a, Near Safed." *Palestine Exploration Fund, Quarterly Statement* 11 (1909) 195–200.

McCown, C. C., and Wampler, J. C. *Tell en-Nasbeh I–II.* Baltimore, 1947.

Mackay, T. S. "More Byzantine and Frankish Pottery from Corinth." *Hesperia* 36 (1967) 249–320.

The Macmillan Bible Atlas. Edited by Yohanan Aharoni and Michael Avi-Yonah. New York, 1968.

Makhouly, N. "Rock-cut Tombs at el-Jish." *Quarterly of the Department of Antiquities in Palestine* 8 (1938) 45–50.

Mann, Jacob. *The Jews in Egypt and in Palestine Under the Fatimid Caliphs.* 2 vols. Oxford, 1920, 1922.

Marmardji, A. Sebastianus, ed. and trans. *Textes géographiques arabes sur la Palestine.* Paris, 1951.

Marmorstein, A. "The Inscription of Er-Rame." *Palestine Exploration Fund, Quarterly Statement* 32 (1933) 100–101.

Mattingly, Harold, and Sydenham, E. A. *The Roman Imperial Coinage,* vol. II. *Vespasian to Hadrian.* London, 1926.

Mazar (Maisler), Benjamin. *Beth She'arim: Report on the Excavations During 1936–1940,* vol. I. *Catacombs 1–4.* Jerusalem, 1973.

Meshorer, Ya'akov. "Coins from the Excavations at Khorazin." Text in Hebrew. *Eretz Israel* 11 (1973) 158–162.

Meshorer, Ya'akov. *Jewish Coins of the Second Temple Period.* Translated by I. H. Levine. Tel-Aviv, 1967.

Meyers, Carol L., Meyers, Eric M., and Strange, James F. "Excavations at Meiron in Upper Galilee, 1971–1972: A Preliminary Report." *BASOR* 214 (1974) 2–25.

Meyers, Carol L., Meyers, Eric M., and Strange, James F. "Excavations at Meiron, in Upper Galilee, 1974, 1975: Second Preliminary Report." *AASOR,* vol. 43.

Meyers, Eric M. "The Ancient Synagogue of Khirbet Shema'." In *Perspectives in Jewish Learning,* vol. V, edited by Byron L. Sherwin. Chicago, 1973.

Meyers, Eric M. "Hurvat Shema'—The Settlement and the Synagogue." Text in Hebrew. *Qadmoniot* 5 (1972) 58–61.

Meyers, Eric M. *Jewish Ossuaries: Reburial and Rebirth.* Biblica et Orientalia, XXIV. Rome, 1971.

Meyers, Eric M.; Kraabel, A. Thomas; and Strange, James F. "Archaeology and Rabbinic Tradition at Khirbet Shema': 1970 and 1971 Campaigns." *Biblical Archaeologist* 35 (1972) 2–31.

Naveh, J. "Dated Coins of Alexander Jannaeus." *Israel Exploration Journal* 18 (1968) 20–25.

Oswald, F., and Pryce, T. D., *An Introduction to the Study of Terra Sigillata.* London, 1920.

Oyama, M., and Takehara, H. *Standard Soil Color Charts.* Revised edition. No place: Japan Color Research Institute, 1967.

Perrot, G., and Chipiez, C. *History of Art in Phoenicia.* London, 1885.

Pinkerfeld, J. "'David's Tomb': Notes on the History of the Building." *Bulletin: Louis M. Rabinowitz Fund for the Exploration of Ancient Synagogues* 3 (1960) 41–43.

Poey d'Avant, Faustin. *Monnaies féodales de France.* Paris, 1858–1962.

Prausnitz, M. W.; Avi-Yonah, M.; and Barag, D. *Excavations at Shavei Zion: The Early Christian Church.* Monografie di Archeologia e d'Arte, 2. Rome, 1967.

Press, Isaiah. *A Topographical-Historical Encyclopaedia of Palestine.* Text in Hebrew. 4 vols. Jerusalem, 1951.

Puttrich-Reignard, O. *Die Palastanlage von Chirbet el Minje.* Deutschen Vereins vom Heiligen Lande, Palästinaheft 17/20 (1939) 9–29.

Rahmani, L. Y. "The Ancient Synagogue of Ma'on (Nirim): The Small Finds and Coins." *Bulletin: Louis M. Rabinowitz Fund for the Exploration of Ancient Synagogues* 3 (1960) 14–18.

Ravani, B., and Kahane, P. P. "Rock-Cut Tombs at Huqoq." '*Atiqot* 3 (1961) 121–147.

Reece, R. *Roman Coins.* London, 1970.

Reisner, G. A., et al. *Harvard Excavations at Samaria, 1908–1910.* Cambridge, 1924.

Robinson, Edward. *Biblical Researches in Palestine and the Adjacent Regions: A Journal of Travels in the Years 1838 and 1852.* 3d ed. London, 1867.

Safrai, S. "Was There a Women's Gallery in the Synagogue?" Text in Hebrew. *Tarbiz* 32 (1963) 329–338.

Saller, Sylvester John. *Excavations at Bethany (1949–1953).* Jerusalem, 1957.

Saller, Sylvester John. *Second Revised Catalogue of the Ancient Synagogues of the Holy Land.* Jerusalem, 1972.

Sambon, Arturo. *Normanni: sulle monete delle provincie meridionale d'Italia dal VII al IX secolo.* N. p., 1916.

Sarre, F. P. T. *Die Keramik von Samarra.* Berlin, 1925.

Sauer, James A. *Heshbon Pottery 1971: A Preliminary Report on the Pottery from the 1971 Excavations at Tell Hesban.* Andrews University Monographs, vol. VII. Berrien Springs, Mich., 1973.

Schermann, Theodor. *Propheten- und Apostellegenden.* Texte und Untersuchungen, 31. Leipzig, 1907.

Schlumberger, Gustave. *Numismatique de l'Orient latin.* Paris, 1876.

Schneider, H. *The Memorial of Moses on Mt. Nebo,* vol. III. *The Pottery.* Jerusalem, 1950.

Seaby, H. A. *Greek Coins and Their Values.* London, 1966.

Seager, A. R. "The Building History of the Sardis Synagogue." *American Journal of Archaeology* 76 (1972) 425–435.

Smith, L. D. "Cluster Analysis and Classification Strategies: An Example from Israel." *Newsletter of Computer Archaeology* 9 (1973) 1–10.

Smith, R. H. *Pella of the Decapolis,* vol. I. *The 1967 Season of the College of Wooster Expedition to Pella.* Wooster, Ohio, 1973.

Squarciapino, M. Floriani. "The Synagogue at Ostia." *Archaeology* 16 (1963) 194–203.

Stekelis, M. "A Jewish Tomb-Cave at Ramat Rachel." Text in Hebrew. *Journal of Jewish Palestine Exploration Society* 3 (1934–1935) 25–27.

Stewardson, Henry C. *The Survey of Western Palestine: A General Index.* London, 1888.

Sukenik, E. L. *The Ancient Synagogue of Beth Alpha.* London, 1932.

Sukenik, E. L. *The Ancient Synagogue of El-Hammeh (Hammath-by-Gadara).* Jerusalem, 1935.

Sukenik, E. L. *Ancient Synagogues in Palestine and Greece.* London, 1934.

Sussman, V. "Ancient Burial Cave at Rehobot." Text in Hebrew; summary in English. '*Atiqot* 5 (1969) 69–72.

Thompson, H. A. "Two Centuries of Hellenistic Pottery." *Hesperia* 3 (1934) 311–450.

Thomsen, Peter. *Loca Sancta.* Reprinted, Hildesheim, 1966.

Tiesenhausen, W. *Moneti vostochnavo khalifata.* St. Petersburg, 1873.

Tsori, N. "The Ancient Synagogue at Beth-Shean." *Eretz Israel* 8 (1967) 149–167.

Tsori, N. "The House of Kyrios Leontis at Beth-Shean." *Eretz Israel* 11 (1973) 229–247.

Tushingham, A. D. *The Excavations at Dibon (Dhiban) in Moab: The Third Campaign, 1952–53. Annual of the American Schools of Oriental Research* 40 (1972).

Tzaferis, V. "Tombs in Western Galilee." Text in Hebrew; summary in English. '*Atiqot* 5 (1969) 72–79.

Urman, D. "Jewish Inscriptions from Dabbura in the Golan." *Israel Exploration Journal* 22 (1972) 16–23.

Vaux, R. de. "Céramique masulmane des Xe–XIe siècles à Abu Gosh (Palestine)." *Bulletin d'Etudes Orientales* 11 (1945–46) 13–30.

Vaux, R. de. "Fouilles au Khirbet Qumrân." *Revue Biblique* 60 (1953) 83–106.

Vaux, R. de. "Les grottes de Murabba'at et leurs documents." *Revue Biblique* 60 (1953) 245–267.

Vaux, R. de, and Steve, A.-M. *Fouilles à Qaryet el-'Enab = Abu Gosh.* Paris, 1950.

Vilnay, Zev. *Holy Monuments in Eretz Israel.* Text in Hebrew. Jerusalem, 1963.

Vogel, E. K. "Bibliography of Holy Land Sites." *Hebrew Union College Annual* 42 (1971) 1–96.

Walker, John. *A Catalogue of the Muhammadan Coins in the British Museum*, vol. II. *A Catalogue of the Arab-Byzantine and Post-Reform Umayyad Coins.* London, 1956.

Watzinger, C. *Denkmäler Palästinas: eine Einführung in die Archäologie des Heiligen Landes.* 2 vols. Leipzig, 1933–1935.

Wright, Thomas, ed. *Early Travels in Palestine, Comprising the Narratives of Arculf, Willibald, Bernard, Saewulf, Sigurd, Benjamin of Tudela, Sir John Maundeville, De La Brocquiere, and Maundress.* London, 1848.

Yadin, Yigael. *The Finds from the Bar Kochba Period in the Cave of Letters.* Jerusalem, 1963.

Yadin, Yigael. *Masada.* London, 1966.

Yeivin, Zev. "Excavations at Khorazin." Text in Hebrew. *Eretz Israel* 11 (1973) 144–157.

Yeivin, Zev. "Survey of Settlements in Galilee and the Golan from the Period of the Mishnah in Light of the Sources." Text in Hebrew. Ph.D. dissertation, Hebrew University, Jerusalem, 1971.

Yeivin, Zev. "The Synagogue at Eshtemoa." Text in Hebrew. *Qadmoniot* 5 (1972) 43–45.

Zlotnick, D. *The Tractate "Mourning."* Yale Judaica Series, vol. XVII. New Haven, 1966.

APPENDIX A. LOCUS INDEX BY AREA AND LOCUS

KEY

*	Homogeneous	MR-LR	Middle Roman to Late Roman	Med	Medieval
†	Few	B	Byzantine		
—	Many	EB	Early Byzantine	UD	Undistinguishable
		LB	Late Byzantine	NS	Not saved
H	Hellenistic	R-B	Roman to Byzantine	TS	Terra sigillata
R	Roman	LR-B	Late Roman to Byzantine	WW	White ware
		A	Arabic	KS rim	Khirbet Shema' rim (Galilean
ER	Early Roman	EA	Early Arabic		bowl)
MR	Middle Roman	LA	Late Arabic	LF	Lamp fragment
LR	Late Roman	B-A	Byzantine to Arabic	Pi	Pithoi fragments
ER-LR	Early Roman to Late Roman				

Area	Locus	Stratum	Bucket	Field Reading	Objects	Description
NW I.25	25007	IV	17	LR*	944 — glass rim 943 — glass rim	Plaster-filled soil just above bedrock, below 25005
		IV	18	LR, EB		
NW I.31	31021	mixed, V–VII	54	LR, B, A†		Layer of soft, powdery earth below 31019 within synagogue
			55	LR, B, A	748 — glass rim 697 — bronze ring 700 — glass rim 699 — glass rim 698 — iron nail 951 — spindle whorl (stone) 701 — glass rim	
			56	LR, B, A		
			57	B, A		
			58	LR, B	800 — glass base 799 — iron knife	
			59	LB	894 — iron ring 895 — glass frag.	
			60	LR†, B		
			61	LR†, LB	803 — iron nail 802 — glass rim 801 — glass rim	
			62	LR, LB	854 — ceramic lamp base 857 — glass rim 856 — glass rim 855 — glass rim 858 — glass neck frag.	
			64	B	860 — ceramic spindle whorl	
			65	LR, B, A	893 — glass rim 892 — glass rim 955 — iron knife blade 954 — iron nail frag. 953 — iron ring 952 — bone 1212 — bronze cosmetic spoon	

Area	Locus	Stratum	Bucket	Field Reading	Objects	Description
			66	LR, B, 1 TS	957 — iron nail 956 — glass rim	
			67	LR, B, 1 TS	1799 — iron nail 1805 — iron nail	
			69	LR, B, A†	959 — glass rim	
			71	LR, B		
			72		1265 — iron nail 1213 — glass rim	
			73	LR, B	1214 — glass body frag.	
			77	1 A†, brown glaze, LR, B	1216 — ceramic lamp frag. 1215 — glass body frag.	
			78	MR-LR		
			81	B, A, 1 LF		
			82	B	1218 — blade frag.	
NW I.32	32024	IV	43	LR		Soil sealed under later wall 32018, west of eagle doorway
			49	LR, many pithoi	1219 — glass body frag.	
			55	UD, pithoi frags.		
			56	UD, NS— many pithoi		
	32022	V	58	LB		Earthen layer immediately overlying floor of frescoed chamber
			64	UD, LR		
	32028 comb. with 32030	mixed, III–VI	51	LR	1221 — glass rim 1220 — glass base	Grayish-brown, clay-like soil found within "genizah"
			53	LR	1688 — lamp frag.	
			54	LR, B, EA	1264 — glass base	
			57	UD, LR		
			59	LB		
			62	LR		
			67	LR†, B, A		
			69	LR, B?	1740 — glass rim	
			70	LR		
			74	LR		
			78	LR		
NW I.33	33003.1	VI	15	LR, B, A, 6 WW, 1 KS rim		Makeup of compact layer 33003 (possible surface)
			41 (or 33020)	R, B, 1A, Pi	3728 — glass rim	
	33015	VI	29	LR*, 1A, Pi*, 1 WW		Loose dry soil overlying bedrock
			31	R, Pi		
			34	LR, Pi*		

Area	Locus	Stratum	Bucket	Field Reading	Objects	Description
	33020	VI–VII	43	B, A, Med, Pi, 5 WW, 2 KS rims		Loose, rubbly soil (10–15 cm) above cobbles 33021
			45	B, 6 WW	3802 – grinder	
	33022	VI	46	R-B, Pi		Fill below cobbles 33021 and over bedrock
			47	LR, A, Pi, 4 WW, 1 KS rim		
	33023	V	48	LR, Pi		Earth equivalent to 33015, below wall 33013
NW I.34	34009	IV	10	R, 1 WW		Possible surface in corner of walls 34003 and 34005
			14	1 MR, LR, 1 WW	3691 – ?	
	34010	V	11	MR, LR, B		Layer of very fine soil
			18	LR, B, 2 WW, 1 KS rim		
			20	LR, B, 2 KS rims		
			19	MR, 1 WW, 2 KS rims		
NW VII.1	1016	IV	21	LR, B?	723 – glass body frag. 725 – glass rim 724 – glass rim	Soil within stairway platform on east face of North Building
			25	LR		
			46	MR-LR	969 – glass rim	
			58	LR, 1 LF		
			62	LR, B		
			71	LR*		
	1022	IV	38	LR	844 – ? 841 – glass body frag. 840 – lead obj.	Dark brown soil with much plaster in southwest corner of area, within synagogue
	1026	IV	34		837 – glass base	Compact soil, north of synagogue east of step 5
	1035	IV–V	41	LR	963 – bronze ring frag. 962 – glass rim 964 – iron nail 961 – glass rim	Soil above flagstone floor north of synagogue
	1035P	IV	43	LR?	965 – stamped ceramic base	Soil between flagstones north of synagogue
	1037.1	IV	48	LR	968 – glass rim	Clay-like soil below 1037 and 1014, in synagogue
	1050	III–IV	77	LR, UD		Bright, yellowish soil below 1049, with 1015
	1052	III–IV				Windblown soil on surface of declivity in northwest corner of synagogue
	1055	III–IV	81	LR*, Pi		Layer below 1054 marl on south side of cavity in northwest corner of synagogue
	1056	III–IV	82	LR, Pi*		Layer below 1054 marl on northern side of cavity

Area	Locus	Stratum	Bucket	Field Reading	Objects	Description
	1058	III–IV	85	LR, Pi*	3293 — ceramic lamp frag. 3369 — metal	Soil layer below 1057 in cavity
	1059	III–IV	86	LR*, Pi, 2 KS rims		Soil layer below 1058 in cavity
			87	Pi	3354 — ceramic lamp frag.	
	1060	III–IV	88	LR, Pi	3379 — glass rim	Rubbly, rocky soil below 1059 in cavity
			89	1 ER, LR, Pi*	3573 — basalt 3572 — basalt	
			90	LR, Pi, 4 KS rims	3520 — ceramic lamp frag. 3528 — object 3429 — glass rim 3502 — metal ring 3519 — ceramic lamp frag. 3518 — glass rim	
			91	MR, LR, Pi, 1 KS rim	3300 — ceramic lamp frag. 3301 — ceramic lamp frag. 3304 — glass rim	
			92	MR, LR, Pi*	3365 — ceramic lamp frag.	
NW VII.3	3011	IV	29	LR*		Decomposed soil above bedrock
	3016	V	21	LR,* B		Clay-like soil below wall 3005
	3017	V	23	LR, B, 1 WW		Clay-like soil below wall 3016, above bedrock and flagstones 3012
	3018	IV	25	R		Soil beneath terrace wall 3013
	3019	V	26	LR, B, 2 WW		Foundation trench (?) of wall 3013
	3021	IV	28	LR* 1 KS rim, 1 TS		Earthen makeup for flagstone surface 3006
NW VII.8	8004	mixed, IV–VI– VII	6	LR, A	1966 — glass rim 1961 — metal hook 1953 — glass rim 1952 — metal jewelry 1954 — stone rim	Soil horizon below 8001 and above bedrock
			7A	A	1967 — stone	
			7B	LR, B, A	1976 — metal arrow tip 1968 — millstone 3796 — ceramic heating stone 3795 — ceramic heating stone	
			8	LR*, B, A*, 4 WW	3002 — glass rim	
			10	LR, B, A, Pi		
			11	LR, B, A* Pi, 1LF, 2 WW, 2 KS rims, 1 TS		
			12	LR, A, Pi, 1 KS rim		
			16	LR(B?), 2 KS rims		
			21	LR, B?, A, Pi, UD, Med		
			23	LR, A, B, 1 TS		

Area	Locus	Stratum	Bucket	Field Reading	Objects	Description
			24	LR, B, A, Pi, Med	3246 — glass base 3278 — iron blade	
			26	LR, A, Pi		
			31	LR, Pi, 1 WW, 3 KS rims		
			33	LR, Pi, UD		
	8007	mixed, IV–VI	27	LR?, B?, A		Yellow clay layer west of wall 8005
	8008	mixed, IV–VI	30	LR, B?, A, Pi	3517 — object 3216 — stone 3238 — glass rim	Compact soil layer, full of limestone chips, below 8007 and above bedrock
NW VII.9	9007	mixed, IV–VI–VII	6	A*, Med		Brownish soil layer below 9006
			13	LR?, Pi		
			14	B, A, Med	3763 — ceramic stopper	
			17	LR, B, A, UD, Med		
	9008	IV	7	LR, Pi		Blackish soil layer below 9007
NW VII.13	13002	VI	29	Pi	3175 — metal ring	Earthen layer below 13001 and over bedrock or 13003
			30	LR, B?, A	3207 — copper cosmetic tool	
			33	LR, 1 A, 1 WW, 1 TS		
			34	LR, B, 2 A	3315 — glass handle	
			35	LR, B, 4 KS rims	3075 — ceramic heating stone	
			36	LR, A*		
		V	37	LR, 1 KS rim		
			38	LR*, 1 B, 1 WW, 2 TS, 3 KS rims	3343 — glass base	
			39	LR*, 1 TS, 4 KS rims	3371 — glass rim 3332 — glass rim	
			40	LR*, Pi, 5 KS rims	3458 — glass rim	
			41	LR*, 2 KS rims		
			43	LR*, Pi, 1 KS rim		
	13003	V	42	LR*, 2 KS rims		Yellowish earth below 13002, in flagstones
			44	LR*, Pi, 8 KS rims		
			45	LR*, 2 KS rims	3546 — glass base	
			46	LR, B, 2 Pi, 1 TS	3584 — ceramic lamp frag. 3583 — ceramic lamp frag. 3548 — glass rim	
			48	LR*, 2 KS rims		
NW VII.14	14005	mixed, IV–VI	21	LR, 1 KS rim		Soil layer below 14004 and above bedrock
			30	LR, B, A, Pi, 3 KS rims	3816 — object	

Area	Locus	Stratum	Bucket	Field Reading	Objects	Description
NE I.19	19070	VI	26	LR,B, EA, 6 WW	3291 — iron nail 3282 — glass base 3281 — glass base 3286 — glass rim 3285 — glass base 3284 — glass base 3283 — glass rim 3277 — iron nail	Dry soil under surface
	19071	VI	27	B,B–A, EA, 3 WW	3368 — ceramic lamp frag. 3367 — hair pin 3388 — metal obj. 3389 — ceramic lamp 3397 — iron nail 3313 — iron nail 3294 — glass base	Dry soil under 19070
	19072	IV	29	LR	3417 — iron nail 3344 — glass bead	Moist soil under 19071, over bedrock
NE I.26	26018.1	VII	26	LR, B, A		Make-up of hard-packed dirt surface 26018, south of synagogue
			28	LR, B, A, Med, 4 WW		
			32	LR, B, A, Med, 1 WW	1945 — iron nail 1914 — iron nail	
	26020	IV	31	LR		Fill in synagogue below surface 26011 and fill 26019
	26022.1	VII	36	LR, B, A		Make-up of paved surface 26022 south of synagogue
			37	B, A, 2 WW		
			38	LR, R–B, B, LA, 1 WW, 2 KS rims	1989 — glass rim	
			62	1 B, UD	3338 — iron nail 3356 — glass neck	
	26023	V	39	LR, B, 4 WW, 5 KS rims	3019 — ceramic button frag. 3016 — glass rim	Moist, yellowish soil under 26022.1, south of synagogue
			42	LR, B, A, UD		
	26024	V	40	B, Pi, 1 WW, 2 KS rims — 5th C.		Moist fill over bedrock under 26023, south of synagogue
			41	LR, B, 1 WW, UD		
			43	LR, 1 KS rim		
			44	LR†, B		
	26027.1	IV	45	LR		Make-up of synagogue floor, east of stylobate wall
	26028	IV	46	LR, H?		Moist fill below 26027.1, east of stylobate wall
	26029	IV	47	LR, Pi	3208 — iron nail	Moist fill below 26028, east of stylobate wall
	26030	IV	48	LR, Pi*		Dry fill under 26027.1 under bench along south wall of synagogue
	26031	IV	50	LR, Pi*		Moist fill below 26029, east of stylobate wall
	26035	V	51	B, Pi		Moist soil under 26031 between wall 26033 and stylobate wall
	26036	IV	59	LR		Moist, compact soil under 26034 along stylobate
	26037	IV	55	LR*		Moist soil under 26034 along 26033

Area	Locus	Stratum	Bucket	Field Reading	Objects	Description
	26038.1	III–IV	58	MR?, 1 TS		Moist soil below synagogue floor, west of stylobate
			68	MR?, LB, Pi, 1 TS, UD		
NE I.32	32014	IV–V	53 70	LR, B?, Pi R, Pi, UD		Windblown soil under 32012.1 near wall 32007
			77	MR, LR, 2 KS rims		
	32015	IV–V	51	LR, B, R		Windblown soil under 32012.1 near wall 32002
			69	MR?, LR, Pi*		
			75	MR, LR		
	32016	IV–V–VI	54	LR, B, Pi	3038 – stone arch. frag. 3028 – glass bead 3048 – basalt	Moist fill on synagogue floor (under 32012.1, 32014, 32015)
			55 55A	LR, 1 B, 1 A Pi*, ER, LR*, Pi* 5 KS rims	3073 – iron nail 3070 – iron nail 3069 – iron nail 3066 – glass rim 3065 – glass rim 3074 – iron nail 3081 – metal ring	
			56	LR*, 1 Pi		
			71	MR?, LR, Pi, UD	3529 – glass rim	
			72	MR, LR, 1 KS rim, many Pi	3565 – ceramic lamp frag. 3558 – glass base 3804 – glass bead	
			73	LR, Pi*, 2 KS rims		
			39	LR, B, A, 1 TS	850 – glass rim 851 – glass rim 852 – glass rim 853 – glass body frag.	
			42		981 – iron nail	
NE VII.2	2019.1	IV	62	LR, UD		Make-up of synagogue floor east of pedestal 2009
			66	LR*		
	2025	IV	63	LR*, many Pi		Rubbly fill beneath 2019.1 beneath synagogue floor
			67	LR*		
	2026	IV	64	LR		Fine fill beneath 2025 beneath synagogue floor
			65	MR–LR	1791 – glass rim	
			70	LR		
	2027	IV	71	LR		Moist fill layer beneath 2026 under synagogue floor, above bedrock
			73	LR*, 1LF	1943 – chert point	
			74	LR*		
	2030	II–III	76	MR–LR, many Pi.	1941 – ceramic lamp frag. 1942 – stone spindle whorl 1946 – ceramic lamp frag.	Fine, compressed fill inside chamber

Area	Locus	Stratum	Bucket	Field Reading	Objects	Description
			77	MR–LR	1939 – glass rim 1940 – ceramic lamp frag. 1938 – glass body frag. 1937 – glass rim	
			78	MR–LR		
			79	MR–LR		
	2032	IV	81	LR*, 1LF, 2 KS rims	3749 – iron nail 3437 – glass rim 3433 – glass rim	Dark brown soil under benches 2006 along north wall of synagogue
	2033	IV	82	LR*	3484 – glass rim	Yellowish-brown soil under 2032 under bench along north wall of synagogue
			83	LR*, 1 KS rim		
	2035	IV	85	LR, Pi, 1 KS rim		Dark brown soil beneath 2034 under bench along north wall of synagogue
			86	MR, LR, Pi		
	2036	IV	87	MR, LR		Light, loose area of soil adjacent to and under 2035
			88	LR, 1 LF		
	2037	III	89	MR, Pi	3660 – ceramic stopper	Dark brown soil under 2035, between outcropping of bedrock and wall 2010
	2038	IV	91	LR, UD		Moist, compact soil above bedrock in NE corner of synagogue
	2042	IV	94	LR		Yellowish-brown soil under benches 2006 west of stylobate
			95	LR, B, 1 KS rim	3741 – object	
	2043	VII	92	LR, A		E-W wall along north balk
			96	A*	3615 – ceramic lamp frag.	
	2045	IV	99	R, 1 KS rim		Moist, hard soil directly under 2020, architrave
			100	MR?, LR		
	2046	IV	102	LR	3735 – glass base	Moist, compact soil in area west of stylobate, above bedrock
NE VII.3	3009.1	IV	11	LR*, 1 KS rim		Soil under pavement 3009 (east of synagogue)
			12	LR*, 1 KS rim		
			13	LR*, 3 TS, 2 KS rims		
			28	LR, B?, 1 LF		
	3014	IV	16	R, 1 MR, UD		Moist, compact soil under 3009.1 and above bedrock
	3015	V	17	LR, B, 4 KS rims		Moist, compact soil south of wall 3020 (under 3011)
	3016	IV–V	20		3817 – frit decoration 3774 – glass rim	Moist soil north of wall 3020 (under 3010)
			21	LR, B 3 KS rims		
			23	LR, 1 LF		
	3017	mixed	24	LR, B, 1 WW, Arab strainer		Moist, compact soil under wall 3020
	3018	IV	25	LR, Pi*		Final soil horizon above bedrock, north of 3020
C-1	C-1:01	V	1	4th C.	690 – glass rim 689 – glass base	Surface material
	C-1:02	V	2	4th–5th C.		Moist, clay-like earth below the surface
			3	LR, 4th C.	623 – glass body frag.	

Area	Locus	Stratum	Bucket	Field Reading	Objects	Description
			4	4th C.	619 — glass rim	
			11	4th C.	714 — glass rim 713 — glass rim	
	C-1:03	V	5	4th C.	620 — glass rim	Layer of moist earth with rock fragments and gray plaster, below C-1:02
			13	LR*	731 — glass base	
			14	LR*	776 — glass base 777 — glass body frag.	
	C-1:04	IV	6	4th C.	642 — glass body frag.	Puddled silt from last use of cistern, below C-1:03
			7	LR*, 4 TS	637 — glass base 688 — glass rim 640 — glass rim 639 — ivory pin	
			9	4th C.		
			10	LR*		
			15	LR*	774 — glass rim 773 — glass rim 772 — glass base 775 — glass base 805 — stone rim 804 — ceramic lamp disc 771 — glass base 770 — glass rim	
			15A	late 4th C*		
			16	LR*	769 — glass rim 768 — glass rim 767 — glass rim	
			17	LR*	784 — glass rim 783 — glass base 782 — glass base 781 — glass rim 778 — glass bead 807 — iron object 806 — glass rim	
			17A	late 4th C.	3843 — glass base	
	C-1:05	IV	18	LR*	809 — iron blade 808 — iron frag.	Pit in cistern floor below cistern opening
			19	LR*		
T17 (*miqveh*)	17:12	IV	23	4th C.*		Surface soil layer within *miqveh*
			24	4th C.*		
			25	4th C.*		
	17:13	IV	26	4th C.*		Fine fill layer, below surface, within *miqveh*
	17:14	IV	27	4th C.*		Clay-like earth layer within *miqveh*, below 17:13
			28	4th C.*		
	17:15	IV	29	4th C.*		Greyish, clay-like layer within *miqveh*, below 17:14 and above bedrock
T29 North	29:06	II	14	NS	490 — ceramic lamp 489 — ceramic lamp 204 — glass	Pale brown layer above floor of tomb, below 20:05
	29:08	III–IV	19	B, UD		Pale brown layer adjacent to 29:06, on floor of tomb
			25	LR–B, UD	366 — ring 367 — bead 505 — ceramic lamp frag. 491 — ceramic lamp frag.	
			26	Small LR†, UD		

Area	Locus	Stratum	Bucket	Field Reading	Objects	Description
	29:10	IV	24	LR–B, UD, 1 KS rim, 1 4th C. jar		Dark brown fill in *kokh* #9
			27	LR–B, UD	368 – iron nail 504 – ceramic lamp frag.	
	29:11	IV	28	UD–NS	369 – iron nail	Pale yellow fill and fall from ceiling in *kokh* #7
			29	UD–NS	479 – ceramic lamp 372 – iron ring 371 – iron ring 370 – iron nail	
	29:13	IV	31	UD–NS	480 – bronze ring link 481 – ring 503 – ceramic lamp frag. 488 – iron nail 487 – bronze ring	Dark, yellowish-brown fill in *kokh* #5
	29:15	IV	32	LR–B, UD, 1 KS rim		Dark brown fill in *kokh* #3
	29:17	IV	34	LR–B, UD, 2 KS rims		Dark brown fill in *kokh* #1
	29:18	IV	37	LR–B, UD, 3 KS rims, Pi	483 – metal ring 482 – iron chain	Dark brown fill in *kokh* #2
T29 South (= T40)	29:06	III–IV	10	B and later		Light, brown air-laid and water-puddled layer upon floor
			13	B, UD	280 – metal 279 – glass spindle whorl	
			14	B, UD	492 – ceramic lamp 360 – iron nail head	
			15	LR–B	484 – ceramic lamp frag. 493 – ceramic lamp 362 – iron nail 361 – glass bead	
	29:12	III–IV	28	LR?, UD, Pi	404 – ceramic lamp 456 – glass	Moist, compact soil under 29:11, over bedrock
SE II.1	10005	IV	5	LR–4th C.*	737 – glass rim 735 – glass rim 736 – glass rim	Compact, clay-like soil above bedrock (surface?)
	10013	IV	50	LR, B	1712 – glass base 1726 – nail frag.	Roughly mettled surface inside walls 10006, 10007, 10021, 10010
			51	LR, B, A†	1727 – glass rim	
	10014	IV				Hard earthen surface, in use with walls 10006, 10007, 10010
	10014 P	IV	26	LR*	1059 – iron nail	
	10014.1	IV	27	LR*	1261 – glass rim	
			54	LR*, TS		
	10016	IV	30	LR		Hard, clumpy soil contiguous to bedrock within walls 10006, 10007, 10010
			31	LR*		
			56	LR*		
			57	B?		
	10017	IV				Hard-packed dirt surface associated with walls 10006, 10007, and 10010
	10017 P	IV	34	LR, B?		
			36	LR	1256 – glass body frag. 1259 – iron nail	
	10017.1	IV	65	LR*		
	10019	IV	44	LR		Moist, clay-like fill and decomposed bedrock under surface 10017

Area	Locus	Stratum	Bucket	Field Reading	Objects	Description
	10020	IV	45	LR*	1260 — glass rim	Lower part of fill 10018 between 10015 and platform 10022
			46	LR*	1613 — glass base	
	10024	IV	59	LR		Hard-packed soil beneath 2nd stage of 10025
			64	LR*		
	10028	IV				Surface below 10017.1
	10028.1	IV	69	LR*	1932 — iron sickle 1862 — bronze ring	
			70	LR*, 1 TS		
	10029	IV	71	LR*		Very hard, clay-like soil below 10028 above bedrock
SE II.17	17009	IV				Firmly-packed, semi-mettled surface, north of wall 17007 and pit 17015. Same as 18007
	17009.1		9	LR*	1774 — glass rim	
	17011	IV	16	ER–LR	1933 — glass base	Loose soil just below bedrock mouth of pit 17015
	17012	IV	17	LR, Pi	1931 — iron nail	Firmly packed soil in pit 17015 beneath 17011
	17014	IV	20	LR*		Moist, loose soil in second chamber of 17015
SE II.18	18007	IV				Hard-packed street or courtyard surface, somewhat mettled, between walls 18002 and 18006.
	18007.1		6	LR*	1851 — glass rim	
			7	LR, B?	1898 — glass base 1896 — glass rim	
	18008	IV	8	LR*	1859 — glass base 1876 — glass rim 1879 — glass rim	Moist, reddish soil below 18007
SE II.22	22002	IV	9	LR	868 — ceramic lamp frag. 867 — glass base 866 — glass base 865 — glass rim 863 — glass rim 864 — glass rim 843 — glass bead	Moist soil below surface layer in pit 22006
	22003	IV	16	LR*, 3 TS	890 — glass rim 886 — glass base 889 — glass rim 888 — glass rim 887 — glass rim	Moist, firmly-packed soil, with much pottery and rock chips, below 22002
			20	LR*	1255 — glass rim	
	22006	IV	23	LR, B?	1065 — glass rim 1064 — glass rim 1063 — glass rim 1062 — glass rim 1061 — glass rim 1060 — glass rim 1072 — glass base 1068 — glass rim 1069 — glass rim 1070 — glass rim 1071 — glass rim	Bottom layer of soil, below 27004, above bedrock, in pit; also, designation for the declivity itself
			28	LR, B?	1263 — ceramic lamp frag.	
	22020	IV	45	LR*	1200 — glass rim	Lower part of fill 22018 between wall 22015, platform 22022, and wall 22031
			46	LR*	1613 — glass base	
SE II.23	23005	IV	5	LR–EB*	737 — glass rim 735 — glass rim 736 — glass rim	Compact, clay-like soil above bedrock (surface?) outside room A

Area	Locus	Stratum	Bucket	Field Reading	Objects	Description
	23013	IV	50	LR, B	1712 — glass base 1726 — nail frag.	Roughly mettled surface inside walls 23006, 23007, 23021, 23010, within room A
			51	LR, B, A	1727 — glass rim	
	23014	IV				Hard, earthen surface, in use with walls 23006, 23007, 12010, inside room A
	23014 P	IV	26	LR*	1059 — iron nail	
	23014.1	IV	27	LR*	1261 — glass rim	
			54	LR*, TS		
	23016	IV	30	LR		Hard, clumpy soil contiguous to bedrock within walls 23006, 23007, 23010, inside room A
			31	LR*		
			56	LR*		
			57	B?		
	23017	IV				Hard-packed, dirt surface, associated with walls 23006, 23007, and 23010, inside room A
	23017 P	IV	34	LR, B?		
			36	LR	1256 — glass body frag. 1259 — iron nail	
	23017.1	IV	65	LR*		
	23019	IV	44	LR		Moist, clay-like fill and decomposed bedrock under surface 23017, inside room A
	23024	IV	59	LR		Hard-packed soil beneath 2nd stage of bench 23035 in northeast of room A
			64	LR*		
	23028	IV				Surface below 23017.1 in room A
	23028.1	IV	69	LR*	1932 — iron sickle	
			70	LR*, 1 TS	1862 — bronze ring	
	230029	IV	71	LR*		Very hard clay soil below 23028 above bedrock in room A

APPENDIX B. INDEX OF COIN FINDS BY AREA AND BY LOCI
by Richard S. Hanson

Northwest I:25

Locus 1
R1305	Roman Ae3: Constantius II/fel temp reparatio	346–361 CE
R1325	Roman Ae2: Licinius I/soli invicto comiti	308–324 CE
R1326	Ptolemaic drachm: Ptolemaios IV or V, king of Cypros?/ Eagle	2 c. BCE
R1340	Unattributable; perhaps not a coin	

Locus 5
R1376	Tyrian tetradrachm: Melqarth/ club with oak leaf	152/3 CE
R1377	Roman Ae3: Constantine II?/fel temp reparatio	346–361 CE
R1379	Tyrian drachm: Tyche/galley	84/5 CE
R1378	Seleucid dilepton: Alexander I?/ Apollo with bow	152–144 BCE

Northwest I:26

Locus 00
R1349	Roman Ae3: Constantius II?/fel temp reparatio	346–361 CE

Locus 1
R1307	Roman Ae4: Valentinian III?/salus reipublicae with cross	425–450 CE
R1308	Roman Ae3: Constans/Victoriae DD Augg Q NN? Two victories facing	341–346 CE

Locus 5
R1306	Roman Ae3: Constantius/gloria exercitus	330–335 CE

Locus 9
R1309	Roman Ae3: Constantius II?/vot xx mult xxx	341–346 CE?
R1310	Tyrian tetradrachm: Claudius II?/col tur met and galley with 3 figures	268–270 CE?

Locus 11
R1327	Roman Ae3 or 2? Unattributable	4 c. CE?

Locus 19
R1410	Roman Ae3: ..../vota type	4 c. CE

Locus 34
R1599	Roman antonianus: Gallienus/securit perpet	260–268 CE
R1600	Roman Ae4: unattributable	Late 4– early 5 c. CE
R2001	Alexander Yannai: anchor/star	103–76 BCE

Locus 35
R2011	Roman Ae3: Constantius II?/fel temp reparatio	346–361 CE
R2012	Roman Ae4: Unattributable	4 c. CE
R2013	Lead; unattributable	

Northwest I:27

Locus 2
R519	Islamic: unattributable	

Locus 6
R520	Ayyubid: al-Kamil Muhammed	1236–1237 CE

Northwest I:28

Locus 00
R2245	Jewish? Possible wreath on rev.	1 c. BCE

Locus 2
R521	Roman Ae3: Licinius I/ soli invicto comiti	308–324 CE
R522	Tyrian hemidrachm: Tyche/palm tree	104–167 CE
R601	Roman Ae3: unattributable	4–early 5 c. CE

Locus 4
R525	Roman Ae4 or 3: unattributable	4–early 5 c. CE

Locus 5
R524	Lead, perhaps a coin of Alexander Yannai	103–76 BCE?
R536	Roman Ae3: Constantius II/fel temp reparatio	346–361 CE

Locus 8
R526	Alexander Yannai: ..../star	103–76 BCE
R527	Roman Ae3: Constantinopolis/gloria exercitus	335–341 CE
R528	Roman Ae4: unattributable	4–early 5 c. CE
R529	Alexander Yannai: anchor/star	103–76 BCE
R530	Roman Ae4: unattributable	4–early 5 c. CE
R531	Roman Ae4: Theodosius I/vot v mult x	379–395 CE
R532	Roman Ae: unattributable	4 c. CE
R533	Roman Ae3 or 4: unattributable	4–early 5 c. CE
R534	Roman Ae3: unattributable	4 c. CE
R535	Roman Ae4: Arcadius/salus rei-publicae	383–395 CE

Northwest I:29

Locus 00
R537	Roman Ae3: ..../gloria exercitus, one standard	337–341 CE

Locus 1
R538	Roman Ae3: Constans/Victoria DD NN Augg	341–346 CE

Locus 6
R539	Ae denaro of Frederick II: ROMIMPR:SEPAUG/eagle with R.IERSL.ET.SICIL	1197–1250 CE

Locus 8
R540	Roman Ae3 or 2: ..../fel temp reparatio	346–361 CE
R541	Roman Ae3: Julian/fel temp reparatio	355–361 CE

Locus 9
R543	Tyrian drachm? Tyche/....	1 c. BCE– 2 c. CE

Locus 11
R542	Roman Ae3: Julian/fel temp reparatio	355–361 CE
R544	Roman Ae4: unattributable	4–early 5 c. CE
R624	Unattributable	

Northwest I:30

Locus 00
R545	Roman Ae2: Constantius II/fel temp reparatio	346–361 CE

R549	Roman Ae4: Valentinian II?/spes reipublicae (Victory with chi-rho)	383–393 CE?
R554	Bahri Mamluk: Baybars I	1260–1277 CE
Locus 1		
R553	Roman Ae4: Julian?/vot x mult xx	361–363 CE?
R547	John Hyrcanus II: Hebrew inscription in wreath/double cornucopiae	76, 63–40 BCE
R548	Roman Ae3: Julian?/spes reipublice (soldier with spear)	355–361 CE?
R550	Roman Ae4: Arcadius/salus reipublicae (Victory with chi-rho)	383–393 CE
R551	Roman Ae3: Constantius II?/fel temp reparatio	346–361 CE
R552	Alexander Yannai: anchor/star	103–76 BCE
R555	Roman Ae3: Constantius II/fel temp' reparatio	346–361 CE
Locus 4		
R556	Roman Ae4: unattributable	late 3–early 4 c. CE?
R557	Abbassid: Al-Ma'mun	829 CE
R558	Byzantine follis: Justinian I	Ca. 527 CE
R559	Roman Ae3: Constantius II/fel temp reparatio	346–361 CE
Locus 6		
R560	Roman Ae2: Constantius II?/fel temp reparatio	346–361 CE
Locus 7		
R562	Roman Ae3: Constantius II?/vot-mult	341–346 CE?
R561	Roman Ae4: ..../Victory moving left	378–394 CE?
R563	Roman Ae3: unattributable	4 c. CE
R564	Byzantine fragment	6–7 c. CE
R575	Roman Ae3: Theodosius I?/salus reipublicae (Victory dragging captive)	383–395 CE
Locus 8		
R565	Roman Ae2: Helena Augusta/securitas reipublice	324–330 CE
R566	Roman Ae3: Theodosius II?/gloria romanorum (three emperors with spears)	408–421 CE?
R567	Jewish or Tyrian: faint palm tree on reverse	1–2 c. C.E.?
R568	Unattributable	
Locus 8.1		
R569	Billon denier: Hugh III, Duke of Burgundy	1162–1193 CE
Locus 9		
R574	Unattributable	
Locus 12		
R570	Roman Ae3: Constantius II?/vot xx mult xxx	341–346 CE?
R571	Likely a coin of Nerva	96–98 CE?
R572	Alexander Yannai? Faint trace of star on reverse	103–76 BCE?
R573	Roman Ae3: Theodosius II?/gloria romanorum (three emperors standing)	402 CE?
Locus 14		
R576	Roman Ae3: ..../Victory moving left	Late 4–early 5 c. CE
R577	Byzantine decanummium: Justin I?	518–527 CE?

Northwest I:31

Locus 1		
R578	Tyrian didrachm: Melqarth/club with inscription	112–184 CE
R1311	Alexander Yannai: anchor/star	103–76 BCE
R580	Roman Ae4 or 3: ..../vot xx mult xxx	341–346 CE

R1496	Roman Ae3: ..../gloria exercitus (one or two soldiers with standard)	335–341 CE?
R1502	Tyrian or Seleucid dilepton: bust of king or Melqarth/palm tree	2 c. BCE?
Locus 2		
R1313	Roman Ae2: Maximian I/concordia militum (Jupiter and Victory)	285–308 CE
R1314	Roman Ae3: Constantius II?/fel temp reparatio	346–361 CE
R1319	Roman Ae3: unattributable	Late 3–early 5 c. CE
Locus 5		
R579	Ayyubid: al-'Adil Abu Bakr	1211–1212 CE
Locus 19		
R1312	Roman Ae3: Constantius II/vot xx mult xxx	341–346 CE
R1381	Roman Ae3: ..../virtus exerc romanor? (emperor spearing victim)	360–363 CE?
Locus 20		
R1328	Abbassid; ar dirham: al-Ma'mun, Isbahan	819–20 CE
R1315	Roman Ae3: ..../gloria exercitus (one standard)?	4 c. CE
Locus 21		
R1329	Roman antonianus: Gallienus?/salus augg	253–260 CE?
R1341	Roman Ae4: Valentinian II, Theodosius I, Arcadius or Flaccilla/salus reipublicae (Victory with captive)	383–392 CE
R1342	Roman Ae3: ..../securitas reipublicae	364–383 CE
R1343	Jewish? Unattributable	1 c. CE?
R1344	Roman Ae2: Licinius I/ providentiae Augg (camp gate)	308–324 CE
R1380	Alexander Yannai: anchor/star	103–76 BCE
R1382	Unattributable. Perhaps a medallion	
R1383	Roman Ae3: unattributable	Late 3–early 5 c. CE
R1384	Roman Ae3: Constantius II/vot xx mult xxx	341–346 CE
R1412	Umayyad fals: unattributable	695–750 CE
R1495	Roman?	Late 3–early 5 c. CE?
R1503	Ptolemaic drachm? Possibly Seleucid: bust/eagle with wings raised	3–2 c. BCE
R1560	Roman Ae4 or 3: unattributable	Late 3–early 5 c. CE?

Northwest I:32

Locus 00		
R581	Roman Ae2: Constantius Gallus/fel temp reparatio	351–354 CE
Locus 1		
R582	Phoenician or Palestinian area: unattributable	1 c. BCE?
R587	Bahri Mamluk: Baybars I (lion/hexagram)	1260–1277 CE
R588	Bahri Mamluk: Baybars I (lion/hexagram)	1260–1277 CE
R589	Bahri Mamluk: Baybars I (lion/hexagram)	1260–1277 CE
R590	Roman Ae3: Constantine/gloria exercitus	335–337 CE
R591	Bahri Mamluk: Baybars I	1260–1277 CE
Locus 4		
R583	Venetian grosso: Marino Morosine, Doge of Venice/Christ seated facing with IC XC inscribed above posts of throne	1249–1253 CE

R584	Bahri Mamluk: Baybars I (lion/hexagram)	1260–1277 CE

Locus 8

R585	Roman dupondius? Septimius Severus?/Minerva with spear	193–211 CE?

Locus 14

R586	Roman Ae4 or 3: Julian?/vot ... mult xx	4 c. CE

Locus 16

R1316	Roman Ae3: Gratian/securitas reipublicae (Victory)	378–383 CE

Locus 22

R1553	Roman Ae3: Valentinian I?/emperor dragging captive	364–378 CE?

Locus 28

R1469	Roman Ae3: unattributable	4–early 5 c. CE
R1548	Roman Ae4: Theodosius II?/gloria romanorum (three emperors standing)	Ca. 408 CE
R1549	Roman Ae3: Constantius II?/fel temp reparatio	346–361 CE
R1550	Roman Ae4: Valentinian II?/salus reipublicae (Victory dragging captive, chi-rho)	383–392 CE?
R1551	Roman coin of Palestine: Trajan/cornucopiae with palm branch	99/100 CE
R1552	Unattributable	
R1554	Roman Ae4: unattributable	4 c. CE
R1555	Roman Ae4: Arcadius/concordia Aug. (cross)	395–408 CE

Locus 29

R2002	Roman Ae4: unattributable	4–early 5 c. CE

Locus 30

R1556	Roman Ae3 or 2: unattributable	4 c. CE
R1557	Roman Ae3: Constantius II/spes reipublicae	355–361 CE
R1558	Roman Ae2: Constantius II/fel temp reparatio	346–361 CE
R1559	Roman Ae3: unattributable	Late 3–early 5 c. CE
R1571	Roman Ae3: Valentinian I/emperor dragging captive	364–375 CE

Northwest I:34

Locus 7

R2268	Byzantine follis: Justin II	565–578 CE
R2269	Bahri Mamluk: Baybars I (lion/hexagram)	1260–1277 CE
R2270	Roman Ae3: Constantius II?/fel temp reparatio	346–361 CE
R2267	Alexander Yannai or John Hyrcanus II: Hebrew inscription in wreath/double cornucopiae	Ca. 76 BCE (103–40 BCE)
R2279	Alexander Yannai or John Hyrcanus II: Hebrew inscription in wreath/double cornucopiae	Ca. 76 BCE (103–40 BCE)

Locus 10

R2296	Hasmonean? Unattributable	1 c. BCE?

Locus 13

R2322	Roman antonianus: Probus/clementia temp (Jupiter giving Victory to emperor)	276–282 CE

Northwest VII:1

Locus 00

R2102	Tyrian tetradrachm: Philip II?/col turo met with Apollo	3 c. CE

R2142	Unattributable	

Locus I

	Roman Ae?	2–4 c. CE?
R1431	Roman Ae?	3–early 5 c. CE?

Locus 11

R1345	Roman Ae4: Constantius II?/vict aug?	341–346 CE?

Locus 16

R1351	Roman Ae3: unattributable	4–early 5 c. CE
R1350	Roman Ae3: Theodosius II?/gloria romanorum (three emperors standing)	393–395 CE?
R1364	Roman Ae4: Theodosius II/salus reipublicae (Victory and chi-rho)	402–408 CE
R1429	Roman Ae3: Theodosius II?/gloria romanorum? (three emperors standing)	402 CE?
R1492	Alexander Yannai: Hebrew inscription in wreath/double cornucopiae	103–76 BCE
R1565	Roman Ae3: urbs roma/wolf with twins	330–335 CE

Locus 16a

R1491	Ayyubid: al-'Adil Abu Bakr	1211–1212 CE

Locus 22

R1386	Roman semis: Severus Alexander/colonia Bostra	222–235 CE
R1387	Alexander Yannai: anchor/star	103–76 BCE

Locus 25

R1385	Roman Ae4? Unattributable	4–early 5 c. CE?

Locus 35

R1413	Roman Ae4: Honorius or Theodosius II/gloria romanorum (two emperors facing)	408–421 CE
R1414	Roman Ae?	2–4 c. CE?
R1415	Roman Ae3: Constantius II?/spes reipublice or reipublice	355–361 CE?

Locus 41

R1493	Roman Ae3 or 4? Unattributable	Late 3–early 5 c. CE?

Locus 47

R1494	Seleucid dilepton? Bust with lion headdress/palm tree with bow	2 c. BCE?

Locus 56

R2157	Roman denarius: Hadrian/Ceres or Venus	117–138 CE

Locus 60

R2183	Roman Ae3: Gratian/securitas reipublicae	378–383 CE

Surface finds

R677	Alexander Yannai or John Hyrcanus II: Hebrew inscription in wreath/double cornucopiae	Ca. 76 BCE (103–40 BCE)
	Roman Ae2: Honorius/virtus exerciti (Victory hailing emperor)	395–408 CE

Northwest VII:2

Locus 1

R1388	Coin of Petra: Elagabalus/bull	218–222 CE
R1389	Roman Ae3: Constantius II?/vot xx mult xxx	341–346 CE
R1416	Sidonian drachma: Tyche/galley	1–2 c. CE?

Northwest VII:3

Locus 2

R2236	Roman Ae3: Jovian?/vot xx mult ...	363–364 CE?

Locus 4

R2234	Roman Ae3: unattributable	4 c. CE

Locus 5

R2235	Roman Ae3: ..../securitas reipublicae	364–383 CE

Locus 23
R2309   Byzantine follis: Justin II   572–573 CE
On second flagstone level
in dirt about floor outside square
R2324   Mamluk?   13 C. CE?

Northwest VII:8

Locus 00
R2325   Ayyūbid Ae fals: al-'Aziz Muhammad
with al-Mostansur   1226–1237 CE
Locus 01
R2071   John Hyrcanus II: Hebrew inscription
in wreath/double cornucopiae   76, 63–40 BCE
Locus 1
R1577   Roman Ae4: ..../salus reipublicae?   Late 4–early
                                             5 c. CE?
R2064   Tyrian didrachm: Melqarth/club with
inscription   155–156 CE
R2072   Roman antonianus: Valerianus/
fortuna redux   253–260 CE
R2080   Roman Ae2: Constantius II/fel temp
reparatio   346–361 CE
R2081   Ayyubid Ae fals: Salah ed-Din with
Fengid al-Sal.h Isma'il b. Maḥmud   1175–1178 CE
R2079   Roman antonianus: Gallienus/virtus
aug   260–268 CE
Locus 2
R2298   Alexander Yannai: anchor/star   103–76 BCE
Bucket 8
R2098   Roman Ae3: ..../vota wreath   4 c. CE

Northwest VII:9

Locus 00
R2323   Roman Ae3: ..../Victory   Latter 4 c. CE
Locus 1
R2241   Roman Ae2: Constantine/soli invicto
comiti   306–320 CE
R2311   Bahri Mamluk, Ar dirham: Baybars I   1268–1274 CE
Locus 4
R2273   Hasmonean?   1 c. BCE?
R2312   Tyrian didrachm: Melqarth/club with
inscription   155–156 CE
Locus 6
R2242   Alexander Yannai: anchor/star   103–76 BCE

Northwest VII:14

Locus 1
R2215   Tyrian or Sidonian drachm:
Tyche/galley   Late 2 c. CE?
R2243   Byzantine follis: Justin I   518–527 CE
R2239   Ayyubid ar dirham: Salah al-Din   1185–1193 CE
R2290   Roman Ae4: Valentinian II,
Theodosius I, Arcadius, Flaccilla or
Honorius/salus reipublicae   383–395 CE
Locus 2
R2281   Roman Ae3: Constantius II?/fel
temp reparatio   346–361 CE
R2299   Roman Ae3: ..../fel temp reparatio   346–361 CE
R2300   Roman Ae3: Roma/wolf with twins   330–335 CE?
R2320   Ayyubid fals: al-Salih Ayyub   1240–1244 CE
Locus 3
R2282   Alexander Yannai: anchor/star   103–76 BCE
Locus 5
R2326   Tyrian drachm: Melqarth or Tyre/
palm tree   1–2 c. CE

Northwest VII:19

Locus 4
R2042   Alexander Yannai or John
Hyrcanus II: Hebrew inscription in   Ca. 76 BCE
wreath/double cornucopiae   (103–40 BCE)
R2043   Roman Ae3? Unattributable   4–early 5 c. CE
Locus 5
R2005   Ayyūbid: al-'Adil Abū Bakr   1200–1218 CE
R2006   Roman Ae: unattributable   4–early 5 c. CE
R2014   Roman Ae: unattributable   4–early 5 c. CE
R2015   Bahri Mamluk: Baybars I   1260–1277 CE
R2016   Half denaro of Frederick II:
IMPERATOR:ROM/IERSP·ET·
SICIL·R   1197–1250 CE
Locus 8
R2044   Roman Ae3: Constantius II?/fel temp
reparatio   346–361 CE
R2060   Byzantine follis: Anastasius I   498–518 CE

Northwest VII:27

Locus 1
R1504   Roman Ae: Hadrian/emperor with
standard   120 CE
R1505   Roman Ae3: ..../......reipublicae   Late 4–early
                                             5 c. CE
R1506   Roman Ae4: Constantius II?/fel temp
reparatio   346–361 CE
Locus 3
R1566   Roman Ae3: ..../Victory moving left Late 4 c. CE
R1567   Seleucid or Tyrian?   2–1 c. BCE?
R1568   Seleucid? Seleucis II?/bull   246–226 BCE?
Locus 6
R2007   Roman Ae3 or 4: Constantine or
Constantius II?/emperor standing   First half of
with spear   4 c. CE?
R2008   Ayyubid fals: al-'Adil Abu Bakr   1201–1203 CE
Locus 7
R2009   Ayyubid fals: Salah ed-Din   1190 CE
Locus 8
R2010   Roman Ae3: unattributable   4 c. CE
Locus 10
R2063   Roman Ae3: Constantius II/fel temp
reparatio   346–361 CE
R2052   Roman Ae3: Julian/fel temp reparatio 355–361 CE

Northwest VII:33

Locus 00
R2090   Billon denier: Jean de Brienne, regent
for Yolanda/cross with IOHEX:REX   1219 CE
R592   Roman antonianus: Probus/clementia
temp   276–282 CE
Locus 1
R2149   Roman Ae4: Arcadius/victoria augg
(two victories facing)   383–408 CE
Locus 7
R2074   Roman Ae4: Valentinian II,
Theodosius I or Arcadius/salus
reipublicae (Victory with captive)   383–392 CE
Locus 10
R2096   Roman-Jewish: Domitian/Agrippa II   Ca. 80 CE
R2097   Roman Ae3: Gratian?/securitas
reipublicae (Victory)   378–383 CE?

Northeast I:19

Locus 2
R593   Roman Ae3: Constantius II/fel temp
       reparatio   346–361 CE
R594   Roman Ae3: Constantine/gloria
       exercitus   335–337 CE
R595   Roman Ae3: Constantius II/gloria
       exercitus   335–341 CE
R596   Mamluk? Unattributable   13–14 c. CE
R597   Seleucid dilepton: Antiochus
       IV/strutting horse   175–164 BCE
R598   Alexander Yannai: ..../star   103–76 BCE
R599   Alexander Yannai?   103–76 BCE
R600   Ptolemaic drachm? Amon Re/eagle
       with thunderbolt   3–2 c. BCE?

Locus 72
R2197 Jewish?   1 c. BCE–1 c.
                                              CE?
R2199 Tyche/Agrippa I?   37–44 CE?

Northeast I:20

Locus 7.1
R2050 Roman Ae3: Valens/gloria
       romanorum   364–375 CE

Northeast I:25

Locus 1
R622   Roman Ae3: Constantine or one of
       his sons/gloria exercitus (one
       standard)   335–341 CE
Locus 6
R601   Roman Ae4: unattributable   Late 4–early
                                              5 c. CE
R602   Roman Ae4: unattributable   4–early 5 c. CE
R603   Roman Ae4: unattributable   4–early 5 c. CE
Locus 7
R604   Roman Ae3: unattributable   3–4 c. CE
Locus 36
R606   Roman Ae3? Unattributable   3–5 c. CE
R607   Roman Ae4? Unattributable   Late 4–early
                                              5 c. CE
R608   Tyrian hemidrachm: Tyche or bust
       of an emperor/palm tree   1–2 c. CE?
R609   Jewish?   1 c. CE?
R610   Roman Ae2: ..../fel temp reparatio   346–361 CE
R611   Roman Ae3: Constantius II?/fel temp
       reparatio   346–361 CE
R612   Roman Ae2: Constantius II/gloria
       exercitus (two standards)   330–335 CE
R613   Roman denarius Ar: Vespasian/
       standing figure on column   75–79 CE
Locus 37
R614   Roman Ae4: Unattributable   4–early 5 c. CE?
R615   Alexander Yannai: ..../star   103–76 BCE
R605   Alexander Yannai: Hebrew inscription
       in wreath/double cornucopiae   103–76 BCE
Locus 40
R616   Jewish?   1 c. BCE?
Locus 41
R621   Alexander Yannai: anchor/star   103–76 BCE
Locus 42
R617   Byzantine follis: Justin II   575 CE
R618   Alexander Yannai: anchor/star   103–76 BCE

R619   Roman Ae4: Constantius II?/vot xx
       mult xxx   341–346 or
                                              ca. 383 CE
R620   Roman Ae2: Probus/clementia temp   276–282 CE

Northeast I:26

Locus 00
R2328 Roman Ae2: Constantius Gallus/fel
       temp reparatio   351–354 CE
R2327 Roman Ae3?   4 c. CE?
R2329 Roman Ae3?   4 c. CE?
R2135 Abbassid, anonymous of Tyre   811–812 CE
Locus 3
R623   Roman Ae3: Theodosius I/gloria
       romanorum   379–395 CE
Locus 4
R1594 Roman Ae3: Constantius II?/victoria
       aug/augg?   341–346 CE?
Locus 5
R1595 Alexander Yannai: anchor/star   103–76 BCE
Locus 6
R1596 Alexander Yannai?   103–76 BCE?
R1597 Islamic? Unattributable   8–14 c. CE?
R1598 Roman Ae4: ..../iovi conservatori?   Late 3–early
                                              4 c. CE?
Locus 31
R2148 Roman Ae: Nero (wreath)/palm
       branch   58 CE
Locus unlisted
R2041 Tyrian hemidrachm: Tyche/palm tree   104–167 CE
R2051 Alexander Yannai: anchor/star   103–76 BCE

Northeast I:27

Locus 00
R1497 Seleucid dilepton: Demetrius II/palm
       tree   143–140 BCE
Locus 2
R1488 Roman Ae4: unattributable   Late 3–early
                                              5 c. CE
R1489 Roman Ae4: Constans/vot xx mult
       xxx   341–346 CE
R1561 Unattributable

Northeast I:31

Locus 1
R625   Roman Ae2: Constantius II/fel temp
       reparatio   346–350 CE
Locus 3
R1411 Tyrian hemidrachm: Tyche/palm tree   Early 2 c. CE
Locus 4
R1317 Unattributable
Locus 9
R633   Roman Ae: Domitian/Agrippa II
       (palm tree)   81 CE
R1318 Roman Ae3: ..../fel temp reparatio or
       Victoria augg.   341–361 CE
Locus 22
R3854 Roman Ae4: Constans   337–341 CE
R3855 Alexander Yannai: anchor/star   103–76 BCE

Northeast I:32

Locus 00
R2070 Roman Ae4: Valentinian III?/Victoria
       aug.   425–455 CE?

Locus 1
R627   Unattributable
R2329 Alexander Yannai: anchor/star   103–76 BCE
Locus 12
R2134 Seleucid dilepton: Demetrius II/palm
       tree   146–138 BCE
Locus 12.1
R2264 Roman Ae4: unattributable   4 C. CE
Locus 14
R2073 Tyrian didrachm: Melqarth/club
       within oak leaf   3–2 C. BCE
Locus 15
R626   Ptolemaic drachm: Euergetes III/
       eagle   247–222 BCE
R2051 Alexander Yannai: anchor/star   103–76 BCE
Locus 16
R2092 Roman Ae4: ..../securitas reipublicae
       (Victory)   364–383 CE
R2093 Tyrian hemidrachm: Tyche/palm tree   64–65 CE?
R2136 Alexander Yannai: anchor/star   103–76 BCE
Locus 19
R2259 Alexander Yannai: anchor/star   103–76 BCE
Locus 20
R2195 Tyrian drachm: Tyche/galley?   98 BCE–85 CE

Northeast I:33

Locus 00
R397   Jewish?   1 C. BCE–1 C.
                                              CE?

R394   Lead; unattributable
R392   Roman Ae2: Constantius II/gloria
       exercitus (two standards)   330–335 CE
Locus 5
R391   Seljuk of Rum: Qilij-Arslan b. Mas'ud 1156–1192 CE
R390   Bahri Mamluk: Baybars I (lion/
       hexagram)   1260–1277 CE
R398   Islamic? Unattributable   8–14 C. CE?
R393   Alexander Yannai: anchor/star   103–76 BCE
Locus 10
R395   Roman Ae2: Maximianus/concordia
       militum   286–310 CE
R396   Roman Ae3: Constantine?/iovi
       conservatori aug.   306–324 CE

Northeast I:34

Locus 00
R628   Roman Ae3? Unattributable   3–early 5 C. CE
R631   Roman Ae3: Unattributable   4 C. CE
Locus 1
R629   Roman Ae2: Constantine/soli invicto
       comiti   308–320 CE
Locus 7
R630   Ayyubid: al-'Adil Abu Bakr   599–607 CE

Northeast VII:1

Locus 2
R632   Alexander Yannai: Hebrew inscription
       in wreath/double cornucopiae   103–76 BCE
Locus 8
R1320 Roman Ae2: Constantine/providentiae
       aug.   324–330 CE
R1321 Mamluk? Unattributable   13–14 C. CE?
Locus 14
R1330 Ayyubid: Ṣalaḥ ed-Din   1169–1193 CE
R1346 Roman Ae2: Constantine/soli invicto
       comiti   306–337 CE
R1352 Roman Ae3: ..../fel temp reparatio   346–361 CE

Surface find
R677   Alexander Yannai or John
       Hyrcanus II: Hebrew inscription in
       wreath/double cornucopiae   Ca. 76 BCE
                                              (103–40 BCE)

Northeast VII:2

Locus 00
R1365 Roman Ae4: Arcadius/salus
       reipublicae (Victory dragging captive,
       chi-rho)   393–395 CE
R1366 Seleucid dilepton: Demetrius II/palm
       tree   162–151 BCE
R1323a Roman Ae4: Constantius II/fel temp
       reparatio   346–361 CE
R1331 Roman colonial: Elagabalus as Mark
       Anthony/eagle   218–222 CE
R1332 Roman Ae4: Theodosius I/salus
       reipublicae (Victory dragging captive,
       chi-rho)   383–392 CE
R1333 Roman Ae4: Theodosius I, Arcadius
       or Honorius/salus reipublicae (Victory
       dragging captive)   393–395 CE
R1334 Roman Ae3: Honorius/gloria
       romanorum (three emperors standing)   408–423 CE
R1335 Roman Ae4: Johannes?/salus
       reipublice (Victory dragging captive,
       chi-rho)   423–425 CE?
R1336 Roman Ae3: ..../gloria exercitus (one
       standard)   335–341 CE
R1337 Roman Ae4: Theodosius I/vot x mult
       xx in wreath   383 CE
R1338 Roman Ae3: unattributable   4–early 5 C.
                                              CE
R1339 Roman antonianus: unattributable   3 C. CE
Locus 2
R1322 Alexander Yannai: Hebrew inscription
       in wreath/double cornucopiae   103–76 BCE
R1323 Roman Ae4: ..../soldier or Victory
       moving left   4–early 5 C. CE
Locus 4
R1353 Roman Ae3: ..../gloria exercitus (one
       standard)   337–341 CE
Locus 5
R1367 Roman Ae4: ..../cross within circle   5 C. CE
R1368 Roman Ae3: Constantine/gloria
       exercitus (one standard)   335–337 CE
Locus 7
R1490 Ayyūbid: al-'Adil Abu Bakr   1204–1208 CE
Locus 14
R1369 Seleucid dilepton: Demetrius II/palm
       tree   145–144 BCE
Locus 15.1
R1392 Alexander Yannai: anchor/star   103–76 BCE
Locus 17
R1370 Billon denier: Guillaume II de
       Charbigny?   1203–1233 CE?
R1391 Roman Ae4: Arcadius/virtus exercitus   393–408 CE
R1393 Tyrian tetradrachm: Elagabalus/
       Astarte placing wreath on trophy   218–222 CE
R1417 Tyrian tetradrachm: Elagabalus as
       Mark Anthony/Astarte placing wreath
       on trophy   218–222 CE
Locus 22
R1432 Roman Ae3: Constantius II?/fel temp
       reparatio   346–361 CE

R1433   Roman Ae4: Valens or Arcadius/
        Victory moving left   364–408 CE
R1434   Roman Ae4: unattributable   4–early 5 c. CE
R1435   Roman Ae3: ..../fel temp reparatio   346–361 CE
R1436   Roman Ae3: Valentinian I or II/salus
        reipublicae   364–392 CE
R1437   Roman Ae4: unattributable   4–early 5 c. CE
R1438   Roman Ae3: ..../fel temp reparatio   346–361 CE
R1439   Roman Ae3: Julian/soldier moving
        right   360–363 CE
R1440   Roman Ae3: ..../securitas reipublicae 364–383 CE
R1441   Roman Ae3: Valens or Valentinian/.... 364–378 CE
R1442   Roman Ae3 or 2: Constantius II?/....   Mid–4 c. CE
R1443   Seleucid dilepton: ..../palm tree   2 c. BCE?
R1444   Roman Ae4: unattributable   Late 4–early
                                                5 c. CE
R1446   Roman Ae3: Constantius II/fel temp
        reparatio   346–361 CE
R1447   Roman Ae3: Arcadius?/Victory
        moving left   383–408 CE?

Locus 23
R1448   Roman Ae4: unattributable   4–early 5 c. CE
R1445   Roman Ae3: Valens or Valentinian I/
        securitas reipublicae   364–378 CE

Locus 30
R2061   Alexander Yannai: anchor/star   103–76 BCE
R2062   John Hyrcanus II: Hebrew inscription
        in wreath/double cornucopiae   76, 63–40 BCE

Northeast VII:3

Locus 00
R2222   Seleucid or Tyrian dilepton?   2 c. BCE?
R2257   Unattributable: likely not a coin
R2266   Tyrian drachm: Tyche/palm tree   108–109 CE

Locus 3
R2221   Roman Ae?   Late 3–early
                                                5 c. CE?

Locus 4
R2260   Roman Ae4: Theodosius I/Victoria
        auggg (Victory dragging captive)   379–395 CE
R2262   Roman Ae3: Constantine?/vn mr?   341–346 CE?
R2316   Roman Ae4: unattributable   4–early 5 c. CE

Locus 10
R2317   Alexander Yannai: anchor/star   103–76 BCE

Locus 12
R2319   Jewish: unattributable   1 c. BCE–early
                                                1 c. CE

Locus 13
R2303   Roman Ae3 or 2: Arcadius or
        Honorius?/concordia aug?   393–408 CE?

Locus 17
R2318   Roman Ae3: Constantius II/fel temp
        reparatio   346–361 CE

On pavement
R2261   Roman Ae3: Valens?/restitur reip?   364–367 CE?

Northeast VII:13

Locus 00
R592   Roman antonianus: Probus/clementia
        temp   276–282 CE
R2240   Roman Ae3: Constantius II/gloria
        exercitus (two standards)   330–335 CE

Locus 1
R2003   Roman Ae3: Constantius II/vot xx
        mult xxx within wreath   341–346 CE
E2164   Roman Ae2: Constantine/vot xxx   324–330 CE

Locus 2
R2099   Roman Ae3: Constantine/gloria
        exercitus (two standards)   330–335 CE
R2207   Abbassid Ar dirham: al-Mansur   768 CE
R2208   Roman Ae4: ..../Victory   4–early 5 c. CE
R2209   Roman Ae3: unattributable   4 c. CE

Tomb 17

Surface
R1303   Alexander Yannai: anchor/star   103–76 BCE

Tomb 29 South

Locus 13.1
        Roman Ae4: unattributable   4 c. CE

Tomb 31

Locus 00
R1304   Tyrian Ar shekel: Melqarth/eagle
        with wings outspread   125 BCE–70 CE

Southwest I:28   Cambridge Probe I

Locus 1
R670   Mamluk?   13–14 c. CE?
Locus 2
R671   Roman Ae3: Constantius II?/fel temp
        reparatio   346–361 CE
R672   Tyrian tetradrachm: Caracalla   196–217 CE
Locus 5
R673   Roman Ae4 or 3: unattributable   4 c. CE?
R674   Roman Ae4: Theodosius I/salus
        reipublicae (Victory dragging captive,
        chi-rho)   379–395 CE
Top of pebble floor
R675   Roman Ae4: ..../aeterna pietas?   First half of
                                                4 c. CE?

Southeast I:24   Cambridge Probe II

Locus 4
R634   Roman Ae2: Theodosius I/gloria
        romanorum   379–395 CE
Locus 5
R635   Roman Ae3: unattributable   4 c. CE?
R639   Roman Ae3: Commemorative issue of
        Constantine/quadriga   337–341 CE
Locus 7
R636   Roman Ae3: Licinius I/iovi
        conservatori   307–324 CE
R637   Roman Ae4: unattributable   4–early 5 c. CE
Locus 7/8
R640   Roman Ae3: ..../felicitas reipublice? 4 c. CE
Locus 8
R638   Unattributable
Locus 10
R641   Roman Ae: unattributable   Late 3–early
                                                5 c. CE
R642   Roman Ae3: unattributable   Late 3–early
                                                5 c. CE
R643   Roman Ae3: Constantius II/gloria
        exercitus (one standard)   337–341 CE
R644   Roman Ae3 or 2: ..../vota wreath   4 c. CE
R645   Roman Ae3: Constantius II?/gloria
        exercitus (one or two standards,
        unclear)   330–341 CE
R646   Roman Ae 2 or 3: ..../gloria exercitus? 330–341 CE?

R658	Roman Ae3 or 4: unattributable	4–early 5 c. CE
Locus 11		
R647	Jewish?	1 c. BCE–early 1 c. CE?
R648	Roman Ae3: ..../securitas reipublicae? (Victory moving left)	364–383 CE?
R649	Unattributable	
R650	Roman Ae4? Unattributable	4–early 5 c. CE?
R651	Roman Ae3: unattributable	4 c. CE?
R652	Roman Ae: unattributable	late 3–early 5 c. CE
R653	Roman Ae3: Constantius II?/fel temp reparatio	346–361 CE
R654	Roman Ae? Unattributable	Late 3–early 5 c. CE
R655	Roman Ae3: Constantius II?/vot xx mult xxx	341–346 CE?
R656	Roman Ae3: Constans?/gloria exercitus	335–341 CE?
R657	Roman Ae? Unattributable	Late 3–early 5 c. CE
R659	Roman Ae3: Constantius II?/....	323–361 CE?
R660	Alexander Yannai: ..../star	103–76 BCE
R661	Roman Ae? Unattributable	Late 3–early 5 c. CE
R662	Roman Ae3: Commemorative coin of Constantine/quadriga	337–341 CE
R663	Roman Ae: unattributable	Late 3–early 5 c. CE
R664	Roman Ae3: Constantine II/gloria exercitus (two standards)	330–335 CE
R665	Unattributable	
R666	Roman Ae3: Roma/wolf with twins	First half of 4 c. CE
R667	Roman Ae3: unattributable	4 c. CE?
Locus 12		
R668	Roman Ae3: Constantius II?/gloria exercitus (one standard)	335–341 CE
R 669	Roman Ae3? Constantine/gloria exercitus (one standard)	335–337 CE
Southeast II:23		
Locus 1		
R1347	Roman Ae3: Constantine II/gloria exercitus (two standards)	330–335 CE
R1348	Roman Ae3: Constantine/gloria exercitus (two standards)	330–335 CE
R1372	Tyrian drachm: Tyche/galley	Late 1–early 2 c. CE
R1394	Roman Ae3: Jovian/vot v	363–364 CE
R1395	Roman Ae3: unattributable	4 c. CE
R1398	Roman Ae4: Theodosius I, Arcadius or Honorius/salus reipublicae (Victory with chi-rho)	393–395 CE
R1400	Roman Ae3: Constantius II?/fel temp reparatio	346–361 CE
R1402	Roman Ae3: Constantius II?/fel temp reparatio	346–361 CE
R1404	Roman colonial: Severus Alexander?/ col Bostra	222–235 CE?
R1476	Roman Ae2: Valentinian II/gloria romanorum	Ca. 385 CE
R1477	Roman Ae3: unattributable	4 c. CE?
R1478	Roman Ae4: unattributable	4–early 5 c. CE
R1514	Roman Ae3: Jovian?/vot v	363–364 CE?
R1515	Roman Ae3: unattributable	4 c. CE

R1516	Roman Ae?	Late 3–early 5 c. CE
R1517	Roman Ae3: unattributable	4–early 5 c. CE
R1518	Roman Ae: unattributable	Late 3–early 5 c. CE
R1519	Unattributable	
R1520	Roman Ae4: ..../Victory	Late 4–early 5 c. CE
R1521	Roman Ae4: unattributable	4–early 5 c. CE
R1522	John Hyrcanus II: Hebrew inscription in wreath/double cornucopiae	76, 63–40 BCE
Locus 2a		
R1405	Roman Ae3: Constantine/gloria exercitus (two standards)	330–335 CE
Locus 3		
R1406	Roman Ae3: ..../gloria exercitus?	Mid–4 c. CE
R1371	Roman Ae3: Valentinian I or Valens/ securitas reipublicae? (Victory with wreath)	367–375 CE
R1420	Roman Ae4: Valentinian I, II or III/ salus reipublicae	375–392 or 425–455 CE
Locus 3a		
R1421	Roman Ae4: Valentinian II?/salus reipublicae (Victory)	383–392 CE
Locus 5		
R1374	Roman Ae3: unattributable	4 c. CE
R1375	Roman Ae4: unattributable	4–early 5 c. CE
Locus 6a		
R1481	Roman Ae3 or 4: unattributable	4 c. CE
Locus 8		
R1396	Roman Ae3: Jovian?/vot v	363–364 CE?
R1397	Roman Ae3: Julian?/securitas reipublicae?	361–363 CE?
R1399	Jewish?	1 c. BCE–early 1 c. CE
R1401	Roman Ae3: unattributable	Late 3–early 5 c. CE
Locus 12		
R1418	Roman Ae3: unattributable	4–early 5 c. CE
R1419	Roman Ae3: Julian/securitas reipublicae (Victory)	361–363 CE
Locus 13		
R1470	Roman Ae3: unattributable	4 c. CE
R1523	Roman Ae3: unattributable	4 c. CE
R1524	Roman Ae?	Late 3–early 5 c. CE?
R1525	Roman Ae3: .... (Victory)	Late 4–early 5 c. CE
R1526	Roman Ae3: ..../fel temp reparatio?	346–361 CE?
R1527	Roman Ae3: ..../victoria aug? (emperor standing with spear)	4 c. CE
R1528	Roman Ae3: .... (Victory)	Late 4–early 5 c. CE
R1529	Roman Ae3: Constantius II?/fel temp reparatio	346–361 CE
R1530	Roman Ae3: Valentinian I, Valens or Gratian/securitas........ (Victory)	364–383 CE
R1531	Roman Ae3: unattributable	4 c. CE
Locus 14		
R1471	Roman Ae4: unattributable	4–early 5 c. CE
R1472	Roman Ae3: Licinius I/iovi conservatori (Victory, eagle, captive)	308–324 CE
R1532	Jewish: Herod Archelaus? Cornucopiae/galley	4 BCE–6 CE?
R1533	Alexander Yannai: anchor/star	103–76 BCE

R1534 Roman Ae4: unattributable — Late 4–early 5 c. CE

Locus 14.1
R1582 Roman Ae4? Unattributable — 4 c. CE?
R1583 Roman Ae3: unattributable — 4 c. CE
R1584 Roman Ae4: Honorius or Theodosius II/gloria romanorum — 410–423 CE
R1585 Roman Ae2: Constantius II?/fel temp reparatio — 346–361 CE
R1586 Roman Ae3: unattributable — 4–early 5 c. CE
R1587 Roman Ae3: unattributable — 4 c. CE

Locus 16
R1473 Roman Ae3: unattributable — 4 c. CE
R1474 Roman Ae3: Constans or Constantius II?/Victoriae DD Augg QNN? — 341–346 CE?
R1475 Roman Ae3: unattributable — 4 c. CE
R1589 Roman Ae4: unattributable — 4–early 5 c. CE
R2017 Roman Ae3: unattributable — 4 c. CE
R2018 Roman Ae3: Constantius II/fel temp reparatio — 346–361 CE
R2019 Roman Ae3 or 2: ..../fel temp reparatio — 346–361 CE

Locus 17
R1479 Roman Ae4: unattributable — 4–early 5 c. CE
R1480 Roman Ae: unattributable — 4–early 5 c. CE

Locus 17.1
R2036 Roman Ae3: unattributable — 4 c. CE

Locus 23
R1588 Roman Ae? unattributable — 4 c. CE

Locus 24
R2020 Unattributable

Locus 26
R2054 Unattributable
R2046 Roman Ae3: ..../fel temp reparatio — 346–361 CE
R2047 Roman Ae? — 4 c. CE?

Locus 28.1
R2048 Roman Ae3: Commemorative issue of Constantine/quadriga — 337–341 CE
R2055 Roman Ae4: Valentinian II?/salus reipublicae (Victory with chi-rho) — 375–392 CE?
R2049 Roman Ae3: unattributable — 4 c. CE
R2056 Roman Ae4: unattributable — 4–early 5 c. CE
R2057 Alexander Yannai: anchor/star — 103–76 BCE
R2058 Roman Ae3 or 4: unattributable — 4 c. CE

Locus 29
R2059 Roman Ae3: ..../fel temp reparatio — 346–361 CE

Southeast II:17

Locus 1
R1498 Roman Ae4: Valentinian I?/salus reipublicae — 364–375 CE
R1499 Roman Ae4: Theodosius I?/.... — 379–395 CE?
R1500 Roman Ae? Unattributable — 4 c. CE
R1501 Roman Ae3: ..../fel temp reparatio? — 346–361 CE?
R1535 Roman Ae3: Constantine/gloria exercitus (one standard) — 335–337 CE
R1536 Roman Ae3: Constantius II or Constans/Victoriae DD NN Augg QNN — 341–346 CE
R1537 Alexander Yannai: anchor/star — 103–76 BCE
R1538 Roman Ae2: Constantine/soli invicto comiti — 308–320 CE

Locus 3
R1539 Roman Ae4? Unattributable — 4 c. CE
R1546 Roman Ae3: ..../fel temp reparatio — 346–361 CE
R1540 Roman Ae3: Constantius II/gloria exercitus (one standard) — 337–341 CE

R1541 Roman Ae3: Constantius II/fel temp reparatio — 346–361 CE
R1542 Roman Ae4: Gratianus, Valentinianus II or Arcadius /Victory — 367–395 CE
R1543 Roman Ae3? Unattributable — 4 c. CE?
R1544 Roman Ae3: Theodosius II?/Victory — 402–450 CE?
R1545 Roman Ae4: ..../Victory — Late 4–early 5 c. CE
R1547 Roman Ae2: Constantius II/fel temp reparatio — 346–361 CE
R1590 Roman Ae4: unattributable — Late 4–early 5 c. CE
R1591 Roman Ae3: unattributable — 4 c. CE
R1592 Roman Ae4: Arcadius?/vot x mult xx — 383–408 CE?

Southeast II:8

Locus 1
R1593 Roman Ae4: ..../virtus exercitus? — 360–363 CE?

Locus 7.1
R2021 Roman Ae3: Constantius II/fel temp reparatio — 346–361 CE
R2022 Roman Ae4: Theodosius I?/victoria aug (Victory) — 383–392 CE?
R2023 Unattributable
R2024 Roman Ae3: Constantius II?/fel temp reparatio — 346–361 CE
R2025 Roman Ae3: ..../fel temp reparatio — 346–361 CE
R2037 Roman Ae3: Constantius II/fel temp reparatio — 346–361 CE
R2038 Roman Ae3: unattributable — 4 c. CE
R2039 Roman Ae4: ..../securitas reipublicae (Victory) — 364–383 CE

Cistern 1

Locus 00
R676 Ayyubid fals: al-'Adil Abu Bakr — 1200–1218 CE

Locus 1
R1301 Roman colonial: Elagabalus/col Bostra — 218–222 CE

Locus 4
R1302 Roman Ae4: Theodosius I/vot x mult xx — Ca. 389 CE
R1354 Roman Ae3: Arcadius/salus reipublicae — 383–408 CE
R1355 Roman Ae4: Valentinian II, Theodosius I, Arcadius or Flaccilla/salus reipublicae — 383–402 CE
R1356 Roman Ae4: Valens or later/salus reipublicae (Victory dragging captive, chi-rho) — 364–402 CE
R1357 Roman Ae4: Arcadius/salus reipublicae — 383–408 CE
R1358 Roman Ae3: Constantius II/vot xx mult xxx — 341–346 CE
R1359 Roman Ae3: Constans?/Victoriae DD Augg — 341–346 CE?
R1360 Roman Ae3: Constantius II/fel temp reparatio — 346–361 CE
R1361 Roman Ae2: Constantius II/providentiae caess — 324–330 CE
R1362 Roman Ae3: Commemorative issue of Constantine/Aequitas — 341–346 CE
R1363 Roman Ae3: Constantius II?/... — 323–361 CE?

GENERAL INDEX
by David P. Lewis

Subentries are listed alphabetically under the main word. One looks up "al-Minah" under "M" and "el-Hammeh" under "H." Coin legends are in small capital letters. The authors wish to thank Mr. David P. Lewis for preparation of this index.

PLATES AND PHOTOGRAPHS

Plate 6.1

R626

R1369

R1497

R1494

R2266

R2312

R1376

R2061

R1533

R1303

R393

R2051

R552

R632

R1332

Plate 6.1. Ptolemaic, Seleucid, Tyrian, and Hasmonean coins. *Top row:* Ptolemaic (R626); Demetrius II (R1369); Alexander (?) (R1497). *Second row:* Seleucid (R1494); Tyrian Tyche of 108/9 BCE (R2266); Tyrian Melqarth of 155/6 CE (R2312). *Third row:* Tyrian Melqarth of 152/3 CE (R1376); Alexander Yannai (R2061, R1533, R1303, R393). *Bottom row:* Alexander Yannai (R2051, R552, R632, R1322).

Plate 6.2

R2148   R633   R613   R1551

R2157   R585   R1331

R1404   R2102   R1310

R2079   R2072   R592

Plate 6.2. Roman coins of the first three centuries CE. *Top row:* Nero (Palestinian – R2148); Domitian (Agrippa II – R633); Vespasian (R613); Trajan (R1551). *Second row:* Hadrian (R2157); Septimus Severus (R585); Elagabalus (R1331). *Third row:* coin of Bostra (portrait unclear – R1404); Philip II (R2102); Claudius II (?) (R1310). *Bottom row:* Gallienus (R2079); Valerianus (R2072); Probus (R592).

Plate 6.3

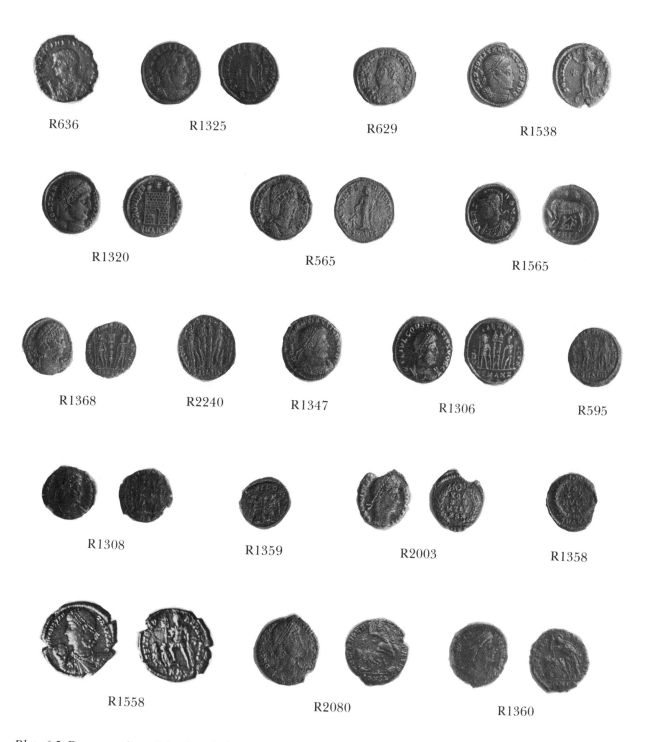

R636   R1325   R629   R1538

R1320   R565   R1565

R1368   R2240   R1347   R1306   R595

R1308   R1359   R2003   R1358

R1558   R2080   R1360

Plate 6.3. Roman coins of the first half of the 4th century CE. *Top row:* Licinius I (R636 and R1325); Constantine the Great (R629 and R1538). *Second row:* Constantine the Great (R1320, R565, and R1565). *Third row:* Constantine the Great (R1368); Gloria exercitus with two standards (R2240, R1347, and R1306); Gloria exercitus with single standard (R595). *Fourth row:* Constans (R1308); Victoria Augustorum (R1359); Vota XX (R2003 and R1358). *Bottom row:* Constantius II (R1558, R2080, and R1360).

Plate 6.4

R2328   R581   R541   R2052

R1557   R1514   R2183   R1571

R1476   R634   R1334   R1498

R674   R1364   R1332   R550   R1335

Plate 6.4. Late Roman coins (mid-4th through early 5th century CE). *Top row:* Constantius Gallus (R2328 and R581); Julian (R541 and R2052). *Second row:* Constantius II and Julian (R1557); Jovian (R1514); Gratian (R2183); Valentinian I (R1571). *Third row:* Valentinian II (R1476); Theodosius I (R634); Honorius (1334); Valentinian II (1498). *Bottom row:* Theodosius I (R674); Theodosius II (R1364); Theodosius II (R1332); Arcadius (R550); Johannes (?) (R1335).

Plate 6.5

R2309 R2207 R2135

R520 R591 R589

R2015 R1382 R2016 R2090

Plate 6.5. Byzantine, Islamic, and Crusader coins. *Top row:* Justin II (R2309); al-Mansur (R2207); Abbassid dirham minted in Tyre (R2135). *Second row:* al-kamil Muhammed (R520); Baybars I (R591 and R589). *Bottom row:* Baybars I (R2015); unattributable early Islamic (?) (R1382); Frederick II (R2016); John of Brienne (R2090).

Plate 7.1. "GALILEAN BOWLS," 1:5

Field, Square, Bucket, Sherd	Locus	Stratum	Selected Colors of Important Loci*	
			Sec.	Ext.
1. NW I.30.24	L.30012	—	7.5 YR 6/4	5 YR 6/8
2. NE I.32	L.32015	IV–V	2.5 YR 6/6	5 YR 2/3 + 6/2
3. MI.2.48.26	L.2019	Ia	2.5 YR 4/3	2.5 YR 5/4
4. T-29 North	L.29010	IV	5 YR 4/1	2.5 YR 6/6
5. NE I.25	L.25035	IV	5 YR 3/1	5 YR 6/4
6. MI.2.49.11	L.2019	Ia	2.5 YR 5/6	2.5 YR 5/6
7. NE I.25	L.000	mixed		
8. NE VII.1	L.1024	V		
9. T-29 South.16.27	L.29007	IV	5 YR 4/8	5 YR 6/6
10. T-29 North.8.5	L.29003	IV	5 YR 5/8	5 YR 7/8
11. NW VII.14.21	L.14005	mixed		
12. SE II.17.7.32	L.17008	IV	2.5 YR 5/8	5 YR 5/8
13. NE I.32	L.32018.1	IV	2.5 YR 5/4	2.5 YR 5/6
14. NW VIII	L.13002	VI		
15. NW VII.13	L.13002	VI		
16. MI.2.37.5	L.2014.1	II.2	2.5 YR 3/1–3/3	2.5 YR 5/6
17. T-29 South	L.29013	IV		
18. T-29 South	L.29004	IV		
19. SE II.22.16.8	L.22003	IV	2.5 YR 5/8	2.5 YR 6/8
20. NE I.32.53	L.32014	IV–V		
21. MII.2.49.12	L.2019	Ia	2.5 YR 5/6–3/1	2.5 YR 5/6
22. NE I.32.53	L.32014	IV–V		
23. NW VII.1.27.6	L.1013	V	2.5 YR 5/8	2.5 YR 6/8
24. T-17.21.41	L.17001	IV	2.5 YR 6/6	5 YR 6/2
25. MI.2.49.10	L.2019	Ia	2.5 YR 5/6	2.5 YR 5/6–3/1
26. NW VII.13	L.13002	VI		
27. MI.2.49.5	L.2019	Ia	2.5 YR 5/6	2.5 YR 6/6
28. MI.2.30.4	L.2011	II.3	2.5 YR 5/6	2.5 YR 4/2
29. T-29 South	L.29007	IV		
30. NE VII.1.5.21	L.1002	mixed	2.5 YR 5/8	2.5 YR 6/8

* For a full discussion of color and ware consult the text, pp. 178–179.

Plate 7.1

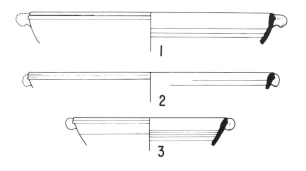
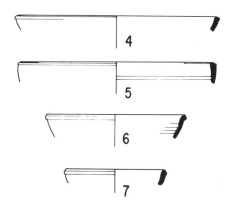
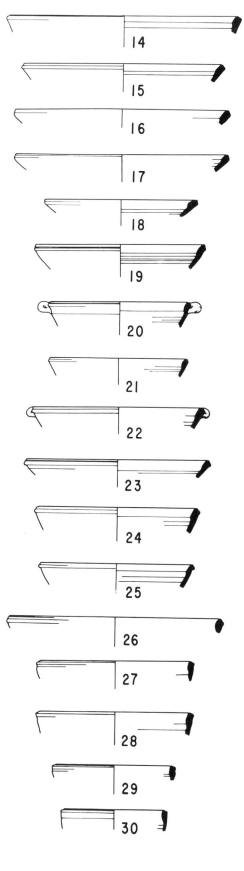
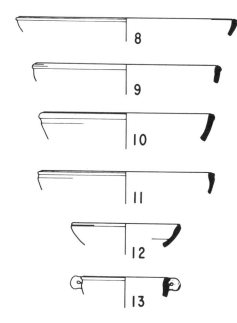

Plate 7.2. "GALILEAN BOWLS," 1:5

Field, Square, Bucket, Sherd	Locus	Stratum	Selected Colors of Important Loci	
			Sec.	Ext.
1. NW VII.1	L.1060	III–IV		
2. NW VII.1	L.1060	III–IV		
3. T-29 South	L.29007	III–VII		
4. NW VII.3	L.3021	IV		
5. T-29 North	L.29008	III–IV		
6. NW I.32.78.8	L.32030	III–VI	2.5 YR 4/8	2.5 YR 6/8
7. NE VII.2.82	L.2003	IV	2.5 YR 4/4	2.5 YR 4/2
8. NW VII.2	L.2002	—		
9. MI.2.44.5	L.2016.1	II.1b	2.5 YR 5/6	2.5 YR 5/6
10. MI.2	L.2011	II.3		
11. MI.2.30.6	L.2011	II.3	10 R 5/6	2.5 YR 5/6
12. NE VII.2.86	L.2035	IV		
13. NW VII.13	L.13003	V	2.5 YR 4/4	2.5 YR 5/4
14. NE I.32.32.12	L.32014	IV–V	2.5 YR 5/8	2.5 YR 5/2
15. T-29 South	L.29006	III–IV	2.5 YR 5/8	2.5 YR 6/8
16. MI.2.30.7	L.2011	II.3	10 R 5/6	2.5 YR 5/6
17. NE I.32.32.8	L.32014	IV–V	2.5 YR 4/8	10 R 5/8
18. NW I.31	L.31000	—		
19. T-29 South	L.29001	VI–VII		
20. MI.2.48.34	L.2019	Ia	2.5 YR 4/2	2.5 YR 4/2
21. NW VII.18	L.8004	mixed		
22. NE I.32	L.32016	IV–VI		
23. NW I.33.48	L.33023	V		
24. NW VII.13	L.13003	V		
25. NW VII.13	L.13003	V		
26. MI.2.44.11	L.2016.1	II.1b	2.5 YR 5/6	5 YR 6/5
27. MI.2.36.10	L.2015	II.2	2.5 YR 5/8	2.5 YR 5/6–6/5
28. NW VII.13	L.13002	VI		
29. SE I.24.6.3	L.24001	IV	2.5 YR 5/8	5 YR 7/6
30. MI.2.36.11	L.2015	II.2	2.5 YR 5/8	2.5 YR 5/5–6/5
31. NW I.32.51.32	L.32028	III–VI	5 YR 5/4	2.5 YR 6/4
32. NW VII.13	L.13003	V		
33. MI.2.48.3	L.2019	Ia	2.5 YR 5/6	2.5 YR 5/6
34. NE I.26.43.2	L.26024	V		

Plate 7.2

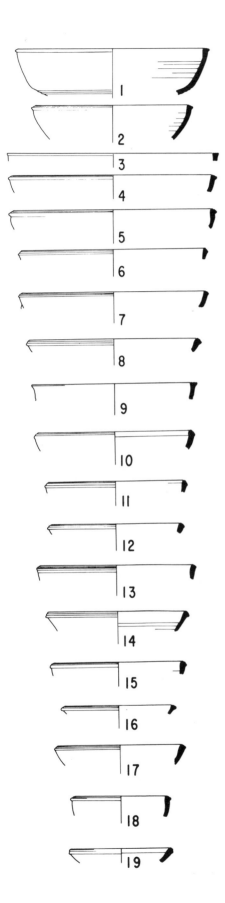
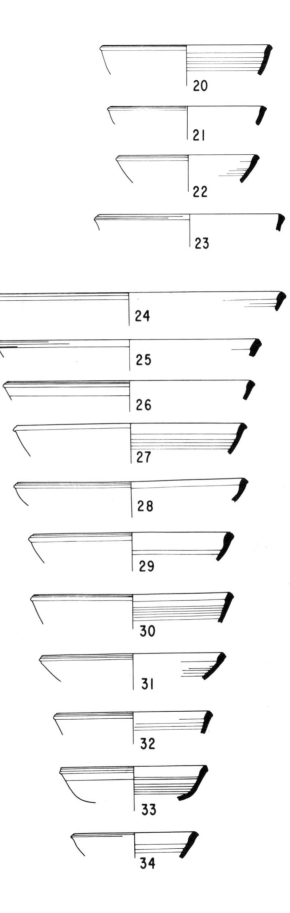

Plate 7.3. "GALILEAN BOWLS," 1:5

Field, Square, Bucket, Sherd	Locus	Stratum	Selected Colors of Important Loci	
			Sec.	Ext.
1. NW VII.13	L.13003	V		
2. MI.2.41.4	L.2015	II.2	2.5 YR 4/8	2.5 YR 5/6–6/4
3. NE I.32.81.5	L.32016	IV–VI	10 YR 5/6	10 YR /6
4. NW VII.14	L.13002	mixed		
5. T-17	L.17010	IV		
6. NE I.26.3.2	L.26003	mixed	5 YR 5/8	2.5 YR 5/8
7. T-29 South.13.12	L.29007	mixed	2.5 YR 6/6	2.5 YR 6/8
8. MI.2.45.1	L.2016.1	II.1b	2.5 YR 4/6	2.5 YR 3/1–4/6
9. NW VII.1	L.1060	III–IV		
10. MI.2.41.6	L.2015	II.2	2.5 YR 4/6	5 YR 4/6
11. MI.2.48.21	L.2019	Ia	2.5 YR 4/6	10 R 5/6
12. T-17.8.31	L.17003	IV	2.5 YR 5/8	2.5 YR 6/6
13. T-29 South	L.29008	mixed		
14. MI.2	L.2016.1	II.1b		
15. T-17	L.17003	IV		
16. NW I.32.70.3	L.32030	III–VI	5 YR 6/6	5 YR 6/6
17. MII.2.48.3	L.2019	Ia	2.5 YR 5/6	2.5 YR 5/6
18. MI.2.44.13	L.2016.1	II.1b	10 R 5/4	10 R 5/6
19. NE VII.2.67.7	L.2025	IV	2.5 YR 5/8	2.5 YR 6/4
20. NE VII.32.2	L.14	IV		
21. MI.2.31.2	L.2011	II.3		
22. MI.2.49.17	L.2019	Ia	10 R 5/6	10 R 5/6
23. NW VII.13	L.13003	V		
24. MI.2.48.4	L.2019	Ia	2.5 YR 5/6	2.5 YR 4/1,3,4
25. NW VII.13	L.13003	V		
26. NW I.28.18	L.28008	—		
27. MI.2.48.27,28,29	L.2019	Ia	10 R 5/6	2.5 YR 5/3

Plate 7.3

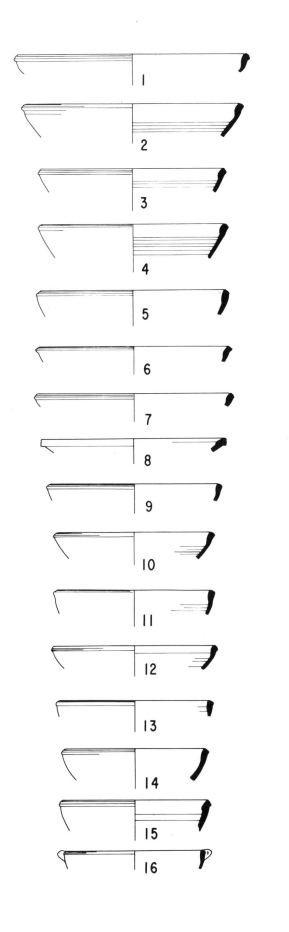

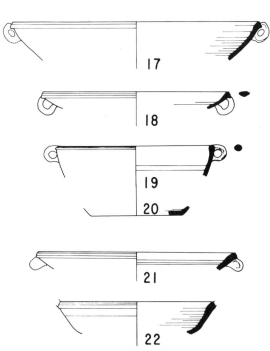

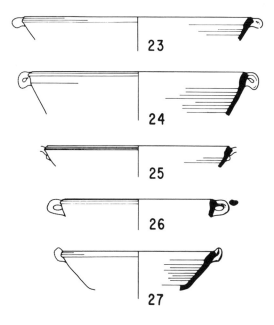

Plate 7.4. "GALILEAN BOWLS," 1:5

Field, Square, Bucket, Sherd	Locus	Stratum	Selected Colors of Important Loci	
			Sec.	Ext.
1. MI.2.41.16	L.2015	II.2	2.5 YR 5/6	2.5 YR 5/8
2. T-29 South	L.29007	mixed		
3. NW I.33.48.2	L.33023	V	2.5 YR 5/6	5 YR 5/6
4. SE II.17.6.4	L.17001	IV	2.5 YR 5/8	2.5 YR 6/8
5. C-1.04.9.2	L.1004	IV	2.5 YR 4/8	2.5 YR 6/8
6. NW VII.1	L.1060	III–IV		
7. NW VII.3	L.3019	V		
8. NE VII.2.63.16	L.2025	IV	2.5 YR 5/8	2.5 YR 6/4
9. NW VII.13	L.13000	mixed		
10. SE II.23.11.12	L.23001	IV	5 YR 5/8	5 YR 5/8
11. NE I.26.42	L.26023	V	2.5 YR 6/6	2.5 YR 6/6
12. NE VII.3	L.3009.1	IV	2.5 YR 4/6	2.5 YR 5/6
13. NE VII.3.17.3	L.3015	V	2.5 YR 6/6	2.5 YR /6
14. NW I.34.14.4	L.34009	IV	2.5 YR 5/6	2.5 YR 5/6
15. NE I.29	L.29000	mixed		
16. NE I.25.27.4	L.25036	IV	2.5 YR 6/8	2.5 YR 6/8
17. T-17.5.19	L.17001	IV	7.5 YR 7/6	7.5 YR 6/6
18. T-29 South.6	L.29005	mixed		
19. T-17.5.23	L.17001	IV	2.5 YR 6/8	5 YR 6/8
20. NE I.26.40	L.26024	V	10 R 5/6	10 R 6/6
21. NW VII.13	L.13003	V		
22. NW VII.33	L.13002	VI		
23. NW VII.13	L.13002	VI		
24. NW VII.13	L.13002	VI		
25. MI.2.30.9	L.2014.1	II.2	2.5 YR 5/6	2.5 YR 6/6
26. C-1	L.1005	IV		
27. SE II.23.11.1	L.23001	IV	2.5 YR 5/8	2.5 YR 6/8
28. NE I.25.36.4	L.25037	—	10 YR 8/2	10 YR 8/2
29. MI.2.35	L.2014.1	II.2	2.5 YR 6/6	2.5 YR 4/1
30. MI.2.41	L.2015	II.2	2.5 YR 4/6	2.5 YR 4/1, 5/6
31. NW VII.14	L.14010	—	2.5 YR 6/8	2.5 YR 6/8
32. NE VII.3.17	L.3015	V	2.5 YR 5/6	2.5 YR 5/4

Plate 7.4

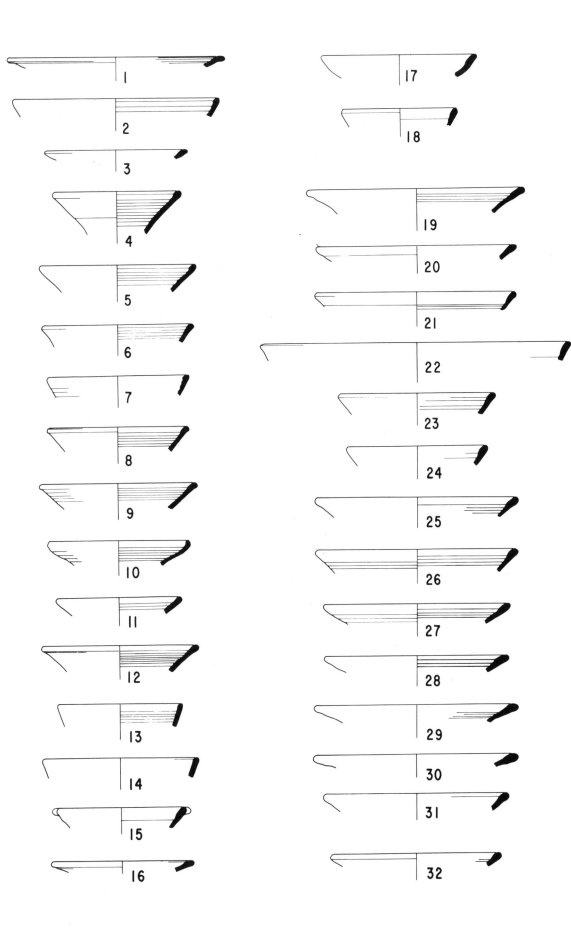

Plate 7.5. "GALILEAN BOWLS," 1:5

Field, Square, Bucket, Sherd	Locus	Stratum	Selected Colors of Important Loci	
			Sec.	Ext.
1. MI.2	L.2015	II.2	2.5 YR 5/6	5 YR 4/4, 5/6
2. MI.2.25	L.2012	—	2.5 YR 6/8	2.5 YR 5/6, 2/1
3. NE I.19.27	L.19071	VI	2.5 YR 5/6	2.5 YR 6/6
4. MI.2.38	L.2014.1	II.2	2.5 YR 6/6	2.5 YR 5/6
5. NW VII.13	L.13003	V		
6. T-17.2.17	L.17000	IV–V	2.5 YR 5/8	2.5 YR 6/8
7. NE I.25.1.2	L.25000	mixed		
8. NE I.26.39.12	L.26023	V	5 RP 3/1	5 YR 7/3
9. NE VII.3	L.3009	IV		
10. NE I.25	L.25036	—		
11. NE I.25.22.9	L.25009	—	2.5 YR 5/8	2.5 YR 6/8
12. NW I.34.19.4	L.34010	V	2.5 YR 5/6	2.5 YR 6/6
13. MI.2.48	L.2019	Ia	2.5 YR 5/6	7.5 YR 5/3
14. T-29 South	L.29005	—		
15. T-29 South.18.3	L.29007	—	2.5 YR 6/8	2.5 YR 5/6
16. T-29 South	L.29013	—		
17. T-29 South	L.29007	—		
18. NW VII.8	L.8004	mixed		
19. NW VII.3	L.3017	V		
20. NW VII.8	L.8004	mixed		
21. NW VII.8	L.8004	mixed		
22. NE I.26.7.6	L.26007	—	7.5 YR 4/4	5 YR 6/6
23. T-29 South	L.29013	—		
24. NW VII.	L.8004	mixed		
25. T-17.19.9	L.17000	III–V	2.5 YR 6/8	2.5 YR 6/8
26. MI.2.38	L.2014.1	II.2	2.5 YR 5/6	2.5 YR 5/6
27. NE I.26.5.6	L.26005	mixed	2.5 YR 4/8	5 YR 5/6
28. T-29 South	L.29004	—		
29. NW VII.13	L.13002	VI		
30. MI.2.36	L.2015	II.2	2.5 YR 4/7	2.5 YR 5/8
31. T-29 South.20.17	L.29008	—	2.5 YR 5/8	2.5 YR 6/8
32. T-29 South.13.20	L.29006	—	5 YR 4/6	2.5 YR 6/8

Plate 7.5

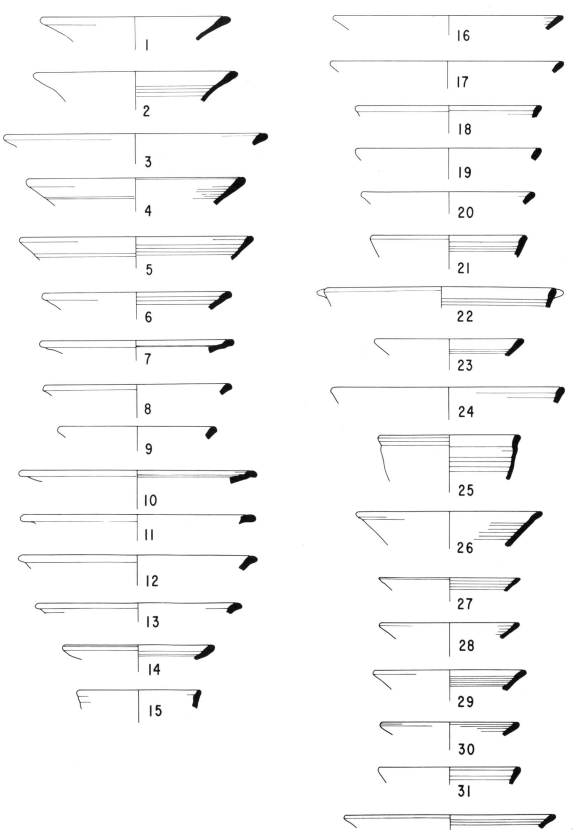

Plate 7.6. "GALILEAN BOWLS," 1:5

Field, Square, Bucket, Sherd	Locus	Stratum	Selected Colors of Important Loci	
			Sec.	Ext.
1. MI.2	L.2015	II.2	2.5 YR 6/8	5 YR 7/6
2. MI.2	L.2015	II.2	2.5 YR 6/8	5 YR 6/4
3. T-17	L.17017	IV		
4. NW VII.13	L.13002	VI		
5. NE I.26.55.2	L.26037	IV	2.5 YR 4/4	2.5 YR 5/2
6. T-29 South	L.29007	—		
7. NE I.25	L.25045	—		
8. T-29 South	L.29007	—		
9. NW VII.14.30	L.14005	mixed		
10. T-29 South	L.29013	—		
11. NW VII.3.36	L.3000	mixed		
12. NW I.34.19.3	L.34010	V	2.5 YR 5/4	2.5 YR 5/1
13. NW VII.13	L.13002	VI		
14. NW VII.3.36	L.3000	mixed		
15. T-29 South	L.29004	—		
16. NE VII.3	L.3015	V		
17. T-29 South	L.29004	—		
18. NW VII.13	L.13003	V		
19. NW VII.8	L.8008	mixed		
20. MI.2	L.2015	II.2	2.5 YR 6/8	2.5 YR 5/6, 6/8
21. NE I.26	L.26007	—		
22. NW VII.1	L.1059	III–IV		
23. NE VII.3.20	L.3009.1	IV	10 R 5/6	10 R 5/6
24. NW I.33	L.33015	VI		
25. T-29 North.34	L.29017	IV		
26. T-17	L.17003	IV		
27. T-17.6	L.17003	IV		
28. NE I.25	L.25042	—		
29. NE I.26.39.3	L.26023	V	2.5 YR 6/6	2.5 YR 6/6
30. NW I.32.54	L.32028	III–IV		

Plate 7.6

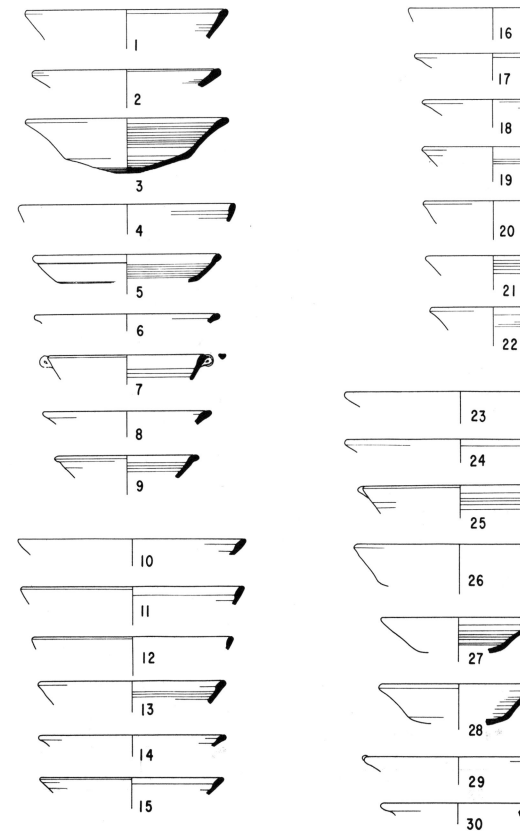
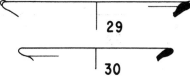

Plate 7.7. "GALILEAN BOWLS," 1:5

Field, Square, Bucket, Sherd	Locus	Stratum	Selected Colors of Important Loci	
			Sec.	Ext.
1. NW VII.13	L.13002	VI		
2. NW VII.23	L.13003	V		
3. T-17	L.27006	IV		
4. NW I.32.54	L.32028	mixed		
5. NW VII.1	L.1059	III–IV		
6. NE VII.3.21	L.3016	IV–V		
7. NE VII.3.21	L.3016	IV–V		
8. NW I.32.78	L.32030	mixed		
9. MI.2.31	L.2011	II.3	5 YR 3/3	5 YR 7/8
10. SE II.23.45	L.23020	IV		
11. T-17	L.17000	IV		
12. T-17	L.17001	IV		
13. T-29 South	L.29004	mixed		
14. T-17	L.17000	IV		
15. MI.2	L.2012	II.3	2.5 YR 6/8	5 YR 7/6
16. NW I.33	L.33022	VI	2.5 YR 4/6	2.5 YR 5/6
17. NE I.26	L.26023	V		
18. NE VII.2	L.2032	IV	2.5 YR 5/6	2.5 YR 6/6
19. T-17	L.17003	IV		
20. NW VII.13	L.13003	V		
21. SE II.23	L.23008	IV		
22. NE I.26	L.26003	mixed		
23. MI.2	L.2011	II.3	2.5 YR 5/6	2.5 YR 5/6
24. NE VII.2	L.2045	IV		
25. T-17	L.17001	IV		
26. NE VII.1	L.1003	mixed		
27. NE VII.13	L.13003	V		
28. NE I.31.18	L.31003	—		
29. T-29 South	L.29008	mixed		
30. NW VII.13	L.13002	VI		
31. NE I.19	L.19070	VI		
32. NE VII.3	L.3009.1	IV		

Plate 7.7

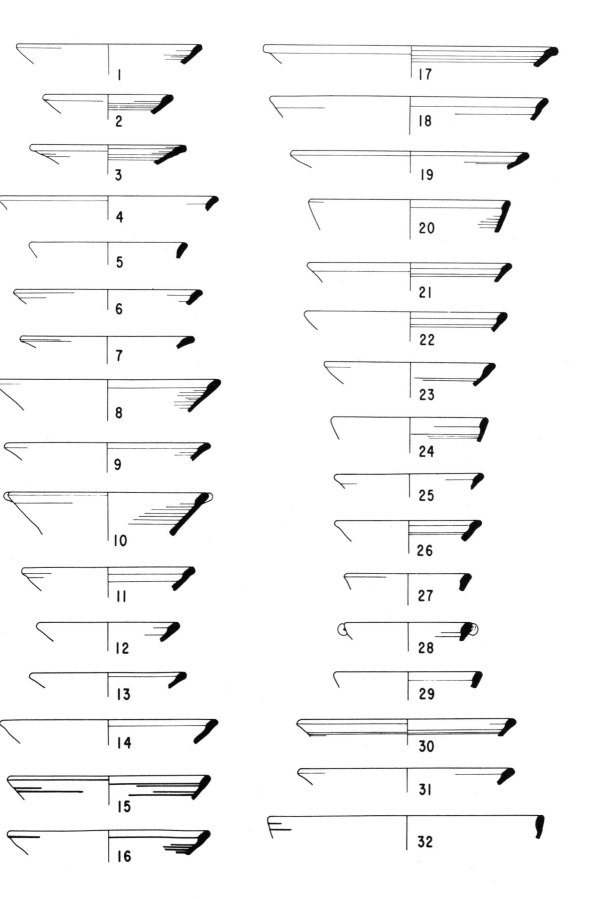

Plate 7.8. "GALILEAN BOWLS," 1:5

Field, Square, Bucket, Sherd	Locus	Stratum	Selected Colors of Important Loci	
			Sec.	Ext.
1. NW VII.13	L.13002	VI		
2. T-17	L.17001	IV		
3. T-17.13.12	L.17001	IV		
4. T-17	L.17006	IV		
5. NW VII.13.38.2	L.13002	VI		
6. T-17.2.11	L.17000	IV		
7. MI.21.30.2	L.3011	—	5 YR 4/2	2.5 YR 5/6
8. NW VII.13.34.9	L.13002	VI		
9. MI.2	L.2014.1	II.2	2.5 YR 5/6	5 YR 6/4, 5/4
10. NE I.26	L.26024	V		
11. NE I.26.39	L.26029	IV		
12. T-29 South	L.29007	mixed		
13. NW I.34	L.34007	—		
14. NW VII.13	L.13002	VI		
15. NW VII.9.6.4	L.9007	mixed		
16. NW VII.13.45.2	L.13003	V		
17. T-29 South.21.17	L.29008	mixed		
18. NW VII.13.42.7	L.13002	VI		
19. T-29 South 3.8	L.29001	—		
20. T-29 South.18.14	L.29007	mixed		
21. NE VII.3.25.2	L.3018	—		
22. T-17.21.9	L.1701	IV		
23. NE I.25.46.3	L.25043	V		
24. T-29 North 24.1	L.29010	—		
25. MI.2.44.14	L.2016.1	II.1b	2.5 YR 5/6	2.5 YR 6/6
26. NW VII.13.44.14	L.13003	V		
27. T-17.4.13	L.17001	IV		
28. T-17.4.14	L.17001	IV		
29. NW I.30.21.8	L.30008.1	—		
30. NW VII.13.39.5	L.13002	VI		

Plate 7.8

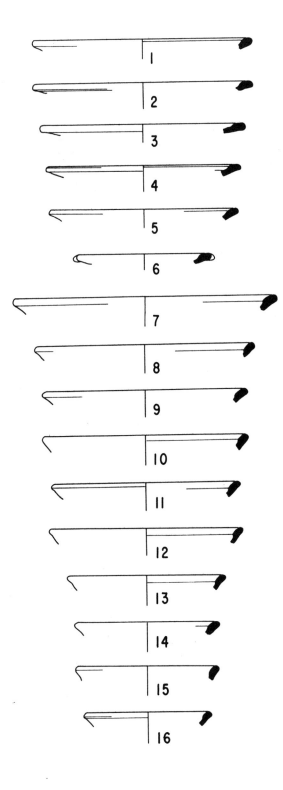

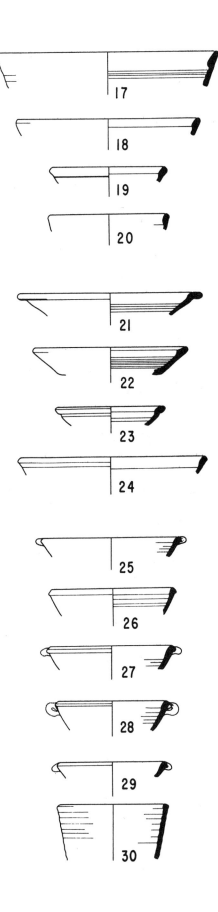

Plate 7.9. "GALILEAN BOWLS," 1:5

Field, Square, Bucket, Sherd	Locus	Stratum	Selected Colors of Important Loci	
			Sec.	Ext.
1. NE I.26.55.1	L.26037	IV	2.5 YR 4/6	2.5 YR 5/6
2. MI.2.48.41	L.2019	Ia	5 PB 3/1	7.5 YR 4/1, 6/4
3. MI.2.48.10	L.2019	Ia	10 R 5/6	10 R 5/6
4. MI.2.49.2	L.2019	Ia	2.5 YR 5/6	2.5 YR 5/6
5. MI.2.46.1	L.2018.1	II.1a	10 R 4/4	10 R 5/4, 5/1
6. SE II.17.6.2	L.17005	IV		
7. MI.2.36.8	L.2016.1	II.1b	5 YR 3/6	5 YR 4/8, 5/8
8. T-29 South.18.10	L.29007	mixed		
9. MI.2.48.23	L.2019	Ia	2.5 YR 5/6	2.5 YR 5/6
10. MI.2.49.8	L.2019	Ia	10 R 4/4	10 R 5/6, 3/1
11. NE I.19.70.6	L.19070	VI	5 P 4/1	5 YR 6/6
12. T-29 South.3.4	L.29001	mixed		
13. MI.2.48.40	L.2019	Ia	2.5 YR 4/4	2.5 YR 6/6
14. T-29 North.9.9	L.29003	mixed		
15. MI.2.48.1	L.2019	Ia	2.5 YR 5/6	2.5 YR 6/6
16. NW VII.34.20.4	L.34010	—		
17. NE I.32.72.3	L.32016	IV–VI		
18. NW I.32.78.8	L.32030	mixed		
19. SE II.17.7.15	L.17008	IV		
20. SE II.17.15.7	L.17006	IV		
21. NE.1.26.36c.3	L.26022.1	VII	2.5 YR 5/6	2.5 YR 5/6
22. NW VII.13.44.11	L.13003	V		
23. MI.2.48.16	L.2019	Ia	2.5 YR 4/2	10 R 5/6
24. NW VII.14130.4	L.14005	mixed		
25. MI.2.41.11	L.2015	II.2	2.5 YR 4/6	2.5 YR 5/6, 4/6
26. SE II.23.42.11	L.23018	IV		
27. NE I.25.45.1,2, 14,46.1.6	L.25042/43	V		
28. T-17.22.12	L.17001	IV		

Plate 7.9

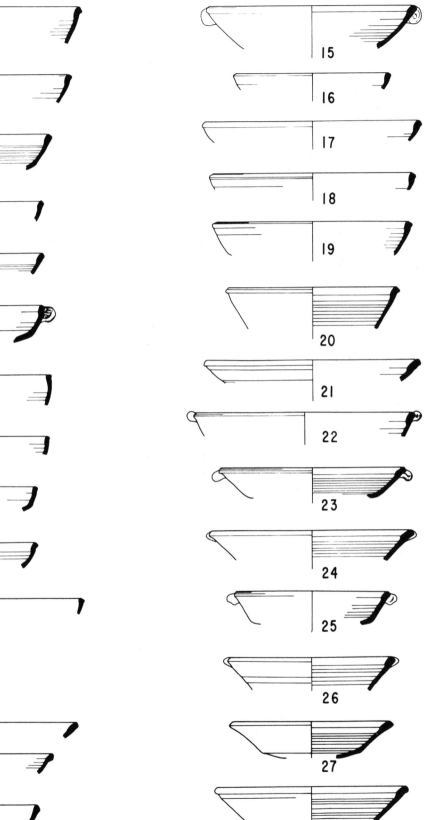

Plate 7.10. "GALILEAN BOWLS" AND BOWLS WITH EVERTED LIP, 1:5

| Field, Square, Bucket, Sherd | Locus | Stratum | Selected Colors of Important Loci | |
			Sec.	Ext.
1. NE I.32.73.2	L.32016	IV–V–VI	10 R 5/6	10 R 5/6
2. NE I.32.80.2	L.32019	III–IV	2.5 YR 5/6	2.5 YR 6/6
3. SE II.23.46.9	L.23020	IV		
4. NW VII.13.40.5	L.14005	mixed		
5. MI.2.41.3	L.2015	II.2	2.5 YR 5/6	5 YR 4/1, 10 R 5/6
6. MI.2.41.7	L.2015	II.2	2.5 YR 5/6	2.5 YR 5/4, 4/1
7. T-29 South 29.9	L.29013	IV		
8. NW VII.13.28.11	L.13002	VI		
9. T-29 South.29.11	L.29012	IV		
10. NW VII.13.44.17	L.13003	V		
11. NW I.32.78.7	L.32030	mixed		
12. SW I.28.8.2	L.28004	—		
13. NE VII.3121.5	L.2016	IIb		
14. T-17.6.25	L.17003	IV		
15. SE II.22.24.3	L.22006	IV		
16. MI.2.36.12	L.2015	II.2	2.5 YR 5/8	2.5 YR 6/7
17. NE I.26.5.11	L.26005	—		
18. T-17.2.5	L.17001	IV		
19. T-29 South.5.8	L.29004	mixed		
20. MI.2.48.17	L.2019	Ia	2.5 YR 5/4	2.5 YR 5/6
21. T-29 South.6.7	L.29004	mixed		
22. NW I.32.57.1	L.32028	mixed		
23. NE VII.2.66.4	L.2019.1	IV		
24. T-29 South.29.15	L.29013	IV		
25. NE I.32.77.1	L.32014	IV–V	2.5 YR 5/6	2.5 YR 5/6
26. NE I.26.46.1	L.26028	IV		
27. NE I.26.43.4	L.26024	V		
28. SE II.17.7.1	L.17008	IV		
29. NE I.32.69.2	L.32015	IV–V	2.5 YR 5/6	2.5 YR 5/6

Plate 7.10

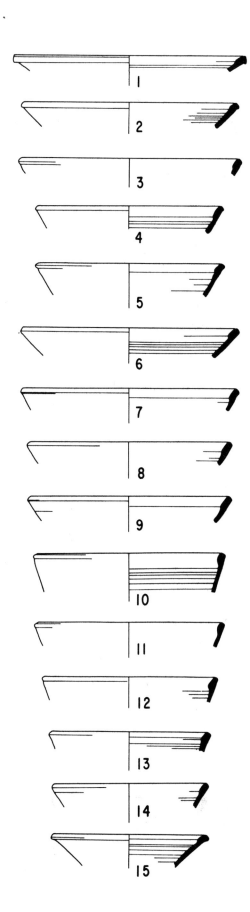

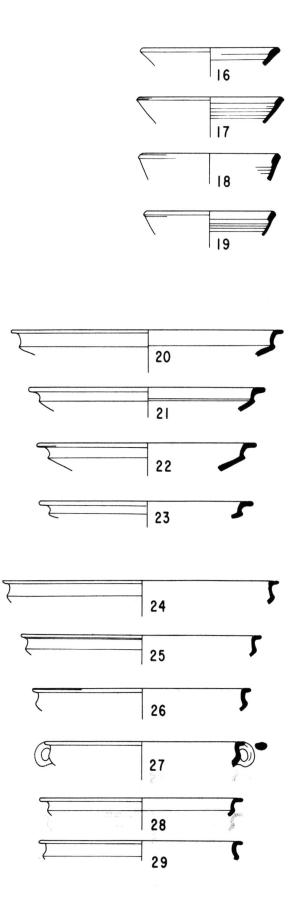

Plate 7.11. BOWLS WITH EVERTED LIP, 1:5

Field, Square, Bucket, Sherd	Locus	Stratum	Selected Colors of Important Loci	
			Sec.	Ext.
1. NE I.32.72.12	L.32016	IV–VI	2.5 YR 5/6	2.5 YR 5/6 + 7.5 YR 7/4
2. NE I.32.77.9	L.32014	IV–V	2.5 YR 4/6	2.5 YR 4/1
3. MI.2.41.9	L.2015	II.2	2.5 YR 5/8	2.5 YR 5/6
4. NE I.26.46.2	L.26028	IV		
5. NW VII.3.28.3	L.3021	IV		
6. T-17.5.27	L.17001	IV		
7. NE I.32.81.6	L.32016	IV–VI		
8. NE I.26.43.1	L.26024	V	10 R 5/6	10 R 5/6
9. NW I.33.45.5	L.33020	VI–VII		
10. NE I.32.81.7	L.32016	IV–VI	10 YR 5/6	2.5 YR 5/4
11. NW VII.3.29.1	L.3011	IV		
12. T-17.18.31	L.17003	IV		
13. NW VII.13.42.10	L.13003	V		
14. T-17.22.32	L.17001	IV		
15. T-17.15.2	L.1700	IV		
16. NW VII.2.86.3	L.2035	—	10 R 6/6	10 R 5/6
17. NW I.32.53.2	L.32028	mixed		
18. NE VII.2.63.1	L.2025	IV		
19. NW VII.1.90.14	L.1060	III–IV		
20. NW VII.13.38.8	L.13002	VI		

Plate 7.11

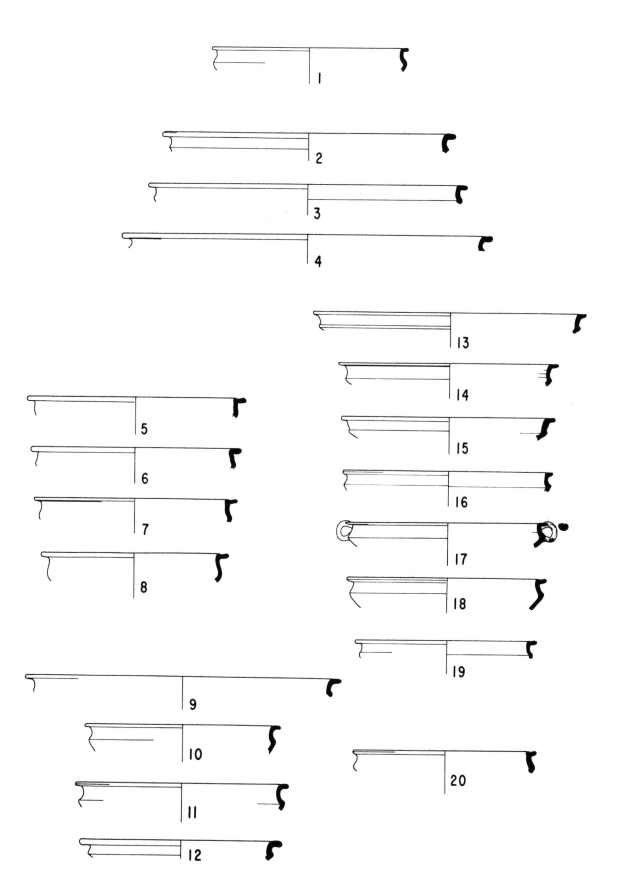

Plate 7.12. BOWLS WITH EVERTED LIP AND COOKING BOWLS
WITH HORIZONTAL HANDLES, 1:5

Field, Square, Bucket, Sherd	Locus	Stratum	Selected Colors of Important Loci	
			Sec.	Ext.
1. NE VII.2.71.1	L.2027	IV		
2. NE VII.2.63.17	L.2025	IV		
3. NE VII.1.4.7	L.1022	VII		
4. NW I.33.47.5	L.33022	VI		
5. NE I.26.59.2	L.26036	IV	10 R 5/6	5 YR 7/3
6. NE VII.2.89.1	L.2037	III		
7. MI.2.55.4	L.2019	Ia	10 R 4/6	10 R 4/4
8. NW I.33.47.18	L.33022	VI		
9. NW I.33.34.3	L.33015	VI		
10. NE I.32.72.4	L.32016	VI	10 R 4/8, 10 R 7/1	2.5 YR 5/6 + 5 YR 7/3
11. NE VII.2.100.1	L.2045	IV	2.5 YR 4/6	7.5 YR 7/3
12. MI.2.36.5	L.2015	II.2	2.5 YR 5/8	2.5 YR 5/6
13. NE I.32.87.6	L.32016	VI	2.5 YR 6/6	2.5 YR 6/6
14. NW I.33.29.8	L.33015	VI		
15. NE I.32.44.4	L.3200	VII		
16. T-17.13.9	L.17006	IV		
17. NW I.32.53.1	L.32028	VI		
18. NW I.33.46.8	L.33022	VI	2.5 YR 5/4	2.5 YR 5/4
19. NE I.32.73.1	L.32016	VI	10 R 5/6	5 YR 7/3 + 2.5 YR 7/1
20. NW I.33.46.1	L.33022	VI	2.5 YR 4/1	2.5 YR 6/4
21. T-29 South.29	L.29013	IV		
22. NE VII.2.86.4	L.2035	IV	10 R 5/6	10 R 5/6
23. SE II.23.19.8	L.23008	IV		
24. NE VII.2.67.9	L.2025	IV		
25. MI.2.35.4	L.2015	II.2	2.5 YR 5/8	5 YR 6/6
26. NW I.33.47.2	L.33022	VI	2.5 YR 4/1	2.5 YR 6/6
27. NW VII.8.33.3	L.8004	VII		
28. NW VII.13.34.2	L.13002	VII		
29. NE I.19.70.3	L.19070	VI	10 R 5/6	5 YR 4/4

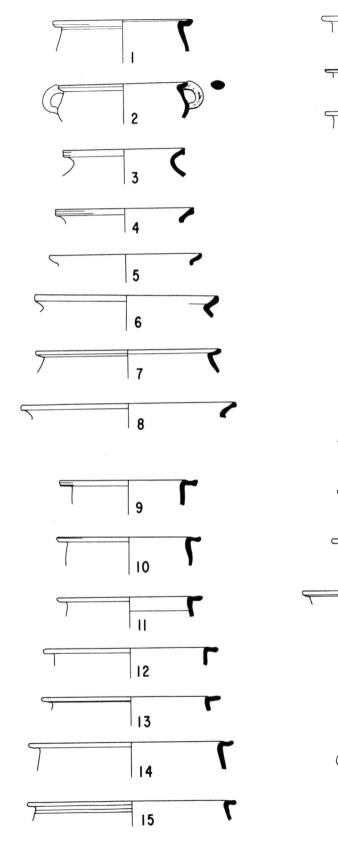

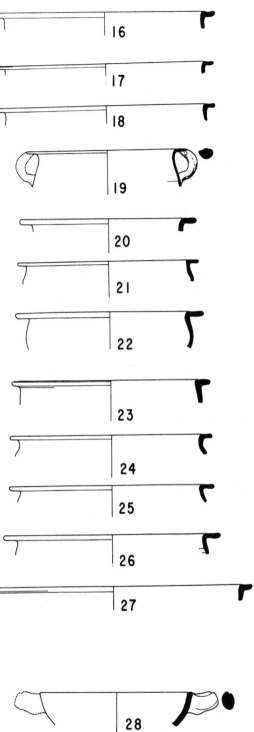

Plate 7.12

Plate 7.13. COOKING BOWLS WITH HORIZONTAL HANDLES
AND GLOBULAR COOKING POTS, 1:5

Field, Square, Bucket, Sherd	Locus	Stratum	Selected Colors of Important Loci	
			Sec.	Ext.
1. NW I.34.3.24	L.34001	VII		
2. NE I.25.30.14	L.25036	VI	5 YR 4/1	5 YR 5/3
3. NW VII.13.42.4	L.13003	V		
4. NE I.25.26.16	L.25036	VI	2.5 YR 5/8	2.5 YR 6/8
5. NE I.19.70.5	L.19070	VI	5 PB 4/1	2.5 YR 6/4
6. SE II.23.11.1	L.23008	IV	10 YR 6/2	10 YR 6/4
7. NW I.33.45.7	L.33020	VI–VII		
8. NW VII.13.44.13	L.13003	—		
9. NE I.19.70.16	L.19070	VI		
10. NE I.19.70.10	L.19070	VI		
11. NW VII.1.90.10	L.1060	III–IV		
12. NE I.26.47.1	L.26029	IV		
13. NE I.26.46.7	L.26028	IV		
14. NW VII.1.92.3	L.1060	III–IV		
15. SE II.17.7.5	L.17008	IV		
16. SE II.22.18.1	L.22004	IV		
17. NE VII.15.23	L.15002	—		
18. NE I.25.49.1.2.3	L.25045	V	2.5 YR 6/8	2.5 YR 6/8
19. MI.2.48.7	L.2019	Ia	10 YR 5/6	10 YR 5/4
20. MI.2.47.1	L.2019	Ia	2.5 YR 4/4	2.5 YR 4/4
21. MI.2.49.1	L.2019	Ia	2.5 YR 4/3	2.5 YR 5/3
22. MI.2.38.3	L.2014.1	II.2	2.5 YR 6/6	2.5 YR 6/4
23. NE I.32.81.3	L.32016	VII		
24. MI.2.52.1	L.2018.1	II.1a	2.5 YR 5/6	2.5 YR 5/6
25. NE I.26.39.9	L.26023	V	2.5 YR 5/6	2.5 YR 6/6 + 5/1
26. MI.2.48.35	L.2019	Ia	2.5 YR 5/6	2.5 YR 5/6

Plate 7.13

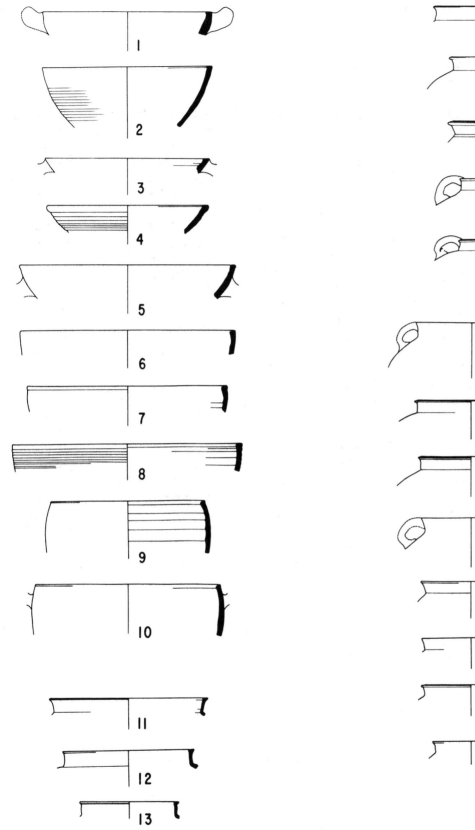
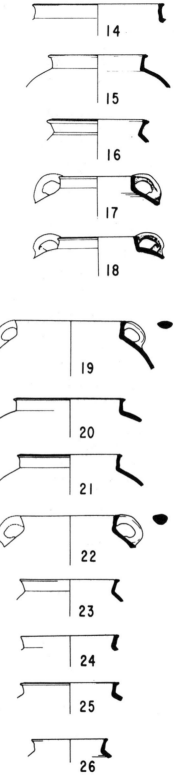

Plate 7.14. GLOBULAR COOKING POTS, 1:5

Field, Square, Bucket, Sherd	Locus	Stratum	Selected Colors of Important Loci Sec.	Selected Colors of Important Loci Ext.
1. MI.2.48.2	L.2019	Ia	2.5 YR 5/6	2.5 YR 6/6
2. MI.2.49.16	L.2019	Ia	2.5 YR 6/6	2.5 YR 5/6
3. MI.2.41.15	L.2015	II.2	10 R 4/8	2.5 YR 5/8
4. MI.2.44.8	L.2016.1	Ia	10 R 5/4	2.5 YR 5/4
5. MI.2.48.5	L.2019	Ia	2.5 YR 5/6	2.5 YR 5/5
6. MI.2.48.38	L.2019	Ia	2.5 YR 6/8	5 YR 6/3
7. MI.2.48.14	L.2019	Ia	2.5 YR 5/6	5 YR 6/4
8. MI.2.31.1	L.2011	II.a	2.5 YR 5/8	2.5 YR 6/8
9. MI.2.48.12	L.2019	Ia	2.5 YR 5/6	2.5 YR 5/6
10. MI.2.44.5	L.20161	II.1b	2.5 YR 5/6	2.5 YR 5/6
11. MI.2.38.4	L.2014.1	II.2	2.5 YR 5/6	2.5 YR 5/6
12. MI.2.48.31	L.2019	Ia	2.5 YR 5/6	5 YR 6/4
13. NW VII.13.44.15	L.13003	V		
14. NW VII.8.24.4	L.8004	mixed		
15. MI.2.38.15	L.2014.1	II.2	10 R 5/6	10 R 6/6
16. MI.2.41.5	L.2015	II.2	2.5 YR 5/8	2.5 YR 4/6
17. T-29.5.29.12	L.2013	III–IV		
18. NE I.32.77.6	L.32014	IV–V		
19. SE II.17.15.5	L.17006	IV		
20. MI.2.29.1	L.2012	II	2.5 YR 5/6	10 R 5/6
21. MI.2.48.22	L.2014.1	II.2	2.5 YR 5/6	2.5 YR 5/6
22. MI.2.45.2	L.2018.1	II.1a	2.5 YR 4/4	7.5 YR 6/3
23. MI.2.45.2	L.2016.1	II.1b	2.5 YR 4/4	2.5 YR 5/6
24. MI.2.55.6	L.2019	Ia	2.5 YR 5/4	2.5 YR 4/2
25. MI.2.25.3	L.2012	II	2.5 YR 6/8	5 YR 7/6
26. MI.2.44.9	L.2016.1	II.1b	2.5 YR 6/6	2.5 YR 6/6
27. MI.2.44.7	L.2016.1	II.1b	2.5 YR 6/6	2.5 YR 6/6
28. NW VII.3.29.3	L.3011	IV		

Plate 7.14

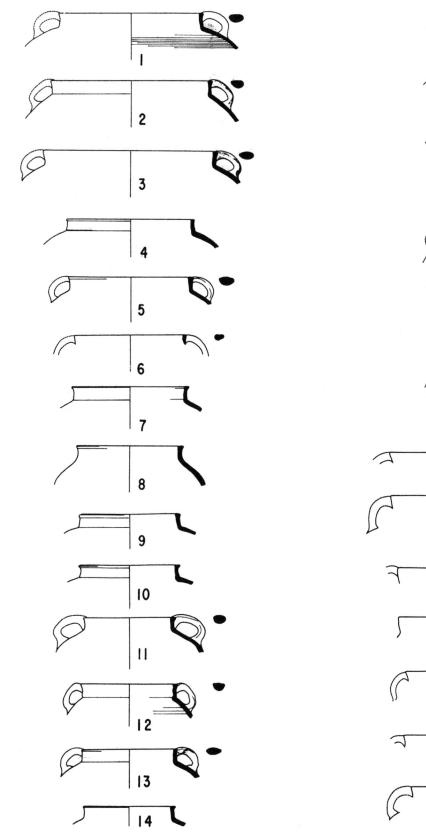

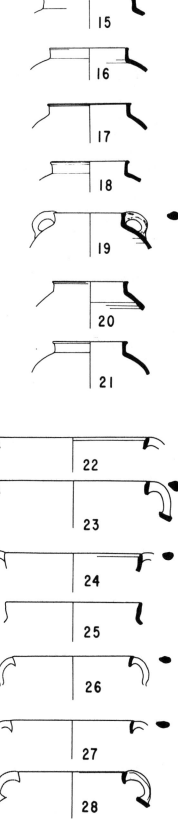

Plate 7.15. GLOBULAR COOKING POTS, 1:5

Field, Square, Bucket, Sherd	Locus	Stratum	Selected Colors of Important Loci	
			Sec.	Ext.
1. MI.2.48.39	L.2019	Ia	2.5 YR 5/6	2.5 YR 5/6
2. MI.2.46.2	L.20181	II.1a	5 YR 4/2	5 YR 4/2
3. MI.2.41.20	L.2015	II.2	2.5 YR 4/6	2.5 YR 5/6
4. MI.2.44.12	L.2016.1	II.1b	2.5 YR 5/6	2.5 YR 6/6
5. MI.2.61.6	L.2019	Ia	2.5 YR 5/6	2.5 YR 5/6
6. MI.2.36.4	L.2015	II.2	2.5 YR 3/6	5 YR 8/3
7. MI.2.48.30	L.2019	Ia	2.5 YR 5/6	2.5 YR 5/6
8. NE I.26.55.5	L.26037	IV	2.5 YR 6/6	2.5 YR 6/6
9. NE VII.2.67.6	L.2025	IV		
10. NE I.26.55.7	L.26037	IV	2.5 YR 5/4	2.5 YR 4/1
11. NW I.33.29.3	L.33015	VI		
12. NE I.32.87.1	L.32016	mixed	10 R 6/6	10 R 5/6
13. NW I.33.47.16	L.33022	VI	10 YR 4/2	10 YR 4/1
14. MI.2.49.15	L.2019	Ia	10 R 5/6	10 R 5/4
15. C-1.19.5	L.1005	IV		
16. T-29 South.18.20	L.29007	IV		
17. NE I.26.44.2	L.26024	V	5 PB 3/1	5 YR 6/2
18. NW I.34.9.11	L.34007	VI	5 R 4/1	7.5 YR 5/3
19. NW I.33.46.5	L.33022	VI	2.5 YR 4/1	2.5 YR 5/4
20. C-1.18	L.1005	IV		
21. C-1.4	L.1002	V		
22. C-1.15	L.1004	IV		
23. C-1.4	L.1002	V		

Plate 7.15

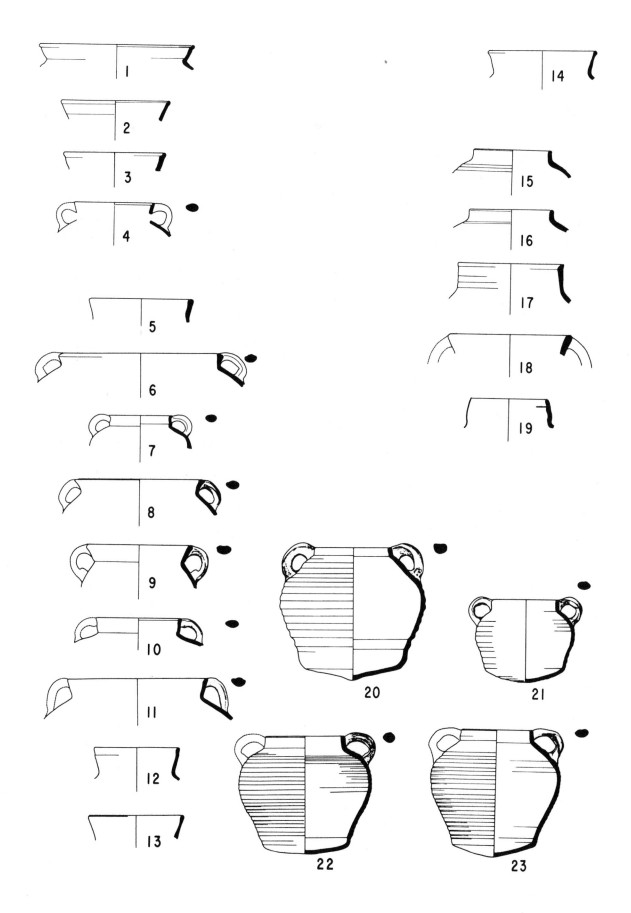

Plate 7.16. GLOBULAR COOKING POTS, 1:5

Field, Square, Bucket, Sherd	Locus	Stratum	Selected Colors of Important Loci	
			Sec.	Ext.
1. MI.4.31.1	L.4017			
2. MI.2.38.13	L.2014.1	II.2	2.5 YR 5/6	2.5 YR 5/4, 6/6
3. SE II.23.11.7	L.23001	IV	2.5 YR 5/8	2.5 YR 6/8
4. C-1.8.3	L.104	IV	2.5 YR 6/2	5 YR 6/6
5. C-1.4.9	L.102	V	2.5 YR 6/2	2.5 YR 6/2
6. C-1.2.3.1	L.102	V	2.5 YR 5/8	2.5 YR 6/8
7. MI.2.41.17	L.2015	II.2	2.5 YR 5/6	5 YR 6/4
8. C-1.8.17	L.104	IV	2.5 YR 5/8	2.5 YR 6/8
9. SE II.23.50.144	L.23013	IV	2.5 YR 4/8	2.5 YR 5/8
10. SE II.22.24.13	L.22006	IV	2.5 YR 4/8	2.5 YR 6/6
11. SE II.23.45.11	L.23020	IV	2.5 YR 5/8	2.5 YR 6/6
12. SE II.23.15.5	L.23011	IV	2.5 YR 4/6	2.5 YR 5/6
13. SE II.23.12.3	L.23008	IV	2.5 YR 5/8	2.5 YR 6/8
14. SE II.22.24.20	L.22006	IV	2.5 YR 5/8	2.5 YR 6/8
15. NW VII.13.35.4	L.13002	VI		
16. T-17.32.8	L.1715	IV	2.5 YR 5/8	2.5 YR 6/8
17. SE II.17.8.2	L.17009.1	IV	5 YR 4/6	7.5 YR 6/4
18. NW VII.1.86.2	L.1060	III–IV		
19. NE VII.2.88.1	L.2036	IV	2.5 YR 5/6 + 2.5 YR 5/1	2.5 YR 5/6
20. SE II.17.6.10	L.17005	IV	2.5 YR 5/8	2.5 YR 6/8
21. NW VII.13.35.5	L.13002	VI		
22. SE II.23.46.4	L.23020	IV	2.5 YR 5/8	2.5 YR 6/8
23. MI.2.31.4	L.2011	II.3	2.5 YR 5/8	2.5 YR 6/8
24. SE II.22.23.16	L.22006	IV	5 YR 5/8	2.5 YR 6/4
25. C-1.2	L.102	V		
26. C-1.8.19	L.104	IV		
27. C-1.2	L.102	V		

Plate 7.16

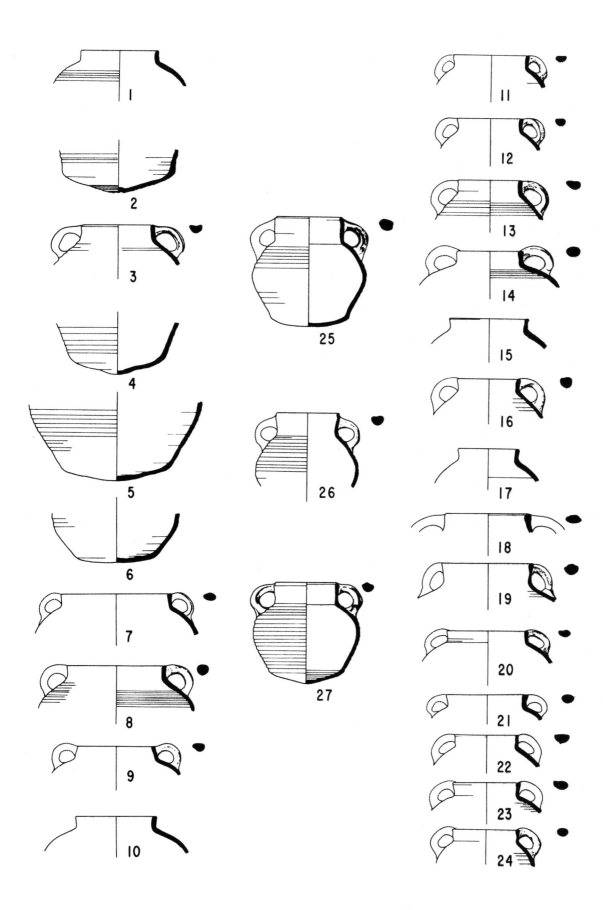

Plate 7.17. LIDS, BASINS WITH FOLDED RIM, AND BOWLS, 1:5

Field, Square, Bucket, Sherd	Locus	Stratum	Selected Colors of Important Loci	
			Sec.	Ext.
1. MI.2.29.4	L.2012	II.3	5 PB 4/1	2.5 YR 6/6
2. T-29 North.25.3	L.29008	IV	2.5 YR 3/0	2.5 YR 6/8
3. NW VII.1.88.6	L.1060	IV		
4. NE VII.3.17.2	L.3015	V	5 YR 5/3	5 YR 5/2
5. SE II.23.44.3	L.23019	IV	2.5 YR 5/6	5 YR 6/8
6. C-1.4.12	L.1002	V		
7. NW I.34.11.4	L.34010	V	7.5 YR 5/1	7.5 YR 5/1
8. NE VII.3.24.8	L.3017	mixed	2.5 YR 3/1	2.5 YR 3/1
9. NE I.19.26.7	L.19070	V		
10. NE I.25.27.13	L.250036	V	5 YR 4/3	2.5 YR 5/4
11. NE I.25.30.15	L.250036	V	2.5 YR 5/4	2.5 YR 5/2
12. NE VII.1.12.20	L.1009	mixed		
13. NW VII.13.36.11	L.13002	VI		
14. NE I.26.39.5	L.26023	V	2.5 YR 5/4	10 R 4/3–6/3
15. SE II.22.24.9	L.22006	IV	2.5 YR 4/8	2.5 YR 5/6
16. SE II.22.23.15	L.22006	IV	2.5 YR 5/8	2.5 YR 6/4
17. T-17.21.50	L.1701	IV		
18. T-17.22.38	L.1701	IV		
19. SE II.23.45.10	L.23020	IV	2.5 YR 5/8	2.5 YR 6/8
20. NE VII.1.11.7	L.1003	mixed		
21. NW I.25.18	L.25007	IV		
22. NW I.25.17	L.25017	IV		
23. NE VII.3.24.4	L.3017	VI	2.5 YR 5/6	2.5 YR 5/6
24. NE I.32.80.1	L.32019	III	10 R 5/6, 10 R 4/1	10 R 6/4
25. T-17.4.14	L.17001	IV	2.5 YR 5/8	2.5 YR 6/8
26. NE VII.2.79.11	L.2030	III	10 R 4/8	10 R 5/6
27. SE II.23.12.5	L.23008	IV	2.5 YR 6/8	2.5 YR 4/8
28. SE II.23.15.1	L.23011	IV	2.5 YR 4/8	5 YR 6/6
29. SE II.22.9.1	L.22002	IV	2.5 YR 5/8	2.5 YR 6/8

Plate 7.17

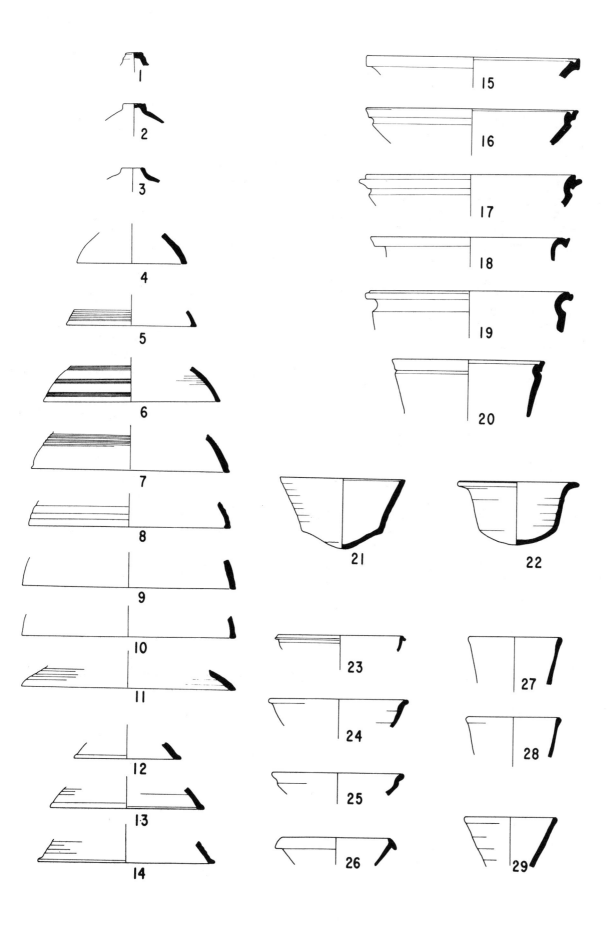

Plate 7.18. MISCELLANEOUS BOWLS, GLAZES, AND NECKLESS COOKING POTS
WITH FOLDED RIMS, 1:5

Field, Square, Bucket, Sherd	Locus	Stratum	Selected Colors of Important Loci	
			Sec.	Ext.
1. NW VII.1.89.1	L.1060	IV	2.5 YR 4/6	2.5 YR 5/3
2. NE VII.1.8.9	L.1004	IV	2.5 YR 4/6	2.5 YR 4/1
3. SE II.22.16.6	L.22003	IV	5 YR 4/2	5 YR 6/6
4. SE II.23.19.1	L.23008	IV	2.5 YR 4/8	5 YR 6/6
5. T-29 North.18.2	L.29007	IV		
6. NW I.33.46.2	L.33022	VI	10 YR 7/4	7.5 YR 8/3 + 7/3
7. NW I.31.16.21	L.31000	VII	10 YR 8/3	10 YR 8/4
8. NE I.25.36.32	L.25037	VII	7.5 YR 8/2	7.5 YR 8/2
9. NE I.19.27.9	L.19071	VI	5 YR 7/4	2.5 YR 6/6
10. NW VII.8.24.7	L.8004	VII		
11. NW I.31.18.20	L.31001	VII	5 YR 7/6	5 YR 6/3 + brown glaze
12. NW I.31.18	L.31001	VII	2.5 YR 5/8	2.5 YR 5/6 + brown glaze, yellow stripe
13. NE VII.2.96.1	L.2043	VII	10 R 6/3	brown glaze with yellow stripes
14. NW I.31.16.20	L.31000	VII	5 YR 7/6	5 YR 6/4 + brown glaze, yellow stripe
15. NW VII.8.27.2	L.8007	VI		
16. NW VII.8.21.1	L.8004	VII		
17. NW VII.14.24.1	L.14002	—		
18. NW I.34.9.15	L.34007	VI	2.5 YR 5/4	5 GY 5/8 + white slip, glazed
19. NW VII.13.34.5	L.13002	VI		
20. NW I.31.19.13	L.31000	VII	2.5 YR 5/6	2.5 YR 5/6 + yellow paint inside
21. NW VII.9.14.5	L.9007	VII		
22. NW VII.8.6.10	L.8001	VII		
23. NW VII.13.34.8	L.13002	VI		
24. NW VII.9.14.2	L.9007	VII		
25. NW I.31.16.18	L.31000	VII	2.5 YR 5/8	2.5 YR 5/4 + green stripes, brown glazed
26. NE I.26.4.6	L.26003	VI	10 YR 3/1	5 YR 5/4
27. NW I.34.11.8	L.34010	V	2.5 YR 5/6	2.5 YR 6/8
28. NW I.34.20.5	L.34010	V	2.5 YR 5/3	2.5 YR 5/3 + 5/1
29. SE II.23.15.4	L.23011	IV	5 YR 4/1	7.5 YR 5/4

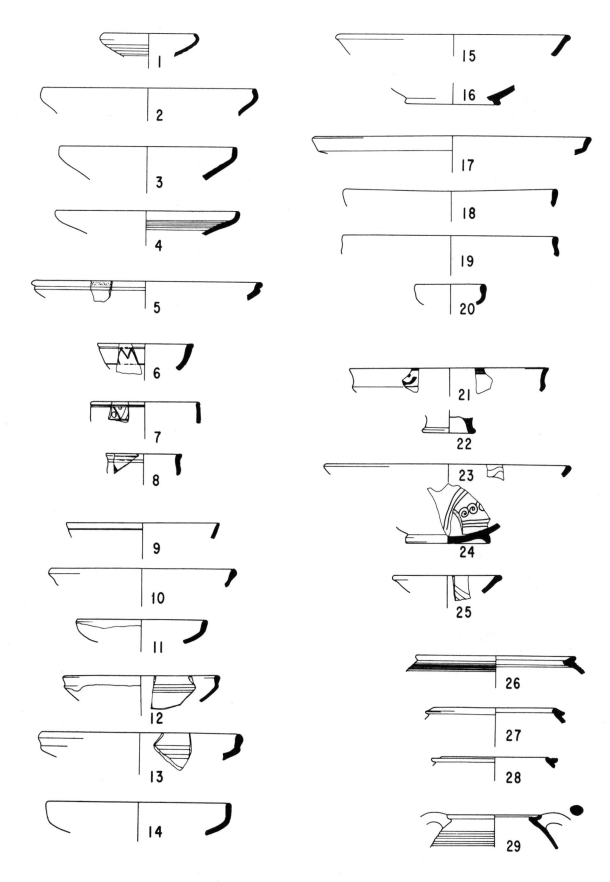

Plate 7.19. MISCELLANEOUS OPEN FORMS, JARS, AND COOKING POTS, 1:5

Field, Square, Bucket, Sherd	Locus	Stratum	Selected Colors of Important Loci	
			Sec.	Ext.
1. C-1.8.13	L.1004	IV	5 YR 6/4	2.5 YR 6/4
2. NE I.26.3.4	L.26003	VII	2.5 YR 5/8	2.5 YR 6/8
3. NW VII.14.30.4	L.14005	VI		
4. NE I.25.25.4	L.25035	VI	7.5 YR 3/2	7.5 YR 6/4
5. NW VII.3.26.4	L.3019	V		
6. MI.2.61.5	L.2019	Ia	5 YR 7/4	5 YR 7/6
7. NW VII or I.32.29.2	L.000	—		
8. NE I.32.56.1	L.32016	VI	2.5 YR 4/4	2.5 YR 5/6
9. NE VII.1.11.1	L.1003	VI		
10. NE I.26.39.13	L.26023	V		
11. T-17.13.4	L.17006	IV	2.5 YR 5/8	2.5 YR 6/8
12. NE I.19.70.9	L.19070	VI	5 PB 2/1	5 PB 2/1
13. NE I.25.30.15	L.25036	VI	2.5 YR 5/4	2.5 YR 5/6
14. NW I.34.9.16	L.34007	VI	2.5 YR 3/1	2.5 YR 3/3
15. C-1.8.10	L.1004	IV	2.5 YR 5/4	5 YR 6/3
16. NE I.25.26	L.25036	VI		
17. C-1.8.2	L.1004	IV		
18. C-1.9.1	L.1004	IV		
19. T-17.22.7	L.1701	IV	2.5 YR 6/8	5 YR 6/6
20. T-17.11.18	L.1703	IV		
21. NE I.19.27.13	L.19071	VI	10 R 7/3	7.5 YR 7/3
22. NE VII.3.25.4	L.3018	IV	2.5 YR 4/6	10 R 4/4
23. NE VII.8.24.2	L.8004	VII		
24. NW VII.13.34.4	L.13002	VI		
25. SE II.23.48.3	L.23001	IV	7.5 YR 3/2	5 YR 5/8
26. NW VII.13.34.1	L.13002	VI		
27. NE VII.1.7.10	L.1003	V	10 R 4/4	5 YR 5/3
28. NW I.32.7.1	L.32007	IV	2.5 YR 5/6	2.5 YR 6/8
29. NW I.32.78.4	L.32030	VI	5 YR 4/8	5 YR 6/4
30. NW I.34.9.6	L.34007	VI	10 R 5/4	2.5 YR 6/6
31. NW VII.8.32.2	L.8008	VI		
32. NW VII.8.24.2	L.8004	VII		

Plate 7.19

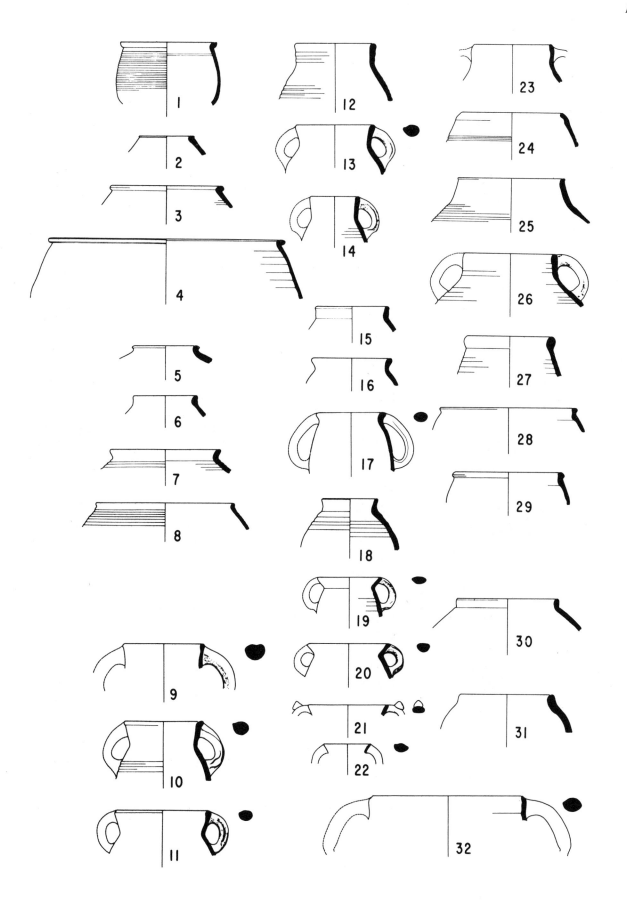

Plate 7.20. JARS, 1:5

Field, Square, Bucket, Sherd	Locus	Stratum	Selected Colors of Important Loci	
			Sec.	Ext.
1. MI.2.48.42	L.2019	Ia	7.5 YR 7/1	7.5 YR 8/4
2. MI.2.61.4	L.2019	Ia	5 YR 8/3	5 YR 7/4
3. MI.2.55.2	L.2019	Ia	7.5 YR 7/2	5 YR 7/3
4. MI.2.49.6	L.2019	Ia	5 YR 5/1	2.5 YR 7/6
5. MI.2.48.8	L.2019	Ia	10 R 5/4	5 YR 6/3
6. NE VII.2.86.1	L.2035	IV	5 YR 5/1	10 YR 7/3
7. NE VII.2.63.11	L.2025	IV	10 YR 5/8	2.5 YR 6/8
8. NW I.32.69.1	L.32028	VI	10 YR 5/2	10 YR 8/3
9. MI.2.36.9	L.2015	II.2	N 5/1	5 YR 6/6
10. NW I.26.25.2	L.26008	IV	10 R 6/6	10 YR 7/2
11. NW I.32.59.2	L.32030	VI	10 YR 6/2	10 YR 5/2
12. MI. 2.41.8	L.2015	II.2	7.5 YR 7/4	7.5 YR 8/4
13. MI.2.35.2	L.2015	II.2	2.5 YR 6/8	2.5 YR 6/8
14. MI.2.36.3	L.2015	II.2	5 YR 4/2	10 YR 7/4
15. SE II.17.15.3	L.17006	IV	2.5 YR 5/8	5 YR 6/6
16. MI.2.36.7	L.2015	II.2	2.5 YR 5/6	5 YR 7/8
17. MI.2.49.14	L.2019	Ia	10 YR 6/4	2.5 YR 6/6
18. MI.2.44.1	L.2016.1	II.1b	10 R 5/6	2.5 YR 6/6
19. MI.2.35.8	L.2015	II.2	10 R 6/6	7.5 YR 8/4
20. MI.2.36.13	L.2015	II.2	2.5 YR 5/6	5 YR 6/4
21. MI.2.36.1	L.2015	II.2		5 YR 6/4
22. T-17.19.7	L.17000	IV	10 R 5/4	5 YR 5/1
23. T-29 South.18.12	L.29007	IV	2.5 YR 6/6	5 YR 6/6
24. MI.2.38.14	L.2014.1	II.2	10 R 5/6	2.5 YR 6/6
25. T-17.4.10	L.17001	IV	2.5 YR 6/6	5 YR 6/6
26. SE II.23.48.2	L.23001	IV	2.5 YR 5/8	5 YR 5/8
27. SE II.23.45	L.23020	IV	2.5 YR 5/6	5 YR 6/6
28. T-29 South.30.1	L.29010	IV		
29. NE I.26.3	L.26003	VII	5 YR 6/8	5 YR 6/8
30. NW VII.13.43.1	L.13002	VI		
31. NE I.32.81.11	L.32016	VI		
32. NE I.25.109.1	L.25010	—	2.5 YR 5/8	5 YR 5/8
33. MI.2.36.2	L.2015	II.2	5 YR 7/8	5 YR 7/8
34. T-17.10.11	L.17010	IV	10 YR 6/2	10 YR 6/3
35. T-17.1.16	L.17001	IV	2.5 YR 6/6	5 YR 7/6
36. T-17.6.30	L.17033	IV	2.5 YR 6/6	5 YR 7/6
37. T-29 South.28.6	L.29012	IV		
38. T-17.32.7	L.17015	IV	2.5 YR 5/6	7.5 YR 5/4
39. SE II.22.16.3	L.22003	IV	2.5 YR 5/6	5 YR 5/8
40. SE II.23.46.3	L.23020	IV	2.5 YR 5/6	5 YR 6/8
41. SE II.23.48.1	L.22001	IV	2.5 YR 5/8	5 YR 6/8
42. NW I.34.14.7	L.34009	IV	5 YR 5/2	2.5 YR 5/6
43. NW VII.13.38.14	L.13002	V	5/2	2.5 YR 5
44. NE I 32.72.5	L.32016	VI		
45. NE VII.1.44.2	L.1018.1	IV		

(continued on verso following)

Plate 7.20

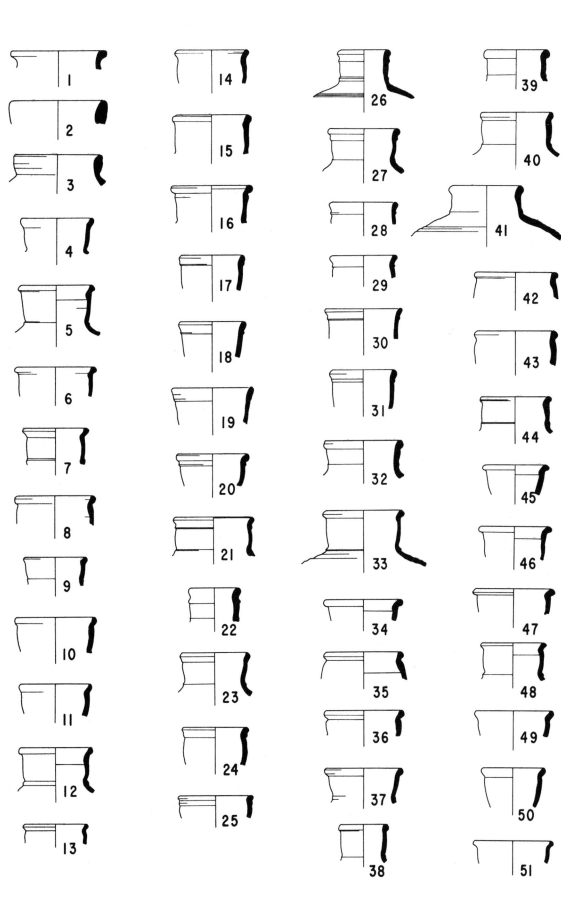

(*Plate 7.20, continued*)

46. SE II.17.17.9	L.17012	IV	10 R 5/6	7.5 YR 6/4
47. NE I.32.72.7	L.32016	VI		
48. NE I.25.49.9	L.25045	V		
49. T-17.7.5	L.17004	IV		
50. T-17.4	L.17001	IV	2.5 YR 5/6	5 YR 6/6
51. T-29 South.29.21	L.29013	IV		

Plate 7.21. JARS, 1:5

Field, Square, Bucket, Sherd	Locus	Stratum	Selected Colors of Important Loci	
			Sec.	Ext.
1. T-29 South.16.31	L.29007	IV	5 YR 6/1	7.5 YR 6/2
2. T-29 South.16.19	L.29007	IV	5 YR 5/1	10 YR 6/3
3. T-17.12.2	L.17006	IV	2.5 YR 6/6	5 YR 6/6
4. T-17.21.41	L.17001	IV	2.5 YR 6/6	5 YR 6/2
5. MI.2.38.5	L.2014.1	II.2	2.5 YR 5/6	2.5 YR 6/6
6. SE II.23.15.3	L.23011	IV	10 YR 4/1	7.5 YR 5/4
7. SE II.17.6.1	L.17005	IV	2.5 YR 5/8	2.5 YR 6/8
8. T-17.6.4	L.17003	IV	5 YR 5/4	5 YR 6/6
9. C-1.15A.1	L.1004	IV	2.5 YR 5/8	2.5 YR 6/8
10. MI.2.27.3	L.2011.1	II.3	2.5 YR 6/6	2.5 YR 6/8
11. SE II.17.9.4	L.17009.1	IV	2.5 YR 5/8	5 YR 6/6
12. SE II.23.1.1	L.23001	IV	2.5 YR 5/8	2.5 YR 6/8
13. T-17.32.4	L.17015	IV	2.5 YR 6/6	5 YR 7/4
14. T-29 North.24.2	L.29010	IV		
15. SE II.23.44.1	L.23019	IV	2.5 YR 5/6	7.5 YR 6/4
16. T-29 South.6.2	L.29004	IV		
17. NW VII.3.26.2	L.3019	V		
18. NE I.19.39.10	L.19072	IV		
19. NW I.34.9.7	L.34007	V	2.5 YR 7/4, 6/1	2.5 YR 7/4
20. NW VII.13.38.12	L.13002	V		
21. NE I.19.27.1	L.19071	VI	5 YR 5/2	5 YR 7/4
22. NE VII.1.12.7	L.1009	VI		
23. NE I.25.30.38	L.25036	V	5 YR 6/1	5 YR 7/2
24. NW I.31.66.5	L.31021	VII		
25. NW I.31.59	L.31021	VII		
26. NW VII.1.38.9	L.1022	IV		
27. NE VII.1.2.3	L.1002	VII	5 YR 5/3	7.5 YR 6/2
28. SE II.23.36.4	L.23017P	IV	5 YR 5/3	10 YR 5/2
29. NE VII.2.79.18	L.2030	III	2.5 YR 5/8	10 R 6/6
30. NW I.33.29.5	L.33015	VI		
31. NE VII.2.91.2	L.2038	IV	5 YR 6/3,1	5 YR 6/3
32. MI.2.41.1	L.2015	II.2	10 R 5/6,1	2.5 YR 6/6
33. NW I.34.9.5	L.34007	V	10 R 5/6 + 10R 5/1	2.5 YR 6/6
34. NW VII.9.6.2	L.9007	VII		

Plate 7.21

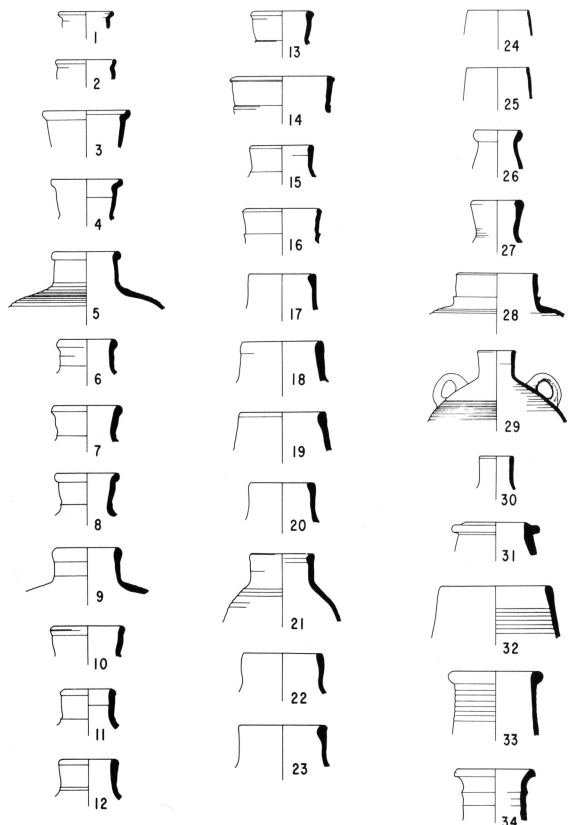

Plate 7.22. JUGLETS AND MISCELLANEOUS CLOSED FORMS, 1:5

Field, Square, Bucket, Sherd	Locus	Stratum	Selected Colors of Important Loci Sec.	Ext.
1. SE II.23.1.2	L.23001	IV	5 YR 6/6	7.5 YR 6/6
2. NE I.32.82.3	L.32016	III	2.5 YR 5/8	5 YR 6/3
3. MI.2.37.2	L.2014.1	II.2	2.5 YR 4/3	5 YR 6/4–5/1
4. NW VII.1.66.1	L.1046	IV		
5. MI.2.45.3	L.2016.1	II.1b	2.5 YR 5/1–5/6	2.5 YR 5/6
6. NW I.26.18.7	L.26008	—	5 YR 4/6	2.5 YR 6/8
7. NW VII.1.44.1	L.1018.1	IV		
8. NW I.33.45.3	L.33020	VII		
9. NW I.25.14.2	L.25005		5 YR 5/8	5 YR 6/6
10. T-29 South.20.11	L.29008	IV	2.5 YR 5/8	2.5 YR 6/8
11. NW I.33.47.14	L.33022	VI	5 PB 3/1	5 YR 4/1
12. SE II.23.64.1	L.23024	IV		
13. NE I.25.29.16	L.25036	V		
14. NE VII.1.13.7	L.1003	mixed		
15. NE I.26.50.3	L.26031	IV		
16. NW VII.1.38.2	L.1022	IV	2.5 YR 5/8	2.5 YR 6/8
17. T-29 North.23	L.2909	IV		
18. NE I.32.82.2	L.32016	III	2.5 YR 5/6–4/1	2.5 YR 5/6
19. NE VII.2.79.32	L.2030	III	5 YR 6/6	5 YR 7/4
20. NW VII.13.38.10	L.13002	IV		
21. NE I.32.73.5	L.32016	IV	2.5 YR 5/6	2.5 YR 5/6
22. SE II.17.19.13	L.17013	IV	2.5 YR 5/8	2.5 YR 6/6
23. MI.2.38.20	L.2014.1	II	2.5 YR 5/6	2.5 YR 6/6
				Slip: 10 R 5/3
24. NE VII.2.79.38	L.2030	III	2.5 YR 5/8	10 R 5/6
25. NE I.26.46.4	L.26028	IV	2.5 YR 6/6	2.5 YR 6/6
26. NW I.34.9.12	L.34007	—	7.5 YR 8/4	7.5 YR 8/4
27. NE VII.1.5	L.1002	mixed	2.5 Y 7/2	2.5 Y 8/2
28. NW I.32.54.1	L.32030	VI	10 YR 8/2	10 YR 8/2
29. T-29 South.25.2	L.29010	IV		
30. NW VII.1.48.1	L.1037	IV	5 YR 6/4	5 YR 7/3
31. NE I.32.72.11	L.32016	IV	2.5 YR 3/1–6/6	10 YR 6–8/1
32. T-17.31.2	L.1714	IV	5 YR 7/6	5 YR 7/4
33. NE I.19.27.5	L.19071	VI	2.5 YR 6/3	2.5 YR 6/4
34. NW I.34.11.3	L.34010	V	7.5 YR 5/1	7.5 YR 6/2
35. T-29 North.18.4	L.2907	IV		
36. NW I.33.29.10	L.33015	VI		
37. T-17.13.1	L.17006	IV	5 YR 7/6	5 YR 7/6
38. T-29 South.3.7	L.29001	IV		
39. NW I.33.45.1	L.33020	VII		
40. NW VII.9.6.8	L.9007	VII		
41. NW I.33.31.4	L.33015	VI		
42. SE II.17.17.3	L.17012	IV	2.5 YR 5/8	5 YR 6/4
43. NW I.31.66.10	L.31021	VII		
44. NE VII.2.81.8	L.2032	IV	5 YR 7/3	5 YR 7/3

(continued on verso following)

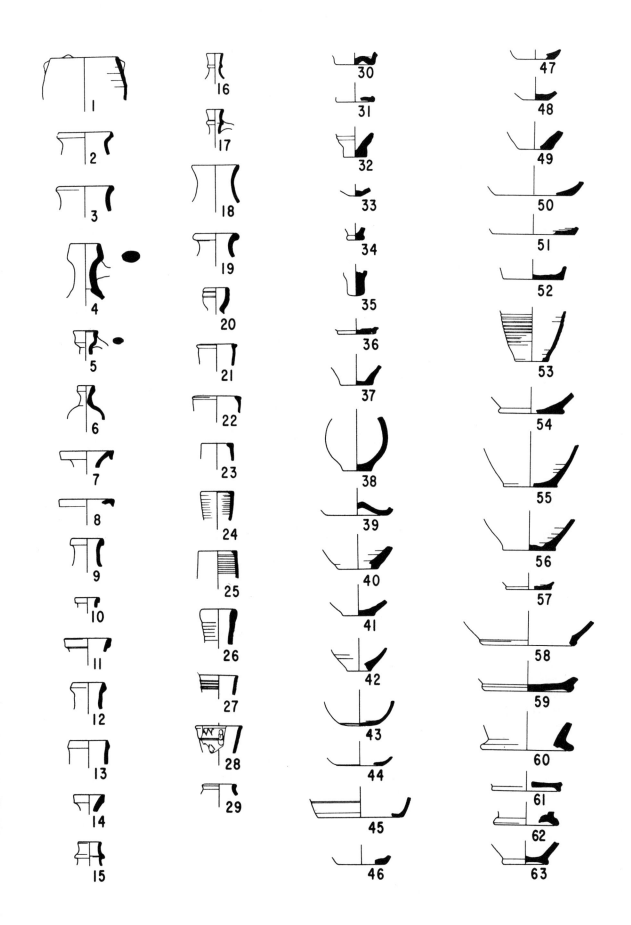

Plate 7.22

45. NE I.25.36.4	L.25037	V	10 YR 8/2	10 YR 8/2
46. NE I.26.40.3	L.26024	V	7.5 YR 8/4	7.5 YR 8/4
47. NE I.26.38.4	L.26022.1	VII	2.5 YR 4/1	2.5 YR 5/6
48. MI.2.61.3	L.2019	Ia	2.5 YR 4/1–7/4	7.5 YR 8/4
49. NE VII.2.63.12	L.2025	IV	5 YR 7/2	5 YR 7/4
50. NW VII.1.90.7	L.1060	IV		
51. NE I.19.26.4	L.19070	VI	7.5 YR 7/4	7.5 YR 8/4
52. NE I.25.44.1	L.25042			
53. SE II.23.66A.1	L.23026	IV	2.5 YR 5/6	5 YR 5/8
54. NE I.25.31.16	L.25036	V	10 YR 7/3	10 YR 7/4
55. NE I.19.26.2	L.19070	VI	10 YR 7/3	5 YR 6/2
56. NE I.19.26.1	L.19070	VI	7.5 YR 7/3	7.5 YR 8/1–5/1
57. NE I.19.27.7	L.19071	VI	7.5 YR 7/3	10 YR 7/4
58. NW VII.3.26.4	L.3019	V		
59. NW VII.3.26.23	L.3019	V		
60. MI.2.55.5	L.2019	Ia	5 P 4/1	10 R 5/1
61. NE I.26.38.7	L.26022	VII	2.5 YR 5/6	2.5 YR 5/4
62. NW I.33.47.4	L.33022	VI	10 R 6/6	5 UR 6/3
63. NW I.31.19.23	L.31000	VII	7.5 YR 8/6	7.5 YR 8/6

Plate 7.23. TERRA SIGILLATA AND AMPHORISKOI, 1:5

Field, Square, Bucket, Sherd	Locus	Stratum	Selected Colors of Important Loci	
			Sec.	Ext.
1. C-1.8.24	L.1005	IV	2.5 YR 6/8	2.5 YR 6/8
2. NW VII.13.46.1	L.13003	V		
3. NW VII.8.23.3	L.8004	VII		
4. NW VII.13.40.2	L.13002B	V		
5. SE II.23.48.6	L.23001	IV	10 YR 5/1	7.5 YR 6/4
6. NE VII.3.7	L.3011	VI		
7. SE II.17.9.6	L.17009.1	IV	5 YR 6/6	5 YR 7/8
8. SE II.23.48.5	L.23001	IV	2.5 YR 6/6	5 YR 7/8
9. SE II.23.2.4	L.23001	IV	2.5 YR 5/4	5 YR 6/6
10. NW VII.13.39.13	L.13002B	VI		
11. NW I.31.58.2	L.31021	VII	2.5 YR 6/6	10 R 6/8
12. SE II.23.70.3	L.23028.1	IV	2.5 YR 4/8	2.5 YR 6/8
13. NE VII.3.13.1	L.3009.1	IV	2.5 YR 6/4	2.5 YR 7/4
14. SE II.22.16.1	L.22003	IV	5 YR 6/4	2.5 YR 6/4
15. SE II.23.48.4	L.23001	IV	5 YR 4/4	5 YR 6/4
16. NE VII.3.13.5	L.3009.1	IV	2.5 YR 6/6	2.5 YR 7/4
17. NW VII.13.38.9	L.13002B	V		
18. NW I.34.9.2	L.34007	VI	2.5 YR 6/4	5 YR 6/4
19. C-1.10.1	L.1004	IV	2.5 YR 6/4	5 YR 5/4
20. NE VII.1.11.2	L.1003	VII	2.5 YR 6/6	2.5 YR 6/6
21. NW VII.3.28.1	L.3021	IV		

(*continued on verso following*)

Plate 7.23

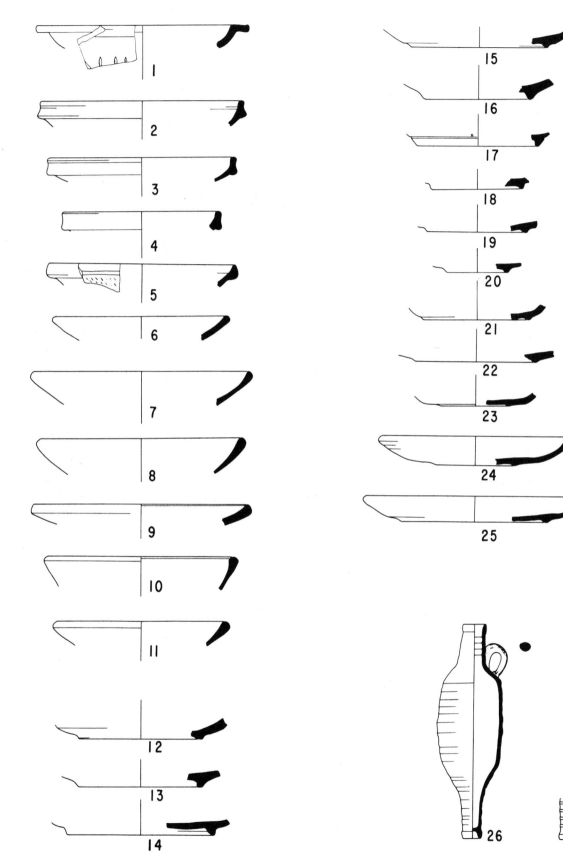

(*Plate 7.23, continued*)

22. NE VII.1.11.12	L.1003	VII		
23. SE II.22.16.5	L.22003	IV	7.5 YR 5/4	7.5 YR 7/4
24. C-1.15A.8	L.1004	IV		
25. SE II.23.54.2	L.23014.1	IV	5 YR 6/6	5 YR 7/6
26. SE II.23.36	L.230017P	IV		
27. SE II.22.24.16	L.22006	IV	5 YR 5/6	7.5 YR 7/4

Plate 7.24. LARGE STORAGE VESSELS AND BASINS, 1:5

Field, Square, Bucket, Sherd	Locus	Stratum	Selected Colors of Important Loci	
			Sec.	Ext.
1. NW VII.1.88.2	L.1060	IV		
2. MI.2.49.7	L.2019	Ia	5 YR 6/2	5 YR 6/3
3. NE I.26.47.9	L.26029	IV	5 YR 5/3	2.5 YR 6/6
4. NE VII.2.81.5	L.2032	IV	5 YR 7/3	5 YR 6/3
5. NW I.33.31.2	L.33015	VI		
6. NE I.32.29.1	L.32008	VI		
7. NW I.33.34.2	L.33015	VI		
8. NW I.33.47.7	L.33022	VI	5 PB 3/1	2.5 YR 6/4
9. MI.2.44.10	L.2016.1	II.1b	5 YR 5/1	5 YR 6/3
10. NW VII.1.92.1	L.1060	IV		
11. NW I.32.83.9	L.32016	VI	2.5 YR 3/1	2.5 YR 5/4
12. NW I.26.33.13	L.26013	IV	2.5 YR 5/6	5 YR 6/6
13. SE II.23.42.4	L.23018	IV	10 YR 6/4	7.5 YR 7/4
14. NW VII.13.36.8	L.13002A	VI		
15. NW VII.13.36.6	L.13002A	VI		
16. NW VII.13.36.5	L.13002A	VI		
17. NW VII.8.31.1	L.8004	VII		
18. NW VII.13.29.2	L.13002A	VI		
19. T-29 South.23.5	L.29009	IV	7.5 YR 6/4	5 YR 6/6
20. NW VII.13.36.1	L.13002A	VI		
21. NW VII.13.36.3	L.13002A	VI		

Plate 7.24

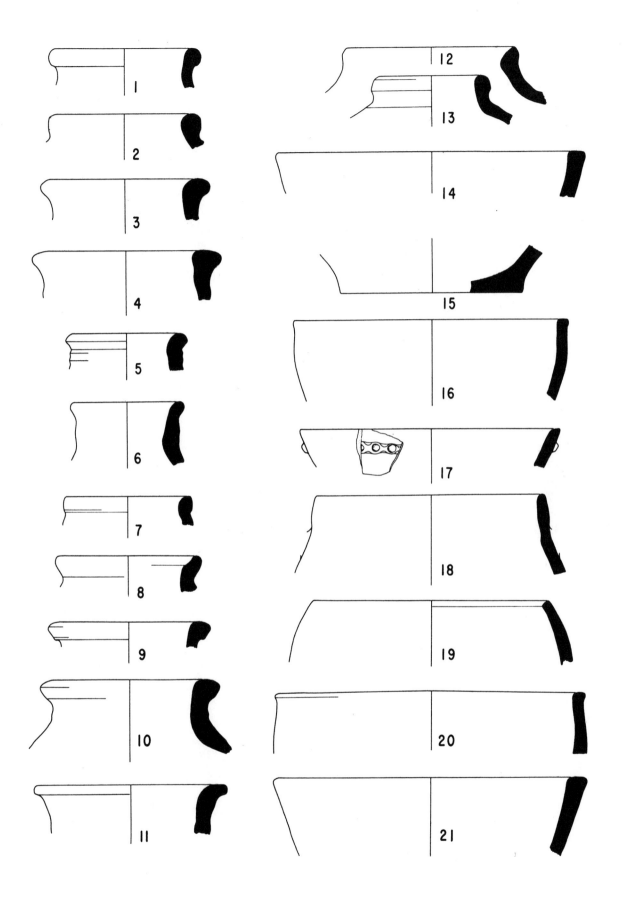

Plate 8.1. IRON AND BRONZE OBJECTS, 1:2.5

No. Reg.	Field, Square Bucket	Locus	Artifact	Parallels
1. 3405	NW VII.8	L.8000	cosmetic tool, bronze	*Nessana* I, pl. XXIII:5–6
2. 120	NE I.33.5	L.3300	cosmetic tool, bronze	
3. 587	NW I.26.10	L.26005	cosmetic tool, bronze	
4. 109	NW I.30.1	L.30001	cosmetic tool, bronze	*Dhiban*, fig. 13:61
5. 427	NW I.30.22	L.30008.1	cosmetic tool, bronze	*Bethany*, pl. 57C
6. 3207	NW VII.13.30	L.13002	cosmetic tool, bronze	
7. 3367	NE I.19.27	L.19071	cosmetic tool, bronze	
8. 3621	NE VII.1	L.1000?	spatula, bronze	
9. 3753	NW VII.14.20	L.14002	spatula, bronze	
10. 3267	NW VII.33.21	L.33012	spatula, bronze	
11. 3175	NW VII.13.29	L.13002	ring, bronze	*Bethany*, pl. 58C10?
12. 739	NW VII.2.26	L.2004	ring, bronze	
13. 3502	NW VII.1.90	L.1060	ring, bronze	
14. 1948	NW VII.13.9	L.13004	engraved ring, bronze	
15. 3376	NW VII.1	L.33001	ball, bronze	
16. 3257	NW VII.33.17	L.33001	clasp, bronze	
17. 114	NW I.3.4	L.3001	arrowhead, iron	*Beth She'arim* III, pl. 73:10
18. 3622	NW VII.1.00	L.1000	arrowhead, iron	
19. 113	NW I.30.1	L.30000	arrowhead, iron	
20. 357	NW I.31.23	L.31001	arrowhead, iron	
21. 3048	NW VII.8.15	L.8001	arrowhead, iron	
22. 1976	NW VII.8.7	L.8001	arrowhead, iron	
23. 40	NW I.29.4	L.29001	arrowhead, iron	
24. 37	NE I.32.7	L.32001	arrowhead, iron	
25. 624	NW I.31.45	L.31002	blade, iron, knife	
26. 3279	NW VII.8.25	L.8003	blade, iron	
27. 121	NW I.31.5	L.31001	blade, iron	

Plate 8.1

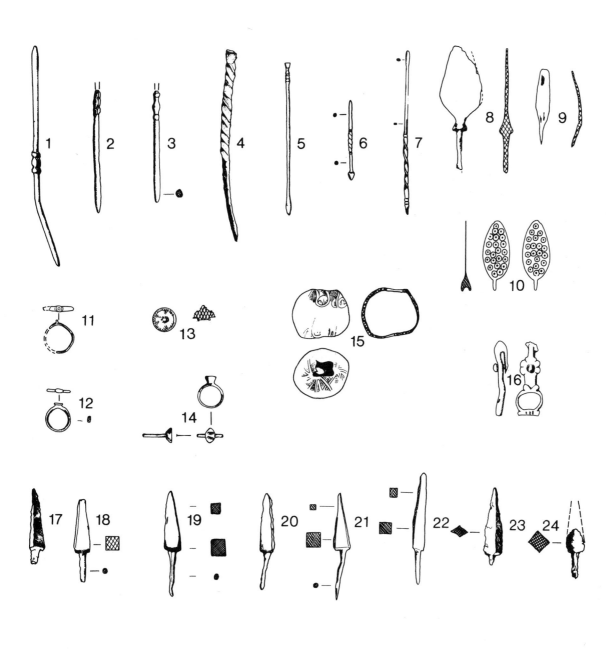

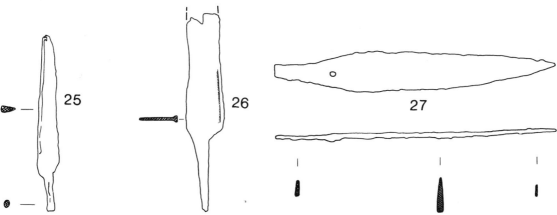

Plate 8.2. IRON AND BRONZE OBJECTS, 1:2.5

No. Reg.	Field, Square Bucket	Locus	Artifact	Parallels
1. 3264	NW VII.3.11	L.3008	blade, iron	*Beth She'arim* III, fig. 102:5
2. 799	NW I.31.58	L.31021	blade, iron	
3. 3032	NE I.26.42	L.26023	blade, iron	
4. 1218	NW I.31.82	L.31021	blade, iron	
5. 355	NW I.31.20	L.21005	iron	
6. 380	NE I.25.35	L.25037	scissors, iron	*Beth She'arim* III, fig. 102:3
7. 419	NE I.33.39	L.33003	scissors, iron	
8. 378	NE I.25.36	L.25037	scissors, iron	
9. 379	NE I.25.35	L.25037	pin, iron	*Beth She'arim* III, pl. 73:3
10. 1212	NW I.31.65	L.31021	cosmetic spoon, bronze	*Pella* I, pl. 64:196
11. 3112	MII.1.21	L.1009	iron	
12. 253	NE I.25.16	L.25006	disc, bronze	
13. 1692	SE II.23.48	L.23001.1	sickle blade, iron	*Khirbat al-Karak*, pl. 48:7
14. 809	C-1.1.18	L.1005	sickle blade, iron	

Plate 8.2

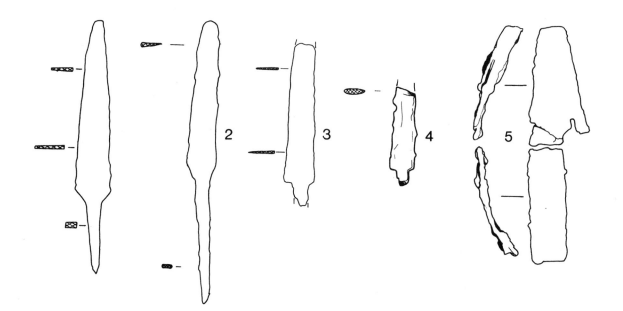

2

3

4

5

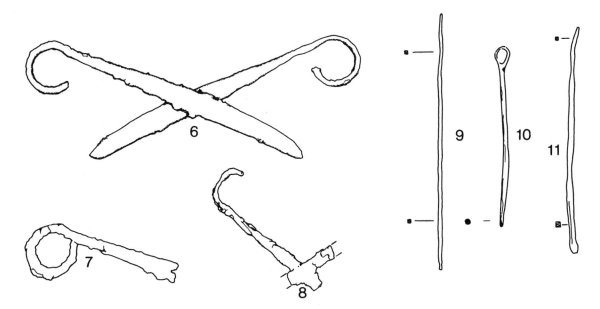

6

7

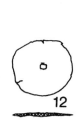

8

9

10

11

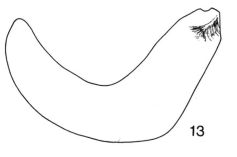

12

13

14

Plate 8.3. IRON AND BRONZE OBJECTS, 1:2.5

No. Reg.	Field, Square Bucket	Locus	Artifact	Parallels
1. 1074	NE VII.1.41	L.1002	bell, bronze	*Beth Sheʻarim* III, fig. 101:6
2. 363	T-29 South.16	L.29007	ring, iron	*Bethany*, pl. 58 C-10
3. 482	T-29 North.37	L.28018	chain, iron	
4. 304	NW I.29.38	L.29001	ring, iron	*Khirbat al-Karak*, pl. 45: 15–17
5. 205	NW I.31.8	L.31001	ring, iron	
6. 697	NW I.31.55	L.31021	ring, bronze	
7. 230	NE I.25.38	L.25036	iron	
8. 894	NW I.31.59	L.31021	ring, iron	
9. 964	NW VII.1.41	L.1035	nail, iron	
10. 720	NE VII.2.23	L.2014	nail, iron	
11. 50	NE I.32.9	L.32001	nail, iron	
12. 236	NE I.31.32	L.31009	nail, iron	*Beth Sheʻarim* III, pl. 73:5
13. 248	SE I.24.28	L.24011	hook and eye	*Pella* I, pl. 60:70
14. 660	NW I.26.27	L.26009	nail, iron	
15. 49	NW I.3.07	L.30006	nail, iron	
16. 3108	NW VII.8.19	L.8001	nail, iron	*Bethany*, fig. 34:13
17. 3208	NE I.26.47	L.26029	nail, iron	
18. 705	NW VII.1.18	L.1013	nail, iron	*Beth Sheʻarim* III, pl. 73:4
19. 405	T-29 South.22	L.29007	ring, iron	
20. 372	T-29 North.29	L.29011	ring, iron	
21. 371	T-29 North.29	L.29011	ring, iron	

Plate 8.3

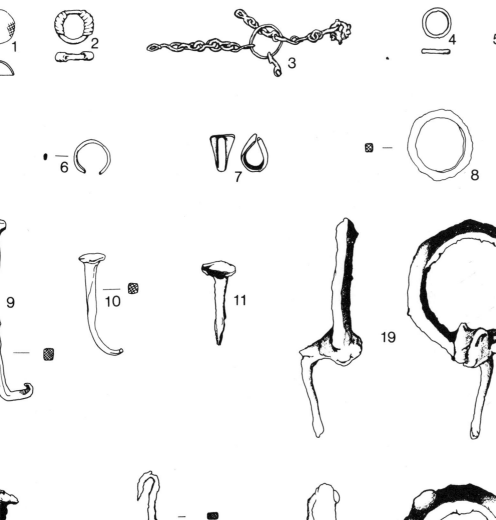
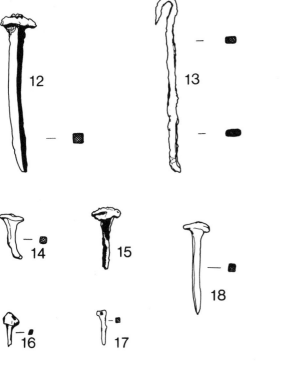
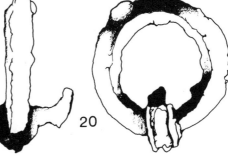
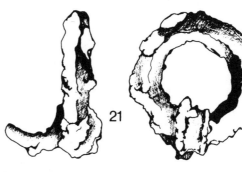

Plate 8.4. GLASS VESSELS, 1:2.5

No.	Reg.	Field, Square Bucket	Locus	Artifact	Parallels
1.	3065	NE I.32.55	L.32016	bowl, molded	*IEJ* 21, fig. 6.1–7
2.	748	NW I.31.55	L.31021	bowl, molded	Ibid.
3.	3609	NE I.32.74	L.32012.1	bowl, molded	Ibid.
4.	817	NW I.25.14	L.25005	bowl, molded	Ibid.
5.	1869	NE I.32.33	L.32014	bowl, molded	*IEJ* 21, fig. 6.11–12
6.	290	NE I.32.24	L.32008	bowl, molded	
7.	3110	NW VII.13.26	L.13000	cup, molded	Ibid. fig. 6.11
8.	3226	NW VII.33.20	L.33011	cup, molded	
9.	3039	NW VII.1	L.1000	cup, bowl?, molded	Ibid. fig. 6.12
10.	943	NW I.25.17	L.25017	bowl	
11.	3518	NW VII.1.90	L.1060	bowl	
12.	813	NW I.25.14	L.25005	bowl	
13.	688	C-1.7	L.1004	bowl	
14.	3433	NE VII.2.81	L.2032	bowl, cup?	
15.	960	NW VII.1.41	L.1035	bowl, cup?	
16.	787	NW I.25.13	L.25013	cup	
17.	790	NW I.26.45	L.26019	bowl	
18.	864	SE II.23.9	L.23001	bowl	
19.	818	NW I.25.14	L.25005	bowl	
20.	3651	NE VII.8.3	L.8003	bowl	
21.	781	C-1.17	L.1004	bowl	*'Atiqot* 5 (H.S.), p. 74:3
22.	865	SE II.23.9	L.23001	bowl	
23.	822	NW I.25.14	L.25005	bowl	

Plate 8.4

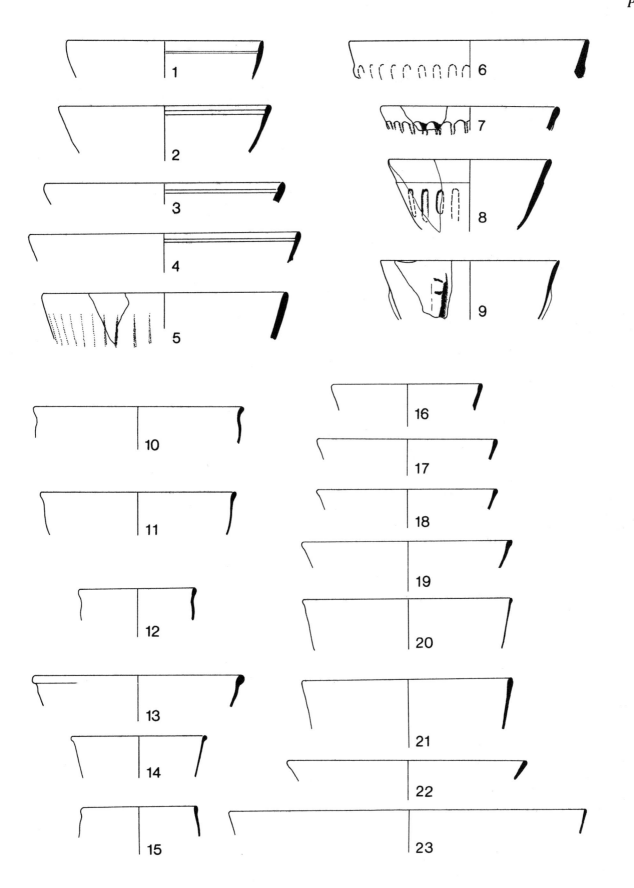

Plate 8.5. GLASS VESSELS, 1:2.5

No. Reg.	Field, Square Bucket	Locus	Artifact	Parallels
1. 3548	NW VII.13.46	L.13003	bowl rim	
2. 3371	NW VII.13.39	L.13002	bowl rim	
3. 714	C-1.11	L.1002	rim	
4. 736	SE II.23.5	L.23005	rim	
5. 949	NW I.25.46	L.25005	rim	
6. 722	NW I.26.43	L.26019	rim	
7. 663	NW I.26.27	L.26009	cup rim	
8. 968	NW VII.1.48	L.1037.1	cup	*'Atiqot* 5 (H.S.), p. 74:6
9. 956	NW I.31.66	L.31021	cup	Ibid.
10. 802	NW I.31.61	L.31021	cup	Ibid.
11. 793	NW I.26.52	L.26019	cup	Ibid.
12. 966	NW VII.1.45	L.1037	bottle	Ibid.
13. 851	NE VII.2.39	L.2017	bowl rim	Ibid.
14. 725	NW VII.1.21	L.1016	bowl rim	Ibid.
15. 619	C-1.4	L.1002	bottle	Ibid.
16. 767	C-1.16	L.1004	bottle	*'Atiqot* 5 (H.S.), p. 74:6
17. 3437	NE VII.20.18	L.2032	bottle	*Khirbat al-Karak*, pl. 59:2
18. 3332	NW VII.13.39	L.13002	cup, bowl, bottle?	*'Atiqot* 5 (H.S.), p. 74:6
19. 828	NW I.26.6	L.26019	bowl rim	
20. 945	NW I.25.46	L.25005	bottle	*Pella* I, pl. 78:306
21. 786	NW I.25.13	L.25005	bottle	
22. 959	NW I.31.69	L.31021	bottle	
23. 664	NW I.26.27	L.26009	bottle	*Khirbat al-Karak*, pl. 59:4 etc.
24. 893	NW I.31.65	L.31021	bottle	Ibid.
25. 856	NW I.31.62	L.31021	bottle	Ibid.
26. 863	SE II.23.9	L.23001	bottle	Ibid.
27. 852	NE VII.2.39	L.2017	bottle	Ibid.
28. 806	C-1.17	L.1004	bottle	Ibid.
29. 784	C-1.17	L.1004	bottle	Ibid.
30. 774	C-1.15	L.1004	bottle	Ibid.

Plate 8.5

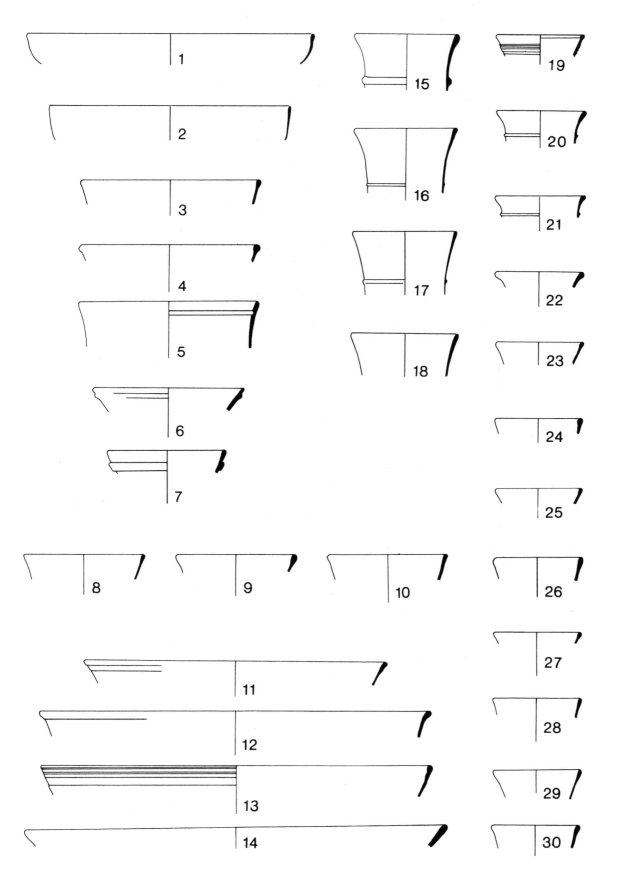

Plate 8.6. GLASS VESSELS, 1:2.5

No.	Reg.	Field, Square Bucket	Locus	Artifact	Parallels
1.	948	NW I.25.46	L.25005	cup rim, 4th c.	
2.	962	NW II.1.41	L.1035	cup rim, 4th c.	
3.	961	NW VII.1.41	L.1035	small bowl, 4th c.	
4.	3253	NW VII.8.32	L.8008	cup, 4th c.	
5.	700	NW I.31.55	L.31021	cup	
6.	839	NW VII.1.37	L.1025	bowl, late 3d, 4th c.	
7.	3356	NW I.26.62	L.26022.1	bottle, late 1st, mid 3d c.	*Pella* I, pl. 78; 309 par.
8.	816	NW I.25.14	L.25005	drinking cup, mal-formed by fire	
9.	817	NW I.25.14	L.25005	cup rim	
10.	1221	NW I.32	L.32028	bottle	*Beth She'arim* III, fig. 97:10
11.	1686	NW I.31.92	L.31021	cup, bowl? rim	
12.	773	C-1.15	L.1004	cup, 4th c.	
13.	770	C-1.15	L.1004	bottle neck	*Bethany*, pl. 57-E
14.	3379	NW VII.1.88	L.1060	bottle, 4th c.	*'Atiqot* 5 (H.S.), p. 63:2
15.	791	NW I.26.52	L.26019	bottle	
16.	862	SE II.23.9	L.23001	bottle	
17.	3611	NW I.34.6	L.34002	bottle, 3d, 4th c.	
18.	3728	NW I.33.41	L.33003.1	late 1st, early 3d c.	
19.	857	NW I.31.62	L.31021	bottle, 6th c.	
20.	610	NW I.26.16	L.26009	4th c.	
21.	737	SE II.23.5	L.23005	bottle neck, late 1st c.	
22.	623	C-1.3	L.1002	bottle, 5th to 6th c.	*Khirbat al-Karak*, pl. 60:13
23.	3484	NW VII.2.82	L.2033	cup, bowl, bottle?, 4th c.	
24.	3016	NE I.26.39	L.26023	cup	
25.	745	NW VII.2.34	L.2017	cup, 4th c.	
26.	855	NW I.31.62	L.31001	cup, 4th to 5th c.	
27.	768	C-1.16	L.1004	cup, 4th c.	
28.	783	C-1.17	L.1004	cup, 4th c.	
29.	792	NW I.26.52	L.26019	cup, 4th c.	
30.	769	C-1.16	L.1004	cup, 4th c.	
31.	3529	NE I.32.71	L.32016	cup, 4th to 5th c.	
32.	969	NW VII.1.46	L.1016	bottle, 4th c.	

Plate 8.6

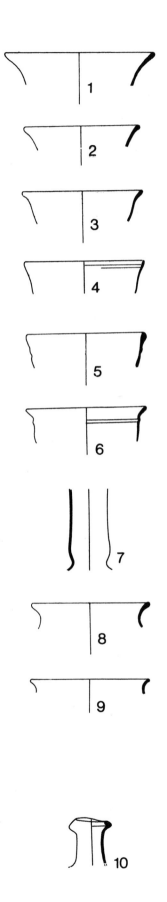

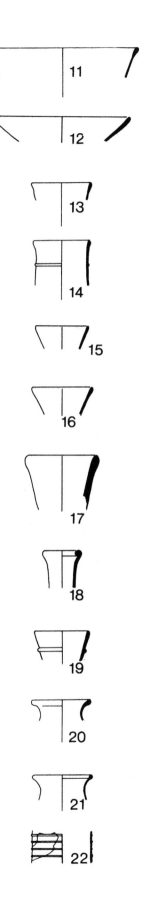

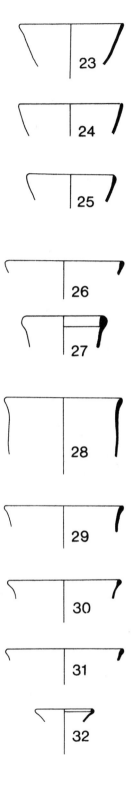

Plate 8.7. GLASS VESSELS, 1:2.5

No.	Reg.	Field, Square Bucket	Locus	Artifact	Parallels
1.	3547	NW VII.13.47	L.13003	bottle	*Pella* I, pl. 79:376
2.	3458	NW VII.13.40	L.13002	cup	*'Atiqot* 3, p. 126:14
3.	3304	NW VII.01.91	L.1060	rim	
4.	724	NW VII.1.21	L.1016	rim	
5.	640	C-1.7	L.1004	bowl	
6.	735	SE II.23.5	L.23005	bowl	
7.	801	NW I.31.61	L.31021	bowl	
8.	3735	NW VII.20.102	L.2045	rim	
9.	746	NW I.25.11	L.25005	bowl	
10.	947	NW I.25.46	L.2505	bottle or jar	
11.	892	NW I.31.62A	L.31021	rim	
12.	3429	NW VII.1.90	L.1060	rim	*'Atiqot* 5 (H.S.), p. 74:1
13.	824	NW I.25.15	L.25005	rim	*'Atiqot* 5 (H.S.), p. 77:1
14.	713	C-1.11	L.1002	bowl	
15.	746	NW I.25.11	L.25005	rim	
16.	850	NW VII.20.39	L.2017	bowl rim	
17.	1072	SE II.22.23	L.22006	base	
18.	3282	NE I.19.26	L.19070	base	*Khirbat al-Karak*, pl. 60:20
19.	621	C-1.6	L.1004	base	
20.	776	C-1.14	L.1003	base	
21.	3546	NW VII.13.45	L.13003	base	
22.	3246	NW VII.8.24	L.8004	base of bottle or jar	
23.	1220	NW I.32.51	L.32028	base	
24.	1687	NW I.31.92	L.31021	base	
25.	815	NW I.25.14	L.25005	bowl base	*'Atiqot* 5 (H.S.), p. 77:2
26.	3558	NE I.32.72	L.32016	base	*Bethany*, fig. 34:17 (4030)
27.	800	NW I.31.5	L.31021	base of bowl or plate	
28.	3343	NW VII.13.28	L.13002	base of plate	
29.	819	NW I.35.14	L.25005	lamp base	*Shavei Zion*, fig. 16:25
30.	823	NW I.25.15	L.25005	lamp base	*'Atiqot* 5 (H.S.), p. 63:5, 7
31.	835	NW I.1.33	L.1013	lamp base	*Rabinowitz Bull.* 3, fig. 9:3
32.	751	NW VII.1.24	L.1018	lamp base	*Khirbat al-Karak*, pl. 60:26 *Beth She'arim* III, fig. 97:25

Plate 8.7

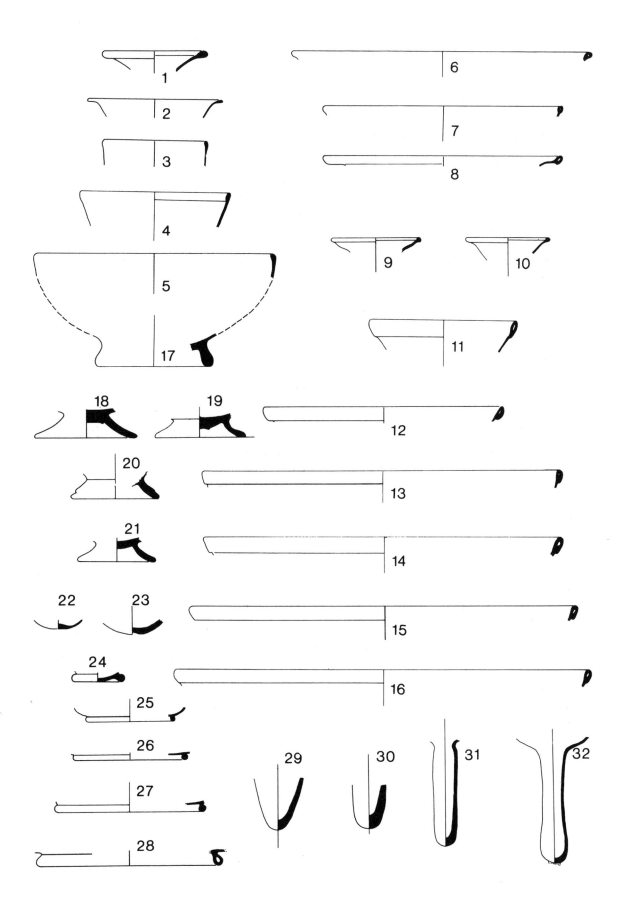

Plate 8.8. GLASS, STONE, CERAMIC, AND BONE (IVORY) OBJECTS, 1:2.5

No. Reg.	Field, Square Bucket	Locus	Artifact	Parallels
1. 689	C-1.1	L.1004	bottle or drinking cup glass, base	
2. 779	NE VII.2.35	L.2017	drinking cup, glass, base	
3. 731	C-1.13	L.1003	drinking cup, glass, base	
4. 3834	C-1.33	L.1004	base, glass	
5. 637	C-1.7	L.1004	base, glass	
6. 3294	NE I.19.27	L.19071	juglet, base, glass	*Dhiban*, fig. 13:29
7. 1685	NW I.31.92	L.31021	bottle rim, base, glass	
8. 3064	NW VII.8.15	L.8001	base, glass	
9. 946	NW I.25.46	L.25005	rod, glass	
10. 3666	NW I.34.19	L.34010	handle, glass	
11. 3804	NW I.32.72	L.32016	rod, glass	
12. 216	NE I.25.26	L.25036	rod, glass	
13. 387	NE I.25.35	L.25037	cosmetic tool, glass	
14. 3454	NE VII.8.32	L.8008	handle, glass	
15. 3315	NW VII.13.34	L.13002	handle, glass	
16. 92	NE I.33.05	L.33000	handle, glass	
17. 661	NW I.26.16	L.26009	loom weight, stone	
18. 1954	NW VII.8.06	L.8001	bowl rim, stone	
19. 3019	NE I.26.39	L.26023	button, ceramic	
20. 1951	NW VII.33.01	L.33000	disc, bone	
21. 3528	NW VII.1.90	L.1060	tool, polished bone	
22. 952	NW I.31.65	L.31021	pin, bone	
23. 869	SE II.23.9	L.23001	pin, bone (ivory?)	
24. 639	C-1.7	L.1004	pin, bone (ivory?)	
25. 3743	NW I.34.23	L.34013	tool, bone	
26. 1252	SE II.23.19	L.23012	needle, bone	*Tyropean Valley*, pl. XXI:46
27. 327	NE I.34.9	L.34000	scarab, ivory (bone?)	
28. 428	NW I.25	L.25000	comb, bone	
29. 536	NE VII.1.18	L.1004	bead	
30. 238	SE I.24.07	L.24004	bead	
31. 951	NW I.31.55	L.31021	spindle whorl, stone	*Pella* I, pl. 78:286; pl. 79: 387
32. 860	NW I.31.64	L.31021	spindle whorl, ceramic	
33. 269	NE I.25.30	L.25036	spindle whorl, stone	*Pella* I, pl. 78:318
34. 3720	NW VII.14.18	L.14002	spindle whorl, stone	Ibid.

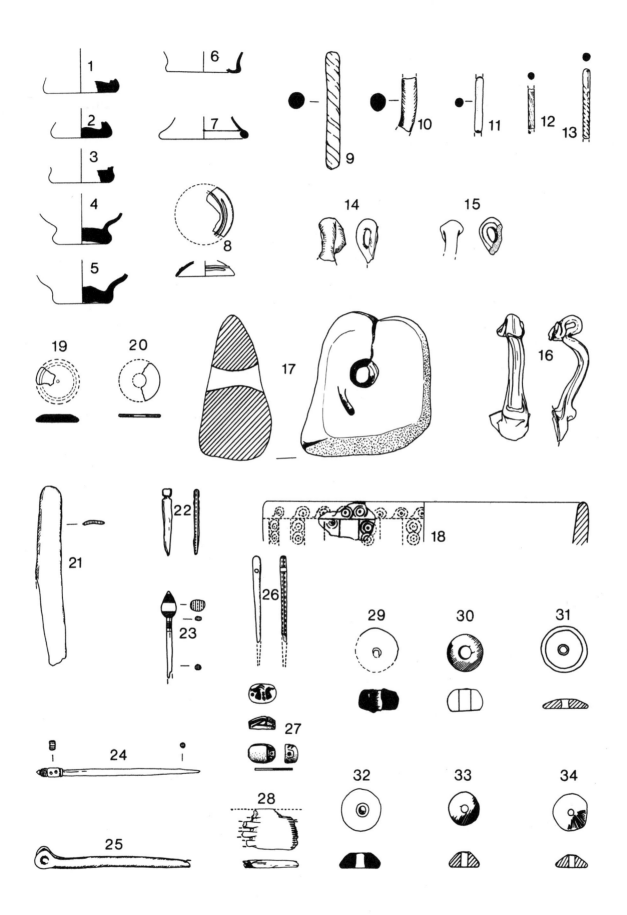

Plate 8.9. CERAMIC LAMPS, 1:2.5

No. Reg.	Field, Square Bucket	Locus	Artifact	Parallels
1. 493	T-29 South.15	L.29006	lamp ceramic	*Beth She'arim* III, pl. 70:4; *'Atiqot* 3, p. 126:24–26; p. 127:5–6
2. 490	T-29 North.14	L.29006	lamp, ceramic	
3. 492	T-29 South.14	L.29006	lamp, ceramic	
4. 485	T-29 South.18	L.29007	lamp fragment, ceramic	
5. 484	T-29 South.15	L.29006	lamp fragment, ceramic	
6. 489	T-29 North.14	L.29006	lamp, ceramic	
7. 1688	NW I.32.53	L.32028	lamp fragment, ceramic	
8. 404	T-29 South.28	L.29012	lamp, ceramic	
9. 3407	NW I.33.17	L.33003	lamp, ceramic	
10. 3565	NE I.32.72	L.32016	lamp, ceramic	
11. 3293	NW VII.1.85	L.1058	lamp fragment, ceramic	
12. 3301	NW VII.1.91	L.1060	lamp, ceramic	
13. 3850	SE II.23.15.10	L.23011	lamp, ceramic	
14. 3252	NW VII.33.18	L.33001	lamp base, ceramic	

Plate 8.9

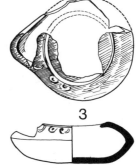

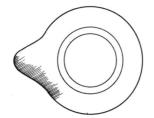

1

2

3

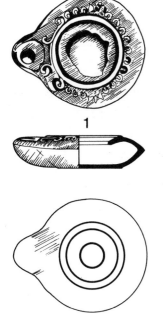

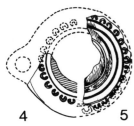

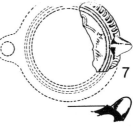

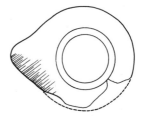

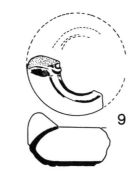

4   5

6

7

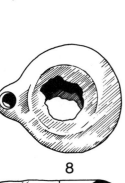

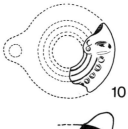

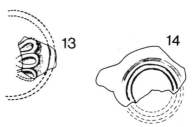

8

9

10

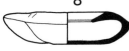

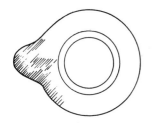

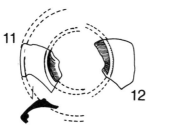

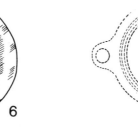

11

12

13   14

Plate 8.10. CERAMIC LAMPS, 1:2.5

No. Reg.	Field, Square Bucket	Locus	Artifact	Parallels
1. 3389	NE I.19.27	L.19071	lamp, ceramic	*Beth She'arim* III, fig. 50:1 *Khirbat al-Karak*, pl. 60: 31
2. 491	T-29 North.25	L.29008	lamp, ceramic	
3. 479	T-29 North.29	L.29008	lamp, ceramic	*Pella* I, pl. 60, obj. 56
4. 3823	NW I.33	L.33018	lamp, ceramic	*Samaria* (Harv.), fig. 191: 1460
5. 320	NE VII.1.08	L.1004	lamp, ceramic	*Beth She'arim* III, pl. 70:24
6. 811	NE VII.2	L.2008	lamp, ceramic	
7. 3736	NE VII.8.03	L.8003	lamp fragment, ceramic	
8. 3268	NW VII.1.52	L.1051	lamp fragment, ceramic	
9. 3851	NW I.31.77	L.31021	lamp base, ceramic	
10. 854	NW I.31.62	L.31021	lamp base with menorah, ceramic	*Beth She'arim* III, fig. 93:2
11. 476	T-29 North.9	L.29003	lamp, ceramic	

Plate 8.10

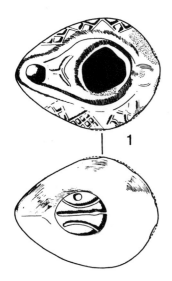

1

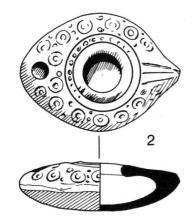

2

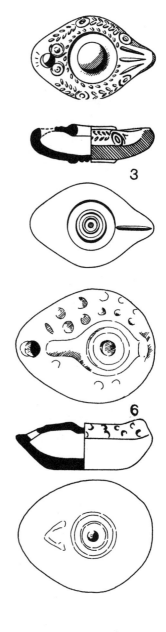

3

6

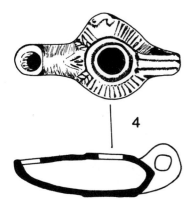

4

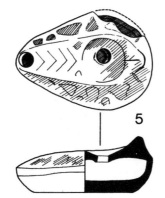

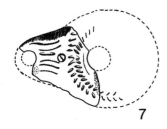

5

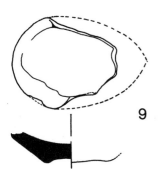

7

9

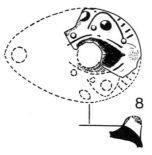

8

10

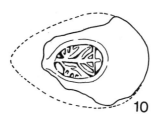

11

Plate 8.11. CERAMIC LAMPS AND CERAMIC, GLASS, AND STONE OBJECTS, 1:2.5

No.	Reg.	Field, Square Bucket	Locus	Artifact	Parallels
1.	3849	Surface find	000	lamp, ceramic	
2.	123	T-22	L.22000	lamp, ceramic	
3.	3583	NW VII.13.46	L.13003	lamp handle	
4.	3820	NE I.1.19.17	L.19070	lamp handle, ceramic	
5.	3520	NW VII.1.90	L.1060	lamp base, ceramic	*Beth She'arim* III, fig. 92: 5–6
6.	3844	NE VII.2	L.2004	lamp, ceramic	
7.	3763	NW VII.9.14	L.9007	stopper, ceramic	
8.	1216	NW I.31.77	L.31021	lamp, ceramic	*Beth She'arim* III, fig. 92:4
9.	3845	NW VII.3.24.1	L.3017	strainer, ceramic	
10.	388	NW I.30.19	L.3001	TS stamp, cross	Hayes, p. 356, type 69
11.	3445	NE VII.2.79.28	L.2030	spatulate lamp nozzle, ceramic	
12.	2000	SE II.23.42.7	L.23018	spatulate lamp nozzle, ceramic	*'Atiqot* 1, p. 126:18
13.	319	NE VII.1.7	L.1003	rim, glass	
14.	1061	SE II.23.23	L.23006	bottle, glass	
15.	1065	SE II.23.23	L.23006	bottle, glass	*Beth She'arim* III, fig. 98:3
16.	1937	NE VII.2.77	L.2030	vessel, glass	
17.	1062	SE II.23.23	L.23006	bottle, glass	*'Atiqot* 5 (H.S.), p. 77:7
18.	331	NE I.34.8	L.34000	bottle, glass	*Tyropean Valley,* pl. 21:30
19.	1625	NW I.32	L.32023	wine glass	*'Atiqot* 5 (H.S.), pl. 74:18 *Dominus Flevit* I, pl. 34:24 *Khirbat al-Karak,* pl. 60:23 *Dhiban,* no. 89 *Shavei Zion,* fig. 16:16 *Pella* I, pl. 79
20.	146	T-29 South.5	L.29004	bead, frit	
21.	361	T-29 South.15	L.29006	bead, glass	
22.	367	T-29 South.25	L.29008	bead, glass	*Khirbat al-Karak,* pl. 46:5
23.	1977	NW VII.33.4	L.33003	bead, carnelian	
24.	458	T-29 South.25	L.29010	bead, glass	*Pella* I, pl. 79:C
25.	457	T-29 South.26	L.29001	bead, glass	
26.	3729	NW VII.3.13	L.3007	vessel, basalt	
27.	413	NE I.25.47	L.25042	gem, carnelia, itaglio	
28.	3481	NW I.34.2	L.34002	grinder, basalt	
29.	1885	NE I.26.11	L.26005	whetstone	
30.	407	T-29 North.2	L.29001	ostracon	
31.	422	NW I.30.29	L.30015	ostracon	
32.	429	NE I.32.27	L.32006	ostracon	

Plate 8.11

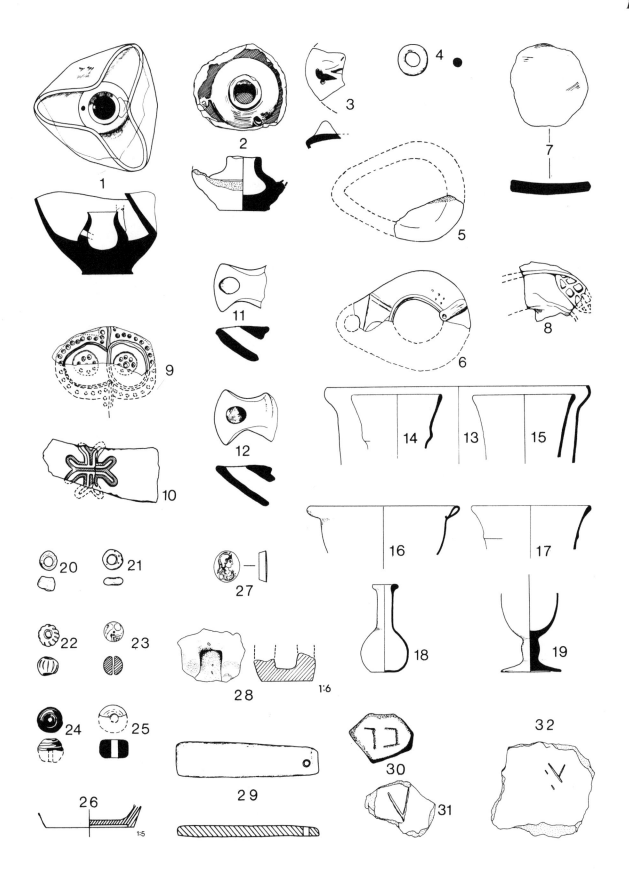

I.1

Photo I.1. Inside the synagogue ruins, view to the north at the beginning of the dig.

Photo I.2. Aerial view of Khirbet Shema' to the south, 1971.

I.2

2.1

2.2

Photo 2.1. Khirbet Shema' as seen from the next spur to the east. The dolomitic limestone forming sublinear outcrops on the eastern face of the hill dip gently to the north and more steeply to the west (away from the view). These strata were quarried on the upper western slope of this hill beyond the site, for architectural purposes. A fault breccia zone follows the line indicated by X and may be traced along the line where the bedrock outcrop is discontinuous (cf. photo 2.7). Higher foothills of Mount Meiron line the horizon.

Photo 2.2. Khirbet Shema' (arrow) and its environment, looking toward the northeast. The surface morphology of the spur on which the site was constructed is clearly shown. Wadis have cut steep-walled valleys to the east and northwest of the site. A striking bedrock erosional remnant (called Elijah's Throne) appears in the right foreground. This columnar rock remnant represents the remains of bedrock strata now lost to erosion. Crustal uplift, largely by faulting, has produced the high relief seen throughout this view.

Photo 2.3. The surface appearance of a local rock quarry site, showing the effects of weathering since the time when materials were quarried for local structures. Some brecciation may be.seen in the left portion of the rock outcrop. Chisel marks still appear on the rock surface above and to the right and left of the scale.

2.3

2.4

2.5

Photo 2.4. A fragment of the dolomitized limestone from the Mausoleum (monument) on the south part of the site. Weathering has etched out the fractured portions of the rock, which were later resealed by calcite cement within the natural rock environment (arrow).

Photo 2.5. Microphotograph of the monument sample shown in photo 2.4. Rhombic dolomite crystals (arrow) can be seen growing at the expense of calcite crystals in the upper left and lower right. The light-toned portion is where calcite cementation is the host area for dolomite crystals which began to develop. The crystal at the arrow is 0.2 mm across.

Photo 2.6. Regolithic weathered bedrock (solution remnants of the parent rock) as seen in typical shapes occurring in the soil immediately above the unweathered rock. Pinnacled remnants of the parent rock become isolated by later solution weathering to form the sculpture-like geometries shown. It is important to realize that these remnants may exhibit forms resembling a range of artifacts varying from cult objects to near perfect worn ax heads.

2.6

2.7

2.8

Photo 2.7. Fault (tectonic) breccia. This local bedrock material has been through several phases of shearing caused by crustal movements along the local fault zones. Such breakage was followed by cementation, only to be shattered again and subsequently healed by cementation again. The calcite cement is rich in hematite-bearing terra rossa particles, giving a brownish-red coloration to the specimen areas between the white or yellow limestone and silicified limestone in the rock mass; both of these appear as the lighter areas.

Photo 2.8. Medium cobble-sized travertine vein fragment composed of calcite crystals. This material occurs in vein fillings in the lower member of the Deir Hana formation outcropping to the southwest higher on the foothill spur which is the site of Khirbet Shemaʿ. This is the raw material observed in certain ceramic materials from the site, as well as that which was used in great abundance in the surface plaster of the synagogue (cf. photo 2.16).

Photo 2.9. The wine press working area, carved into the local dolomitic limestone bedrock. Crushing areas, wine channels, and sump receivers may be observed as clearly cut into the local rock surface. Subsequent weathering has etched these work surfaces to produce the peculiar expression to be observed. The local dip (8° to the west) of the bedrock of Khirbet Shemaʿ was utilized in the cutting of this utility, located to the south of the synagogue structure.

2.9

Photo 2.10. Circular lime kiln constructed in the valley of the wadi immediately to the east of Khirbet Shema'. Calcination of the walls of this pyrotechnical feature illustrates the lime-burning function of its structure. The view looks in the loading doorway on the south side. The walls of the kiln were supported by earth piled around to preserve the shape.

Photo 2.11. Exotic basalt scoria cobble. Lithic surface material of this composition and fabric was observed in the area north and northeast of Gush Halav and Sasa in surface flows which occur in that area. This material could serve as a rasper, scraper, or rubbing stone. Several specimens of varying size occurred on the site of Shema'.

Photo 2.12. Microphotograph of alkaline olivine basalt. This extrusive igneous material is characteristic of most Galilean lava flows. The light-colored lathlike crystals are plagioclase distributed throughout the ground mass of pyroxene crystals forming the darker background. All of the basalt objects occurring in the excavation were made up of this mineral assemblage, with minor variation in crystal size and gas bubble inclusions. The bright crystal near the center is 0.1 mm long.

2.11

2.12

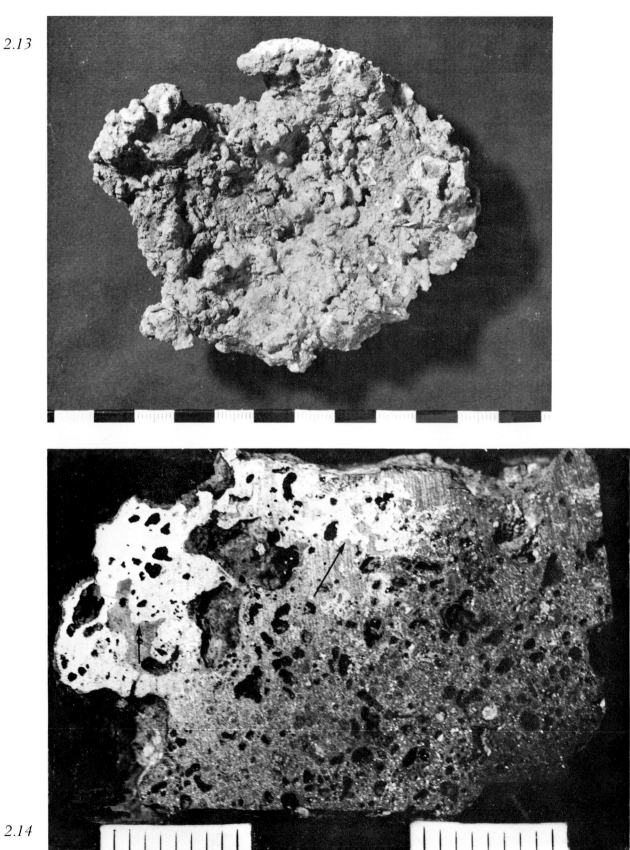

2.13

2.14

Photo 2.13. Slag showing the concave crucible form in which iron smelting had taken place. The presence of slag materials such as this and others is evidence of a small-scale local iron industry, probably connected with the occupation of the environment of the site.

Photo 2.14. Polished section of the slag shown in photo 2.13. The bright, highly reflective areas (arrows) of the section are proof that the iron-smelting operation was a success, for they represent metallic iron in the midst of a glassy slag having a composition close to that of the olivine fayalite.

Photo 2.15. Tufa. This exotic lithic material from the surface of the site is a hot-spring carbonate deposit formed around plants (for example, at arrow) which grow in an area where lime-bearing hot-spring waters emerge from their underground passage. This tufa probably came from Tiberias, where thermal springs are known in the history of the area. The use of this material may have been the same as for the basalt scoria found among the lithic material of the site (cf. photo 2.11).

2.15

2.16

2.17

Photo 2.16. Type I surface plaster (A) and type III subsurface plaster backing (B). This surface plaster is composed of nearly pure white calcium oxide (slaked lime, now recarbonated) with an aggregate of crushed vein calcite (at arrow), much of which cleaves to form the typical calcite cleavage rhombs (cf. photo 2.17). The type III backing varies from place to place in the architectural structure of the synagogue. Here the material is seen containing lithic fragments of fault breccia, limestone, dolomitized limestone, ceramic fragments, quartz crystals, with minor straw binding. The composition of the calcined lime varies, and in some specimens charcoal is present. This subplaster varies in color depending upon the amount of terra rossa included and the amount of yellow dolomitized bedrock fragments.

Photo 2.17. Straw binding molds on the surface on type III subsurface plaster. The binding was necessary to form a strong wall plaster which would remain in place and endure the stress of the walled areas.

Photo 2.18. Calcite cleavage fragments which were mechanically extracted from a 3-cm-square section of type I plaster. See photo 2.8 for the parent lithic material for this plaster aggregate.

2.18

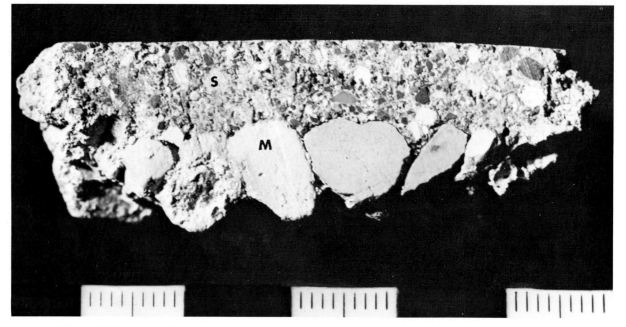

Photo 2.19. Type VI plaster composed to two distinct preparations. The surface material(s) contains fine to coarse sand-sized limestone, lithified terra rossa, dolomitized limestone, most of which shows evidence of some wadi transport and sorting. This material is laid upon a subsurface make-up (M) composed of small pebble-to-granule-sized limestone and chalk in a matrix of white calcined lime mortar. This material could serve as a surface of a floor or a basin or a pool in which water or other liquids might be contained.

Photo 2.20. Fragment of a surface portion of a terra rossa mudbrick. The matrix is the deep red soil color with dolomitized limestone fragments, probably from the regolith or the alluvial wadi terraces from which the brick material was probably quarried. The horizontal curving lineations are straw molds.

2.21

Photo 2.21. Section of a body sherd from the surface of the synagogue site. Abundant grass binding was used in this ceramic material, composed of the kaolinitic terra rossa clays of the area.

Photo 2.22. Section of a body sherd from the surface of the synagogue site. The ceramic paste is composed of rendzinate field clay in which the tests of numerous silicified foraminifera are preserved. The lithic aggregate is taken from a wadi which contained silicified limestone, chalk, and basalt lithic sediment.

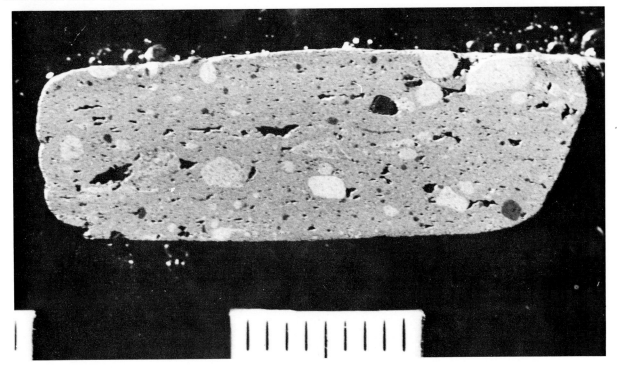

2.22

3.1

Photo 3.1. Probe inside the *bema*, showing the early plastered bench along the plastered south wall of the synagogue, looking east.

Photo 3.2. A view of the early bench on the south wall under the *bema*.

Photo 3.3. Probe beneath the plaster floor east of the Stylobate Wall.

Photo 3.4. Architectural fragments from fill east of the Stylobate Wall. *From left to right,* (1) fragment of acanthus-leaf decoration = NE VII.2, AF 21; (2) fragment of acanthus-leaf decoration = NE I.32, AF 41; (3) fragment of a Corinthian capital (with the lower bearing surface preserved) = NE VII.2, AF 23; (4) fragment of a Corinthian capital (with the lower bearing surface preserved) = NE VII.2, AF 22; and (5) fragment with bead-and-reel molding (with the lower bearing surface preserved) = NE I.32, AF 30.

Photo 3.5. Entrance of the pre-synagogue *miqveh,* to the west.

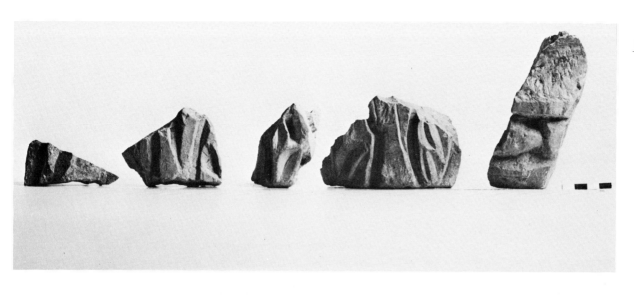

3.4

3.5

3.6

Photo 3.6. Bedrock in the adjoining room north of the synagogue.

Photo 3.7. Inside the *genizah*, looking north.

3.8

Photo 3.8. A column fragment in the Stylobate Wall.

Photo 3.9. North doorposts with the entrance court.

Photo 3.10. Molding on the eagle doorpost (of the western entrance), identical to northern door-way molding.

3.9

3.10

3.11

3.12

Photo 3.11. A column base of the Torah shrine.

Photo 3.12. Benches in the southeast corner of the synagogue.

Photo 3.13. Early benches against the north wall of the synagogue, with reused ashlars of Synagogue I as a second bench.

3.13

3.14

Photo 3.14. Bedrock in the northwest corner of the synagogue.

Photo 3.15. Eastern half of reconstructed Synagogue II, with earlier benching visible on the western side of the *bema*.

3.16

Photo 3.16. Detail of the eastern end of the *bema*, with an earlier bench running behind.

Photo 3.17. The western entrance with stairway. Note the late bench to the left, and the find spot of the rosette capital.

Photo 3.18. The Menorah Lintel to the north entrance of Synagogue II.

3.17

3.18

Photo 3.19. West end of the reconstructed Synagogue II, showing the Frescoed Room and entrance to the *genizah.*

Photo 3.20. Detail of the outside stairway north of the synagogue under excavation. Note the plaster on the north face of the synagogue wall and ashlars in the background.

Photo 3.21. Synagogue II as excavated at the end of the 1971 season.

3.21

Photo 3.22. The east face of the North Building.

Photo 3.23. The North Building, to the west, showing the north stairway.

Photo 3.24. Interior of the North Building, to the west.

3.23

3.24

3.25

3.26

Photo 3.25. Overall view of the western terrace to the north, synagogue to the right.

Photo 3.26. Late standing pillar on exposed bedrock after excavation in the western terrace, looking south.

Photo 3.27. Rooms south of the synagogue, looking west-northwest.

3.27

3.28

3.29

Photo 3.28. Detail of cobbled floor L.26018 south of the synagogue.

Photo 3.29. Detail in the easternmost room south of the synagogue, floor 26022.

Photo 3.30. The synagogue, showing areas to the north, including the North Room.

3.30

3.31

3.32

Photo 3.31. Detail of the North Room, showing paving partially removed and with storage bin L.2017 exposed.

Photo 3.32. Rooms to the east of the synagogue = NE I.33 and NE I.34.

Photo 3.33. Panoramic view of the reconstructed synagogue, to the south.

3.33

3.34

Photo 3.34. View of the reconstructed synagogue, to the northeast.

Photo 3.35. Reconstructed synagogue, to the west.

Photo 4.1. View of the bottom of the cistern, showing the collection basin.

Photo 4.2. View upward within the cistern, showing a millstone in the neck.

Photo 4.3. Balk within the cistern, showing stratification.

4.2

4.3

Photo 4.4. View to the north inside Room A in SE II.

Photo 4.5. A whole amphoriskos lying on floor 23017 in SE II.23.

Photo 4.6. View of platform 22022 in SE II with staircase and wall 22031. Fill 22018 was between 22022 and 22031.

4.5

4.6

4.7

4.8

Photo 4.7. Composite photo from above of SE II.

Photo 4.8. The *miqveh*, to the north.

Photo 4.9. The pre-lavatorium, to the west. Below and to the left is a sump and an opening into the *miqveh* proper.

Photo 4.10. Entry to the *miqveh* proper, to the north, showing steps.

Photo 4.11. Inside the *miqveh*, looking out to the south.

Photo 4.12. The *miqveh* chamber, looking north, showing plaster.

4.11

4.12

Photo 4.13. The screw press post northeast of the wine press.

Photo 5.1. View of the Mausoleum (TM) to the northwest.

5.2

5.3

Photo 5.2. View of the Mausoleum to the north, showing the exposed foundation.

Photo 5.3. Southwest corner of the Mausoleum, with plastered foundation.

Photo 5.4. The Mausoleum, to the west, showing relationship to Tomb 1 beneath.

5.4

Photo 5.5. Rock-cut graves in Tomb 22.

Photo 5.6. The central chamber of Tomb 22, showing graves in the rear and the *kokh* to the right.

Photo 5.7. Both sets of graves in Tomb 22.

5.6

5.7

Photo 5.8. Tomb 29 North, *kokh* 1.

Photo 5.9. Bones and a lamp on the floor of the main chamber of Tomb 29 North.

Photo 5.10. Interior of the main chamber of Tomb 29, north to west, toward the bone chamber. *Kokhim* in the south wall to the left.

Photo 5.11. Bones inside the bone chamber of Tomb 29 North.

5.12

Photo 5.12. View straight up to stone slabs covering the shaft into Tomb 29 South.

Photo 5.13. Bones in the fill in Tomb 29 South, looking east.

5.13

unclosed

5.14

Photo 5.14. View to the west of Tomb 31.

Photo 5.15. Tomb 31: false doorway to the left of the entrance.

7.1

Photo 7.1. A bowl with yellow glaze and brown line.

Photo 8.1. Iron scissors, pl. 8.2:6.

8.1

Photo 8.2. Engraved bronze ring, pl. 8.1:14.

Photo 8.3. Menorah lamp base, pl. 8.10:10.

Photo 8.4. Terra sigillata cross stamp, pl. 8.11:10.

Photo 8.5. Agate bead.

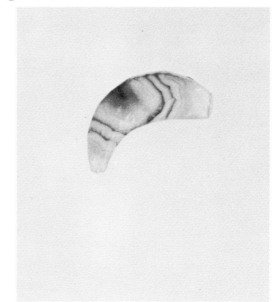

8.6

Photo 8.6. Hellenistic scarab, pl. 8.8:27.

Photo 8.7. Engraved carnelian gem, pl. 8.11:24.

8.7